GANGS AND GANG BEHAVIOR

GANGS AND GANG BEHAVIOR

G. Larry Mays, Editor

New Mexico State University

Nelson-Hall Publishers
Chicago

Project Editor: Dorothy Anderson
Typesetter: Precision Typographers
Printer: Capital City Press
Cover Painting by Jane Meredith

Library of Congress Cataloging-in-Publication Data

Gangs and gang behavior / G. Larry Mays, editor.
     p.   cm.
    Includes bibliographical references (p.   ) and index.
    ISBN 0–8304–1457–6
     1. Gangs—United States.   2. Juvenile delinquency—United States.
 I. Mays, G. Larry.
 HV6439.U5G3595   1997
 364.1'06'60973—dc20   96–38332
                                                   CIP

Manufactured in the United States of America.

10   9   8   7   6   5   4   3   2   1

TM The paper used in this book meets the minimum requirements of American National Standard for Information Sciences—Permanence of Paper for Printed Library Materials, ANSI Z39.48-1984.

Contents

CONTENTS

CONTENTS

Introduction

This book represents one effort in what has become a life-long devotion to the problems of youngsters and the situations in which they find themselves. The topic of gangs seems to be one that holds a great fascination for the public. In this regard, college students, as part of the general public, find the discussion of gangs both frustrating and fascinating.

When the public is confronted with gang activity, reactions range from morbid attraction to utter revulsion. The success of movies like *Colors, Boyz in the Hood, New Jack City*, and other popular portrayals of gang life shows how the entertainment industry has exploited the public's curiosity about gangs and gang behavior. We can always debate whether these movies provide accurate portrayals or not, but we cannot debate whether they have been financially successful, for virtually all of them have been.

Why, then, a book on gangs and gang behavior? My odyssey into the world of gangs began with a stint as a municipal police officer in the early 1970s. During that time, I had the opportunity to witness ganglike activity, but nothing compared to gang activity today. My police career gave me the chance to work with juvenile offenders, and the interest that was developed there was carried over into my teaching and research activities.

In the midst of my academic career—during the early 1980s—there seemed to be a nationwide resurgence in gang activity and a corresponding interest by students and researchers in learning more about the "new" gangs. The gangs of the 1980s seemed to be bigger, more powerfully armed, and more violent than their predecessors. It was, as someone noted, "not *West Side Story* any longer." Therefore, my interest and involvement with the topics of gangs and gang behavior was as a criminal justice educator who treated gangs in the broader context of juvenile delinquency and juvenile justice.

In 1990 my involvement became much more personal. At that time two graduate students in my department expressed an interest in doing thesis research on gang activity in southern New Mexico. The town in which my university is located had seen an increase in what was assumed to be gang activity: assaults in the high schools and middle schools, high levels of graffiti in several neighborhoods, the display of "colors" by groups of adolescents, and the appearance of drive-by shootings. In fact, the local newspaper and the police department both began to attribute a number of criminal and delinquent acts to gangs.

The response by the police department was initially that indicated by Ron Huff in his book *Gangs in America* (Sage, 1990): there was a fairly substantial level of denial. However, as the drive-by shootings escalated and the amount of graffiti increased, the police department reluctantly acknowledged the presence of gangs and created a "gang unit." To aid police efforts and to assess the level of gang activity in the community, the city council created a gang task force comprised of individuals from a variety of interests and perspectives. As the local juvenile crime "expert" I was pressed into duty and served on the gang task force for about eighteen months. At that point, my interest in gangs passed from being *merely* academic to being real world and problem-solving in nature.

As a result of the gang research by our graduate students and my service on the gang task force, my research and teaching increasingly moved to the area of understanding and addressing gang problems. As this happened, my students and the groups I was asked to speak to wanted to know more. Particularly, the question "Why do these youngsters join gangs?" kept arising. In an effort to deal with the why, especially for those students who anticipate careers in the criminal justice system, I designed a selected topic class on gangs and gang activity. In that class I have had some students scour the literature to see what has been written that improves their knowledge of why gangs form, why certain youths join gangs when others do not, and what can be done about the web of gang problems. This book is the result of that effort. It contains the articles and original papers that my students and I feel are representative of the body of literature on gangs.

Briefly, I want to say what this book is and what it is not. First, most of the articles presented here are reprinted from scholarly academic journals in a variety of social science fields—principally criminal justice, criminology, and sociology. As such, they represent peer reviewed examinations of phenomena associated with gangs and their activity. Every effort has been made to choose those articles most usable by the instructor in the class and most intellectually accessible to the students. It is not possible for any one book to include everything on gangs, so this book does not attempt to be all things to all people.

INTRODUCTION

Second, the major sections of the book are arranged by topic, addressing the most common student questions, such as "What is a gang, anyway?" My colleagues and undergraduate and graduate students (who served as unofficial advisors on this project) shaped the book's organization.

Third, this book seeks to address a number of specific needs. It can be used in a course specifically on gangs or to study the topic of gangs in juvenile delinquency and/or juvenile justice courses.

Finally, I look at this book as a work in progress. I do not feel that the final word has been spoken or written about gangs, and interest in gangs will continue for the foreseeable future. This book is not *the* definitive work on the subject of gangs, but should serve as a useful reference source of the most recent, dependable, and enlightening writings on gangs in the late twentieth century. With this in mind, it should be obvious why the "classics" on gangs have been omitted. The articles and books by some of the leading criminologists of this century have been reprinted often and should be readily available to most students. The articles included here are meant to supplement, not supplant, those that have gone before.

I look forward to your comments and criticisms. If you are a faculty member or student using this book and want to correspond with me via e-mail, my address is glmays@nmsu.edu. I will try to answer all of your inquiries and suggestions in a timely manner.

Part 1

Definitions—A Struggle for Understanding

What is a gang? That would seem to be an easy question facing us as we launch out into a study of gangs and gang behavior, but as you will see from the readings in this section, there is no universal agreement over what constitutes a gang. As you read the selections in this section, remember one fundamental point: all gangs are groups, but not all groups are gangs.

In the first article, Ball and Curry discuss the problems of definition in criminology generally, and particularly how these problems make the areas of gang research more difficult. They note that the label "gang" has taken on a variety of meanings for researchers, for practitioners, and for youngsters who are members of youth groups that might be considered gangs. Such confusion has some suggesting that the label "gang" should be abandoned altogether. Ball and Curry, however, suggest a number of definitional methods that should contribute to our understanding of the various activities normally identified as gang-related phenomena.

The second article, by Winfree, Fuller, Vigil, and Mays, takes the approach of definition suggested by Horowitz (1990). That is, rather than imposing a strict definition as to what constitutes a gang, Winfree and his colleagues, in a survey of ninth and eleventh grade high school students, let the respondents self-report their level of gang involvement (from none up to a great deal). Any youngsters reporting gang involvement described features associated with their gangs. In this research, gang membership was associated with groups having: a name; an identifiable leadership component; initiation rituals (particularly physical initiations like ''jumping in''); the use of identifiable ''colors,'' often including wearing the logos of certain professional sports teams; and methods of visual communication of gang identity, such as tattoos, jewelry, and hand signs.

The final article in this section comes from a National Institute of Justice document. While this piece is on law enforcement recordkeeping, it also focuses on definitions. It summarizes the results of a survey of seventy-nine large U.S. metropolitan police departments. Curry, Ball, and Fox—the principal investigators for the gang research project—discuss defining gangs, assessing the scope of the gang problem nationwide, and the dilemmas facing law enforcement agencies in recording gang information. A primary objective of this project was to identify (or develop) effective anti-gang strategies for law enforcement agencies.

Questions for Consideration

As you finish reading this section, ask yourself the following questions:

1. Is it clear when a group becomes a gang and when it is not a gang?
2. Who does the defining, and what difference does that make?
3. Can we define a gang in the abstract or must we make references to other known entities about which we can agree on definitions?
4. Do the entertainment and news industries help in our understanding of what gangs are and what they do, or do they merely cloud the issue further?

1

The Logic of Definition in Criminology: Purposes and Methods for Defining "Gangs"

Richard A. Ball and G. David Curry

Problems of definition in criminology are more serious than many admit, for as Maxson and Klein (1990:71) quote an anonymous attorney, "Let me make the definitions and I'll win any argument." This article examines the term *gang*, which is the subject of the quotation, as a case in point. When surveyed in the early 1980s, 50 percent of the 44 largest cities in the United States reported gang problems (Needle and Stapleton, 1983). The most recent national survey shows that by 1992 this figure had grown to 91 percent, and approximately the same percentage of the next 35 largest cities also now reported such problems (Curry et al., 1994). Yet as far back as the middle 1970s, one of the most experienced gang researchers stressed that, "At no time has there been anything close to consensus on what a gang might be—by scholars, by criminal justice workers, by the general public" (Miller, 1975:115). Later researchers added that definitions "have varied over time according to the perception and interests of the definer, academic fashions, and the changing social reality of the gang" (Spergel et al., 1989:13).

The confusion is so great that some advocate abandoning the term, maintaining that it can never be standardized because it is not a term used by youth themselves to reflect the actual empirical reality of their involvements but rather a relatively meaningless label thrown about by the adult community (Conly, 1993). Others insist that everyone should be allowed to define it according to personal preferences to avoid closing off exploration of a rich variety of alternative possibilities (Horowitz, 1990). Finally, some maintain that everyone already understands the meaning intuitively (National Institute of Justice, 1992).

Reprinted with permission from *Criminology*, Vol. 33, No. 2 (1995): 225–245.

This last position may amount to saying, "I can't define 'gang,' but I know one if I see one." Logically, it is an appeal to "ostensive definition," the method by which a phenomenon is defined by physical introduction, such as by pointing at it (Harney, 1984). It poses the same problem faced by the courts with respect to terms such as obscenity or pornography, the problem of passage from a *clear* to a *distinct idea*. Although one has a clear or vivid idea of a thing when one can recognize examples of it immediately, the idea is not yet distinct until one can enumerate one-by-one the features that distinguish the thing from others. Even when the courts are able to arrive at a reasonably clear idea of pornography in the sense that they can recognize examples, they have not been successful in developing a distinct definition. Much the same is true of the term gang, which has led some gang researchers to the nominalistic position suggesting that there can never be a satisfactory definition (Horowitz, 1990).

Despite the insistence of the nominalists, however, words are not merely circular terms defined by other words in an endless cycle. Most terms are linked to empirical reality by having been defined ostensively in the first place (Makau, 1990). Part of the difference between a scientific and a literary approach to criminology lies in the persistent effort to clarify key terms from time to time by the ostensive method, pointing directly to empirical reality, so that definitions do not stray too far from their empirical referents. Still, verbal definitions are needed precisely because the researcher or theorist cannot take everyone to the phenomenon in question. And even if that were possible, when one pointed at a complex phenomenon and called it a gang, (1) meaning would have to depend entirely on visible characteristics and (2) it might not be clear which of all the visible characteristics were considered salient (Harney, 1984). As many logicians have shown (Baker and Hacker, 1984), those pointing at some phenomenon ostensively are usually drawing on a body of implicit knowledge extrinsic to it, including heuristic rules for what to see as well as how to see it, even if they are unable to articulate the implicit rules that guided observation and interpretation.

Definitions are necessary (Robinson, 1950), some definitions are better than others (Ayer, 1971), and criteria exist by which their relative value can be assessed (Bentley and Dewey, 1947; Quine, 1970). Some definitions can be considered superior because they prove more useful for certain purposes. This may involve, for example, something as simple as the level of generality. Destro (1993:280) seems to have had this in mind when commenting on gang definitions, noting that, "in legal parlance' sociological definitions tend to be both overinclusive ('overbroad') and underinclusive ('discriminatory'), and if they are adopted for criminal law purposes, they are in danger of being held unconstitutional because they are not specific enough." He could have added that legal definitions of *gang* tend to be both overly narrow and overly broad for sociological purposes because they neglect the social dimensions that make the phenomenon sociologically meaningful.

Logically, approaches to the problem of definition may be classified in terms of purposes, types, and methods, which makes possible a multitude of definitional styles. Theorists may seek a definition that will provide a term logically integrated into a larger postulatory framework, while researchers seek sufficient standardization to guide them toward the same phenomena and allow for comparison of findings. Administrators may care less about the theoretical power or empirical applicability of a definition than the fact that it is simple enough to impose bureaucratic standardization for purposes of recordkeeping, and police may be interested primarily in an expedient definition allowing them to hold the collectivity responsible for criminal acts of individual members or vice versa (Moore, 1993). To complicate matters further, even those with the same purpose may be working with either a lexical or stipulative type of definition, depending upon whether they wish to report customary meanings or establish a more specific definition by fiat. Much of the confusion stems from different definitions of *definition* and logical errors in their comparison.

Methods of Lexical Definition

Criminology texts (e.g., Bynum and Thompson, 1992; Seigel and Senna, 1994) and courts (Destro, 1993) sometimes begin their search for a gang definition with the dictionary. Unfortunately, however, dictionary definitions are less a summary of customary speech than what one logician has called "the history of use by a preferred class" (Robinson, 1950:36). In dictionary definitions, the term *gang* tends to designate collectivities that are (1) marginal, (2) loosely organized, and (3) without a clear, social purpose. Like other forms of deviance, gangs are defined not in their own terms but in terms of what they are not. Because definitions should never be expressed in the negative (Stebbing, 1933), the result is that dictionary definitions of *gang*, which tend to be veiled expressions of bourgeois disapproval, may actually impede efforts to arrive at a standardized definition intrinsic to the phenomenon in question.

Faced with the problem of studying gang participation without a definition, some have asked respondents whether they belonged to a collectivity that *they* defined as a gang. As Fagan (1989:634) has stressed, "This strategy was chosen specifically to avoid the problems in definitions that have confounded gang research." Yet Spergel and Curry (1988, 1990) found that participation indicators scaled differently for Hispanics and African Americans, meaning that lexical gang definitions seem to vary even among those who define themselves as gang members. In an effort to put together a lexical definition that could be used by law enforcement agencies, Miller (1975) asked a national survey of youth service agency workers, police officers, community outreach workers, judges, criminal justice planners, probation officers, prosecutors, public defenders, educators, city council members, state legislators, ex-convicts, and past and present members of gangs for their definition of the term. Although the result was a list of 1,400 different characteristics, 85 % agreed on 6 items defining a youth gang as

> a self-formed association of peers, bound together by mutual interests, with identifiable leadership, well-developed lines of authority, and other organizational features, who act in concert to achieve a specific purpose or purposes which generally include the conduct of illegal activity and control over a particular territory, facility, or type of enterprise. (Miller, 1975:121)

Klein and Maxson (1989:205) argue that this is a "discouraging" approach, insisting that definitions based on a vote have no special validity. In terms of the logic of definitions, they are correct and incorrect, depending on the type of definition, Voting is an appropriate approach for determining the *lexical* definition held by a particular segment of the population. Such definitions may seem unsatisfactory because they are inconsistent and vary from one segment of society to another, but the fact is that the more complex and changing the society, the more varied and shifting will be their lexical definitions. At the same time, voting is certainly a poor method for establishing a *stipulative* definition, especially when the subject is highly emotional and different segments of society seem to be approaching the question from different perspectives with different purposes.

Methods of Stipulative Definition

Methods of stipulative definition include the implicative method, the denotative method, definition by analysis, and definition by synthesis. The implicative method is also called the contextual method because it implies a definition through use of the word in a context that suggests its meaning (Baker and Hacker, 1984). Sometimes called the exemplification method, the denotative method cites specific examples denoted by the term. Definition by analysis is the method through which a phenomenon is defined by breaking it into component parts, either by listing properties or subtypes (Ayer, 1971). The method of definition by synthesis is also called the relational method because it proceeds by showing how something relates to other things already known (Robinson, 1950).

Often what is taken for an analytic definition is really one form of synthetic definition. This conflation leads to several common errors of logic, some of which have affected criminological research and theory. Correlational

6

definition, for example, which is one substrategy of the synthetic method, defines a term by locating it in terms of its correlates (Hall, 1943:162–165), as when an "alligator" is defined as "a large reptile *associated with tropical rivers and marshes of the U.S. and China.*" Unfortunately, it is easy to confuse correlates with properties, thus mistaking what is really a synthetic definition for an analytic definition delineating intrinsic properties. Another form of the synthetic method is causal or genetic definition, such as when a "circle" is defined geometrically as "that figure produced by drawing a line in a plane with one end fixed" (Robinson, 1950:133). Still another is definition by description (Lewis, 1929:231), such as when "gold" is defined as "the most precious metal," giving not a chemical analysis but a socioeconomic description that locates the substance by its socioeconomic meaning. Much confusion has resulted from tangling these methods.

The Implicative Method

Such gang researchers as Moore (1978), Vigil (1988), Hagedorn and Macon (1989), and Horowitz (1990) tend to rely upon implicative definition. In some ways the implicative method can provide a richer sense of the meaning of a particular term, because actual use of a term illustrates dimensions of meaning in a way that a succinct definition may never match (Stebbing, 1933). As a method capable of portraying the phenomenon as a dynamic process in a way that cannot be captured by a list of defining characteristics, it is either the equivalent of the "process definition" advocated but not entirely clarified by such gang researchers as Hagedorn and Macon (1989) or an especially useful strategy for developing such definitions. But the richness of implicative defini- tion is bought at the price of precision, and the method tends to be unsatisfactory for purposes of standardizing definitions. Because implications convey differ- ent meanings to different people, latent connotations tend to escape theoretical debate and empirical research (Ayer, 1971).

To the extent that succinct definitions are provided, they tend to take their meaning from the general context. Thus, one of Hagedorn and Macon's (1989:5) shorter definitions describes the gang as a

> friendship group of adolescents who share common interests, with a more
> or less clearly defined territory, in which most of the members live. They
> are committed to defending one another, the territory, and the gang name
> in the status-setting fights that occur in school and on the street.

The meanings of such subsidiary terms as "friendship" are implied within the book-length context.

The implicative method of definition directs theory toward an emphasis on the way in which the gang fits as a natural part of the everyday life of a community. It encourages an *emic* methodology that tries to see through the eyes of the gang rather than an *etic* methodology that examines the gang through the lens provided by official data (Hagedorn and Macon, 1989). Theorists and researchers defining the gang through the implicative method are in greater danger of "going native" because anything begins to seem more acceptable when one defines it through the worldview of its adherents. By implying a definition through continued usage of the term within a conceptual framework rooted in a certain sociopolitical perspective, it also implies acceptance of this perspective. Thus, Hagedorn and Macon (1989) not only charge those using other methods with a "courthouse criminology" that sides with the authorities but also insist that only a researcher who already shares the worldview of the gang neighborhood is equipped to understand either it or the gang as defined within its context. In the same way, the implicative method leads Moore (1977) to advocate a "collaborative model" that relies on current or former gang members as informants and requires that the research design and all research instruments be developed in collaboration with them,

The contextuality through which implicative definition is constructed amounts to an elaborate set of tautologies, which are then reinforced by rules that define only those accepting them as qualified to study gangs. Such definitions serve to support the preexisting assumptions of those who share the perspective but fail to satisfy those who do not share it. By emphasizing local ambiance with empathic stress on such aspects as ethnic life, implicative definitions provide more literary texture than theoretical generalization, something that is both strength and weakness.

The Denotative Method

Knox's (1991) gang definition counters the implicative method with the denotative method, multiplying detailed example after detailed example, complete with constitutions and by-laws, to show what he means by a gang. Like the ostensive method, the denotative method seems at first glance to nail down meaning in a way that eliminates ambiguity. Logically, however, the method tends to be unsatisfactory as a strategy for defining gangs, in part because precise denotation of a term requires indication of all the particular examples to which it is applied or at least all of the classes to which it is applied (Ayer, 1971), and in part because the method works poorly for defining terms that are not primarily or exclusively denotative but highly connotative as well (Cooper, 1986).

The denotation/exemplification method is most effective for standardizing the definitions of terms carrying only a few denotations, such as the term *continent*, for which there are only seven examples, but there are thousands of different examples of gangs, with new ones appearing almost every day. Actually, presentation of examples in minute detail tends to favor the particular

8

over the general, and no matter how many examples are presented, there may always be others that are quite different. Further, "The term 'gang' is notoriously imprecise [in denotation], but there is no question that it has a generally pejorative connotation" (Destro, 1993:178). Indeed, in many ways *gang* seems to be not an indicative term (e.g., a denotative noun) at all but an expressive term (e.g., a connotative expletive) uttered either when certain emotions are evoked or in order to evoke such emotions in others.

Part of the problem in defining many terms is that the emotional dimension of meaning may be stronger than the indicative dimension. That is why the difficulty in developing a denotative definition of *gang* is so similar to that faced in developing denotative definitions of terms such as obscenity or pornography, which also seem to be primarily connotative (expressive) rather than denotative (indicative). *Art* can be distinguished from *pornography* in no objective sense but only by the emotional response it evokes. Unfortunately for denotative definition, this means that what serves as art for one person may serve as pornography for another. To the extent that the difference between a "friendship group" (Hagedorn and Macon, 1989) and a pathological "near-group" (Yablonsky, 1959) lies in the eye of the beholder, gang definition will continue to depend on the characteristics of the definer rather than the defined.

Definition by Analysis

Many have approached the problem of gang definition through the analytic method, and the sorts of properties they have elected to focus upon have led them in certain directions. Both research and theory have been heavily influenced by the resulting definitions. Used to good effect by such gang researchers as Knox (1991) and Jankowski (1991), the comparison-and-contrast substrategy of analytic definition is especially useful for moving from clear to distinct ideas (Ayer, 1971). By providing a series of examples with overlapping but differing properties, such as in sharpening gang definitions through comparison-and-contrast with phenomena such as the crew or posse, this substrategy solves some of the problems of the denotative method, especially through its capacity to clarify the meaning of many different but related terms simultaneously.

When definition by analysis of properties is used most precisely, it yields a listing of properties each of which is itself not only defined specifically but also weighted according to an analytic formula. The fact that criminal law requires specific charges demands that police-based definitions proceed by analysis of properties, and the general rule that individuals are not to be punished for what they are (e.g., gang members) but for what they do (e.g., gang activities) tends to require that such definitions focus on illegal behavior. Thus, it is not surprising that when Miller (1975) attempted to develop a standardized definition by constructing both a list of key properties and an ordinal weighting from lexical definitions supplied by multiple informants in five "gang-problem cities," the result included in rank order (1) violent or criminal behavior as a major activity, (2) group organization with functional role division and chain-of-command, (3) identifiable leadership, (4) continuing and recurrent interaction of members, and (5) identification with and/or claims of control over identifiable community territory.

Many other gang researchers also stress illegal behavior in their definitions. Gardner (1993:5), for example, emphasized that "the key element [analytic property] that distinguishes a gang from other organizations of young people is delinquency; its members regularly participate in activities that violate the law." Such definitions have had a profound impact on gang research, theory, and policy, with the result that "the sociological literature on gangs offers a number of theories, but a close look at each of these indicates that they are really theories about delinquency and not theories about gangs" (Jankowski, 1991:21). The apparently irrational tendency to move from almost total denial when gangs first appear to overreaction when they can no longer be ignored (Huff, 1990) is to some extent a logical consequence of the fact that by this definition they are not gangs until lawbreaking has become their primary characteristic, by which time drastic measures seem necessary.

Definitions including illegal activity as an intrinsic defining property, especially those in which it is defined as the dominating property, also tend to minimize any theoretical distinctions among gangs except for degree of delinquency. In fact, because illegal activity tends to be the only normative property included, properties such as friendship and common interests, which are usually considered positive qualities, are excluded from gang definitions. The results include (1) tacit acceptance of the law enforcement perspective (Morash, 1983) and (2) tautological inclusion by definition of the very delinquency that researchers and theorists may be trying to explain (Short, 1990).

The function of a definition is to explain the meaning of a term, and analytic definitions, by tearing it out of context, may actually deprive it of much of its meaning. If the only salient property of a "gang member," for example, is his or her membership in a gang, one result may be that any illegal activity involving such a person is defined as "gang related." This is the case in Los Angeles, where the definition produces twice as much "gang-related" violence as would be produced by the Chicago definition, which acknowledges that gang members may have motives unrelated to their gang membership (Maxson and Klein, 1990).

Further, analytic definitions, by assigning the same properties to all gangs, deflect theoretical and research interests away from gang variations. Some (e.g., Cloward and Ohlin, 1960; Jankowski, 1991; Knox, 1991; Taylor, 1990; Thrasher, 1927) have countered this by defining the gang entirely or partly in terms of constituent subtypes rather than constituent properties. By emphasizing the variety of different forms subsumed under the concept *gang*, this definitional substrategy tends to yield a looser definition than that obtained by analysis of properties, and the covering term *gang* becomes more of a linguistic convenience. One result is that theory often moves more in the direction of explaining how different subtypes develop than in the direction of generalizing about gang development, while research tends to examine the way in which different subtypes function rather than the way in which the gang functions *sui generis*.

Synthetic Definition

While analytic definition defines by reduction to constituents, the synthetic method defines by locating a phenomenon in a larger and presumably better-understood context. Thus, the earliest gang definition in criminology (Puffer, 1912:7) defined the gang as "for the boy one of the three primary social groups . . . [which include] the family, the neighborhood, and the play group, but for the normal boy the play group is the gang," further defining all three primary groups as "restrictive human groupings, formed like flock and pack and hive." Successful synthetic definitions open fruitful new avenues for theory and research, while misplaced synthetic definitions direct both into blind alleys. Puffer's definition incorporated the assumption that primary groups in general and the gang in particular were outmoded evolutionary remnants and that ganging was a stage through which boys recapitulated the evolution of their species, emerging from that primitive state as they matured.

Although they are much less laden with biological assumptions, most gang definitions agree in treating the gang as one type of group and are therefore in part synthetic definitions. Short (1990:239), for example, defines it as "a group whose members meet together with some regularity over time, on the basis of group-defined criteria of membership and group-determined organizational structure." This method of definition has had a profound effect upon research and theory from the days of Puffer (1912) through the work of Short and Strodbeck (1965) to Goldstein's (1991) recent work approaching gangs through the group dynamics tradition. Yet, synthetic definitions treating the gang as a group are also somewhat tautological, assuming what ought to be researched and ignoring the data suggesting that gang organization ranges across a considerable continuum.

Yablonsky's (1959) synthetic definition located the gang as a "near-group" midway between the stable, cohesive, and relatively permanent group with fixed membership and the spontaneous, chaotic, temporary mob with shifting membership. Horowitz's (1983) differentiation of "gangs," "groups" and "pseudogroups" provides a more recent example of an effort to define the gang by comparison-and-contrast to organizational types that are similar in some ways but different in other respects. Most gang researchers

11

tend to characterize them as "loosely organized" (Spergel, 1989:2) or "characteristically unstable as a form of association and organization" (Short, 1974: 16). Klein and Maxson (1989:100) capture some of this in their description of the gang as a "shifting, elusive target, permeable and elastic, not a cohesive force but a spongelike resilience," and the data suggest that gangs tend to slide back-and-forth along an organizational continuum. At some point, a "pre-gang" (Knox, 1989) becomes a gang, but it may slide back to "pre-gang," perhaps even dissolving, or it may become increasingly stable, cohesive, and permanent, crossing the definitional boundary from "gang" to "organized crime," as Taylor (1990) has characterized the El Rukns in Chicago.

Process definitions capture some of these dynamics, but they remain vague, while analytic typologies tend to reify the types and deflect attention from the organizational fluidity of gangs. Unfortunately, efforts at synthetic typologies may also fail because of this same fluidity. When Miller (1980), frustrated with earlier efforts to construct a standardized definition through the analytic method he had been following implicitly to that point, turned toward a synthetic method that located three types of "gangs" within a larger typology of 20 different "law-violating youth groups," the definition proved unworkable for police departments surveyed, most of which could not distinguish the gang subtypes from the other 17 subtypes (Needle and Stapleton, 1983).

That part of Thrasher's (1927:46) influential definition that terms the gang an "interstitial group" reflects the synthetic method both by defining the gang as a group and by locating it in a transitional phase between childhood and adulthood and a transitional zone between central business district and more stable residential areas. His definition was motivated in part by an urge to combat theorists such as Puffer (1912), but it too led in certain directions, in this case toward concentration on the social disorganization that was presumed to characterize interstitial areas and provide a natural breeding ground for both gangs and delinquency. Some later theorists such as Cohen (1955), Bloch and Niederhoffer (1958), and Miller (1958), along with researchers such as Yablonsky (1959), Spergel (1964), and Miller (1975), tended to treat the relationship as one in which the milieu produced the gang, which was characterized as having delinquent properties. Others tended to see the milieu as less disorganized and to focus upon the way in which the gang fit into the community structure (Suttles, 1968; Whyte, 1943), treating gang involvement in illegal activity as another part of the scene but not as the major focus of the gang. Still others (Hagedorn and Macon, 1989; Horowitz, 1983; Moore, 1978; Sullivan, 1989; Vigil, 1988) have minimized causal relationships between gangs and illegality, explaining any association as the consequence of a common source—long-term poverty. Vigil's (1988) explanation of barrio gangs in terms of "multiple marginality" manifesting itself in "choloization" (a term originally meaning a racial or cultural marginal between Indian and colonial Spanish ways of life but broadened to cover many aspects of sociocultural interstitiality), shows the impact of Thrasher's (1927) synthetic definition on gang theory even after 60 years.

Correlational Synthetic Definitions. Much of the confusion over gang definition seems to be the result of conflating correlates with intrinsic, analytic properties. This is most obvious in definitions treating illegal activity as an intrinsic property of the gang, because they tend to produce the theories based on the assumption that the forces leading to gang formation—whether the instinctive need to run in a pack (Puffer, 1912), status frustration (Cohen, 1955), or the lack of structured rites of passage (Bloch and Niederhoffer, 1958)—are the same as those leading to delinquency. Other correlates that have been confused with properties include adolescent male membership, lower socioeconomic status, urban areas, territoriality, violence, and drug dealing.

Gang definitions (Huff, 1990; Klein, 1971; Miller, 1975) frequently use the terms *adolescent* or *youth*: Puffer (1912) specified the early teens; Thrasher (1927) added somewhat older members; and Miller (1975), Vigil (1988), and Goldstein (1991) specified age ranges of 10–22, 13–25, and 9–30, respectively. Curry et al. (1994) report that the modal age of gang members has increased considerably, from about 16 to over 19 with some cities estimating that 80 percent of those involved in gangs are adults over age 18. If "adolescence" is used as it once was to refer to the teen years from 13 to 19, it is clearly not to be regarded as an intrinsic property of the gang. Only if the term is used loosely to refer to that interstitial age period between childhood and maturity, and is regarded as beginning earlier and ending later than was once the case, is it still possible to defend a position defining adolescence as an analytic property of the gang.

Puffer (1912), who defined early adolescent, male membership as an intrinsic property of the gang, could only conclude that boys were manifesting a primordial instinct that disappeared in later adolescence. Noting the increasing numbers of young adult "adolescents," and impressed with the trend toward drug dealing and violence, Goldstein (1991), who seems to see adolescence as more of a correlate than a defining property, is led to treat age as a dependent variable with respect to the former and an independent variable with respect to the latter. He hypothesizes that gangs now retain older members primarily because of a shift to drug-dealing activity, with the increasing lethal violence then resulting from the tendency of these older "youth" to use more sophisticated weapons. Gang researchers such as Hagedorn and Macon (1989) do not define violence or drug dealing as either intrinsic properties or significant correlates, define age as more of a correlate than a property, and trace the shift toward older membership to economic changes that have eliminated jobs for the young adults who would once have aged-out of the gang.

Troublesome collectivities of youth have always been much more likely to be defined as gangs if they were of lower socioeconomic status and happen to be located in large cities (Bursik and Grasmick, 1992; Huff, 1990; Vigil, 1988). Yet similar activity has existed for many years among middle-class youth and in rural areas, suburbs, and small towns (Muchlbauer and Dodder, 1983; Salisbury, 1958: Vigil, 1988). Since Puffer (1912) and Thrasher (1927), definitions have focused on males manifesting territoriality, but considerable evidence shows that females are now frequently involved in these activities and that territoriality is less important and differently defined (Campbell, 1984; Vigil, 1988).

On the other hand, some (Curry et al., 1994; Klein and Maxson, 1989) have cited evidence indicating that Yablonsky's (1959) stress on violence may be more appropriate to definitions today than when it was first proposed in the 1950s. Others (Taylor, 1990) have insisted that the same is true of drug dealing, which was not a part of early definitions at all. Logic suggests that socioeconomic status, urban setting, adolescent male membership, territoriality, violence, and drug dealing should not be included as properties defining a gang, although definitions might cite these characteristics as correlates. When correlates are mistaken for properties, gang definitions tend to include many incorrect assumptions. Definitions treating both violence and illegal activity as intrinsic properties of the gang, for example, led logically to the assumption that the association between an increase in cocaine dealing and growing violence in Los Angeles could be traced to gangs, assuming that when gangs extended their illegal activity into the cocaine trade, they brought their violence with them. The fact that the only research into the question proved this assumption wrong (Klein et al., 1988) emphasizes once again the need for greater attention to the logic of definition.

Causal Synthetic Definitions. Causal definition was once more common in gang research than it is today. Unfortunately, however, the residual effects have lingered, and the problem here is even more serious than with correlational definition. Not only does causal definition run the risk of confusing correlations with properties, but it falls further into tautology by treating as logically genetic, a priori characteristics what are really hypotheses.

Puffer's (1912:7) definition of the gang as "one of the three primary social groups . . . formed like pack and flock and hive" went on to add, *"in response to deep-seated but unconscious needs"* (emphasis added), thus initiating the tradition of causal definitions. Thrasher (1927) devoted considerable effort to countering these Darwinian assumptions, but that part of his classic definition terming the gang a group that is "first formed spontaneously, and then integrated through conflict" (p. 46) represents another causal definition. Thirty years later, Miller's (1958) first gang definition incorporated a teleological hypothesis, defining the gang as "a stable and solitary primary group *preparing the young male for an adult role in lower-class society"*

14

(emphasis added). Although correlational definitions are acceptable and can be useful if clarified, causal definitions should be confined to axiomatic systems such as geometry, where tautology is proof of consistency rather than a source of error, and should be strictly avoided in any field wishing to develop through empirical research (Robinson, 1950).

Synthetic Definitions by Description. Definitions by description are pragmatic definitions that seek not intrinsic properties, correlates, or causes but a means of defining in terms of consequences (Bentley and Dewey, 1947). Working in this tradition, labeling theory stressed that "deviance" is not defined by any inherent properties of the phenomenon but by social reactions to it. The tradition maintains that the "definition of the situation" is more important than its intrinsic properties because, "if men define situations as real, they are real in their consequences" (Thomas and Thomas, 1928:572).

Major parts of Sarnecki's (1985:11) definition of the gang as a "group of individuals *who are linked together because the police suspected them of committing crimes together"* (emphasis added) represent synthetic definition by description, as do other definitions (Cartwright, 1975:4) which indicate that the gang is an "interstitial and integrated group of persons who meet face-to-face regularly *and whose existence and activities as a group are considered an actual or potential threat to the prevailing social order"* (emphasis added). Each begins by defining the gang as a group but focuses its definition on the negative reactions.

The same is true of those parts of Klein's (1971:1428) influential definition of the gang as "any denotable adolescent group of youngsters who (a) are *generally perceived as a distinct aggregation* by others in their neighborhood, (b) *recognize themselves* as a denotable group (almost invariably with a group name), and (c) have been involved in a sufficient number of delinquent incidents to call forth a *consistent negative response from neighborhood residents and/or law enforcement agencies"* (emphasis added). Klein (1971:1428) notes that, "this is not meant as a definitive denotation of the label, gang, [but] is merely designed to say that a group is a gang when it is reacted to as a distinctly anti-social group of genuine concern and accepts itself as a group apart." Despite all disclaimers, however, there has been a persistent tendency to take such synthetic definition for analysis of intrinsic properties. That part of Klein's (1971:1428) definition referring to "a sufficient number of delinquent incidents" seems to be defining a property of the gang, partly because "delinquent incidents" are being taken for granted as a property, and partly because it is easy to overlook the fact that the term "sufficient" is being defined by social reactions. To say that the delinquent incidents were sufficient to call forth consistent negative reactions from either the neighborhood or the police is to imply that they were serious and prevalent.

That part of Klein's (1971:1428) disclaimer that points out that his definition is "not meant as a definitive denotation" has been largely ignored and the definition has been treated as if substantial delinquent activity were in fact an intrinsic property of the gang. Because it tends to shift the emphasis from the way in which the gang fits into its milieu toward a focus on negative characteristics arousing community opposition, it deflects attention from the data showing that communities are usually ambivalent about their gangs, partly because the members are their children, partly because either they or their friends may have once been gang members themselves, and partly because the gangs do offer recreation, protection, and other services. The tendency to mistake synthetic definition by description for analysis of properties is the real source of Hagedorn and Macon's (1989) complaint that definitions such as Klein's (1971:1428) somehow tend to make the basic question one having to do with why its members are delinquent rather than whether they are delinquent. Such problems make it clear that concern for the logic of definition is not a matter of hairsplitting among those interested in the philosophy of science but an issue vital to progress in gang research, theory, and public policy.

Conclusion

Even when older definitions have proved acceptable, new definitions often become necessary, either because of changes in the phenomenon itself or changes in the purposes for which definition is required. As Bridgeman (1928) pointed out in his well-known discussion of "operational definitions, any research definition is likely to require periodic respecification, partly because it will tend to include some false implications that arose as a consequence of the serendipitous process that produced it. Definitions tend to be based on those aspects of the phenomena in question that were most visible and most salient at the time. As the relative visibility of various phenomenal features changes with research progress, and the salience of these various features shifts with new perspectives and purposes, redefinition often becomes necessary.

Each of the methods of definition examined above has its strengths and weaknesses. The analytic method is best for defining intrinsic features, and the synthetic method is best for locating within a framework of cumulative knowledge. The implicative method adds breadth and depth, while the denotative method sharpens meaning by specific examples. Avoiding the causal method entirely, the best definitions tend to combine the remaining methods according to the most powerful heuristic rules available.

Thrasher's (1927:46) definition undoubtedly remains so influential in part because he complemented his synthetic method with the analytic method, terming the gang not only an "interstitial group" but specifying that it was characterized by properties such as "meeting face-to-face, milling, moving through space as a unit, conflict, and planning," then subsuming these properties under the framework of "collective behavior" and adding the further analytic properties of "tradition, unreflective internal structure, espirit de corps, solidarity, morale, group awareness, and attachment to a local territory." Klein's (1971:1428) widely used definition combines reference to the denotative and synthetic method in his definition of the gang as "any denotative group of youngsters" while stressing synthetic definition by description, and Miller (1975, 1980) was driven to complement his earlier analytic method (Miller, 1975) with the synthetic method (Miller, 1980). Unfortunately, however, few if any gang researchers and theorists have been sufficiently conscious of their own definitional strategies, with the result that their definitions have carried too many latent connotations, treated correlates or consequences as properties or causes, or contributed to similar errors of logic. It is crucial that definitions combining different methods make it clear whether they are advancing lexical or stipulative definitions and whether defining characteristics are considered properties, correlates, or consequences.

One methodological key lies in discovering and clarifying the tacit rules used for determining which of the innumerable features of a particular phenomenon are most salient for definitional purposes. Although a familiar strategy for establishing such rules is operational definition itself, which defines a particular phenomenon entirely in terms of whatever operational rules are used to measure it (Bridgeman, 1928), there are more general strategies. One of these is *formalism*. The strength of formalism lies in its focus upon the recurring *forms* or patterns of social life rather than upon the changing *content*, its "preponderance of the logical over the normative" (Wolff, 1964:xviii).

As a general rule, the logic of definition suggests that gang definitions would do better to focus upon the abstract, formal characteristics of the phenomenon rather than connotative, normative content. For reasons such as those already outlined, it is preferable that illegal activity not be part of the definition unless clearly specified as a correlate rather than a property. The general use of the term suggests that the essence of the gang lies in the weakening of conventional norms rather than a commitment to their opposite. Legal definitions can always add a further term to specify the more extreme, *delinquent gang*. A normatively neutral definition also focuses attention on the distinction between such similar collectivities as the gang and the crew, the latter sharing many properties, correlates, and consequences with the former but differing in that it is committed to crime and *is* organized for that purpose.

Among all the possible formal approaches to gang definition, one can be taken for illustrative purposes. One formal approach to gang definition that appeals to the logic of definition is the abstract view of the gang as combining a view of it as a social system (synthetic method) with a stress on its most salient organizational properties (analytic method). Heuristic rules for determining salience might yield something like the following: The gang is a spontaneous, semisecret, interstitial, integrated but mutable social system whose members share common interests and that functions with relatively little regard for legality but regulates interaction among its members and features a leadership structure with processes of organizational maintenance and membership services and adaptive mechanisms for dealing with other significant social systems in its environment. If the differences between properties, correlatives and consequences are stressed, such an illustrative definition might be supplemented with a statement of correlates indicating that it is traditionally but not exclusively male and territorial and is often associated with lower-class, urban areas. Descriptive consequences including perceived antisocial behavior calling forth negative reactions from significant segments of society should add further specification, which could be further supplemented with a range of examples and used within a larger context illustrating this meaning more fully.

The first part of this definition is somewhat similar to Jankowski's (1991). Like Arnold's (1966) definition, it focuses on abstract system properties. To a much greater extent than either of these, however, it is guided by the logical distinctions between the various methods of defamation, as well as rules as to the salience of various systemic dimensions, or what has been termed the "developmental logic of social systems" (Teune and Mlinar, 1978: 16). Those heuristic, methodological rules focus greater attention, for example, on *adaptation* and *accommodation* processes (Bailey, 1994; Colomy, 1992), the first involving mutual adjustments with other key social systems within the external environment, and the second with management of tensions and disruptions arising internally.

Space limitations preclude a more elaborate effort at a defensible definition of *gang*. Here we have tried only to clear the ground somewhat. We suggest that gang research and theory might make more consistent progress through greater attention to the logic of definition. It is important that researchers and theorists become increasingly aware of the differences among their implicit methodological approaches to definition so as to avoid at least the more obvious sources of confusion. Our hope is to have contributed in some small part to clarification of the problems.

References

Arnold, William R. (1966). The concept of the gang. *The Sociological Quarterly* 7: 59–75.

Ayer, A.J. (1971). *Language, Truth and Logic*. 2d ed. New York: Pelican.

Bailey, Kenneth D. (1994). *Sociology and the New Systems Theory: Toward a Theoretical Synthesis*. Albany: State University of New York Press.

Baker, G. P. and P.M.S. Hacker. (1984). *Language, Sense and Nonsense*. Oxford: Basil Blackwell.

Bentley, Arthur F. and John Dewey. (1947). Definition. *The Journal of Philosophy* 34:281–306.

Bloch, Herbert A. and Arthur Niederhoffer. (1958). *The Gang: A Study in Adolescent Behavior*. New York: Philosophical Library.

Bridgeman, P.W. (1928). *The Logic of Modern Physics*. New York: Macmillan.

Bursik, Robert J., Jr. and Harold G. Grasmick. (1992). *Neighborhoods and Crime: The Dimensions of Effective Community Control*. New York: Free Press.

Bynum, Jack E. and William E. Thompson. (1992). *Juvenile Delinquency: A Sociological Approach*. Boston: Allyn & Bacon.

Campbell, Anne. (1984). *The Girls in the Gang: A Report from New York City*. New York: Basil Blackwell.

Cartwright, Desmond, Barbara Tomson and Hersey Schwartz. (1975). *Gang Delinquency*. Monterey, CA: Brooks/Cole.

Cloward, Richard A. and Lloyd E. Ohlin. (1960). *Delinquency and Opportunity*. New York: Free Press.

Cohen, Albert. (1955). *Delinquent Boys: The Culture of the Gang*. Glencoe, IL: Free Press.

Colomy, Paul. (1992). *The Dynamics of Social Systems*. Newbury Park, CA: Sage.

Conly, Catherine H. (1993). *Street Gangs: Current Knowledge and Strategies*. Washington, DC: National Institute of Justice.

Cooper, David E. (1986). *Metaphor*. Oxford: Basil Blackwell.

Curry, G. David and Irving Spergel. (1988). Gang homicide, delinquency and community. *Criminology* 26:381–405.

Curry, G. David, Richard A. Ball, and Robert J. Fox. (1994). Final Report: National Assessment of Law Enforcement Anti-Gang Information Resources. Washington, DC: National Institute of Justice.

Destro, Robert A. (1993). Gangs and civil rights. In Scott Cummings and Daniel J. Monti (eds.), *Gangs: The Origin and Impact of Contemporary Young Gangs in the United States*. Albany: State University of New York Press.

Fagan, Jeffrey. (1989). The social organization of drug use and drug dealing among urban gangs. *Criminology* 27:633–669.

Gardner, Sandra. (1993). *Street Gangs*. New York: Franklin Watts.

Goldstein, Arnold P. (1991). *Delinquent Gangs*. Champaign, IL: Research Press.

Hagedorn, John and Perry Macon. (1989). *People and Folks*. Chicago: Lakeview Press.

Harney, Maurita J. (1984). *Intentionality, Sense and the Mind*. Boston: Martinus Nijhoff.

Horowitz, Ruth. (1983). *Honor and the American Dream: Culture and Identity in a Chicano Community*. New Brunswick, NJ: Rutgers University Press.

———. (1990). Sociological perspectives on gangs: Conflicting definitions and concepts. In C. Ronald Huff (ed.), *Gangs in America*. Newbury Park, CA: Sage.

Huff, C. Ronald (ed.). (1990). *Gangs in America*. Newbury Park, CA: Sage.

Jankowski, Martin Sanchez. (1991). *Islands in the Street: Gangs in American Life*. Berkeley: University of California Press.

Klein, Malcolm W. (1971). *Street Gangs and Street Workers*. Englewood Cliffs, NJ: Prentice Hall.

Klein, Malcolm W. and Cheryl L. Maxson. (1989). Street gang violence. In Neil A. Weiner and Marvin E. Wolfgang (eds.), *Violent Crime, Violent Criminals*. Newbury Park, CA: Sage.

Klein, Malcolm W., Cheryl L. Maxson, and Larry Cunningham. (1988). *Gang Involve-*

ment in Cocaine "Rock" Trafficking. Final Report for National Institute of Justice. Los Angeles: University of Southern California.

Knox, George. (1991). *An Introduction to Gangs*. Berrien Springs, MI: Vande Vere.

Lewis, C.I. (1929). *Mind and the World Order*. New York: Scribner.

Makau, Josina M. (1990). *Reasoning and Communication*. Belmont, CA: Wadsworth.

Maxson, Cheryl L. and Malcolm Klein. (1990). Defining and measuring gang violence. In C. Ronald Huff (ed.), *Gangs in America*. Newbury Park, CA: Sage.

Miller, Walter B. (1958). Lower class culture as a generating milieu of gang delinquency. *Journal of Social Issues* 14:519–529.

_____. (1975). *Violence by Youth Gangs and Youth Groups as a Crime Problem in Major American Cities*. Washington, DC: National Institute for Juvenile Justice and Delinquency Prevention.

_____. (1980). Gangs, groups, and serious youth crime. In David Schicor and Delos H. Kelly (eds.), *Critical Issues in Juvenile Delinquency*. Lexington, Mass: D.C. Heath.

Moore, Joan. W. (1977). The Chicano Pinto research project: A case in collaboration. *Journal of Social Issues* 33:144–158.

_____. (1978). *Homeboys: Gangs, Drugs, and Prisons in the Barrios of Los Angeles*. Philadelphia: Temple University Press.

_____. (1993). Gangs, drugs, and violence. In Scott Cummings and Daniel J. Monti (eds.), *Gangs: The Origins and Impact of Contemporary Youth Gangs in the United States*. Albany: State University of New York Press.

Morash, Merry. (1983). Gangs, groups and delinquency. *British Journal of Criminology*, 23:309–331.

Muehlbauer, Gene and Laura Dodder. (1983). *The Losers: Gang Delinquency in an American Suburb*. New York: Praeger.

National Institute of Justice. (1992). National Institute of Justice Conference on Action Plan Development for the Gangs Initiative. *Summary of Proceedings*. Washington, DC: National Institute of Justice.

Needle, Jerome and W. Stapleton. (1983). *Police Handling of Juvenile Gangs*. Washington, DC: National Institute for Juvenile Justice and Delinquency Prevention.

Puffer, J. Adams. (1912). *The Boy and His Gang*. Boston: Houghton Mifflin.

Quine, W. V. (1970). *Philosophy of Logic*. Englewood Cliffs, NJ: Prentice Hall.

Robinson, Richard. (1950). *Definition*. Oxford: Clarendon.

Salisbury, Harrison. (1958). *The Shook-Up Generation*. New York: Harper.

Sarnecki, John. (1985). *Delinquent Networks*. Stockholm: Swedish National Council.

Seigel, Larry J. and Joseph J. Senna. (1994). *Juvenile Delinquency*. St. Paul, MN: West.

Short, James F. (1974). Youth gangs and society. Micro- and macrosociological process. *The Sociological Quarterly* 15: 3–19.

_____. (1990). New wine in old bottles? In C. Ronald Huff (ed.), *Gangs in America*. Newbury Park, CA: Sage.

Short, James F. and Fred L. Strodbeck. (1965). *Group Process and Gang Delinquency*. Chicago: University of Chicago Press.

Spergel, Irving. (1964). *Racketville, Slumtown, Haulburg*. Chicago: University of Chicago Press.

_____. (1989). *Youth Gangs: Problems and Response*. Chicago: University of Chicago School of Social Service Administration.

Spergel, Irving, G. David Curry, R.A. Ross, and Ron L. Chance. (1990). *Survey of Gang Problems in 45 Cities*. Chicago: School of Social Service Administration, University of Chicago.

Stebbing, L.S. (1933). *A Modern Introduction to Logic*. 2d ed. London: Methuen.

Sullivan, Mercer. (1989). *Getting Paid: Youth Crime and Work in the Inner City*. Ithaca, NY: Cornell University Press.

Suttles, Gerald D. (1968). *The Social Order of the Slum: Ethnicity and Territory in the Inner City*. Chicago: University of Chicago Press.

Taylor, Carl S. (1990). *Dangerous Society*. East Lansing: Michigan State University Press.

Teune, Henry and Zdravko Mlinar. (1978). *The Developmental Logic of Social Systems*. Beverly Hills, CA: Sage.

Thomas, W.I. and Dorothy Swaine Thomas (1928). *The Child in America: Behavior Problems and Programs*. New York: Knopf.

Thrasher, Frederic. (1927). *The Gang*. Chicago: University of Chicago Press.

Vigil, J. Diego. (1988). *Barrio Gangs: Street Life and Identity in Southern California*. Austin: University of Texas Press.

Whyte, Willaim F. (1943). *Street Corner Society*. Chicago: University of Chicago Press.

Wolff, Kurt H. (1964). *The Sociology of George Simmel*. New York: Free Press.

Yablonsky, Lewis. (1959). The delinquent gang as a near-group. *Social Problems* 7: 108–117.

2

The Definition and Measurement of "Gang Status": Policy Implications for Juvenile Justice

L. Thomas Winfree, Jr., Kathy Fuller, Teresa Vigil, and G. Larry Mays

Recently the general public's perception of youth gang problems has become what best can be described as a phobia. Although youth gangs are not a unique aspect of contemporary American society, their prevalence in the late-1980s and early-1990s has spurred public interest and concern. Extensive media coverage and apparent increase in both gang sophistication and violence have led the public to perceive youth collectivities as major threats to public safety and order.

Historically, gang research has followed an unusual, almost schizophrenic, path. Considerable gang research was conducted in the United States from the 1920s (e.g., Bogardus, 1926; Thrasher, 1927) through the 1950s (e.g., Cohen, 1955; Miller, 1958), and this research was influential in shaping many of the early theories on delinquent behavior. However, from the late-1960s until the mid-1980s gang research all but disappeared from the criminology literature. This dearth of research led Bookin-Weiner and Horowitz (1983) to examine the question of whether we were facing the "end of the gang." Their conclusion was that gangs had not disappeared, research focus simply had shifted away from them.

As a result of the shifting political ideologies predicted by Bookin-Weiner and Horowitz (1983) and the recent "re-emergence" of gangs in the United States, public concern about the problem has led to calls for law enforcement officials to "do something." Gang research and gang intervention strategies seem to be especially compelling at this point for several reasons: (a) the emergence of youth gangs in smaller and medium sized communities, (b) the

Reprinted with permission from *Juvenile & Family Court Journal*, Vol. 43, No. 1 (1992): 29–38.

increased diversity of gang composition, (c) the increased sophistication in weaponry and the greatly elevated levels of violence associated with some gangs, and (d) the controversy surrounding the role of gangs in drug trafficking and the associated violence (Huff, 1990). The "gang problem," however, is not simply a police or policy-makers' problem, but a societal problem. While the police and policy-makers are part of the solution, it is important for society to recognize that the answers they demand will have to come from their own communities.

This article is designed to supplement our still-expanding knowledge base on gangs and recent gang activity. This effort was aimed at an at-risk population of junior and senior high school students in the ninth and eleventh grades. The population of interest is situated in a county along the border between the United States and Mexico, an area which experiences a great deal of immigration (both legal and illegal).

Before going further, however, it is important to establish a few definitional ground rules. Of particular interest will be the definitions of "gang," "gang members," and "gang behavior."

Defining Gangs and Gang Activity

One of the most difficult tasks for gang researchers is agreeing on acceptable definitions. Even with the most basic concept, such as "gang," there can be disagreement over meanings. For example, the Los Angeles Police Department (1988:3) defines a criminal street gang as "a group of persons working to an unlawful or antisocial end." Klein (1971:111) defined a gang as "any denotable adolescent group of youngsters who (a) are generally perceived as a distinct aggregation by others in the neighborhood, (b) recognize themselves as a denotable group (almost invariably with a group name), and (c) have been involved in a sufficient number of delinquent incidents to call forth a consistent negative response from neighborhood residents and/or law enforcement agencies." Spergel (1990:181) adds further that "The term 'youth gang' is generally used here to refer to groups and behaviors that represent an important subset of delinquent and sometimes criminal groups and their behaviors."

Unlike many other social scientists who have searched for gang definitions, Horowitz (1990) suggested that having a preconceived definition may not be necessary and, indeed, may be undesirable. She concludes that "restricting the boundaries of what constitutes a gang may limit the types of questions asked, and looking for invariant properties and generating highly abstract categories to explain social experiences may not be as useful as many sociologists assume" (Horowitz, 1990:42).

Not only are gangs and gang members difficult to define, but so are "gang behaviors" or "gang-related offenses." Maxson and Klein (1990) struggle with this issue in looking at reports of gang-related offenses in Los Angeles and Chicago. They point out the fact that non-gang members can commit "gang crimes," and that gang members could commit "non-gang crimes" (i.e., offenses not associated with or furthering gang goals and objectives).

Miller (1990:265–66) suggests that five features of gangs and gang behaviors are particularly salient: (1) gang activity by locality varies over time, (2) in some communities (for whatever reasons) gang activities are at low levels or are totally absent, (3) most gang members are relatively young, (4) gangs provide positive functions for youths involved in them, and (5) most gang activity is not visible.

To deal with the definitional problems in the present research, we have chosen to steer a middle course. On the one hand, the survey instrument utilized allowed youngsters to designate themselves as gang members. On the other hand, we also employed an alternative, more restrictive definition— one that somewhat comports with Klein's (1971)—which mandates that gang members must be "ranked in" or have to undergo certain initiation rites, and that they must manifest some outward symbols of gang membership (such as "colors," tattoos, or handsigns). In terms of gang-related activity, we focus on those types of offenses *traditionally* associated with gangs: painting graffiti, engaging in group (i.e., gang) fights, and shooting at someone (see, e.g., New Mexico Governor's Organized Crime Prevention Commission, 1991). While these definitional approaches may be unsatisfying to some, they at least provide a starting point for the analysis in this study.

Research Methods

Sample

Early in March 1991, two independent public school districts in southern New Mexico were approached about a survey of gang-related activities. After several months of discussion, four schools in the two districts, two junior high schools and two high schools, agreed to participate in the proposed survey. Students in the ninth and eleventh grades were targeted for the study to provide the necessary stratification by grade level. From lists provided by both school districts a total of 590 names were randomly selected, with each school district contributing to the sample proportionate to its total number of students. Within each school males were overselected in a ratio of at least three to one; however, the sample included the names of 140 females.

During the month of April 1991, questionnaires were distributed by members of the research team in a separate area in the school to which the students were called from their classrooms. Nearly four-hundred students whose names were provided to the schools showed up to participate in the study. The general purpose of the study was explained, and students were offered the opportunity to withdraw from the study; only three students elected not to complete a questionnaire. A total of eighteen questionnaires was eliminated from consideration owing to incompleteness of responses or the nonresponsiveness of the students; another eighty-one students selected for the sample (roughly 15% of the total) were absent on the administration day. The remaining 373 completed questionnaires represented 74 percent of the students selected for the sample who were in attendance on the administration day.

Two-thirds of the sample (235 youths) attended the more rural schools, which was nearly identical to the population parameter. The ratio of males to females was 2.7 to 1, only slightly lower than called for by the sampling protocol. Indeed, there were 103 females and 270 males in the sample. The sample was heavily (75.3%) Hispanic. Among the remaining students there were but a few African- and Asian-American, with Anglos accounting for eighty-five of the remaining ninety-two students. Again, given the oversampling of the county schools, these statistics suggest a fairly representative sample on the key demographic variables.

Variables

Involvement in Gangs. We employed two methods of defining "gang involvement." The first method—the "self-definition"—divided the sample into three groups, each one with successively more activity in gangs. First, students who responded positively to a question about whether they had ever been interested in joining a gang were classified as "wannabes." Second, students who indicated that they had at sometime been gang members but were no longer involved with the gang were defined as "former gang members." Third, those individuals who indicated continued membership in a gang were accorded "active member" status. By the self-definition method, the following levels of gang involvement were observed: sixty-eight wannabes (lowest involvement), forty-five former gang members, and fifty-six current gang members (highest involvement).

The second definition was more restrictive. In this case active and former gang members were defined first. In both cases, gang membership was determined by a series of questions that addressed (a) initiation rites and (b) gang symbols. A person was considered to be, or have been, a gang member only if he or she was initiated into the group and indicated that the gang endorsed one or more external symbols of membership, including the following: "colors," tattoo(s), or handsigns. Active gang members were distinguished from former gang members in terms of a positive response to the question of current gang status. All other members of the sample who indicated that they had considered joining a gang at some time or belonged to a gang did not share the requisite characteristics were considered wannabes. By this more restrictive definitional process, the following levels of gang involvement were observed: 116 wannabes (lowest involvement), eighteen former gang members, and thirty-one active gang members (highest involvement).

Self-Reported Delinquency. The questionnaire included twenty-two items describing criminal events. The students could indicate whether they had engaged in these acts since grade school (0 = did not report committing the act; 1 = committed the act at least once since grade school). Given the focus of the study, we selected the three "offenses" that are frequently described in the literature as interpersonal, "gang-related" offenses, recognizing that they are not the exclusive domain of gang members. That is, students were asked how often they had: (1) taken part in a fight involving more than two people where only fists were used, (2) taken part in a fight involving more than two people where weapons other than fists were used, and (3) ever shot at someone because they were told to by someone else. By summing the responses to the three items, we created an index of gang-related crime. This index ranged from 0 (engaged in none of the acts) to 3 (engaged in all three at least once).

Personal-Biographical Characteristics. Among the 169 students who indicated some gang involvement or aspirations, the ratio of males to females was nearly identical to that for the sample as a whole: males accounted for 77.5 percent of the gang subsample and 72.4 percent of the sample. Gang activity is generally considered an urban phenomenon. In the border southwest, however, gangs have existed in rural and urban areas for decades, particularly ethnic-Hispanic gangs. Again, rural students were oversampled—63.4 percent of the sample and 70.4 percent of the subsample—to provide sufficient numbers for an adequate analysis. For similar reasons, we were not surprised to find that the gang-involved subsample consisted of 81.1 percent Hispanic Americans.

We were interested in discerning the impact of a series of school—and family—based variables on gang involvement, however it was defined, and self-reported criminal activity. Only looking at those sample members with gang involvement and aspirations resulted in a subsample that was even more heavily weighted toward the ninth grade. That is, six in ten members of the sample were in the ninth grade, compared to seven in ten members of the gang-involved subsample. We find this statistic to be consistent with previous research on gangs: gang members either "age out" of their interest in and involvement with gangs or they fail/drop out of school. Only one-quarter of the subsample reported no time spent per day studying for school; equal numbers of students (63) reported spending one or two hours a day studying as reported studying three or more hours. These breakdowns were not significantly different from the sample as a whole. The grade distribution for the subsample was not significantly different from the total sample. Nearly one-half of the subsample reported mostly C grades; one in three indicated that they received mostly B grades; mostly A or mostly D grades were the minority, being reported, respectively, by 8.3 percent and 13 percent of the subsample.

Findings

Who's in the Gangs? One Question, Two Answers?

We were interested in the extent to which altering the definition of gang alters our ability to predict the level of criminal involvement reported by those youth who, by self-admission, are more than a little interested in gangs and gang activity. As a consequence, we employed two operational definitions of gang memberships. Table 2.1 presents a cross-tabular analysis of gang involvement defined two ways, by seven student personal-biographic characteristics. As previously noted, using the more restrictive definition clearly reduces the number of former and active gang members, who for analytic purposes, were accorded the status of wannabes. Place of residence was not significantly related to self-defined gang membership. That is, irrespective of where they lived, roughly equal percentages of the gang-oriented youth were classified as wannabes, former gang members or active members. However, the more restrictive definition yielded a different picture by place of residence: there were significantly more former and active gang members in the city than in the county.

Males are far more likely to report being gang members or to be so classified by the more restrictive definition. However, it is interesting to observe that once the requirement that the youth be initiated into the gang and that symbols of involvement be included in the definition, only about 8 percent of the females qualify as active gang members, and there are no former female gang members! Under the far more liberal self-definition, 21.1 percent of the females report that they are former members, and 15.8 percent say they are active members. This finding suggests that large numbers of the young women in our sample may identify with gangs but that they are not necessarily accepted as members by these male-dominated groups.

No matter which definition is used, being Hispanic does not mean that one enjoys a higher probability of gang membership than other ethnicities. In short, in this sample, gang problems are not the unique province of one ethnic group.

The fourth variable is the type of living arrangement reported by the youth. The chi-square analysis does not support the idea that children from single parent households are significantly more likely to be involved in gangs, again, no matter how gang membership is defined.

By the restrictive definition there are roughly equal proportions of the students at each grade level who report being active gang members, but more eleventh graders than ninth graders who report being former members. A

Table 2.1 Personal-Biographical Variables by Gang Involvement, Self-Report versus, in Parentheses, Restrictive Definitions

Variable	Gang Involvement			N
	Wannabe	Former	Active	
Gang Members	39.5	26.9	33.5	169
	(71.0)	(10.9)	(18.3)	
Place of Residence:[1]				
City	37.0	32.6	30.4	40
	(58.0)	(18.0)	(24.0)	
County	41.5	24.4	34.1	119
	(76.5)	(7.6)	(16.0)	
Gender:[2]				
Female	63.2	21.1	15.8	38
	(92.1)	(0.0)	(7.9)	
Male	33.6	28.2	38.2	131
	(64.9)	(13.7)	(21.4)	
Ethnic Groups:[3]				
Hispanic	37.5	34.4	28.1	137
	(73.0)	(8.8)	(18.2)	
Other	40.9	24.8	34.3	32
	(62.5)	(18.8)	(18.8)	
Living Arrangement:[4]				
Single Parent/Guardian	37.0	32.6	30.4	46
	(73.2)	(8.1)	(18.7)	
Two Parents/Guardians	41.5	24.4	34.1	123
	(65.2)	(17.4)	(17.4)	
Year in School:[5]				
9th Grade	40.2	24.6	35.2	122
	(73.0)	(8.2)	(18.9)	
11th Grade	40.4	31.9	27.7	46
	(66.0)	(17.0)	(17.0)	
Hours Spend Studying:[6]				
None	32.6	14.0	53.5	43
	(58.1)	(4.7)	(37.2)	
1 to 2	36.5	30.2	33.3	63
	(74.6)	(11.1)	(14.3)	
3 or More	49.2	31.7	19.01	63
	(76.2)	(14.3)	(9.5)	
Grades:[7]				
Mostly A Grades	57.1	35.7	7.1	14
	(85.7)	(7.1)	(7.1)	
Mostly B Grades	46.2	34.6	19.2	52
	(76.9)	(15.4)	(7.7)	
Mostly C Grades	40.7	22.2	37.0	81
	(70.4)	(8.6)	(21.0)	
Mostly D Grades	13.6	18.2	68.2	22
	(50.0)	(9.1)	(40.9)	

1. Self-Definition: $x2 = .63$; df = 2; p = .73/Restrictive: $x2 = 6.5$; df = 1; p = .04
2. Self-Definition: $x2 = 11.4$; df = 2; p = .003/Restrictive: $x2 = 11.2$; df = 2; p = .004
3. Self-Definition: $x2 = 1.3$; df = 2; p = .53/Restrictive: $x2 = 2.8$; df = 2; p = .24
4. Self-Definition: $x2 = 1.2$; df = 2; p = .56/Restrictive: $x2 = 3.02$; df = 2; p = .22
5. Self-Definition: $x2 = 1.3$; df = 2; p = .53/Restrictive: $x2 = 2.8$; df = 2; p = .25
6. Self-Definition: $x2 = 14.8$; df = 4; p = .005/Restrictive: $x2 = 15.2$; df = 4; p = .004
7. Self-Definition: $x2 = 22.6$; df = 6; p = .009/Restrictive: $x2 = 14.2$; df = 6; p = .027

similar pattern was observed for the self-definition analysis by grade level. These findings suggest that the youth in the sample began to turn away from gangs in the higher grades. However, in neither case are these differences significant.

The hours the youths spend studying is significantly related to the question of gang membership, no matter how gang membership is defined. Among those youths who spend no hours a day studying, over one-half self-report being active gang members and over one-third exhibit the same level of gang involvement by the more restrictive definition. Also by the more restrictive definition, three-quarters of those who study at least one hour a day are wannabes. By the self-definition, one or two hours per day does not appear to make much difference, but three or more hours does: active gang members account for only one in five such youths. This fact is all the more significant since every member of this group has shown at least an interest in joining a gang, if not outright membership.

Finally, grades also exhibited strongly significant ties to gang involvement, but more so for the more liberal definition. Only about 7 percent of the students earning mostly A grades reported being gang members; over two-thirds of the students reporting mostly D grades self-reported the same level of gang involvement. Using the more restrictive definition did not change the percentage of mostly A students reporting gang membership. Only about 41 percent of the mostly D students were placed at the same level of involvement by the restrictive definition. The cross-tabular analysis using the two definitions of gang membership yielded similar results. By both definitions, males earning lower grades and spending less time studying report the highest levels of gang involvement. The more restrictive definition yielded one additional significant relationship: youth in the city report higher levels of gang involvement than those in the rural part of the county.

Predicting Gang-Related Crime:
An Ordinary Least Squares Regression Solution

Table 2.2 summarizes two regression equations. These analyses extend the preliminary cross-tabular findings: the two definitions provide rather similar insights in gang-related behavior. That is, the model which includes the more liberal, self-definition method explains one-third more variance than the model with the more restrictive definition. Before focusing on the unstandardized and standardized effects of these variables in their respective equations, we turn to a brief examination of the effects of the other variables.

There are only minor variations in either the standard beta (β) values, understandardized β values, or standard error of the β values for all seven of the personal biographical variables. Place of residence, year in school, hours spent studying, ethnicity, and living arrangement provide virtually no

Table 2.2   Predicting Gang-Related Crime: Self-Report Versus, in Parentheses, Restrictive Definitions of Gang Membership

Independent Variables	B	SE B	ß	T	Significance Of T
Currently Active in Gang	.91	.16	.40	5.55	.0000
	(.48)	(.19)	(.17)	(2.51)	(.013)
Previously Active in Gang	.33	.16	.14	2.04	.043
	(.16)	(.23)	(.05)	(.6)	(.491)
Residence (City)	−.22	.15	−.09	−1.43	.155
	(−.16)	(.17)	(−.07)	(.95)	(.343)
Living Arrangement	.15	.15	.06	1.00	.32
	(.15)	(.16)	(.06)	(.93)	(.35)
Gender (Male)	.55	.16	.22	3.39	.0009
	(.68)	(.17)	(.27)	(3.92)	(.0001)
Ethnicity (Hispanic)	.02	.18	.005	.09	.93
	(.04)	(.19)	(.015)	(.21)	(.83)
Academic Grades	.39	.09	.29	4.49	.0000
	(.48)	(.09)	(.36)	(5.26)	(.0000)
Study Hours	−.02	.07	.12	−.23	.82
	(−.04)	(.07)	(−.04)	(−.60)	(.55)
Year in School	.14	.07	.12	1.89	.06
	(.13)	(.08)	(.11)	(1.61)	(.11)
Multiple R	.652				
	(.583)				
R Square	.426				
	(.340)				
Adjusted R Square	.393				
	(.303)				

insights as to the level of self-reported gang activity in either equation. However, in both equations, youth earning lower grades reported significantly more gang activity. [It is also interesting to observe that hours spent studying was not related to gang activity; furthermore, these two variables, grades and hours spent studying, were only slightly ($r = -.22$) correlated.] Finally, gang activity is a decidedly male activity; however, grades provide as much if not more insight into gang activity as the individual's gender. In short, besides present or former gang membership, gang-related criminal activity is best understood, in declining order of importance, in terms of academic grades (lower grades) and gender (male).

Allowing the youths to self-define the level of their involvement in gangs appears to be a more fruitful method than employing a definition that requires youths to (a) undergo an initiation (e.g., being "jumped" or "ranked" into the gang) and (b) some external symbols showing that one is a member of a particular gang or gangs in general. Comparing the unstandardized regression weights for gang membership reveals that those self-defined as active gang members reported .43 more units of gang-related criminal activity than those youths defined as active gang members by the restrictive method. No other cross-equation difference approached this magnitude. Within their respective equations, the standardized regression weight (ß) for self-reported active member (dummy coded) clearly made the greatest single contribution, while active membership defined by the restrictive method (also dummy coded) was more on par with academic grades and gender (male). Self-reports of previous gang activity made a significant impact only when the less restrictive definition was used.

Summary

Among those youths in our sample with a predisposition toward gangs and gang behavior, the level of involvement in a gang appears related to gender, the amount of time spent studying, and grades, with being a male, spending less time studying, and lower grades signifying higher involvement in gangs. If one employs a more restrictive definition, one that required an initiation rite and the adoption of symbols signifying gang membership, living in the city was more conducive to higher levels of gang involvement than county residence.

Self-reported involvement in gang-related crime, including drive-by shootings and multiple-partner fights, was better understood in terms of the less restrictive definition of gang membership. Among the other personal-biographical characteristics, only gender and grades made significant contributions, along with gang membership, to our understanding of gang-related crime. Specifically, this type of activity was highest for male, active gang members with low grades.

These findings lead us to the following speculations about why the self-report definition of gang memberships proved to be a better predictor of gang-related crime than the more restrictive definition. First, a self-report definition is more inclusive and incorporates many youngsters who probably should be classified as wannabes. These youngsters may have high levels of internal motivation (success or self-esteem goals) or high levels of external motivation (fear from gang members or rival gangs) to be identified with a gang and participate in gang activities. As a result, they may be criminally active to demonstrate their gang-worthiness. Second, given the ages and academic statuses of the students included in this research, the most gang-involved youngsters may not have been reached by this effort. Many of these youngsters are no longer in school because they have dropped out or aged out (i.e., they are eighteen or nineteen years old). Third, those youngsters meeting the most restrictive gang definition may not have been present the day the survey was administered. They also may have chosen not to participate in the study simply by not coming to the central location once they were dismissed from class.

There is also the possibility that those youths with the highest level of gang involvement answered cautiously given their acknowledged identification as gang members in some of the schools.

Policy Implications

The results from this research leave us pondering two questions: (1) How should we define "gang status?" and (2) What difference does it make? These questions are critical given the gang intervention strategies being employed in some jurisdictions in the United States. For example, some police departments are utilizing aggressive gang-suppression strategies including stopping suspected gang members and completing field interrogation reports on them and, in some instances, photographing them. Also, there has been discussion of courts providing sentence enhancements for any crime committed by a gang member, based on the factor of "gang status."

The problems associated with such approaches are manifest. First, these kinds of system responses give gangs and gang members one of the things they seek the most: recognition. Many of these youngsters have not distinguished themselves in their families, schools or neighborhoods. Therefore, gangs help provide a definition of who they are: individual and collective identities are intertwined. Second, an even more troubling aspect of gang intervention programs may be that they miss most of the non-gang youths who may commit a great deal of delinquency (including the types of offenses we typically label as "gang-related").

What we have been describing is a problem of definition. A restrictive definition—such as that proposed by Klein (1971:111) and other gang researchers (cf. Short, 1989:246; Spergel, 1990:181), and employed in this research—imposes social structural dimensions on gangs that may or may not have much to do with the reality of the current gang phenomenon. If it is gang violence we wish to understand, then this approach may be less fruitful than the self-definitional method. After all, as William I. and Dorothy S. Thomas (1928), writing on the state of children in America, observed many years ago, "If men define situations as real, they are real in their consequences." Our study suggests that this may be the case for self-defined gang membership and related interpersonal violence, a position also advanced by Horowitz (1990).

Clearly gang researchers are just beginning to appreciate the multi-dimensionality of what is viewed by some policy-makers and implementers as a monolithic structure, the gang problem. Normally, we would call for more research, inside and outside of schools. Yet more research on the prevalence of this problem—however it is defined—without attention to its conceptual definition may provide little usable information upon which to base new anti-gang policies and strategies. We may learn a lot or little about some classes of activities that are only tangentially linked to gang membership and gang-crime.

References

Bogardus, E.S. (1926). *The City Boy and His Problems*. Los Angeles: House of Ralston.

Bookin-Weiner, H. and R. Horowitz. (1983). "The End of the Youth Gang: Fad or Fact?" *Criminology*, 21(4): 585–602.

Cohen, A.K. (1955). *Delinquent Boys: The Culture of the Gang*. Glencoe, IL: Free Press.

Horowitz, R. (1990). "Sociological Perspectives on Gangs: Conflicting Definitions and Concepts." In *Gangs in America*, ed. C. Ronald Huff. Newbury Park, CA: Sage.

Huff, C.R. (1990). "Introduction: Two Generations of Gang Research." In *Gangs in America*, ed. C. Ronald Huff. Newbury Park, CA: Sage.

Klein, M.W. (1971). *Street Gangs and Street Workers*. Englewood Cliffs, NJ: Prentice Hall.

Los Angeles Police Department. (1988). "Street Gang Eradication Program." Report presented to the Board of Police Commissioners, November 14.

Maxson, C.L. and M.W. Klein. (1990). "Street Gang Violence: Twice as Great, or Half as Great?" In *Gangs in America*, ed. C. Ronald Huff. Newbury Park, CA: Sage.

Miller, W.B. (1958). "Lower Class Culture as a Generating Milieu of Gang Delinquency." *Journal of Social Issues*, 14:5–19.

Miller, W.B. (1990). "Why the United States Has Failed to Solve Its Youth Gang Problem." In *Gangs in America*, ed. C. Ronald Huff. Newbury Park, CA: Sage.

New Mexico Governor's Organized Crime Prevention Commission. (1991). *New Mexico Street Gangs*. Santa Fe, NM: Author.

Short, J.F. (1989). "Exploring Integration of Theoretical Levels of Explanation: Notes on Gang Delinquency." Pp. 243–259 in S.F. Messner, M.D. Krohn and A.E. Liska (eds.), *Theoretical Integration in the Study of Deviance and Crime Problems and Prospects*. Albany: SUNY Press.

Spergel, I.A. (1990). "Youth Gangs: Continuity and Change." In *Crime and Justice: A Review of Research,* eds. M. Tonry and N. Morris. Chicago: University of Chicago Press.

Thomas, W.I. and Thomas W.S. (1928). *The Child in America*. New York: Knopf.

Thrasher, F.M. (1927). *The Gang: A Study of 1,313 Gangs in Chicago*. Chicago: University of Chicago Press.

3

Gang Crime and
Law Enforcement Recordkeeping

G. David Curry, Richard A. Ball, and Robert J. Fox

Gangs and crime committed by gang members are now pervasive in numerous American cities, presenting a challenge to law enforcement. A National Institute of Justice (NIJ)-sponsored survey of metropolitan police departments in the seventy-nine largest U.S. cities showed that in spring 1992 all but seven were troubled by gangs, as were all but five departments in forty-three smaller cities.

In 110 jurisdictions reporting gangs, the survey found that over the previous twelve-month period there were:

- 249,324 gang members.
- 4,881 gangs.
- 46,359 gang-related crimes.
- 1,072 gang-related homicides

A problem of this magnitude calls for the development of law enforcement strategies that are flexible enough to meet local needs while possessing sufficient uniformity to make it possible to compare results across different communities. To do this requires accurate statistics on gangs in the United States and the crimes gang members commit.

The NIJ-sponsored survey findings detailed in this Research in Brief represent a first step toward the development of national-level data on gangs, their members, and their criminal activities. Results of the NIJ Gang Survey suggests some fruitful preliminary actions jurisdictions can take to improve the information on gangs available to policymakers and officials:

- Develop a centrally based collection of data on gang-related incidents. This could be part of the new National Incident Based Reporting System (NIBRS)

U.S. Dept. of Justice, *National Institute of Justice Research in Brief*, Aug. 1994.

being implemented by the Federal Bureau of Investigation (FBI) as a replacement to its Uniform Crime Reports.

- Provide technical assistance to help local law enforcement agencies contribute to this central data collection. Accomplishing this would involve continuing to develop uniform definitions across jurisdictions of what constitutes a gang, a gang member, and a gang-related crime.
- Assess the level of gang-related crime problems in terms of gang-related crimes or incidents rather than numbers of gangs and gang members. This would recognize that the gang crime problem is not about young men and women forming groups with names and symbols but about groups and individuals in these groups committing crimes against persons and property.

These actions would further the formation of comprehensive, effective policies to curb gangs and gang membership, especially among juveniles, in all our nation's cities.

Obstacles to Gathering Dependable National Data on Gangs

What is described under the general term, "gang problem," varies greatly from city to city. For the purposes of this survey, to be counted as a gang, law enforcement officials had to identify the group as a "gang" that was involved in criminal activity and included youth in its membership. As will be seen in this report, a universally accepted definition of "gang" does not exist, making it difficult to gather national statistics that accurately portray the extent of the gang problem.[1] Previous national-level surveys and numerous recent research studies have led to a greater uniformity in identifying what organizations are gangs, however.

Law enforcement agencies need help in reporting gang-related information accurately and routinely. While some manual or computerized records are maintained by all local departments reporting gang crime problems, not all local departments conduct annual tabulations that include the number of gangs, gang members, *and* gang-related crimes—as few as twenty-seven of the large city police departments surveyed.

The appropriate statistic for assessing the magnitude of gang-related crime problems is not the number of gang members but the crimes they commit.

Previous Estimates

National estimates of gang-related crimes have been generated by periodic studies conducted by university researchers under cooperative agreements with the Office of Juvenile Justice and Delinquency Prevention (OJJDP) or the National Institute of Justice (NIJ). In the first national-level study of the gang problem published in 1975,[2] an OJJDP-sponsored research project studied twelve large cities, six of which were found to have gang crime problems.

Estimates for the six cities ranged from 760 to 2,700 gangs and from 28,500 to 81,500 gang members. An expansion of the original study in 1982 estimated 97,940 gang members in 2,285 gang in 286 cities[3] Within a year, two other OJJDP-sponsored researchers,[4] using a random sample of police departments in cities with populations over 100,000, reported that twenty-seven (45 percent) of the sixty cities had gang crime problems.

The next effort to gather national-level data was begun in 1988 when the University of Chicago, with funds from OJJDP, conducted a survey of community-level gang programs that might serve as prototypes for a national-level gang program initiative.[5] From 35 jurisdictions with organized responses to gangs, the OJJDP/University of Chicago survey reported 1,439 gangs and 120,636 gang members, but some jurisdictions provided only estimates rather than exact data.

Distribution of Gang Problems

Figure 3.1 shows survey results on the officially reported presence of gang problems for the cities in the study. Of the large city police departments, seventy-two (91%) reported the presence within their jurisdictions of criminally involved groups with youths as members that they labeled as ''gangs.'' Of the seven jurisdictions not reporting gang problems, three (4%) reported the presence of gang-like, criminally involved, youth-based groups that were officially identified by some label other than ''gangs.'' Baltimore, Maryland, reported a ''drug organization'' problem; Raleigh, North Carolina, a ''posse'' problem; and Washington, D.C. a ''crew'' problem.[6] Police departments in Memphis, Tennessee; Newark, New Jersey; Pittsburgh, Pennsylvania; and Richmond, Virginia, reported they had no officially acknowledged gang or gang-like problems.

If the three cities with ''gang-like'' crime problems are combined with the seventy-two reporting gang problems, 95 percent of large U.S. city police departments reported that gangs or gang-like organizations engaged in criminal activity and involved youths within their jurisdictions. Figure 3.2 lists the large cities in the study by presence of reported gang crime problems as of spring 1992.[7]

In addition, the NIJ Gang Survey also gathered updated information on gang crime problems in forty-three smaller city police departments.[8] A total of thirty-eight cities (88%) reported gang crime problems in 1992. Figure 3.3 lists the smaller cities in the study by presence of reported gang crime problems as of spring 1992.

Changes since 1988

Many of the cities surveyed by this project (the forty-three smaller cities and fifty-one of the seventy-nine largest cities) were included in the screening

Figure 3.1: Gang Crime Problems by Site, 1992

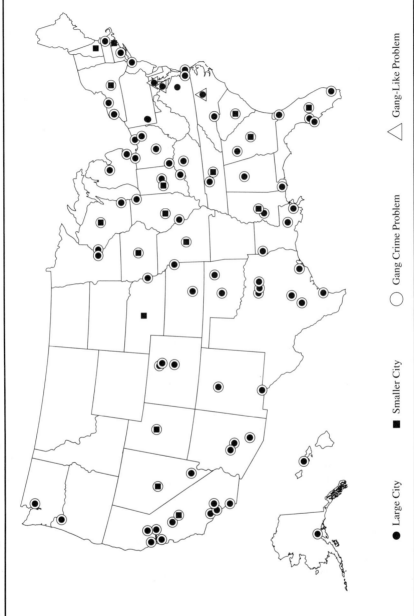

● Large City   ■ Smaller City   ○ Gang Crime Problem   △ Gang-Like Problem

Source: NIJ Gang Survey.

Figure 3.2: 79 Largest U.S. Cities by Type of Officially Reported Gang Problems as of Spring 1992

Reported Gang Problem

Akron (OH)
Albuquerque (NM)
Anaheim (CA)
Anchorage (AK)
Arlington (TX)
Atlanta (GA)
Aurora (CO)
Austin (TX)
Baton Rouge (LA)
Birmingham (AL)
Boston (MA)
Buffalo (NY)
Charlotte (NC)
Chicago (IL)
Cincinnati (OH)
Cleveland (OH)
Colorado Springs (CO)
Columbus (OH)
Corpus Christi (TX)
Dallas (TX)
Denver (CO)
Detroit (MI)
El Paso (TX)
Fort Worth (TX)
Fresno (CA)
Honolulu (HI)
Houston (TX)
Indianapolis (IN)
Jackson (MS)
Jacksonville (FL)
Jersey City (NJ)
Kansas City (MO)
Las Vegas (NV)
Lexington (KY)
Long Beach (CA)
Los Angeles (CA)
Louisville (KY)
Mesa (AZ)
Miami (FL)
Milwaukee (WI)
Minneapolis (MN)
Mobile (AL)
Nashville (TN)
New Orleans (LA)

New York (NY)
Norfolk (VA)
Oakland (CA)
Oklahoma City (OK)
Omaha (NE)
Philadelphia (PA)
Phoenix (AZ)
Portland (OR)
Riverside (CA)
Rochester (NY)
Sacramento (CA)
San Antonio (TX)
San Diego (CA)
San Francisco (CA)
San Jose (CA)
Santa Ana (CA)
Seattle (WA)
Shreveport (LA)
St. Louis (MO)
St. Paul (MN)
St. Petersburg (FL)
Stockton (CA)
Tampa (FL)
Toledo (OH)
Tucson (AZ)
Tulsa (OK)
Virginia Beach (VA)
Wichita (KS)

"Drug Organization" Problem Only

Baltimore (MD)

"Posse" Problem Only

Raleigh (NC)

"Crew" Problem Only

Washington (DC)

No Reported Problem

Memphis (TN)
Newark (NJ)
Pittsburgh (PA)
Richmond (VA)

Source: NIJ Gang Survey.

38

Figure 3.3: Smaller Cities by Presence of Officially Reported Gang Problem as of Spring 1992

Reported Gang Problem

Albany (NY)	Joliet (IL)
Benton Harbor (MI)	Kansas City (KS)
Berkeley (CA)	Madison (WI)
Cambridge (MA)	Orlando (FL)
Chattanooga (TN)	Pasadena (CA)
Chino (CA)	Peoria (IL)
Cicero (IL)	Pomona (CA)
Compton (CA)	Racine (WI)
Decatur (GA)	Reno (NV)
Des Moines (IA)	Rockford (IL)
El Monte (CA)	Salt Lake City (UT)
Evanston (IL)	San Bernadino (CA)
Flint (MI)	Spartansburg (SC)
Fort Lauderdale (FL)	Sterling (IL)
Fort Wayne (IN)	Tallahassee (FL)
Garden Grove (CA)	
Gary (IN)	
Glendale (CA)	*No Reported Gang Problem*
Greenville (MS)	Charleston (SC)
Hartford (CT)	Lincoln (NE)
Hialeah (FL)	Portsmouth (NH)
Huntington Beach (CA)	Springfield (MA)
Inglewood (CA)	Wilmington (DE)

Source: NIJ Gang Survey.

process for the 1988 OJJDP/University of Chicago survey. The presence of gang crime problems in these ninety-four cities could therefore be compared for 1988 and 1992. Figure 3.4 shows the increase that occurred over these four years, in both large and small cities.

Defining Gangs

Of the seventy-two police departments in large cities reporting gang problems, seventy completed a questionnaire on what constitutes a gang or supplied researchers with a copy of an official definition or regulation pertaining to gangs. Police departments in smaller cities were less likely to supply official definitions than departments in larger cities. All prior national surveys of gang crime problems have encouraged police departments to move toward more uniform definitions. Previous researchers have refined the criteria for defining gangs to include violent behavior, group organization, leadership, territory, and recurrent interaction, but some have also included symbols worn or used by particular gangs to identify themselves.[9] In this report dress decoration and graffiti are labeled as "symbols," and police departments are counted as using this criterion if their definition includes wearing certain colors, sharing a common set of signs and symbols, or writing graffiti.

Violent behavior trailed symbols as a defining criterion in both large and smaller cities, according to the NIJ Gang Survey. For large cities, 93 percent included some reference to symbols in their definitions; for the

Figure 3.4: Cities Reporting Gang Crime Problems in 1988 and 1992

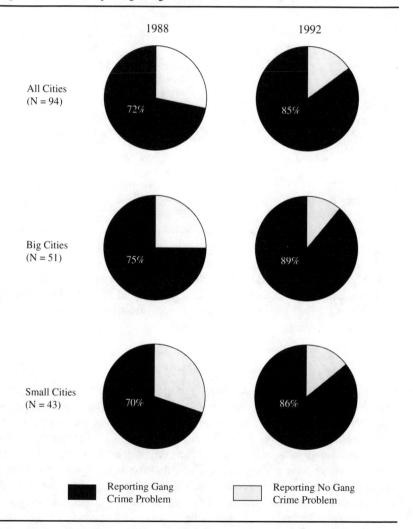

1988   1992

All Cities
(N = 94)

72%   85%

Big Cities
(N = 51)

75%   89%

Small Cities
(N = 43)

70%   86%

■ Reporting Gang
Crime Problem

☐ Reporting No Gang
Crime Problem

Source: NIJ Gang Survey.

Figure 3.5: Criteria for Defining Gangs

Criteria Used	Large Cities*	Smaller Cities*
Use of Symbols	93%	100%
Violent Behavior	81%	84%
Group Organization	81%	88%
Territory	74%	88%
Leadership	59%	48%
Recurrent Interaction	56%	60%

*Of the cities surveyed, 70 (89%) of the large cities and 25 (58%) of the smaller cities indicated the criteria used to define gangs.
Source: NIJ Gang Survey.

smaller cities, all with definitions included one or more references to symbols (figure 3.5).

There is a growing convergence of definitions of gangs. In 1992, more departments were using similar definitions than in 1988.

Recording Gang Information

All departments that reported the presence of gang-related crime problems keep some kind of official record of these gangs, their members, or their specific gang-related criminal activity. For all 110 departments in large and smaller cities reporting gang crime problems, 85 percent (ninety-three cities) record data on these three measures of the gang crime problem: 90 percent of the largest cities keep records of all three measures compared to 78 percent of the smaller cities. In another 12 percent (thirteen cities), police departments keep records on gangs and members but not incidents. Of the remaining four departments, one department keeps records on members and incidents, one on incidents only, and two on members only.

Reporting Gang Information

Policy administrators and policymakers who must develop and conduct responses to gang crime need to know the magnitude of the problem. The ability of the police departments included in the NIJ Gang Survey to report this information in terms of the number of gangs, the number of gang members, and the number of gang-related crimes varied considerably. While a majority of the respondents, regardless of city size, recorded all three measures of gang crime information, reporting capability on these three different statistical measures of jurisdictional gang crime problems did not match the degree of recording.

Only thirty-four departments (31%) were able to report the number of gangs, number of gang members, and number of gang incidents for their jurisdictions for 1991. Another fifteen (14%) reported numbers of gangs, members, and gang-related homicides. The capability of reporting numbers of gangs and members, but not incidents, was found in thirty-seven (34%) of the departments.

In the remaining 21 percent of cities, information reporting varied.

Akron, Ohio, with a newly recognized gang problem, reported only the number of gang-related homicides for 1991 (forty incidents). San Jose, California, with its computer system, could provide only information on the number of gangs. St. Petersburg, Florida, with a manual recordkeeping system, provided detailed statistics on incidents but could produce no estimates of the number of gangs or gang members in the jurisdiction.

Fresno, California, maintains manual records but does not tabulate any of the three kinds of requested gang information. New York City and Philadelphia have recently limited their local gang crime problems to only Asian gangs; gang-like crime problems among ethnic groups other than Asian are treated as "drug organizations." The only available statistic for New York City for 1991 was nineteen homicides attributed to Asian gangs.

Additional difficulties encountered in reporting on the scope of gang problems varied considerably across cities. In Jacksonville, Florida, a shortfall in staffing committed to dealing with a growing gang problem means the tabulation of annual gang statistics is given lower priority. In San Diego, California, two computers are used to store gang information, but summary reports are extracted from paper files. In Honolulu and Miami, data are input into regional GREAT (General Reporting, Evaluation, and Tracking)[10] systems, but the departments themselves do not have the capability to generate reports.

Gang Members and Gang Incidents

In the majority of jurisdictions that reported both numbers of gang members and numbers of gang-related crimes (in addition to gang homicides), far more gang members were reported than gang-related incidents. For example, the Los Angeles Police Department reported 503 gangs and 55,258 gang members yet only 8,528 gang-related crimes in 1991. The Chicago Police Department reported that 29,000 gang members in 41 gangs accounted for only 4,765 gang incidents in 1991. The Louisville Police Department reported 250 gang members in 20 gangs and only one gang-related incident (an assault) in 1991.

In the largest cities reporting gang problems, 26 reported statistics on gang members and gang-related incidents for 1991. Of these twenty-six departments, only three reported more gang-related incidents than gang members— Denver (5,100 members, 6,109 incidents), Seattle (800 members, 1,083 incidents), and Tucson (1,377 members, 2,607 incidents). None of these three cities reported more than two incidents per gang member. Statistics on gang-related incidents were less likely to be reported in the smaller cities, but of the ten reporting numbers of gang members and gang-related incidents, only Flint, Michigan, reported more incidents for 1991 than members.

Two explanations for this apparent imbalance are possible. One is that gang member files are maintained from year to year, while gang incident files are year-specific. Thus gang members may be tracked in the files even though they have not recently committed gang-related incidents. It has been suggested that gang members' names be routinely purged from files after a given time period has elapsed without an additional offense.

A second reason for this ratio is the degree to which gang crimes involve multiple offenders, particularly when the Chicago definition is used. The Chicago definition is based on a crime's being related to gang function. Another definition, the Los Angeles definition, is based on a crime's involving a gang member either as an offender or a victim.[11] The 1988 University of Chicago/OJJDP national survey revealed an even greater variation in the definition of gang incidents across cities than that constituted by the difference between Chicago and Los Angeles.[12]

An examination of the data currently available on gang incidents reveals their utility. As can be seen in figure 3.6, gang-related crime, as reflected in

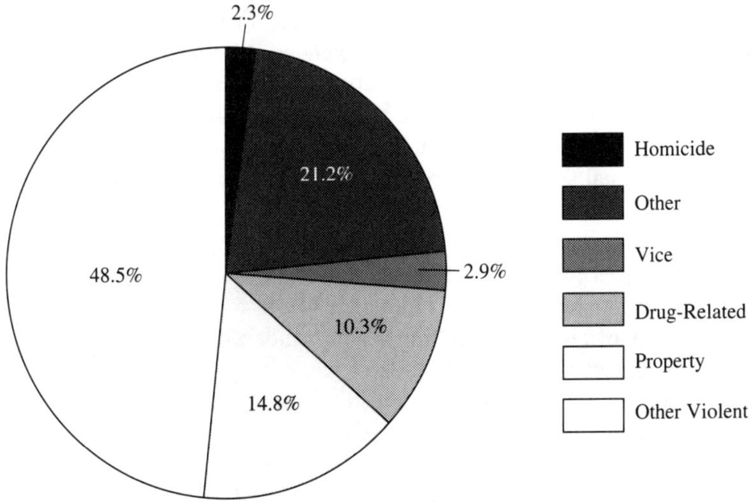

Figure 3.6: Gang-Related Crime by Type as Percent of Total Recorded

available law enforcement statistics, is above all a violent crime problem. Homicides and other violent crimes account for about half of all recorded gang-related crime incidents. Crimes that are usually thought of as explicitly motivated by profit, such as property crimes, drug-related crimes, and vice, represent comparatively smaller portions of the national gang crime problem as measured by law enforcement statistics.

Gender and Gangs

The NIJ Gang Survey specifically requested available official record data on females involved in gang-related criminal activity. Yet in a number of cities females, as a matter of policy, were never classified as gang members.[13] In other jurisdictions, females were relegated statistically to the status of "associate" members. In all, twenty-three (31.9%) of the largest city police departments with reported gang crime problems did not provide statistics on female gang members, and nine (12.5%) reported no female gang members. Forty large city police departments reported a total of 7,205 female gang members. Including numbers from the twenty-one smaller cities and county jurisdictions brings the total to 9,092 female gang members in sixty-one law enforcement jurisdictions across the Nation.

This figure represents only 3.65 percent of the total number of gang members reported to the researchers. If, in an effort to control for law enforcement policies that officially exclude female gang members, gang members are counted only from cities reporting some number of both male and female gang members, this percentage increases to 5.7 percent.

The survey also requested that available statistics on gang-related crimes be broken down by type of crime and by gender. Although a number of law enforcement agencies were not able to report annual statistics for gang-related crimes, fifty-nine large and smaller cities and selected counties did report the most commonly available gang-related crime statistic—number of gang-related homicides. Annual statistics for other types of gang-related crimes were reported by smaller numbers of cities.

Figure 3.7 indicates the major differences in the types of crimes officially attributed to males compared to females. Proportionally almost twice as many female gang-related crimes were homicides (4.5% for females and 2.3% for males). Violent offenses not resulting in a homicide were proportionally much more common for male gang offenders, while property crimes were more common for female offenders.

Looking at raw national totals, only the percentage of gang-related property crimes (1.1% or 75 of 6,880) attributed to females exceeds 1 percent of the total number for any type of crime. Only 8 (0.7%) of the total of 1,072 gang-related homicides were attributed to females. If one limits the analysis to jurisdictions reporting gang-related crimes for females, the percentages

Figure 3.7: Gang-Related Crime by Type as Percent of Total Recorded by Gender

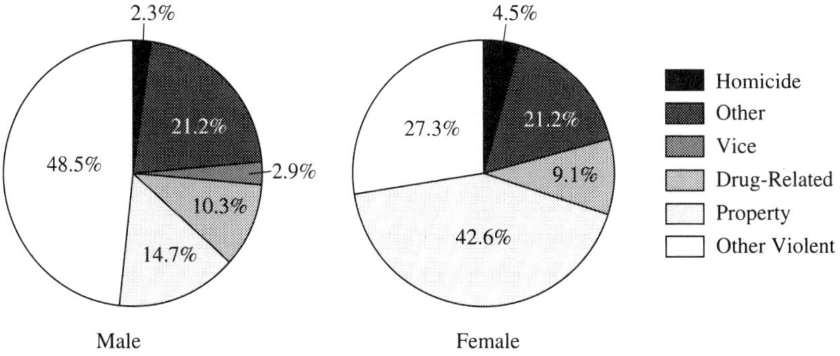

Note: No gang-related crime was reported in the Vice category for females.
Source: NIJ Gang Survey.

attributed to females for each type of crime increase substantially. In these jurisdictions the respective percentage for females for each type of crime are 11.4 percent for gang-related homicides, 3.3 percent for other violent crimes, 13.6 percent for property crimes, 12.7 percent for drug-related crimes, and 16.7 percent for other crimes.

The 1988 OJJDP/University of Chicago survey received reports of the existence of twenty-two independent female gangs in 1987 from its sample of communities with organized responses to gang crime problems. The 1992 NIJ Gang Survey received reports of ninety-nine independent female gangs spread over thirty-five law enforcement jurisdictions in 1991. (Although it did not count the number of female gang members, Birmingham, Alabama, recorded the existence of two independent female gangs; in addition, Portland, Oregon, had one; and St. Paul, Minnesota, and Wichita, Kansas, each reported three.)

Because of changes in the way gangs are defined and identified, as well as differences in national survey methodologies, it is difficult to determine if female involvement in gang-related crimes rose between 1987 and 1991. Only twenty-three of the thirty-four law enforcement agencies offering 1987 estimates to the 1988 OJJDP/University of Chicago survey provided official annual statistics on the number of female gang members in their jurisdictions to the 1992 NIJ Gang Survey.

Ethnicity and Gangs

In the early part of this century, gang involvement in criminal activity was viewed as a social phenomenon associated with ethnic Americans, most commonly second-generation white immigrants from Eastern and Southern Europe and African-Americans recently arrived from the South. More recent studies have increasingly focused on the growth of involvement in gangs by Central and South American and Asian immigrants. Although most research in the last few decades has focused on minority involvement in gang activity, the study of involvement of white youths in gang-related crime has continued.[14] The NIJ Gang Survey, like previous research, indicates that involvement in gang-related crime remains for the most part associated with African-American and Hispanic youths, although the proportion of white and Asian youths appears to be increasing. Of the police departments reporting gang crime problems, almost all said they recorded the race or ethnicity of gang members. As with other types of data noted above, there was a difference between *recording information* and *being able to report* that information in summary form. Of the seventy-two large city police departments reporting gang crime problems, only twenty-five (35%) provided statistics on the ethnicity of identified gang members; of the thirty-eight smaller cities, only twelve (32%) provided statistics on ethnicity. As figure 3.8 shows, the ethnic composition of gang members in these cities remains predominantly black (48%) and Hispanic (43%). The black groups were made up primarily of African-Americans but also included Jamaicans and blacks of other countries.

Figure 3.8: Gang Members in 1991 by Ethnicity

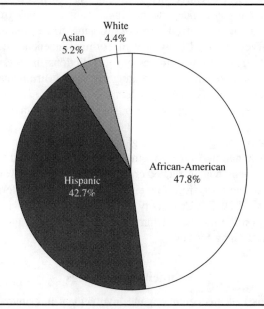

Source: NIJ Gang Survey.

Only sixteen cities (eleven of them among the largest cities) provided ethnic breakdowns on gang members for both 1990 and 1991 (The 1992 NIJ survey asked for ethnicity data for both 1990 and 1991.) From the data for these cities, it is possible to gain a limited idea of how the ethnicity of gang involvement may be changing. While the reported number of black gang members for these cities increased by 13 percent between 1990 and 1991, the number of Hispanic gang members increased by 18 percent over the same period. Although significantly smaller in terms of actual numbers of gang members, the numbers of gang members identified as Asian or white were increasing at a significantly higher rate. From 1990 to 1991 for the cities where data were available, the number of Asian gang members increased by 66 percent and the number of white gang members by 55 percent.

Law Enforcement Anti-Gang Strategies

Having analyzed the scope of gang activity and the composition of gangs, the survey sought to identify the primary and secondary law enforcement strategies cities used to respond to gang problems. It also sought to analyze the links, if any, between the strategies used and the department's perceived effectiveness in dealing with gangs.

Analysis of law enforcement agency strategies for dealing with gang crime problems was modeled after the analysis conducted by the OJJDP/ University of Chicago researchers,[15] who identified five primary categories of response strategies:

- *Community organization:* contact with community organizations, provision of speakers to these organizations, sharing of information, help in the organization of community watches and graffiti cleanup campaigns.
- *Social intervention:* cooperation with social service agencies, particularly counseling programs.
- *Opportunity provision:* cooperation with school tutoring and jobs programs.
- *Suppression:* identification of gang members, special case management, special intelligence operations, increased law enforcement, increased incarceration, and increased liaison between law enforcement agencies.
- *Organizational change/development:* identification of additional resources and funding, advocacy of new laws.

All respondents to the 1992 NIJ Survey mentioned suppression as one of their response strategies, and 44 percent identified it as their primary response strategy. When researchers compared the perceived effectiveness of gang response programs and the prevalence of each primary strategy, the researchers found that only in cities that had adopted opportunity provision and community organization as their primary strategies was there greater perceived agency effectiveness in dealing with gang-related crime problems.

In the NIJ Gang Survey, of the seventy-two large cities with gang-related crime problems, sixty-four (89%) completed the strategy-effectiveness questionnaire requested by the survey. Of the thirty-eight smaller cities reporting gang-related crime problems, twenty-seven (71%) completed this portion of the survey. All responding departments reported trying at least one special suppression strategy and at least one community organization strategy. Most had tried more than one of each. In the large city departments, all had tried at least one organizational change strategy; in the smaller cities, a majority (78%) had.

Ways of preventing the formation of gangs, such as social intervention and opportunity provision strategies, were less commonly used in both large and small cities. In the large cities, social intervention strategies were used by thirty-one (48%) of the reporting departments and opportunity provision strategies by twenty-six (41%). Among the smaller cities, a majority of departments did, however, report cooperating with social service programs (63%) and tutoring and job programs (51.9%).

No law enforcement agency reported relying completely on suppression strategies. This may reflect recommendations being made in recent years including those found in the OJJDP/University of Chicago research and development products that grew out of the 1988 survey.[16] Those findings strongly recommended balanced programs that employ a wide range of strategies, and that is the approach that most local law enforcement agencies responding to the NIJ Gang Survey seemed to be following.

Conclusion

In summary, this study showed the need to work toward standardizing the meaning of ''gangs'' around the Nation to improve collection and reporting of national data on gang-related crime. On the basis of accurate data, the effectiveness of multiple intervention strategies could then be better assessed.

Notes

1. J.M. Hagedorn, *People and Folks: Gangs, Crime and the Underclass in a Rustbelt City*, Chicago: Lake View Press, 1988; and R. Horowitz, ''Sociological Perspectives on Gangs: Conflicting Definitions and Concepts,'' in C.R. Huff (ed.), *Gangs in America*, Newbury Park, CA: Sage Publications, 1990, are advocates of more open, local definitions of what constitutes a gang. On the other hand, citing the need for national-level assessments and comparisons needed by law enforcement practitioners and policymakers, W.B. Miller, *Violence by Youth Gangs and Youth Groups as a Crime Problem in Major American Cities*, Washington, DC: U.S. Government Printing Office, 1975; J. Needle and W.V. Stapleton, Reports of the National Juvenile Justice Assessment Centers, *Police Handling of Youth Gangs*, Washington,

DC: Office of Juvenile Justice and Delinquency Prevention, U.S. Department of Justice, 1983; C.L. Maxson and M.W. Klein, "Street Gang Violence: Twice as Great or Half as Great?" in C.R. Huff (ed.), *Gangs in America*, Newbury Park: Sage, 1990; and I.A. Spergel and G.D. Curry, "The National Youth Gang Survey: A Research and Development Process" in A.P. Goldstein and C.R. Huff (eds.), *Gang Intervention Handbook*, Champaign, IL: Research Press, 1993, have called for a greater emphasis on uniform definitions.

2. W.B. Miller, 1975.

3. W.B. Miller, *Crime by Youth Gangs and Groups in the United States*, Washington, DC: U.S. Department of Justice, National Institute of Juvenile Justice and Delinquency Prevention, 1982.

4. J. Needle and W.V. Stapleton, 1983.

5. I.A. Spergel and G.D. Curry, 1993:361–402.

6. Operational definitions for "posse" and "crew" correspond to the operational definition for "gang" in that each is involved in criminal activity and includes youth in its membership. At this level of analysis, the only difference between a posse, a crew, and a gang is the local law enforcement agency's official label for each.

7. Pittsburgh officially recognized its gang crime problem in June 1992 and subsequently formed a gang response task force within the city police department.

8. These cities were screened in 1988 by the OJJDP/University of Chicago survey (see "Survey Methodology"). One additional small city, Glendale, CA was included in the OJJDP/University of Chicago screening process. It was identified as having a gang crime problem but having no organized community response.

9. J. Needle and W.V. Stapleton, 1983. The additional criterion that Needle and Stapleton added was "dress including body decoration and identifying graffiti."

10. Developed in the Los Angeles Sheriff's Department and Los Angeles Police Department. See C.R. Huff and W.D. McBride, "Gangs and the Police," in A.P. Goldstein and C.R. Huff (eds.), *The Gang Intervention Handbook*, Champaign, Research Press, 1993.

11. The difference between the Chicago and Los Angeles definitions has been discussed by I.A. Spergel, "Youth Gangs: Continuity and Change," in N. Morris and M. Tonry (eds.), *Crime and Justice: An Annual Review of Research*, Chicago: University of Chicago Press, 1990; C.L. Maxson and M.W. Klein, 1990; and R. Block and C.R. Block, "Lethal and Nonlethal Street Gang Crime in Chicago," NIJ Draft Report, 1992.

12. I.A. Spergel and G.D. Curry, 1993.

13. Miller, 1975, estimated that 90 percent of gang members in cities with gangs were male.

14. For studies of white ethnics and gang involvement in the first half of the 20th century, see F.M. Thrasher, *The Gang*, Chicago: University of Chicago Press, 1927; and W.F. Whyte, *Street Corner Society*, Chicago: University of Chicago Press, 1943. For studies on Hispanic gang involvement, see J.W. Moore, *Going Down to the Barrio: Homeboys and Homegirls in Change*, Philadelphia: Temple University Press, 1991; J.D. Vigil, *Barrio Gangs*, Austin, TX: University of Texas Press, 1988; and F. Padilla, *The Gang as an American Enterprise*, New Brunswick, NJ, 1992. For studies of Asian gangs, see K.L. Chin, *Chinese Subculture and Criminality: Non-*

traditional Crime Groups in America, Westport, CT; Greenwood Press, 1990; and J. Fagan, K.L. Chin, and R. Kelly, *Lucky Money: Paying Lucky Money to Little Brothers*, Washington DC: U.S. Department of Justice, National Institute of Justice. For a description of the role of race relations in the emergence and development of African-American gangs, see J.M. Hagedorn, *People and Folks: Gangs, Crime and the Underclass in a Rustbelt City*, Chicago: Lake View Press, 1988. W.B. Miller described the continued involvement of whites in gangs in the late 1960's in "White Gangs," *Transaction 6*, 1969:11–26. A more recent description of the criminal involvement of white youths in gangs is provided by M. Sanchez-Jankowski, *Islands in the Street*, Berkeley: University of California Press, 1991.

    15. I.A. Spergel and G.D. Curry, 1993.

    16. A complete list of the products of the OJJDP/University of Chicago project can be found in I.A. Spergel and G.D. Curry, 1993.

Funding for this research was provided by Cooperative Agreement number 91–IJ–CX–K003 from the National Institute of Justice, U.S. Department of Justice. *The National Institute of Justice is a component of the Office of Justice Programs, which also includes the Bureau of Justice Assistance, Bureau of Justice Statistics, Office of Juvenile Justice and Delinquency Prevention, and the Office for Victims of Crime.*

    Findings and conclusions of the research reported here are those of the researchers and do not necessarily reflect the official position or policies of the U.S. Department of Justice.

Part 2
Theories—A Search for Explanation

This section examines several of the theories associated with the study of gangs and gang activity. Theory is one of those words almost certain to turn off the minds of many students.

Psychologist and philosopher Kurt Lewin said that nothing is as practical as a good theory. In an applied social science field like criminal justice, theories should be tied to both research and policies. This connection can be illustrated by the following propositions (with thanks and acknowledgements to my colleague Tom Winfree):

1. Theories are constructed to help us do a variety of things, but in the social sciences primarily to describe, explain, predict, and control (Babbie, 1992).
2. Theories are not good or bad, but useful or not useful. To be a useful theory, the various concepts and propositions must be testable (Akers, 1994).
3. Theory testing is one of the important components of much social science research (Bernard, 1990).
4. If the theory proves to be useful, it should be applied to policies concerning the social problem being examined—in the present case, gangs (Winfree and Abadinsky, 1996).

Many of the theories related to crime and deviant behavior were developed by studying adolescent behavior. This section examines a variety of the theories (or near-theories) that can aid in our understanding about how youth gangs form, why they persist, and what we can do to intervene with gangs and gang members.

In the first section, Winfree, Bäckström, and Mays look at social learning theory to understand gang behavior. This article utilizes the form of social learning theory developed by Ronald Akers (and colleagues) and examines the process by which social behaviors are learned, and particularly how certain behaviors are rewarded and reinforced or punished and diminished. This particular theory has been used to study a number of adolescent behaviors including smoking, and drug and alcohol use (Akers et al., 1979; Winfree and Griffiths, 1983; Winfree, Griffiths, and Sellers, 1989).

The second article deals with the notion of social dislocation. Here Jackson examines concepts traditionally associated with theories like social disorganization and others that came from the Chicago School in the 1930s, 1940s, and 1950s. Specifically, Jackson is interested in the degree to which economic changes and population shifts impact the amount of violence and property crimes. She finds that changes in many major cities—for instance, from manufacturing to service-based economies—have undermined the economic opportunities available to the unskilled urban poor. Thus, gang development may be one among many factors related to the nature of America's postindustrial economy.

Lasley, in his article on the age of gang members, examines the question of whether youth gang members are getting older and, thus, are becoming adult gang members. Several others writers have suggested that as gangs age they also become more violent. To test this notion, Lasley gathered self-reported data from 445 active street gang members in Los Angeles. His findings, in this piece, indicate that, contrary to the conventional wisdom, most gang members are adolescents and not adults, and that street gangs are still primarily youth gangs. The examination of age is an important factor in understanding gangs and gang behavior, and it will be considered further in part 4.

The final article in this section looks at the relationship between perceived occupational opportunity and involvement in delinquent activities. The authors of this article apply the theoretic framework developed by Cloward and Ohlin to a national sample of 2,500 males. Simons and Gray found that the four race groups (black/white X lower class/upper class) did not differ significantly in their perceived opportunities to obtain the jobs they desired. In response to criticisms of opportunity theory, Simon and Gray also note that much of the previous research done on this theory has oversimplified the original notions developed by Cloward and Ohlin. This article and others related to research on employment prospects and delinquent activity continue to be important because, in many communities, programs aimed at gang intervention are often based on the assumption that employment can make a difference in reducing the amount of gang delinquency in which youngsters will engage.

Questions for Consideration

As you finish reading this section, consider the following questions:

1. What do we mean when we use the word theory, and to what extent does theory relate to the "real world?"
2. Are most programs dealing with delinquent youngsters based on one or more theories? Do the people who run these programs always think in terms of theories? What other words might be used that really are substitutes for "theory?"
3. What kinds of factors—social/environmental, personal/psychological, economic and so on—can help us better understand the world of gangs? Which ones are the most appealing to you, and why?
4. Is there any one theory that best helps us understand gangs? Do some theories distinguish between what we might call "normal" delinquency and gang activity?

References

Akers, Ronald L., Marvin D. Krohn, Lonn Lanza-Kaduce, and Marcia Rado-sevich. (1979). "Social Learning and Deviant Behavior: A Specific Test of a General Theory." *American Sociological Review* 44: 635–655.

Akers, Ronald L. (1994). *Criminological Theories: Introduction and Evaluations*. Los Angeles, CA: Roxbury.

Babbie, Earl. (1992). *The Practice of Social Research*. 6th ed. Belmont, CA: Wadsworth.

Bernard, Thomas J. (1990). "Twenty Years of Testing Theories: What Have We Learned and Why?" *Journal of Research in Crime and Delinquency* 27: 325–347.

Winfree, L. Thomas, Jr. and Howard Abadinsky. (1996). *Understanding Crime: A Guide to Crime Theory*. Chicago: Nelson-Hall.

Winfree, L. Thomas Jr. and Curt T. Griffiths. (1983). "Social Learning and Marijuana Use: A Trend Study of Deviant Behavior in a Rural Middle School." *Rural Sociology* 48: 219–239.

Winfree, L. Thomas, Jr., Curt T. Griffiths, and Christine S. Sellers. (1989). "Social Learning Theory, Drug Use, and American Indian Youths." *Justice Quarterly* 6: 395–417.

4

Social Learning Theory, Self-Reported Delinquency, and Youth Gangs: A New Twist on a General Theory of Crime and Delinquency

L. Thomas Winfree, Jr., Teresa V. Bäckström, and G. Larry Mays

Gang researchers typically describe the "costs" and "rewards" of gang behavior and the social context—complete with initiation rituals—in which one become a full-fledged member; concurrently, they describe the gang's primacy for its members, the intensity that terms like "the 'hood'" and "*mi barrio*" have for many gang members, and the priority of loyalty to the gang, a loyalty bordering on that normally expressed for one's family (cf. Curry and Spergel, 1988; Horowitz, 1983; Spergel, 1990, pp. 208–217, 223–226; Torres, 1980; Vigil, 1988). That is, without specifically mentioning either differential association theory or social learning theory, many observers of the gang scene, but especially the subcultural/cultural transmission writers, have used the basic terminologies and causal processes of both theories to describe and explain the gang problem (cf. Cloward and Ohlin, 1960; Cohen, 1955; Miller, 1958; Shaw and McKay, 1931; Thrasher, 1927).[1] We believe, therefore, that elements of social learning theory hold much promise for providing insights into the process of becoming and continuing as a gang member. To this end, we address the following question: To what extent are attitudes toward gangs and gang activity, social reinforcers and punishers, and differential associations linked to self-reported gang involvement and gang-related delinquency? Before addressing this question, however, an examination of the ties between social learning theory and youth gangs is in order.

Reprinted by permission of Sage Publications, Inc. from *Youth & Society*, Vol. 26, No. 2 (December 1994): 147–177.

Social Learning Theory and Youth Gangs: Conceptual Links

Ronald L. Akers' variant of social learning theory represents a merger of Edwin Sutherland's differential association theory and operant conditioning (Akers, 1985, 1992; see also Burgess and Akers, 1966; Sutherland and Cressey, 1974). The theory not only specifies the general social learning mechanisms by which the rationalizations, norms, rules, and motivations of non-normative behavior are learned—this was the heart of Sutherland's "generic" theory—but it also specifies the roles of positive and negative social mechanisms, all of which work to condition the "learner" toward or away from crime (Akers, 1985, 1992; Bandura, 1977). An important element in social learning theory is instrumental conditioning. Behavior is "acquired or conditioned by the effects, outcomes, or *consequences* it has on the person's environment" (Akers, 1985, p. 42; emphasis in the original). Further, Akers believes that the primary processes by which instrumental conditioning are achieved are reinforcement and punishment. Behavior is said to be reinforced when repeated episodes are met with a response by others that influences the actor to engage in the behavior again under similar circumstances; as a result, the behavior increases (Akers, 1985, pp. 43, 45). Behavior is punished when the response of others is such that the actor is discouraged from engaging in the conduct again under similar circumstances; as a result, the behavior decreases (Akers, 1985, pp. 44, 45). This description of rewards and punishments is nearly identical to those provided by qualitative gang research (Horowitz, 1983; Johnstone, 1981, 1983; Moore and Vigil, 1989; Torres, 1980; Vigil, 1988). Gang members reward certain behaviors in their peers and punish others, employing goals and processes that are indistinguishable from those described by Akers.

Like Sutherland, Akers (1985) believes that definitions are "normative meanings which are given to behavior; that is, they define an action as right or not right" (p. 49). Unlike Sutherland, Akers (1985) sees social learning theory as "viewing [these definitions] as verbal behavior (overt and subvocal), which can be reinforced, and by viewing them in a class of stimuli called *discriminative stimuli* (p. 49; emphasis in the original). Discriminative stimuli are themselves a source of reinforcements; they are differentially reinforcing. We view differential definitions as a construct, which implies that an individual learns, through close, intimate interactions with others, evaluations of orientations and behaviors as appropriate or inappropriate, good or bad. Delinquent conduct is more likely to ensue when young people develop, through reinforcements and punishments, definitions favorable rather than unfavorable to delinquency. For example, defending the neighborhood or the gang's honor—by whatever means necessary—is a discriminative stimuli with high moral authority.

Another point of convergence with Sutherland is found in differential associations, perhaps the single most important explanatory variable (cf. Akers, Krohn, Lanza-Kaduce, and Radosevich, 1979; Krohn, Lanza-Kaduce, and Akers, 1984; Sellers and Winfree, 1990). The concept of differential associations—typically operationalized as the proportion of one's best friends that engages in some illicit act—has a natural linkage to gang research. Gangs typically do not encourage active members to have friends, especially close friends, outside of the gang (cf. Horowitz, 1983; Miller, 1977; Spergel, 1990, pp. 223–226). We suspect that the ties between differential associations and both gang membership and self-reported juvenile misconduct should be as strong as that previously reported between drug-using peers and self-reported illicit drug use (cf. Akers et al., 1979; Goe, Napier, and Bachtel, 1985; Johnson, Marcos and Bahr, 1987; Orcutt, 1987; Winfree and Griffiths, 1983). Following both Sutherland and Akers, then, the greater the proportion of one's best friends who are youth-gang members, the greater the social forces impelling the youth to become a gang member.

Data and Measures

Sample

In early 1991, two independent public school districts in a single southern New Mexico county were approached about a survey of gang-related activities. The county had been experiencing what could be described as gang-related activities: the appearance of graffiti on fences and buildings, group fights involving youngsters displaying certain "colors," and, especially, drive-by shootings. The local newspaper had given this "gang activity" prominent coverage; the police department had formed a gang unit; and the city council had created a gang task force to assess the nature and scope of the local gang problem. Clearly, in this community, there was, at the time of the school-based survey, much apprehension concerning the perceived level and seriousness of youth-gang activity (Mays, Fuller, and Winfree, 1994; Mays, Winfree, and Jackson, 1993).

After much negotiation, the administrators of three area schools agreed to a limited, stratified random sample of ninth- and eleventh-grade students. This research reports on the ninth-grade students only, of which there were approximately 1,000 in attendance at the three schools. This emphasis is justified for two reasons. First, prior youth-gang research suggests that much gang recruitment occurs in the middle or junior high schools (Johnstone, 1983; Lasley, 1992; see also Spergel, 1990); ninth-grade students, then, represent a high-risk group for gang recruitment and gang activity. Second, by the eleventh grade, many active youth-gang members may not be in school (Curry and Spergel, 1992; Spergel, 1990). For both of these reasons, a study of gang recruitment and gang activity among ninth graders seems warranted.[2]

The names of 340 ninth-grade students, roughly one in three, were drawn from attendance lists provided by both school districts. Within each school, male students were purposefully oversampled at a ratio of three to one: the sample included the names of 80 females and 260 males. On the administration days, absentees numbered 52, decreasing the maximum sample size to 288 students. Another 40 students elected not to report to the administration sites. Questionnaires were distributed to 248 students, after which the study's general purpose was explained and the students offered the opportunity to withdraw; only two students exercised this option. Fourteen questionnaires were later eliminated from consideration due to incompleteness of responses or nonresponsiveness. The remaining 234 questionnaires represented 81.3 percent of the students selected for the sample who were in attendance on the administration day or 68.8 percent of the students originally selected for the study. In discussions with schools administrators, we learned that perhaps 10 percent of the ninth-grade students had repeated at least one class, and many were two or three years older than their peers. Because we were exclusively interested in the younger members of the ninth-grade cohort, we next deselected anyone over the age of sixteen from the sample. Therefore, we dropped another thirty-seven students. The remaining 197 individuals formed the final sample for this study.[3]

Nearly two-thirds of the youths (62.9%) attended two rural junior high schools located within a few miles of the Mexican border and characterized by a high Mexican-American population. The remaining students (37.1%) lived in a city of 62,000 residents some twenty miles northwest of the rural school district. The final ratio of males to females was 2.3 to 1, slightly lower than called for by the sampling protocol: There were 138 males and 59 females. Three fourths of the sample were Spanish surnamed. Among the remaining students there were very few African and Asian-Americans; Anglos—an indigenous term used to refer to all nonminorities—accounted for 80 percent of the remaining students. The average student was 15.5 years of age, and the range was 12 to 16 years. Again, with the exception of oversampling males, these statistics suggest that the sample was representative of the communities.

Measures

Delinquency. We employed a self-report delinquency (SRD) inventory.[4] Each respondent was asked to indicate his or her involvement in a list of twenty-two different activities, the specific content for which was based on research by Gold (1970); Hindelang, Hirschi, and Weis (1981); and Osgood, O'Malley, Bachman, and Johnston (1989). Recent SRD studies, including Fagan's (1989) study of New York City gang youth and Osgood et al.'s (1989) examination of a national sample of high school seniors, examined variations by offense-specific indices. The current study focuses on serious youthful misconduct; consequently, seven self-reported behaviors, including general status offenses (e.g., running away from home, curfew breaking), school-based non-normative conduct (e.g., skipped school, been suspended from school), and minor misconduct (e.g., spreading rumors about another youth), were dropped from the analysis.

The respondents were asked to indicate, using the following fixed categories, how often they had "broken these rules" since leaving the eighth grade; (1) never, (2) one or two times, (3) three to five times, (4) six to ten times, (5) more than ten times. This self-report anchoring point proved to be problematic. The time frame reflected by the phrase, "since leaving the eighth grade," was slightly less than one calendar year, as the data were collected in February and March. However, it is possible that some students sampled failed a grade, that is, "since leaving the eighth grade" translated into nearly two years, which is another reason that we limited our focus to youths under seventeen years old. It is possible that we have included some individuals who are being asked to recall information over a two-year period. We believe that the odds of a recall period greater than eighteen to twenty months is slight and that the number of youths affected is fairly small.

To further minimize the effects of this shortcoming, we also elected to focus on the level of criminal involvement as opposed to the specific rates of offending. To this end, we assigned a value of "1" to each offense, for which the self-reported offending exceeded "once or twice." Individuals who did not report any offending or reported involvement only once or twice were accorded a value of "0." Next, the fifteen offenses were grouped into five composite indices: (1) *Theft Crimes* (taken things worth less than $2; taken thing worth between $2 and $50; taken things worth over $50); (2) *Other-Property Crimes* (borrowed someone's car without his or her permission; destroyed public property; destroyed private property); (3) *General Personal Crimes* (had a fist fight with one other person; "beat up" on kids who hadn't done anything to you; hurt or inflicted pain on someone else to see them squirm); (4) *Drug-related Crimes* (bought or drank beer, wine, liquor; used illegal drugs like marijuana or cocaine; sold illegal drugs like marijuana or cocaine); and (4) *Group-Context Personal Crimes* (taken part in a fight involving more than two people where only fists were used; taken part in a fight involving more than two people where weapons other than fists were used; shot at someone because you were told to by someone else). Using this procedure, the composite scores reflected how many of the offense-specific crimes the youth reported committing three or more times. For each of the five separate indices, the summated scores ranged from 0 to 3. Cronbach's alpha provided a measure of scale reliability: theft crime ($\alpha = .68$), property crime ($\alpha = .79$), personal crime ($\alpha = .60$), drug-related crime ($\alpha = .54$), and group-context crime ($\alpha = .72$). Summary statistics for each SRD offense index—and the rest of the variables—are reported in table 4.1.

Table 4.1   Variables and Attributes with Unweighted Sample Distribution

Variable	Attributes	% (frequencies)/Mean (δ)
Hispanic	0 = Non-Hispanic	24.9 (49)
	1 = Hispanic	75.1 (148)
Male	0 = Female	29.9 (59)
	1 = Male	70.1 (138)
Urban	0 = County	62.9 (124)
	1 = City	37.1 (73)
Age	In years	$\bar{X}$ = 15.5 (δ = 0.57)
Differential Associations:	1 = None	59.3 (105)
Peer Gang Members	2 = Less than ½	20.3 (40)
	3 = More than ½	11.7 (23)
	4 = All	14.7 (29)
Differential Associations:	−1 = gang disapproval	37.1 (73)
Peers' Approval	0 = no difference	43.1 (85)
	+1 = gang approval	19.8 (39)
Differential Associations:	−1 = gang disapproval	74.4 (146)
Adults' Approval	0 = no difference	16.2 (32)
	+1 = gang approval	9.6 (19)
Differential Reinforcers:	−1 = net punishers	6.1 (12)
Reinforcers-Punishers Index	0 = no difference	26.9 (53)
	+1 = net reinforcers	67.0 (32)
Differential Reinforcers:	−1 = negative reactions	42.6 (84)
Peers' Reactions	0 = no differences	14.2 (28)
	+1 = positive reactions	43.1 (85)
Differential Reinforcers:	1 = negative reactions	68.0 (134)
Parents' Reactions	0 = no differences	6.6 (13)
	+1 = positive reactions	25.4 (50)
Differential Definitions:		
Pro-Gang Attitudes	Scale score	$\bar{X}$ = 6.46 (δ = 2.29)
Youth Gang Members	0 = Nongang	81.7 (161)
	1 = Gang	18.3 (36)
Theft Crime	Index score	$\bar{X}$ = 1.31 (δ = 1.05)
Other-Property Crime	Index score	$\bar{X}$ = 1.21 (δ = 1.14)
Personal Crime	Index score	$\bar{X}$ = 1.27 (δ = 0.89)
Drug Related Crime	Index score	$\bar{X}$ = 1.04 (δ = 0.94)
Group Context Crimes	Index score	$\bar{X}$ = 0.70 (δ = 0.95)

Gang Membership. We employed a combination of the self-definitional and criterion methods to determine whether the youth was a *youth gang member* (cf. Curry and Spergel, 1992; Klein, 1971; Miller, 1990; Short, 1989). The instrument included a series of questions related to the respondents' gang involvement. At one point, we asked the following questions: "Have you ever been in a gang?" There were three additional criteria that the gang had to possess before we included the youth as a present or former gang member. First, there had to be a group name and at least one of the following cultural elements: (a) an initiation, (b) a specific leader or leaders, and (c) gang "nick-names" for members. Second, the gang had to employ at least one of the following symbols: (a) "colors," (b) tattoo(s), (c) hand signs, and (d) jewelry. Finally, we asked the youths to rank the five most important activities engaged in by the gang. To qualify as a youth gang, at least one illicit activity (i.e., sex, drugs, or drinking) or one illegal activity (i.e., fighting, committing crimes, vandalism) had to appear on this list. By this restrictive definitional process, we identified thirty-six current or former gang members, or 18.3 percent of the sample of ninth-grade students in the three schools surveyed.

Social Learning Measures.

Differential associations. Akers specified that besides coming first in the causal nexus, at a minimum, differential associations have at least two sources: peers and significant others (Akers et al., 1979, p. 638; see also Akers, 1985). Peer influence is by far the most common indicator of differential associations. It would be a misinterpretation of both Sutherland and Akers to assume that these ties simply reflect a restatement of the old saw "birds of a feather flock together." Rather, as observed by Sutherland and Cressey (1974), "the theory of differential association is concerned with ratios of associations with patterns of behavior, no matter what the character of the person representing them" (p. 79). Indeed, we defined *differential association* as a proportion of one's best friends (i.e., reflecting the intensity dimension) who were involved in gang activity, and measured it by the following question: "About how many of your *best friends* are gang members?" We provided the following response categories for our first measure of differential associations, *peer gang members*: (1) none or almost none, (2) less than half, (3) more than half, and (4) all or almost all. Most of the students sampled (53.3%) had no friends who were gang members.

The second aspect of differential associations, often tied to the construct of norm qualities, is defined as the perceived values of one's significant others and parents.[5] Peers, significant-other adults, and parents are part of what Akers and associates (1979, p. 638) describe as the groups that "provided the social environments in which exposure to definitions, imitation or models, and social reinforcements . . ." takes place. *Norm qualities* traditionally have been defined as either prescriptive (telling you what to do) or proscriptive (telling you what not to do). More recently, additional aspects of norm qualities have been included in studies of misconduct: ascriptive norms fail to provide guidance or matters of moral decision-making; and permissive norms may not only approve of certain forms of misconduct but may even encourage participation (Sellers, Winfree, and Griffiths, 1993).

In the present context, both the norm qualities of significant-other adults and peers were measured. The following question tapped the permissiveness ɔf significant-other adult norm qualities: "What is the attitude toward gangs of most of the adults whose opinions you value or think are important?" The youths were asked to select one of the following responses: (1) strongly disapprove, (2) disapprove, (3) depends on the circumstances, (4) approve, and (5) strongly approve; the higher the score reported, the greater the approval. The identical question was asked about ". . . teenagers whose opinions you value or think are important." For this analysis, strong approval and approval were collapsed into one category and assigned a value of +1. Similarly, strong disapproval and disapproval were collapsed and coded as −1. The response that depends on circumstance was coded as 0. As a general observation, the youths surveyed reported higher levels of *peer approval* than *adult approval*.

Differential reinforcements. Social reinforcers constitute a major component of Akers' variant of social learning theory. As Akers (1985) notes, "sometimes our behavior is met by reactions from others (or has some other consequence attached to it) which influence us to do the same again under similar circumstances" (p. 44). Reinforcers are either positive (a reward is received) or negative (a punisher is removed.) Akers further differentiates between social and nonsocial reinforcers, the basic distinction being that the latter are rewarding at an unconditioned or physiological level, while the former require other human beings to aid in their interpretation as desired states or outcomes. Similarly, Akers' social learning theory places considerable emphasis on the role of punishers to extinguish the behavior. As with reinforcers, "punishment may be brought about by either the addition or subtraction of stimulus events" (Akers, 1985, p. 44). Akers also recognizes that punishers may be social and nonsocial, or even combined social/nonsocial differential reinforcements (Akers, 1985; Akers et al., 1979).

We asked the subjects to review two lists of what were arbitrarily defined as good and bad things associated with gang membership. The good things included the following: (1) be "cool" (positive social reinforcer), (2) feel successful (positive social reinforcer), (3) be more like someone else (positive social reinforcer), (4) for the excitement (positive nonsocial reinforcer), and (5) for the money (positive nonsocial reinforcer). The list of bad things included the following: (1) get in trouble with the police (negative social punisher), (2) get in trouble with my parents (negative social punisher), (3) lose friend (negative social punisher), (4) feel guilty (negative social/nonsocial punisher), (5) get hurt (negative nonsocial punisher). The respondents were asked to check those outcomes that they believed could or would happen to gang members. For the purposes of this analysis, we assigned a value of −1 to all punishers and +1 to all reinforcers checked by the students and summed across the 10 items. In cases where the sum of all items was negative, we assigned a value of −1, whereas those students who perceived as many pluses as minuses received a score of 0, and those cases in which the pluses outnumbered the minuses were accorded a score of +1. The uncollapsed *reinforcers/punishers index* was reasonably reliable ($\alpha = .62$).

The second set of differential reinforcers measures was also derived directly from Akers and associates (1979); it reflected the probable rewarding and punishing reactions of friends and family members when faced with the prospect that the respondent was a gang member. To measure *parents' reactions*, we asked the following question: "What would your parents or guardians most likely do if they thought you were a member of a gang?" Respondents were asked to select one of the following possible responses: (1) encourage you, (2) disapprove but do nothing, (3) scold or punish you, (4) kick you out of the house, and (5) turn you over to the police. In addition, they could give other possible reactions. This latter group, along with the five other responses, was collapsed into a continuum that include negative responses (-1), neutral responses (0), and positive responses ($+1$). In order to obtain *peers' reactions*, the identical question was asked about ". . . the teenagers whose opinions you value or think are important." As a general observation, the youths surveyed reported more negative reactions among their parents and guardians than was the case for peers.

Differential definitions. The expression of pro-deviance attitudes has been used in a number of studies to measure differential definitions (cf. Akers et al., 1979; Sellers and Winfree, 1990). It has been borrowed directly from Sutherland's differential association theory and is conceived to be a product of the process whereby the individual, through interactions with others, learns evaluations of behavior as good or bad. Deviant behavior is more likely to result when individuals develop definitions that are favorable rather than unfavorable to that behavior. The pro-deviance differential-definition measure used in this study was grounded in the "gang experience." The subjects were asked whether they disapproved, neither approved nor disapproved, or approved of the following: (1) having friends in gangs, (2) being in a gang yourself, (3) taking part in illegal gang activities such as fights, and (4) doing whatever the gang leaders tell you to do. The higher the scale score, the more pro-gang the attitude. The *pro-gang attitudes* scale exhibited a high level of reliability ($\alpha = .84$).

Personal-Biographical Characteristics.

Gender. Gang behavior, especially gang-related crime, is largely a male phenomenon (cf. Bowker, Gross, and Klein, 1980; Campbell, 1987, 1990, 1991; Spergel, 1986, 1990). Campbell (1990) notes that females in gangs have typically been used "to carry weapons (being immune to search by male officers), provide alibis, act as spies and lures, and provide sex for male members'' (p. 168). We acknowledged this differential status and involvement by oversampling males to guarantee sufficient gang members to provide a meaningful analysis. The final sample included 138 males (70.1%) and 59 females (29.9%). For analytic purposes, however, we weighted the females' responses so that the ratio of males to females approximated the actual population; that is, each female's response was accorded a weight of 2.3. We coded gender as *male* (1) or *female* (0).

Residence pattern. Gangs are often viewed as a large city phenomenon, although recent studies have called this generalization into question (cf. Johnstone, 1981; Maxson, Klein, and Gordon, 1987; McKinney, 1988; Takata and Zevitz, 1987, 1990). Students were coded as one (1) if they resided in the city or urban setting and zero (0) if they resided elsewhere. As previously noted, most of the sample was non-urban (62.9%).

Ethnicity. The gang phenomenon in the Southwest has long been associated with the Hispanic-American culture (Spergel, 1990, p. 212), although critics point to the fact that there is nothing endemic to the Chicano barrio to support the view that it is more gang- or violence-prone than other cultural communities (Erlanger, 1979). For example, as Vigil (1988, p. 7) maintains, although Chicano gangs are notable because of their prevalence and persistence, only about 4 percent to 10 percent of barrio youngsters—the population perhaps at greatest risk—are associated with gangs. However, most studies of youth gangs focus on the minority status of the gang membership (cf. Fagan, 1989; Fagan, Piper, and Moore, 1986; Miller, 1975, 1982; Spergel, 1990). Given the relatively small number of non-Hispanic minority-group members in the samples, ethnicity was coded as *Hispanic* (1) and non-Hispanic (0). Again, over three quarters of the sample (75.1%) was Hispanic.

Age. Older youths typically report far more extensive crime histories and a broader range of self-reported delinquencies (Spergel, 1986, 1990). *Age* was treated as an interval-level variable. The average age was 15.5, with a standard deviation of 0.57.

Design of the Analysis. As a result of the variable operationalizations, we employed two different analytic techniques: logistic regression and ordinary least squares regression. First, we were interested in whether the youth had ever been involved in a gang. Our intent was to demonstrate that, knowing certain information about all members of our study, we could predict group membership. To this end, we employed the SAS logistic regression analysis (Harrell, 1986). Logistic regression (Cox, 1970) is a nonlinear regression procedure that requires far fewer assumptions than linear classification methods such as discriminant analysis.[6] That is, the logistic model makes no assumptions about the normality of the classification variables, nor about the quality of the dispersion matrices for the several populations; it is often preferred to discriminant analysis (Cox, 1970). The data were also analyzed using the linear discriminant analysis program found in SPSS^x (SPSS, Inc., 1983) with qualitatively similar results.

Second, we were interested in the level of youthful involvement in five types of criminal conduct: theft crime, joy-riding/destruction crime, personal crime, drug-related crime, and group-context crime. We employed z-score transformations for the measures of delinquency. Thus, using ordinary least squares (OLS) regression, we provide a test of the linkages between social learning theory, gang involvement, and five forms of illegal behavior whereby the unstandardized coefficients can be compared across all forms of illegal behavior.

Results

Youth Gang Membership: Predicting Involvement in Gangs

The logistic regression equations summarized in table 4.2 address the first part of the research question: To what extent is the level of self-reported gang involvement linked to personal-biographical characteristics, social reinforcers, social punishers, attitudes toward gangs and gang activity, and differential associations? The first model in table 4.2 summarizes the logit created by the personal-biographical variables.[7] The relatively small Somers' d for this logit ($d_{yx} = .359$) suggests that the model provides a poor means of classifying gang members. It would appear that, although Hispanics and males are more likely to be gang members than nongang members, we should not make too much of this conclusion.

The second model includes social learning theory's differential association elements, only one of which made a significant contribution to the logit. That is, gang members, more than uninvolved youths, exhibit differential associations (i.e., peers in gangs). The Somers' coefficient ($d_{yx} = .591$) is nearly twice that observed in the model for personal-biographical variables alone. It would appear that knowing something about one's friends' involvement in gangs is a better predictor of a youth's own gang involvement than are considerations such as race, sex, or residence pattern. Interestingly, neither the norm qualities of peers or significant-other adults are important in distinguishing gang members from those who eschew such groups.

The third model summarizes the classification results for the logit that employs the three differential reinforcement variables. The strength of these social learning variables is reflected in the fact that the unstandardized coefficient, model chi-square results, and Somers' d coefficient are similar to those reported in the model for differential associations. This latter finding is particu-

Table 4.2   Logistic Regression: Current Youth Gang Members by
Person-Biographical Characteristics and Social Learning Variables,
with Unstandardized Coefficients, Standard Errors (in parentheses),
and Somers' Coefficients

Variables	Personal-Biographical Variables	Differential Associations	Differential Reinforce-ments	Differential Definitions	All Variables
Hispanic	1.10*				0.70
	(0.55)				(0.67)
Male	1.26*				
	(0.52)				0.79
					(0.60)
Urban	0.07				
	(0.43)				0.34
					(0.55)
Age	0.56				
	(0.33)				−0.38
					(0.45)
Differential Associations:		1.07*			0.57*
Peer Gang Members		(0.19)			(0.26)
Differential Associations:		−0.11			−0.16
Peers' Approval		(0.29)			(0.35)
Differential Associations:		0.31			0.07
Adults' Approval		(0.31)			(0.37)
Differential Reinforcers:			1.06*		0.38
Reinforcers/Punishers Index			(0.33)		(0.42)
Differential Reinforcers:			0.31		0.05
Peers' Reactions			(0.25)		(0.31)
Differential Reinforcers:			0.39		0.27
Parents' Reactions			(0.23)		(0.28)
Differential Definitions:				0.57*	0.30*
Pro-Gang Attitudes				(0.10)	(0.13)
Model Chi-Square	13.76*	43.04*	28.81*	46.15*	61.06*
Somers' d_{yx} Coefficient	0.359	0.591	0.541	0.626	0.702

*$p \leq .05$.

larly intriguing because much of the previous research on peer influences supports the overwhelming primacy of deviant peers. However, neither peer nor parental reactions to gang membership provide insights into actual membership.

Knowing the extent to which a youth possesses pro-gang attitudes provides the single best method of discriminating between gang and nongang youth. The results of the logistic analysis reported in the fifth equation suggest that this variable alone is a better discriminator than either differential associations or differential reinforcements. Simply put, youth possessing pro-gang attitudes are very likely to be youth-gang members.

The final equation examines all eleven independent variables. First, the model chi-square value ($\chi^2 = 61.06$) and Somers' coefficient ($d_{yx} = .702$) suggest that the logit created from the combined model provides a better method of discriminating between gang and nongang youth than any of the previous logits. Second, none of the personal-biographical variables makes a significant contribution to the logit. Third, the peer-as-gang-members variable, whereas half that observed in the differential-associations-alone model, still exerts a significant influence in this equation. Unlike the impact of gang-member peers, which continues to be significant and direct, the influence of the reinforcer/punisher index is no longer significant. The contribution of this variable to the logit drops with the inclusion of gang attitudes, suggesting that the former's influence is either indirect, through the creation of pro-gang attitudes, or suppressed by gang attitudes (see Rosenberg, 1968). These data, unfortunately, cannot distinguish between these effects.[8] Finally, the influence of gang attitudes is, like gang-member peers, significant and direct. Gang members appear to possess very pro-gang attitudes.

Juvenile Crime: Predicting Crime-Specific Offense Involvement

We present five separate ordinary least-squares regression equations in table 4.3, one each for the SRD subscales, to determine the extent to which social-learning variables are differentially linked to the crime-specific subscales. Given the literature of "gang-related" criminal activity, we suspect that the social learning variables will be of greatest importance for offenses committed in a group context and less so for the more garden-variety SRD offenses. More-over, the key social learning variables are all grounded in the "gang experience." It is possible that involvement in these other nongroup-context activities is also related to either gang membership or social learning factors or both.

Theft-Crime Offending. Three variables make significant contributions to the prediction of theft crimes. Specifically, theft crimes are highest among urban, male youths with pro-gang attitudes. This form of offending is not linked in any significant way to the remaining personal-biographical variables or social learning variables. In particular, it is not linked to gang membership. Although possession of the same generally negativistic attitudes as gang members helps us understand this form of offending, gang membership is not critical. The eleven-variable solution accounts for a respectable 23.3 percent of the variance in the level of self-reported theft crime, with pro-gang attitudes making at least four times the relative contribution of the other two significant factors, gender and residence pattern.

Other-Property Crime Offending. The adjusted coefficient of determination for the second equation ($R^2 = .292$) was 30 percent greater than that reported for the theft crimes. Most of this increased explanatory power was derived from personal-biographical variables: higher instances of other-property crimes, including joy-riding and vandalism, were reported by males and urban residents than by females and those subjects in rural areas. Indeed, unstandardized coefficients for both residential pattern and gender were higher in this equation, with the coefficient for gender being nearly 50 percent higher.

We also observed significant unstandardized coefficients for only one of the six social learning variables. Like theft crimes, other-property crime offending was tied to the possession of pro-gang attitudes. The relative and

Table 4.3 Ordinary Least Squares Regression: Self-Reported Crime-Specific Offenses by Person-Biographical Characteristics, Social Learning Variables, and Gang Involvement, with Unstandardized Coefficients and (in parentheses) Standardized Coefficients

Variables	Theft Crime	Other-Property Crime	Personal Crime	Drug-Related Crime	Group-Context Crime
Hispanic	0.08	0.10	−0.36*	0.06	−0.14
	(0.03)	(0.04)	(−0.16)	(0.02)	(−0.06)
Male	0.27*	0.43*	0.23*	0.15	0.40*
	(0.13)	(0.21)	(0.12)	(0.08)	(0.20)
Urban	0.23*	0.28*	0.05	0.46*	0.21*
	(0.11)	(0.14)	(0.03)	(0.22)	(0.10)
Differential Associations:	0.06	0.01	0.08	0.03	0.28*
Peer Gang Members	(0.07)	(0.02)	(0.08)	(0.03)	(0.30)
Differential Associations:	0.09	0.006	−0.02	0.11	−0.008
Peers' Approval	(0.07)	(0.004)	(−0.01)	(0.08)	(−0.006)
Differential Associations:	−0.09	−0.11	−0.0001	−0.23*	−0.03
Adults' Approval	(−0.05)	(−0.07)	(−0.006)	(−0.14)	(−0.02)
Differential Reinforcers:	−0.03	0.15	0.17	0.18*	0.18
Reinforcers/Punishers Index	(0.05)	(0.09)	(0.09)	(0.09)	(0.10)
Differential Reinforcers:	0.0006	−0.007	−0.08	−0.06	0.05
Peers' Reactions	(−0.0004)	(0.006)	(−0.07)	(−0.06)	(0.05)
Differential Reinforcers:	0.11	0.05	0.13	−0.01	−0.11
Parents' Reactions	(−0.09)	(−0.04)	(−0.11)	(−0.01)	(−0.09)
Differential Definitions:	0.21*	0.19*	0.20*	0.15*	0.12*
Pro-Gang Attitudes	(0.45)	(0.41)	(0.45)	(0.32)	(0.26)
Youth-Gang Member	−0.03	0.16	−0.31	0.31	0.38*
	(−0.01)	(0.06)	(−0.11)	(0.11)	(0.14)
Multiple R	0.516	0.568	0.528	0.509	0.704
Multiple R^2	0.266	0.323	0.279	0.259	0.495
Multiple R^2 (Adjusted)	0.233	0.292	0.245	0.226	0.472

*$p \leq 0.05$.

absolute contributions of this variable to the other-property crime solution are virtually identical to those reported for theft crime.

Personal-Crimes Offending. Attitudinally, high personal-crimes offending is best understood in terms of pro-gang attitudes. However, no other social learning variable made a significant impact in the second regression equation. Two personal-biographical variables did come into play: gender exhibited a significant link, with males reporting more instances of offending than females; and Spanish-surnamed youth reported significantly lower levels of offending than other youths. The explained variance for personal-crime offending ($R^2 = .245$) was in between the variance reported in the previous two equations.

Drug-Related Crime. The coefficient of determination for drug-related crime ($R^2 = .226$) is similar to that for the other "garden-variety" forms of criminal misconduct. However, some different forces appear to be at work. For example, adult approval is inversely and significantly related to offending: The lower the significant-other adult approval of gangs and gang behavior, the greater the offending. We suspect that this observation is related to the fact that those who engage in a wider variety of drug-related offenses also know that the significant-other adults in their lives would disapprove of such conduct. This knowledge, however, does not equate to the lower levels of criminal involvement. What we could be seeing in this equation is a problem with the time-order sequencing of the data: Those youths who already engage in higher levels of offending also view parental approval with disdain. Alternately, this could also be a case of "reaction formation" (Cohen, 1955), in which drug-law-violating youths are rejecting adult norm qualities. What is interesting about this finding is its crime-specific nature: It only appears for drug-related offenses. For their part, pro-gang attitudes contribute roughly twice as much to the explained variance as does adult approval: Youths with high pro-gang attitudes also exhibit higher levels of involvement in drug-related crime.

Only place of residence among the personal-biographical variables makes a significant contribution to the regression equation. In fact, the unstandardized coefficient for residence pattern in this equation is far greater than those observed for any of the other equations; moreover, in terms of the other variables in this equation, its contribution lies above both the reinforcers/ punishers index or adult approval and below gang attitudes. Thus it would appear that to a far greater extent than for any other offense, drug-related offenses may be part of a larger urban crime phenomenon, perhaps even a reflection of the absolute opportunity to buy, sell, and use drugs, including alcohol.

Group-Context Personal Crimes. Group-context offenses have two main characteristics that together distinguish them from the previous crime indexes. First, they are violent crimes, ranging from various forms of assault to attempted murder. Second, the offenses are by definition either committed in a group setting or at the command of someone else. For example, the two fight scenarios, one with only fists and the other with weapons other than fists, both involve more than two participants; the third offense, shooting at someone, occurred because of a third party's command or order.

The fifth and final regression equation in table 4.3 examines the links between the key independent variables and group-context personal crime. Besides the highest corrected coefficient of determination among the four equations ($R^2 = .472$), there are three distinct features to this equation. First, being male is not only significantly linked to the conduct, but the coefficient equals the best this variable achieved in any previous equation (see other property crimes). Thus, with the exception of drug-related crimes in which gender is relatively unimportant, males reported higher levels of involvement in theft crimes, personal crimes, other-property crimes, and group-context crimes.

Second, urban residence pattern makes a significant contribution in this equation, just as it has in three of the four others; however, its contribution is more like that reported for theft and other-property crime than for drug-related crime. Thus, to the extent to which group-context is a proxy measurement of "gang-related" crime, illicit gang activity is significantly more likely to occur in an urban setting than a rural one. The relative impact of this variable, however, is between one half and one third of the other significant factors, including gender.

Finally, group-context personal crimes exhibited strong and significant ties to gang attitudes and, for the first time, both differential associations and gang membership. Pro-gang attitudes and differential associations make very similar contributions to the explained variance. Higher levels of involvement are associated with pro-gang attitudes and higher proportions of gang-member peers. Gang membership makes roughly half the contribution of either of these social learning variables. Clearly, gang members are more likely to report higher levels of group offending.

Summary and Discussion

This research takes a somewhat unique approach to the study of delinquency by applying social learning theory concepts to youth gang membership and related juvenile misconduct. Specifically, we begin with the premise that involvement in youth gangs by ninth-grade students can be understood in terms of variables derived from Akers' (1985, 1992) variant of social learning theory. Indeed, this was the case: Gang members were distinguishable from nongang youths more in terms of variables derived from social learning than personal-biographical characteristics, including ethnicity, gender, and place of residence.

The level of involvement in offense-specific crimes, including theft crimes, general personal crimes, other-property crimes, and group-context personal crimes, constituted our second focus. We included various crime-specific offenses because previous gang researchers have implied that self-reported incidence rates may depend upon personal involvement in gangs. We found that three variables were consistently and significantly related to the level of self-reported misconduct. Respondents who had higher identification with progang attitudes, which are by definition antisocial and antilegal, reported more misbehaving. Second, except for personal crimes, city youths reported higher levels of offending than rural youths. Finally, with the exception of drug-related offenses, males were more likely than females to report higher levels of SRD.

Three sets of findings are of particular interest to the question of social learning theory's viability to gang research. First, differential associations, gang attitudes, *and* active gang membership all made significant contributions only in the case of group-context personal crime. This finding configures well with the social learning perspective: This crime type consists of offenses that are committed with a group or at the behest of others. Reinforcing this view is the observation that this offense subscale is the only one in which membership in a gang exhibits a direct and independent link to the rate of offending. Second, along with other recent reports on youth gangs, we did not find a link between gang membership and theft or general personal crimes (Altschuler and Brounstein, 1991; Fagan, 1989; Klein, Maxson, and Cunningham, 1991; cf. Taylor, 1990a, 1990b). Finally, variables derived from social learning performed differently depending upon the form of offending. Peer norm qualities and both peer and parental reactions revealed virtually nothing about youthful offending, or, for that matter, about gang membership. Drug-related and group-context crimes, the two forms of offending that exhibited the closest empirical ties to social learning theory, involved different combinations of social learning variables: Drug-related offending was understood largely in terms of the reinforcers/punishers index, adult approval, and pro-gang attitudes; group-context offending added differential associations and youth-gang membership to pro-gang attitudes, while exhibiting no significant ties to the punishers/reinforcers index or to adult approval. In short, only pro-gang attitudes exhibited consistent insights into youthful misconduct. Future studies of crime-specific offending and social learning theory should address the implications of these anomalies for social learning theory's ability to provide insights into gang recruitment and retention.

We acknowledge that this study has certain sample size, regional, and ethnicity-based limitations as to generalizability; moreover, because we only addressed gang membership and delinquency by ninth-grade students attending school, we did not have access to a significant group of potential subjects: those youths who have dropped out of school prior to or during the ninth grade. Nonetheless, we also believe that the analyses contain several noteworthy theoretical and policy implications. First, applying a theory not normally associated with gangs proved substantively and theoretically fruitful. We suggest that the youths in our sample viewed gang behavior much like their peers in other tests of social learning theory have viewed their youthful misconduct (Akers, 1985, 1992), but perhaps with greater connectivity owing to the social nature of gangs (see also Curry and Spergel, 1992). Second, this research runs counter to the conventional police truism that gang members are heavily involved in theft crimes (McKinney, 1988). Along these same lines, although gang members appear to be no more likely than nongang youths to engage in general personal crimes, they are more likely to engage in group-context violence, much of which typically takes the form of intergang or intergroup confrontations. Besides emphasizing the social roots of gangs, this finding may mean that youths predisposed to personal assault crimes may be recognized (and perhaps even recruited) by gangs for their fighting and risk-taking behaviors (i.e., fearlessness) a conclusion supported by other gang researchers (cf. Johnstone, 1983; Moore and Vigil, 1989; Vigil, 1983).

Problems with causal sequencing remain unanswered. Since its inception, social learning theory has faced criticism about what comes first—associations, definitions, or reinforcement (cf. Akers, 1993; Akers and LaGreca, 1991; Gottfredson and Hirschi, 1990; Hirschi, 1969; Lanza-Kaduce, Akers, Krohn, and Radosevich, 1982; Stafford and Ekland-Olson, 1982; Strickland, 1982). This research has not addressed these concerns. Perhaps it has added to the controversy because it appears that certain associations (e.g., adult norm qualities) are inversely related to at least one form of offending, drug-related crime. We suspect that because we are measuring offending and these variables at the same time, we may be seeing an example of "reaction formation," whereby the youths who have higher levels of offending are also rejecting the values of significant-other adults. Only additional research will be able to determine the validity of these rather speculative observations.

We further suspect that prevention and intervention programs that specifically target gangs as the source of property crimes or even general personal crimes may meet with limited success in slowing either the crimes in question or the proliferation of local gangs. As Curry and Spergel (1992, pp. 288—289) observed, there are differences not only between being gang-involved and committing gang delinquency, but also between nongang and gang delinquency. They further note, "Attempting to use prevention techniques tailored for gang delinquency in an effort to quell nongang delinquency or vice versa may prove uninformed and unfruitful" (Curry and Spergel, 1992, p. 289).

Appendix Intercorrelation Matrix (Pearson's *r* to the right of the diagonal; one-tailed significance to the left)

	(A)	(B)	(C)	(D)	(E)	(F)	(G)	(H)	(I)	(J)	(K)	(L)	(M)	(N)	(O)	(P)	(Q)
(A) Hispanic[1]	—	-.17	-.37	.07	.04	.03	.11	.11	.12	.18	.04	.11	-.02	-.02	-.17	-.04	.06
(B) Male[2]	.00	—	-.03	-.05	.20	.06	.16	-.10	.16	.12	.15	.19	.16	.27	.19	.12	.31
(C) Urban[3]	.00	.32	—	.03	-.02	.05	-.08	-.18	-.13	-.14	.00	-.06	.10	.12	.09	.20	.08
(D) Age[4]	.18	.22	.31	—	-.17	-.04	.03	.01	-.05	-.07	-.07	-.09	-.03	.03	.05	.02	-.06
(E) Reinf/Pun[5]	.23	.00	.36	.00	—	.13	.40	.13	.20	.39	.45	.38	.18	.30	.22	.26	.30
(F) PeerReact[6]	.28	.18	.21	.27	.00	—	.17	.16	.03	.27	.38	.18	.22	.11	.18	.15	.29
(G) ParReact[7]	.04	.00	.08	.32	.00	.00	—	.07	.29	.22	.22	.23	.01	.11	.01	.09	.12
(H) PeerAppr[8]	.03	.05	.00	.44	.02	.00	.11	—	.11	.26	.23	.07	.14	.11	.06	.11	.11
(I) AdltAppr[9]	.03	.00	.01	.21	.02	.32	.00	.03	—	.24	.22	.17	.04	.07	.08	-.04	.14
(J) BestFrs[10]	.00	.02	.00	.12	.00	.00	.00	.00	.00	—	.68	.42	.34	.34	.31	.28	.56
(K) AttGang[11]	.27	.00	.47	.13	.00	.00	.00	.00	.00	.00	—	.46	.48	.50	.45	.41	.60
(L) GangMbr[12]	.04	.00	.18	.07	.00	.00	.00	.00	.00	.00	.32	—	.20	.30	.12	.28	.43
(M) Theft[13]	.39	.00	.06	.30	.00	.00	.42	.01	.00	.00	.00	.00	—	.57	.41	.40	.42
(N) Othp[14]	.39	.00	.02	.31	.00	.00	.03	.12	.15	.00	.00	.00	.00	—	.43	.55	.55
(O) Person[15]	.00	.00	.08	.19	.00	.04	.46	.15	.11	.00	.00	.03	.00	.00	—	.31	.48
(P) Drug[16]	.23	.02	.00	.36	.00	.00	.07	.03	.27	.00	.00	.00	.00	.00	.00	—	.47
(Q) Group[17]	.18	.00	.09	.15	.00	.00	.02	.03	.01	.00	.00	.00	.00	.00	.00	.00	—

Note: 1. Ethnicity: Non-Hispanic (0), Hispanic (1); 2. Gender: Female (0), Male (1); 3. Residence: Rural (0), Urban (1); 4. Age: In years; 5. Reinforcers/Punishers Index: (-1) More Punishers, Equal (0), More Reinforcers (+1); 6. Peer Reactions: (-1) Negative, (0) Neutral, (+1) Positive; 7. Parents' Reactions: (-1) Negative, (0) Neutral, Positive (+1); 8. Peer Gang Approval: (-1) Disapprove, (0) Neutral, (+1) Approve; 9. Adult Gang Approval: (-1) Disapprove, (0) Neutral, (+1) Approve; 10. Proportion of Best Friends in Gangs; 11. Pro-Gang Attitudes: Higher score, more pro-gang; 12. Gang Member: (0) No. (1) Yes; 13. Theft Crime: Involvement Level; 14. Other Property Crime: Involvement Level; 15. Personal Crime: Involvement Level; 16. Drug Crime: Involvement Level; 17. Group-Context Crime: Involvement Level.

The fact that gangs are prevalent in the schools surveyed, as determined by independent examinations of school and police records, might explain why "gang attitudes" have effects, even when gang membership's efforts are largely limited to group-context personal crimes or crimes of aggression generally. That is, to resurrect Sutherland once more, definitions favorable to misconduct may be more prevalent in an environment where gang members exist than where they do not exist because such definitions may be learned through modeling or other vicarious experiences. Further, this suggestion raises a policy implication: reducing gangs may reduce crime not only by limiting crime by gang members but also by diminishing the power of "gang reinforcers" (pro-gang attitudes) on nongang members.

By contrast, if the target behavior is the violence commonly associated with youth gangs—for example, gang fights or drive-by shootings—then addressing the processes by which school-age children join gangs takes on greater significance. Gang interventionists may wish to explore the learning process— the reinforcers and punishers, along with the differential associations and definitions—linked to gang membership. For example, negative social punishers exhibited an inverse and independent relationship to gang membership. Consequently, getting out the specific message that gangs create problems for youths with their parents and with the law may make gang membership less appealing. It may be possible to use these same forces to "unlearn" gang motivations and definitions, or prevent the process from occurring (cf. Peat and Winfree, 1992; Thompson and Jason, 1988; Winfree, Sellers, and Clason, 1993).

Even assuming we are to classify correctly all gang and nongang youths in an area, there is much about even gang-related offenses that defies our relatively strong classificatory model. As Johnstone (1983), in his study of gang recruitment, observed, strategies designed to target and arrest gang leaders may meet with limited success. "A much more viable long-term strategy of gang control is to concentrate on drying up the sources of recruitment. The long-term survival of a youth gang just as for any other social group depends on its ability to attract new members" (Johnstone, 1983, p. 298). In order to accomplish this goal, however, we must better understand the recruitment and retention process. We suggest that a primary goal must be the development of better typologies of gang involvement and the application of theories such as social learning to their evolution.

Notes

1. Thompson and Jason (1988) provide an evaluation of an intervention program designed to combat street gangs. They do not explicitly reference learning theory; indeed, they tie the program to "social development theory" (Weis and Hawkins, 1981). What they describe is a "community psychology" approach to gang interven-

tion, including the individual and community costs of gangs and drugs, reinforcements and alternatives to pro-drug definitions, and values clarification. Peat and Winfree (1992) also describe an institutional-based rehabilitation program that uses social learning concepts that define the inmate therapeutic community as an agent of pro social change.

2. Fifty years of gang literature provides a relatively uniform image of the ties between education and youth gangs, at least regarding active gang membership: Gang members rarely attend or graduate high school (cf. Bogardus, 1926; Cohen, 1955; Johnstone, 1983; Lasley, 1992; Miller, 1958; Spergel, 1990; Takata and Zevitz, 1987). It appears that gang members prematurely leave school, but especially high school, in fairly large numbers and for a variety of academic and legal reasons. Therefore we acknowledge that this study only addresses the question of school-based gang involvement.

3. Comparison of the individuals who failed to complete their questions ($n = 14$), those dropped because they were over 16 years of age ($n = 37$), and the remaining 9th-grade students ($n = 197$) on all key behavioral, attitudinal, and sociodemographic indicators failed to reveal significant differences.

4. Nettler (1978) is critical of self-report studies of deviant behavior. As he has observed, "asking people questions about their behavior is a poor way of observing it" (Nettler, 1978, p. 107). This study, as we have noted, is not without its design problems, which we have acknowledged and corrected by offering a conservative view of youthful misconduct. Moreover, we employed a SRD measurement technique that has consistently shown reliable and valid results (cf. Gold, 1970; Hirschi, 1969; Hindelang et al., 1981; Osgood et al., 1989).

5. The study of norm qualities is not limited to social learning theory. Norm qualities are an integral part of social control theory's beliefs (Hirschi, 1969) and deterrence theory's "inhibitory variables" (Grasmick and Green, 1980). See Sellers et al. (1993) for a complete review of the literature and the links between legal attitudes, permissive norm qualities, and juvenile misconduct.

6. We let Y_i be the dependent variable (group indicator) for the ith observation, and let $X = (X_{i1}, X_{i2}, \ldots, X_{in}')$ be the vector of the independent variables for the ith observation. In binary logistic regression the model used is

$$P(Y_i = 1 = 1/(1 - \exp (X_i'B)) \qquad (1)$$

where $P(Y_i =)$ is the probability that the ith observation belongs to the group i, and B is the vector of unknown parameters that may or may not include the intercept term. If $P(Y_i = 1)$ is abbreviated as pi, straightforward manipulation shows

$$\text{logit}(p_i = \log (p_i/(1 - p_i)) = X_i'B \qquad (2)$$

Model parameters are interpreted in a manner similar to partial regression parameters: assuming that all other variables remain constant, a change of one unit in X_{ik} results in an increase of b_k units in the logit for case i. The nonlinear nature of the logit transformation must be remembered. A change of one unit from, say, 1 to 2 is not equivalent on the probability scale to a change of one unit from 20 to 21.

Somers' d, a product of SAS's logistic analysis procedure, is a measure of association that generalizes to Goodman and Kruskal's (1979) gamma. The logistic procedure reports this measure of association between the predicted ($X_i''\hat{B}$) and the population indicator, as in the correlation coefficient $-1 \leq d \leq 1$, with $| d | = 1$ implying perfect concordance. Somers' d is reported becaue it generalizes to multiple population situations better than parametric measures like R^2.

Finally, we conducted inspections for collinearity for both the logistic and ordinary least squares regression techniques. Both techniques are sensitive to collinearities among the model's independent variables. Hosmer and Lemeshow (1989) suggest that while collinearity analysis should be helpful in identifying the dependencies among the covariates, one would not normally employ these analyses for logistic analysis unless the estimated coefficients and standard errors provide evidence of degradation in the fit. There was no such evidence in the present analyses. In the case of the ordinary least squares analyses, we also saw no evidence of collinearity in the intercorrelation matrix (see Appendix) or the adjusted R^2 values.

7. Technically, the term *logit* was originally defined as a particular metametric transformation in quantal bioassays:

$$\text{logit}(\pi) = \log_e(\pi/1 \ \pi).$$

It is in this sense that the term *logit* is used throughout this article.

8. An ordinary least squares solution involving gang attitudes and the 10 independent variables is instructive (data not shown). First, it achieves a rather robust coefficient of determination ($R^2 = .534$). Second, two differential reinforcement variables, friends' reactions and the net reinforcers/punishers index, make similar significant contributions ($\beta = .15$ and $\beta = 17$, respectively). However, the strongest direct contributor to this equation is proportion of best friends in gangs ($\beta = .567$). No other personal biographical or social learning variables provide significant insights into personal definitions of gangs and gang behavior.

References

Akers, R. L. (1985). *Deviant behavior: A social learning approach* (3rd ed.). Belmont, CA: Wadsworth.

Akers, R.L. (1992). *Drugs, alcohol, and society: Social structure process and policy.* Belmont, CA: Wadsworth.

Akers, R.L. (1993). *Criminological theories: Introduction and evaluation.* Los Angeles: Roxbury.

Akers, R.L. and La Greca, A.J. (1991). Alcohol use among the elderly: Social learning, community context, and life events. In D.J. Pittman and H.R. White (Eds.), *Society, culture, and drinking patterns re-examined* (pp. 246–262). New Brunswick, NJ: Rutgers Center on Alcohol Studies.

Akers, R.L., Krohn, M.D., Lanza-Kaduce, L., and Radosevich, M. (1979). Social learning and deviant behavior: A specific test of a general theory. *American Sociological Review, 44*(4), 635–655.

Alschuler, D. and Brounstein, P.J. (1991). Patterns of drug use, drug trafficking and other delinquency among inner city adolescent males in Washington, D.C. *Criminology, 29*, 589–622.

Bandura, A. (1977). *Social learning theory.* Englewood Cliffs, NJ: Prentice-Hall.

Bogardus, E.S. (1926). *The city boy and his problems.* Los Angeles: House of Ralston.

Bowker, L.H., Gross, H. S., and Klein, M.W. (1980). Female participation in delinquent gang activity. *Adolescence, 15*, 509–519.

Burgess, R.L., and Akers, R.L. (1966). A differential association-reinforcement theory of criminal behavior. *Social Problems, 14*, 228–247.

Campbell, A. (1987). Self definitions by rejection: The case of gang girls. *Social Problems, 34*, 451–464.

Campbell, A. (1990). Female participation in gangs. In C.R. Huff (Ed.), *Gangs in America* (pp. 163–182). Newbury Park, CA: Sage.

Campbell A. (1991). *The girls in the gang* (2nd ed.). Cambridge, MA: Basil Backwell.

Cloward, R.A., and Ohlin, L.E. (1960). *Delinquency and opportunity: A theory of delinquent gangs.* New York: The Free Press.

Cohen, A. (1955). *Delinquent boys: The culture of the gangs.* Glencoe, IL: The Free Press.

Cox, D.R. (1970). *The analysis of binary data.* London: Methuen.

Curry, G.D., and Spergel. I.A. (1988). Gang homicide, delinquency, and community. *Criminology, 26*, 381–405.

Curry, G.D., and Spergel, I.A. (1992). Gang involvement and delinquency among Hispanic and African-American adolescent males. *Journal of Research in Crime and Delinquency, 29*, 273–291.

Etlanger, H.S. (1979). Estrangement, machismo, and gang violence. *Social Science Quarterly, 60*, 236–247.

Fagan, J. (1989). The social organization of drug use and drug dealing among urban gangs. *Criminology, 8*, 633–661.

Fagan, J., Piper, E., and Moore, M. (1986). Violent delinquents and urban youths. *Criminology, 24*, 439–471.

Goe, W.R., Napier, T.L., and Bachtel, D.C. (1985). Use of marijuana among rural high school students: A test of a facilitative-constraint model. *Rural Sociology, 50*, 409–426.

Gold, M. (1970). *Delinquent behavior in an American city.* Belmont, CA: Brooks/Cole.

Goodman, L.A., and Kurskal, W.H. (1979). *Measures of association for cross-classification.* New York: Springer-Verlag.

Gottfredson, M., and Hirschi, T. (1990). *A general theory of crime.* Palo Alto, CA: Stanford University Press.

Grasmick, H., and Green, D. (1980). Legal punishment, social disapproval, and internalization as inhibitors of illegal behavior. *Journal of Criminal Law and Criminology, 71*, (3), 325–335.

Harrell, F.E. (1986). The LOGIST procedure. *SUGI Supplementary Library Users' Guide, Version 5* (Chapter 23). Cary, NC: SAS Institute.

Hindelang, M.J., Hirschi, T., and Weis, J.G. (1981). *Measuring delinquency.* Beverly Hills, CA: Sage.

Hirschi, T. (1969). *Causes of delinquency*. Berkeley, CA: University of California Press.

Horowitz, R. (1983). *Honor and the American dream*. New Brunswick, NJ: Rutgers University Press.

Hosmer, D.W., Jr., and Lemeshow, S. (1989). *Applied logistic regression*. New York: John Wiley.

Johnson, R.E., Marcos, A.C., and Bahr, S.J. (1987). The role of peers in the complex etiology of adolescent drug use. *Criminology, 25*, 323–329.

Johnstone, J.W.C. (1981). Youth gangs and black suburbs. *Pacific Sociological Review, 24*, 355–375.

Johnstone, J.W.C. (1983). Recruitment to a youth gang. *Youth and Society, 14*, 281–300.

Klein, M.W. (1971). *Street gangs and street workers*. Englewood Cliffs, NJ: Prentice-Hall.

Klein, M.W., Maxson, C.L., and Cunningham, L.C. (1991). "Crack," street gangs, and violence. *Criminology, 29*, 623–650.

Krohn, M.D., Lanza-Kaduce, L., and Akers, R.L. (1984). Community context and theories of deviant behavior: An examination of social learning and social bonding theories. *Sociological Quarterly, 25*, 353–372.

Lanza-Kaduce, L., Akers, R.L, Krohn, M.D., and Radosevich, M. (1982). Conceptual and analytical models in testing social learning theory. *American Sociological Review, 47*(1), 169–173.

Lasley, J.R. (1992). Age, social context, and street gang membership: Are "youth" gangs becoming "adult" gangs? *Youth and Society, 23*, 434–451.

Maxson, C.L., Klein, M., and Gordon, M.A. (1987). *Gangs in smaller cities*. Unpublished manuscript.

Mays, G.L., Fuller, K., and Winfree, L.T., Jr. (1994). Gangs and gang activity in southern New Mexico: A descriptive look at a growing rural problem. *Journal of Crime & Justice, 17*(1), 25–44.

Mays, G.L., Winfree, L.T., Jr. and Jackson, S. (1993). Youth gangs in southern New Mexico: A qualitative analysis. *Journal of Contemporary Criminal Justice, 9*(2), 134–145.

McKinney, K.C. (1988, September). Juvenile gangs: Crime and drug trafficking. *Juvenile Justice Bulletin*, pp. 1–8.

Miller, W.B. (1958). Lower class culture as a generating milieu of gang delinquency. *Journal of Social Issues, 14*, 5–19.

Miller, W.B. (1975). *Violence by youth gangs and youth gangs as a crime problem in major American cities*. Washington, DC: National Institute of Juvenile Justice and Delinquency Prevention, U.S. Justice Department.

Miller, W.B. (1977). *Conceptions, definitions, and images of youth gangs*. Cambridge, MA: Harvard Law School, Center for Criminal Justice.

Miller, W.B. (1982). *Crime by youth gangs and groups in the United States*. Washington, DC: National Institute of Juvenile Justice and Delinquency Prevention, U.S. Justice Department.

Miller, W.B. (1990). Why the United States has failed to solve its youth gang problem.

In C.R. Huff (Ed.), *Gangs in America* (pp. 263–287). Newbury Park, CA: Sage.

Moore, J.W., and Vigil, J.D. (1989). Chicano gangs: Group norms and individual factors related to adult criminality. *Aztlan, 18*, 27–44.

Nettler, G. (1978). *Explaining crime.* New York: McGraw-Hill.

Orcutt, J.D. (1987). Differential association and marijuana use: A closer look at Sutherland (with a little help from Becker). *Criminology, 25*, 341–358.

Osgood, D.W., O'Malley, P.M., Bachman, J.G., and Johnston, L.D. Time trends and age trends in arrests and self-reported illegal behavior. *Criminology, 27*, 389–417.

Peat, B.J., and Winfree, L.T., Jr. (1992). Reducing the intra-institutional effects of prisonization: A study of a therapeutic community for drug-using inmates. *Criminal Justice and Behavior, 19*, 206–225.

Rosenberg, M. (1968). *Logic of survey analysis.* New York: Basic Books.

Sellers, C.S., and Winfree, L.T., Jr. (1990). Differential associations and definitions: A panel study of youthful drinking behavior. *The International Journal of the Addictions, 25*, 755–771.

Sellers, C.S., Winfree, L.T., Jr., and Griffiths, C.T. (1993). Legal attitudes, permissive norm qualities, and substance use: A comparison of American Indian and non-Indian youth. *The Journal of Drug Issues, 23*(3), 493–513.

Shaw, C.R., and McKay, H.D. (1931). Social factors in juvenile delinquency. In *Report of the National Commission on Law Observance and Law Enforcement* (Vol. 2, No. 13: *Report on the causes of crime*, pp. 192–198). Washington, DC: U.S. Government Printing Office.

Shaw, C.R., and McKay, H.D. (1942). *Juvenile delinquency in urban areas.* Chicago: University of Chicago Press.

Short, J.F. (1989). Exploring integration of the theoretical levels of explanation: Notes on gang delinquency. In S.F. Messner, M.D. Krohn, and A.E. Liska (Eds.), *Theoretical integration in the study of deviance and crime: Problems and prospects* (pp. 243–259). Albany: SUNY Press.

Spergel, I.A. (1986). The violent gang in Chicago: A local community approach. *Social Science Review, 60*, 94–131.

Spergel, I.A. (1990). Youth gangs: Continuity and change. In M. Tonry and N. Morris (Eds.), *Crime and justice: A review of research* (pp. 171–275). Chicago: University of Chicago Press.

SPSS, Inc. (1983). *SPSS^x user's guide: A complete guide to SPSS^x language and operations.* New York: McGraw-Hill.

Stafford, M.C., and Ekland-Olson, S. (1982). On social learning and deviant behavior: A reappraisal of the findings. *American Sociological Review, 47*(1), 167–169.

Strickland, D.E. (1982). Social learning and deviant behavior: A specific test of a general theory: Comments and critique. *American Sociological Review, 41*(1), 162–167.

Sutherland, E., and Cressy, D. (1974). *Criminology.* Philadelphia: J.B. Lippincott.

Takata, S.R., and Zevitz, R.G. (1987). Youth gangs in Racine: An examination of community perceptions. *Wisconsin Sociologist, 24*, 132–141.

Takata, S.R., and Zevitz, R.G. (1990). Divergent perceptions of group delinquency in a midwestern community: Racine's gang problem. *Youth and Society, 21,* 282–305.

Taylor, C.S. (1990a). Gang imperialism. In C.R. Huff (Ed.), *Gangs in America* (pp. 103–115). Newbury Park, CA: Sage.

Taylor, C.S. (1990b). *Dangerous society.* East Lansing: Michigan State University Press.

Thompson, D.W., and Jason, L.A. (1988). Street gangs and preventive interventions. *Criminal Justice and Behavior, 15,* 323–333.

Thrasher, F.M. (1927). *The gang: A study of 1,313 gangs in Chicago.* Chicago: University of Chicago Press.

Torres, D.M. (1980). *Gang Violence Reduction Project evaluation report.* Sacramento: California Youth Authority.

Vigil, J.D. (1983). Chicano gangs: One response to Mexican urban adaptation in the Los Angeles area. *Urban Anthropology, 12,* 45–75.

Vigil, J.D. (1988). *Barrio gangs.* Austin, TX: University of Texas Press.

Weis, J., and Hawkins, J.D. (1981). *Preventing delinquency.* Washington, DC: National Office of Juvenile Justice and Delinquency Prevention, U.S. Department of Justice.

Winfree, L.T., Jr., and Griffiths, C.T. (1983). Social learning and adolescent marijuana use: A trend study of deviant behavior in a rural school. *Rural Sociology, 48,* 219–239.

Winfree, L.T., Jr., Sellers, C.S., and Clason, D. (1993). Social learning and adolescent deviance abstention: Toward understanding the reasons for initiating, quitting, and avoiding drugs. *Journal of Quantitative Criminology, 9*(1), 101–125.

5

Crime, Youth Gangs, and Urban Transition: The Social Dislocations of Postindustrial Economic Development

Pamela Irving Jackson

Policy makers and scholars recently have provided detailed testimony of the transformation of the U.S. economy from manufacturing-based to service-based (Berg, 1981; Bradbury, Downs, and Small, 1982; Stanback and Noyelle, 1981). Current analyses have begun to explore the impact of this transformation on the urban center and the largely minority populations left behind within its boundaries. Evident in this new urban reality (cf. Peterson, 1985) are the dislocations associated with economic decline, including increases in the rate of violent crime and in reliance on government-provided income assistance programs (cf. Wilson, 1987). Development and exacerbation of urban youth gang problems have been traced to recent declines in opportunities for unskilled labor (cf. Hagedorn and Macon, 1988). Several other types of anecdotal evidence also have illustrated the problems resulting from a national economic transformation that left in its wake unskilled laborers without access to opportunities for retraining at the level required for success in the new technological environment (cf. Berry, 1985; Downs, 1985; Kasarda, 1985).

Thus far, however, a national analysis of the effect of recent economic and social transitions on the level and nature of crime in cities and on the development of youth gangs throughout the United States has not been undertaken. Some researchers have investigated Wilson's (1987) arguments concerning class-related changes in the residential segregation of minority groups—for example, Massey and Eggers's (1990) analysis of whether middle-class minority members in sixty U.S. metropolitan areas really have removed themselves spatially from the poor. Studies also have addressed the effective-

Reprinted with permission from *Justice Quarterly*, Vol. 8, No. 3 (September 1991): 379–397.

ness of varying types of city-level response to youth gang problems (cf. Spergel, Curry, Ross, and Chance, 1989). Yet the impact of recent well-recognized demographic and economic transitions (cf. P. Peterson, 1985) on crime and youth gangs has not been scrutinized directly in U.S. urban centers nationwide, or with appropriate attention to the influence of regional variations in these transitions.

This study fills that gap. Its central thesis is that demographic and economic transition have contributed to crime and to the presence of youth gangs in U.S. cities, even in the presence of controls for the following possibly competing explanations: opportunity factors related to the ease and profit of crime, age structure, racial and income heterogeneity, and economic deprivation. I also investigate the impact of regional variations in growth and decline on the crime rate in accordance with Wilson's prediction that such differences should be reflected in the severity of urban social dislocations.

Population, Data, and Hypotheses

The research is based on a multivariate analysis of quantitative data from all U.S. cities of 25,000 or more in 1970 and 1980. Further investigation of a subset of the cities in this analysis yields information on the impact of these shifts for the development of youth gangs. Data were obtained from the U.S. Census of Population (1970, 1980), the Uniform Crime Report (Federal Bureau of Investigation, 1980), and the 1981 National Juvenile Assessment Center survey regarding youth gangs (Needle and Stapleton, 1983).

I use ordinary least squares regression and logistic regression. The dependent variables of the analysis are urban crime rates and the presence of urban youth gangs. In this paper I devote primary attention to the influence of population and economic transition on the level of crime and on the presence of youth gangs. I also include the following independent variables to test the competing theoretical explanations noted above: city population size and density, climate, household activity ratio, ratio of blacks' to whites' median income, percent poor, percent unemployed, racial composition measures, and percent youth (ages fifteen to twenty-four). The operationalization of each variable is described below.

Demographic and Economic Transition

Taken together, recent work by Wilson (1987) and by Hagedorn and Macon (1988) directly advances the proposition that crime and youth gangs are among the social dislocations resulting from the U.S. transition from a manufacturing-based to a service-based economy. Wilson argues that a rise in the proportion of female-headed households, increased reliance on welfare, and greater level of violent crime are all, in one way or another, manifestations of the social disorganization consequent to urban losses in opportunities for unskilled workers. Hagedorn, with Macon, applies this argument to his analysis of current trends in gang development in Milwaukee; he predicts that youth gangs will assume an increasing presence throughout the United States in those urban centers most affected by the demographic and economic decline inherent in the nation's postindustrial economic transition.

These propositions advanced by Wilson and Hagedorn have solid foundations in the now-classic work of Durkheim ([1893] 1965, [1895] 1965, [1897] 1951) and of Shaw and McKay (1942), in which crime and youth gangs are treated directly as consequences of the impact of demographic and economic transition on anomie and social disorganization. More current research provides further support for these links. Work by both Chamlin (1989) and Sampson and Groves (1989, for example, underscores the continued criminogenic importance of urban change. Chamlin (1989) studied the determinants of robbery and homicide in 109 large cities and demonstrated the criminogenic impact of urban structural changes that weaken social cohesion. Sampson and Groves's (1989) research on British localities provides evidence of the influence of community social disorganization on criminal victimization and offending.

Urban centers declined economically during the 1970s with the movement of manufacturing and wholesale operations, their initial reason for existence, to foreign and suburban locations, and with the national economic shift toward a service-based economy requiring technologically sophisticated training for many of the new positions it created. Kasarda's (1985) recent study of the growth of jobs with low educational requirements demonstrates that the suburbs and the exurbs have absorbed most of these positions. Herbert Jacobs (1985) examines the criminogenic implications of these changes.

In their recent book on gangs, crime, and the underclass, after reviewing the literature on gang information, Hagedorn and Macon (1988: 21) note that we do not know why gangs form in some cities but not in others, or how gangs in smaller cities are similar to or different from gangs in larger cities. They point to the drastically changed economic conditions in poor, minority urban neighborhoods as having contributed to the ''institutionalization of gangs as a means for young adults to cope with economic distress and social isolation'' (Hagedorn and Macon, 1988: 111).

Theories stressing economic and social marginality as triggers of gang formation (cf. Cloward and Ohlin, 1960; Miller, 1975; Moore., et al. 1978, 1983) still apply, but because adulthood does not bring new opportunities for achievement, the movement up and out of the zone of transition does not occur for minority group members as it did for the European immigrants studied by the earliest researchers in this area. Hagedorn and Macon stress that ''the significance of the formation of a minority urban underclass and the simultaneous emergence and entrenchment of gangs is completely overlooked'' (1988:

25-26). The interstitial nature of gangs—as a bridge between youth and adulthood occurring in the transitional zones between disorganized and stable communities—may have changed, insofar as the gang experience for many continues with joblessness and meaningless part-time work into the adult years. Work by Curry and Spergel (1988) and by Sampson and Groves (1989) underscores the effect of socioeconomic disorganization on gang activity, supporting Hagedorn and Macon's argument that recent demographic and economic changes have contributed to the development of youth gangs.

Because they reflect demographic and economic transition, economic instability and population decline are expected to be significant predictors of higher crime rates in this study, especially for crimes of violence (cf. H. Jacobs, 1985: 230), and to contribute to the presence of youth gangs. The percentage change in civilian labor force opportunities in manufacturing and in wholesale and retail trades between 1970 and 1980 are included in the investigation as indicators of economic instability. Their decline represents a diminution of employment opportunities for unskilled, less educated city residents (cf. Kasarda, 1985; Wilson, 1987).

Percentages of city residents born in the state where they are now living (1980) and percentage of population change (1970–1980) provide indicators of long- and short-term demographic change in the city. Population decline has been viewed as indicative of "a declining city syndrome" (Clark, 1985: 254; Muller, 1975; G. Peterson, 1976) and as a measure of "urban distress" (Clark, 1985: 259; Nathon and Dommel, 1977). Throughout the United States, particularly in the northeastern and north central regions, large central cities lost population during the 1970s. The declines may have reflected the loss of employment opportunities in these regions, a loss that triggered urban fiscal and social problems.

Competing Theoretical Explanations

Routine activities (cf. Cohen and Felson, 1979), economic deprivation and relative deprivation (cf. Danziger and Wheeler, 1975; D. Jacobs, 1982; Massey and Eggers, 1990; Shelley 1980), heterogeneity (cf. Blau and Blau, 1982), and the age structure of a city (cf. Hindelang and McDermott, 1981) may explain any observed impact of demographic and economic transition on both crime and youth gang presence. To test the influence of these competing explanations in comparison to that of the central proposition of this analysis, I bring into the analysis indicators of economic deprivation, the age structure of the population, routine activities related to the ease and profit of crime, and population heterogeneity.

Percent poor and percent unemployed in 1980 represent long- and short-term conditions of economic deprivation; the ratio of blacks' to whites' median income reflects relative deprivation. Percent black and percent Hispanic indicate population heterogeneity. In addition to these variables I include the household activity ratio—"the sum of the number of married, husband-present, female labor-force participants and the number of non–husband-wife households, divided by the sum of the total number of households." This is Cohen and Felson's (1979: 200) indicator of the number of households likely to be without guardians because of the occupants' employment. The index provides a measure of the dispersion of activities away from the home; as a measures of the absence of guardians, I expect it to be related positively to the level of crime in cities. In addition, I expect this index to have increased along with recent urban population and economic transitions because economic instability increases the proportion of female-headed families (cf. Sampson, 1987), which contribute to the number of non–husband-wife households.

I include city population size, density, and climate in the analysis as structural indicators of the ease of crime commission in a city and because they are associated with population and economic transition, the main independent variables of this investigation. The largest, most densely settled U.S. cities are known to have experienced the greatest demographic and economic decline, especially in the northeast and north central regions, where the mean January temperature is lowest. The link between these demographic characteristics and crime is also well established. For example, I expect population size and density to influence the ease of crime commission because they heighten anonymity, reduce social cohesion, and strain law enforcement resources (cf. Boggs, 1965; Harries, 1975, Jackson, 1984; Reppetto, 1974). Climate, measured here by mean January temperature, may influence the likelihood of larceny, burglary, robbery, auto theft, and arson because milder temperatures encourage more socializing outside the home, thus increasing the vulnerability of dwellings and vehicles.

Dependent Variables

This analysis includes two dependent variables: urban crime rates and the development of urban youth gangs. I obtained information on urban crime rates from the Uniform Crime Report (Federal Bureau of Investigation, 1980). Wilson's analysis of the determinants of urban social dislocations focuses on rates of violent crime in cities. In the present analysis, however, I investigate separately the determinants for each of the eight Part I index offenses because each of these direct contact predatory crimes (cf. Cohen and Felson, 1979: 589) may respond to different social pressures. For example, the frustration produced by anomie and social disorganization may result in a link between crimes of violence and economic and social transition (cf. Bernard, 1990). Although property crimes also may be influenced by transition, as deviant subcultures replace conventional normative structures eroded by change, different causal processes are at work (cf. Messner and J. Blau, 1987). Hence the strength of these links may differ.

To test the effect of economic and population transition on gangs, I use as a dependent variable data gathered in 1981 by the National Juvenile Justice Assessment Center (Needle and Stapleton, 1983) on the existence of gangs in a random, representative sample of sixty U.S. cities of 100,000 or more. In each city police department, the authors interviewed gang control and youth personnel as to the existence of gangs in the city. The investigation of recognized urban gangs was based on analysis of these sixty cities which the authors selected "using population size and geographic region as major criteria for sampling" (Needle and Stapleton, 1983: 1).For this subgroup of the present study's larger population of cities, I investigate the determinants of the existence of gangs recognized by the police using a dichotomous indicator of gang presence, where 0 = no police-provided evidence of gangs in the city and 1 = police-provided evidence of gangs.[1] Unfortunately the small size of this subsample precludes investigation of the regional differences that I explore in the prediction of urban crime rates.

Results

Table 5.1 contains associations among pairs of the urban socio-political characteristics included in the study. Although they are a useful starting point, these Pearson's correlation coefficients reflect only bivariate associations without controls for other possible determinants of the association. The multivariate equations in a later table are a more accurate gauge of the extent to which each independent variable influence specific crime rates and the incidence of gangs after other urban characteristics are controlled.

The bivariate associations, however, provide reason for continuation of the analysis. For example, a statistically significant relationship exists between higher crime rates and decline in the percentage of the civilian labor force employed in wholesale and retail trades ($r = -.17$). A bivariate relationship also exists between the percentage of residents born in the state who still live there and the total rate of index crimes; higher crime rates are found in cities with more population transition ($r = -.24$). This measure of long-term population transition is associated with increases in the number of manufacturing positions ($r = -.25$), lower levels of poverty ($r = .14$), and higher mean January temperatures ($r = -.53$).

Decline in the percentage of the civilian labor force employed in wholesale and retail positions also predicts increases in the crime rate ($r = -.17$), as do greater unemployment ($r = .23$), greater income inequality between blacks and whites ($r = -.21$), dispersion of activity away from the home ($r = .37$), and climate conducive to recreation outside the home ($r = .23$).

Table 5.1 Zero-Order Correlation Matrix with Means and Standard Deviations (All cities ≥ 25,000, N = 561) (Pearson's rs)

	1	2	3	4	5	6	7	8	9	10	11	12	13	14	15	16	$\bar{X}$	SD
Percent black	—	.12[b]	-.17[c]	-.05	.41[c]	.40[c]	.13[b]	-.24[c]	.11[b]	.69[c]	-.27[c]	-.21[c]	-.07	.10[a]	.44[c]	-.13[b]	15.5	17.1
Density		—	.28[c]	-.11[b]	.15[c]	.25[c]	-.15[c]	-.22[c]	.25[c]	.18[c]	.11[b]	-.13[b]	-.15[c]	-.03	.03	.21[c]	4324.4	3722.9
Percent Hispanic			—	-.06	-.03	-.21[c]	-.34[c]	.22[c]	.07	.21[c]	.20[c]	-.07	.24[c]	.44[c]	.06	.47[c]	8.3	13.4
Population age 15–24				—	-.06	.28[c]	.00	.09[a]	-.05	.02	-.12[b]	.18[c]	.05	-.12[b]	-.10[a]	-.01	2.1	.5
Percent unemployed					—	-.02	.23[c]	-.29[c]	.05	.58[c]	-.03	.08[c]	-.28[c]	-.26[c]	.23[c]	-.01	7.0	3.0
Household activity ratio						—	-.02	-.21[c]	.10[a]	.23[c]	-.25[c]	-.18[c]	.01	-.11[b]	.37[c]	-.07	.7	.1
Residents born in state							—	-.38[c]	-.05	.14[c]	-.05	.08[a]	-.25[c]	-.53[c]	-.24[c]	-.37[c]	60.0	16.2
Percent population change								—	-.03	-.19[c]	.07	.06	.21[c]	.38[c]	-.06	.05	7.3	22.0
Population size									—	.12[b]	-.08[a]	-.06	-.01	.01	.09[a]	.27[c]	129.1	370.2
Percent poor										—	-.25[c]	-.11[b]	-.05	.17[c]	.44[c]	.11	10.3	5.4
Blacks'/whites' income											—	-.04	-.05	-.12[b]	-.21[c]	.14[c]	.7	.2
Wholesale/retail change												—	-.25[c]	-.08[a]	-.17[c]	-.23[c]	-.1	2.25
Manufacturing change													—	-.28[c]	.11[b]	.20[c]	-2.6	4.1
January temperature														—	.23[c]	.28[c]	36.6	13.6
Index crime rate															—	.07	80.1	27.8
Gang presence[d]																—	.5	.5

a. $p < .05$
b. $p < .01$
c. $p < .001$
d. gang presence correlation based on 51 cases.

With regard to gangs, the bivariate associations suggest that they are more likely to be present in large (r = .27), densely settled (r = .21) cities with a large Hispanic population (r = .47), greater long-term population transition (r = −.37), and greater declines in the number of wholesale and retail positions (r = −.23). The multivariate equations presented below test the theoretical importance of these associations, providing evidence of the impact of economic and demographic transition on crime and gang presence when the influence of other independent variables is controlled.

Table 5.2 suggests that the relationship between demographic and economic transition and urban crime rates withstands controls for other, possibly competing explanatory variables. Long-term population change, as reflected in the percentage of city residents born in the state where they are now living, has a statistically significant impact on the total rate of index crimes and on each of the individual crime rates except arson. This measure of long-term population change is one of the strongest predictors of each type of crime, an indication that the lower the percentage of city residents born in the state, the greater the rate of crime. The socially disorganizing effects of such population change appear to be reflected in urban crime levels.

Percentage of city population change during the decade (1970–1980), an indicator not only of social disorganization but also of urban socioeconomic decline, has a statistically significant impact on the rates of robbery, burglary, and auto theft; population decline predicts higher crime rates. In addition, decline in labor force opportunities in manufacturing between 1970 and 1980 contributes to higher rates of robbery and auto theft; similar declines in wholesale and retail trades trigger increases in rape, robbery, auto theft, and arson rates.

The contribution of other characteristics of city structure in explaining variations in crime rates also merits attention. Unemployment, for example, short-term by its official definition, is socially disorganizing and disrupts individuals' major link with conventional society. This variable is a positive significant predictor of the total rate of index crime and of each of the individual rates of direct contact predatory crime except larceny, even after other sociodemographic characteristics of cities have been controlled. Percent poor, reflecting the extent of longer-term economic detachment in the city, also has a positive significant impact on the total crime rate, as well as on the rates of homicide, robbery, assault, burglary, larceny, and auto theft. Sampson's (1987) work suggests that this influence may result in part from the impact of economic deprivation on family structure.

Percent black and percent Hispanic, indicators of population heterogeneity, do not have a significant impact on the total rate of crime when the indicators of demographic and economic transition and the other control variables are held constant. Both, however, have a positive, statistically significant impact on the rates of three violent crimes: homicide, rape, and robbery.

Table 5.2 Regression Equations for Index Crimes Rates (1980) on Transition, Social Disorganization, Opportunity, and Other Social Characteristics of Cities (All Cities ≥ 25,000, N = 561)

	Total Crime Rate	Nonnegligent Homicide	Forcible Rape	Aggravated Assault	Robbery	Burglary	Larceny	Auto Theft	Arson
Constant	-31.310	-.060	-.654	-2.420	-6.564	-9.011	-9.546	2.738	-1.839
Mean January Temperature, Standardized Coefficient (S)	.073	.099[b]	.068	.118[a]	.018	.156[c]	.029	-.063	.118[a]
Population Size S	.029	.143[c]	.081[b]	.009	.144[c]	.010	-.001	.053	.062
Percent Change in Wholesale/Retail S	-.031	-.045	-.063[a]	.004	-.083[a]	-.050	.021	-.115[b]	-.111[b]
Ratio of Blacks' to Whites' Median Income S	-.031	-.007	-.027	.009	.053[a]	-.018	-.080[a]	.098[b]	.089[a]
Proportion Age 15-24 S	-.204[c]	-.078[b]	-.032	-.045	-.129[c]	-.212[c]	-.163[c]	-.135[c]	-.064
Percent Unemployed S	.164[c]	.142[c]	.294[c]	.102[a]	.136[c]	.124[b]	.140[b]	.071	.275[c]
Density S	-.239[c]	-.132[c]	-.233[c]	-.097[a]	.083[b]	-.109[b]	-.397[c]	.221[c]	-.042
Percent Change in Manufacturing S	.019	-.044	-.018	-.039	-.105[c]	.026	.068	-.084[a]	-.018
Percent Population Change (1970–1980) S	-.057	-.043	-.040	-.037	-.104[c]	-.081[a]	-.005	-.085[a]	-.018
Household Activity Ratio S	.381[c]	.068[a]	.252[c]	.110[b]	.247[c]	.298[c]	.369[c]	.165[c]	.172[c]
Percent City Residents Born in State S	-.314[c]	-.104[b]	-.271[c]	-.154[c]	-.302[c]	-.227[c]	-.256[c]	-.232[c]	-.047
Percent Hispanic S	.017	.206[c]	.130[b]	.064	.147[c]	.025	-.060	.125[b]	.070
Percent Black S	.053	.489[c]	.375[c]	.290[c]	.309[c]	.128[b]	-.116[a]	.057	-.093
Percent Poor S	.271[c]	.145[b]	.020	.244[c]	.132[b]	.268[c]	.187[b]	.210[c]	-.012
R^2	.44[c]	.60[c]	.51[c]	.38[c]	.63[c]	.47[c]	.29[c]	.42[c]	-.10[c]

a. p (one-tailed test) < .05

b. p < .01

c. p < .001

Percent black also has a positive impact on the rates of assault, burglary, and larceny; percent Hispanic influences the rate of auto theft.

Greater similarity of average blacks' and whites' incomes appears to contribute to the rates of robbery, auto theft, and arson in a city, even after other known crime determinants are controlled. Meriting future investigation is the question of whether this occurs because greater equality between racial groups reflects the greater criminal opportunity association with affluence or because greater interracial equality reflects widespread poverty and its associated criminogenic conditions.

City population size contributes to the rates of homicide, rape, and robbery even after demographic change, economic transition, and other predictors of the urban crime rate are controlled. The higher levels of anonymity, lower social cohesion, and weaker informal surveillance associated with large city size may undermine social restraints and provide greater opportunity for violent crime. Population density has a statistically significant negative impact on the total crime rate and on the homicide and rape rates, as well as on the rates of assault, burglary, and larceny; this finding suggests criminogenic conditions in cities with lower levels of density. Such cities were slightly more likely to be experiencing population transition in 1980 (Pearsons's r for density and population change $= -.22$) (cf. Frey and Speare, 1988).

Dispersion of activities away from the home, as measured by the household activity ratio, has a positive significant impact on the total crime rate as well as on the rate of each individual index crime. Mean January temperature, a measure of climatic conditions conducive to interaction outside the home (cf. Cheatwood, 1988), is a positive significant predictor of the rates of homicide, assault, burglary, and arson.

In summary, the multivariate equations show that urban crime rates are influenced by both long- and short-term city population change, as well as by declines in manufacturing and wholesale/retail positions, even in the face of controls for competing explanatory variables. The data support the central thesis of this paper regarding the impact of postindustrial change on crime in urban centers. Although competing explanations do not undermine this support, they shed additional light on the importance of urban characteristics that reflect the opportunity for crime. The anonymity and the household dispersion of modern life, as well as climatic conditions that encourage the pursuit of leisure and interaction outside the home, appear to be related to specific rates of urban crime.

Regional Variations

Wilson's analysis of urban deterioration in the 1970s suggests regional contextual differences that could affect the development of crime. For example, he writes that urban centers have undergone ''an irreversible structural transition from centers of production and distribution of material goods to centers of administration, information exchange, and higher order provision,'' and notes that in northern areas in particular, city labor markets have been transformed from "centers of goods processing to centers of information processing,'' with consequent shifts in the educational requirements for employment (Wilson, 1987: 39).

In the northeast and the midwest especially, Wilson illustrates that the jobless rate among to sixteen- to twenty-four-year-old black males increased sharply during the 1970s. At the same time, information processing centers have replaced jobs in manufacturing and other blue-collar industries in the north (Wilson, 1987: 40). In the south and the west, he points out, the jobless rates among young black males in the central city has not risen as sharply; jobs with low educational prerequisites have not left these communities as consistently, and business migration to these areas has added others. Work by Massey and Eggers (1990: 1170) also suggests regional variations in the cumulative overall effect of these changes on urban centers, with the greatest dislocations in the northeast and the midwest.

One measure of decline in northeastern and north central cities is reflected in their 3.4 percent average population loss between 1970 and 1980. Cities in the south and the southwest, on the other hand, grew 16.4 percent on average during that decade. This growth was reflected in the fact that only 54 percent of the residents of these cities in 1980 were born in the state (44% in urban centers of the west, 62% in cities of the south). For northeastern and north central cities the figure is 68 percent, reflecting less population transition there during the decade. The average decline in manufacturing and in wholesale/retail employment was greater in northern/north central cities, 4.18 percent and .083 percent respectively, than in southern and western cities, which showed declines of only 1.3 percent and .07 percent. Even so, both population decline in the north and population growth in the south and the west manifest transition, a condition known to be criminogenic in and of itself.

Despite some differences in the extent of unemployment, youth, poverty, and minority status—all conditions conducive to the development of anomie—in 1980 the regional groupings of cities on average were not far apart on most of these control variables. Cities in the northeastern and north central regions averaged about 8 percent unemployment in 1980; the mean figure was 6 percent for southern and western cities. About 10 percent of the central city population was below the poverty level in the north, and about 11 percent in the southern/western group of cities. There was no appreciable difference in the relative size of the population aged fifteen to twenty-four, which averaged about 2 percent in each group. The proportion minority varied in expected directions. Northern cities had, on average, 14 percent black population and 4 percent from Hispanic groups. Cities in the south and west on average were 17 percent black and 12 percent Hispanic.

In 1980 the ratio of blacks' to whites' median income averaged .76 in northern cities and .68 in cities of the south and the west. Mean city population size in the north was 137,000, while it averaged about 123,000 in southern and western cities. Dispersion of activities away from the home, however, showed no major regional variation. Population density, at 5,367 persons per square mile, was considerably greater in cities of the north/north central region than in the south and the west, where cities averaged about 3,437 persons per square mile. Mean January temperature, 25 degrees in northern cities and 47 degrees in southern and western cities, indicates greater climatic conduciveness to recreation outside the home in cities of the west and the south.

In the multivariate equations for each of the regional groupings, the statistical influence of the indicators of demographic and economic transition, as well as the impact of most of the individual control variables, showed similar patterns across the regional divide. (The regional regression results are not shown in tabular form, but are available upon request.) Regional differences in the predictive ability of the model itself stand out, however. With regard to the total crime rate, for example, the model's predictive ability is more than 15 percent greater for northern cities than for southern and western cities; for homicide the difference is 18 percent; for rape, 35 percent; for robbery, 11 percent; for assault, 21 percent; for burglary, 20 percent; for arson, 12 percent. (For larceny and auto theft, there is no appreciable explanatory difference.) In every case, the explanatory difference shows that the model predicts the level of crime more accurately in northeastern and north central cities, where the greatest demographic and economic decline has occurred. In the south and the west, regions characterized by urban population growth rather than by decline, the model's predictive deficit suggests the need to look for additional determinants of crime in the nation's growth regions.

Urban Gangs

The logistic regression equation in table 5.3 demonstrates the impact of demographic and economic transition on gangs after other competing explanatory variables are controlled.[2] The logit model shows that decline in the economic prospects for unskilled workers, as measured by the percentage of change in the number of wholesale and retail jobs, is a statistically significant determinant of metropolitan urban gangs. The only other significant predictor of gangs is the size of the population aged fifteen to twenty-four, the group most vulnerable to anomie and to the consequences of social disorganization.

These findings provide some support for Hagedorn and Macon's (1988) contention that modern urban gangs are one consequence of the inability of urban teens and young adults to achieve a firm foothold in the unskilled labor market. The anomie and the free time characteristic of youths in cities with

Table 5.3   Logistic Regression Model of Gang Presence (N = 51)

Predictor	Logistic Coefficient	Standard Error
Intercept	4.666	6.895
Mean January temperature	.028	.029
Population size	.001	.001
Percent change in wholesale/retail	−.525[a]	.293
Ratio of blacks' to whites' median income	2.175	2.451
Proportion age 15–24	.031[a]	.015
Percent unemployed	−.005	.162
Density	.000	.000
Percent change in manufacturing	−.093	.086
Percent population change (1970–1980)	−.014	.015
Household activity ratio	−12.208	−10.852
Percent city residents born in state	−.011	.025
Percent Hispanic	.041	.035
Percent black	−.020	.030
Percent poor	−.001	.118
Total crime rate	.007	.015

a. p < .05

declining economic prospects for unskilled labor may be conducive to the development and persistence of urban youth gangs—and to police reports of their presence.

Conclusions and Discussion

Overall the results provide support for the central thesis of this paper. Demographic and economic transition seem to have some influence on crime and on the presence of youth gangs in U.S. cities even in the presence of controls for possibly competing explanations: opportunity factors related to the ease and profit of crime, age structure, racial and income heterogeneity, and economic and relative deprivation. Although the impact of demographic and economic change on crime rates remained stable across regions, regional differences in the model's predictive ability point to the need for further study of the impact of growth and decline on urban crime in cities.

The results of the logit model developed to explain gang presence show that decline in wholesale and retail positions was a significant predictor of gang presence, as was the size of the fifteen- to twenty-four-year-old population. In the multivariate model other indicators of urban conditions, including race, ethnicity, inequality, population size, and density, did not have a statistically significant impact on urban gangs.

In investigating the influence of recent population and economic shifts in cities throughout the United States, as well as separately in regional subpopu-

93

lations of cities where the nature of economic and population changes has diverged, I have focused on the criminogenic impact of population and economic transitions known to disorganize communities by reducing social cohesion and creating a mismatch between labor and jobs (cf. Kasarda, 1985). The extent to which the level and the nature of urban crime have been influenced by the transitions of recent postindustrial economic development had not been investigated previously, either for cities of 25,000 or more nationally or comparatively in regions with differing patterns of urban transition. Similarly, researchers had neglected multivariate studies of the determinants of youth gangs' presence in large samples of cities.

Several other pieces of current research support and elaborate on the findings reported in this paper. They suggest that crime and youth gangs are likely consequences of the patterns of sociodemographic change recently experienced by U.S. urban centers. Work by Sampson (1987) and Sampson and Groves (1989) has investigated the influence of varying patterns of economic opportunity on the social organization and criminal involvement of specific groups and populations. With data for 150 of the largest U.S. cities, Sampson (1987: 375) demonstrated that economic deprivation and the dearth of employed black men increased the percentage of female-headed black households, and then developed a simultaneous model showing the impact of family disruption on both juvenile and adult adjusted arrest rates among blacks for robbery and homicide. The finding that family disruption influenced the juvenile offending rate even more than the adult offending rate led Sampson to suggest that "the effects of family structure are related to macrolevel patterns of social control and guardianship, especially regarding youths and their peers" (1987: 37).

In their study of 11,000 residents in 300 British localities, Sampson and Groves (1989) addressed social disorganization, a related theme, linking it to its roots in Shaw and McKay's theory and to its consequences in terms of criminal victimization and offending. They found that measures of social organization linked community structural characteristics, including socioeconomic factors, residential mobility, ethnic heterogeneity, and family disruption, to criminal victimization and offending rates based respectively on victim and self-reports. Overall the Sampson and Groves (1989) study suggests that elements which weaken a community's social cohesion thereby breed delinquency and crime.

The study described here adds to this body of research by demonstrating in U.S. cities of 25,000 or more the impact of the nation's recent postindustrial demographic and economic changes on both direct-contact predatory crime rates and reports of urban youth gangs. The influence of urban decline on urban crime rates and on gang presence survives controls for other criminogenic structural characteristics of cities, and highlights the importance of social change on the quality of life in urban centers.

The long-term consequences of crime, youth gangs, and other social dislocations resulting from the impact of these changes merit careful scrutiny. Much evidence suggests that the problems of cities have only begun. Zatz's (1985) work, for example, demonstrates the long-term criminal justice consequences for youths with gang identity and criminal involvement. In light of recent figures showing that one black male in four and one Hispanic male in ten in the United States is under criminal justice supervision, the influence of gang involvement in channeling youths into inmate social systems cannot be ignored. It may be that without improvement in the economic prospects of urban youths, the transience of gang involvement noted by Thrasher (1927) and others will become a thing of the past. Combined with Hispanic migration to urban centers, *los cholos* and dim economic prospects may give gang involvement a permanent allure (cf. Moore, 1985; Zatz, 1985).

Urban decline, with its associated economic stress and social disorganization, may weaken the social cohesion and social control processes of cities, resulting in the social dislocations discussed by Wilson (1987), Hagedorn and Macon (1988), and others. As a result, higher crime rates and more youth gangs may be among the unintended consequences of the nation's postindustrial growth and development.

Notes

1. Complete data on all independent variables are available for 51 of Needle and Stapelton's cities.
2. Because the dependent variable, presence or absence of police-reported gangs in a city, is dichotomous, the logit model is appropriate in that it is designed to provide for assessment of the impact of several interval-level independent variables on a truncated dependent variable.

References

Berg, Ivar. (1981). *Sociological Perspectives on Labor Markets*. New York: Academic Press.

Bernard, Thomas J. (1990). "Angry Aggression among the 'Truely Disadvantaged.' " *Criminology* 28: 73–96.

Berry, Brian J.L. (1985). "Islands of Renewal in Seas of Decay." In Paul E. Peterson (ed.), *The New Urban Reality*. Washington, DC: Brookings Institution, pp. 69–98.

Blau, Judith R. and Peter M. Blau. (1982). "Metropolitan Structure and Violent Crime." *American Sociological Review* 47: 114–28.

Boggs, Sarah L. (1965). "Urban Crime Patterns." *American Sociological Review* 30: 899–905.

Bradbury, Katherine L., Anthony Downs, and Kenneth A. Small (1982). *Urban Decline and the Future of American Cities*. Washington, DC: Brookings Institute.

Chamlin, Mitchell B. (1989). "A Macro Social Analysis of the Change in Robbery and Homicide Rates: Controlling for Static and Dynamic Effects." *Sociological Focus* 22 (4): 275–86.

Cheatwood, Derrel. (1988). "Is There a Season for Homicide?" *Criminology* 26 (2): 287–306.

Clark, Terry Nichols. (1985). "Fiscal Strain: How Different Are Snow Belt and Sun Belt Cities?" In Paul E. Peterson (ed.), *The New Urban Reality*. Washington, DC: Brookings Institute, pp. 253–80.

Cloward, Richard A. and Lloyd E. Ohlin. (1960). *Delinquency and Opportunity: A Theory of Delinquent Gangs*. New York: Free Press.

Cohen, Albert K. (1955). *Delinquent Boys: the Culture of the Gang*. New York: Free Press.

Cohen, Lawrence E. and Marcus Felson. (1979). "Social Change and Crime Rate Trends." *American Sociological Review* 44: 588–607.

Curry, G. David and Irving A. Spergel. (1988). "Gang Homicide, Delinquency, and Community." *Criminology* 26: 381–405.

Danziger, S. and D. Wheeler. (1975). "The Economics of Crime: Punishment of Income Redistribution." *Review of Social Economy* 33 (October): 113–31.

Downs, Anthony. (1985). "The Future of Industrial cities." In Paul E. Peterson (ed.), *The New Urban Reality*. Washington, D.C.: Brookings Institute, pp. 281–94.

Durkheim, Emile. ([1893] 1951). *The Division of Labor in Society*. New York: Free Press.

———. ([1895] 1965). *The Rules of Sociological Method*. New York: Free Press.

———. ([1897] 1951). *Suicide*. New York: Free Press.

Federal Bureau of Investigation. (1980). *Uniform Crime Report*. Washington, DC: U.S. Government Printing Office.

Frey, William H. and Alden Speare, Jr. (1988). *Regional and Metropolitan Growth and Decline in the United States*. New York: Russell Sage Foundation.

Hagedorn, John M. and Perry Macon. (1988). *People and Folks: Gangs, Crime and the Underclass in a Rustbelt City*. Chicago: Lake View Press.

Harries, Keith D. (1974). *The Geography of Crime and Justice*. New York: McGraw-Hill.

Hindelang, M.J. and M.J. McDermot. (1981). *Juvenile Criminal Behavior: An Analysis of Rates and Victim Characteristics*. Washington, DC: U.S. Government Printing Office.

Jackson, Pamela Irving. (1984). "Opportunity and Crime." *Sociology and Social Research* 2: 172–92.

Jacobs, David. (1982). "Inequality and Economic Crime." *Sociology and Social Research*. 66: 12–28.

Jacobs, Herbert. (1985). "Policy Responses to Crime." In Paul E. Peterson (ed.), *The New Urban Reality*. Washington, DC: Brookings Institute, pp. 225–52.

Kasarda, John D. (1985). "Urban Change and Minority Opportunities." In Paul E. Peterson (ed.), *The New Urban Reality*. Washington, DC: Brookings Institute, pp. 33–68.

Massey, Douglas S. and Mitchell L. Eggers. (1990). "The Ecology of Inequality: Minorities and the Concentration of Poverty, 1970–1980." *American Journal of Sociology* 95 (5): 1153–88.

Merton, Robert K. (1968). *Social Theory and Social Structure*. New York: Free Press.

Messner, Steven F. and Judith R. Blau. (1987). "Routine Leisure Activities and Rates of Crime: A Macro-Level Analysis." *Social Forces* 65: 1035–51.

Miller, Walter B. (1975). *Violence by Youth Gangs and Youth Groups as a Crime Problem in Major American Cities*. Washington, DC: U.S. Department of Justice.

Moore, Joan W. (1985). "Isolation and Stigmatization in the Development of the Underclass: The Case of Chicano Gangs in East Los Angeles." *Social Problems* 33 (1): 1–12.

Moore, Joan, Diego Vigil, and Robert Garcia. (1983). "Residence and Territoriality in Chicano Gangs." *Social Problems* 31 (2): 182–94.

Moore, Joan with Robert Garcia, Carlos Garcia, Luis Cerda, and Frank Valencio. (1978). *Homeboys*. Philadelphia: Temple University Press.

Muller, Thomas. (1975). *Growing and Declining Urban Areas: A Fiscal Comparison*. Washington, DC: Urban Institute.

Nathan, Richard P. and Paul R. Dommell. (1977). "The Cities." In Joseph A. Peckman (ed.), *Setting National Priorities: The 1978 Budget*. Washington, DC: Brookings Institute, pp. 283–316.

Needle, Jerome A. and Wm. Vaughan Stapleton. (1983). *Report of the National Juvenile Justice Assessment Centers: Police Handling of Youth Gangs*. Washington, DC: U.S. Department of Justice.

Peterson, George E. (1976). "Finance." In William Gorham and Nathan Glazer (eds.), *The Urban Predicament*. Washington, DC: Urban Institute. Pp. 35–118.

Peterson, Paul E., ed. (1985). *The New Urban Reality*. Washington, DC: Brookings Institute.

Reppetto, Thomas. (1974). *Residential Crime*. Cambridge, MA: Ballinger.

Sampson, Robert J. (1987). "Urban Black Violence: the Effect of Male Joblessness and Family Disruption." *American Journal of Sociology* 93 (2): 348–82.

Sampson, Robert J. and W. Byron Groves. (1989). "Community Structure and Crime: Testing Social-Disorganization Theory." *American Journal of Sociology* 94 (4): 774–802.

Shaw, Clifford R. and Henry D. McKay. (1942). *Juvenile Delinquency and Urban Areas*. Chicago: University of Chicago Press.

Shelley, Louise. (1980). *Crime and Modernization*. Carbondale: Southern Illinois University Press.

Spergel, Irving A., G. David Curry, R.A. Ross, and R. Chance. (1989). "Survey of Youth Gang Problems and Programs in 45 Cities and 6 Sites." Technical report. Chicago: University of Chicago, School of Social Service Administration.

Stanback, Thomas M., Jr. and Thierry J. Noyelle. (1981). *Metropolitan Labor Markets in Transition: A Study of Seven SMSAs*. Washington, DC: U.S. Department of Commerce.

Thrasher, Frederick M. (1927). *The Gang*. Chicago: University of Chicago Press.

U.S. Bureau of the Census. (1970). *Characteristics of the Population*. Washington, DC: U.S. Government Printing Office.

_____. (1980). *Characteristics of the Population*. Washington, DC: U.S. Government Printing Office.

Wilson, William Julius. (1987). *Truly Disadvantaged: The Inner City, the Underclass and Public Policy*. Chicago: University of Chicago Press.

Zatz, Marjorie. (1985). "Los Cholos: Legal Processing of Chicano Gang Members." *Social Problems* 33 (1): 13-30.

6

Age, Social Context, and Street Gang Membership: Are "Youth" Gangs Becoming "Adult" Gangs?

James R. Lasley

Recent accounts of violence and criminal sophistication associated with contemporary street gangs have produced a growing number of policymakers and social scientists who believe that the "youth" gang may no longer be a valid concept in today's society (Horowitz, 1990; Huff, 1989, 1990; Klein and Maxon, 1989, 1990; Short, 1990). This position, however, is not without a theoretical foundation. Specifically, some gang theorists suggest that inner-city gang members are growing progressively older (Fagan, 1990; Horowitz, 1983; Huff, 1989; Klein and Maxon, 1985) in response to decaying institutional controls and inadequate opportunity structures within the lower class. However, despite such claims, the effect of class differences on the aging process of modern street gang members has yet to be systematically examined.

Within the social context of lower-class, inner-city Los Angeles neighborhoods, the present study investigates the extent to which street gangs are the domain of youth or adulthood. Self-report field data gathered from 445 active street gang members representing both lower- and middle/upper-class backgrounds are used to explore empirically hypotheses generated from the latter research question.

Age and Gang Membership

Although a great deal of research has been directed toward explaining the relationship between age and crime (Hirschi and Gottfredson, 1983), the effect of age on gang membership has received comparatively little attention. Since

Reprinted by permission of Sage Publications, Inc. from *Youth & Society*, Vol. 23, No. 4 (June 1992): 434–451.

Thrasher's (1927) pioneering study of Chicago gangs, age has been considered a constant rather than a variable in that calculus of gang behavior. That is, a majority of gang studies have adopted the traditional etiological notion that collective deviance is largely an adolescent phenomenon that seldom persists beyond early adulthood (see, e.g., Short and Strodtbeck, 1965; Yablonsky, 1966).

By and large, most first-generation gang research (i.e., conducted prior to the 1970s; e.g., Cohen, 1955; Cloward and Ohlin, 1960; Miller, 1958) indicates that there are distinct age-linked boundaries defining the onset and desistence of street gang involvement: this is what Klein (1971) terms the "gang age." For Kantor and Bennett (1968), the gang age ranged from ten to twenty-five years. It was eleven to twenty-five years for Cooper (1967), and twelve to twenty-two years for the New York City Youth Board (1960).

Adult roles in gangs have, however, been identified in a handful of first-generation studies, but most of the accounts have been rationalized conceptually as adolescent "outliers" (Geis, 1965; Spergel, 1983). For example, early investigations of subcultural deviance patterns conducted by Thrasher (1927), Whyte (1943), and Short (1964) revealed marginal adult participation in established street gangs. However, these observations were interpreted within the context of their respective analytic frameworks as an "extension of youth" rather than a significant trend worthy of a unique theoretical explanation.

Second-generation gang studies conducted during the early and mid-1970s added further support to the thesis that gangs are fundamentally youthful primary groups (e.g., Klein, 1971; Miller, 1975). Klein (1971), who compiled extensive self-report data on Los Angeles street gangs, noted the following "typical" age profile of the gangs he observed:

> The typical gang has two to five age-graded subgroups. Thus there may be a small group of twelve- and thirteen-year olds, a large group of fourteen–fifteen-year olds, a still larger group in the sixteen–eighteen-year old bracket, and a smaller disintegrating group of older boys. (P. 65)

In addition, he found no evidence suggesting that experience in youth gangs was in any respect a precursor to adult criminality. Thus the typical "gang boy," according to Klein (1971, p. 83), "is first and foremost, an adolescent with all the problems and advantages accruing to that age group in our society."

On a national level, Miller (1975) specifically examined the notion of "age expansion" among street gangs in major U.S. cities; that is, that gangs are recruiting younger members as well as retaining older members. Using longitudinal arrest data spanning a five-year period, he failed to confirm either the expansion or the reduction in gang-prone ages:

> Of 807 gang-member arrests reported for the four largest U.S. cities 93 percent fell within the fourteen–twenty-one age-span, and 82 percent

within the fourteen–nineteen range. Only 6 percent of those whose arrests
were reported were younger than thirteen or older than twenty-three.
(Miller, 1975, p. 22)

On the basis of these findings, Miller (1975) concluded the following: "It
seems likely that claims of significant age-range expansion derive from over-
generalizations from a relatively small number of striking but atypical cases"
(p.22).

Within the past decade, there has been an emerging third generation of
gang literature that has called into question the "caricature of adolescence"
(Klein, 1971) stance born from the work of prior generations of gang study.
Ideologically speaking, third-generation researchers claim that recent ecological changes producing increased social and economic disorder within urban
underclass neighborhoods have given rise to a generation of adult "new gang"
members (Fagan, 1990; Hagedorn, 1988).

The New Gang

The conceptual profile of new gangs is quite different from that found
in most existing studies of gang behavior, and especially so from those
representing the early Chicago school. In particular, the "new gangster"
is conceived as noticeably older than Shaw's "Jack Roller" (1930) or
Thrasher's delinquent "boys" (1927). New gang theorists argue that this
age trend (i.e., the emergence of "adult" gang members) is the direct
result of an urban underclass that has become entrenched in conditions of
economic deprivation.

Age and the New Gang

According to new gang theory, dramatic increases in urban poverty levels
occurring over the past decade (Taylor and Covington, 1988; Wilson, 1987)
have resulted in the systematic failure of inner-city youths to "mature out"
of their gang member roles. This trend, it is further assumed, is perpetuated
by the economic inability of inner-city gang members to establish and maintain
legitimate adult life-styles in lower-class communities and subcommunities.
Hypothetically speaking, the end result of this process has been the creation
of a new cohort of adult lower-class gang members—which has not been
evidenced in past generations of gang research.

Increases in postadolescent new gang membership have been linked to
increasing conditions of economic deprivation within numerous geographic
as well as ethnic boundaries. Perhaps the first clue of a significant "aging"
gang population was provided by Moore (1978) in her life-course typology
of a Chicano youth growing up within a Los Angeles barrio:

> He develops in response to reference groups that include the traditional barrio gang in adolescence. . . . In young adulthood, he moves into veterano status in the gang. His reference group includes Chicano factions in prison. . . . In maturity and middle age, the gang remains a reference group, but his prestige in the gang drops. (P. 159)

More recent studies have also suggested a similar association between increasing patterns of protracted gang membership and a growing Mexican-American underclass in the Los Angeles area (Erlanger, 1979; Vigil, 1990).

Interestingly, the etiological picture painted for aging Chicano gang members is quite similar to that for the black delinquent subculture. In Milwaukee, for example, Hagedorn (1988) discovered a disproportionate number of young adult gang members in their early twenties:

> We did not expect to find such high levels of continuing adult gang involvement. The gang founders, faced with harsh economic conditions, have maintained their gang ties and continued to hang out together. (P. 125).

Furthermore, Hagedorn (1988) echoes the economic deprivation perspective of new gang theorists in explaining these findings: "Rather than maturing out of the gang into a job, or raising a family, Milwaukee gang founders have just kept hanging out together" (p. 125).

Structural linkages between economic deprivation factors and the aging of gang membership have also been noted among underclass black populations in Los Angeles (Klein and Maxon, 1989) and Chicago (Rosenbaum, 1983; Spergel, 1983) in addition to Chicago's Hispanic underclass (Horowitz, 1983).

The Study

This study explores the basic etiological foundation of the new gang: the aging inner-city gang member. Thus the primary objectives of this investigation are to determine (a) whether or not inner-city gang members have, in fact, gotten older and (b) to what degree the growing urban underclass has contributed to this trend. Answers to these research questions are of critical importance for providing an empirical linkage between hypothesized aging pattern and class origins of the new gang.

Data used here were taken, in part, from a large-scale study of unofficial gang behavior conducted in Southern California. The sampling and measures contained in these data are unique to the issues at hand because, unlike other gang data sets, they capture statistically the age structure of lower- as well as middle/upper-class gang members. Specific methods of data collection and use related to the present study are described below.

102

Sampling

The probability sampling of gang members is, at best, problematic (Short and Strodtbeck, 1965). Most notable problems encountered in this process include how to define the unit of analysis (i.e., gang members), identifying an appropriate sampling frame, and minimizing estimation error due to selection bias.

The gang member population represented in this study was operationalized according to the following definition, which was adapted from Miller (1975)[1]:

> A gang is a group of recurrently associating individuals with identifiable leadership and internal organization, identifying with or claiming control over territory in the community, and engaging either individually or collectively in violent or other forms of illegal behavior. (P. 9)

Selection of this definition was guided by both theoretical and practical concerns. Theoretically, it captured the crime-specific orientation of the new gang—in contrast to a more crime-neutral concept of gang behavior, similar to that originated by Thrasher (1927). From a practical standpoint, this definition was highly compatible with the collective focus of the study sampling frame.

Because the primary sampling objective was to target and select gang membership within low, middle, and upper socioeconomic (SES) levels, a sampling frame was derived by combining officially recognized street gangs located within selected Los Angeles and Orange County standard metropolitan statistical areas.[2] Gang populations from these particular counties were pooled and sampled because of their contrasting demographic qualities. On one hand, Los Angeles gang members are characteristically urban and represent lower-class, minority backgrounds. Orange County, on the other hand, is host to a growing number of nonminority street gangs that are rooted by territory in both lower- and middle/upper-class inner-city neighborhoods.

Selection of the gang member sample was carried out using a stratified two-stage cluster procedure. Stratification was performed by dividing the full sampling frame into low, medium and high social class strata on the basis of income estimates for census tracts specific to each gang's territory. To improve within-cluster homogeneity—as well as limit the potential for confounding race effects—the Los Angeles frame was restricted to black gangs and the Orange County frame to white gangs.

Initial clusters, that is, street gang "sets," were created by randomly selecting gangs from each of the three predetermined class stratums. This process resulted in the formation of the following clusters: twenty-one black gang clusters from low-income neighborhoods within South Central Los Angeles; thirteen and seven white gang clusters, respectively, representing low-income and middle/upper-income neighborhoods within Orange County at large.

At first, my associates and I attempted second-stage selection of individual gang members within each cluster through attending planned collective gatherings (i.e., meetings, initiations, and so forth) of each target gang. However, difficulties encountered in locating or gaining entry into such situations resulted in the abandonment of this strategy and led to the adoption of a more traditional "snowball" gang member identification method.

Briefly, the particular snowballing procedure used here involved both the vertical and horizontal linking of gang associational networks. The first step in this process was the identification of distinct age-graded layers within each target gang.[3] Second, through a variety of informal networks,[4] initial contact was made with gang members representing cliques within each age layer. These preliminary contacts were then requested to contact for potential interview other gang members—also active within their respective gangs— who were within as well as above and below their particular age cliques, hence ensuring both within-age (vertical) and between-age (horizontal) sample representation.

Represented in the final sample were thirty-six (88%) of the forty-one clusters originally selected. From these, a sample of 435 gang members was obtained. (A descriptive summary of each cluster and its relative contribution to the total sample is presented in the appendix.)

Data

Data used in this study were drawn, in part, from extensive personal interviews with gang members that my associates and I carried out between October 1989 and June 1990. For the most part, interviews were conducted one-on-one with each gang member and typically took place within a "natural" gang setting specific to the territorial boundaries of each group examined.[5] Substantively, the interview focus was on determining the relative importance of social, physical, and psychological factors affecting gang membership over the life course. However, the present analysis is restricted to the preliminary empirical examination of age and socioeconomic data derived from these interviews.

The self-reported age (in years) of individual gang members, recorded at the outset of each interview, was used as the study criterion. Socioeconomic status, the sole study predictor, was measured by a standardized scale reflecting the joint effects of self-reported educational attainment and relative occupational prestige. Both education and occupation variables were measured at the parental rather than the individual level. This was due to the general finding that nearly all gang members, regardless of age, resided permanently with either one or both parents at the time of this study.

Not surprisingly, class rankings of gang members developed by census tract income during the sampling phase were nearly identical to those generated by the composite SES measure of parental income and occupation. This parallel between aggregate and individual class positions was due, in large part, to two factors: (a) the extreme homogeneity of social and economic conditions within each of the target census tracts and (b) the fact that most gang members were extremely dependent on their families for food, shelter, and other necessities of life. Interestingly, the latter condition of familial dependence was strikingly evident for gang members across all SES levels.[6]

To ease comparative analyses and to sustain subgroup sample sizes, SES was reduced from its original interval metric to a simple dichotomy (low and middle/upper). The assignment of individual gang members to either low- or middle/upper-SES categories was guided by several indices of relative class position. In all, the SES level of approximately 78 percent ($N = 338$) of the total gang sample was classified as low.

An interaction measure, gang member race (black or white), was included to explore probable joint effects between ages, SES, and ethnicity. By combining the SES and race measures, three discrete gang samples were formed: black, low SES ($N = 206$); white, low SES ($N = 132$); and white, middle/upper-SES ($N = 97$). Unfortunately, only the low-SES was represented within the black subsample.[7]

Methods and Assumptions

This study employs a cross-sectional research design; thus analytic conclusions of gang membership age characteristics made here are—statistically speaking—based on static rather than dynamic differences. There are several reasons that justify the use of this design for exploring the new gang age hypothesis, considering that the investigation of age trends inherently falls within the empirical realm of longitudinal methodology.

First, and most important, it is here assumed that the question of whether or not a growing inner-city underclass is producing adult gang members can be answered by comparing the age distribution of gang membership between low- and middle/upper-SES neighborhoods. If time-linked economic deprivation within urban centers has indeed produced protracted gang membership, the age distribution of gangs originating in low-SES neighborhoods should be more positively skewed (i.e., favoring the aged) than that evidenced for neighborhoods classified as middle/upper-SES. It is also assumed that cross-sectional analyses are a valid means for exploring the likely impact of race on the relationship between gang member age and SES. Specifically, this assumption is necessary for examining the new gang proposition that social pressures to stay in the gang are greatest within urban minority underclass neighborhoods. This new gang interactional hypothesis is probed here by contrasting the age structure of black and white gangs, while controlling for neighborhood SES.

Perhaps the most unique design feature of the present data set is its inclusion of SES controls. Methodologically, this allows the direct examination of how age affects gang membership apart from class influences. Comparable examinations of age and class effects on gang membership are nonexistent in previous new gang research (e.g., Fagan, 1990; Hagedorn, 1988; Vigil, 1990), because these studies, unlike the present one, relied exclusively on data acquired from lower-class gang samples.

Findings

Age distributions for both low- and middle/upper-SES members are presented in table 6.1. Also shown in table 6.1 are results from numerous univariate and bivariate analyses used to determine statistical commonalities as well as differences between each gang member age distribution. In concert, the data in table 6.1 suggest that gang membership is still, as Klein (1971) observed, "a caricature of adolescence." Findings on several empirical levels provide support for this conclusion.

On a univariate level, central tendency and dispersion measures revealed striking similarities between the age distributions for low- and middle/upper-SES gang members. Most important, these analyses revealed no indication of distributional skew that would suggest overrepresentation of adult gang membership among the low-SES sample. In general, findings from these analy-

Table 6.1   Age Distribution of Gang Membership Within Socioeconomic Status Categories

| | Gang Member Age (in Years) | | | | | | | | | | | | |
| | < 13 | | 14-15 | | 16-17 | | 18-19 | | > 20 | | Total | |
SES	%	(N)	%	(N)	%	(N)	%	(N)	%	(N)	%	(N)
Low	6.5	(22)	23.1	(78)	37.3	(126)	19.8	(67)	14.8	(50)	100	(338)
Middle/upper	4.1	(4)	23.7	(23)	43.3	(42)	16.5	(16)	12.4	(12)	100	(97)

| | Summary Statistics | | | | | |
	Mean	SD	Skew	Kurtosis	Median	Min-Max (Age)
Low	16.81	2.69	1.21	5.87	17	9-33
Middle/upper	16.77	2.76	1.95	7.51	16	11-31

Distributional Difference Tests

t ratio = .674 (ns) x^2 = 2.16 (ns)   D = .109

Note: Row percentages may not sum to 100 due to rounding error.

Figure 6.1: Age, Socioeconomic Status, and Gang Membership

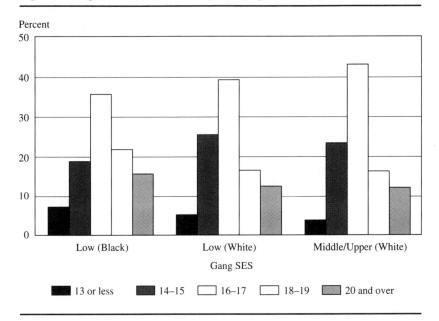

Percent

ses indicated that gang membership tends to peak between the ages of sixteen and seventeen years and tends to decline monotonically thereafter—irrespective of class differences.

Furthermore, bivariate analyses failed as well to demonstrate statistical invariance between the two gang samples. Both continuous and categorical tests of distributional difference yielded nonsignificant results ($t = .674$, ns; $X^2 = 2.16$, ns, respectively) for age comparisons between gang members classified as low and middle/upper SES. This finding was further supported by the relatively low Index of Dissimilarity score ($D = .109$) associated with the age distribution of gang members across categories of social class.[8]

In general, then, the new gang hypothesis that increases in urban economic deprivation have resulted in protracted gang membership cannot be confirmed by these findings. Contrary to new gang theory, findings reported here suggest that adult gang membership is as statistically rare in neighborhoods where opportunities are few as it is in neighborhoods where opportunities are many. Hence, according to results from this study, pressures concomitant with life in urban underclass environments do not appear to be forcing a majority of adolescent gang members to remain in their deviant roles upon entering adulthood.

Joint effects of race and SES on the age distribution of gang membership are explored graphically in figure 6.1. As this figure illustrates, holding gang member race constant appears to produce a negligible interactive effect on the zero-order relationship between gang member age and SES. Results of additional, more detailed, analyses of this three-way interaction are presented in table 6.2.

Overall, distributional trends reported in table 6.2 reveal only slight empirical differences in gang member age as a function of race and class. These differences were, however, in the direction predicted by new gang theorists: That is, gang members who were both low SES and black appeared to be, on average, slightly older than either their low- or middle/upper-SES white counterparts. Results from statistical tests used to examine the significance of this finding are presented in table 6.3.

Statistically speaking, and contrary to new gang theory, significant differences were not discovered between the ages of gang members while controlling for race and SES (see table 6.3). Interestingly, bivariate comparisons

Table 6.2   Age Distribution of Gang Membership Within Socioeconomic Status and Race Categories

Age (in Years)	Black: Low SES		White: Low SES		White: Middle/Upper SES	
	%	(N)	%	(N)	%	(N)
13 or less	7.3	(15)	5.3	(7)	4.1	(4)
14–15	18.9	(39)	18.9	(39)	23.7	(23)
16–17	35.9	(74)	39.4	(52)	43.3	(42)
18–19	21.8	(45)	16.7	(22)	16.5	(16)
20 or more	16.0	(33)	12.9	(17)	12.4	(12)
Total	100.0	(206)	100.0	(132)	100.0	(97)
Summary statistics						
Mean	17.02		16.68		16.77	
SD	2.88		2.42		2.76	
Skew	1.12		1.04		1.95	
Kurtosis	5.88		3.06		7.51	
Median	17		16		16	
Min-max (age)	9-33		11-28		11-31	

Note: Column percentages may not sum to 100 due to rounding error.

Table 6.3   Distribution Tests for Gang Subgroups

Gang/(Socioeconomic Status)	X^2	p	t ratio	p	Index of Dissimilarity
Black (low) vs. White (low)	4.10	ns	1.90	ns	.14
Black (low) vs. White (upper/middle)	4.25	ns	.97	ns	.15
White (low) vs. White (middle/upper)	0.48	ns	.61	ns	.02

between low-SES black gang members and white gang members at both low- ($t = 1.90$, *ns*; $X^2 = 4.10$, *ns*; $D = .14$) and middle/upper-SES levels ($t = .97$, *ns*; $X^2 = 4.25$, *ns*; $D = .15$) failed to indicate reliable differences in age structure. Furthermore, similar age invariance was discovered when middle/upper-SES white gang members were contrasted with their underclass counterparts ($t = .61$, *ns*; $X^2 = 0.48$; $D = .02$).

Again, but this time with regard to the combined impact of race and SES, the age structure of gang membership found here did not agree with that hypothesized under new gang paradigms. To the contrary, the immediate findings support the traditional notion that race and SES do not condition the length of time one spends in a street gang. In a general sense the findings from this study suggest that whether or not gang members are white or black, rich or poor, they tend to "age out" of collective deviance on the way to achieving adult status.

Conclusion

Throughout decades of gang research, one assumption regarding the etiology of street gang membership has remained largely unchallenged: specifically, that gang membership is primarily a youthful activity. Recently, however, a growing number of theories have claimed that the traditional notion of youth gangs is an idea whose time has come and gone (see, e.g., Fagan, 1989). At the nucleus of this alternative argument is the claim that inner-city streets are now being increasingly occupied by adult gang members who have aged into their subcultural identities as the result of institutionalized poverty within ghettos, barrios, and slums.

The purpose of the present study was to examine the tenets of new gang theory by determining the incidence and prevalence of aging gang membership within and across various levels of class and ethnicity. Overall, the findings from this investigation failed to provide empirical evidence that was congruent with new gang concepts of the aging gang member.

In this study, the tendency toward adult gang membership was clearly the exception and not the rule. For the most part, gangs investigated here were composed primarily of adolescents—regardless of differences in race or socioeconomic status. The following statement, obtained from a member of the South Central Los Angeles sample, represents the general opinion of most study participants with regard to the aging pattern of modern gang membership:

> Gang members are just like everybody else, when it comes to age we have a generation gap. Every new generation that comes along brings with it something else. Young gangsters coming up always seem to be a little tougher than the rest. By the time the "BG's" [baby gangsters] become "OG's" [original gangsters] the old guys leave on their own or

get pushed out. If you are old and a "High-roller" you leave the gang and make it on your own. Most of the old guys leave the gang because they are not respected or just can't keep up anymore.

All things considered, the final conclusion that must be drawn here is that streets gangs are still very much youth gangs. This general finding does not, however, summarily dismiss the new gang proposition that ecological decay within inner-city neighborhoods has resulted in the expansion of gang membership. Instead, it suggests that if growing urban underclass conditions have indeed been instrumental in expanding gang membership, such expansion—with regard to age—has likely been in a horizontal rather than a vertical direction. In other words, social and economic conditions may be pressuring more same-aged youths to join gangs instead of causing more adolescents to retain their gang roles as adults.

In sum, general findings from data examined here indicate that most street gang members are likely to be adolescents who give up their street gang affiliations upon reaching adulthood. Substantively, this conclusion does not rule invalid the new gang economic deprivation hypothesis for explaining the youthful onset of gang membership; however, it is the *desistence* of such behavior among adults that this theory fails to account for fully. As the present study suggests, social context factors do not appear to be producing street gang members who "mature-in" rather than "mature-out" of adult collective deviance roles.

Appendix: Description of Sample and Sampling Strata

Gang Origin	Race	SES	Gangs Sampled	Gangs Contacted	Contact Rate	Total Gang Members Contacted
South Central Los Angeles	Black	Low	21	17	80.9%	206
Orange County, at large	White	Low	13	12	92.3%	132
Orange County, at large	White	Middle/ upper	7	7	100.0%	97
Total	—	—	41	36	87.8%	435

Notes

1. Other general definitions of gang membership were examined for possible use; however the present definition (Miller, 1975) was ultimately selected for its compatibility with the general law enforcement definition of gang behavior that guided the study's sampling frame.

2. All gangs examined here were "officially" recognized by law enforcement. Specifically, Los Angeles gangs were randomly selected from Los Angeles Police

Department intelligence records; similarly, Orange County gangs were selected from information supplied by the Orange County Sheriff's Department.

3. The identification of number and size of age layers within each target gang was assessed through police records indicating age ranges of past and active members. Although this method provided, at best, a rough estimate of age grading, it was helpful for estimating the probable number of cliques within each gang.

4. Many official as well as unofficial sources were used to gain initial entry into the target gangs; high school counselors, clergy, probation officers, teachers, and friends of friends, were among some of the more fruitful methods.

5. Efforts were made to conduct all interviews within locations and areas selected by the individual gang members. This included such locations as restaurants, churches, schoolyards, and convenience stores.

6. Seven members of the middle/upper-SES white sample, 4 of the low-SES white sample and 18 of the low-SES black sample were excluded from the present analyses because their SES could not be determined through the general method used here. The age characteristics of these subjects, however, did not appear to differ systematically from those representative of the total gang sample.

7. Repeated efforts were made to identify and interview middle/upper-SES black gang members; however, such a population could not be located within the greater Los Angeles area.

8. The following formula was used to compute D, the Index of Dissimilarity:

$$D = \frac{1}{2} \sum_{i=1}^{m} \left| \frac{B_j}{B} - \frac{W_j}{W} \right|$$

where B_j = frequency of black gang members within SES categories in which black gang members are overrepresented, B = total population of black gang members, W_j = frequency of white gang members within SES categories in which white gang members are overrepresented, and W = total population of white gang members.

Within the context of the present study, D indicates the relative proportion of low-SES gang members (black or white, in bivariate analyses including race effects) required to exchange position with middle/upper-SES gang members to achieve evenness in categories in which middle/upper-SES gang members are overrepresented. Although the value of this measure is clearly relative in nature, a D score below .20 is here considered to represent relative dissimilarity between age distributions. For a further explanation of D and its interpretation, see Steffensmeier, Allan, Harer, and Streifel (1983).

References

Cloward, R.A., and Ohlin, L.E. (1960). *Delinquency and opportunity: A theory of delinquent gangs*. New York: Free Press.

Cohen, A.K. (1955). *Delinquent boys: The culture of the gang*. Glencoe, IL: Free Press.

Cooper, C.N. (1967). The Chicago YMCA detached workers: Current status of an action program. In M.W. Klein (Ed.), *Juvenile gangs in context: Theory, research and action*. Englewood Cliffs, NJ: Prentice-Hall.

Erlanger, H.S. (1979). Estrangement, machismo and gang violence. *Social Science Quarterly, 60*, 235–249.

Fagan, J. (1989). The social organization of drug use and drug dealing among urban gangs. *Criminology, 27*, 633–669.

Fagan, J. (1990). Social processes of delinquency and drug use among urban gangs. In C.R. Huff (Ed.), *Gangs in America*. Newbury Park, CA: Sage.

Geis, G. (1965). *Juvenile gangs*. Washington, DC: President's Committee on Juvenile Delinquency and Youth Crime.

Hagedorn, J.M. (1988). *People and folks: Gangs, crime and the underclass in a Rustbelt city*. Chicago: Lakeview.

Hirschi, T., and Gottfredson, M. (1983). Age and the explanation of crime. *American Journal of Sociology, 89*, 552–584.

Horowitz, R. (1983). *Honor and the American dream*. New Brunswick, NJ: Rutgers University Press.

Horowitz, R. (1990). Sociological perspectives on gangs: Conflicting definitions and concepts. In C.R. Huff (Ed.), *Gangs in America*. Newbury Park, CA: Sage.

Huff, C.R. (1989). Youth gang and public policy. *Crime & Delinquency, 35*, 524–537.

Huff, C.R. (1990). *Gangs in America*. Newbury Park, CA: Sage.

Kantor, D., and Bennett, W.I. (1968). Orientation of street-corner workers and their effect on gangs. In S. Wheeler (Ed.), *Controlling delinquents*. New York: Wiley.

Klein, M.W. (1971). *Street gangs and street workers*. Englewood Cliffs, NJ: Prentice-Hall.

Klein, M.W., and Maxson, C. (1985). Rock sales in South Los Angeles. *Sociology and Social Research, 69*, 561–565.

Klein, M.W., and Maxson, C. (1989). Street gang violence. In N.A. Weiner & M.E. Wolfgang (Eds.), *Violent crime, violent criminals*. Newbury Park, CA: Sage.

Klein, M.W., and Maxson, C. (1990). Street gang violence: Twice as great, or half as great? In C.R. Huff (Ed.), *Gangs in America*. Newbury, CA: Sage.

Miller, W.B. (1958). Lower class culture as a generating milieu of gang delinquency. *Journal of Social Issues, 14*, 5–19.

Miller, W.B. (1975). *Violence by youth gangs and youth groups as a crime problem in major American cities*. Report submitted to the National Institute for Juvenile Justice and Delinquency Prevention, Washington, DC.

Moore, J.W. (1978). *Homeboys*. Philadelphia, PA: Temple University Press.

New York City Youth Board. (1960). *Reaching the fighting gang*. New York: Author.

Rosenbaum, D.P. (1983). *Gang and youth problems in Evanston: Research findings and policy options*. Evanston: Illinois Center for Urban Affairs.

Shaw, C. (1930). *The jack-roller: A delinquent boy's own story*. Chicago: University of Chicago Press.

Short, J.F. (1964). Adult-adolescent relations and gang delinquency. *Pacific Sociological Review, 7*, 59–65.

Short, J.F. (1990). New wine in old bottles: Change and continuity in American gangs. In C.R. Huff (Ed.), *Gangs in America*. Newbury Park, CA: Sage.

Short, J.F., and Strodtbeck, F. (1965). *Group process and gang delinquency*. Chicago: University of Chicago Press.

Spergel, I. (1983). *Violent gangs in Chicago: Segmentation and integration*. Chicago: University of Chicago Press.

Steffensmeier, D., Allan, E. Harer, M., & Streifel, C. (1983). Age and the distribution of crime. *American Journal of Sociology, 94*, 803-831.

Taylor, R.B., and Covington, J. (1988). Neighborhood changes in ecology and violence. *Criminology, 26*, 553-589.

Thrasher, F. (1927). *The gang*. Chicago: University of Chicago Press.

Vigil, J.D. (1990). Cholos and gangs: Culture change and street youth in Los Angeles. In C.R. Huff (ed.), *Gangs in America*. Newbury, CA: Sage.

Whyte, W.F. (1943). *Street corner society*. Chicago: University of Chicago Press.

Wilson, W.J. (1987). *The truly disadvantaged*. Chicago: University of Chicago Press.

Yablonsky, L. (1966). *The violent gang*. New York: Irvington.

7

Perceived Blocked Opportunity as an Explanation of Delinquency among Lower-Class Black Males: A Research Note

Ronald L. Simons and Phyllis A. Gray

While once the most widely accepted explanation for delinquent behavior, opportunity theory has fallen out of favor in recent years (Kornhauser, 1978; Nettler, 1984; Elliott, Huizinga, and Ageton, 1985). To a large degree this decline in popularity has been in response to an accumulation of evidence that discrepancy between occupational aspirations and expectations is only modestly related to involvement in delinquent behavior (Eve, 1978; Elliott and Voss, 1974; Johnson, 1979; Simons, Miller, and Aigner, 1980). This finding is taken as disconfirmation of Cloward and Ohlin's (1960) thesis that the strain of differential access to occupational opportunity causes lower-class youth to experiment with socially illegitimate means for pursuing success and venting frustration.

Unfortunately, most researchers have failed to take into account the way in which Cloward and Ohlin's (1960) distinction between self and system blaming leads to the prediction that occupational strain will be associated with delinquent behavior only among youth of certain social strata. Most studies of the relationship between occupational strain and delinquency fail to examine differences by race and class, and hence do not provide a true test of Cloward and Ohlin's theory. As Bernard (1984) notes, the evidence is more supportive of strain theory when one focuses upon lower-class youth.

Critics of opportunity theory tend to reduce Cloward and Ohlin's (1960) view to the hypothesis that perceived lack of occupational opportunity causes delinquency (Nettler, 1984; Kornhauser, 1978; Hirschi, 1969). Such an interpretation treats opportunity theory as essentially the same as the econometric

Reprinted by permission of Sage Publications, Inc. from *Journal of Research in Crime & Delinquency*, Vol. 26, No. 1 (February 1989): 90–101.

perspective on crime that posits that people choose the most expedient means for achieving material success, that individuals engage in criminal behavior when it is perceived as more profitable than legitimate alternatives (Becker, 1968). However, this amoral, rather psychopathic view of human beings is quite incompatible with Cloward and Ohlin's work. They contend that

> a theory of "pressures leading to aberrant acts" is not sufficient. . . . The question of legitimacy occupies a place of crucial importance in this inquiry. (P. 41)

Cloward and Ohlin observe that most delinquents accept traditional morality. Most delinquents, for example, accept the moral validity of the norm prohibiting stealing and become quite indignant when someone takes something that belongs to them. Hence one is faced with the seeming inconsistency of individuals experiencing little guilt or remorse over violating norms that they generally view as desirable. Cloward and Ohlin resolve this paradox by introducing the concept of system blaming.

They maintain that failure to achieve one's aspirations does not necessarily lead to delinquent behavior. Delinquent behavior will lead to feelings of guilt and anxiety, and termination of the behavior, unless the legitimacy of the social system's rules is somehow negated. This negation becomes possible when the person perceives the reasons for his failure as rooted in the unjust organization of the social order. "The most significant step in the withdrawal of sentiments supporting the legitimacy of conventional norms is the attribution of the cause of failure to the social order rather than oneself" (Cloward and Ohlin, 1960, p. 111). Individuals feel justified in challenging the legitimacy of the rules associated with an unfair system.

Cloward and Ohlin distinguish between perceived moral validity and perceived legitimacy of norms. They note that individuals who perceive the system as inequitable may grant the moral validity of law-abiding behavior but challenge the legitimacy of such behavior given their life circumstances. A person may regard conformity with the law as generally morally superior to delinquent behavior but view deviance as necessary or justified given the unfair situation or circumstances created by the social system.

According to Cloward and Ohlin, perceptions of system injustice and system blaming are likely to occur whenever individuals experience significant discrepancies between the criteria upheld by the formal ideology of the social order and those actually employed by authorities in making choices, decisions, and judgments. They note that

> even in a democratic society, for example, where the dominant ideology stresses criteria based on social equality, talent, skill, knowledge, and achievement, many competitive selections and judgements take account

of such nonuniversalistic criteria as race, religion, family prestige, wealth, social class, and personal friendship. (P. 115)

Of course, persons in certain social positions are more likely to experience these discrepancies than persons in other positions. Individuals in lower-status positions, especially lower-class minorities, are more apt than persons of higher status to encounter situations in which opportunities are blocked based upon what are perceived to be unjust and arbitrary institutional arrangements. Thus, when faced with actual or anticipated failure to achieve occupational success, lower-class persons are likely to blame the system for their failure. And, this sense of system injustice encourages such persons to become alienated from the social system and to vent their frustration and pursue success through expedient deviant means.

In contrast, higher-status individuals are likely to blame themselves when they fail to achieve occupational goals. Such persons remain committed to the legitimacy of conventional norms and feel pressure to change themselves rather than the system. Cloward and Ohlin (1960, p.130) contend that

> people who violate rules which they accept as valid are likely to experience strong feelings of guilt. . . . With repeated violations the accumulated anxiety tends to become so intense that the offender gives up his deviant conduct unless he can develop some defense against feelings of guilt.

The lower-class person has a defense in the form of perceived injustice and illegitimacy of the system. The higher-status individual lacks this justification for violating conventional morality.

Based upon this logic, Cloward and Ohlin's strain theory predicts a positive association between anticipated failure to achieve desired occupational goals and involvement in delinquency for lower-class young people, especially lower-class minority youth. This relationship is not predicted, however, for higher-status adolescents. The theory predicts that while higher-status youth may experiment with delinquency, they are unlikely to sustain their involvement as they have no defense against the guilt and anxiety created by such actions. Thus, based upon the work of Cloward and Ohlin, it was hypothesized that the relationship between perceived blocked occupational opportunities and delinquency would be rather strong for lower-class blacks, somewhat lower for lower-class whites, and insignificant for middle-class whites and blacks.

Methods and Procedures

Sample

The data used in this analysis were collected by the Behavioral Research and Evaluation Corporation (BREC) in the mid-1970s for the Office of Youth

Development of the U.S. Department of Health, Education, and Welfare (Brennan, Huizinga, and Elliott, 1975). Data were obtained from youth in grades seven through twelve in nine sites: Dallas, Detroit, Kansas City, Las Vegas, Portsmouth, South Bronx, Tallahassee, Portland, Oregon, and Fallen, Nevada (Brennan, 1974). A combination of random and cluster sampling was utilized to construct the sampling frame. Both door-to-door and school administered surveys were employed. Care was taken to include dropouts from each of the study sites.

The data were collected as part of the National Strategy for Youth Development Project, and hence communities were selected at least in part because they were open to the initiatives that were associated with the study. Hence the locations might be viewed as atypical in this respect. Be this as it may, the heterogeneity of the sites with regard to size, location, race/ethnicity, and social class suggests that they might be considered to approximate a national representative sample (Brennan, Huizinga, and Elliott, 1975).

Given sex-role socialization in our society, Cloward and Ohlin (1960) contend that female adolescents are less likely to be concerned with occupational chances and opportunities than males. Hence they present their theory as an explanation of male delinquency. In keeping with their theoretical statement, analysis for the present study focused only upon the males in the sample. Unfortunately, almost one-fourth of the sample contained missing data on one or more of the variables included in the study. In most cases this was for the variable SES where either no information was provided or the description of parents' occupation was so sketchy as to preclude coding. Complete data were available for 1,906 whites and 531 blacks. The correlation matrix produced using listwise deletion was compared to the matrix for pairwise deletion to determine the extent to which the large number of missing cases might serve to modify the results obtained from multiple regression analysis. The two matrixes were quite similar, suggesting that the missing data did not function to bias the results.

Measures

Respondents completed the Youth Needs Assessment questionnaire, which was designed to provide baseline data concerning the problems of youth. The instrument focused upon various perceived needs, concerns, attitudes, and feelings. The following measures were employed in the present study.

Socioeconomic Status. SES was measured by head of household's educational and occupational status. Educational attainment ranged from a score of one that indicated graduate/professional training to a score of seven that indicated a grade school education. Occupational status also varied along a seven-point continuum ranging from professional to welfare/subsistence.

Past research on strain theory has been criticized for not focusing upon lower-class samples (Bernard, 1984). While Cloward and Ohlin posit that blocked occupational opportunities lead to delinquency among lower-class youth, most delinquency studies have employed samples consisting largely of working- and middle-class youngsters. In an effort to address this problem, respondents were dichotomized into lower and middle class. A respondent was defined as lower class if the head of his household had less than a high school education and either worked at a semiskilled or unskilled job or was on welfare. The remaining higher-status respondents were defined as middle class. Dichotomizing the groups in this fashion produced subsamples with 177 lower-class whites, 1,729 middle-class whites, 146 lower-class blacks, and 385 middle-class blacks.

Blocked Opportunities. Most studies purporting to test strain theory operationalize blocked opportunities as the difference between an individual's desired and expected occupational outcomes. This method of measurement is problematic, however, in that respondents may cite occupational aspirations that they consider unrealistic, though desirable, in the best of all possible worlds. A person may cite a particular occupational outcome as a desired goal but feel that in actuality very few people are likely to attain this position. Importantly, if the aspiration is seen as unrealistic, as an outcome that most people are unlikely to achieve, an individual will feel little frustration as a consequence of not expecting to attain it. Little strain is created by failure to reach a goal that very few people have a chance of attaining.

In contrast, when a person perceives that his chances of achieving a desired occupational outcome are less than that of others (i.e., that the goal is a realistic aspiration for others but not for oneself), he is likely to feel disappointed and frustrated. It is under these circumstances that the individual suffers strain, with some individuals locating the cause in the social system while others attribute the cause to themselves.

Given these considerations, access to occupational opportunities was measured by the following statement:

> Some people say that every person in the United States has an equal chance to get the job he wants. Others say some persons have a better chance to get the jobs they want. How about you? Do you have a worse, equal, or better chance than do others to get the job you want?

Rather than merely measuring whether the respondent expected to obtain the job he desired, this statement assessed the degree to which the individual perceived that his chances differ from those of other people.

Self-reported Delinquency. Delinquency was measured by a nineteen-item report scale developed by BREC. The items varied from minor offenses such as skipping school or using alcohol to more serious offenses such as using force to get money from another person or stealing something worth more than $50. Response categories were "never," "once or twice," "several times," and "very often." The scale has been shown to have excellent reliability across various categories of race, age, and social class. Coefficient alpha has been shown to vary from .85 to .96 (Brennan, Huizinga, and Elliott, 1975).

Some have contended that delinquency scales that contain a number of minor deviant acts fail to provide a fair test of strain theory as Cloward and Ohlin were concerned with explaining serious crime (Bernard, 1984; Vold and Bernard, 1986). Certainly it is true that Cloward and Ohlin considered their theory to be an explanation of serious crime among lower-class youth. They contended, however, that alienated lower-class adolescents begin by experimenting with non-serious deviance. "These first acts are usually minor and often impulsive expressions of resentment against the apparent injustice of the established social order" (Cloward and Ohlin, 1960, p. 126). They go on to argue that over time, in response to the hostile reactions of conventional society and the support provided by deviant peers, this minor delinquency escalates to serious crime. Thus Cloward and Ohlin posit a relationship between perceived blocked opportunity on the part of lower-class youth and an increase in both minor and serious delinquency. And, therefore, the BREC scale, which covers a wide range of delinquent acts, would seem to be an appropriate measure for testing their theory.

Results

Table 7.1 provides the means and standard deviations for each of the variables by race and social class. The table shows that the four groups score very

Table 7.1   Distributions for Delinquency and Perceived Opportunity by Race and Social Class

Subsample	Delinquency		Occupational Chances	
	$\overline{X}$	S.D.	$\overline{X}$	S.D.
Lower-Class Whites	25.80	8.44	2.09	.51
Lower-Class Blacks	23.20	6.66	2.09	.60
Middle-Class Whites	24.61	7.77	2.13	.54
Middle-Class Blacks	23.58	7.65	2.11	.63

similarly on self-reported delinquency. This is consistent with several other studies that report no relationship between social class and delinquency when self-report measures of the type used in the present study are employed (Tittle, Villemez, and Smith, 1978). The standard deviation for lower-class blacks is somewhat lower than for the other three groups suggesting that there is less variability, or more consistency, with regard to deviant behavior across persons in this group. Mean scores for perceived opportunity differ very little across groups. As one might expect, the means for the two lower-class groups are lower than for the two middle-class groups, but the differences do not approach statistical significance.

Turning to a consideration of the relationships between the variables, table 7.2 provides the zero-order correlations for the four groups. Given the way the opportunity variable is coded, a negative correlation indicates that as perceived opportunity becomes less delinquency increases. The table shows that perceived occupational opportunity has a very small association with delinquency for lower- and middle-class whites and for middle-class blacks. Indeed, for two of the groups the coefficient is not even statistically significant. The correlation for middle-class whites is statistically significant given the large N for this group, but the small magnitude of the coefficient suggests little substantive significance. In contrast, there is a moderate correlation of $-.24$ for lower-class blacks. Tests for the difference between correlations

Table 7.2   Correlations Between Perceived Occupational Opportunity and Delinquency by Race and Social Class

	Social Class	
Race	*Lower*	*Middle*
Whites	$-.07$	$-.12*$
Blacks	$-.24*$	$-.09$

*p ≤ .01.

Table 7.3   Beta Coefficients for Delinquency Regressed on Perceived Occupational Opportunity Controlling for Parental Rejection and Family Structure

	Lower-Class Whites	*Lower-Class Blacks*	*Middle-Class Whites*	*Middle-Class Blacks*
Occupational Chances	$-.01$	$-.25*$	$-.07*$	$-.07$

*p ≤ .01.

showed that the coefficient for lower-class blacks is significantly higher ($p \leq .05$) than the coefficients for the other three groups.

One might speculate that the correlation between blocked opportunity and delinquency for lower-class blacks is spurious. Family factors, such as living in a single-parent household or having rejecting parents, have been found to be related to delinquency (see Loeber and Stouthamer-Loeber, 1986) while there is also evidence that such variables influence a youth's occupational aspirations and performance in school (Furstenberg, 1974). Table 7.3 presents the standardized regression coefficients between occupational opportunity and delinquency for the four groups with the variables family structure and parental rejection partialed out.[1] The pattern of findings remains the same after controlling for these variables: The coefficient for lower-class blacks is moderately strong and significantly higher than for the other three groups.

Discussion

The four class by race groups did not differ from each with regard to perceived opportunity to achieve the job they desired. Although the mean scores on perceived opportunity were slightly lower for lower-class than middle-class respondents, the differences were not statistically significant. Similarly, there was no evidence of a difference in perceived opportunity by race. Previous studies have found that lower-class youth of both races tend to have lower aspirations than youngsters of higher status (Kornhauser, 1978). Perhaps it is because they aspire to less prestigious jobs that lower-class adolescents in the present study perceived no more blocked opportunity than did higher-status youth.

Some have argued that the finding that lower-class youngsters aspire to more humble occupations than higher-status youth, or the finding that they often perceive little or no more blocked opportunity than higher-status adolescents, is a fatal blow to opportunity theory (Hirschi, 1969; Kornhauser, 1978; Liska, 1971; Nettler, 1984). These conclusions are legitimate if, as is frequently done, opportunity theory is boiled down to two contentions: First, that youth of all social strata are oriented toward the same success goals, and, second, that young people become delinquent in response to frustration over their inability to achieve these goals. While these two statements are usually taken to be the essence of opportunity theory, they would seem to be an oversimplification of Cloward and Ohlin's arguments.

First, while Cloward and Ohlin assume that young people of all social classes are oriented toward material success, it is not essential to the theory that they aspire to jobs of equal status or prestige. Second, and more important, it is not merely an anticipated inability to achieve occupational goals that causes delinquency, but the perception that the system is not operating fairly, that some people have an opportunity to obtain valued jobs while others do

121

not. Thus to some degree youth of all social classes are likely to anticipate failure to realize their occupational aspirations; and given their realistically lower aspirations, lower-class youth may anticipate no more failure than higher-status youth. However, and this we take to be the crux of the theory, lower-class youngsters are likely to respond to anticipated failure in a different fashion than middle-class young people.

Given the everyday experiences of lower-class life, youth from such neighborhoods are likely to perceive the system as unjust, as not treating people such as themselves fairly. Hence they are more likely than higher-status persons to blame the system for their anticipated failure. And, blaming the system rather than themselves allows them to withdraw sentiments supporting the norms of the system and to experiment with delinquent behavior. Thus the theory posits a relationship between anticipated occupational success and delinquency only for lower-class youth, and particularly lower-class minority youth, as these are the individuals whose life experiences are apt to lead to system blaming.

The results of the present study provide some support for this hypothesis. Contrary to opportunity theory, perceived chance for occupational success was not related to delinquency for lower-class whites; however, there was a moderate association for lower-class blacks. It may be that lower-class whites have difficulty countering the equal opportunity ideology of U.S. society, and, like middle-class persons, blame themselves for their failure. In contrast, lower-class blacks, who experience the effects of racism in addition to class barriers, may be more predisposed to blame the system for their failure.

Other studies provide additional evidence concerning the significance of perceptions of injustice in explaining deviant behavior. In a laboratory study, Stephenson and White (1968) showed that young males were more apt to cheat on a test to win prizes if they felt they had been treated unfairly by the experimenter. Simons and Harrod (1979) used the ratio of black to white unemployment as a rough indicator of racial discrimination and argued that when the ratio was high there should be more system blaming and crime. Consistent with this prediction, they found that even after controlling for levels of unemployment among blacks and whites, there was a substantial association between the ratio of black to white unemployment and various measures of property crime. Thus it appears that perceptions of injustice may pave the way for experimentation with deviant behavior, and anticipated occupational failure combined with such perceptions may be one of the factors involved in the etiology of delinquency among lower-class blacks.

These conclusions need to be tested, however, through studies that measure important processes only assumed in the present study. System blaming was not a variable in the analysis reported above. A thorough test of Cloward and Ohlin's thesis requires a longitudinal design where one examines the relationship between anticipated occupational success, system blaming, and delinquency over time.

Note

1. Parental rejection was measured with the five-item Parental Rejection Scale developed by BREC (Brennan, Huizinga, and Elliott, 1975). Family structure was a dichotomous variable with living in a father-headed household coded one and all other situations coded zero.

References

Becker, G.S. (1968). "Crime and Punishment: An Econometric Approach." *Journal of Political Economy* 2:176.

Bernard, T.J. (1984). "Control Criticisms of Strain Theories: An Assessment of Theoretical and Empirical Adequacy." *Journal of Research in Crime and Delinquency* 21:353-372.

Brennan, T. (1974). *Evaluation and Validation Regarding the National Strategy for Youth Development: A Review of Findings.* Boulder, CO: Behavioral Research and Evaluation Corporation.

_____, D. Huizinga, and D.S. Elliot. (1975). *Theory Validation and Aggregate National Data: Integration Report of OYD Research FY1975.* Vol. 12. Boulder, CO: Behavior Research and Evaluation Corporation.

Cloward, R. and L.E. Ohlin. (1960). *Delinquency and Opportunity: A Theory of Delinquent Gangs.* Glencoe, IL: Free Press.

Elliott, D.S., D. Huizinga, and S.S. Ageton. (1985). *Explaining Delinquency and Drug Use.* Beverly Hills, CA: Sage.

Elliott, D.S. and H. Voss. (1974). *Delinquency and Dropout.* Lexington, MA: D.C. Heath.

Eve, R.A. (1978). "A Study of the Efficacy and Interactions of Several Theories for Explaining Rebelliousness Among High School Students." *Journal of Criminal Law and Criminology* 69:115-125.

Furstenberg, Frank F., Jr. (1974). "The Transmission of Mobility Orientation in the Family." *Social Forces* 49:595-603.

Hirschi, T. (1969). *Causes of Delinquency.* Berkeley: University of California Press.

Johnson, R.E. (1979). *Juvenile Delinquency and Its Origins.* Cambridge, MA: Cambridge University Press.

Kornhauser, R.R. (1978). *Social Sources of Delinquency.* Chicago: University of Chicago Press.

Liska, A.E. (1971). "Aspirations, Expectations, and Delinquency." *Sociological Quarterly* 12:99-107.

Loeber, R. and M. Stouthamer-Loeber. (1986). "Family Factors as Correlates and Predictors of Juvenile Conduct Problems and Delinquency." Pp. 29-149 in *Crime and Justice: An Annual Review.* Vol. 7, edited by M. Tory and N. Morris. Chicago: University of Chicago Press.

Nettler, G. (1984). *Explaining Crime*. 3rd ed. New York: McGraw-Hill.

Simons, R.L. and W.J. Harrod. (1979). "Unemployment, Legitimation, and Property Crime: The Sociological Versus Econometric Model of Exchange." *Journal of Social Service Research* 2:387–404.

Simons, R.L., M.G. Miller, and S.M. Aigner. (1980). "Contemporary Theories of Deviance and Female Delinquency." *Journal of Research in Crime and Delinquency* 17:42–57.

Stephenson, G.M. and J.H. White. (1968). "An Experimental Study of Some Effects of Injustice on Children's Moral Behavior." *Journal of Experimental Social Psychology* 4:460–469.

Tittle, C., W. Villemez, and D. Smith. (1978). "The Myth of Social Class and Criminality." *American Sociological Review* 63:643–656.

Vold, G.B. and T.J. Bernard. (1986). *Theoretical Criminology*. 2nd ed. New York: Oxford University Press.

Part 3
The Demographics of Gangs—Gender, Race, and Ethnicity

No study of gangs would be complete without an examination of the issues of gender, race, and ethnicity. These topics are among the most fascinating, and frequently controversial, factors associated with gangs and gang behavior. There is always the fear that certain groups are going to be branded "crime-prone" based on where the people live, their socioeconomic status, or their racial/ethnic makeup. No matter how much we would like to sidestep these criticisms (or potential criticisms), gender and race/ethnicity have played a prominent role in the study of delinquency in general and of gangs in particular.

Gender is a difficult issue to address adequately in crime related studies, and especially those relating to gang delinquency. Most authors start from the position that virtually all gang activity is a male domain. This means that little research has been done on females in gangs or female gangs. Anne Campbell is one who has contributed greatly to our understanding of girls in gangs. Her research, and that by others, indicates that girls typically do not find liberation or equality in gangs. In fact, they occupy "traditional" roles—sex objects, lures, spies, weapons and drug couriers—in virtually all gangs. The article included here reports on the results of a two-year participant observation study of Puerto Rican girl gang members in New York and particularly focuses on their rejection of certain aspects of their social identities based on class, race, and gender.

The second article, by Harris, is based on interviews of twenty-one present and former girl gang members from Los Angeles. Like Campbell, Harris combines the dimensions of gender and race/ethnicity in trying to explain gangs and gang behavior. Harris presents these gang girls the opportunity to describe their world to outside observers.

In the United States, especially, the study of gangs and gang activity has concentrated on certain racial or ethnic groups (and certain cities as well). Curry and Spergel examine gang activity by Hispanic and African-American adolescent males. These groups often are identified as being at-risk populations, especially in inner cities. Curry and Spergel took as their research subjects 139 Hispanic and 300 African-American males enrolled in grades six through eight in four inner-city Chicago schools. They found that while gang involvement was a relatively good predictor of delinquency, delinquency was not a good predictor of gang involvement.

Zatz, like Campbell, Harris, and Curry and Spergel, looks at the involvement of Hispanic youngsters in gangs. Unlike the other authors, however, she examines the legal processing of 1,916 court referrals in Maricopa County (Phoenix), Arizona. Maricopa County has a substantial Hispanic population, and Phoenix is among the seventy-nine largest U.S. cities with a reported gang problem. In this research, Zatz reports that, contrary to expectations, there is no correlation between Hispanic youngsters' reported gang membership and their juvenile court records. However, other factors do show differences in influence if the youngster is alleged or acknowledged to be a gang member. These findings may have policy implications for those state and local jurisdictions that consider sentence enhancements or more severe treatment for youths accused of committing gang-related crimes.

The final two articles deal with Asian gangs. Chin, Fagan, and Kelly note that while extortion against Chinese businesses by Asian gangs is acknowledged to exist, there is very little information on the exact scope and nature of the problem. These authors surveyed 603 Chinese-owned businesses in three New York City Chinese neighborhoods. They conclude that three social and economic factors sustain extortion of Chinese businesses: the unique political economy of the neighborhoods, the cultural norms of Chinese communities, and the relationship between the youth gangs and adult criminal organizations.

Calvin Toy examines the Chinese immigration from Hong Kong into San Francisco in the late 1960s and the integration of Asian gangs into the community's criminal subculture. He concludes that gangs composed of recent immigrants from Hong Kong were frustrated in their efforts to find legitimate employment and, thus, many turned to utilitarian crimes in order to survive. These youngsters also faced harassment from existing Chinese gangs and so formed their own gangs. Toy warns that recent immigration from the Southeast Asian nations of Laos, Thailand, and Cambodia also portends a difficult period of adjustment for those Asian youths settling in San Francisco. This may mean that Asian youngsters will form gangs, carve out territories geographically and economically, and turf wars will escalate.

Questions for Consideration

As you finish reading this section, consider the following questions:

1. What are the possible connections between gender and gang activity (or other forms of delinquency)? Are males inherently more delinquent than females?
2. Why does the general public associate gang activity with certain racial or ethnic groups? Are minorities more prone to gang activity or is there an error in perception?
3. What features distinguish gang activity for various racial and ethnic groups? In other words, are all gangs alike or do Hispanic youth gangs differ in significant ways from African-American or Asian gangs?
4. Do different demographic characteristics cause gang involvement, or do they predict likely involvement?
5. How would various theories on crime and delinquency help us understand the potential impact of gender, race, and ethnicity on gang activity?

8

Self Definition by Rejection: The Case of Gang Girls

Anne Campbell

Although there is evidence that young women have participated in urban street gangs since the mid-nineteenth century (Asbury, 1970; Salisbury, 1958; Thrasher, 1927), it is only recently that they have received attention as a topic of study in their own right. Prior to the 1970s, female gangs were usually treated as journalistic curiosities (Hanson, 1964; Rice, 1963) or as footnotes to the study of male gangs (Cohen, 1955; Cohen and Short, 1958; Short and Strodtbeck, 1965; Thrasher, 1927). Two themes are apparent in much of this early work: the psychological problems and inappropriate sex-role behavior of female gang members.

Psychological studies portrayed female gang members as immature, anxious, and maladjusted (Thompson and Lozes, 1976), as relatively low in intelligence (Rice, 1963), and as socially inept and sexually promiscuous (Ackley and Fliegel, 1960; Cohen, 1955; Welfare Council of New York City, 1950). Thus, this early research attributed many of the same characteristics to gang members which were used to describe female delinquents in general (Smart, 1976). However, Bowker and Klein (1983) reanalyzed data from the 1960s and found only trivial differences between gang and non-gang girls on a variety of psychological tests.

Early studies by social workers and sociologists tended to decontextualize the behavior of ghetto girls and to compare it unfavorably with middle-class stereotypes of femininity. Social workers placed particular emphasis upon gang girls' slipshod appearance, their preference for pants over skirts, and their poor personal hygiene, posture, and manners (Ackley and Fliegel, 1960; Hanson, 1964). Girls' failures in these areas were taken as indications of low self-esteem, prompting remedial efforts to turn them into young ladies (Short

Reprinted with permission from *Social Problems*, Vol. 34, No. 5 (1987):451–466. © 1987 by the Society for the Study of Social Problems.

and Strodtbeck, 1965). These departures from appropriate feminine behavior were also seen as the surface manifestations of a more profound problem: their promiscuity. Although the evidence for this was drawn from a highly questionable source—reports of male gang members—the promiscuity of gang girls was highlighted in Cohen's (1955) theoretical analysis of working-class delinquency. He argued that because emotional and romantic conquests are the female counterpart of societal achievement among boys, these young women expressed their rejection of the "middle-class measuring rod" by freely dispensing sexual favors. Thus, while boys boast about delinquent acts in order to achieve masculine status within their own oppositional subculture, girls should logically flaunt their promiscuity as a badge of their oppositional female identity.

Examination of the slim quantity of ethnographic work on delinquent and gang girls in fact suggests that this is not the case. The social talk of delinquent girls generally shows that they not only reject sexual activity outside the context of a steady relationship but even reject friendships with "loose" girls whose reputation might contaminate them by association (Smith, 1978; Wilson, 1978). Horowitz (1983) reinforces this point in her examination of barrrio lifestyles of teenage girls in Chicago. As part of the Chicano culture, they must maintain the appearance of virginity and restraint even though the broader U.S. culture encourages and condones sexual experience. The girls manage this contradiction by ascribing pregnancy to momentary passion in the context of a love relationship (the use of contraception would imply a cold-blooded and more permanent commitment to sexual experience). They can maintain their "virgin" status even after motherhood if their public demeanor continues to emphasize their commitment to motherhood and rejection of casual sexual adventures.

Female members of New York street gangs described in this paper had club rules which explicitly required serial monogamy, and girls who spread their sexual attentions too far were disciplined by the gang's "godmother." The pejorative potency of terms such as "whore" and "slut" is clearly seen in the way these teenage girls used such terms to characterize their enemies and rivals, and epithets such as these are often the triggers which spark female fights (Campbell 1986). It was this observation that gave rise to the present study: The words and typifications we use to characterize our enemies are often an important guide to the ascriptions we most reject in ourselves. By extension, our self concept may evolve from our rejection of such negative personal attributes rather than from the active construction of a social identity.

Using data from Puerto Rican gang members, I show how the girls' sense of self as gang members is derived from their rejection of various aspects of membership of three interlocking societal identities: class, race, and gender. They arrive at a female gang identity by default rather than by affirmation. The fragmented and reactive nature of their self definition helps to make sense of many of the contradictions which are present in the social talk of the gang girl. By "backing away" from one aspect of an assigned role, she may run the risk of being cast in another unacceptable role from which she must also extricate herself. For example, in rejecting women's passivity toward men, a girl may endorse her support for abortion. However, in doing so, she risks being seen as cheap or as a bad mother. Her support for abortion in one context may be withdrawn in another. To achieve self-presentational consistency, the individual must have formed a coherent schema of her ideal self to which she refers. As long as her self presentation depends upon rejecting an interlocking set of actions or qualities, she is likely to find herself escaping from one rejected identity but risking entry into another. The point is that not all components of a given role are rejected; indeed, it is hard to imagine what the result of such a total rejection would be. The girls accept the desirability of some aspects of femininity, class, or ethnicity but reject others. Essentially they are saying, "I am not *that* kind of woman," which is very different from saying, "I am not a woman."

In focusing upon self presentation through the words of the social actors themselves, the present study has much in common with the study of accounts (Goffman, 1959; Scott and Lyman, 1968). Accounts are usually given by actors in anticipation of or in response to listeners' negative evaluation of the actors' behavior. They are the means by which actors excuse or justify instances of untoward behavior. Stokes and Hewitt (1976) go further to argue that accounts serve to reconcile prevailing norms with innovative or deviant behavior and, over time, can alter group norms. In the case of delinquency, Sykes and Matza (1957) describe various "techniques of neutralization" which deny the wrongfulness of crime or justify it with respect to some superordinate value. My analysis of gang girls' accounts differs in three major respects from this tradition. First, I focus on social identities rather than on discrete actions. Girls see actions as characteristic of certain types of person and they vilify these behaviors not for their own sake but because they are the manifestations of a rejected identity. This idea is tacitly embodied in some of Sykes and Matza's (1957) justifications and excuses. For example, an "appeal to higher loyalties" often invokes reference to the overriding importance of group solidarity, which can be seen from the present perspective as colloquially indicating "I am not the kind of person who deserts my buddies." Second, the accounts I describe are not directed only at anti-social behaviors. The qualities which gang girls reject include passivity, submissiveness, and provincialism as well as drug addiction and prostitution. Tension exists not only between deviance and respectability but also between old-fashioned and modern values, between poverty and glamour. Third, while accounts are usually efforts to justify the speaker's own behavior, I focus mainly on disparagement of others' behavior. That is, I am concerned with gossip and "put-downs." As Moore (1978:52) notes: "Gossip, heavily judgmental, is at the heart of much sociability at the frequent parties. Gossip is fun. It also means that everybody—adult and adolescent—has a 'reputation' that is continuously shifting and renewed.''

This putting-down of others is a crucial component of the establishment of a self image. To accuse neighboring gang members of being ''whores'' or ''glue sniffers'' clearly announces that the speaker denies the applicability of such terms to herself. Analysis of the vilification of others is not only a useful methodological tool, but this process of symbolic rejection may be at the heart of how gang girls arrive at their own self definition. They do not actively work at constructing a coherent female group image but rather arrive at one by default as they reject components of the identities they attribute to others.

Method

Between 1979 and 1981 I attached myself to three New York City female gangs as a participant observer. During the first six months of research, I made initial contacts with a number of city gangs through site visits to gang outreach programs and introductions arranged by the New York Gang Crimes Unit. At the end of this period, I selected three gangs for in-depth observation and subsequently spent six months with each of them. In each case, I selected one girl as the focus of the research and spent approximately four days-a-week with her in day-to-day activities—during the course of which I came to meet her fellow gang members, family, and neighbors. Whenever possible I tape-recorded dialogues between individual girls and myself, as well as group interactions between the girls and between female and male members. I augment my analysis of these recordings with material from my field notes.

One of the three groups I studied was the Five Percenters, a black Islamic movement organized into gang-like structures in a number of East Coast cities. However, I restrict my focus here to the accounts of Puerto Rican gang members, the majority of whom belonged to the Sex Girls and the Sandman Ladies.[1] As with female gangs described in other major cities (Miller, 1975; Quicker, 1984), both gangs were affiliated with previously established male gangs and adopted a feminized version of the male gang's name. Female members constituted approximately 10 percent of gang membership in the city (Collins, 1979). The girls had their own leader and made most of their decisions independently of the males, including the acceptance, initiation, and discipline of their members. Gang members ranged in age from twelve to twenty-eight.

The Sandman Ladies were located on the west side of Manhattan with headquarters in the apartment of the female and male leaders (a married couple) in a housing project. They referred to themselves as a club or a family rather than as a gang, and identified themselves as ''bikers''—although the twenty male and eleven female members possessed only one working motorcycle between them. Their primary source of income was from street sales of marijuana, augmented by burglary and by hiring themselves out to protect cocaine sellers in the mid-town area.

The Sex Girls were located in the East New York section of Brooklyn and most of the members lived within a few block, of their clubhouse—one of the many abandoned buildings in the neighborhood. Their male counterparts named themselves the Sex Boys in honor of one of the local streets (Essex Street) when they split from the Ghetto Brothers in 1972. The male and female gangs were in a state of decline by 1979. A number of members were dead or imprisoned, and the formal structure of the gangs was in disarray. Although the Sex Girls allegedly had fifty members in the mid-1970s, their numbers had declined to about ten by the time of my research. The gangs' main source

Figure 8.1: The Female Gang Member in Relation to Definition-by-Rejection Qualities of Alternative Membership Groups

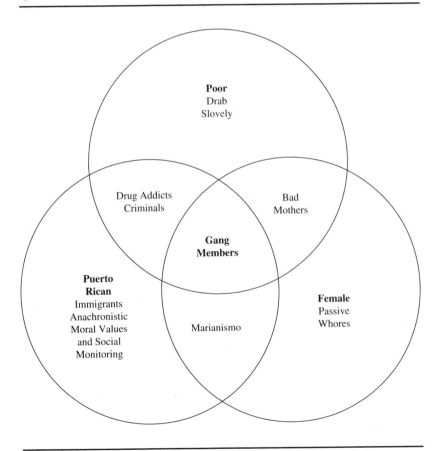

of revenue was drug dealing. During my field work, they were involved in a dispute with an Italian group of dealers over territorial rights to selling, which resulted in the deaths of three of the male members. Their income was augmented by petty criminality such as stripping cars and abandoned buildings.

A content analysis of the verbal "put downs" that appeared in the social talk of gang girls revealed ten recurrent topics. In each of these, the girls expressed rejection of specific behaviors or qualities and clearly identified themselves as distinct from individuals who could be characterized by them. For ease of presentation, I have conceptualized them as shown in figure 8.1 as locations in a matrix of three interlocking structural variables: poverty, ethnicity, and gender. It should be stressed that this conceptualization is mine and did not arise explicitly from the girls themselves. Rather these topics of social talk occurred sporadically throughout my field work and the girls themselves did not specifically relate any given "put-down" to these sociological categories. It should also be noted that the diagrammatic representation is not meant to imply that all three components contribute equally to self definition. For some girls, being female seemed superordinate to being poor or Puerto Rican while for others it was not.[2]

Ethnicity

Anachronistic Values and Social Monitoring

Many gang members were born in Puerto Rico or have visited the island frequently to stay with relatives. As with any immigrant group, their feelings for the homeland tend to be mixed. Often the gang members would talk nostalgically of the sunshine and the fruit growing wild on the trees. Such positive recollections were usually tempered with less pleasant memories of poverty: the lack of indoor plumbing, the perpetual diet of rice and beans, the lack of new clothes or shoes. Aside from the material deprivation they associated with the island, gang members often expressed the views that Puerto Rico continued to adhere to anachronistic moral values and that islanders were old fashioned in comparison with New Yorkers. For example, many of the gang members who returned to the island for vacations were shocked at the great importance local police attached to marijuana possession. The girls saw the tough enforcement and stiff penalties as indicative of the old fashioned attitude of their homeland. In contrast, they viewed the ready availability of "herb" in corner stores in New York City as an indication of a more progressive and liberal attitude toward marijuana on the mainland. The rigid moral values in Puerto Rico prohibited many of the activities that the girls found most attractive in New York—hanging out in the street, dressing fashionably, flirting, drinking, getting "high," and attending parties. When they stayed with relatives on the island, they were required to come home early and to help with household chores. Some girls said their New York clothing caused consternation among their Puerto Rican kin. The girls' parents seemed to share such views, in that a frequent response to the girls' misbehavior was to send them to stay with relatives on the island. Girls who were associating with undesirable boys, who became pregnant, or who were beyond the control of their parents were often shipped back to Puerto Rico where they would be less tempted by the freedom of the mainland.

The girls also noted that these traditional conceptions of appropriate behavior were enforced by claustrophobic social monitoring which was conspicuously absent in their life in New York. The girls viewed the anonymity and mobility of city life as reflections of the progressive values of the United States. Gang members often complained about the confining tightness of social controls on the island. As one girl put it:

> Puerto Ricans are very simple minded and the atmosphere is very, very close—and that's ideal for whoever likes to be close to people. Not me, I personally like New York. It's very cold and people think twice about speaking to you. I don't like being watched. Over there close communities everywhere you go. Everybody knows everything. I can't deal with that. This is the only place where you can come here and be yourself to an extreme but you can still be a faggot—that's an extreme. Or bitch. Dress that way, and I'm not saying it's going to be accepted by everybody, but you can still survive. Feel your identity—whether it be religion or whatever.

The tension between the sense of belonging associated with these extended networks and discomfort with their tight social monitoring has also been noted by Horowitz (1983) in her ethnographic research on Chicanas.

Immigrants

Gang members more than anything else see themselves as American and identify strongly with the special reputation of New York. They are not "hicks" but street-wise people who cannot be tricked, conned, or fooled. They know all the hustles and are not taken in by them. They strongly reject the old superstitions of the island which they see as evidence of its backward status. For example, many villagers in Puerto Rico continue to believe in "esperititas"—that curses can be placed upon individuals and only be removed through consultation with mediums who locate the source of the curse. The curse can then be lifted by the use of candles and herbs purchased from the local bontanica. Although botanicas exist in New York City, they are supported by older Puerto Ricans who are unwilling to openly discount the supernatural. However, gang members saw these beliefs as anachronistic and provincial. In seeking revenge over a rival, they were far more likely to fight it out or "drop a dime" (inform on them) to the police.

In stressing their status as Americans and their superiority over other more recently arrived immigrants, gang members took particular pride in the commonwealth relationship between Puerto Rico and the United States. They viewed the fact that they could come and go from the island without visas as evidence that they were not "immigrants." They saw other newcomers to the city such as Haitians, Dominicans, and Cubans as naive, provincial, and backward in their outlook. As one girl observed:

> America doesn't really want foreigners like me coming in, but right now Puerto Rico isn't foreign. Yeah. Dominican. Cuban. All those kinds of people. They came by boat. They can come on a boat from Santo Domingo or Puerto Rico. A lot of them get caught though, but a lot of them get in. And that's what fucks up the country. . . . Well, now the blacks and Puerto Ricans don't have anything to worry about—it's the Cubans now. You know I saw a movie and it said if there were no niggers, we'd have to invent them. Do you know what? The Cubans are taking over the oppressed group now.

A source of particular irritation was the inability of some of these newly arrived groups to speak English. This was particularly striking because many of the gang members themselves spoke "Spanglish," switching from one language to another—sometimes in mid-sentence. Nevertheless, their pride in their children's ability to speak and write standard English was evident, and they were often apologetic about their parents' inability to converse in anything but Spanish. For gang members, assimilation into mainstream American life was demonstrated by fluency in English which at the same time indicated the acquisition of "advanced" material values and skills.

Poverty

Drabness

The majority of gang members came from families that received welfare assistance and lived in communities where this was the norm. The families of many gang members were female-headed, and the mother often represented the only constant parent in the girl's life. Many of the girls themselves had their first child during their teenage years, after which they either lived at home, sharing child-rearing duties with their mother, or moved into a local apartment with the child's father. Gang girls with children were in the more secure position of receiving AFDC checks, but they still relied on their wits (or those of their boyfriends) to provide for any unanticipated expenses. Consequently, males who had successful hustles were a prized commodity and addicted males were considered a liability since any income they might obtain was spent on heroin. The boys would hustle money on a day-to-day basis by stripping abandoned buildings, selling marijuana, or rolling drunks. Girls did not draw distinctions between legal and illegal income—provided the latter did not invite police attention. The frequent crises of poverty were managed by circles of relatives and neighbors who relied on one another to borrow and lend food or money until the arrival of the next check (Lewis, 1965; Sheehan, 1976). Life on a shoestring budget meant that there were frequent trips to corner stores to buy items of food, often at inflated prices.

After motherhood, the girls rarely considered taking up employment. They saw their duty as first and foremost to their children, and their role as mothers not only provided a measure of dignity but a legitimate reprieve from the alien world of work. Their low level of literacy and lack of high school diploma meant that they would be eligible only for manual work paying minimum wages. Such jobs would not add sufficiently to the quality of their life to justify leaving their children. Besides, the girls were clearly apprehensive about employment, since most of them had never held a job and doing so would mean leaving their immediate neighborhood. Gang members rarely ventured beyond a few blocks radius from their homes, and the principal source of influence from beyond the neighborhood was television. The girls avidly watched soap operas and game shows during the day. Their favorite shows were filled with images of glamour and conspicuous consumption in which women were either kept in limitless luxury by men or worked in highly attractive jobs. It is perhaps not surprising that, when queried about the kind of job they would like, gang members frequently cited dancing, singing, and modeling (see McRobbie, 1978). The contrast between these aspirations and their actual job opportunities was striking and typified their rejection of any image of themselves as poor or drab. If work entailed menial labor, they would rather remain at home where their role as mothers engendered a measure of respect.

A good deal of their self presentation involved an image of devil-may-care casualness about the reckless spending of unanticipated income. They spent unexpected money immediately on drugs or alcohol and on trips to movies and steak houses. Many commentators on ghetto life have taken this as evidence of an inability to plan, save, or defer the gratification of immediate pleasure (see Meissner, 1966). When viewed as part of the development of self image by rejection, the spending of money on glamorous leisure experiences represents the denial, albeit temporary, or the conception of themselves as poor.

Slovenliness

Gang members also place considerable emphasis upon the purchase of the "right" brand names in jeans, sneakers, alcohol, and stereo equipment. They considered it particularly important that their children dressed well, especially at Easter, and they spent large sums of money on clothes that children would outgrow within a few months. They refused secondhand clothes as indicative of the poverty which they made every effort to deny:

> Your kid might come home and say, "Mom, you got to buy me $30 sneakers, $2.99 sneakers ain't doing it for me. I just can't stand criticism any more. You have to buy me $30 sneakers." What do you do? You go out there and you try to get them for your kids—the best way you can, the best way you know how or something.

Their effort to distance themselves from poverty stereotypes was reflected in great concern about cleanliness in appearance. Although they sometimes referred to themselves as "outlaws," they never displayed the disregard for personal hygiene and appearance that has been described among biker groups like the Hells Angels (Thompson, 1967). Getting ready to "hang out" often took some time because the girls were so meticulous about their clothing and make-up. Jeans were dry cleaned rather than washed, and boots were oiled and sneakers whitened every day. Some gang girls rejected the wearing of "colors" because they felt it made them look cheap and dirty. They wore the full uniform of boots, jackets, and scarves only when they anticipated a run-in with a neighboring girl gang:

> We used to wear hankies over here, hankies over here. Pockets, on necks, pants, hats, all over. I used to think "Oh that's bad. That's nice." But then I realized, "Look at me. I'm a girl. That doesn't look right." Like, "Look at that little tramp or whore". . . . You know—my jacket, my jacket, my clothes. I never like to wear them. Only when I'm going to fight or rumble, something like that.

Drug Addicts

The poverty-level Puerto Rican neighborhoods in which these gang members lived had high levels of crime and drug addiction. The fact that the girls belonged to highly visible gangs meant that they were viewed by the police and the community as being involved in both of these activities. The girls denied this. When they talked about drug abuse, they drew a clear line between recreational use and addiction. Marijuana was both used and sold by gang members and its place in their life was as uncontroversial as that of alcohol. They occasionally used LSD and amphetamines at parties. However, heroin use was strongly condemned. While some girls had experimented with "skin popping," they viewed intravenous injection of the drug as the index of real dependence. The girls took pains to distance themselves from any such involvement. Heroin users were seen as undependable, capricious, and irresponsible, and they were generally not welcome within the gang. They frequently stole from other members, failed to pay back loans, and were unavailable when needed for defense of the neighborhood. In spite of such vocal condemnation of heroin users, a number of the gang members were enrolled in methadone programs and had relapses into heroin use.

The gang placed firm demands for reform upon such members. As one female leader told an addict who wanted to rejoin the gang after leaving temporarily during a bout of heroin use:

> It's harder coming back the second time. I watch you more. You were fucking up a lot before, you were always nodding. Always told to shut up and you didn't listen. If you blend, you blend. If you don't, you don't. You've been to a different place. So just pretend you never left. Don't be talking about it. I don't want to hear nothing you've got to say.

A few days later, the girl stole three pairs of jeans and disappeared, confirming once again the gang's mistrust of an addict's commitment to anyone but herself. Significantly, a term of disparagement frequently leveled against rival gangs was that they were "dope fiends" or "glue sniffers."

Criminals

The girls did not consider many victimless offenses as criminal in spite of the fact that they might be against the law. These included drug selling, inter-gang warfare, organized crime, prostitution, domestic violence, stripping of abandoned buildings and automobiles, shoplifting, and burglary of businesses. Nevertheless, gang members assumed a condemnatory stance toward people they defined as "criminals." To affirm their own exclusion from this category, they employed a number of self-presentation devices. They symbolically distanced themselves from criminals by reserving the term for "crazy" people—for example, Charles Manson or David Berkowitz. Criminals also included rapists and child molesters.[3] Nevertheless, gang members were still left with the problem of accounting for their residential burglaries and robberies which by their own definition were wrong. They achieved this through the use of two favored techniques of neutralization: appeal to necessity and denial of responsibility (see Sykes and Matza, 1957). In the first case, they often justified property offenses with reference to a temporary financial crisis which left them no other option. In the second, they argued that they were "crazy" from drugs or alcohol while committing the act. However, neither of these justifications was accepted if the crime was committed on the gang's own turf:

> It was this old lady, she had a bunch of money in her pocket and we was on the corner, you know. We seen the money and I told Little Man,

"Come on, Little Man, you want to do it? Let's take the money." So this old lady we know for a long time. She was a little bit crazy. I said "Come on Little Man, let's do it." Then she walked to the corner and we walked to the corner, right? And then we grab her and took the money but it was on the same block. The cops came and everything but we did it wrong because it was on the same block, so then Danny didn't like it. He started to scream at me, but he wasn't my [the girl gang's] leader, he can't do nothing.

Members accounted for their gang's existence by pointing out the jungle-like quality of city life. Similarly to male members of the Lions in Chicago (Horowitz, 1983), they noted the high local crime rate and the need for some form of protection for themselves and their children. Frequently, the presence of rival gangs was given as their raison d'etre. They reasoned that since the other gang had "hardware" they had no option but to arm themselves also. As they saw it, they represented a vigilante force on behalf not only of themselves but of friends and neighbors too. In this regard, they felt a sense of cooperative rivalry with the police. The gang too was in the business of maintaining security, and the police frequently came to them to seek information on the perpetrators of neighborhood crime. As one member boasted:

What the community cannot get to, I can get to. Sometimes the cops come in and nobody will tell them a goddamn thing. Nobody is going to tell nothing—even to save their hide, they won't tell them—but I will come along and they will tell me. They will open up to me because they know, having gone through that shit, everybody opens up willing. They let me know what's up and that way I bring up what happened [to the police].

Because of their cooperation—at least in instances where the crime in question was not committed by them and especially where it was perpetrated by another gang or by competing drug sellers—they saw themselves as undercover assistants. Accordingly, they were outraged when the police arrested one of them. They felt betrayed and pointed out that the local precinct house would be unable to keep order in the neighborhood without their help.

The Guardian Angels represented a major thorn in their side. The media portrayed the Angels as "good" kids, but the gang members believed that this group received disproportionate credit for its crime control efforts. They often accused the Angels of perpetrating as much crime as they prevented:

The Guardian Angels got media recognition, they got everything now. They say they're this and they are that, that they're protecting the subway. That's bullshit, man. That's bullshit. right. They've already gotten busted for ripping somebody off on the subway, with their shit on, with their berets and their Magnificent Thirteen T-shirts and all their bullshit.

At the same time, gang members resented their own media image as "bad kids" and believed the press was conspiring to deny them appropriate publicity.

Femininity

Bad Mothers

Much has been written about motherhood as an important rite of passage among disadvantaged teenage girls (Rainwater, 1960; Stack, 1974; Staples, 1971; Sullivan, 1985). From an early age gang girls assisted in the raising of their younger siblings, although often with considerable ambivalence, and their own sexual experimentation began early. Many gang girls had their first intercourse at or before puberty and, consequently, pregnancy by the age of fifteen was not uncommon. In New York City, about half of all teen pregnancies result in the birth of a child.[4] Although the girls' parents may initially react with anger, they usually come to accept the situation and provide practical, if not financial, support. Motherhood means that the girl may now legitimately leave school and receive her own welfare check (although in the case of minors it may be paid through her mother). The young couple may marry but more often they do not: in Puerto Rico there is a long tradition of consensual unions (Fitzpatrick, 1971). Although the teenage father takes pride in this public demonstration of his manhood, his commitment to the mother and child is often temporary. Consequently, many teenage mothers face a future on public assistance in which men come and go, offering varying degrees of support or exploitation. As Horowitz (1983) points out, the Hispanic girl is likely to be deeply concerned about her identity as a good mother. To avoid any imputation of irresponsibility as a mother, she must make every effort to demonstrate her dedication to the welfare of her child. A good deal of gossip among gang members centered on girls who failed to take adequate care of their children. Motherhood did not require abandonment of the gang, but it did entail making satisfactory arrangements for the child. Girls who brought their children with them to the corner to hang out were considered irresponsible (also see Horowitz, 1983:128). The appropriate course of action was to leave the child with the grandmother for the night. After an all-night party, the girls would conscientiously return home in the early hours to get their children ready for school. Child care revolved very heavily around physical appearance, and the children's clothes were washed and ironed carefully. Especially with daughters, considerable sums were spent on "cute" dresses and on straightening or perming their hair. Keeping their children in school and off the streets preoccupied the gang members, and much shame was attached to having a child in a "special class." Any failure on the child's part that might be traced back to inadequate motherhood was strongly condemned.

Passivity

Even as they extolled the importance of being a good mother, the girls opposed any view of themselves as being at the mercy of men. They took pride in their autonomy and rejected any suggestion that they could be duped or conned by males, especially in the area of having children. For many of the boys, parenthood symbolized the couple's commitment to one another, and the males would often express their desire to father a child as evidence of their warm regard for the girl. After their first or second child, the girls objected, realizing that ultimately they would be left "holding the baby":

> In Puerto Rico those ladies, boy, they have to suffer a lot. Those men, they play you dirty. All having a bunch of kids. All dirty and shit. And you see a man like that, why you going to keep having kids? For the same fucking man? Having four, six, seven kids like women do in Puerto Rico? I say "Uh-uh, that's not me." I do me an abortion. And like I tell you, I do four abortions already.

Abortion was a problematic issue for most of the girls. Wholehearted support might be construed as callous disregard for human life and place them in jeopardy of being seen as "bad mothers." On the other hand, too many children could lead to a male-dependent lifestyle and suggest that they were vulnerable to being "conned" by men. Consequently, abortion was accepted as legitimate after the first or second child but was generally condemned in a first pregnancy. Adding fuel to their justification for abortion was the strongly condemnatory stance taken toward it in Puerto Rico; having an abortion was also an acceptance of being a modern American woman.

Whores

Because of the local public perception of the "loose" sexual morality of female gang members, the girls were faced with particular problems of self presentation in this sphere. The cultural context of Hispanic life places considerable emphasis upon the purity of young women before marriage although sex in the context of an exclusive love relationship is acceptable (Acosto-Belen and Christenson 1979; Pescatello, 1973). In the gang, serial monogamy was the norm and sexual promiscuity was frowned upon. One of the most frequent disparagements of rival gang members was that they were "nothing but a bunch of "ho's" (whores).[5] This epithet was one about which the girls were very sensitive:

> People say I'm a whore? They got to prove that. They can't say "You're a whore" just like that. They got to prove a lot of things. They ain't got no proof, so what's up? Right. So I say I don't live with the people no more. I live by myself. What the people say, I don't care. You know. Let it go.

Although it was in no way a requirement of membership, attachment to the gang often resulted in the girl becoming sexually involved with one of the male members. Once an exclusive romantic relationship had been established, the male would feel free to exert control over her public behavior and demeanor. At parties, for example, girls would sometimes get "high" and flirt mildly with other boys. This behavior usually provoked severe disapproval from their partners. During the summer, the boys would not allow their girlfriends to wear shorts or low cut T-shirts on the street. The girls chafed against these kinds of restrictions since they believed that flirting and fashion did not betoken promiscuity; however, they did accept the general premise that sexually suggestive behavior was inappropriate. Controls which males exerted in their role as boyfriends would certainly have been rejected by the girls had the males tried to impose them as a gang on the female affiliate.

The girls also exerted a good deal of social control over one another's sexual behavior. New girls in the group who, unaware of the prevailing norms, slept around with a variety of men were called to account for their behavior at meetings and instructed that serial monogamy was required. While this was in part motivated by the girls' own self interest in protecting their exclusive relationship with their boyfriends, members also referred to the danger of losing male respect by this kind of unselective sexuality:

> We think that she's a whore? She's a tramp? We just call her and we tell her "You got to get down with that one. But don't let everyone go to you. You're going to play with that one? Play with one, but the other ones, they're like friends." They [the boys] used to talk about her. We used to tell her, "Look, they talk about you—this and that. You think you're doing it right, but you doing it wrong. Because they're talking about you like a dog." She cool out in the end.

Marianismo

In their effort to avoid the stigma of cheapness through serial monogamy, the girls ran the risk of becoming overdependent on men. The term *marianismo* describes the qualities of femininity which are reciprocal to those of machismo in men. It refers to the cult of the Virgin Mary. A good woman accepts the dominance of men, values her own compliance and nurturance, and consistently places the needs of her family, especially her husband, above her own (Pescatello, 1973). Gang girls, socialized in the United States, strongly rejected

143

this subordinate view of female life. Most girls had seen their mother tolerate, for various periods of time, the blatant abuse and infidelity of their fathers. They frequently expressed disgust that their mothers had remained in the situation:

> Yeah—Puerto Rican women they hurt a lot. Some women they hurt a lot. They suffer a lot because of the man. Or because of their kids. I don't know. Like my mother—I say "Mommy, why don't you leave Poppy?" "Ah, because I love him at the time and I don't want you to have a stepfather." I used to tell her, "Oh man, sometimes you're stupid."

The right of the Puerto Rican male to exercise physical control in his own house has been noted frequently, and the girls' history of physical abuse from their fathers and stepfathers made them unwilling to tolerate similar beatings from their own partners. After violent domestic confrontations, when they saw their boyfriend repeating the same cycle of abuse that their mothers had accepted, they often made exaggerated efforts to assert their own independence:

> I said, "Don't think because I have kids I'm going to put up. I'm not." Like some women will put up, I won't. I'll leave him. I don't have to put up with him. I'll find somebody else that will give me more. I try not to aggravate him so what I do is I worry him a lot. I'll leave him even if it takes killing myself to do it. If I have to escape and that's the only way because he's watching, because he doesn't want me to get away, I'll do it. I'll kill myself.

Infidelity on the part of the male represented an ever present threat to the stability of their social arrangements. Puerto Rican culture emphasizes male autonomy in many spheres including that of extra-marital affairs (Acosto-Belen and Christenson, 1979; Pescatello, 1973). Although the males' traditional role as breadwinners and the exclusive rights it gave them have eroded, the double standard of sexual morality continues to exist in many New York communities. Puerto Rican women regard men with both fear and condescension as violent, sexual, free, and childish. Men's immaturity and irresponsibility are part of their nature for which they cannot be held fully accountable. Nongang girls in the neighborhood were often attracted by the boys' outlaw image. The boys felt that to refuse an offer of sex was tantamount to admitting homosexuality and argued that if a girl "put it in his face" they had no choice but to go along. The girls accepted this rogue male image and so had to exert their own control over rival girls. They did this vigorously as if to underline their unwillingness to repeat the marianismo of their mother:

> We'll still find out. We'll always find out. They'll swear on their mother, their father, their sister, their brother "I didn't do it. I didn't do it with

that bitch. I wouldn't make good with that bitch.'' They try to soup. But I already know the deal with them, ''Alright, yeah, yeah, yeah.'' And that's when I go. Then I go up to the girl. And they don't even bother hitting us 'cos they know they're gonna get worse. I would just go up, ''Hey, I hear you made it with my old man.'' This and that. And blat, that's it. The whole thing is over 'cos they don't even raise their hands. They put their head down and they cut out fast.

In this way many romantic disputes involving couples were actually resolved between the young women. The necessity of being attached to a male in order to have sexual relations, combined with a reluctance to challenge the boy directly over his infidelity, had a very divisive effect upon the girls' relationships with one another. As Horowitz (1983) also notes, disputes over men constituted a major source of aggression among the girls.

However, gang girls do take pride in their ability to fight. In rejecting passivity, they stress their aggressiveness and work hard at developing a reputation as a fighter:

Girls around here they see a girl that's quiet, they think that she's a little dud. Yeah—let's put it that way. They think they don't know how to fight. . . . Round here you have to know how to fight. I'm glad I got a reputation. That way nobody will start with me—they *know*, you know. They're going to come out losing. Like all of us, we got a reputation. we're crazy. Nobody wants to fight us for that reason—you know. They say ''No, man. That girl might stab me or cut my face or something like that.''

Among the Chicana girls studied by Horowitz (1983), aggression was only acceptable when it was directed against other females. Even here, it was seen by the community as an untypical behavior flying in the face of the self control that was expected of young women. However, Quicker's (1984) description of Chicana gang members in Los Angeles reveals strong similarities with the girls in Puerto Rican gangs. Although aggression was most often directed at females, either ''squares'' or members of rival gangs, the girls I studied took particular pride in recounting episodes in which they had fought with male gang members from neighboring groups. Hispanic gang boys express considerable ambivalence about the girls' aggression. On one hand they are proud of the girls' ''heart,'' while at the same time they will often intervene in a female fight to prevent injury to the girls (also see Horowitz, 1983). Whatever the boys' attitude, the Puerto Rican girls clearly took pride in their willingness to fight and saw it as an indication of their commitment to the gang, to their relationships, and to their self-respect. More than winning a fight, it was important to be ready to enter one. Before a fight they prepared by tightly securing their hair with oil (so that opponents could not grab it) and donning boots and jeans. Rival gang members were disparaged as hanging out with their men only when times were good and failing to support them during gang wars:

> Tramps. All they think about is screwing. It's true. It's true, shit. They don't fight. They don't go to rumbles with their guys. Nothing. They're punks. They're a bunch of punks. Cuiso, right? The Cheeseburgers are a bunch of punks? They're not tough. They're a bunch of dope fiends.

The importance of not "ranking out" or backing down from a fight was frequently stressed. It was seen as indicative of moral weakness. Fighting was sufficiently highly valued that the initiation of new "prospects" required them to demonstrate their fearlessness in the face of physical attack.

> Well when we started it was like initiating people—when you take them to the park, like, to see. Like there's some girls that join, like "I get in trouble, I got backup." Now for us this wasn't that. We used to take a new girl to the park. Now that girl had to pick one of our girls, and whoever she wanted, she had to fight that girl to see if she could take the punches. Now if she couldn't, she wouldn't fight. Then we wouldn't take her. Because then we know that someday—you know, somewhere in the streets—she's going to wind up getting hurt. So we knew that she could fight her battles and we used to let her join. She had to fight first. Without crying.

Discussion and Conclusions

Previous work on female gang members has placed considerable emphasis upon their sexuality either as an area for reform through social work, as a symptom of their rejection of middle-class values, or as the single most important impression management problem which they face. While any examination of self concept clearly must include attention to the management of appropriate male or female identity, I believe it is a disservice to girls in gangs not to recognize other salient features of their self definition. These young women are stigmatized by ethnicity and poverty as well as gender.

By virtue of their marginal position, both economically and socially, they live their lives within a bounded geographical area where the major sources of influence and support are likely to be families, friends, and neighbors. Without the opportunity to fulfill themselves in mainstream jobs beyond the ghetto, their sense of self must be won from others in the immediate environment. Within this context, gang girls see themselves as different from their peers. Their association with the gang is a public proclamation of their rejection of the lifestyle which the community expects from them. Sociological portraits that deny the girls' sense of differentness from other neighborhood youth deny the validity of the way the girls see themselves.

The sense of differentness experienced by the girls is fragmented and diffuse—as indeed it must be since they do not fully embrace an oppositional deviant identity. They do not buy into a countercultural role that is well-articulated and wholly coherent. Rather they reject bits and pieces of the conventional lifestyle that is expected of them in the local community. Inevitably, the girl finds herself in a contradictory and vulnerable position as she attempts to retain her integrity within her shifting self definition. She is Puerto Rican but neither provincial nor unAmerican. She may be poor but her life is neither drab nor criminal. She enjoys her femininity but rejects passivity and suffering.

My evidence suggests that much can be learned from examining how we vilify the traits and actions of others. Much of our social life is spent in talk, and a significant portion of it is concerned not with our own behavior but with that of others. The terms of condemnation in gossip reveal a good deal about our own preoccupations and values. When we criticize others' behavior we assure the listener and ourselves that we are exempt from similar accusations—we set ourselves apart from the object of our derision. Sometimes we level our criticism at figures beyond our acquaintance such as media personalities or politicians; but the most salient reference point for our self definition are those individuals or groups whose social niche we share. This is particularly true for disadvantaged groups who are caught in a restricted social environment with little hope of mobility.

Important questions remain to be answered about the present approach, as about other sociological analyses of accounts. The chronology of gang membership and self definition by rejection remains uncertain. Do gangs act as clearing houses for those who have already felt their distance from "straight" lifestyles, or does gang membership encourage and articulate this kind of self definition? What changes occur in the evaluation of previously rejected qualities when the girl falls away from the gang? Answers to these questions will only be found if researchers continue to take disparaging social talk as a legitimate focus of enquiry. Closer examination of the vilification of others may indicate that gossip is a strategic resource for the development of a sense of selfhood.

Notes

1. For a fuller account of these gangs see Campbell (1984).

2. There is, of course, considerable scholarly debate as to the primacy of each of these factors, and researchers in women's studies, minority studies, and economics would certainly disagree as to the relative influence of gender, race, and class on lifestyles and self-conceptions.

3. It should be born in mind that gang members themselves are not exempt from victimization. When one of the gang girls was the victim of an attempted rape, it was clear to gang members that the perpetrators were "criminals."

4. Personal Communication with Planned Parenthood of New York City, Inc., January, 1984.

5. None of the girls I spoke with admitted to prostitution in their past. Where money was accepted from men after a date, it was treated as an unanticipated act of generosity. For example, one girl occasionally met men outside a Manhattan swingers club and went in with them. This lowered the men's admission price. The money they gave her at the end of the evening was considered a gift.

References

Ackley, Ethel and Beverly Fliegel. (1960). A social work approach to street corner girls. *Social Work*, 5:29–31.

Acosta-Belen, Edna and Elia H. Christenson. (1979). *The Puerto Rican Woman*. New York: Praeger.

Asbury, Herbert. (1970). *The Gangs of New York*. New York: Capricorn Books.

Bowker, Lee H. and Malcolm W. Klein. (1983). The etiology of female juvenile delinquency and gang membership: a test of psychological and social structural explanations. *Adolescence*, 8:739–51.

Campbell, Anne. (1984). *The Girls in the Gang*. New York: Basil Blackwell.

Campbell, Anne. (1986). Self report of fighting by females. *British Journal of Criminology*, 26:28–46.

Cohen, Albert K. (1955). *Delinquent Boys: The Culture of the Gang*. New York: Free Press.

Cohen, Albert K. and James F. Short. (1958). Research in delinquent subculture. *Journal of Social Issues*, 14:20–37.

Collins, H. Craig. (1979). *Street Gangs: Profiles for Police*. New York: New York City Police Department.

Fitzpatrick, Joseph P. (1971). *Puerto Rican Americans: The Meaning of Migration to the Mainland*. Englewood Cliffs, NJ: Prentice Hall.

Goffman, Erving. (1959). *The Presentation of Self in Everyday Life*. New York: Doubleday Anchor Books.

Hanson, Kitty. (1964). *Rebels in the Streets: The Story of New York's Girl Gangs*. Englewood Cliffs, NJ: Prentice Hall.

Horowitz, Ruth. (1983). *Honor and the American Dream*. Chicago: University of Chicago Press.

Lewis, Oscar. (1965). *La Vida: A Puerto Rican Family in the Culture of Poverty: San Juan and New York*. New York: Vintage Books.

McRobbie, Angela. (1978). *Jackie: An Ideology of Adolescent Femininity*. Birmingham, England: Centre for Contemporary Culture Studies.

Meissner, Hanna H. (1966). *Poverty and the Affluent Society*. New York: Harper and Row.

Miller, Walter B. (1975). *Violence by Youth Gangs and Youth Groups as a crime Problem in Major American Cities*. Washington, DC: U.S. Government Printing Office.

Moore, Joan. (1978). *Homeboys*. Philadelphia: Temple University Press.

Pescatello, Ann. (1973). *Female and Male in Latin America*. Pittsburgh: University of Pittsburgh Press.

Quicker, John C. (1984). *Homegirls: Characterizing Chicano Gangs*. San Pedro, CA: International Universities Press.

Rainwater, Lee. (1960). *And the Poor Get Children: Sex, Contraception and Family Planning in the Working Class*. Chicago: Quadrangle.

Rice, Robert. (1963). A reporter at large: The Persian Queens. *The New Yorker* 39: 153–87.

Salisbury, Harrison E. (1958). *The Shook-Up Generation*. New York: Harper and Bros.

Scott, Marvin and Stanford Lyman. (1968). Accounts. *American Sociological Review*. 33:46–62.

Sheehan, Susan. (1976). *A Welfare Mother*. Boston: Houghton Mifflin.

Short, James F. and Fred Strodtbeck. (1965). *Group Process and Gang Delinquency*. Chicago: University of Chicago Press.

Smart, Carol. (1976). *Women, Crime and Criminology*. London: Routledge and Kegan Paul.

Smith, Lesley S. (1978). Sexist assumptions and female delinquency: An empirical investigation. Pp. 74–86 in Carol Smart and Barry Smart (eds.), *Women, Sexuality and Social Control*. London: Routledge and Kegan Paul.

Stack, Carol B. (1974). *All Our Kin: Strategies for Survival in a Black Community*. New York: Harper and Row.

Staples, Robert (ed.). (1971). *The Black Family: Essays and Studies*. Belmont, CA: Wadsworth.

Stokes, Randall and John P. Hewitt. (1976). Aligning actions. *American Sociological Review* 41:838–45.

Sullivan, Mercer L. (1985). *Teen Fathers in the Inner City: An Exploratory Ethnographic Study*. New York: Vera Institute of Justice.

Sykes, Gresham M. and David Matza. (1957). Techniques of neutralization: A theory of delinquency. *American Sociological Review* 22:664–70.

Thompson, Hunter. (1967). *Hell's Angels*. New York: Ballantine.

Thompson, Robert J. and Jewel Lozes. (1976). Female gang delinquency. *Corrective and Social Psychiatry and Journal of Behavior Technology Methods and Therapy* 22:1–5.

Thrasher, Frederick. (1927). *The Gang*. Chicago: University of Chicago Press.

Welfare Council of New York City. (1950). *Working with Teenage Groups: A Report on the Central Harlem Project*. New York: Welfare Council of New York City.

Wilson, Deidre. (1978). Sexual codes and conduct: a study of teenage girls. Pp. 65–73 in Carol Smart and Barry Smart (eds.), *Women, Sexuality and Social Control*. London: Routledge and Kegan Paul.

9

Cholas, Mexican-American Girls, and Gangs

Mary G. Harris

Urban sprawl, population growth, high unemployment, changing immigration patterns, and urban recession have moved street gangs out of low-income, inner-city neighborhoods where poverty, racial division, and high unemployment contributed to their formation. Today, there are at least 600 gangs with an estimated 100,000 gang members operating in Los Angeles County, and their impact is felt throughout the city including the once more affluent suburban areas. Los Angeles has been dubbed the "gang capital of the world," where every school and community is impacted in some way. In 1991, 770 murders were gang related, making 1991 the seventh consecutive year of record gang killings. While many of these were attributed to black gangs, the incidence of violent crimes and gang activity on the part of Mexican-American gangs is also on the increase.

Mexican-American gangs have existed in the barrios of Los Angeles for as long as seventy years, and females have been active within those gangs since that time. The Pachucos, active in the twenties and thirties, the forerunners of today's Mexican-American gangs, developed styles and rituals concerning dress, manners, and social attitudes, which have become inherent in the social world of the barrios today. It is interesting to note that the modern version of the Pachuco, today's Cholos and Cholas (gang members) have developed a lifestyle and dress similar to the Pachuco innovators. The difference today is that cultural patterns have become far more debilitating including more frequent drug use and violence which has escalated to include far more gang killings.

This study focuses on Mexican-American gang girls as they act within the Mexican-American gang milieu in the San Fernando Valley of Los Angeles.

Reprinted with permission of Pleneum Publishing Corporation from *Sex Roles*, Vol. 30, No. 3/4 (1994): 289–301.

Twenty-one female present and former gang members were interviewed concerning participation in and attitudes toward gang activities. The interviews were extensive, on-going over a year period, sometimes individually and sometimes in groups, and took place in many different locales—homes of the gang girls, the neighborhood center, my home, street corners, the barrio, the park—to provide an in-depth view of the world of the Chola, the gang girl. The study attempts to understand this subculture from the world-view of the Chola.

Females form an intricate, cohesive and significant sub-group within all Mexican-American gangs. In some cases, the female cliques appear to be stronger and more active than the male cliques; in other cases, female gang members are subservient to the more dominant male members.

Mexican-American gangs as they operate in the San Fernando Valley of Los Angeles are loosely organized groups of young people who become deeply involved in a subculture that leads to gang membership, enabling core members to achieve the highest awards of power, esteem, and a strong sense of identity. The most active members range in age between thirteen and sixteen; younger persons may have the affect—the dress and behavior—in preparation for becoming core gang members, older members begin to decrease their involvement in intense gang activity while maintaining identification as a gang member as they enter into adulthood. Gangs are usually named after the street, housing project, or barrio from which the gang originates. Members identify closely with their neighborhood or "hood" and it is this name they tattoo on themselves and write on walls throughout the city.

Gangs are composed of divisions of cliques (klikas), roughly based on age cohort with divisions of either males or females. In a sense, the gang is similar to the army, the divisions operating with some autonomy yet loyal to the hood, ostensibly operating to protect the neighborhood but in actuality operating to promote prized violent behaviors. Several of the females in this study were members of Pacas Flats, for example, which contains three female divisions, loosely based on age, Tiny Locas, Chiquitas, and Juanitas. In this gang, membership in the original clique is maintained. The entire clique moves from being the youngest clique, through their most active period to eventually become the "veteranas." Parents who had been gang members as youngsters continued to identify themselves as members of a particular clique and gang.

The size of the gang roughly correlates to the size of the barrio or neighborhood of low-income segregated, neighborhoods of Mexican-Americans, with gangs ranging in size from thirty to three-hundred. Gang boundaries are dynamic, changing as members move in and out, often in response to the specific situation. All-out war with a rival gang will elicit a large response of members; walking, talking, drinking in the park will call out fewer.

The Mexican-American females become members of a gang in a manner similar to becoming a member of any teenage group. For core members, the gang becomes a total institution, much like a commune or military unit, completely absorbing the individual into the subculture. The gang members expressed a strong sense of belonging to the gang, and compared gang membership to a family. In many cases, the gang took precedence over the family even when the family was endangered.

Core members of the gang interact with one another according to established patterns which are binding on them as gang members, and are clearly identifiable both by other gang members and by persons who are not in the gang. Interaction within the gang is specific and ritualistic in form, with sanctions applied whenever someone does not adapt to the patterned forms of gang behavior.

Members from rival gangs perversely challenge each other to test group fidelity and to clearly establish membership. The challenge is one of the rituals which clearly identifies gang membership and intensifies the sense of belongingness to the group. It is formalized in this way:

> *Sonya:* Like if you go somewhere. Like we go to the park and a bunch of girls from SanFer [a rival gang] are there, and us Blythe Street Girls. And they're going to give us hard looks, and we're going to give them hard looks, and that's where it's going to start. And they'll say, "Where are you from?" "Blythe Street. Where are you from?" "Well, fuck you." And then we go. Just for the street. Uno Blythe. Blythe Street's number one. That's all it is.

Membership

As a gang member becomes increasingly entrenched in the gang, she internalizes its values. The ability and willingness to fight, facing the enemy not running, to be "bad," to be "crazy," to be tough and to use drugs are all prized behaviors. Girls who exhibit these qualities are most desired as gang members:

> *Reselda:* We don't take everybody. We'll see how she takes care of business. If she can back up her shit. If she fits in with what we're doing. If you're in a gang you're supposed to back it up because they're your homegirls.

Eligibility for membership is both ascribed and achieved. It is ascribed in that a girl must live in the barrio or very close to the center of gang activity:

> *Reselda:* Well, like our neighborhood is the projects. They don't have to live in the projects; as long as they live like in the city of Pacoima, they can join. As long as they were raised in Pacoima they can hold up Pacoima.

It is also ascribed in that a girl, with rare exceptions, must be of Mexican-American descent. In response to the question, "Was your gang only Chicanas?" one gang member responded:

Cindy: We had a black chick and a couple of white chicks. They were wannabe's [want to be's]. If I were white, I wouldn't want to be a Chicana. Because, shit, they're the one's who end up getting their ass kicked the most. Chicanas don't like gabachas [white girls] that try to back up Chicanas. Be what you are. Don't try to be somebody else.

Membership is achieved by adopting manners and dress of gang members. Younger girls copy the dress and actions of gang members, become part of the gang support group and are fringe members before actually becoming initiated into the clique. They "claim the hood," that is, identify themselves as gang members, and are invited to join after they have proven their loyalty by demonstrating their ability to fight.

Benita: Well, if you live where I live, you want to be a gang member. It's what you do. You want to be like your older sister or your cousin. So when I was young I started dressing like them. And then I'd go to the park and start hanging around. I used to sneak out my bedroom window at night to hang with them so my father wouldn't know, so I could go to the park and get high and have fun. And then it was too late—I was in it.

A girl is often socialized to the group before joining. She selects the clique as her reference group as early as age six, engages in conforming behavior, and is apt to be rewarded by the gang for doing so:

Nona: I was already dressing and wearing the eyelashes and the makeup. Right after my brother was killed, I was wearing the makeup. I had nobody to tell me you can't be wearing this and you can't be wearing that. My mom used to tell me but I didn't care. What was running through my mind was my brother. Besides, I was starting to get jumped. That's when I realized, "Hey, I'm not going to take anymore of this shit." Cause if you fuck with me, I'm going to fuck right back. I don't have to put up with this shit.

If a member repudiates the values of the gang, or is unable or unwilling to fight, she is rejected.

Reselda: You can belong as long as you can back up your shit and don't rat on your own homegirls or back away. If you don't back them up and you run we'll jump that girl out because she ain't going to take care of nothing. All she wants is our backup and our support but she ain't going to give us none of hers, so what's the use of her being around. She has to be able to hold up the hood.

Reasons for Joining

Perception of a common destiny, a sense of belonging and identity, a need for group support and cohesiveness, and a need for revenge, were reasons given for joining the gang.

Reselda: Everybody's fighting and everybody's against each other because everybody's trying to be the same. Everybody's in the same ball, like, doing the same thing. A lot of them don't have a job, drugs, everybody wants to be the same. They're all into gangs. They're all trying to be alike.

Anita: There's a lot of reasons why I wanted to get in it. I wanted to roam with more girls. A lot of things used to happen like with my family and stuff, and I grew up with anger in me. Like with hate and stuff. So when this gang came along I didn't care.

Cindy: What makes a gang member is that you live in that environment and at some time, in some place, you're going to get into it because you're going to be with a homegirl or a friend who gets into a fight so you're going to have to back her up.

Reselda: Other gang girls are going to hit you up and ask where you're from. So in order to say Pacoima or something you're going to have to have some kind of clique and girls together to back you up instead of walking yourself. That way you have back up.

I went in the gang because of my friends, you know, they told me if I was a Chicana why didn't I dress like one and why didn't I back up the barrio. I started dressing when I was in the seventh grade. My older sisters were in. They used to back up the barrio all the way.

Benita: All it really is that you want to be a Chola because you see the other girls that want to be a Chola and it looks as if they have fun and everything. You want to put the make-up on like them too.

Who are these girls and what are their backgrounds that would propel them toward membership in a culture that demands total compliance, forces them outside of the forms of the dominant culture and creates a lifestyle that usually culminates in jail, on drugs, or dead? While the reasons given for joining a gang often center around belongingness needs and identification, for many the violent nature of their lives may provide another answer. They have seen their brothers shot, their sisters raped, or been raped themselves.

Vicki: I got raped by a gang called Canoga Ala—Alabama Street, and it was bad. See right here? [Points to scar on chin.] They hit me in the face and I was just all full of blood. I was bloody, my shirt was ripped, they took off my bra, my underwear. They took me to a doctor right away. I was scared in there.

Nona: I've gotten raped twice. I've gotten doped up. I lost my legs. I wasn't able to walk or to talk for three weeks.

I got raped by my homeboy's father. He doped me up one time. I was babysitting for him and his wife. They went to a show. When they came back he asked me if I wanted some hot chocolate before I came home, and I said "Yeah." I drank it. It tasted just like ordinary chocolate. It didn't taste like he put anything in it. He asked if I wanted a ride home and I said no, I could walk. I lived on one side of the projects and he lived on the other side. I took the long way around to stop by my friend's house. As I was walking, I was feeling kind of dizzy. I started staggering. So when I went to my friend's house, my mind—I was fucked up. My friend's mother asked, "What's wrong, Nona?" She was watching me as she seen me walking home, and she seen him pull me into the car. After that I don't remember anything. All I remember is him taking me to Hansen Dame and he was beating my ass and putting downers down me. I was trying to spit them out but as I was spitting them out they were going down. I don't remember what happened: My mother and my sister and my brothers found me in an abandoned house. I was crawling out. I couldn't walk, I couldn't talk for a long time.

After that I turned into a big pill taker. Then I was on heroin.

I got almost raped another time. I got beat up really really bad. I got knocked out. After that I was in the hospital for a week.

Many of these girls reported abusive relationships in their homes, abusive fathers who beat their mothers when they come home "all boozed up."

Benita: I've been mostly on my own since I've been twelve. I wasn't really too much of a member of my family. I don't know what goes on in my family. We don't talk to each other. Before I was twelve I lived with my grandparents. My parents left. They did their own thing. My dad got married to someone else, my mom got married to someone else.

Maryann: I haven't live with my mom all my life. I've been from home to home. To my grandma's house, back to my mom's. From my mom's back to my grandma's. When I was little my mom was not married because she was a widow. My father died two months before I was born. I had to make it for myself. My mom would bring home boyfriends and they used to beat on me. I've still got marks all over me. Here [showed mark on arm] and burns here [scar on upper leg].

Reselda: I used to hate my dad because of what he did to my mom. I grew up with this hatred and anger because I couldn't hit my dad and take care of my mom.

A lot of them do come from families that are messed up. A lot of girls, like they ain't got back up in their families. If they get into a gang they got more back up. They've got more girls to really hang around with. More girls to hustle with, to pull this and pull that, and maybe get money. They come from low families, a lot of them. Or families that are messed up. They ain't got too much love in the family. So they don't care what's going on. If their family don't care, she don't care. Nothing's going right in her house so what should she care about what's going on out there.

For most core gang members, bonds to both family and school are weak. Generally they have low aspirations and are isolated from dominant institutions. None of the females in this study completed high school. The gang provides a source of status, identity, cohesion, esteem needs and sense of belonging. It is the most prevalent peer group association in the barrio, the one most readily available, and provides a strong substitute for weak family and lack of conventional school ties.

Gang Identification

Gang members report that they identify with the gang, assimilate the sentiments and conform to the values. Interaction among members shapes the attitudes and behaviors of the girls as they come to accept the organizational and normative schemes. Their behavior reflects their role relations and their adherence to the set of norms standardized among them. The gang enhances its power over members to control behavior through socialization and sanctions. As a primary reference group, the gang elicits stronger loyalty than friends or family:

Reselda: Another thing the gang causes is family situations between parents and the kids. Cause we'd go out with the homeboys and the homegirls and we'd get in fights and come back beat up or high or something. They worry. Parents worry. We even had shootouts at our house. It almost got my dad killed. We used to have to fight with gangs on the street, and then they can go shoot at your house, or shoot at your mom or dad. They don't care.

Once a girl becomes a member of the gang and this membership is part of her self-definition, she will work to maintain that membership. Girls will support each other in any fight or conflict, and will prove their loyalty regard-

156

less of risk. Supporting the "hood" and identification as a gang member are two norms of great consequence, with strong sanctions applied if a girl is shown to be disloyal.

> *Sonya:* If someone asks me "Where are you from?" I'm not going to say "Nowhere." That's why you get shot. Because if you're in it you're not going to say "Nowhere" cause if you do they'll find out and they'll know you ranked out and you're going to get your ass jumped. That's how it is. So you have to say "Delano."

Homeboys and Homegirls

While the girls purport to be independent of their male counterparts, they clearly allowed male dominance in many instances.

> *Sonya* They don't let us go [when the gang is retaliating against a rival gang and they expect to kill someone]. They have to be careful, cause as soon as they start shooting the police are going around looking. They have to hide their guns and everything. Especially when they go to Corona, they don't like us to go.

The homeboys themselves exhibited an attitude of territoriality toward the girls.

> *Nona:* They guys from the Flats, they'd be disappointed when they'd see homegirls with guys from other hoods. That would cause another gangbang.

Gang Activities

Members interact frequently, both formally and informally. Informally they "hang around" together, everywhere, and constantly, always in groups. More formally, the clique meets to hold policy discussions and planning sessions. When asked what was talked about at the meetings, Reselda said:

> It wasn't always bad things. Sometimes good things like maybe a dance. Like we have our territory. We have the park and we have like a gym and we can use it for a dance hall. We also talk about like if something came down like the weekend before like say we had a gang fight and this homegirl didn't back up her shit or backed away then we decide what we're going to do like kick them out. Like if they don't take care of business then we don't want them around, We'll talk about say like somebody got stabbed and so we'll make plans how to get them back. You know, make plans how we're going to return the battle. You know, revenge. Just

revenge. We just talk about revenge, revenge, revenge. Just for a street name.

Without exception, the girls interviewed had engaged in heavy drug use. Meetings and gatherings are places where drugs are shared, and often the money-raising activities, both legal and illegal, are to raise money to purchase drugs. In some interviews, the girls seemed more willing to discuss their drug use than their gang activities, as if somehow the drugs were the reality:

> *Lydia:* Most of them, they'd get so high that when something comes down, they don't know what they're doing. Like I seen one of my homeboys. He got killed, stabbed. He was so loaded he couldn't even move.

> *Nona:* In the park everybody used to just kick back, get loaded, keep each other warm. It was our place.

> *Vicky:* Most of us were high because when you're high you feel more brave and you can do more. I noticed most gang members who have gotten killed are always loaded.

Violence

The norms of the gang demand violence and violent acts. Being "bad," "crazy," or "wild" earn respect and status. The leader of the clique is usually the fiercest fighter.

> *Maryann:* It's not that you like to fight. You have to fight. But I like fighting.

As violence escalates, use of weapons increases.

> *Cindy:* We had to hurt others to take care of ourselves. Mostly I carried a switchblade in my sock. The only time I used to use it is when I used to get ganged up on.

> *Reselda:* Most of us in our gangs always carry weapons. Guns, knives, bats, crowbars, any kind. One of my homeboys had a machine gun. Whatever we can get hold of that we know can hurt then we'll have it.

Four distinguishable motives for engaging in gang violence—honor, local turf-defense, control and gain—operate within the gang subculture. Machismo, even for girls, is involved in the value system that promotes the ready resort to violence upon the appearance of relatively weak provoking stimuli.

Nona: I shouldn't have stabbed the mother of a homeboy, but she shouldn't have hit me. I was at a party, and when my homeboy fell, I looked at him and said, "You motherfucker." And she said "Don't call my son a fucker." She looked very young. She shouldn't have been in the house. Crazy old lady. But I regret it. I swear I regret that. I stabbed three people that night, and my sweater—I had a brand new sweater and it got all full of blood. I gave it away. When I got out of jail that time my mother had a big box full of all the knives I used to collect. I threw all of them away.

This subculture of violence crosses generations—the parents of many of the girls in this study are or had been gang members. Core gang members share a commitment to the use of physical aggression as a major mode of personal interaction and a device for solving problems. The girls described here will fight instead of flee, assault instead of articulate, and kill rather than control their aggression.

The following story related by one of the girls illustrates the manner in which gang gatherings escalate into violent acts. The story typifies gang gatherings, the use of the park as a gathering place, the nature and importance of identity with the "hood," the use of gang rituals, and demonstrates the patois of the gang subculture:

Anna had been committed to a drug placement center for drug abuse at the time of this incident. At the placement center she met a girl who had been a member of a rival gang in Venice, about twenty miles from Pacoima, and the two girls decided they would leave the placement center without permission in order to attend a dance:

Anna: This girl, she awol'd with me. I called my sister up. I didn't know they were going to jump her at all. I didn't have no idea. About two years before that, about four of the homegirls, they went to Venice and they got jumped with their homegirls by all Venice. They got jumped and they didn't do nothing. They got jumped and they found their way out, so they all wanted to get Venice.

So I called my sister and I told her to wait because I remember they were going to a dance that day, so I called her to wait for us. She asked me who was coming down.

Why you're in a gang, you don't want nobody to have your name. My sister asked, "Who's with you?" and I said, "Blanca from Venice." Blanca from Pacoima, our homegirl, was there.

I guess when I hung up they said, "All right, Venice is coming!" The three other girls that had got jumped in Venice, they were there that night. They were at my house. So you know how their minds thought. When we went down to their barrio, we got jumped. Plus she's carrying the name of the barrio that we had business with.

So we went to the dance and all of a sudden everybody changed their mind. "Let's go to the park." Everybody was always game to go to the park. They didn't mind how late it was, or when it was.

So my sister got real loaded that day. We went to the park and there was a lot of people. There was over 50 guys and there was about like 30 girls. Just packed. Guys from Van Nuys, another barrio, were there. And all the Flats [Pacoima] were there.

All of a sudden my sister, man, she was rowdy. She used to have a mouth. She used to start anywhere at any time. When she got drunk she used to go off. Not meaning to, but she used to. All of a sudden she just got up and hit that girl up where she was from. And that girl said, "Hey, I just want to come to party with you people. I don't want no hassle." And my sister just pushed her.

So one of the guys asked one of the girls, "Hey, where's she from?"

And the guy goes louder, "She's from Venice! Jump her! Jump her!"

And that's when all the girls just went for her. Not all of them but the four main girls and my sister. My sister had cracked a bottle and cracked her head open. She had her arm halfway sliced off. Just beat up. Totally beat up. They kicked her in the ribs a few times. She was all dazed down. Her face was all bruised up.

Everybody at placement knew she left with me. It would have been my fault. And I would get a girl from the hair and pull her back. By the time I had one girl pulled back, this girl would be on her all over again. There was nobody on my side. Everybody was going for her.

So finally, I don't know how she got away. And I told her, "Run, Run."

She goes, "Come with me."

And I told her, "No. I can't." Cause if I would have, they would have thought I'm a ranker for taking care of her and splitting.

Somehow she got away. When I went back the story was that I had set her up. But I told her, "I didn't set you up. If I had set you up, I would have took you in the heart of the projects. You would have gone through a maze." Cause when you're in the projects, you got to know your way around to get out of there.

I didn't set her up. But that's how the story goes. She was really hurt. When I went back, that was eight days later, her eyes were all bruised up still. Her face was all bruised up. She had stitches on her arm. She had stitches on her head.

After that I turned myself in. I went to juvie for awhile.

Symbols

The gang members interpret the behavior of other gang members through specific dress, language and symbols such as tattoos and places (both names given to gang members, and signs written as graffiti on walls and buildings, claiming territory), which are required to maintain membership and which have specific meaning and value for gang members. The gang uniform, including specific tattoos and sometimes makeup, referred to as "gangstered down" is a clear announcement of gang membership.

> *Reselda:* The reason I put my hood on me [she had the name of her gang, Pacas Flats, tattooed on her fingers and toes] was because I wanted them to know where I was from. When you're in your hood, you love your hood. So you love it enough to put it on you. That's why what I got on me is my neighborhood. I started to put my name on my back when I was dusted. Anita put my teardrop on [teardrop was on left cheek and signifies a boyfriend in jail] with India ink by hand. She did my teardrop and my Pacoima on my arm. And I did this [Pacas] one time when I was all wired up on whites.

All members have placas or nicknames, which they write on the walls. Assigned gang names, placas, in many instances are an appropriate and accurate description of the person—Lonely, Stranger, Clyclona, Gata, Smokey, Dusty, Loca, Sad Girl. In other instances they signify prized attributes such as toughness, wildness, and craziness—Joker, Bad Girl, Mala, Cyclona. Writing your gang placa in a rival territory is an invitation to a gangbang.

Leaving the Gang

Girls who are fringe members of the gang are not as firmly enmeshed in the gang milieu as core members. For them, leaving the gang can be as uncomplicated as simply not participating in gang activities:

> *Evelyn:* I just backed away from it. That's it. I hung around with all of them and I did everything that they did. When I wanted to get out, you can't tell them, "Oh, I want to get out." They'll jump you. You just start backing away from them. You still talk to them when you see them, but don't hang around with them or nothing. That's what I did. If you're cool with them, they'll be cool with you all the way. But if you're not, forget it. Don't even mention you want to get out. Just move.

For others, leaving the gang is not as simple:

Sonya: There's this girl, Gina. She was jumped in and everyday she was having fights with her parents. So she told us she wanted to be jumped out. So one day she was just coming from school. We were there waiting for her. And when she came, we just told her, "So you still want to get out." And she said, "Yeah," and we told her, "O.K., we're going to jump you out right now." She just said "All right." We jumped her out. We wouldn't let her walk out—I didn't like her, either. See I let two other girls out cause they were like my best friends. See there's other homegirls and they won't back you up or nothing. If you need a backup, they won't do it. They're just different than others.

Often by the age of seventeen and eighteen, interests and activities of individual members are directed outward toward the larger community rather than toward the gang, and girls begin to leave the active gang milieu. Some become pregnant, some get married, some go straight, some are institutionalized, others graduate to heroin use where "getting a fix" overrides all other interests and considerations.

Reselda: A lot of the girls, they got pregnant and they're with their old mans. Mostly all of them. All of the girls that were in the Flats. They all got old mans, or pregnant or OD's or shot.

Detention Centers

Most of the girls in this study reported having been in a detention facility of one kind or another, drug rehab centers, jail, juvenile camps. In no instance were these centers seen as deterrents, and in many instances they were seen as safer, more secure environments:

Benita: I was fifteen and a half when I was in Ventura Youth Authority. After that I was in Pride House [a drug rehabilitation center]. Altogether it was a year and nine months. I liked it at Pride House. When it was time for me to come home, I wasn't sure I was ready. I was afraid. I had Dogs. They hadn't found out, but when I was busted done a robbery at Danny's they found out. But I had OD'd, that's why they decided to put me away.

Reselda: I was busted most of my life. When I was sixteen I had did one GTA [grand theft auto] and a burglary. I was supposed to be there for about two years until I turned 18, but then I AWOL'ed again and GTA'd again. So they got me and I AWOL'ed again and I took about four other girls with me and I got busted again. And I almost got shot that day too from the cops. They chased me for a mile. We were in the car and we were getting all loaded. . . . They came that next day and put me in a camp.

Jail ain't nothing for me. I've been raised in it most of my life, so I can kind of hack what's going on in there. . . . You know what helped me slow down a little bit is when I was in camp. I used to have my own little room in there. I used to sit in there. I used to get lock-up—for fighting, and one time they caught me getting high in there. So when I was in lock-up I used to think a lot. So I know I have good feelings in here somewhere. Sometimes I wanted to go back in there. It's easy in there.

Conclusion

This study focused on the group as an important factor in the motivations of human behavior, and illustrated how the core gang member's behavior is determined by social structures and group culture by defining the perspective and attitudes of the girl gang. It showed how the peer group exerts a powerful influence on the gang girl by developing norms and values of interaction and affective support, and described the sanctions applied when a group member departs from those norms. The girls report that their motivation is a desire for a common destiny, a sense of belonging and identity, and a need for group support and cohesiveness. They identify with the gang, assimilate its sentiments, and conform to its values. Their behavior reflects their roles within the subculture, and the group controls the behavior of the girls by socialization and sanctions. The group elicits stronger loyalty as a reference group than does the family or any other institution. For these girls, violence is conforming behavior shaped by the normative standards of the subculture with which the Chola identifies.

10

Gang Involvement and Delinquency among Hispanic and African-American Adolescent Males

G. David Curry and Irving A. Spergel

With the perceived spread and growing seriousness of the youth or street gang problem in the United States in recent years (Huff 1990; Miller 1990; Spergel 1990), there is now increasing policy and program interest at local and national levels in issues of prevention as well as intervention and suppression of gangs. Ecological approaches have identified the social and economic characteristics of community areas in which the residents experience a greater likelihood of gang involvement or delinquency (Shaw and McKay, 1972; Bursik and Webb, 1982; Reiss and Tonry, 1986; Curry and Spergel, 1988). Fagan (1989, 1990) has demonstrated that gang-identified youths exhibit higher levels of delinquency and drug involvement than other youths. A key question for prevention or early intervention is who is at risk to become a gang member and participate in antisocial acts. Here we attempt to extend the individual-level research by (a) obtaining measures of the degree to which "at risk" preadolescents or younger minority (Hispanic and African-American) adolescents, who reside in gang crime areas, are involved in gang activity; (b) using regression analysis to compare structural models of gang involvement and delinquency for Hispanic and African-American youths; and (c) using structural equation modeling to examine the relationship between gang involvement and delinquency.

Delinquency and Gang Involvement

The terms youth gang or street gang are highly value laden and are sometimes used indiscriminately (Horowitz,1990; Spergel, 1990; Decker and Kempf,

Reprinted by permission of Sage Publications, Inc. from *Journal of Research in Crime & Delinquency*, Vol. 29, No. 3 (August 1992): 273–291.

1991; Spergel and Chance, 1991).Theorists, researchers, and practitioners have not used the terms consistently. The definition of what is a gang, who is a gang member, and what is a gang incident varies within jurisdictions, across cities, and over time. For many, youth gangs and delinquency have become synonymous. This has not always been the case. Although delinquent and criminal gangs were certainly included, the 1,313 gangs studied by Frederick Thrasher (1927) were not universally involved in criminal behavior. Thrasher's gang grew out of the childhood play group, lived in the interstitial niches of the social world, and thrived on conflict. Doc and William F. Whyte's (1943) other Corner Boys were more involved in bowling, a drama club, and even local politics than in illegal activity. Spergel (1964) describes gangs as one among several varieties of street groups and delinquent subcultures and notes that youth gangs can vary in social structure and function across neighborhood settings. For Suttles (1968), gangs are part of the social order of impoverished neighborhoods. The change in research perspective comes in the 1950s. For Cohen (1955) and Miller (1958), gangs are explicitly delinquent groups. Specifically defining contemporary gangs as groups with a delinquent focus has been attributed by Hagedorn (1988) to Klein (1971) and Miller (1975).

Previously we (Curry and Spergel, 1988) have distinguished gangs from delinquent groups. Group delinquency is "law-violating behavior committed by juveniles in relatively small peer groups that tend to be ephemeral, that is, loosely organized with shifting leadership. The delinquent group is engaged in various forms of minor or serious crime'' (p. 382). Gang delinquency or crime is

> law-violating behavior committed both by juveniles and adults in groups that are relatively enduring and completely organized, usually with leadership and membership structure. The youth gang member engages in a range of illegal acts that are significantly more violent and intimidating than those of the delinquent non-gang member. The gang member acts more often within a framework of mutual peer support or commonality, conflict relations with other gangs, and sometimes a tradition of turf, colors, signs, and symbols. It is important to observe that subgroups, associated groups, and different kinds of members of the gang may be deferentially committed to various delinquent activities such as drug trafficking, drug use, gang fighting, burglary, or non-delinquent activities such as hanging around and partying. The attributes of social group, delinquent group, and youth gang are not exclusive of each other but represent distinctive constellations of activity. It is important that while we can expect to find some overlap of gang involvement and delinquent behavior, we do not expect the two phenomena to be perfectly correlated. (Curry and Spergel, 1988, p, 382)

Here we extend our analysis of the problematic nature of the relationship between gang involvement and delinquency to individual-level data.

Ethnic/Racial Differences, Delinquency, and Gang Involvement

A major research objective is to determine whether the gang socialization process, or at least precursors to it, are different for African-American youth and for Hispanic youth in the same locality. Many researchers have observed dissimilarities in patterns of gang involvement across ethnic groups. Spergel (1964) found differently structured youth gangs or delinquent groups in three ethnic communities that he studied. In particular, he noted differences in patterns of Puerto Rican, Italian, and mixed European ethnic gang involvement. In his picture of slum society as an ordered segmentation, Suttles (1968) also describes distinctions in behavior across the socially parallel worlds inhabited by Italian, Mexican, Puerto Rican, and African-American youth gangs. Although her primary concern is female gang involvement, Campbell (1984) draws on differences in family organization between African-Americans and Puerto Ricans to explain differences in patterns of gang involvement across the two ethnic groups. Curry and Spergel (1988) delineate differential patterns of gang crime and delinquency across communities that can be to some extent attributed to the differential distribution of ethnic and racial populations as well as economic and social factor. Hagedorn (1988) and Moore (1988) outline a number of ways that the predominantly African-American gangs studied by Hagedorn in Milwaukee differ from the Hispanic gangs studied by Moore (1985; Moore, with Garcia, Garcia, Cerda, and Valencia, 1978) in Los Angeles. In a collection by various authors (Huff 1990) using participant observation methods to study African-American, Hispanic, Chinese, and Vietnamese gangs, an array of ethnically distinct patterns of gang formation, organization, and crime are reported.

The data examined here encompass socialization information on Hispanic and African-American youths growing up on the near west side of Chicago in the late 1980s. Underclass theory (Wilson, 1987; Hagedorn, 1988) and adolescent subculture theory (Vigil, 1988) offer promise in explaining differences, respectively, in African-American and Hispanic gang socialization processes.

While Wilson's (1987) conceptualization of the contemporary underclass involves both Hispanics and African-Americans, he emphasizes significant differences between poor inner-city Hispanic and African-American populations by comparing their levels of poverty, family structure, and experience of crime. African-Americans appear to be closer to the bottom of the socioeconomic or class ladder. Institutional racism and the more pervasive alienated status of African-Americans, especially males in American society, more than poverty per se could possibly explain the more encompassing gang influence circumstances of African-American gang youth (Oliver, 1989).

For Chicago, a tradition of participation in youth gang activity that is limited to early adolescence could explain a shorter, more intense period of gang commitment among low-income Hispanic youth in comparison to African-American youth in near-by communities (Curry and Spergel, 1988). This is in sharp contrast to the multigenerational gang participation of Chicanos in the different sociohistorical setting observed by Moore (1978) in Los Angeles. Vigil (1988) emphasizes the concept of multiple marginality in the explanation of Mexican-American youth gang formation in the southwest over time. The youth gang serves for a period of time as surrogate for family, school, employer, and police (Vigil, 1988).

In summary, the literature strongly suggests that the orientation, activities, and structure of lower income Hispanic and African-American communities and gangs are different. These differences should be reflected in the preconditions for and processes by which youths become involved in gangs. These early socialization differences should also be precursors of the distinctive character of the gang subcultures into which some of these youths will mature. Modeling these early differences is one of our purposes here, using information on individual youths, their family and school contexts, and their community as they experience it in a comparatively poor, population-dense, inner-city neighborhood.

Data

The Socialization to Gangs data set was constructed in 1987 by surveying all attending male students in the sixth through eighth grades at four middle schools from a low-income neighborhood in the near northwest area of Chicago. The selection of schools was made by Chicago Public Schools administration as middle schools with serious gang problems. The communities that surround the schools are marked by disproportionate numbers of gang homicides in Chicago's police records (Block, 1991). The schools are in a contiguous neighborhood, each within nine city blocks of one of the others. The greatest distance between any two schools is a little over one mile. Three of the schools are integrated Hispanic and African-American, and the fourth has a totally African-American student body. Survey data were supplemented with information from police records and school disciplinary and other records.

Available research, police data, and community concern are in agreement that males constitute the primary gang problem (Spergel, 1990; Campbell, 1984). Because of limited resources, we are unable to consider here issues of the development of a gang involvement scale for females. We assume there would be distinctions, different factors, or at least differently weighted factors, contributing to socialization of females to gangs.

The school records that we use do not distinguish between Puerto Rican and Mexican students in our study, but we know from school and census records that the breakdown between Puerto Rican and Mexican students for the community is approximately fifty-fifty. Hispanic students were given the option of answering the survey in Spanish or English. Although research distinguishing between Puerto Rican and Mexican adolescents and gangs might be worth pursuing, our inability to distinguish between the two groups in Chicago has also been experienced by other researchers (Block, forthcoming) and remains a weakness in our data.

The conduct of a survey of school children is always subject to the requirements of parental consent and attendance. Akers, Krohn, Lanza-Kaduce, and Radosevich (1979) describe a similar sampling process. Although they obtained a greater percentage of response based on school record estimates of the population, they did not seek a sample of strictly inner-city minority youths in a school jurisdiction with a 50 percent high school dropout rate. Of the cohort population of 975 males between eleven and fifteen years of age, 439, or 45 percent, completed our survey instruments. Approximately fifty parents did not give written consent for their children to participate in the study. The majority of nonparticipation, however, can be attributed to nonattendance at school. Statistical comparisons of students surveyed with the entire population of students as represented in school and police records show those not surveyed to have significantly lower achievement scores in math and reading and significantly higher rates of absence from school and arrest. Even at the early age targeted by our study, there was already a subpopulation of male minority students who did not regularly attend school and who had significantly greater levels of officially recorded delinquent behavior. There are no significant differences between the two groups in average age or grade in school. Thus it appears that the male adolescents participating in our study represent that portion of their cohort relatively in conformity with potential achievement of middle-class conventional success as measured by school attendance, no record of arrest, and higher levels of academic achievement.

The survey data set[1] consists of 139 Hispanic students and 300 African-American students. In order to understand the process by which adolescents become involved in youth gangs, we obtained self-report data on a variety of factors including student aspirations and values, family composition, perceptions of the gang problem, participation in gang and nongang antisocial events, as well as contacts and relationships with a variety of peer and adult significant others.

Measuring Gang Involvement

Selection of Gang Involvement Items

We selected items from the self-report survey questionnaire that might reveal a set of attitudes, perceptions, associations, symbolic behaviors and activities that could most directly indicate gang involvement or readiness to be further involved in gang activity. For example, two items were intended to measure attitude or disposition toward gangs. "In general, are there any advantages to someone being in a gang? (Circle one item only.)" The choices are "yes, many," "yes, some," "maybe a few," and "no, none at all." We treat any of the first three answers as seeing something attractive about gang membership. A second item asked, "How many times in the last two months have you worn gang colors at school?" Wearing gang colors, usually combinations of black and bright solid colors, is often forbidden in Chicago Public Schools. We regard the practice when committed with intentionality as a positive identification with youth gangs.

Further, three items were designed to measure differential association. The first read, "Among the places around here, what are the places where you and your friends hang out most of the time?" As a supplement to that question, the following item asked, "What kind of people mainly hang around there? (Check all that apply.)" One of the choices under that item was "gang members." We assumed that having gang members as friends entails a different kind of social involvement than hanging out in the same places that gang members do. A second differential association item asked, "Which words do adults use to describe your friends? (Check all that apply.)" One option was "gang members." A third associational item was constructed from a series of items eliciting self-reports of deviant acts in the last two months committed in the company of gang members.

Finally, three items specifically involved gang-related conflict and violence. The first of these items asked "How many times in the last two months have you flashed gang signs at school?" In the Chicago youth culture flashing gang signs can be regarded as a serious challenge that can lead to physical conflict, submission, or flight. The other two measures of gang involvement concern student respondent participation in incidents of gang-related conflict. One question, where the respondent was viewed as a possible gang victim, read, "in the neighborhood in the last two months, did anyone attack or threaten to attack you or hurt you? (List where.)" The item also probed, "What was the reason for this attack or threat? (Check all that apply.)" One of the choices was "gang related." In the last item, the respondent was asked to view himself as the aggressor or offender. This item read, "In and around school, in the last two months, did you threaten or hurt someone in any of the following places? (Check all that apply.)" A subsequent item probed, "What was the reason for this attack or threat? (Check all that apply.)" "Gang related" was one of the choices.

The empirical issue of how youth in the data set used here define a gang is at least partially addressed. Each youth was asked to list the gangs that he knew to be operating in his school or neighborhood. The groups listed were predominantly segments of high profile gangs known to the police. Clear and consistent definitions of gang and gang incident have been established by the Chicago Police Department and the Chicago Public Schools.

Following Hagan (1989) and Babbie (1990), transformation of an index into a scale should follow a few preliminary steps. An examination of the tetrachoric correlation coefficients for each pair of measures showed all items to be positively (but not perfectly) related. Another consideration is the "power" of the matrix of correlation coefficients. When certain items in a set of measures are redundant or too heavily related to each other, this is reflected in the eigenstructure of the matrix. When this occurs, one can expect to find what is sometimes called a "scree" or point at which the eigenvalues of the matrix markedly approach zero. Such a scree indicates that the matrix is composed of items that are linear combinations of one another. Both matrices of tetrachoric correlations produce sets of eight eigenvalues that do not approach zero. This suggests that each of our eight items for both of our populations measures a unique aspect of the social process of gang involvement. (Examining the eigenstructure of a matrix should not be confused with factor analysis. In fact, our finding here indicates that our sets of variables are unsuitable for factor analysis.)

A Rasch Model of Gang Involvement

The Rasch model was developed for research on test design (Rasch, 1960; Wright and Stone, 1979; Wright and Masters, 1982). An example of the nature and purpose of the model might be a test to measure an individual's knowledge of elementary mathematics. A "good" test would measure differences among individuals taking the mathematics test. Some items should be "easy"—that is, correctly answered by a large number of individuals. Some items should be "difficult"—that is, correctly answered by only a few individuals. An aberrant or ill-fitting individual would be one who gets an odd combination of easy and difficult items correct or incorrect. Although we are attempting to measure gang involvement rather than mathematics knowledge, patterns of responses to items should still conform to a scaling "logic," measuring what we are trying to measure. The computer program MSCALE (Wright, Congdon, and Rossner, 1988) was used to fit the Rasch model to our eight items for each population of youths.

MSCALE isolates and identifies items and respondents as well as "good" fitting items and respondents. Our scale does seem to be a "good" measure for seven of our items and for 138 of our Hispanic respondents. One Hispanic student's responses to the eight items, however, does not fit the mathematical logic of a measure of gang involvement. That student answered only two of our gang items affirmatively. In the last sixty days, he reported being attacked in a gang-related incident and being the attacker in a gang-related incident, but he also responded to all six other items negatively. The computer program rejected this individual's behavior as not conforming to the answer patterns to our items by the other respondents. However interesting a case study of this student might be, a reasonable measure of his gang involvement, based on the logic of the

Rasch model, is negated. This student was the only Hispanic respondent who reported being attacked in a gang-related incident. Consequently, one of our potential items for measuring gang involvement among Hispanic youth, being attacked in a gang incident, had to be dropped from the analysis.

Whereas the rejection of one Hispanic respondent cost us an item, another item answered by a relatively large proportion of African-American respondents (34.7%) also does not withstand application of the Rasch model analysis. A nonfitting item can occur when a number of individuals who appear to be highly involved on the other items appear to be not involved on the basis of an item or when a number of individuals who appear to be not involved on the other items appear to be involved on the item. A t test is used to test whether each item is statistically "in line" with other items in the set (Wright and Stone, 1979). The particular item that asked students about the existence of an advantage in gang membership is identified in this way as not fitting the Rasch model. This may have been the result of a number of students' not understanding the English version of the questionnaire, a condition unfortunately not caught during extensive pretesting of the instrument.

The Rasch model analysis produces a calibrated ordering of the strength of each of our gang involvement measures for the two subpopulations. A Rasch model is similar to a Guttman scale (1950) in that it involves a joint ordering of persons and items and is concerned with the development of a unidimensional scale of items that is independent of so-called person parameters. Rasch modeling is not subject to the restriction of a completely determined structure of response that limits the application of Guttman scales (Andrich, 1985, 1988). The percentage of each subpopulation for which the item response

Table 10.1 Frequency of Gang Involvement Scale Elements by Ethnicity

	Hispanic			African American		
	n	Percentage	Calibration	n	Percentage	Calibration
Wear gang colors	43	30.9	−1.52	82	27.3	−0.67
Advantage in gang membership	37	26.6	−1.24	104	34.7	Dropped
Hang out with gang members	38	27.3	−1.29	112	37.3	−1.27
Deviancy with gang members	22	15.8	−0.43	66	22.0	−0.32
Gang member friends	22	15.8	−0.43	46	15.3	−0.02
Flash gang signs	11	7.9	0.45	54	18.0	0.21
Attacked in gang incident	1	0.7	Dropped	20	6.7	1.24
Attacker in gang incident	4	2.9	1.54	11	3.7	1.94
Item separable reliability		0.93			0.97	

is affirmative and the Rasch calibration are shown in table 10.1. These calibrations are standardized and can be conceptually considered a continuum measuring level of gang involvement. Items at the negative extreme of the continuum, such as wearing gang colors and hanging out with gang members, can be thought of as indicating a lower level of gang involvement. Items at the positive extreme, such as being an attacker in a gang incident, indicate a greater level of gang involvement. Based on the assumptions of Rasch modeling, it is possible to consider the ordering of the items as an important analytic result. Here, we clearly see a different ordering of gang involvement behavior for each of the two subpopulations. Still, no two items are more than two ordinal positions removed across ethnic groups when dropped items are taken into account.

Wright and Masters (1982) recommend separate measures of reliability, one for items and one for persons. The item-separable and person-separable coefficient of reliability are also shown in table 10.1. Based on these results, we conclude that it is legitimate to treat these scales as additive measures of gang involvement for these populations of youths.

Modeling Gang Involvement and Delinquency

Measuring Delinquency

Just as we developed a measure for gang involvement, we use official and self-reported measures for delinquency to generate a single interval-level measure of delinquency. We enter the values one or zero for each of the six variables: arrested once, arrested twice or more, any school discipline report, any self-reported violence, any self-reported property offense, and any self-reported substance abuse. The frequencies and the Rasch modeling calibrations of each item by ethnicity are shown in table 10.2. African-American youths

Table 10.2 Delinquency Scale Items by Ethnicity

| | *Hispanic* | | | *African American* | | |
	n	Percentage	Calibration	n	Percentage	Calibration
Self-reported violence	53	38.1	−2.28	142	47.3	−1.94
Self-reported substance abuse	32	23.0	−0.94	62	20.7	0.00
Self-reported property crime	27	19.4	−0.60	69	23.0	−0.19
School discipline	13	9.4	0.58	67	23.0	−0.14
Single arrest	9	6.5	1.10	49	16.3	0.39
Multiple arrest	4	2.9	2.14	17	5.7	1.90
Item separable reliability		0.95			0.93	

are significantly more likely to have a single arrest and significantly more likely to have a school discipline record. The computerized modeling process reveals that all of the six variables can be regarded as fitting a Rasch model and can therefore be summed to form a delinquency scale. The different ordering of the items for the two subpopulations is indicative of different patterns of delinquency. In comparative ranking, substance abuse is more common among Hispanic youths than is property crime or school discipline problems. As measured here, delinquency is significantly higher among our population of early adolescent African-American males than our population of early adolescent Hispanic males.

Models of Gang Involvement and Delinquency by Ethnicity

We have used the approach of multiple regression analysis to derive sets of exogenous variables for modeling gang involvement and delinquency for each of our ethnic subpopulations. The coefficients[2] shown in tables 10.3 and 10.4 were produced by two-stage least-squares analysis involving our measures of gang involvement and delinquency as endogenous variables. The chi-square goodness-of-fit measures and multiple R-squared values show both models to be acceptable.

Most important for our concern here are the differences in the two sets of self-reported measures for delinquency to generate a single interval-level exogenous variable for the two ethnic groups. The only common exogenous variable for the two models is an associational one, the reported presence of drug distributors who hang out in the same places as youths as a significant estimator of gang involvement. In the model for Hispanics, the remaining estimators include a developmental variable age, an attitudinal measure of educational frustration, and two measures of self-esteem, one peer-based and

Table 10.3   Two-Stage Least-Squares Regression Model for Gang Involvement and Delinquency for Hispanics

Dependent Variable	Independent Variable	b	Beta
Gang involvement	Educational frustration	0.385	0.220*
	Peer self-esteem	1.045	0.348**
	School self-esteem	−1.357	−0.442**
	Drug distributors hang out	1.179	0.312**
Multiple R squared = 0.394			
Delinquency	Age	0.212	0.199*
	Gang involvement	0.550	0.653**
Multiple R squared = 0.448			
Chi-square goodness-of-fit statistic = 5.11		Probability = 0.403	

*Level of statistical significance = .01; **level of statistical significance = .001.

Table 10.4   Two-Stage Least-Squares Regression Model for Gang Involvement and Delinquency for African-Americans

Dependent Variable	Independent Variable	b	Beta
Gang involvement	Female gang members in class	0.153	0.199**
	Male gang members in class	0.120	0.180**
	Drug user friends	0.460	0.153**
	Family gang member	1.390	0.297**
	Drug distributors hang out	0.542	0.193**
Multiple R squared = 0.313			
Delinquency	Family gang member	0.430	0.171**
	Gang involvement	0.428	0.479**
Multiple R squared = 0.256			
Chi-square goodness-of-fit statistic = 5.18		Probability = 0.270	

*Level of statistical significance = .01; **level of statistical significance = .001.

the other school-based. The measure that we label "educational frustration" is the difference between a student's desire to attend college and his expectation of doing so. The greater the distance between aspiration and expectation, the greater the level of gang involvement. Weak attachment to school in conjunction with a strong attachment to peers as sources of self-esteem support theories of social control.

Associational variables dominate our model for gang involvement and delinquency among the African-American students. Hanging out where drug distributors hang out and having friends who use drugs are statistically significant estimators of gang involvement. The presence of gang members—both males and females—are also significant estimators. One of the most powerful exogenous variables in this model is the reported presence of a gang member in the youth's family. It is a significant estimator of both gang involvement and delinquency.

Modeling the Relationship Between Gang Involvement and Delinquency

Both of the models constructed above include gang involvement as an estimator of delinquency. Alternative models that can be tested by fitting two-stage least squares include models that estimate gang involvement from delinquency and models that employ the two variables as mutual estimators. Table 10.5 shows the chi-square goodness-of-fit estimates for each of these alternative models for each ethnic subpopulation. The goodness-of-fit statistic is a measure of the degree to which an estimated covariance matrix generated by the hypothetical model "fits" the observed covariance matrix for the data (Hayduk, 1987). The

Table 10.5   Chi-Square Goodness-of-Fit Statistics for Alternate Models of Gang Involvement and Delinquency

Models			Chi-Square	Probability	Decision
Hispanic					
Gang Involvement	→	Delinquency	5.11	0.403	Not reject
Delinquency	⇉	Gang involvement	21.17	0.001	Reject
Gang Involvement	←	Delinquency	39.78	0.000	Reject
African-American					
Gang Involvement	→	Delinquency	5.18	0.270	Not reject
Delinquency	⇉	Gang involvement	20.51	0.000	Reject
Gang Involvement	←	Delinquency	63.48	0.000	Reject

probability associated with the goodness-of-fit statistic allows the researcher to reject hypothetical models that produce estimated covariance matrices that differ from the observed covariance matrix to a degree that is greater than can be attributed to chance. In this case, all the models except the two that estimate delinquency from gang involvement for the two populations can be rejected at the 0.10 level of statistical significance.

An additional empirical finding should also be noted. Although the measures of gang involvement and delinquency are significantly correlated for both Hispanics and African Americans, the correlations are by no means perfect. These are proportions of both subpopulations who show an above-average level of gang involvement but no delinquency (14.4% for Hispanics; 14.0% for African Americans). Almost one-fifth (19.7%) of African-American respondents show a greater than average level of delinquency but no gang involvement. A much smaller proportion of Hispanic youths (5.8%) show similar results. This result illustrates one additional difference across the two groups in patterns of gang involvement and delinquency.

Conclusions

Using self-report and official data on a set of subpopulations of inner-city minority adolescents, we constructed scalar measures of gang involvement and delinquency. We assumed it was important to develop such measures for younger adolescents because gang commitment and more serious involvement in antisocial gang activity occurs in middle and late adolescence. Based on available data, it seemed appropriate to construct such a scale based on the responses of minority youth, particularly males in the poorest high-gang-crime areas we could find.

For gang involvement, two different seven-item scales were developed—one for Hispanics and one for African Americans. Both withstand tests of scalability. We believe that the construction of this set of measures demonstrates the possibility of measuring levels of gang involvement among adolescent males. This possibility increases the viability of pursuing meaningful prevention strategies, especially through first identifying youth at individual as well as social risk of further gang involvement.

Also of note is that patterns of youth gang involvement are different for Hispanic and African-American male adolescents. Although this outcome is in keeping with the research literature on ethnicity and gang involvement, our finding lays the groundwork for further theoretical refinement and research precision. Our attempt to develop an instrument to measure gang involvement, we believe, has succeeded in an exploratory fashion. In addition, it facilitates modeling the social and individual parameters of the youth gang socialization process. Finally, the differences in patterns of gang involvement between Hispanics and African Americans underscore the need for taking culture and social context into account in the development of differential antigang programs whatever the more general policy strategy and goals may be.

In order to construct models relating youth gang involvement and delinquency, we have used Rasch modeling to construct an interval-level measure of delinquency to complement the scales for gang involvement. The exogenous variables for our models are selected from variables associated with the major institutions of young adolescence—the family, the school, and the peer group. The sets of exogenous variables that are associated with delinquency and gang involvement vary considerably across the models for Hispanic and African-American youths. Gang involvement and delinquency among Hispanic youths is closely associated with intrapersonal variables (e.g., self-esteem and educational frustration). Gang involvement among African-American youths is more closely associated with social or interpersonal variables (e.g., exposure to gang members in the school and home). These differences underscore the need for theoretical attention to cultural factors in attempts to explain gang involvement and delinquency and in the development and evaluation of prevention programs.

An additional aspect of our derived models is the nature of the relationship between gang involvement and delinquency. More specifically, can gang involvement be modeled as an estimator of delinquency? Can delinquency be modeled as an estimator of gang involvement? Most authors concur that the connection between gang involvement and delinquency must to some degree be reciprocal over the duration of adolescence (Spergel, 1990). We do not have in the data being analyzed here the kind of longitudinal information necessary to test this hypothesis. We have used a statistical modeling technique (two-stage least squares) that makes it possible to test the efficacy of a reciprocal connection for these cross-sectional data on early adolescence. Our findings are that for these data, the only models that cannot be rejected at the 0.01 level of statistical significance are those that estimate delinquency from gang involvement. We consider this result evidence of the institutional or quasi-institutional role of the gang as an intervening variable between other social variables and delinquency. We do not, in fact, cannot, assume that gang involvement (especially as measured here) always chronologically precedes involvement in delinquency. The chronological sequence of gang involvement and delinquency is a process that we hope to investigate as longitudinal data become available.

An additional observation is that we do find youths who exhibit some level of involvement in gangs, yet no involvement in delinquency (about 14% of each subpopulation). We also observe youths who are involved in delinquent behavior for whom our data indicate no gang involvement. These nongang delinquents are, however, more common among African-American respondents (19.7%) than Hispanic respondents (5.8%). This finding supports the conclusion of earlier researchers (Spergel, 1964; Miller, 1966; Moore and Vigil, 1987) that gangs do not exist for the sole purpose of engaging in delinquency. This finding is in accord with our earlier finding (Curry and Spergel, 1988) on the absence of a perfect correlation between gang involvement and delinquency at the community level of analysis.

Policy Recommendations

Lundman (1984) pointedly notes, "And although it is true that additional research would be very useful, it is necessary at some point to use what is known as a foundation for recommending what might be done in the future" (p. 223). In that spirit, we offer the following suggestions on the basis of our findings.

Continue to treat gang delinquency as a social and not an individual problem. Our findings show that ecological factors are especially important in the etiology of gang delinquency. This is found to be especially true among our African-American respondents where gang involvement and delinquency are found to be associated with the presence of gang members in classroom and home. Gang and delinquent involvement appeared to be more pervasive social phenomena among African-American youth when compared to Hispanic youths. For Hispanic adolescents, social bonds to school are especially important in the face of the gang as an alternative source of status and self-esteem from peers. Programs that enhance the positive role of the school and family or household unit in the lives of adolescents are recommended. At the same time, however, gang prevention must retain some of its historical attachment to the "area" project concept (Shaw and McKay, 1972) and emphasis on social change at an ecological or community level. This is particularly important in African-American low-income communities that often are ghettos where more significant structural change is required.

Develop and test procedures for measuring gang involvement. Our gang involvement measure serves as a useful starting point. In fact, our scale can, with relative ease, be transformed from a self-report instrument into an informant scale. Parents, teachers, and other significant observers of the lives of adolescents can generate indicators of the level of risk experienced by specific adolescents. Only when it is measured and identified can gang involvement be prevented. Under conditions where destructive labeling, intended or unintended, does not occur, similar scales should be developed for locales where gang activity is decidedly different in scope from that of Chicago. For example, colors and symbols have not been reported as characteristics of group or organized delinquency among African-Americans in a number of cities especially on the East Coast. White and Asian gangs often do not make use of colors and symbols, although name identifiers are frequently used.

Distinguish between gang involvement and gang delinquency. Regardless of race/ethnic community, we have identified portions of the gang-involved community of adolescents who are not involved in delinquency. The existence of this group of youths has long been hypothesized by researchers on youth gangs. Their existence lends credence to the possibility of channeling selected gang youth or even certain gangs into constructive youthful participation for the good of the greater community.

Distinguish between nongang and gang delinquency. Although a relatively rare occurrence among Hispanics, nongang delinquency is much more common among our African-American respondents. Examination (Curry and Spergel, 1990) of the delinquency prevention literature reveals a model of delinquency prevention that does not take into account differences between nongang and gang delinquency that emerge from our empirical investigations. Attempting to use prevention techniques tailored for gang delinquency in an effort to quell nongang delinquency or vice versa may prove uninformed and unfruitful.

Differences in gang delinquency associated with ethnicity must be taken into account in the development of gang delinquency prevention programs. Most immediately, inroads into curbing gang delinquency in the African-American community must focus on who is visible or not visible in the community. The visibility of noncriminal elements, the availability of conventional or positive role models and legitimate opportunities (Cloward and Ohlin, 1960) in the community must be encouraged in an effort to override the currently pervasive visibility of illegitimately organized activity as epitomized by the overly evident activity of organized drug distribution and youth gang activity reported by the youths in our study. Among Hispanics, programs must focus more on building ties between youths and their schools. (This recommendation echoes the concerns of Moore, 1989.) The involvement and acculturation of immigrant parents may be particularly important. In Chicago, where this research has been conducted, the disillusionment of Hispanic students with the operation of schools and the failure of schools to meet the emotional, social, and educational needs of Hispanic students have gone hand-in-hand to produce an environment conducive to the growth of delinquent youth gangs as social alternatives to traditionally legitimized forms of social organizations.

Notes

1. More detailed description of the data-gathering process and comparisons of survey respondents with all same-grade enrollees in the four schools are provided in Spergel and Curry (1987). A more recent and more comprehensive analysis of these data appears in Curry and Spergel (1990).

2. The two-stage least-squares models presented here were constructed using SIMPLIS, Version 1.3, for microcomputers by Jöreskog and Sörbom (1987).

References

Akers, R.L., M.D. Krohn, L. Lanza-Kaduce, and M. Radosevich. 1979. "Social Learning and Deviant Behavior: A Specific Test of a General Theory." *American Sociological Review* 44:636–55.

Andrich, D. 1985. "An Elaboration of Guttman Scaling with Rasch Models for Measurement." Pp. 33–80 in *Sociological Methodology*, edited by N. Brandon-Tuma. San Francisco: Jossey-Bass

_____. 1988. *Rasch Models for Measurement*. Newbury Park, CA: Sage.

Babbie, E. 1990. *Survey Research Methods*. Belmont, CA: Wadsworth.

Block, C.R. 1991. "Gang Homicide in Chicago: Patterns Over Time, Area of Chicago, and Type of Victim." Paper presented at the Annual Meetings of the Midwest Criminal Justice Association. Chicago, October.

_____. Forthcoming. "Lethal Violence in the Chicago Latino Community." Chapter 17 in *The Dynamics of the Victim-Offender Interaction*, edited by A.V. Wilson. Cincinnati: Anderson.

Bursik, R.J., Jr. and J. Webb. 1982. "Community Change and Patterns of Delinquency." *American Journal of Sociology*, 88:24–42.

Campbell, A. 1984. *Girls in the Gang*. New York: Blackwell.

Cloward, R.A. and L.E. Ohlin. 1960. *Delinquency and Opportunity: A Theory of Delinquent Gangs*. New York: Free Press.

Cohen, A.K. 1955. *Delinquent Boys: The Culture of the Gang*. Glencoe, IL: Free Press.

Curry, G.D. and I.A. Spergel. 1988. "Gang Homicide and Delinquency." *Criminology* 26:381–405.

Curry, G.D. and I.A. Spergel with R.W. Thomas and W.Q. Pan. 1990. *Preventing Involvement in Youth Gang Crime*. Research Paper/Technical Report. School of Social Service Administration, University of Chicago/Office of Juvenile Justice and Delinquency Prevention. (Also available from the Department of Sociology and Anthropology West Virginia University)

Decker, S. and K. Kempf. 1991. *Constructing Gangs: The Social Definition of Youth Activities*. St. Louis: Department of Criminology and Criminal Justice and Center for Metropolitan Studies, University of Missouri, St. Louis.

Fagan, J. 1989. "The Social Organization of Drug Use and Drug Dealing among Urban Gangs." *Criminology* 27:633–67.

_____. 1990. "Social Processes of Delinquency and Drug Use Among Urban Gangs." Pp. 183–219 in *Gangs in America*, edited by C.R. Huff. Newbury Park, CA: Sage.

Guttman, L. 1950. "The Basis for Scalagram Analysis." Pp. 60–90 in *Measurement and Prediction*, edited by S.A. Stouffer. New York: Wiley.

Hagan, F.E. 1989. *Research Methods in Criminal Justice and Criminology* 2nd ed. New York: Macmillan.

Hagedorn, J.M. 1988. *People and Folks*. Chicago: Lakeview.

Hayduk, L.A. 1987. *Structural Equation Modeling with LISREL: Essentials and Advances*. Baltimore: Johns Hopkins University Press.

Horowitz, R. 1990. "Sociological Perspectives on Gangs: Conflicting Definitions and Concepts." Pp. 37–54 in *Gangs in America*, edited by C.R. Huff, Newbury Park, CA: Sage.

Huff, C.R. 1990. *Gangs in America*. Newbury Park, CA: Sage.

Jöreskog, K.G. and D. Sörbom. 1987. *SIMPLIS*. Version 1.3. Monroeville, IN: Scientific Software.

Klein, M.W. 1971. *Street Gangs and Street Workers*. Englewood Cliffs, NJ: Prentice-Hall.

Lundman, R.J. 1984. *Prevention and Control of Juvenile Delinquency*. New York: Oxford University Press.

Miller, W.B. 1958. "Lower Class Culture as a Generating Milieu of Gang Delinquency." *Journal of Social Issues* 14:5–19.

_____. 1966. "Violent Crimes by City Gangs." *Annals of the American Academy of Political and Social Science* 364:96–112.

_____. 1975. *Violence by Youth Gangs and Youth Groups as a Crime Problem in Major American Cities*. Washington, DC: U.S. Department of Justice.

_____. 1990. "Why the United States Has Failed to Solve Its Youth Gang Problem." Pp. 263–87 in *Gangs in America*, edited by C.R. Huff, Newbury, CA: Sage.

Moore, J.W. 1985. "Residence and Territoriality in Chicano Gangs." *Social Problems* 31:182–94.

_____. 1988. "Gangs and the Underclass: A Comparative Approach." Introduction, pp. 3–17 in *People and Folks* by John Hagedorn. Chicago: Lakeview.

_____. 1989 "Is There a Hispanic Underclass?" *Social Science Quarterly* 70:265–84.

Moore, J.W. with R. Garcia, C. Garcia, L. Cerda, and F. Valencia. 1978. *Homeboys*. Philadelphia: Temple University Press.

Moore, J.W. and J.D. Vigil. 1987. "Chicano Gangs: Group Norms and Individual Factors Related to Adult Criminality." *Aztlán* 18:27–44.

Oliver, W. 1989. "Sexual Conquest and Patterns of Black-on-Black Violence: A Structural-Cultural Perspective." *Violence and Victims* 4:257–73.

Rasch, G. 1960. *Probabilistic Models for Some Intelligence and Attainment Tests*. Copenhagen: Danmarks Paedogogiske Institut (Chicago: University of Chicago Press, 1980).

Reiss, A.J., Jr and M. Tonry, eds. 1986. *Crime and Justice: A Review of Research.* Vol. 8, *Communities and Crime.* Chicago: University of Chicago Press.

Shaw, C.R. and H.D. McKay. 1972. *Juvenile Delinquency in Urban Areas.* Chicago: University of Chicago Press.

Spergel, I.A. 1964. *Racketville, Slumtown, Haulburg.* Chicago: University of Chicago Press.

_____. 1990. "Youth Gangs: Continuity and Change." Pp. 267–371 in *Crime and Justice: A Review of Research*, Vol. 12, edited by M. Tonry and N. Morris. Chicago: University of Chicago Press.

Spergel, I.A. and R.L. Chance. 1991. "National Youth Gang Suppression and Intervention Program." *National Institute of Justice Review* 224:21–24.

Spergel, I.A. and G.D. Curry. 1987. "Socialization to Gang: School-Community Gang Prevention and Control Study." Research Report, School of Social Service Administration, University of Chicago.

Suttles, G. 1968. *The Social Order of the Slum.* Chicago: University of Chicago Press.

Thrasher, F.M. 1927. *The Gang.* Chicago: University of Chicago Press.

Vigil, J.D. 1988. *Barrio Gangs: Street Life and Identity in Southern California.* Austin: University of Texas Press.

Whyte, W.F. 1943. *Street Corner Society.* Chicago: University of Chicago Press.

Wilson, W.J. 1987. *The Truly Disadvantaged.* Chicago: University of Chicago Press.

Wright, B.D., R.T. Congdon, and M. Rossner. 1988. *MSCALE: A Rasch Program for Rating Scale Analysis.* Chicago: Department of Education.

Wright, B.D. and G.N. Masters. 1982. *Rating Scale Analysis: Rasch Measurement.* Chicago: MESA Press.

Wright, B.D. and M.H. Stone. 1979. *Best Test Design.* Chicago: MESA Press.

11

Los Cholos: Legal Processing of Chicano Gang Members

Marjorie S. Zatz

A central theme in sociological research on crime and deviance is that social control involves a *process* of social definition. This theme is especially prominent in work within the labeling and conflict paradigms. The labeling approach places especially heavy emphasis on process, stressing "the ways in which deviance is 'created' through processes of social definition and rule-making, through processes of interaction with individuals and organizations, including agents and agencies of social control" (Schur, 1971:3). More emphatically, it views deviance "not as a static entity but rather as a continuously shaped and reshaped *outcome* of dynamic processes of social interaction" (Schur, 1971:8).

The process of social definition is particularly clear in the juvenile court. Its substantive justice orientation reinforces the socially-contingent nature of case processing, with the deviant label potentially altering interpretations of other status characteristics and, thereby, affecting legal decision-making. A key to this socially-contingent processing, and to the creation of deviance more generally, is what Hawkins and Tiedeman (1975:182–85) call "processing stereotypes." These stereotypes are categorical systems used to order and make sense of a wide variety of behaviors so as to efficiently, smoothly, and unambiguously process persons through bureaucratic organizations.

One such processing stereotype evident in juvenile court decision-making is gang membership. A number of studies have examined the legal reactions to gangs and gang members. Generally these studies have found that class-based differences in visibility, demeanor, and dress result in inferences about the "moral character" of youths—inferences which contribute to variation in official responses (Chambliss, 1973: Morash, 1983; Pearson, 1983; Werthman and Piliavin, 1967). However, within a given minority group popu-

Reprinted with permission from *Social Problems*, Vol. 33, No. 1 (October 1985): 13–30.

lation—such as young Chicano males—differences based on visibility, demeanor, and dress may be less noticeable. It then becomes an empirical question whether the label "gang member" is an important contingency in the legal processing of juveniles, or whether belonging to a gang has little effect on decision-making involving youths who are already disadvantaged and disvalued due to ethnicity and social class biases.

An adequate understanding of how gang membership or other factors affect the movement of juveniles through the legal system requires a dual focus on court processing time and on the outcome of that process. That is, the rate at which a case moves through the system to a given disposition must be considered along with the severity of that disposition. Prior research on adult courts shows that lengthy processing can itself serve as punishment (Feeley, 1979) and that the timing of court decisions differs for members of diverse social groups (Hagan and Zatz, 1985; Zatz, 1985). However, this processual focus on the timing of legal decision-making has not carried over to studies of juvenile court.

The research presented here uses event-history methods to examine how court-processing time and outcomes differ for Chicano gang members and nongang Chicano youths,[1] in addition to assessing the effects of direct bias or discrimination against gang members, this study considers how the gang label might operate as a "master status" or contingency that alters the interpretation and influence of other personal, offense, or case characteristics. For instance, evidence of an offender's success in school might weigh more (or less) heavily in the legal processing of gang members than of nongang youths. Therefore, this research seeks to answer the following questions:

1. Does alleged gang membership have an independent effect on the rate at which cases move through the system to various dispositions, controlling for other factors?
2. Does gang membership alter the effects of characteristics of the offender, the offense, and the case on rates of movement to these case dispositions?

In the next section, I focus on the perceptions of Chicano gang members held by social control agents and outline the significance of this deviant identity for juvenile court processing time and outcomes. Then, I describe the samples, variables, and analytic technique. After presenting results of the analyses of gang membership on rates of transition through the juvenile court system, I discuss these findings and their implications for research on gangs and on court processing.

Official Responses to Gang Membership

While most research on official responses to gang-related crime in the last decade has been drawn from deterrence theory (e.g., Dahmann, 1981; Maxson and Klein, 1983), labeling and conflict theories suggest a different approach. From this set of perspectives, official responses to gang members stem from and reflect injustice and oppression of lower-class and minority group members (e.g., Chambliss, 1973; Horowitz, 1983; Moore et al., 1978). In reference to such structural factors, Moore et al. (1978:179) observed that "Barrio gangs are known and harassed by the police."

Police and Court Staff Perceptions of Chicano Gang Members

Police in the Phoenix area, the setting of this study, have very negative perceptions of Chicano gang members. This is evidenced by a newspaper interview
with the Chief of Police for the City of Phoenix (*Arizona Republic*, 1980:
A6):

> There is no question about who's involved in the growing problem of
> youth gangs: Mexican-American teenagers. . . . Make no mistake. Youth
> gangs are not just bands of young people who take off their coats and
> have little scraps over a girl on a side street. They are armed. Vicious.
> Drunken. They rob and burglarize. They cruise the streets spoiling for
> blood. They kill. If the gangs grow, and their contempt for law deepens,
> they will rule the streets.

Regardless of the validity of this stereotypic image, it forms the basis for
official responses to Chicano youth. Attributions of gang membership by social
control agents depend in part on the youth's family, neighborhood, and dress.[2]
Indeed, the Latin Gang Member Recognition Guide for the City of Phoenix
(Juvenile Gang Reduction Unit, 1981) states: "The Latin Gang Member will
usually dress in a manner that almost immediately will identify him as a
member of a gang and that a crime in which he is involved may be gang
related."

The police are not the only official actors to hold such perceptions.
Juvenile court social files include a plethora of statements like the following:

> [He] continues to involve himself with the Mexican-American youths.
> . . . in the neighborhood in which he lives.

> Given the awareness of the type of neighborhood where [the youth] lives,
> leaves me a bit surprised that [the youth] has not been involved in more
> serious crimes.

> The majority of the male members of [the youth's] family are involved
> in gang activity. . . . It is a part of the family that [he] is in to be involved
> with the [gang name] and to gain their acceptance from this involvement.

> [He] presents himself as a street dude, a "cholo."

The concept of a "cholo" is closely connected with the barrio and gangs, and is a socially-significant deviant identity in this research setting. The cholo, always male, presents himself as the protector of his family, resists Anglo authority, is viewed by social control agents as antisocial, and is a heavy alcohol and drug user. This "tough" image—along with tattoos and such gang-like attire as a white t-shirt, jeans or khaki pants, and a red bandanna tied around his head—indicates to the police and court staff that the youth is a gang member.

Gang Membership and Processing Time and Outcomes

Gang membership can potentially influence case processing in two ways. First, by simple virtue of their gang status, cholos may receive different dispositions or be processed more or less quickly than nongang boys who, on the face of it, had engaged in the "same" behavior. Here, the system would be openly discriminating against gang members. Since membership in a gang is not itself illegal, such discrimination would constitute a violation of the youth's constitutional rights.

Where such an effect, known in statistical terminology as a "main" effect, is not found, a second form of bias could still exist. Attribution of the gang label could alter the interpretations of other offense, offender, and case characteristics, resulting in differences in court processing for gang and non-gang youths. That is, the gang label (and the police perceptions and stereotypes consistent with this label) might operate as a "master status" or contingency that influences the workings of the legal process and rates of movement through it. Thus, even if the consequences of labeling are not manifested in direct discrimination, the gang label may change the meanings attached to schooling (and other background factors) and the perceived relevance of the complaint type and other case and offense characteristics. This type of "interaction" effect is quite common in research on legal decision-making (Dannefer and Schutt, 1982; Welch et al., 1984; Zatz, 1984a, 1985). One way of assessing such an effect is to include product terms for gang/nongang status in a full model. A related approach which is more useful here is to examine gang and nongang cases separately to see how the legal process differs for "cholos" and those who are not so labeled.

Some examples should clarify how the effects of other characteristics may be contingent on gang membership. First, the juvenile court social files show that gang members are often detained immediately following arrest as a direct consequence of having their names on the police Gang Squad's list. But, the social files alone do not tell us whether gang members are detained *longer* than nongang boys, whether differences due to gang membership only arise for certain types of offenses, or whether the effect of detention on later decisions or the speed of case processing operates differently for gang and nongang youths. For instance, gang boys arrested for minor offenses typically resulting in a warning or probation could be held in detention and then processed slowly. Thus, pretrial detention would serve as an additional punishment beyond any formal sanctions. Or, if their prior record or the seriousness of the charged offense warrant commitment to the Department of Corrections (DOC) or remand to adult court, their detention time could be reduced as they are quickly processed through the system. Studies of adult court processing suggest that pretrial detention increases the likelihood of conviction and of a harsh sentence (Feeley, 1979; Lizotte, 1978; Rankin, 1964). If this also is found in juvenile court, then one consequence of the label "gang member" would be harsher outcomes for gang youths than for their nongang counterparts.

The gang label may also alter the meaning attached to schooling. Prior research has shown the salience of school achievement to juvenile justice dispositions, particularly as school achievement reflects the substantive justice orientation of the court (Cohen and Kluegel, 1979a, 1979b; Horwitz and Wasserman, 1980; Thomas and Cage, 1977). However, remaining in school past the compulsory age or other signs of success in school could be interpreted differently for gang and nongang youths. For instance, completion of one grade and promotion to the next suggests adherence to the dominant value system's stress on education as a mechanism for assimilation and, for gang members, the possibility that the teacher's influence could realistically compete with that of the gang. As a result, gang members who succeed in school may be treated leniently. One source of leniency would be the case outcome if school attendance and promotion make it more likely for gang members to receive less severe dispositions than nongang members. Another source of leniency might lie in the speed of processing. Compared to nongang youths, gang members may be processed especially quickly in an attempt to minimize the disruption of the "school routine," particularly where school is seen as a mechanism through which the cholo can "straighten himself out." In contrast, boys who belong to gangs and perform poorly in school might be viewed as particularly troublesome and unamenable to reform. Then, speedy processing aimed at getting them off the streets may ensue. In this situation, swift processing is likely to be towards the most severe sanctions available—commitment to the custody of the Department of Corrections or remand to adult court.

Gang members also might be arrested for different types of offenses than other youths (Hindelang, 1976; Miller, 1982). On the one hand, they may be disproportionately arrested for violent crimes due to stereotypic perceptions of their behavior. Thus, police may react especially punitively to Chicano gang members as a response to community concern about violent crime. On the other hand, they may be arrested for minor offenses as a strategy of social control. For example, police might suspect that gang boys who are roaming the streets at night are likely to commit a burglary or get into a fight. They may arrest these boys for curfew violations or other minor offenses either as a means of deterring more serious crimes or out of simple harassment. Thus, the perceived relevance of the offense may be contingent on application of the deviant label, with arrest used as a scare tactic to get gang members off the streets while nongang boys are not watched as carefully.

If intake and probation officers share such "processing stereotypes," gang boys may be kept in detention for a long time, even when the formal sanction is only a warning or probation. Or, probation officers could recommend commitment to the DOC or remand to adult court. If the judge concurs with these perceptions, he or she could initiate a hearing to decide on remand, using an administrative hold to keep the boy in detention until the hearing. In this way, interagency processing stereotypes can result in organizational embellishment of deviant roles (Hawkins and Tiedeman, 1975). However, since conflict in sequential processing is most apt to occur at transfer points from one agency to another, it is also plausible that court officials will not share the perceptions of social control agents at earlier processing stages. If so, the rates of processing to the various outcomes should be very similar for both groups.

As these examples demonstrate, gang membership may alter interpretations of other characteristics of the offense, offender, and case. As a consequence, both the final outcome (e.g., probation, commitment to DOC) and the time that it takes to traverse the justice system from initial referral through to case disposition may differ for gang and nongang boys. Unless dynamic analyses that explicitly consider the role of time are conducted, such intricacies cannot be unraveled. The modeling technique used here provides the information needed to properly mirror court processing. These analyses inform us of the increase or decrease in the time it takes to traverse the system (from referral to *each* potential disposition) attributable to gang membership, thereby shedding light on the socially-contingent nature of legal processing.

Data and Methods

Samples

The two samples consist of 172 youths identified by social control agents as gang members and 85 youths not identified as gang members. Although the Phoenix police would not allow me access to their list of gang members, the Department of Corrections and three smaller police departments in the Phoenix metropolitan area provided me with their lists. Thus, the determination of who is and is not a gang member was made by social control agencies. Whether or not the boys identify themselves as gang members is a different question, beyond the scope of the present inquiry.

Since the vast majority of the names of gang members were obtained from the Department of Corrections (DOC), the comparison group was taken from juvenile court listings of boys who were committed to the DOC. More specifically, the comparison group consists of all Chicano boys under age eighteen committed to the DOC during the period January 1981 through May 1983 (the end of data collection) and who were not identified as gang members by the DOC or the police departments participating in the study.[3] Drawing the control group from DOC commitments served to make the two samples similar on the number of prior referrals, as the pattern in this court was to reserve commitment for the youth's fifth or later referral. This similarity was confirmed by a nonsignificant difference-of-means test. In addition, the two groups are quite close in age, with the gang boys averaging 14.18 and the nongang boys 14.50 years. Complete histories of the youths' earlier court processings were made available by the Juvenile Court. From these, information was collected and coded on *all* juvenile court referrals for boys in both samples from their earliest arrests (in 1972) through May, 1983.[4]

The data consist of longitudinal histories of processing events for all court referrals for the 172 gang and 85 nongang boys. Since any given youth could be arrested and processed several times, event-histories of the processings of each individual were created. These event-histories were constructed from the earliest through the most recent referrals for each boy, and included information on a variety of offense, offender, and case characteristics, the dates of entrance and exit from the system, and the disposition for each case. The total number of court processings resulting was 2,228. With listwise deletion of missing data on social and family history variables, this was reduced to 1,263 referrals for the 172 gang boys and 653 referrals for the 85 nongang boys. Following Zatz (1982, 1985) and Zatz and Hagan (1985), I would have preferred to analyze each arrest separately (i.e., all first arrests, then all second arrests, then all third arrests, and so forth). However, this approach was precluded by the small number of nongang youths in the sample relative to the number of variables and possible outcomes. As a result, all referrals were combined and a variable indicating the number of priors was included in the model. The unit of analysis was drawn from these referrals, rather than from the individuals. More specifically, it is the processing "event," or movement of a case through the system from initial referral to disposition.

Variables

The dependent variable was final case disposition. Categories included: (1) dismissal; (2) informal processing; (3) probation; (4) commitment to the Department of Corrections; and (5) remand to adult court. Informal (i.e. noncourt) processing refers to action that does not involve formal adjudication, including judicial warnings, unresolved complaints, and referrals to other

Table 11.1   Descriptive Statistics on All Variables

		Gang		Nongang		Signif.
Variable	Coding	Mean	s.d.	Mean	s.d.	t-value[a]
Social and Family History Characteristics						
Age in years at time of offense	4 – 18	14.18	2.72	14.50	2.69	**
Present or last grade in school	1 – 12; 13 = college	8.89	1.31	8.87	1.29	
Currently attending school	1 = Yes 0 = No	0.39	0.49	0.39	0.49	
Currently employed	1 = Yes 0 = No	0.05	0.22	0.13	0.34	***
Live with at least one parent	1 = Yes 0 = No	0.93	0.26	0.94	0.25	
Percent of siblings with juvenile court records	0 – 100%	10.04	22.22	17.47	30.50	***
Alias used	1 = Yes 0 = No	0.15	0.36	0.15	0.36	
Gang member	1 = Yes 0 = No	1.00	0.00	0.00	0.00	
Offense Characteristics						
Number of accomplices	0 – 11	0.42	0.99	0.38	0.85	
Weapon used	1 = Yes 0 = No	0.02	0.13	0.02	0.15	
Complaint charge seriousness	1 – 9; (1 = low; 9 = high)	5.10	2.82	5.29	2.81	
Court charge seriousness	0 – 9 (1 = low; 9 = high; 0 = no court charge)	2.25	3.34	2.38	3.35	
Type of offense charged						
Violent	1 = Yes 0 = No	0.10	0.30	0.09	0.28	
Grand theft	1 = Yes 0 = No	0.25	0.43	0.30	0.46	**
Obstruction of justice	1 = Yes 0 = No	0.07	0.26	0.08	0.27	
Fighting	1 = Yes 0 = No	0.05	0.22	0.04	0.18	
Narcotics	1 = Yes 0 = No	0.04	0.20	0.05	0.22	
Public peace	1 = Yes 0 = No	0.10	0.30	0.09	0.28	
Status	1 = Yes 0 = No	0.11	0.31	0.11	0.31	
Administrative hold	1 = Yes 0 = No	0.11	0.31	0.11	0.31	

(continued next page)

Table 11.1   continued

Variable	Coding	Gang Mean	s.d.	Nongang Mean	s.d.	Signif. t-value[a]
Case Characteristics						
Type of complaint:						
Immediate detention	1 = Yes	0.33	0.47	0.31	0.46	
	0 = No					
Immediate service (brought	1 = Yes	0.06	0.23	0.04	0.19	
to detention but released)	0 = No					
Citation	1 = Yes	0.01	0.12	0.02	0.15	
	0 = No					
Number of days in pretrial detention	0 – 284	5.96	16.62	6.22	16.21	
Number of counts on complaint	1 – 9; (greater than 9 coded as 9)	1.26	0.75	1.34	0.92	*
Number of counts on court charge	1 – 9; (greater than 9 coded as 9)	0.61	0.99	0.69	1.07	
Number of prior juvenile court referrals	0 – 32	5.57	4.75	5.49	4.96	
Number of days from complaint to case disposition	1 – 1289	91.66	101.10	89.87	92.56	

Notes:

a. t-tests refer to differences of means for the gang and nongang samples.

*Significant at $p \leq .05$.

**Significant at $p \leq .01$.

***Significant at $p \leq .001$.

agencies. The typical pattern of sanctioning in this court was informal judicial warnings for the first few referrals, then probation, and finally commitment to the DOC on the fifth or sixth referral. Remand to adult court was typically used for youths charged with property offenses who were nearing their eighteenth birthdays (Bortner, 1986).

The independent variables included information on the youth's *social and family history* (age, last grade completed in school, whether or not he is currently attending school, employed, lives with at least one parent, percentage of siblings with juvenile records, and whether or not he uses an alias[5]); the *offense* (number of accomplices, use of a weapon, seriousness of the arrest offense, and seriousness of the final offense); and the *case* (type of complaint, number of days in detention pending case disposition, number of complaint counts, number of court counts, and number of prior referrals.)

The four possible types of complaints included: (1) immediate detention following arrest; (2) immediate service, whereby the youth was brought to detention but released prior to serving any detention; (3) citation; and (4) "paper," meaning that the youth was never brought to detention. Paper complaints served as the reference category. A nine-point ordinal scale ranging from an administrative hold on the youth to a violent offense was used to tap offense seriousness. This scale was created by the juvenile court to reflect judges' perceptions of the severity of diverse offenses, and thus should accurately measure the views of judicial officers in this particular court. When a complaint involved more than one count, the most serious offense was used in the seriousness scales. Since the scale was based on the type of offense, offense type was not included as a separate variable in the first set of analyses. It was used in the later analyses, with petty theft serving as the reference category and the seriousness of the complaint omitted. Descriptive statistics and t-tests of differences between gang and nongang means are presented in table 11.1. Very few of the differences were statistically significant and, even among those that were, the differences do not indicate that gang members were always worse than nongang members.

Analyses

Continuous-time data and methods are needed whenever a case can move from one point in a system (e.g., entrance into the court at referral) to another (e.g., case disposition) at any moment in time. Cross-sectional data (which assume the system is at equilibrium) and panel data (with measurements taken at two or more points in time) are not appropriate when processing decisions can occur at any time rather than, for example, on the first day of each month. Similarly, analytic techniques such as ordinary least-squares regression that assume equilibrium or changes only at discrete times do not adequately mirror the dynamics of court processing.

This modeling technique and estimation procedure have several advantages: (1) full utilization of all of the available event-history data; (2) excellent properties including insensitivity to sampling and measurement error with moderate-sized samples (as shown in Monte Carlo simulations by Tuma and Hannan, 1978); and (3) tests of the effects of covariates on movement to several potentially interdependent outcomes. The particular model used here is a Gompertz model, which allows for an exponentially changing hazard rate. It allows movement from one stage of processing to a finite number of outcomes to occur at any point in time, incorporates the effects of time already in the system on the likelihood of quickly moving to the next stage, and controls for the effects of other variables in the equation. This is one of a class of models described in detail by Tuma et al. (1979) and has the form:

$$r_{jk}(t) = \exp(\beta_{jk}X + yZt),$$

where X is a vector of independent variables, β_{jk} is a vector of parameters associated with X, and yZ captures time-dependence.[6]

Restated in more familiar terms, this model, which I will call MODEL A, is:

$$\log r = a + b\,X + c\,GANG + d\,DURATION$$

where r is the rate, X is a vector of characteristics of the person, offense, and case, GANG is a variable coded 0-1 indicating gang membership, and DURATION is the length of time between the initial complaint and disposition of the case. The other symbols denote parameters to be estimated. This rate is computed for each of the possible case dispositions.

Maximum likelihood estimates of the rates of movement through the system from initial referral to the final case dispositions were obtained through the program RATE (Tuma and Pasta, 1979). The rate of transition from the origin state j (referral) to the outcome states k (dismissal, informal processing, probation, commitment, remand) is multiplicative and time-dependent. A log-linear functional form of relations between each transition rate and the exogenous variables was chosen because it has the advantage of constraining rates to be positive for each individual.[7]

The parameters of interest represent the effects of exogenous variables on unobserved rates of transition through the system from referral to each of the five possible destinations or categories of the dependent variable. These rates were modeled as functions of the social and family, offense, and case variables described above. Effects of exogenous factors on movement to *all* five outcomes were analyzed simultaneously. Thus, the parameters inform us of the effects of variables on the timing of court processing from referral to case outcome for *each* disposition, holding constant the other possible outcomes.

For reasons of clarity, antilogs of estimated parameters are reported rather than the parameters themselves. For exponential models such as these, antilogs are readily interpretable as *multipliers* of rates of change from referral to case disposition. Values greater than 1.0 reflect increases in these rates, and values less than 1.0 reflect decreases. For continuous variables, the parameters represent the fractional change in the rate due to an infinitesimal change in the variable. Strictly speaking, the antilog is then the effect of a marginal, rather than a unit, change in the exogenous variable. Since these are generally quite close, and unit changes are more readily understood by sociologists and criminologists familiar with regression analysis, antilogs for continuous variables are interpreted here as multipliers of the rate corresponding to unit changes in the variables. For dummy variables, the percentage change in the rate for one group relative to the control group is just $100\,(e^{\theta} - 1)$, where e^{θ} represents the antilog (see Tuma et al., 1979:835, Tuma and Hannan. 1984: 157–61). This allows us to interpret the antilogs for dummy variables in terms of the percentage increase or decrease in the likelihood of moving to each outcome in the next instant of time (measured here in days) due to the variable under consideration.

For example, looking ahead to table 11.2, age has significant effects on all of the transition rates, controlling for other factors. The antilog for cases that are dismissed is 1.15. Substituting 1.15 into the above formula for e^θ, this means that each additional year of age increases the likelihood of the case being dismissed the next day by $100(1.15 - 1)$, or 15 percent. Similarly, age increases the rate of movement through the system to non-court outcomes by a factor of 1.07. Translated into a percentage, this is $100(1.07 - 1)$, or a 7 percent increase. For cases resulting in probation, however, each additional year of age decreases the likelihood of quickly moving through the system to disposition, as is evidenced by the antilog of 0.89. Once again translating this into a percentage effect, this is $100(0.89 - 1)$, or an 11 percent decrease. Finally, age increases the rate of transition through the system to sanction of commitment and, especially, remand. For cases resulting in commitments to the DOC this increase is on the order of 50 percent $[100(1.50 - 1)]$, and for remands it is 607 percent $[100(7.07 - 1)]$.[8]

Summary

To restate the above, the dependent variable for these analyses was case disposition. It had five categories. The unit of analysis was the event, or movement of a case from one qualitative state (referral) to another (disposition). A given individual could have several events, each corresponding to a new case processing. The modeling technique allows for changes of state to occur at any time. This is particularly appropriate for processing models since processing, by definition, involves movement through time. The unit of time was days. Finally, the parameters of interest tell us about the effects of independent variables on the rate of movement to each category of the dependent variable.

Results

Looking first at the main effects of exogenous variables on rates of movement from referral to case disposition, table 11.2 shows that gang membership did not exhibit any significant effects. That is, when legal and extra legal factors were held constant, application of the label ''gang member'' did not have an independent influence on judicial decision making. This finding is not surprising, given that gang membership is not itself illegal and that less obvious interaction effects of extralegal variables are more typical in the recent sentencing literature.

Most other factors also operated as anticipated by prior research. Generally, characteristics of the offense and of the case had greater impacts on processing decisions than characteristics of the offender. Of the *offender* characteristics, schooling had the most intriguing effects. Youths who were in school tended to be quickly processed to commitment or dismissal. As the

Table 11.2   Estimated Effects of Variables on the Rates of Transition from Referral to Case Dispositions: Full Model[a]

Variables	Dismiss	Non-court	Probation	Commitment	Remand
Social and Family History Characteristics					
Age	1.15*	1.07***	0.89***	1.50***	7.07***
Grade in school	0.89	1.05	1.20***	0.82***	0.76
Attending school	1.45*	1.11	0.96	1.60***	0.11
Employed	0.87	0.80	1.19	0.76	0.18
Live with parents	0.80	1.06	1.08	1.14	1358.00
% Sibs with records	1.00	1.00	0.99	1.00	1.01
Alias	0.95	1.00	0.78	1.10	3.08
Gang member	0.81	1.02	0.83	0.87	1.35
Offense Characteristics					
# accomplices	1.12	0.94*	1.01	0.82*	0.85
Weapon	1.15	0.01	0.77	0.64	6.63*
Complaint seriousness	0.81***	0.90***	0.90***	1.00	1.01
Court seriousness	1.31***	0.71**	1.26***	1.25***	1.57**
Case Characteristics					
Type of complaint (Paper is reference category):					
Immediate detention	3.89***	3.63***	2.33***	1.43*	0.36
Immediate service	2.26**	1.13	1.14	1.17	0.00
Citation	0.00	1.42	0.00	0.00	0.00
# days detained	0.99*	0.99***	1.00	1.01**	1.01
# complaint counts	0.84	0.88*	0.93	0.96	1.48
# court counts	0.71*	0.13***	1.19*	1.30***	0.92
# priors	1.04*	0.99	0.94***	1.04**	1.14**
Duration	0.002*	−0.001***	0.004***	0.004***	0.007
(Constant)	0.00***	0.01***	0.00***	0.00***	0.00
Estimated rate	0.001	0.007	0.002	0.002	0.001
Maximum log of L (alternative hypothesis)	−1116	−6045	−1854	−2027	−131
Pseudo R^2	0.05	0.14	0.06	0.12	0.35
Chi-square[b]	116	2000	249	530	140
Chi-square[c]	115	1913	211	527	138
% of cases	7.57	61.27	13.80	16.34	1.00

Notes:

  a. Effects are expressed as antilogs of the estimated parameters for reasons of clarity. Tests of significance refer to the estimated parameters. A coefficient of 1.0 means that the variable has no effect on the rate.

  b. Test against the null hypothesis of a single time-independent rate for each transition, 20 degrees of freedom.

  c. Test against the null hypothesis of a Gompertz model (exponential hazard rate) with no covariates, 19 degrees of freedom.

    * Significant at $p \le .05$.

  ** Significant at $p \le .01$.

 *** Significant at $p \le .001$.

number of grades completed became larger, though, the rate of movement to probation increased (by a factor of 1.20 for each grade), while processing to commitments was reduced by a factor of 0.82. As was noted earlier, age also affected movement to these dispositions, with each increase in age reducing the rate of movement to probation and increasing the rates to dismissal, informal processing, commitment, and remand.

Of the *offense* variables, perhaps the most interesting finding is that use of a weapon resulted in a speedy remand to adult court. That is, when a weapon was used the likelihood of speedy processing to remand was increased by a factor of 6.63, or 563 percent. Also, each increase in the seriousness score of the arrest (complaint) offense decreased the rate of movement to the most lenient outcomes by factors of 0.81 to 0.90, and increasingly serious conviction (court) offenses slowed the rate of informal processing (by a factor of 0.71) and hastened movement to the other outcomes by factors of 1.25 to 1.57.

Several characteristics of the *case* are also interesting. In particular, the rate of commitment to the Department of Corrections increased with each additional day of pretrial detention, while the rates to dismissal and noncourt decisions were reduced. Also, immediate detention significantly increased the likelihood that a case would quickly move to all outcomes except remand. Increases were on the order of 43 to 289 percent. However, when the boy was brought to detention and then released right away (immediate service), the case tended to be quickly dismissed. Thus the type of complaint was closely related to whether or not the youth was detained. This was reflected in the correlation of 0.52 between the number of days in detention and a complaint calling for immediate detention. Although probation officers and parents, among others, can file a complaint, it is important to recognize that, with the exception of administrative holds, the type of complaint is primarily a police decision. Of the 613 referrals involving immediate detention, 15 percent were for violent offenses, 23 percent for grand theft, 15 percent for obstruction of justice, and 33 percent were administrative holds. Restated in terms of the offense, 49 percent of the violent offenses, 29 percent of the grand thefts, 62 percent of the obstructions of justice, and all of the administrative holds resulted in immediate detention.

Also, each additional count on the court charge increased the rate of processing to commitment and probation by factors of 1.30 and 1.19, respectively, and decreased the rate of movement to dismissal and informal processing by factors of 0.71 and 0.13. Finally, as was expected given both the extant literature and the practice of this court, a long string of prior arrests increased the rate of processing to commitment and remand, and decreased the rate to probation. The likelihood of a speedy dismissal also increased, perhaps due to the police mistakenly arresting boys known to them from previous arrests, even when evidence was clearly lacking.

Given these results, the second question to be explored in this study becomes particularly salient. Allegations of gang membership did not have independent (i.e., main) effects. Thus, direct discrimination is not occurring. However, it may still be the case that other factors influence decision-making differently, contingent on whether or not the youth has been labeled as a gang member. This second issue was investigated through separate analyses for gang and nongang youths.

Two sets of analyses were performed. First, the same model that generated the results shown in table 11.2 was reestimated, once for referrals of gang members and again for nongang referrals. That is, MODEL A was broken down into separate models for gang and nongang referrals, resulting in:

MODEL B_0: log r = a0 + b0 X + d0 DURATION (for nongang) and
MODEL B_1: log r = a1 + b1 X + d1 DURATION (for gang).

These models were estimated simultaneously for each type of case outcome. Results indicated differences in the factors influencing movement to each of the five outcomes for gang and nongang boys. Some of these differences only became visible when all five outcomes were considered. For instance, use of a weapon or an alias increased the transition rate to remand to adult court for gang members and to commitment to the DOC for nongang boys, thus keeping nongang boys within the protection of the juvenile system.

The most interesting differences involved the contingent effects of gang membership anticipated earlier. The length of detention operated similarly for gang and nongang boys. However, a complaint calling for immediate detention increased the likelihood of a speedy commitment to the DOC for gang youths, while this effect was not significant for their nongang counterparts. Also, each additional year of schooling increased the likelihood of quickly receiving probation for gang members, and reduced rates to commitment and remand. For nongang boys, grade in school had no effect. However, attending school (holding constant the grade) made speedy dismissals more likely for them.[9]

Second, the type of offense was included in the model and the dependent variable was collapsed into two categories: (1) outcomes that were less severe than placement outside the home (probation, dismissal, informal processing); and (2) more severe outcomes resulting in placement outside the home (commitment, remand). This simplification of the model from the original five categories arose from both substantive and methodological concerns. Substantively, the contrast between outcomes in which the boys stay at home and those in which they are removed from the home clarifies the options available to the court. Methodologically, with the addition of nine dummy variables for the specific offense types, the loss of degrees of freedom due to the relatively small number of nongang youths, and the large number of variables (26) prohibited simultaneous analysis of movement to all five outcomes when the sample was stratified by gang membership.

As before, the effects of all other variables in the model were held constant when estimating the effect of each variable on movement to these outcomes. The offense types were dummy coded, with petty theft serving as the reference category to which all other offenses were compared. Since the court's seriousness scale was based on the type of offense, the seriousness of the arrest offense was omitted to allow inclusion of the type of offense at arrest. As the arrest and court offenses could differ (typically due to dropping a count or reducing the charge in a manner analogous to plea bargaining in adult court), the seriousness of the court offense was still included in the model. Results are presented in table 11.3

Differences between groups became even clearer when the outcomes were dichotomized in this fashion. Once again, results showed that the effect of a complaint calling for immediate detention on movement to harsh outcomes was only significant for gang members. As table 11.3 shows, it increased this rate by 104 percent for gang boys and was not significant for the control group. Entering the system by a citation was not significant in the earlier analysis, yet when its effects were allowed to diverge for gang and nongang boys it increased the rate to lenient outcomes by 100 percent for gang members.

Grade in school again was only significant for gang youths, while attending school was only significant for boys who were not members of gangs. With promotion to each new grade, the rate of movement to more severe sanctions decreased (by a factor of 0.71) and promotion increased the rate of movement toward less severe sanctions (by a factor of 1.08) for gang boys. For nongang boys, attending school increased processing speed, whatever the outcome. Again, these effects were found controlling for all other variables in the model.

Of particular interest are the findings that arrests for violent, narcotics, and status offenses did not significantly affect outcomes for either group when the severity of the court charge, use of a weapon, and other factors were held constant. Moreover, only two types of offenses exhibited significant effects. Obstruction of justice increased the rate of processing to harsh outcomes for nongang boys (by 280 percent) and, along with administrative holds, to more lenient dispositions for both gang and nongang youths.

Considering other factors, the number of prior referrals was only significant for gang boys receiving harsh sanctions (with each prior increasing this rate by 6 percent), and the only effect of age for gang boys was to increase their rate of movement through the system to harsh outcomes by a factor of 1.70 per year. This effect was similar for nongang boys, but older nongang boys were also more likely to quickly receive less severe sanctions. Whether or not the youth lived with at least one parent (rather than some other relative or in a foster home) and the percentage of siblings with juvenile court records

Table 11.3 Estimated Effects of Variables on the Rates of Transition from Referral to Disposition for Less Severe (Dismissal, Non-court, Probation) and More Severe (Commitment, Remand) Outcomes for Full, Gang, and Nongang Models[a]

Variables	Less Severe			More Severe		
	Full	Gang	Nongang	Full	Gang	Nongang
Social and Family History Characteristics						
Age	1.03**	1.02	1.05***	1.58***	1.70***	1.68***
Grade in school	1.07**	1.08**	1.04	0.81***	0.71***	0.90***
Attending school	1.09	1.03	1.24*	1.53**	1.38	2.49***
Employed	0.90	0.89	0.84	0.69	0.81	0.72
Live with parents	1.08	1.20	0.79	1.30	1.31	0.98
% Sibs with records	1.00	1.00	1.00	1.00	1.00	1.00
Alias	1.03	0.97	1.29	1.10	1.00	1.72*
Offense Characteristics						
# accomplices	0.95	0.96	0.94	0.84*	0.94	0.70**
Weapon	0.85	0.92	0.71	0.83	0.82	0.63
Court seriousness	0.94***	0.94**	0.91**	1.27***	1.28***	1.25***
Type of offense (petty theft is reference category):						
Violent	0.91	0.87	0.93	1.00	0.76	1.46
Grand theft	0.93	0.89	1.05	1.27	0.87	1.99
Obstruction of justice	2.02***	1.99***	2.09***	2.35**	1.59	3.80*
Fighting	0.90	1.02	0.60	1.49	1.31	1.02
Narcotics	0.96	0.98	0.86	1.31	1.20	0.86
Public peace	1.10	1.00	1.38	1.52	1.42	1.80
Status	1.08	1.04	1.12	0.65	0.75	0.34
Administrative hold	8.36***	10.50***	5.31***	0.01	0.02	0.00
Case Characteristics						
Type of complaint (paper is reference category):						
Immediate detention	1.88***	1.76***	2.43***	1.54**	2.04***	0.96
Immediate service	1.03	0.97	1.33	1.12	1.55	0.38
Citation	1.89**	2.00**	1.72	0.02	0.03	0.00
# days detained	0.98***	0.98***	0.97***	1.01**	1.01*	1.01*
# complaint counts	0.93	0.92	0.91	0.98	1.00	0.99
# court counts	0.68***	0.67***	0.70**	1.25***	1.24**	1.34**
# priors	1.00	0.99	1.00	1.06***	1.06***	1.03
Duration	0.000	0.000	0.001	0.004***	0.004***	0.005***
(Constant)	0.00***	0.00***	0.01***	0.00***	0.00***	0.00***
Estimated rate	0.009	0.009	0.009	0.002	0.002	0.002
Maximum log of L (alternative hypothesis)	−8419	−5591	−2810	−2110	−1325	−767
Pseudo R^2	0.007	0.007	0.007	0.13	0.13	0.15
Chi-square[b]	1215	849	402	616	382	266
Chi-square[c]	1200	834	400	614	381	265
% of cases	82.62	83.60	80.70	17.38	16.40	19.30

Notes:
a. Effects are expressed as antilogs of the estimated parameters for reasons of clarity. Tests of significance refer to the estimated parameters. A coefficient of 1.0 means that the variable has no effect on the rate.
b. Test against the null hypothesis of a single time-independent rate for each transition, 27 degrees of freedom for the full model and 26 for the gang and nongang models.
c. Test against the null hypothesis of a Gompertz model (exponential hazard rate) with no covariates, 26 degrees of freedom for the full model and 25 for the gang and nongang models.
* Significant at $p \leq .05$.   ** Significant at $p \leq .01$.   *** Significant at $p \leq .001$.

did not affect the rate of processing for either group, in any analyses. Also, employment status did not have a significant effect, though in additional analyses it increased the rate to probation and decreased the rate to informal processing for nongang boys.

The final variable of interest was duration in the system. Its effects were generally positive and significant across both sets of analyses. Since unobserved heterogeneity always downwardly biases estimates of duration-dependence, this is not a plausible alternative interpretation (see McFarland, 1970). Rather, true duration-dependence exists, indicating that the longer the case was in the system, the greater the likelihood that it would swiftly reach disposition.[10]

Discussion and Conclusions

The research presented in this paper sought answers to two critical questions. The first was whether alleged gang membership has an independent effect on the rate of movement through the system to a variety of case dispositions. The answer is no. That is, there is no evidence of direct bias against gang members in the court system. The second question asked whether the effects of other factors on these rates are contingent upon gang membership. The answer to this question is yes. More specifically, characteristics of the offense, offender, and the case operate differently on court processing to various outcomes, depending upon whether or not the defendant was labeled as a gang member by social control agents.

In particular, complaints calling for immediate detention following arrest significantly increased the rate of movement to more severe outcomes for gang boys, but not for their nongang counterparts. Grade in school decreased the rate of movement to more severe dispositions and increased the rate to less severe dispositions for gang boys, but this was not significant for nongang boys. However, attending school was only significant for nongang boys, serving to increase the rate to all outcomes for them. Also, the rate of movement through the system to harsh sanctions was increased for gang boys with many prior referrals (and, in additional analyses not shown here, remand to adult court was swift for gang boys who used weapons or aliases). The detrimental effect of prior record found for gang members is intriguing, since gang and nongang boys did not differ significantly in their *number* of priors. Thus, this finding indicates that a lengthy prior record was interpreted differently for gang and nongang boys.

Based on media reports of police and community sentiment and prior research findings, I expected arrests for violent, narcotics, and status offenses to have different effects on court processing for gang and nongang boys. This was not found. Related research has discovered that gang and nongang boys were not arrested for different types of offenses (Zatz, 1984b). Put together, these two sets of results suggest either that Chicano boys in the Phoenix area are arrested for similar types of offenses (whether or not they are known to belong to gangs) or that the perception of gang members as heavily involved in the use of drugs and "cruis[ing] the streets spoiling for blood" is in error.

The research findings as presented in this paper are informative for labeling and conflict theories and for emerging theories of court processing. The deviants in this study (the "cholos") were identified as troublemakers largely on the basis of dress and the families and neighborhoods to which they belong. As a consequence of this labeling, their processing differed from that of similar nongang boys. Furthermore, earlier decisions (e.g., detention status) based largely on allegations of gang membership had ramifications for the youths later in the system. The most striking example is the finding that, while entry into the juvenile court system by a complaint calling for immediate detention increased the rate of movement to *less* severe outcomes for everyone, it also increased the rate to the more severe outcomes for gang members.

Prior research suggests that some of the deleterious effects of labeling youths as gang members are not unique to Chicanos. For example, Chambliss (1973) observed that class-based differences in visibility and demeanor were responsible for variation in police responses to boys in two white gangs. Similarly, Werthman and Piliavin's (1967) study of police interactions with black gangs found that the police infer "moral character" from the youths' appearances and neighborhoods. Morash (1983:329) concluded from her study of a white working-class community and a more heterogeneous community that "definition may lead to severe treatment of individuals because their gang-like peer group is mistaken to be a strong influence towards serious delinquency." Finally, Pearson's (1983) historical analysis of "hooliganism" in England shows that social control agents responded to lower-class youths largely on the basis of dress and demeanor.

While most of the effects of gang membership reported here reflect harsher treatment of gang boys, a few do not. In particular, gang members who went furthest in the educational system were treated more leniently. This suggests that the substantive justice orientation of the juvenile court results in favorable assessment of boys who "fell in with a bad group" but still retain a commitment to school achievement and the dominant value-system that it implies.

It must also be stressed that belonging to a gang did not in and of itself result in harsher treatment. The lack of independent effects of gang membership may indicate that Chicano youths are already so disadvantaged and disvalued due to ethnicity or social class biases that gang membership, by itself, makes little difference. Future research which considers gang and nongang boys who differ in racial/ethnic and social class group membership could address this issue. In addition, gang membership did not alter the effects of all of the factors considered. Indeed, while the police may be especially likely to arrest gang members and bring them to court on a complaint calling for immediate detention, judges did not process their cases differently from non-gang youths unless they appeared committed to behaviors that depart greatly from the dominant, Anglo value-system. This reinforces the importance of looking at how extralegal factors can alter the effects of other variables when the influence of membership in a social group—be it class, race/ethnicity, or a gang—is not manifested in obvious ways (Dannefer and Schutt, 1982; Welch et al., 1984; Zatz, 1984a). Where overt discrimination against a particular group is not expected, analysis of contingent effects reveals how particular factors are interpreted and responded to differently, depending on class or status characteristics.

These findings are also of central importance to the emerging body of work on court processing time. Research in this area has focused either on the organizational factors influencing the speed of case processing (e.g., Balbus, 1973; Eisenstein and Jacob, 1977; Neubauer, 1983) or on differences in the processes to which social and racial groups are subjected (e.g., Farnworth and Horan, 1980; LaFree, 1980). Yet, research which ties together processing time and processing outcomes to address differences between social groups is relatively new, and many questions remain unanswered. For example, Hagan and Zatz (1985) and Zatz (1985) have used continuous-time methods and event-history data to explore differences in processing based on race/ethnicity for adults. However, those data did not include measures of detention status, and results presented here indicate that detention results in an increased rate of transition through the system to severe outcomes for gang members.

Finally, the question of whether speedy or slow processing is preferred by social control agents and defendants needs further clarification. Thus far, research has told us little more than that for some outcomes, in some situations, speedy processing is desirable, while in other instances it is not. What the current state of research in this area does tell us, however, is that the dual elements of processing—time and outcomes—must be considered jointly if a realistic picture of court processing is to emerge.

Notes

1. All boys in this study were of Mexican ancestry. Youths of other Hispanic ancestry were not included, and results may not be generalizable to them.

2. The official criteria for determining membership in local Chicano gangs include: (1) self-admission; (2) tattoos; (3) dress; (4) informant information; (5) written communication (e.g., gang literature, bylaws); and (6) officer's identification based on knowledge of the gang.

3. A related study (Zatz, 1984b) compared the gang and nongang samples to assess differences in the type of charge for which they were referred to court, the seriousness of the charge, and the number of charges on the referral. Analyses were conducted using t-tests for differences between means, OLS regression, and structural

equation modeling. The only significant difference found was that gang members were more likely to be arrested for fighting than nongang boys.

4. If boys in the two groups were arrested or processed at different times a "history" effect could inadvertently be introduced, resulting in a biased sample. This was checked by comparing the percentage of referrals and dispositions for gang and nongang boys for each year from 1972 (the earliest referral for any boy) through May of 1983. The patterns of the two groups were quite similar. Although there was a very small but significant difference in mean values (of two months for referrals and six months for dispositions), this is of little or no practical consequence and can be attributed to the small standard errors and the large number of boys (and thus referrals) in the gang sample. To further investigate any differences between the samples, I compared the percentages of *boys* sent to the DOC and of *referrals* resulting in commitment to the DOC for each group. They were generally quite similar, suggesting that the two samples were drawn from the same population.

5. Anglicizations of Spanish names were not coded as aliases.

6. It is an extension of the simple Markov model involving relaxation of the discrete-time, population homogeneity, and time-stationarity assumptions. The discrete-time assumption means that individuals move from one state to another only at certain times. Relaxation of this assumption allows for changes of state (from referral to disposition) at any point in time, resulting in a model that better fits the reality of legal processing. The assumption of population homogeneity is relaxed to assume only that the same rates of change apply to every individual with the same values on variables. Multivariate analyses are thus enabled. Time-stationarity means that the parameters are constant over time. Since causal relations can change over time, rates may well be some specific function of time (Sorensen and Tuma, 1981; Tuma, 1976). For example, willingness to admit to an offense rather than go through the formal adjudication process (the juvenile court's equivalent to plea bargaining) may be patterned by the length of time the person has been in the system. Accordingly, duration-dependence is modeled.

7. The instantaneous rate of transition is defined as:

$$r_{jk}(t) = \lim_{\Delta t \downarrow 0} \frac{p_{jk}(t,\, t + \Delta t)}{\Delta t}, \, j \neq k$$

where Pjk(t, t + Δt) is the probability of a change from state j at time t to state k at time t + Δt. The instantaneous rate of transition $r_{jk}(t)$ is the limit, as Δt approaches zero, of the probability $P_{jk}(t,\, t + \Delta t)$, per unit of time.

8. The estimated parameter is reported for the duration variable, rather than its antilog. All tests of statistical significance were conducted on the RATE parameters themselves, rather than the antilogs. Significance levels are based on two-tailed distributions. RATE calculates F-ratios as the square of the estimated parameter divided by the square of its estimated standard error. These F-ratios tell us whether the parameters differ significantly from zero. In addition, two likelihood chi-square statistics were calculated for each model. The first tests the models against the null hypothesis of a single time-independent rate for each transition. The second tests the models against the null hypothesis of a Gompertz model (exponential hazard rate) without any covariates. Results of both tests are reported in tables 11.2 and 11.3. All chi-square values obtained are significant at the p = .001 level, indicating that the models analyzed improved

significantly upon the null hypotheses. Finally, nested models were compared by calculating the likelihood ratio λ. For large samples -2 in λ has a chi-square distribution with degrees of freedom equal to the number of independent variables. The calculation involves adding the maximum log of L for the nongang and gang models (models B_0 and B_1), subtracting the maximum log of L for the full model (Model A), and multiplying the result by two. The value obtained for the *less* severe outcome is 35.96, meaning that Model B improves significantly on Model A (the full model) at the p = .10 level. The value obtained for the *more* severe outcome is 35.32, which borders on statistical significance, suggesting that the hypotheses deserve future research.

9. Results from this analysis of five outcomes, eighteen variables, and two groups are quite cumbersome and are not presented here. Tables are available from the author upon request.

10. Additional analyses were also conducted with time-independent models. Equations were rerun with models in which the rate was a log-linear function of the independent variables but was not allowed to vary over time and in which the rate was allowed to depend on a random disturbance term (in addition to the observed variables). The χ^2's, pseudo R^2s, and overall estimated rates for all of the models were quite similar.

References

Arizona Republic. (1980). Teen-age gangs: will Phoenix surrender, or battle punks? June 18:A6.

Balbus, Isaac, D. (1973). *The Dialectics of Legal Repression: Black Rebels before the American Criminal Courts.* New York: Russell Sage.

Bortner, M.A. (1986). Traditional rhetoric, organizational realities: remand of juveniles to adult court. *Crime and Delinquency, 32*: Forthcoming.

Chambliss, William J. (1973). The saints and the roughnecks. *Society, 11*:24–31.

Cohen, Lawrence E., and James R. Kluegel. (1979a). The detention decision: a study of the impact of social characteristics and legal factors in two metropolitan juvenile courts. *Social Forces, 58*:146–61.

————. (1979b). Selecting delinquents for adjudication: An analysis of intake screening decisions in two metropolitan courts. *Journal of Research in Crime and Delinquency, 16*:143–63.

Dahmann, Judith. (1981). Operation hardcore: A prosecutorial response to violent gang criminality. Interim report. McLean, VA: MITRE Corp.

Dannefer, Dale, and Russell K. Schutt. (1982). Race and juvenile processing in court and police agencies. *American Journal of Sociology, 87*:1113–32.

Eisenstein, James, and Herbert Jacob. (1977). *Felony Justice: An Organizational Analysis of Criminal Courts.* Boston: Little, Brown.

Farnworth, Margaret, and Patrick M. Horan. (1980). Separate justice: Analysis of race differences in court processes. *Social Science Research, 9*:381–99.

Feeley, Malcolm M. (1979). *The Process Is the Punishment: Handling Cases in Lower Criminal Court.* New York: Russell Sage Foundation.

Hagan, John, and Marjorie S. Zatz. (1985). The social organization of criminal justice processing: an event history analysis. *Social Science Research, 14*:103–25.

Hawkins, Richard, and Gary Tiedeman. (1975). *The Creation of Deviance: Interpersonal and Organizational Determinants*. Columbus, OH: Merrill.

Hindelang, Michael J. (1976). With a little help from their friends: group participation in reported delinquent behavior. *The British Journal of Criminology,16*:109–25.

Horowitz, Ruth, (1983). *Honor and the American Dream: Culture and Identity in a Chicano Community*. New Brunswick, NJ: Rutgers University Press.

Horwitz, Allen, and Michael Wasserman. (1980). Formal rationality, substantive justice, and discrimination. *Law and Human Behavior, 4*:103–15.

Juvenile Gang Reduction Unit. (1981). *Latin Gang Member Recognition Guide for the Field Police Officer*. Phoenix, AZ: Community Services Division, Phoenix Police Department.

LaFree, Gary D. (1980). The effect of sexual stratification by race on official reactions to rape. *American Sociological Review, 45*:842–54.

Lizotte, Alan J. (1978). Extra-legal factors in Chicago's criminal courts: testing the conflict model of criminal justice. *Social Problems, 25*:564–80.

Maxson, Cheryl L., and Malcolm W. Klein. (1983). Agency versus agency: Disputes in the gang deterrence model. In James R. Kluegel (ed.), *Evaluating Contemporary Juvenile Justice*. Beverly Hills, CA: Sage.

McFarland, David D. (1970). Intragenerational social mobility as a Markov process: Including a time-stationary Markovian model that explains observed declines in mobility rates over time. *American Sociological Review, 35*:463–76.

Miller, Walter B. (1982). *Crime by Youth Gangs and Groups in the United States*. National Institute for Juvenile Justice and Delinquency Prevention. Washington, DC: U.S. Department of Justice.

Moore, Joan W., Robert Garcia, Carlos Garcia, Luis Cerda, and Frank Valencia. (1978). *Homeboys: Gangs, Drugs, and Prison in the Barrios of Los Angeles*. Philadelphia, PA: Temple University Press.

Morash, Merry. (1983). Gangs, groups, and delinquency. *The British Journal of Criminology, 23*:309–35.

Neubauer, David W. (1983). Improving the analysis and presentation of data on case processing time. *The Journal of Criminal Law and Criminology, 74*:1589–1607.

Pearson, Geoffrey. (1983). *Hooligan: A History of Respectable Fears*. London: Macmillan.

Rankin, Anne. (1964). The effects of pretrial detention. *New York University Law Review, 39*:641–55.

Schur, Edwin M. (1971). *Labeling Deviant Behavior: Its Sociological Implications*. New York: Harper and Row.

Sorenson, Aage B. and Nancy B. Tuma. (1981). Labor market structures and job mobility. *Research in Social Stratification and Mobility, 1*:67–94.

Thomas, Charles W. and Robin J. Cage. (1977). The effect of social characteristics on juvenile court dispositions. *The Sociological Quarterly, 18*:237–52.

Tuma, Nancy B. (1976). Rewards, resources, and rates of mobility: a nonstationary, multivariate, stochastic model. *American Sociological Review, 41*:338–60.

Tuma, Nancy B., and Michael T. Hannan. (1978). Approaches to the censoring problem in analysis of event histories. Pp. 209–40 in Karl Schuessler, (ed.), *Sociological Methodology*. San Francisco: Jossey-Bass.

_____. (1984). *Social Dynamics: Models and Methods*. Orlando, FL: Academic Press.

Tuma, Nancy B., and David Pasta. (1979). *Invoking RATE*. Stanford, CA: Stanford University.

Tuma, Nancy B., Michael T. Hannan, and Lyle T. Groeneveld. (1979). Dynamic analysis of event histories. *American Journal of Sociology, 84*:820–54.

Welch, Susan, John Gruhl, and Cassia Spohn. (1984). Sentencing: The influence of alternative measures of prior record. *Criminology, 22*:215–25.

Werthman, Carl, and Irving Piliavin. (1967). Gang members and the police. Pp. 56–98 in David Bordua (ed.), *The Police: Six Sociological Essays*. New York: Wiley.

Zatz, Marjorie S. (1982). Dynamic models of criminal justice processing. Pp. 91–114 in John Hagan (ed.), *Quantitative Criminology*. Beverly Hill, CA: Sage.

_____. (1984a). Race, ethnicity, and determinate sentencing: a new dimension to an old controversy. *Criminology, 22*:149–72.

_____. (1984b). Gang membership and crime: An analytic model. Paper presented at the Annual Meetings of the American Society of Criminology, Cincinnati, OH.

_____. (1985). Pleas, priors, and prison: racial/ethnic differences in sentencing. *Social Science Research, 14*:169–93.

Zatz, Marjorie S., and John Hagan. (1985). Crime, time, and punishment: an exploration on selection bias in sentencing research. *Journal of Quantitative Criminology, 1*:103–26.

12

Patterns of Chinese Gang Extortion

Ko-Lin Chin, Jeffrey Fagan, and Robert J. Kelly

Since immigration laws were relaxed and quotas were expanded in 1965, the number of Chinese in the United States has increased from 236,084 in 1960 to 1.6 million in 1990 (Barringer, 1991). Like other immigrant groups before them, most Chinese coming to the United States were law-abiding and hard-working (Kwong, 1987; Zhou, 1992). Nevertheless, some were alleged to be involved heavily in profitable criminal activities such as extortion, gambling, and prostitution (Bresler, 1981; Kinkead, 1992; Posner, 1988). By 1984, U.S. law enforcement authorities observed increased involvement of Chinese criminals in illegal smuggling of aliens, heroin trafficking, and money laundering (President's Commission on Organized Crime, 1984). Also as with other immigrant groups before them, youth gangs appeared in neighborhoods where Chinese immigrant families settled (see, for example, Moore, 1991 on Mexican and Central American immigrants, Padilla, 1992, on Puerto Rican migrants to the U.S. mainland, and Thrasher, 1927, on European immigrants).

Chinese street gangs first appeared in the United States in San Francisco and New York City in the 1960s, soon after the changes in the immigration laws (Chang, 1972; Loo, 1976; Sung, 1977). Formed by young immigrants, the gangs soon became the street "muscle" of the tongs[1] hired to protect gambling, prostitution, and other illegal operations sanctioned by the tongs and other adult organized crime groups (Attorney General of California, 1972). The gangs gained power in Chinese communities through their association with the tongs, their use of violence to intimidate their victims and enemies, and their growing wealth.

By the late 1970s, fueled by the influx of young immigrants, Chinese gangs were involved in serious violent and property crimes, mostly within

Reprinted with permission from *Justice Quarterly*, Vol. 9 No. 4 (December 1992): 625–646.
© 1992 Academy of Criminal Justice Sciences.

the social boundaries of the Chinese communities (U.S. Department of Justice, 1985). The gangs expanded their activities and income sources to include exploitation of Chinese business owners (Chin, 1990). They also developed multiple enterprises to diversify their income sources. For example, some gang members opened legitimate businesses such as restaurants and nightclubs to provide both legal sources of income and a vehicle for laundering illegal income (Meskil, 1989). Competition for turf or disagreement about distribution of income from legal and illegal businesses often led to lethal intergang or intragang violence (U.S. Department of Justice, 1988).

Extortion is acknowledged to be the most prevalent form of crime committed by Chinese gang members, and the mainstay of their incomes (Kerber and Gentile, 1982; Louttit, 1982; Penn, 1980). Through extortion, the gangs exert their firm control on certain territories in the Chinese community (Chin 1990). Police estimate that more than 90 percent of Chinese business owners regularly pay one or more gangs (Meskil, 1989). When retail businesses refuse to pay, their shops may be vandalized, burglarized, robbed, or set on fire. Less often, businessmen and retail store owners have been beaten, shot at, or killed for refusing to pay (Scilla and Locksley, 1985). Resistance to gang extortion has instigated violence by business owners: gang members have been killed by merchants who refused to make extortion or protection payments (McFadden, 1988; Ruffini and Cotter, 1980). Accordingly, intimidation by gangs creates a "subculture of fear" (Wu, 1977) for merchants.

Prior research (Chin, 1990; Sung, 1977; Kwong, 1987) describes four types of gang victimization in the Chinese business community. The first type is "protection." Protection denotes a gang's demand for a fixed amount of money from a business owner to ensure that the business will not be disturbed by that gang or other gangs. The amount is negotiated between the owner and the gang member; the money then is paid regularly. This practice is related closely to territorial rights because theoretically, only members of a gang that control the area where the victim operates his or her business are supposed to ask for protection money.

The second type of victimization, "extortion," is the sporadic and spontaneous demand for money from business owners by gang members.[2] The amount of payment is negotiated on each occasion, and the perpetrators do not promise to provide any service in return. This type of victimization is a manifestation of the parasitic relationship between the offender and the victim, which transcends gang turf. Gang members, like parasites, prey on any member of the business community for "help," regardless of where he or she operates.

In the third type of victimization, gang members sell items to business owners at exorbitant prices. The Chinese custom of consuming or displaying certain items on major holidays, coupled with the Chinese norm of ensuring "harmony" at all costs on these occasions, offers gang members culturally reinforced criminal opportunities for exploiting the community's commercial sector.

In the last type of victimization, gangs refuse to pay for food and services or ask for heavy discounts. Although this type of behavior could be legally called "theft of goods or services," it is culturally regarded as "reciprocal face-giving" behavior between the offender and the victim. That is, the material gain is only secondary to the symbolic meaning.

In sum, extortion is a system of coercive exchange and symmetrical reciprocity. The capacity to impose such a system depends on the power of gangs to carry out credible threats of violence in a social milieu shaped by the cultural norms and values of the victimized community.

Despite allegations of widespread and costly extortion by gangs, few merchants file complaints with law enforcement agencies or prosecutors. Many victims fear gang reprisals and adapt to the burden of extortion payments rather than risking their safety or the well-being of their businesses. Others are cynical about the American criminal justice system; their failure to report extortion shows merchants' lack of trust in the ability of legal institutions to protect them (Song, 1988; Weikel, 1990). Given this inclination to resist open discussion of crime problems in the community, police have complained that the Chinese are "the most uncooperative ethnic group [when it] pertains to police investigations" ("Precinct Chief," 1985:20). The fear of the gangs, coupled with cynicism and ignorance about the criminal justice system, has increased the isolation of the Chinese commercial sector and has increased its vulnerability to extortion. This isolation also has complicated the efforts to study and explain victimization patterns.

Background of This Study

Although extortion and other racketeering activities targeted at businesses appear to be widespread in Chinese communities, few studies have described its prevalence or seriousness, or have analyzed the factors that create vulnerabilities to victimization. No systematic data are available with which to validate claims about its prevalence, the dynamics and processes of extortion, or the severity and persistence of extortion-related problems. Because the phenomenon is relatively recent, few opportunities have arisen to develop theories for explaining the patterns of recurring victimization, to refine methods for its study, or to accumulate empirical knowledge. Extortion of Chinese businesses by youth gangs started only about twenty years ago; only within this decade has it attracted attention from the public, legal institutions, and researchers. Most information about Chinese gangs and their activities comes from law enforcement authorities and the media. Although some studies have analyzed data from a small number of gang members or youths at risk (Chin, 1990;

Robinson and Joe, 1980; Sung, 1977; Toy, 1992), no research has addressed patterns of extortion based on data gathered from representative samples of gang members or their victims.

Accordingly, no systematic research has been conducted on the prevalence of gang extortion, on the monetary loss, or on the characteristics of businesses and business owners who are victimized. The consequences of these recurring patterns of extortion for the economic and social life of Chinese immigrant communities also are not understood. In addition, researchers have not examined the unique social processes in Chinese immigrant communities that may contribute to or mitigate these patterns. For example, we have little information on Chinese business owners' responses and resistance to extortion, or on their attitudes and expectations about victimization and about the remedies at hand.

To examine the patterns of extortion[3] by Chinese gangs, we interviewed owners and managers of businesses in three Chinese neighborhoods in New York City. The interviews addressed the forms and patterns of gang exploitation of businesses, the social processes of victimization, the social and cultural meanings of extortion, and the business community's reactions to the gang problem.

Methods

Sample

Interviews were conducted with owners or managers of businesses in three socioeconomically different "Chinatowns" in the Manhattan, Queens, and Brooklyn boroughs of New York City.[4] We constructed a sample of 888 businesses from the *Chinese Business Guide and Directory* (1990) and adopted a multistage cluster sampling strategy to ensure adequate representation of 10 types of Chinese-owned businesses.[5] Businesses uniquely vulnerable to extortion attempts were oversampled. These included businesses that (1) primarily involve cash transactions, (2) serve primarily Asian customers, (3) receive frequent visits by customers, and (4) are located at street level. The estimates of extortion activities were limited to businesses engaged in legal enterprises, although they may have violated administrative laws regarding work conditions. In view of the difficulty in approaching respondents, and because of concerns about interviewers' safety, we excluded locations in the sex (massage parlor) and gambling industries. Because these are tong-affiliated businesses guarded by gangs (Chin, 1990; Kinkead, 1992), it is unlikely in any case that they are subject to random extortion.

Response rates were high; 580 of the 888 subjects (65.3%) completed the interview. The refusal rate was 11.0 percent (n=98). The remainder (23.6%) were not interviewed because they could not be found. Some businesses had moved or closed (n=93). For others we had a wrong address (n = 27), or the owner was not Chinese (n=38).[6] In some cases, the business could not be reached by telephone (n=52). When these cases were excluded from the original sample, 580 of the 678 remaining subjects (85.5%) were interviewed.

To supplement the relatively small number of business owners from Brooklyn's Chinatown in the original sample, we interviewed an additional twenty-three business owners in that area. Interviewers went door-to-door along Eighth Avenue in Brooklyn and interviewed owners whose business fit the ten categories selected for the study.[7] The Chinese population in this neighborhood is more diffuse than the Chinese populations in Queens and the centrally located

Table 12.1   Respondents' Personal and Business Characteristics (N = 603)

Personal	N	Percent	Business	N	Percent
Sex			Type of Business		
Male	472	78.3	Restaurant	211	35.0
Female	131	21.7	Retail food store	101	16.7
Age			Retail nonfood store	95	15.8
Mean	43		Professional office	33	5.5
Median	42		Service	69	11.4
Mode	41		Wholesale/retail supply	46	7.6
Country of Origin			Garment factory	37	6.1
Hong Kong	324	53.8	Others	11	1.8
Taiwan	104	17.3	Location		
China	85	14.1	Manhattan's Chinatown	335	55.6
Other	89	14.8	Queen's Chinatown	129	21.4
Ethnicity			Brooklyn's Chinatown	42	7.0
Cantonese	332	55.8	Outside Chinatown	97	16.1
Fukienese	44	7.4	Age of Firm		
Chiu Chao/Hakka	29	4.9	Mean	8	
Taiwanese	44	7.4	Median	5	
Shanghainese	45	7.6	Mode	3	
Other Chinese	73	12.3	Size of Firm		
Others	28	4.7	Very Small	55	9.3
Education			Small	172	29.1
No formal schooling	8	1.3	Medium	253	42.8
6th grade or less	55	9.3	Large	111	18.8
7th to 9th grade	68	11.5	Sole Owner of Business?		
10th to 12th grade	198	33.4	Yes	282	48.1
College	230	38.8	No	305	51.9
Graduate school	34	5.7	Also Own the Property?		
Number of Years in the U.S.			Yes	80	13.6
Mean	16		No	508	86.4
Median	14				
Mode	10				

Chinatown in Manhattan. We hypothesized that the symbiotic relationship between the gangs and the ethnic community would lead to higher victimization rates, particularly in areas where the Chinese population and commercial activity were concentrated. The final sample thus included 603 businesses.

Most respondents were well-educated young Cantonese males from Hong Kong who had lived in the United States for about ten years. The businesses were mostly restaurants or retail food or nonfood stores located in the Manhattan and Queens Chinatowns, and were relatively new. Interviewers classified most businesses as small or medium-sized on the basis of their physical size and self-reported volume of activity. Table 12.1 shows the personal and business characteristics of the business.

The data also showed that the Manhattan and Brooklyn Chinatowns were dominated by businessmen from Hong Kong, whereas merchants from Taiwan were most active in Queens and in mid- or upper Manhattan. Respondents from China, the newest group, tended to congregate in areas of Brooklyn outside Chinatown. In comparison with subjects from Hong Kong and China, business owners from Taiwan were better educated and spoke better English. Owners of restaurants and supply firms were less well educated than owners of professional offices. Factory and supply businesses were located mostly in Manhattan's Chinatown, whereas professional offices were situated mostly in Queens' Chinatown. Female respondents were involved predominantly in service-oriented businesses or the garment industry.

Data Collection

To initiate contact with the interviewee, we sent a bilingual letter to the respondent's business address. The letter described the purpose of the study, how the business had been chosen, the confidentiality of the study, and the voluntary nature of participation. It also stated that a $20 stipend would be paid upon completion of the interview. To reassure business owners of the legitimacy of the study, a bilingual letter endorsed by the director of the sponsoring agency (the National Institute of Justice) was included with the notification letter. After the letters were mailed, interviewers contacted business owners by telephone, reminding them of the letter and asking for an appointment for an interview.

Six of the seven interviewers were female college students or social workers. The questions were read aloud to the respondents, who were encouraged to respond in their own words. Responses were recorded in Chinese and were summarized later by bilingual analysts. The interviews took place from April to September 1990.

Gang victimization was measured for each of the four types of gang exploitation of businesses: protection, extortion, forced sale of goods, theft of goods or services. The prevalence, frequency, and amount of payment for each type were recorded, as was any violence associated with each of these dimensions. We also asked respondents to recount the patterns of typical encounters with gangs.

Validity and Reliability

The measurement of gang victimization appeared to have high face validity and reliability. The interviewers were asked to rate the subjects' honesty and memory; interviewers' ratings thus provided assessments of the respondents' honesty in answering the questions. The interviewers reported that most subjects were either "very honest" or "honest" in their accounts of their victimization and appeared to have a clear recall of specific events and interactions. According to the interviewers, many owners kept records of extortion payments or received a receipt from the gang members for each payment. These records or receipts help the owners keep track of their payments and (for the purpose of this study) their victimization. Because few merchants report gang intimidation to the police, and because only victims who are heavily extorted or physically assaulted are likely to contact law enforcement authorities, the police do not maintain any systematic data on gang extortion in the Chinese community. Accordingly it is almost impossible to cross-validate self-reports of victimization with official statistics.

We computed reliability (Cronbach's alpha) for each of the three dimensions of victimization: prevalence, frequency, and monetary costs. For each dimension, we computed the coefficients for the reliability among the four types of extortion. Coefficients were satisfactory: .697 for prevalence of victimization, .601 for frequency, and .633 for monetary costs.

Results

Social Processes of Gang Victimization

The patterns of Chinese gang extortion reported in the qualitative literature were consistent with survey responses. Most respondents in the Chinese commercial sector reported patterns of victimization including protection, extortion, forced sales, and theft of goods and services. No other forms of Chinese gang victimization were reported. Although some subjects stated that their stores were robbed (8.8%) or burglarized (26.9%), most of them said the offenders either were non-Chinese or were not affiliated with Chinese gangs.

Protection. In the Chinese community, protection money is known as *po hoo fay* (protection fee), *tor tay fay* (territory fee), or *Heung yau chin* (incense oil money). The money is paid by merchants to an individual, a gang, or an association that controls the area in which the merchants conduct their business. In this way they obtain the "blessing" of those who are in a position to disrupt commercial activities or damage business property. The practice of paying protection money to gang members is pervasive in Hong Kong and Taiwan, especially among store owners and street vendors (Chi, 1985; Chin, 1990; Zhang, 1984).

The process of asking for protection money often begins when an owner is accosted by a group of gang members at the opening ceremony of his or her business. Younger members remain outside the store and watch the street while older members talk to the owner. Customarily, gang members first congratulate the owner, saying, *"Hoi mun tai gat"* ("Best luck to your business on opening day"). Then they go on to say, "We are from Mott Street; we own this area. If you want to avoid trouble, you have to pay us *po hoo fay*. We want 360 dollars as initial payment for the grand opening ceremony and 100 dollars a week for protection."[8] Because Chinese merchants are well aware of this gang practice, most of them come prepared; they sit down with the perpetrators and discuss how much they can pay. This process is known as *kong su* (negotiating the figures or cutting a deal). The owner may say, "The store is just opened. I am not sure how the business is going to turn out. Give me a break; let me pay you 100 dollars now and 100 dollars a month in the future." More often than not, the gang members accept the offer; in return, more for symbolic purposes than for anything else, they give the owner nicknames and a beeper number, urging him or her to call the beeper number if they have "trouble."

From then on, gang members arrive monthly to collect the protection money. When the collectors show up, the owner or an employee hands them an envelope containing the cash. As the practice becomes routine, few words are needed between the gang member and the victim. In some cases, after handing over the envelope, the owner is offered a receipt, indicating that the protection money for a specific month has been duly paid.

Extortion. Extortion money also is known as *cha chin* (tea money), *hung bao* (red envelope), or *lai si* (lucky money; literally, "good for business"). Unlike protection practices, extortion is a sporadic, spontaneous act committed irregularly by young gang members, mostly on major holidays such as the Chinese New Year. Typically, a group of gang members approaches a business. Two or three older members enter the store while the rest remain outside. Gang members often give the following reasons when asking for money:

"Please lend me some money. I will return the money as soon as possible."

"One of our brothers is *sway jor* [literally "hit by misfortune;" could mean being killed, arrested, or jailed]. We need some money."

"A brother was killed. We need money for his funeral."

"We need money to *yum cha* [to drink tea or eat]."

The amount of money requested often has a peculiar meaning. For example, some owners were asked for $188, to be interpreted as "double prosperity all the way" for the victim. In some cases, gang members demanded $108 or $360.[9] More often than not, however, they asked for about $100, and an owner offered $50. The perpetrators usually took whatever was offered and left.

Forced Sales. Gang members often sell expensive items only on major holidays. The gangs sell tangerine plants and firecrackers during Chinese New Year, mooncakes during the Moon Festival, and Christmas cards or whiskey during the Christmas holidays.[10] A thirty-four-year-old proprietor described this type of gang practice:

> During the past Chinese New Year, a group of teenagers who appeared to be gang members came to me and said, "Happy New Year. Please take this New Year card and pay us $180. It means that you will prosper in the coming year." You know the first digit denotes "one whole year" and the second digit pronounce the same as the word "prosperity" in Cantonese. They said that and they all laughed at me.

Some bakery stores are forced to buy mooncakes from gangs, though these stores also sell mooncakes. A manager of a bakery store was placed in an awkward situation when asked to buy items of which he already had too many:

> During the Moon Festival, two young gang members came and said, "Today is Moon Festival. Please buy this box of mooncakes." I said, "We sell mooncakes too. Why should we need this?" They said, "We have an understanding with your boss. You've got to buy our mooncakes on Moon Festival." I asked, "How much is a box?" They said, "Well, $100 a box, no big deal."[11]

Generally a gang places a large order of mooncakes with the bakery stores in Chinatown before the Moon Festival, anticipating that they will have little trouble selling the commodity during the festival. Sometimes they pay for the items; sometimes they do not.

Theft of Goods or Services. In the Chinese communities, the practice of asking for free goods or services is called *saik pa wong fun* (eating the villain's meal) or *tai pa wong hey* (watching the villain's movie), denoting the perpetrator as a "villain" who cannot be refused. Victims are mostly owners of restaurants, bakery shops, barber shops, videotape rental stores, and other retail enterprises such as groceries and optical stores. Restaurants and video rentals are most likely to be the object of gangs' interest because gang members need to eat and they watch videotapes obsessively.

Gang members believe that restaurant owners should let them eat for free to show respect. The following restaurateur describes how gang members view their behavior:

> During Chinese New Year, more than ten gang members came to my restaurant and ate. Later, they said they had no money. You cannot prevent this because you can't ask people at the door whether they are going to pay or not. They said, "We are from Pell Street. This is our New Year dinner party. We didn't bother you over the year. It is your honor that we come here to eat during the New Year." They left after they said that; they didn't even give me a chance to respond.

Videotape rental stores sometimes are asked to provide a special account for the gang, free of charge. When gang members walk in and tell the clerk about the gang account, they are entitled to check out as many tapes as they like and to keep them for as long as they wish. Some owners said they felt fortunate when the tapes were returned.

It appears that some gangs use this practice to compel store owners to pay protection money instead of harassing them constantly for free or discounted food and services. Some owners stated that when they agreed to pay protection money, they explicitly asked the gang leaders to tell their followers that their business was paying protection money and they should be left alone. Even so, paying protection money by no means assures immunity from young gang members who defy their leaders' orders.

Gang members enjoy watching Chinese martial arts films, which often are shown in movie theaters in Chinatown. Gang violence sometimes erupts inside or in front of theaters in the Chinese community. A respondent who owned a movie theater in Chinatown told an interviewer how he dealt with gang members who frequented his place:

> My theater is the only theater in Chinatown that insists that gang members must buy tickets—at half price, of course—given that they could identify which gang they belong to. I can do that because I hire a non-Asian guard. Even so, they came in a bunch two to three times a week, and I figure I lost at least $1,200 a month because of this. However, from what I know, other theaters in the community fare worse than me. They are letting the gang kids go in free after 10 P.M. It's like the theaters are being taken over by the gangs in the late evening.

Extent of Gang Exploitation

Table 12.2 shows that for all four types of gang victimization, 416 (69%) of the 603 respondents indicated that they had been approached by Chinese gang members and 330 (54.7%) had been victimized; that is, they had paid money or had provided free or discounted goods or services to the offender. The victims were exploited on the average of ten times a year, and these incidents cost them an average of $615 a year (see table 12.2).[12]

The rates, however, vary by type of extortion activity. For example, 130 respondents (21.6%) were approached by gang members for protection money. Sixty-nine (11.4%) of those respondents paid. Among those who paid, the average frequency of payment was fourteen times a year. Most paid once a month or three to four times a year. The average payment was $129; for each store, the average annual monetary loss for this type of crime was about $1,140. Gangs approached 246 subjects (40.8%) for extortion money, and victimized 158 (26.5%). The victims were extorted about five times a year, and paid the gangs an average of $75 on each occasion. Most victims were approached only two to three times a year, most paid about $50 per incident.

Forced sales are the most pervasive type of gang exploitation. Among the 603 respondents, 308 (51.1%) were approached by gang members with items for sale, and 246 (40.8%) bought items at exorbitant prices. On the average, this happened twice a year; the average financial losses for the owners were $51 per occasion and $117 annually. Among the subjects, 103 (17.1%) were approached by members of Chinese gangs for free or discounted goods or services. Ninety-four respondents (15.7%) were victimized in this way. These incidents occurred on an average of seventeen times a year; they cost the victims $119 on each occasion and $1,440 annually.

Table 12.2   Patterns and Extent of Gangs' Victimization of Chinese Business Owners (N = 603)

	Approached (%)	Victimized (%)	Average Annual Frequency (times)	Average Monetary Loss per Incident ($)	Average Monetary Loss per Year ($)
All Four Types of Victimization	69.0	54.7	10		615
Protection	21.6	11.4	14	129	1,140
Extortion	40.8	26.5	5	75	251
Forced Sales	51.1	40.8	2	51	117
Theft of Goods or Services	17.1	15.7	17	119	1,440

Table 12.2 suggests three important aspects of Chinese gang victimization. First, it is evident that Chinese gangs have diversified their patterns of victimization from overt extortion to subtler means—namely selling items to business owners. Before 1980, selling items to business owners was relatively rare among gang members (Chin, 1990), but this now appears to be the most popular form of extortion. The reason for the increased involvement in forced sales may be business owners' relative lack of resistance. Although merchants are least likely to defy gang members' demand for free or discounted goods and services, many businesses are spared this form of victimization. Either these businesses do not carry goods (such as professional offices), their goods are not easily portable (as in garment factories and wholesale or retail supply houses), or their services are needed only occasionally (as in dental offices or funeral homes). As a result, they are unlikely to be the targets of theft of goods and services.

Second, these patterns challenge popular conceptions and contradict police intelligence that Chinese merchants are forced to pay the gangs thousands of dollars a year (see, for example, Brestler, 1981; Posner, 1988). The discrepancy between law enforcement estimates and the rates in table 12.2 may reflect the social processes of negotiation between gang members and business owners. Police estimates may reflect the asking price, but table 12.2 shows the amounts actually paid or the dollar value of goods or services.

Third, except for a few restaurants that pay protection money weekly or monthly, and the nonfood retail stores that are forced more frequently to buy goods, most victims are exploited no more than three or four times a year. Attempts at victimization are more frequent, however. Most merchants refuse to satisfy all the demands of the gangs, and have adopted a variety of ruses to deflect gang members. Store owners may ask gang members to come back another time, or they may pretend that they are not the owners and therefore cannot agree to pay. Thus, although, Table 12.2 suggests relatively low rates of completed victimizations, gang members may attempt harassment more often.

Vulnerability to Gang Demands

Table 12.3 provides the data on the association between gangs' approaches and victimizations and the subjects' personal and business characteristics. Subjects who had more education and who spoke fluent English were less likely to be approached and victimized. Other personal characteristics such as sex, age, country of origin, length of stay in the United States, and affiliation with community associations were not associated with vulnerability to extortion attempts.

Restaurants, food retail stores, and other businesses (cultural recreation, vocational training, and entertainment) were most likely to be approached and victimized by gang members, while professional offices and garment factories were less likely to be the targets. Also, a higher percentage of merchants in Brooklyn's Chinatown than in Manhattan's and Queens' Chinatown were approached and victimized. The gangs appeared more often to have approached and victimized businesses which were owned by more than one person, and

Table 12.3 Gangs' Approach and Victimization, by Personal and Business Characteristics (N = 603) (percentages)

Personal Characteristics	Approached	Victimized	Characteristics	Approached	Victimized
Sex			Type of Business		
Male	69.3	55.7	Restaurant	83.9	73.5
Female	67.9	51.1	Food retail	75.2	54.5
Age			Nonfood retail	67.4	48.4
35 and younger	70.0	53.6	Office	18.2	9.1
36 to 45	72.4	57.3	Service	53.6	43.5
46 and older	69.4	57.3	Wholesale	65.2	50.0
Country of Origin			Factory	45.9	29.7
Hong Kong	71.0	58.0	Others	81.8***	63.6***
Taiwan	65.4	50.0	Chi-square:	81.6	72.7
China	70.6	56.5	Location		
Other	65.2	47.2	Manhattan's Chinatown	71.6	58.2
Education			Queens' Chinatown	58.9	42.6
Low	79.4	73.0	Brooklyn's Chinatown	76.2	61.9
Median	71.8	57.1	Non-Chinatown	70.1*	55.7*
High	64.4*	48.9***	Chi-square:	8.2	10.1
Chi-square:	6.7	12.7	Sole owner?		
English Proficiency			Yes	64.0	48.8
Low	80.1	64.0	No	73.8**	61.0**
Somewhat	75.1	58.7	Chi-square:	6.6	8.8
Fluent	59.7***	47.6**	Have Branch?		
Chi-square:	22.3	11.4	Yes	76.9	64.5
Length of time in U.S.			No	67.9	53.1*
10 yrs. or less	72.0	59.8	Chi-square:		5.0
11 to 20 yrs.	71.1	55.8	Profitability		
21 yrs. or more	65.9	52.3	Good	75.0	61.5
Affiliation with			Moderate	66.7	50.0
Community Association?			Poor	61.2*	49.3*
Yes	69.3	52.6	Chi-square:	8.5	8.2
No	69.2	55.5	Age of Firm		
			3 yrs. or less	63.1	53.3
			4 to 7 yrs.	71.5	57.0
			8 yrs. or more	74.6*	55.7
			Chi-square:	6.9	

   * p < .05
  ** p < .01
*** p < .001

which seemed to be more profitable. In addition, older businesses were more likely to be the targets of Chinese gangs, as were stores that had branches.

Vulnerability also varied by the specific gang that controlled the streets and subneighborhoods within each Chinatown (data are not shown). About 82 percent of businesses within the territory of a particular Chinese gang in Manhattan were targeted by the gang, but only 24 percent of the stores at the outskirts of Manhattan's Chinatown were "shaken down." About 85 percent of the restaurants in Manhattan's Chinatown were exploited by Chinese gangs, but all of the restaurateurs in the core area of the community indicated that they were victimized (data not shown).

Overall, table 12.3 suggests that assimilation may protect against victimization by gangs. Owners who are better educated and who speak fluent English are less likely to be victimized. The lower rates of victimization among these persons may reflect decisions by gangs to avoid businesses owned by people more familiar with U.S. culture and institutions, or may indicate that more highly assimilated people are more able to resist extortion attempts. Nevertheless, the results in table 12.3 confirm the hypothesis that certain types of Chinese-owned businesses are more vulnerable to gang victimization. Merchants in Manhattan's Chinatown, however, where most of the Chinese gangs have their headquarters and where the Chinese population is densest, are not more vulnerable to gang extortion than merchants elsewhere. This finding suggests that extortion is not more likely where there is a greater concentration of Chinese businesses and population. Businesses outside the three Chinese communities are harassed by Chinese gangs as often as are businesses in the "traditional" Manhattan Chinatown. Chinese merchants active outside Chinatowns are almost as vulnerable as business owners in Manhattan's Chinatown and substantially more vulnerable than those who operate their businesses in Queens' Chinatown. These patterns suggest that extortion by Chinese gangs has followed the expansion of the Chinese population beyond the dense confines of Manhattan's Chinatown, often into non-Chinese neighborhoods.

Resistance to Gang Victimization

Resistance to extortion and other forms of victimization by Chinese gangs is rare. Table 12.4 shows that only about one subject in five (20.1%) approached by Chinese gang members did not yield to their demands. Restaurants and service-oriented stores were less resistant to gangs than were professional offices or garment factories. The personal or business characteristics discussed in table 12.3 were not associated with resistance to approaches by gangs.

Business owners or managers use a variety of strategies to avoid victimization, but few can resist outright. Some merchants denied that they were the owners of the establishment. A thirty-four-year-old grocery store owner from Hong Kong told how he avoided paying protection money to a gang:

Table 12.4   Resistance to Gang Demands, by Type of Business (N = 603)

Type of Business	Total N	Approached	Resisted	Percent Resisted
Restaurant	211	177	22	12.4
Retail food store	101	76	21	27.6
Retail nonfood store	95	64	18	28.1
Office	35	6	3	50.0
Service	69	37	7	18.9
Wholesale/retail supply	46	30	7	23.3
Garment factory	37	17	6	35.3
Others	11	19	2*	22.2
Chi-square			17.3	

* p < .05

When the store was opened, a group of teenagers came and said, "Congratulations. We are the Flying Dragons; we want protection money." I replied, "I am not the owner. I cannot make any decision. Please come back some other time." They left, but came back the following day. I told them I am still trying to get in touch with the owner. They came the third time, and I kept telling them that I can't do anything about it. After that, they never came for protection money again.

On most occasions, when a business owner refused to pay protection money, gang members cursed and threatened the owner as they left but rarely returned to attack. If the business was a well-established restaurant or retail store, however, located at the heart of a tightly controlled gang turf, the owner had few opportunities to defy the gang's demands. The following interview, conducted with the well-educated manager of a large store, attests to this point:

When they came and asked for $500 a month for protection, I refused. I said, "I know a lot of people in Chinatown." They replied, "It doesn't matter. You still have to pay." I asked them to let me think about it, and they left. I called 911 right away, but the police didn't even bother to show up. What's the point of calling the police? When they returned the next day, I said I needed more time. In the next few days, they robbed a customer in the toilet room; asked a customer who was sitting in the dining area to lend them his wallet, and took all the cash; stood in front of the store in the evening (about twenty of them) and stared at the employees as they left the business premises. Finally, when one gang member threw a jumbo firecracker behind the counter and burnt the leg of an employee, I got so perturbed that I chased them with a knife. However, after that, I decided to pay them exactly what they asked for.

Some merchants were determined not to submit to the gangs. A store owner who appeared to be closely connected to a gang claimed that he was not intimidated at all:

> A group of Ghost Shadows came and wanted extortion money from me. I said, "No money. Get lost right away." They left the store immediately. They should have figured out who I was before they approached me for money. I am amazed that they have the guts to come before they even know anything about me. These Shadows are all garbage.

Among most of the respondents, who were not part of the Chinese underworld, many believed that they had little choice but to pay the gang. In some cases, when an owner refused, gang members sent a message to the owner pressuring him to pay. One owner found bags of garbage piled up in front of his store after he refused. He paid the gang members when they showed up again. On other occasions, gang members occupied the dining area of a restaurant and made a scene by constantly asking the waiters for chopsticks and spoons.

Chinese business owners' compliance with gang demands may be attributed to three factors. First, explicit threats and coercion were infrequent: among those who had paid protection money, only one in three reported specific threats. Fewer than 20 percent who reported extortion were threatened, as were fewer than 10 percent of those suffering other types of victimization. Specific threats of violence to the business owner or to his or her family were very rare. Weapons were shown to fewer than 2 percent of the victims. When gang members make their approaches in a cultural context laden with symbolic language, business owners may feel less threatened and may be able to justify their victimization more easily.

Second, most victims estimated the annual financial loss from gang victimization at less than $1,000. Small business owners reported losses due to gang extortion of less than $200 in the past year. In relation to other costs of doing business, Chinese entrepreneurs are not hurt significantly by gang members in financial terms. Thus cooperation with gang demands is far less costly than resistance. Merchants who regarded their compliance with gang demands as prudent often gave the following reasons:

> "I paid because I am afraid of their retaliation. I own a small business; I cannot afford to pay for any damage to the store."

> "I was afraid that if I refuse to pay, they will come and sit in the restaurant. If that happened, customers will be afraid to come into my restaurant."

Third, some businessmen construed extortionate demands not as criminal per se but as consistent with Chinese customs and social traditions. Many merchants seemed willing to comply, as long as gang members behaved politely and made demands deferentially, and as long as the items sold by gang members were considered indispensable for Chinese holidays.

Discussion

We theorized that three social and economic factors caused and sustained the pervasiveness of extortion in the Chinese community. First, Chinese communities reflect a unique political economy: they are small, congested, and isolated from the dominant American mainstream culture. The interaction of a small, congested physical space, language barriers that exclude English speakers, cultural rituals that are distinct from those of the surrounding society, and preferences for doing business with other Chinese leads to a physically, socially, and economically isolated and self-contained community. Routine social and economic interactions are concentrated among the members; they call upon the community's social and economic institutions for social regulation and control (Kinkead, 1992; Kwong, 1987). Interactions between offenders and victims are not restricted to rule-breaking behaviors, but also involve other day-to-day routines in which gang members patronize the business premises without criminal intent. Thus the social distinction between offenders and victims is blurred.

Because business competition within the community is fierce and because the family networks of most Chinese immigrants are truncated (Sung, 1987), the business owners have an enormous workload. When threatened by a gang, few merchants have the inclination, time, knowledge, or presence of mind to seek help from formal social control agencies such as the police and the district attorney. Compounding the difficulties in reaching out to such agencies are powerful adult organizations within the community that somehow discourage local people from approaching the authorities, the latter are defined as "outsiders." Because outsiders are distrusted, such an act is considered a betrayal of the community (Kuo, 1977). Some of these adult organizations tend to condone rather than deploring or opposing extortionate activities. In these circumstances, extortion can become institutionalized.

Second, community cultural norms may facilitate the spread and pervasiveness of extortion in the community and may provide gang members with opportunities to engage in predatory acts that are unique to the social context of Chinese communities. For example, certain items are necessary for most Chinese celebrations and holidays (Mano, 1988). The gangs take advantage of this fact and sell these items to business owners at inflated prices. During the Chinese New Year, adults give *hung bao* (red envelopes containing cash) to family members, relatives, and even strangers, as the custom dictates (Henican, 1987). Gang members seize this opportunity and exploit the custom by asking business owners for *hung bao* during this holiday. Thus the gangs manage to use customs as a shield against police and legal sanctions.

Third, a symbiotic relationship exists between the gangs and the adult organizations that provide the community with illegal services (e.g., gambling, prostitution, and loan sharking) (Meskil, 1989). Despite the illicitness of these services, many community residents view these organizations as legitimate and important parts of the social and economic networks that make up the community. Association with these organizations enables the gangs to present themselves as their "youth groups." Thus the gangs attempt to "legitimize" themselves by associating with these organizations.

These patterns are relevant to efforts to develop criminological theories that can explain more adequately the formation of youth gangs and their often ambiguous status in specific communities. A theory that is limited to constructs such as the presence or absence of gangs or adult criminal groups, the level of isolation of the community, and the personal characteristics of the residents may not be sufficient to explain why the patterns and processes of gang victimization differ across ethnic communities. Certain processes appear to sustain youth gangs; these result from the interaction of physical space, the social organization of adult groups engaged in both legal and illegal activities, routine economic activities, and the rules and organizing principles fostered by language and culture. Although the intentions of gangs or gang members to generate gains by illegal means may be similar across ethnic groups, spatial, social, economic, and cultural differences among communities may contribute to quite varied patterns and processes of gang activity.

Notes

1. Tongs were established as self-help groups by the first wave of Chinese immigrants in the United States and southeast Asia during the mid-nineteenth century (Dillon, 1962; Leong, 1936; Trocki, 1990). Vicious group conflicts among the tongs are known as "tong wars" (Gong and Grant, 1930). Historically, the tongs have been active in operating or providing protection for opium dens, gambling places, and houses of prostitution in the Chinese communities (U.S. Senate, 1978). The tongs have thousands of adult members, predominantly male, from all walks of life, but only a few are involved in criminal activities.

2. Chinese business owners made a distinction between "extortion" and "protection," whereas the New York State Penal Code does not.

3. Demanding money or the provision of goods and services to avoid violence or harassment is the working definition of extortion adopted in this study. Chinese gangs use different methods to extort, but all involve the use of threats of violence or mayhem to illegally obtain money, services, and other property of value.

4. The Chinatown in Manhattan is a well-established social and commercial center. It is located on the lower east side of Manhattan and is surrounded by City Hall, "Little Italy," and the East River. Approximately 80,000 persons now live here;

the population is growing rapidly as a result of China's open door policy and the political instability in Hong Kong. Residents are mostly working-class Cantonese-speaking immigrants from China or Hong Kong (Kwong, 1987; Zhou, 1992). The Chinatown in Queens is located in the Flushing section, where thousands of Chinese have settled along Main Street and the No.7 subway route through Jackson Heights and Elmhurst. Residents are predominantly new immigrants from Taiwan or Korea (Chen, 1992). Brooklyn's Chinatown is situated along Eighth Avenue in the Sunset Park section and in neighboring Bay Ridge and Borough Park. It is connected to Manhattan's Chinatown by the N and the B subway trains, which serve as social and economic lifelines between the two communities (Smith,1988).

5. More than 5,000 predominantly Chinese-owned businesses were listed in the 1990 edition of the *Directory*. The ten types of business included in the study were restaurant, retail food store, retail nonfood store, professional office, service, wholesale/retail supply, garment factory, entertainment, vocational training, and cultural recreation. In the *Directory*, 4,290 firms were listed under these business categories for Manhattan, Queens, and Brooklyn.

6. We intended to interview only Chinese business owners, assuming that Chinese gangs victimize only Chinese businesses. After the sample was drawn, we tried to exclude businesses that were apparently non-Chinese or were known to the researchers to be owned by non-Chinese. Even so, we encountered several businesses that we learned were non-Chinese only after we arrived for the interview. As a result, a number of non-Chinese firms were included in the sample.

7. This study initially planned to interview about fifty subjects from Brooklyn's Chinatown. Because that Chinatown's commercial center is relatively small (no more than several blocks along Eighth Avenue), only about one-hundred firms from the area were listed in the *Directory*. As a result, only thirty-six businesses in Brooklyn's Chinatown were included in the original target sample. Of these thirty-six firms, nineteen were interviewed. We decided to supplement the original sample with stores located in the area that were not included in the original sample. The interviewers were instructed to approach one of the ten types of business selected for the study. Eventually we included twenty-three additional stores in Brooklyn's Chinatown in the sample. A comparison between sampled and nonsampled businesses in Brooklyn's Chinatown reveals no difference in subjects' characteristics, such as age, sex, country of origin, length of residence in the United States, English proficiency, and educational level. Also, we found no difference in business characteristics, such as type of business, age of the firm, and size of the firm.

8. On many occasions, gang members do not identify themselves as members of a gang. Instead they simply tell the owner which street they are from. Because most merchants in the community know which gangs control specific streets, mentioning the street name is equivalent to identifying the gang. In this case the owner would have known that the perpetrators belonged to the Ghost Shadows.

9. The number 1, pronounced *yat* in Cantonese, is taken for *yat lu*, meaning "all the way." Eight, pronounced *part*, sounds like the word *fart*, which means "prosperity." The numbers 108 and 36 are both very significant in the Triad legend; they denote the 108 monks who established the first Triad society and the 36 oaths a new recruit takes when joining the society. Triad organizations began as secret societies formed by patriotic Chinese three centuries ago to fight the oppressive and corrupt

Ch'ing dynasty (1644–1911). When the Ch'ing government collapsed and the Republic of China was established in 1912, some of these societies degenerated into criminal groups (Chesneaux, 1972; Morgan, 1960). Most Triad societies now have their headquarters in Hong Kong, but their criminal operations have no national boundaries (Booth, 1990).

10. During the Chinese New Year celebration, the tangerine plant is a necessity for every Chinese household and place of business. The pronunciation of the Chinese word for "tangerine" is similar to the word for "good fortune." The Moon Festival, an event similar to Valentine's Day, is a popular celebration among the Chinese.

11. A box of mooncakes costs about $10–$15 in the supermarket or bakery store in Chinatown.

12. Because owners in certain businesses (e.g., gambling clubs, houses of prostitution) were not sampled, the figures presented in this study may underestimate Chinese gangs' involvement in extortion activities, and the extent of violence in extortion. Yet because gambling locations and the sex industry are controlled by the tongs that employ the gangs to guard these lucrative businesses, they are unlikely to be victims of extortion. To obtain a full measure of the extent of Chinese gang victimization, future research should include businesses that operate in the informal economy as well as in the illicit economy.

References

Attorney General of California. (1972). *Proceedings of the Conference on Chinese Gang Problems*. Sacramento: California Organized Crime and Criminal Intelligence Branch.

Barringer, F. (1991). "Immigration Brings New Diversity to Asian Population in the U.S." *New York Times*, June 12, p. A1.

Booth, M. (1990). *The Triads*. New York: St. Martins.

Bresler, F. (1981). *The Chinese Mafia*. New York: Stein and Day.

Chang, H. (1972). "Die Today, Die Tomorrow: The Rise and Fall of Chinatown Gangs." *Bridge Magazine 2*, 10–15.

Chen, H.S. (1992). *Chinatown No More*. Ithaca: Cornell University Press.

Chesneaux, J. (1972). *Popular Movements and Secret Societies in China, 1840–1950*. Stanford, CA: Stanford University Press.

Chi, Z-X. (1985). (in Chinese) *Gangs, Election, and Violence*. Taipei: Jiao Dian Publishing Co.

Chin, K-L. (1990). *Chinese Subculture and Criminality*. Westport, CT: Greenwood.

Chinese Business Guide and Directory. (1990). New York: Key Publications.

Dillon, R.H. (1962). *The Hatchet Men*. New York: Coward/McCann.

Gong, Y.E., and B. Grant. (1930). *Tong War!* New York: N.L. Brown.

Henican, E. (1987). "Chinatown Hops with the Rabbit." *New York Newsday*, January 30, p. 17.

Kerber, F., and D. Gentile. (1982). "The Tongs' Hammer Lock: Merchants Silent in Face of Extortion." *New York Daily News*, December 26, p. 5.

Kinkead, G. (1992). *Chinatown*. New York: HarperCollins.

Kuo, C-L. (1977). *Social and Political Change in New York's Chinatown*. New York: Praeger.

Kwong, P. (1987). *The New Chinatown*. New York: Hill and Wang.

Leong, G.Y. (1976). *Chinatown Inside Out*. New York: Barrows Mussey.

Loo, C.K. (1976). "The Emergence of San Francisco Chinese Juvenile Gangs from the 1950s to the Present," Master's thesis, San Jose State University.

Louttit, N. (1982). "Toronto Extortion Gangs Play on Chinese Traditions." *Toronto Star*, February 18, p. 4.

Mano, D.K. (1988). "There's More to Chinatown." *New York Times Magazine*, April 24, pp. 42–61.

McFadden, R.D. (1988). "A Chinatown Businessman Is Charged in a Slaying." *New York Times*, June 12, p. 34.

Meskil, P. (1989). "In the Eye of the Storm." *New York Daily News Magazine*, February 5, pp. 10–16.

Moore, J. (1991). *Going Down to the Barrio*. Philadelphia, PA: Temple University Press.

Morgan, W.P. (1960). *Triad Societies in Hong Kong*. Hong Kong: Government Printer.

Padilla, F.M. (1992). *The Gang as an American Enterprise*. New Brunswick, NJ: Rutgers University Press.

Penn, S. (1980). "Youth Gangs Plague Chinatown Merchants with Payoff Demands." *Wall Street Journal*, August 18, p. 1.

Posner, G. (1988). *Warlords of Crimes: Chinese Secret Societies—The New Mafia*. New York: McGraw-Hill.

"Precinct Chief Complains about the Lack of Cooperation." (1985). *Centre Daily News* (in Chinese), June 7. p. 20.

President's Commission on Organized Crime. (1984). *Organized Crime of Asian Origin: Record of Hearing III—October 23–25, 1984, New York, New York*. Washington, DC: U.S. Government Printing Office.

Robinson, N., and D. Joe. (1980). "Gangs in Chinatown: The New Young Warrior Class." *McGill Journal of Education*, 15: 149–62.

Ruffini, G., and J. Cotter. (1980). "Merchant Kills Teen Gangster." *New York Post*, May 7, p.3.

Scilla, S.S., and L. Locksley. (1985). "Chinese Restaurateur Threatened: 5 Charged in Extortion." *The Record*, August 27, p. C1.

Smith, P. (1988). "B-Line to Chinatown." *New York Post*, April 28, p. 55.

Song, J. H-L. (1988). "Chinese Immigrants and Vietnamese Refugees' Adaptation to American Legal Institutions." Paper presented at the annual meeting of the American Society of Criminology, Chicago.

Sung, B.L. (1977). *Gangs in New York's Chinatown*. New York: Department of Asian Studies, City College of New York, Monograph No. 6.

———. (1987). *The Adjustment Experience of Chinese Immigrant Children in New York City*. New York: Center for Migration Studies.

Thrasher, F.M. (1972). *The Gang*. Chicago: University of Chicago Press.

Toy, C. (1992). "Coming Out to Play: Reasons to Join and Participate in Asian Gangs." *The Gang Journal*, *1*(1): 13–29.

Trocki, C.A. (1990). *Opium and Empire: Chinese Society in Colonial Singapore, 1800–1910*. Ithaca: Cornell University Press.

U.S. Department of Justice. (1985). *Oriental Organized Crime: A Report on a Research Project of the Organized Crime Section.* Washington, DC: Federal Bureau of Investigation. Criminal Investigation Division.

_____. (1988). *Report on Asian Organized Crime.* Washington, DC: U.S. Department of Justice, Criminal Division.

U.S. Senate. (1978). *Report of the Joint Special Committee to Investigate Chinese Immigration.* New York: Arno Press.

Weikel, D. (1990). "Crime and the Sound of Silence." *Los Angeles Times*, October 21, p. A1.

Wu, R. (1977). "What the ***** Is Goin On?" *Bridge Magazine*, Fall, pp. 5–11.

Zhang, S. (1984). (in Chinese) *Organized Crime Activities in Hong Kong.* Hong Kong: Tien Ti Book Co.

Zhou, M. (1992). *Chinatown.* Philadelphia, PA: Temple University Press.

13

A Short History of Asian Gangs
in San Francisco

Calvin Toy

Introduction

On September 4, 1977, the worst mass murder in San Francisco's history occurred at the Golden Dragon restaurant in the heart of San Francisco's Chinatown. After five were killed and eleven wounded, all of whom were innocent bystanders, Chinese gangs were recognized as a public threat. The San Francisco Police Gang Task Force was created and funding for social service agencies in the Chinese community increased. However, little has been written or is known about Chinese gangs in San Francisco prior to this event. After the initial concern, which lasted only a few years, attention once again flowed away from these gangs. As a result, there have been few documentations of the formation and development of Chinese gangs in San Francisco.

Today, gangs in San Francisco's Chinese community are no longer exclusively ethnic Chinese. During the past ten years, there has been an enormous increase of Chinese-Vietnamese and Vietnamese gang members. More recently, Cambodian gangs are appearing in various parts of San Francisco. Although some literature (Montero, 1979; Haines, 1981; Henkin and Nguyen, 1981) concerning the migration of Southeast Asians into the United States' urban centers exists, how these groups became integrated into the structure of the Chinese community is a topic that has been virtually ignored. Recent developments among San Francisco's Asian gangs have once again attracted public attention and concern. Knowledge of the development of these gangs is necessary in understanding current events. The purpose of this paper is, therefore, to briefly describe the historical events which took place in San Francisco's Asian communities over the past three decades and the development of its Asian gangs.

Reprinted with permission from *Justice Quarterly*, Vol. 9 No. 4 (December 1992): 647–665.
© 1992 Academy of Criminal Justice Sciences.

Literature Review

Compared to the large body of literature on African American and Hispanic gangs, work on Asian gangs is scarce. Early on, sociologists and psychologists, such as Sollenberger (1968), studied Chinese child-rearing practices for clues to their remarkable socialization capacities. With the dawning of Chinese gangs, however, focus shifted to gang delinquency and organized crimes of Asian origin.

In 1972, the Attorney General of California held a hearing in which many issues concerning the emergence of Chinese gangs were discussed and documented. It was not until after the Golden Dragon Massacre in 1977 that the issue of Chinese gangs in San Francisco was again studied. Takagi and Platt (1977) found that the exploitation of immigrant workers in Chinatown led to a breakdown in traditional family ties and crime. Rice (1977) found that the excitement and financial rewards discovered through Chinese gangs often outweighed legitimate opportunities available to youths, causing an increased likelihood for gang participation. Three years later, Joe and Robinson (1980) found adjustment problems and culture conflict to be the main cause of gang participation (see also Sung, 1987).

Throughout the 1980s many authors were fascinated with organized crime of Asian origin. Many sought to link Asian gangs with what they refer to as the "Chinese Mafia." In 1986, the Attorney General of California conducted another hearing on organized crime, predicting that future influxes of Asian immigrants would exacerbate the Asian gang problem in California. Authors, such as Bresler (1981) and Posner (1988), explored in depth the international organization of the Chinese criminal syndicate and its relation to the heroin trade. Recently, Ko Lin Chin (1990) elaborately discussed the tradition of secret societies in China which are believed to be critical to the development of Asian street gangs in the United States. Today, the thrust of much literature on Asian gangs focuses on organized crime.

Research Methods and Sources of Data

Data for this paper were obtained from face to face interviews from an ongoing study of gangs in San Francisco, California. Interviews consisted of two parts: an in-depth tape recorded section used to obtain qualitative data and a pre-coded schedule of questions used for quantitative purposes. A field observation guide was also used to record information obtained from first hand observations of gang activities.

Respondents were located by means of snowball sampling techniques (Biernacki and Waldorf, 1981). Gang members were initially recruited through personnel of neighborhood-based, social service agencies[1] which provide counseling and psychiatric evaluations for gang members and troubled youths.

After each completed interview, gang members were asked to refer others within the gang or friends in other Asian gangs. Concurrently, intermediaries from social service agencies were recruiting gang members for interviews. Respondents were paid a stipend of $50 for each completed interview, and individuals were paid $40 for each successful referral. The snowball strategy took effect as respondents and social workers recruited gang members for interviews.

After eighteen months of data collection, seventy-three were completed. Sixty-four of those interviewed were active gang members, and nine interviews were considered historical. Specifically, data were collected and analyzed from the following gangs: various factions of the Wah Ching, the Suey Sing, the Hop Sing, the Asian Invasion, the Eddy Boys, the Chinese Playground Boys (a.k.a. CP boys), and the Ping Boys. The first three gangs are thought to be linked with local tongs,[2] and have been established in San Francisco's Chinatown for over fifteen years. These gangs generally consist of foreign born Chinese and ethnic Chinese from Vietnam. The remaining gangs are neighborhood groups which are involved in delinquent activities as well as some drug distribution. They consist of either American born Chinese, foreign born Chinese, or Chinese Vietnamese. Individuals within these groups are sometimes recruited by the established gangs. All of the preceding gangs reside in San Francisco and often use Chinatown as the focus of many activities.

Ideally, a researcher would prefer to speak to those who originally formed the gangs. However, many of these individuals are either dead, incarcerated, or in hiding. Historical interviews were thus most useful for this paper. These interviews consist of information obtained from former gang members, nongang members, and social workers, concerning the formation and development of Asian gangs in San Francisco. Only one respondent was actually involved in creating the gangs. Hence, the data sources may be incomplete or biased, and thus the findings should be viewed with some caution. Given these limitations, I have attempted to trace the factors giving rise to contemporary Asian gangs in San Francisco.

Definition of "Gang Member"

Since there is no consensus among researchers, social workers, and law enforcement agencies, as to what constitutes a "gang," we did not use a specific definition during the preliminary stages of this study. In order to qualify, prospective respondents were asked whether they belonged in a gang and to which specific gang. This strategy of self selection avoided imposing an academic definition of "gang" or "gang member" on respondents. By avoiding the possibility of utilizing an inapplicable definition, this method did not restrict the pool of respondents to what other researchers or law enforcement officials deem to be gangs and gang members. This strategy, however, relied upon the subjective definitions of "gang" by respondents (Fagan, 1990: 8).

Self selection during the preliminary stage of the study allowed the author to conceptualize what a "gang" and what being a "gang member" means to respondents. After fifteen interviews, a workable definition, one offered by Malcolm Klein, was applied. According to Klein (1969: 1427), a gang is:

> any denotable adolescent group of youngsters who (a) are generally perceived as a distinct aggregation by others in their neighborhood, (b) recognize themselves as a denotable group (almost invariably with a group name), and (c)have been involved in a sufficient number of delinquent incidents to call forth a consistent negative response from neighborhood residents and/or enforcement agencies.

Although Klein's definition describes the majority of Asian gangs, it requires some modification to encompass all Asian gangs existing in San Francisco. First, our study has shown that many Chinese gangs cannot be considered "groups of youngsters," since the age range is greater than adolescence fourteen to thirty-four, and many participants are in their twenties and thirties. In addition, we give greater weight to Klein's second requirement than to the other two. Since many Chinese gangs, especially those involved in organized crimes, are discreet with their activities, neither neighborhood residents nor law enforcement officials may always be aware of their existence. However, if a gang considers itself a "denotable group" and, more important, if they have a gang name, we considered the group to be a gang.

Historical Contexts

The Beginnings

Due to a series of Chinese Exclusion Acts, few Chinese women and children were allowed to immigrate to the United States prior to 1965. The Chinese community thus mainly consisted of adult males, who were primarily bachelors. Consequently, there were only a small number of children, which stifled the development of gangs in San Francisco's Chinatown.

Despite the absence of gangs, a tradition of organized criminal activities, which utilized able young men, developed in the late 1800s. Gambling and the use of opium were popular respites from work among the men who lived in Chinatown. Since there were few Chinese women in the United States, prostitution rings formed to serve the needs of bachelors. Many of these activities were run by members of tongs, who sought to ease some of the difficulties recent immigrants faced. Since these activities are considered illegal in the United States, young men were often used as lookouts (a.k.a. "looksees"), guards and enforcers (a.k.a. "hatchetmen") of house rules to assure smooth

231

operations.[3] The predominantly male population, the nature of their preferred activities, and the organization of the community, gave birth to a tradition of organized crime in San Francisco's Chinatown, a subculture having profound impacts on the development of modern Asian gangs.

Groups of youths, which can be considered delinquent youth gangs under certain definitions (Miller, 1958; Yablonsky, 1958; Cloward and Ohlin, 1960), arose in the late 1950s and early 1960s with the subtle increase in youths in Chinatown. Gangs, such as the Raiders, the Continentals, and 880's, can be paralleled with the American gangs that existed during that time. Much like the gangs portrayed in movies such as "The Wild One" and "West Side Story," these groups were preoccupied with committing minor delinquent acts and the thrill of the "rumble." According to one former gang member of that era:

> (R) The gangs were just social groups, like any other group of boys that hung out together and got into fights and stuff. We never even did much drugs. That was considered bad. We never carried any handguns or shot at people. Because we all hung out together in large groups, the police called us a gang.

These gangs were not unique entities uncommon to American culture. Lacking any connections with organized criminal networks, these gangs generally resembled Cloward and Ohlin's (1960) "conflict gang." They often consisted of a few rebellious adolescents who used the gang as a means to release frustration. These gangs can also be paralleled with what Yablonsky (1959) terms as "near-groups." According to Yablonsky (1959: 109), near-groups are characterized by the following factors: (1) diffuse role definitions, (2) limited cohesion, (3) impermanence, (4) minimal consensus of norms, (5) shifting membership, (6) disturbed leadership, and (7) limited definitions of membership expectations. In short, there was a lack of organization and utilitarian purpose within these early gangs.

When members became adults, they usually abandoned the gang since it had little to offer adult life. Like other youths in America at that time, many went to college while others were drafted for the conflict in Vietnam. As members quit, no new generations replenished the gangs, and by the late 1960s, these gangs became virtually extinct.

Formation of Chinese Gangs in the 1960s

Modern Chinese gangs possess distinct behavior patterns and unique organizational structures radically different from earlier Chinese gangs. In comparison to the gangs previously discussed, the modern Chinese gang has "violated all of the so-called traditional norms" (Sung, 1977: 5). Unlike the gangs of the past, who were mainly involved with petty crimes and gang fights, this new wave of gangs were involved with extortion, strong-armed robberies, other violent crimes, and organized crime. Since many more illegal opportunities were open to this group of newcomers, many remain active in the gang as adults. Modern Asian gangs consist of both adult and teenage members, thus, they can no longer be considered "youth gangs." In addition, the gangs of the fifties and early sixties only consisted of ten to twenty members per gang, while contemporary Chinese gangs may have memberships ranging up to three hundred members (President's Commission on Organized Crime, 1984). Therefore, they can be considered an entirely different type of gang, with different sets of norms and values.

Several factors sparked and fueled a collaborative effort among immigrant youths leading to the development of modern Chinese gangs. First, the rescision of immigration quotas during the Kennedy and Johnson administrations provided an influx of Chinese immigrant families from Hong Kong and mainland China into San Francisco. A large pool of immigrant youths in San Francisco provided the individuals needed to create gangs.

Second, new immigrants faced several social problems upon arriving in San Francisco. Neither the Chinese community nor the city of San Francisco generally was prepared to accommodate and provide for needs of its new immigrants. Job opportunities and adequate housing were severely lacking. As a result, many immigrant families lived in extreme poverty.

Third, the general population of San Francisco failed to accept the arrival of new immigrants. Due to overcrowded housing, many immigrants were forced to move into the outskirts of Chinatown. Many of these individuals encroached upon predominantly white neighborhoods, particularly Italian areas, in which individuals greeted the Chinese with hostility and violence. Immigrants youths encountered verbal and physical abuse within Chinatown. The already existing American born Chinese (referred to as A.B.C.'s) gangs resented the idea of this new group of recent immigrants (often referred to as F.O.B.'s, meaning "fresh off the boat") coming into Chinatown demanding jobs and territory. Due to cultural differences, the immigrants were perceived by the A.B.C.'s as an embarrassment to the Chinese community. Abuse and assaults from existing Chinese gangs and other ethnic groups encouraged the new immigrant youths to band together and defend themselves.

Finally, the political attitude among youth in America played a part in influencing young Chinese immigrants. The 1960s were a time of rebellion and demand for social change, especially in the area of civil rights. Groups of Chinese college students, who advocated community empowerment, prompted immigrant youths to organize and demand help from wealthy family associations and tongs. In an attempt to improve conditions, immigrant youths banded together to form an official boy's club called the "Yow Yee," which translates to "Have Righteousness."

Within a short period of time, the Yow Yee's popularity grew among immigrant youths since it was perceived to be their only viable outlet in fulfilling their dreams in a foreign society. The Yow Yee had the crucial elements needed to transform into a small army. At that time, the membership had grown so large (over one-hundred active members), they overshadowed any other organized youth group within San Francisco. Furthermore, they were backed by funding provided through donations collected from Chinatown stores which sympathized with the group.

By the late 1960s, the Yow Yee converted from an assertive position to an offensive, aggressive standing. The group grew impatient with the lack of positive responses from the city and the community. In 1968, the Yow Yee flexed its arms, challenging the "Six Company," the voice and sole power source of the Chinese community since the 1800s, by demanding they take effective measures to influence changes within City Hall. Neither community leaders nor local politicians appreciated such an advancement. After the president of the Yow Yee was threatened by "elders" in the community and forced to resign (Takagi and Platt, 1972), the group understood that they had to rely on illegal sources of money.

Members realized they had power in numbers, yet they still lacked sufficient resources to instill social and economic change. Disillusioned with conventional means and left with few other choices for survival, the group turned the collection of donations into a form of extortion—stores and restaurants were coerced into paying "protection money." Refusal to comply resulted in the destruction of property. This change in the Yow Yee's behavior and attitude propelled them to the status of a criminal street gang.

Certain tongs grew intolerant of the Yow Yee's advancements and feared that violent youths would threaten the tourist industry in Chinatown. The Bing Kung Tong issued a public notice that stated if the gang interfered with any of its member's stores or restaurants, they would be dealt with severely. The Suey Sing Tong took under its aegis a group comprised of other immigrant youths with no allegiance to the Yow Yee in order to combat these aspiring youths. While this gang adopted the name Suey Sing, which is a tong name, it did not necessarily mean that gang members were tong members. A small war took place between the Yow Yee and the Suey Sing in which several Suey Sing gang members were killed. After suffering defeat, the Suey Sing moved its illegal operations across the bay to Oakland's own growing "Chinatown." This victory increased the Yow Yee's power in San Francisco, while certain individuals in the gang believed the primary goal of the gang had not yet been achieved. They neither had a respectable position within the community nor did they have adequate resources to continue.

A crucial turning point occurred when some members of the Yow Yee and the Hop Sing Tong came to an agreement. The Hop Sing witnessed the rise of the Yow Yee and seized the opportunity to influence and use the group to carry out its illegal activities. Certain tongs needed youths to ensure the smooth operation of the gambling houses—they needed guards, escorts for gamblers with large sums of money, lookouts for police raids, and especially people to collect gambling debts (Sung, 1987: 138).

Traditionally, the tongs hired "hatchetmen," who gained their title from splitting heads with hatchets (Posner, 1988), but the Hop Sing realized that the youths would be more efficient in dealing with the growing number of other youth gangs. Members of the Yow Yee were proven to be quick-tempered, street smart, and willing to kill. Moreover, many were under the age of eighteen so that, if caught, they received leniency from the juvenile justice court. In turn, the tong provided gang members with housing, food, and money. When asked if gangs were necessary in the Chinese community, a person who works closely with gang members replied:

(R) Without a doubt. You have to have them.
(I) For?
(R) What do you do, hire the cops to protect your gambling parlor? If you find Chinese people, you find gambling. There's no fucking doubt. What are they going to do, go to the police and say, "Can you check my gambling joint after 2:00 in the morning?" There's no way. And when they gamble, they don't gamble like the old people with $2 or $5. The real gamblers, they gamble big stakes, so you need protection. Along with gambling, there's always the drinking. You don't find gambling without Hennessy or Courvoisier. You would never survive. So along with the drinking, you always find the quaaludes, the downers, and on and on. Cause where there's gambling there's drinking, where there's drinking there's drugs, where there's drugs there's women, where there's women, there's prostitution, and it goes on and on, and there's a business. So you can't believe that there will never be gangs in Chinatown.

Prior to any further discussion of the events which followed, it is necessary at this point to clarify the organization of the Asian criminal structure which exists in San Francisco. Chin (1990) outlined four components which made up Asian organized crime: secret societies, triads,[4] tongs, and gangs. Only the two latter elements, however, played any essential part in the history and development of Asian gangs in San Francisco. As described earlier, Asian gangs first appeared when Chinese youths were forced into self reliance when faced with a lack of legitimate opportunities combined with hostility and violence from local youths. This birth occurred with no assistance from any type of organized crime.

However, criminally influenced tong members did play an essential part in changing the activities of gangs by offering them avenues toward different types of illegal activities. This connection between the two entities has been purely financial. Contrary to popular belief, tongs do not have direct control of gangs nor are the arrangements permanent. Tongs members often use certain respectable gang leaders as liaisons between the tong and the gangs in order to carry out specific criminal activities. More often than not, the average gang member is not aware of the particulars of this connection. Tongs have had little to do with the actual recruitment of gang members; they only play a part in financing the gang. In doing so, they enable selected gangs to become recognized and powerful.

In certain instances, tongs have played a pivotal role in the survival of certain gangs. Older gang members who advise less experienced members are essential in the perpetuation of a gang. Often, though, elder gang members are tempted to quit the gang in order to pursue conventional lives. However, tongs offer opportunities to young men that are almost irresistible. Hence, gang leaders will continue the recruitment process in order to further their own interest and thus the gang will survive.

Warfare in the 1970s

Some members of the Yow Yee refused to be associated with the Hop Sing. Receiving financial backings from a tong meant that the group was under the indirect leadership and control of the tong concerning illegal activities. According to one member of the opposing party:

(R) Some of us wanted the action, the backings from the associations. That was where all the money was at. But if you have the backing of the associations, you had to do everything that they said or they can cut you off. We were Yow Yee. We wanted to do what's right, to have the guts to do what's right. Many of us didn't believe that working for the tong was what's right.

The group broke into two factions after serious disputes. The faction which opposed any ties with the tongs renamed the group "Chung Yee," which stands for "Guts and Righteousness," or "to have the guts to do what's right." The police and the media referred to the gang as the "Joe Fong Gang" or the "Joe Boys" after Joe Fong, one of the "elders" in the group. Members of the Chung Yee refused to acknowledge any name other than Chung Yee. The other faction, which decided to join forces with the Hop Sing Tong, called themselves "Wah Ching," which simply means "Chinese Youth." This split was followed by a decade of war between the two groups.

Since the Wah Ching had the backing of the Hop Sing Tong, the Wah Ching was able to take control of the illegal businesses in Chinatown, such as extortion and the protection of gambling houses. The Wah Ching had their establishments and places of business well protected with foot soldiers. The Chung Yee was no longer able to benefit from the extortion of businesses in

Chinatown, and thus, they had little choice but to leave Chinatown. However, these new areas were not lucrative for this gang since they were generally residential neighborhoods without illegal opportunities; therefore, the group had severe financial difficulties.

Gang warfare became a way of life for gang members. For about ten years, the Chung Yee attempted to regain control of Chinatown to reap its financial rewards. Wars were fought in the public high schools, on the streets, and at local nightclubs. By the mid-1970s, the battles reached enormous proportions. By this time, many gang members carried weapons with them twenty-four hours a day, and were ordered to shoot any opponent they encountered regardless of consequences. A member of the Wah Ching during this time describes the situation:

> (R) Well, to tell you the truth, we were on ludes most of the time. We were luded out. We would get up and go out and try to shoot these people. We didn't even know them. Never spoke to them, they never done nothing to us . . . We didn't have much of a choice. We were supposed to take care of them, and the thing that we did then was, it was called Joe Boy hunting. We woke up and dropped a few ludes, take off in a car, and we would hunt for these guys.

Gang members from both groups were being killed, and others were being incarcerated. In addition, many of the original gang members were now in their mid to late twenties and soon realized the cost of gang participation was becoming too great. Thus, they decided to abandon the gangs and lead conventional lives. However, some hard core members, who were successful with the gang lifestyle and saw that legitimate work had little to offer, continued participation in the gang. Some of these individuals escalated in the hierarchy of the organized criminal network in Chinatown, became tong members, and may be the leaders of gangs today.

As the gangs decreased in number, especially among the Chung Yee, new recruits were needed to replenish the groups. Gang membership became fashionable in the mid 1970s so many youths were eager to belong to one gang or another. The Chung Yee recruited from Washington and Lincoln high schools while the Wah Ching selected youths primarily from Galileo High. Since mostly America born Chinese lived in the Richmond and the Sunset Districts, the areas surrounding Washington and Lincoln High, the Chung Yee started recruiting America born Chinese. Many of these youths were the children of immigrants who had migrated to the United States in the mid-1960s. Concurrently, the Wah Ching were recruiting mostly foreign born Chinese and some American born Chinese from Galileo High. As we will see later, some individuals from this younger generation became active in the 1980s.

The situation came to climax with the Golden Dragon Massacre in 1977.

By this time, the Wah Ching had switched allegiance to the Hip Sing Tong, who had given the gang a better financial offer, while the Hop Sing financed yet another group which now went under the tongs name. On July 4, 1977, the Chung Yee attempted to extort groups of youth selling fireworks in Chinatown. The Wah Ching had already established control over the extortion of fireworks dealers, and thus conflict resulted when the Chung Yee attempted to invade Wah Ching territory. A shootout occurred on Pacific Avenue in which one Chung Yee was killed and another was injured.

As a result of the killing, the Chung Yee conspired to kill as many Hop Sing and Wah Ching as possible at one time. An opportunity arose when a group of Wah Ching and Hop Sing boys were seen eating at a local restaurant, the Golden Dragon. The Chung Yee went into the restaurant and haphazardly opened gunfire, killing five and injuring eleven, none of whom were gang members. This incident proved to be the turning point for both gangs.

The shooting brought swift attention from the police, the mayor, and local Chinatown leaders. The risk of remaining in the gangs soon outweighed the benefits. The chances of getting killed were great, and indeed the death rate was high. Hence, more and more gang members decided to become inactive. In addition, the San Francisco Gang Task Force was formed to specifically deal with the situation in Chinatown. As a result of increased police patrol and surveillance, hard-core gang members as well as criminally influenced Tongs were forced to decrease the visibility of many of their activities. This included the elimination of visible street gangs. At the same time, foot soldiers were constantly harassed by the police, and once arrested, many were banned by the police from returning to Chinatown. Therefore, some members of the Wah Ching and the Hop Sing went underground while others disappeared entirely.

The atmosphere immediately after the Golden Dragon massacre was relatively quiet. The Chung Yee, who lacked financial support from any associations, dispersed entirely, and the Wah Ching decreased in numbers. While some remained active in the Wah Ching, many who fought during the power struggle dropped out of the gang. However, some who were recruited during the end of the war remained in the gang. In the late 1970s, the Wah Ching had a group of foreign born youths and a group of American born Chinese who were eager to be trained and to participate in gang activities. These two groups matured and flourished in the early 1980s.

New Waves of Gangs in the 1980s

Many American born Chinese who were recruited by the Wah Ching several years earlier as youths were ripe for certain gang activities in 1980s. Since they spoke English fluently, the gangs and the associations found certain activities which suited their talents. Some of these jobs included counterfeiting, smuggling, and especially drug dealing. The bulk of the monies to the gang soon came through the distribution of cocaine and quaaludes. The efficiency of drug distribution drew little police attention and therefore allowed this faction of the Wah Ching to exist and prosper in the early 1980s.

Since there was no opposing gang during this time, this group ran amuck in the mid-1980s. These individuals were unfamiliar with the rules and norms of respect and honor that were expected by the older generations of gang leaders and tong members, and many started using the drugs they sold. Consequently, they lost much of the backing of the association. According to an influential member of the Wah Ching at the time:

> (R) Yeah, you know we didn't know any better. We just turned adults. Here we are running loose and there is no one to control us. And everything is just there for the picking. We had all these younger guys that looked up to us. If we told them to do something, they would do it. So all of a sudden, life became one big party.
> (I) You became a big fish in a little pond?
> (R) Yeah, they opened up the vault in the bank and left the doors open, and we walked around and helped ourselves. But our problem was we didn't get along with the "old men." And we never got into position where we got any kind of funding. So that is why, most of the . . . gangs, talking about Chinese, the F.O.B.'s, they usually make their money in gambling and extortion and kickbacks from the older people, whereas the A.B.C.'s are mainly involved in drugs, selling drugs. I mean if you can't communicate, you can see all these old men right, they have a lot of power, and they would fund your group. They would kick back money to you just to keep you in line.

Nevertheless, the financial gains from drug dealing allowed some from this group to venture into more profitable, legitimate businesses while others became independent drug dealers. This faction of the Wah Ching disappeared by the mid 1980s.

Another group of foreign born Wah Ching, mostly from Hong Kong, co-existed with the American born gang. These individuals, who were recruited earlier from Galileo High School, reached their early twenties by this time. Because they spoke Chinese fluently and were more reliable, they were given other tasks by the Hip Sing Tong which suited their unique abilities. This included much of the extortion of Chinatown stores and the guarding and protection of gambling houses. Since the American born group and the foreign born group had different jobs, there was little conflict of interest. The Hip Sing found these youths to be more cooperative and familiar with Chinese codes of behavior than the American born gang members so they received continued support. The foreign born group, with the guidance of the Hip Sing, realized that they needed new recruits in order to replenish the gang and continue its existence.

With the guidance of certain gang leaders, new generations of gangs were born in the early 1980s, and the Wah Ching began to splinter off once again. In the mid-1970s, there was an enormous influx of ethnic Chinese refugees from Vietnam into San Francisco's Tenderloin district. Many children who immigrated at this time reached their teens in the 1980s. These refugees often felt as though they were social outcasts amongst Anglo-Americans as well as with the Chinese community. This group of youths were eager to please and sought a sense of belonging. Many in the Chinese community thought of these youths as fearless and "ruthless" individuals. Certain gang leaders realized their attributes and took the opportunity to recruit and train certain Chinese Vietnamese youths for gang activities.

In the early 1980s, the Wah Gay, a Chinese Vietnamese group, was created as a splinter group of the Wah Ching to expand certain illegal activities. By the mid 1980s, this group matured and prospered. Many oriental massage parlors and gambling houses were opened in the Tenderloin by this group. They were also efficient in committing executions due to their willingness to kill and relocate in other states immediately after the task. Like the Chinese youths in the late 1960s, many Chinese Vietnamese youths saw the gangs as a way to improve their own living conditions and to find a place in American society. By the late 1980s, most of the foot soldiers for the Wah Ching were primarily made up of these new immigrants. They were allowed by gang leaders to come into Chinatown to help collect extortion money and guard gambling houses. Certain competent individuals started to deal cocaine for the gang.

As more and more Chinese Vietnamese youths joined gangs, the situation became very disorganized. The Wah Ching splintered off into many different groups with different leaders. With many power struggles taking place, the groups started to fight amongst each other. As members of the Wah Ching recruited youths independently for their own interest, the name Wah Ching (Chinese Youth) no longer had any meaning, since so many opposing groups were once considered Wah Ching. Today, these groups are often identified by the name of their leader.

The early 1980s also saw the rebirth of the Suey Sing gang in San Francisco. Following the lead of the Wah Ching, the Suey Sing Tong began to utilize groups of youths from the same pool of immigrants. Since there was little tension and conflict in the Chinatown during the early 1980s, the Suey Sing saw the opportunity to support a group which frequented local playgrounds in Chinatown. The Suey Sing's intent was to re-establish its illegal gambling operations in Chinatown. In order to do so, they needed a gang to deter opposition from the proprietors of other gambling halls.

Since the Suey Sing gang was a small and tight knit group, they soon grew in strength and power. By the late 1980s, the Suey Sing Tong had opened several gambling houses in Chinatown and was intent on taking over all the illegitimate businesses in Chinatown.

The 1990s

More recently, the Suey Sing gang is a power to be reckoned with since taking over the extortion and protection of several other gambling houses, which were run by Wah Ching. The Suey Sing, under the direction of young gang leaders aspiring for powerful positions, began its reign in 1990 by brutally executing several influential Wah Ching leaders and threatening the lives of any opposing groups. Although several incidences of retaliation were attempted, none of the array of "Wah Ching" groups were able to organize its forces to prevent the advances of the Suey Sing. Today, this group dominates virtually all the gambling and protection operations in the San Francisco Bay Area.

Over the past two years, journalists, police officials, and political leaders have speculated that triads, presented as strictly criminal syndicates from Hong Kong, are attempting to move into the San Francisco Bay Area before Hong Kong reverts back to Chinese communist rule in 1997. Law enforcement officials insist that these Hong Kong groups, the Wo Hop To in particular, are currently moving into San Francisco's and Oakland's Chinatowns and attempting to take control of illegal activities in Asian communities, and this may be the cause of recent acts of violence. Most observers consider the Suey Sing to be this new organization.

The results of this study, however, indicate that recent reports may be exaggerated. The Suey Sing gang is currently financed by an alleged member of a triad, the Wo Hop To, and some new members who have been recently recruited into the gang may refer to the gang as the Wo Hop To, but there is little evidence to indicate an intricate connection between the entire triad organization in Hong Kong and the gang in San Francisco. The suggestion that a sophisticated network controlled from abroad exists ignores the logistical problems inherent in exercising minute control of the activities of gang members in San Francisco. A far more likely scenario would not preclude the ability of triad membership from having profound influences on general trends among criminal activities in San Francisco.

While there may be some actual Wo Hop To triad members in San Francisco, there are few new players in the Chinese community. Those who are active in the gang today are the same individuals who have been living in San Francisco for at least the past decade. There is no evidence in this investigation to indicate that the Wo Hop To is moving en masse to control street gangs. The Suey Sing gang was already on the rise while the Wah Ching was in decline before the Suey Sing ever received any support from a triad member.

Conclusion and Discussion

With the exception of a few American born Chinese gangs, the history of Asian gangs in San Francisco has been profoundly influenced by patterns of immigration combined with American society's rejection of its new immigrants. In the mid 1960s, San Francisco's inability to accommodate the needs of a new influx of Chinese from Hong Kong spurred a joint effort among immigrant youths to improve living conditions. After several futile attempts to gain funding from the City and the Chinese community, these youths were left with few opportunities. Disillusioned, many turned to utilitarian crime in order to survive. Incidents of violence and harassment from existing Chinese gangs and other ethnic groups also contributed to the perceived necessity amongst certain immigrant youths to band together. Modern Chinese gangs were born from resistant and oppressive forces in San Francisco which were reluctant to allow recent Chinese immigrants to become a part of the community.

Another factor which has impacted the history of Asian gangs is the intervention of organized crime. Tong members refused to support the gangs until they realized that they could receive a service in return. Certain gangs committed crimes for specific tong members who in turn supported the gang, provided for its needs, and gave gang members many additional illegitimate opportunities. This intervention of organized criminal influence changed the face of Asian gangs. The objective of gang leaders and, in turn, the existence of gangs became mostly financial.

Power struggles between gangs were often the indirect result of a single tong's attempt to dominate illegal operations in the Chinese community. Opposition can come from other tongs who financed another gang or from gangs with no allegiance to tongs. Dominant tongs often chose to financially support gangs which were powerful. However, this relationship is usually tenuous, depending on the reliability of the gang. Gangs which received continued backing from criminally influenced tongs survived while those with no basis of financial support dispersed.

Historically, gangs tend to recruit youths with little to gain from legitimate routes and who were apt to commit crimes. In the early 1980s, Chinese immigrant children from Vietnam immigrated to America bringing with them the experiences of a war torn country. Chinese Vietnamese encountered similar social problems and blocked opportunities which the Chinese youths from Hong Kong in the 1960s endured. Throughout the 1980s, gang leaders found that ethnic Chinese from Vietnam were most suited for criminal activities. As more and more Chinese Vietnamese youth immigrated to San Francisco in the late 1980s, participation in Asian gangs drastically increased. Hence the face of Asian gangs now includes many Chinese Vietnamese.

Today, a new wave of immigrant children from Southeast Asian countries such as Laos, Thailand, and Cambodia are facing similar, if not worse, adjustment problems in San Francisco. There has been evidence that a Cambodian gang is on the rise in various parts of the Bay Area. Although the data are inconclusive, Cambodian youths may be forming some connections with traditional Chinese groups. If more and more immigrant youths are unable to find a niche in conventional American society, and if we adhere to the cliche that history repeats itself, new generations of Southeast Asian gangs will arise in San Francisco, power struggles will continue, and people will die.

Notes

1. The author worked closely with the Asian Youth Center, the Chinatown Youth Center, and the Vietnamese Youth Development Center.

2. The English translation of the word "tong" is simply a gathering place or hall. Tongs were first established in the United States in San Francisco by one of the first wave of Chinese immigrants during the mid 1880s. Prior to the emergence of tongs, the Chinese community was controlled by family or district associations. Immigrants who were not accepted by these associations banded together and formed tongs. Due to the secretive nature of the tongs and the strong alliance among them, they soon overpowered the elite family associations (Chin, 1990). According to the Attorney General (1972, 1986) and law enforcement officials, tongs are now criminal organizations involved in heroin smuggling, prostitution, opium smoking, gambling, extortion, and blackmail (Chin, 1990).

3. The primary purpose for the formation of tongs was to help recent immigrants with the difficulties of adjusting to a new country and foreign culture. Activities which were considered illegal in the United States were not thought of as being illegal to the Chinese. It should also be noted that tongs do not exist solely for organized crimes; they are considered by many to be social clubs. Not all tongs are involved with illegal activities, and for those that are, only certain individuals are heavily involved. The FBI terms these tongs as "criminally influenced tongs."

4. Triads are secret societies formed in the seventeenth century by Chinese officials and the alienated poor in China (See Chin 1990, for a detailed discussion). Although triads were founded for political and revolutionary purposes, they are thought to have evolved into intricate criminal organizations which focus on the production and distribution of heroin and opium.

References

Abbot, K. And E. Abbot. (1968). "Juvenile Delinquency in San Francisco's Chinese American Community." *Journal of Sociology* 4:45–46.

PART 3 / THE DEMOGRAPHICS OF GANGS

Attorney General, State of California. (1972). *Proceedings of the Conference on Chinese Gang Problems*. California Organized Crime and Criminal Intelligence Branch (March).

Biernacki, P. and D. Waldorf. (1981). "Snowball Sampling: Problems and Techniques of Chain Referral Sampling." *Sociological Methods and Research* 10:141–63.

Chin, K. (1990). *Chinese Subculture and Criminology: Non Traditional Crime Groups in America*. Westport, CT: Greenwood Press.

Chin, S. (1991). "Viet Youths Find a Niche in Crime." *San Francisco Examiner*. April 29: A1.

Cloward, R., and L. Ohlin (1960). *Delinquency and Opportunity: A Theory of Delinquent Gangs*. New York: Free Press.

Cohen, A. (1955). *Delinquent Boys: The Culture of the Gang*. New York: Free Press.

Fagan, J. (1989). "The Social Organization of Drug Use Among Urban Gangs." *Criminology* 27:633–99.

Furillo, A. (1991). "Reputed Gang Leader Slain." *San Francisco Examiner*. April 20: A1.

Haines, D., D. Rutherford, Dorothy and P. Thomas. (1981). "Family and Community among Vietnamese Refugees." *International Migration Review* 15:310–19.

Haskell, M. And L. Yablonsky. (1970). *Crime and Delinquency*. Chicago: Rand McNally and Company.

Henkin, A., and L. Nguyen. (1981). *Between Two Cultures: The Vietnamese in America*. Saratoga, CA: Century Twenty-One Publishing.

Jackson, P.G. (1989). "Theories and Findings about Youth Gangs." *Criminal Justice Abstracts* June: 31–32.

Joe, D., and N. Robinson. (1980). "Chinatowns Immigrant Gangs." *Criminology* 18:337–45.

Joe, K. (1981). "Kai-Dois (Bad Boys) Gang Violence in Chinatown." Presented Sixth Annual Undergraduate Research Conference, Rho Chapter, California Alpha Kappa Delta, University of California, Los Angeles: May 9. (Unpublished)

Klein M. (1969). "Violence in American Juvenile Gangs." In Mulvihill and Tumin (ed.), *Crimes of Violence*. National Commission on the Causes and Prevention of Violence. Pp. 107–22.

Kwong, P. (1987). "Tongs, Gangs, and the Godfather." In *The New Chinatown*. New York: Hill and Wang.

Montero, I. (1979). *Vietnamese Americans: Patterns of Resettlement and Socioeconomic Adaptation in the United States*. Boulder, CO: Westview Press.

O'Connor, J. (1991). "U.S. City Cops Brace for Asian Gang Wars." *San Francisco Examiner*, July 31: A1.

Posner, G.L. (1988). *Warlords of Crime*. San Francisco: McGraw-Hill.

President's Commission on Organized Crime. (1984). "Organized Crime of Asian Origin." *Record of Hearing III*, New York.

Rice, B. (1977). "The New Gangs of Chinatown." *Psychology Today* 10: 60–69.

Sollenberger, R.T. (1968). "Chinese-American Child-Rearing Practices and Juvenile Delinquency." *Journal of Social Psychology* 74:13–24.

Sung, B. (1977). *Gangs in New York's Chinatown*. New York: Center for Migration Studies.

_____. (1987). "The Deviants-Chinatown Gangs." In *The Adjustment Experience of Chinese Immigrant Children in New York City*. New York: Center for Immigration Studies. Pp. 136–163.

Takagi, P., and A. Platt. (1978). "Behind the Gilded Ghetto: An Analysis of Race, Class, and Crime in Chinatown." *Crime and Social Justice* Spring-Summer: 2–25.

Thrasher, F. (1927). *The Gang: A Study of One Thousand Three Hundred Thirteen Gangs in Chicago*. Chicago: University of Chicago Press.

Van de Kamp, J., Attorney General, State of California (1986). "Organized Crime in California." Annual Report to California Legislature.

Yablonsky, L. (1959). "The Delinquent Gang as a Near-Group." *Social Problems* 7:108–17.

_____. (1962). *The Violent Gang*. New York: Macmillan.

Part 4

Gang Activity— Drugs and Violence

If you ask a member of the general public how drugs and violence relate to gang activity, that person might be surprised that you would even ask. To most people, drugs and violence are synonymous with gangs. However, the articles in this section show that the picture is a little more complicated than that.

Esbensen and Huizinga begin this section with an examination of the relationships between gangs, drugs, and delinquency. Their article is based on research resulting from the Denver Youth Survey and they explore the prevalence of gang activity, the demographic composition of the gangs in the Denver area, the amount of illegal activity engaged in by gang members, and the temporal relationship between delinquency and gang involvement. Esbensen and Huizinga found in their research that gang involvement is a relatively rare event, even among at-risk youngsters. As was discussed in part 1, if the definitions are changed, different levels of gang activity result. Unlike previous researchers, Esbensen and Huizinga found females to constitute as much as 25 percent of gang membership. Finally, these authors found that while gang members were more delinquent than their nongang counterparts, the tendency toward delinquent activity begins at least two years prior to gang identification and involvement. Therefore, gang intervention strategies must be aimed at youngsters heading toward delinquent careers and not wait until formal gang identification has been established.

In the second article, Klein, Maxson, and Cunningham examine the relationship of "crack" cocaine, street gangs, and violent behavior.

Their research project examined the files of the Los Angeles Police Department and the Los Angeles County Sheriff's Department to determine the extent of gang involvement in crack trafficking and the connection between the crack cocaine trade and gang violence. Klein and his colleagues found that crack sales grew dramatically from 1983 to 1985 in the City of Los Angeles and in Los Angeles County and, although there was an increase in gang members distributing this drug, most of the increase in gang involvement was in what the authors characterized as the "street level of sales." The most important conclusion of this article, although not one well-received by many law enforcement authorities, is that drugs and gang activity may occur together (what researchers call correlations), but they are not "a single, comprehensive social problem."

The next article is part of the larger gang research effort out of Southern California. Maxson, Gordon, and Klein return to an issue addressed in part 1: a search for definitions. Here they probe the distinction between gang and nongang homicides and how these events are treated by law enforcement agencies. They examined the records of over seven hundred gang and non–gang-related homicides (as classified by the Los Angeles Police Department and the Los Angeles County Sheriff's Department) to determine the differences in how these events were classified and how they were responded to. Maxson and her colleagues found that gang-related homicides were qualitatively and quantitatively different from nongang homicides. In particular, gang homicides were more likely to occur in public, to involve the use of automobiles and firearms, and to result in other offenses and injuries to other victims. However, these researchers found relatively few "innocent bystanders" as victims in these offenses.

David Curry and Irving Spergel have been among the most prolific of the recent authors and researchers on gangs. In their article, they analyze the differences between gang crime and other forms of delinquency and the relationships among social disorganization, poverty, and gang activity. They conclude that gang homicide rates and general delinquency rates are distinct social phenomena. In fact, gang homicide rates were much more related to theories of social disorganization and poverty than were other types of delinquency. Therefore, the growth and spread of gangs may be much more a function of notions associated with social disorganization and poverty than some type of criminal conspiracy. If this is indeed the case, then gangs develop and grow because of factors in the immediate social environment much more than through "franchising."

In the final chapter in this section, Kennedy and Baron examine the extent to which routine activities theory helps us understand the subculture of violence found in a delinquent street group. This group, while not specifically identified as a gang, was comprised of punk rockers associated with violence. The data gathered came from unstructured interviews and field observations of thirty-five members of a punk group from a mid-size city in Western Canada. The authors of this article found that routine activities theory was not sufficient to explain how this group's interactions turned violent. Instead, they recommend for such studies that researchers combine routine activities with a choice component and then to integrate these elements with a subcultural approach to studying group activity. Again, all of these efforts provide us with other ways of understanding gangs and gang behavior and with other small pieces of the gang puzzle.

Questions for Consideration

As you finish reading this section, consider the following questions:

1. Are drugs a necessary part of youth gang activity?
2. What types of drug involvement might differing gangs exhibit?
3. If one or more gang members are involved in drug trafficking, does this make the drug activity a "gang" activity?
4. Which comes first, drug use, violence, or gang identification? How can we know?
5. What purposes would violence serve in the context of gang involvement?
6. What do the various theories or the recent research undertaken tell us to help us understand how drugs and/or violence play a part in the gang mosaic?

14

Gangs, Drugs, and Delinquency in a Survey of Urban Youth

Finn-Aage Esbensen and David Huizinga

Gang-related research can be traced back to the early part of this century (e.g., Asbury, 1927; Puffer, 1912; Thrasher, 1927) and has been closely associated with the development of criminological theory. During the 1950s, coinciding with the media coverage of gangs, social science researchers and theorists such as Cohen (1955), Miller (1958), and Cloward and Ohlin (1960) paved the way for subsequent researchers in the scientific study of gangs (e.g., Klein, 1971; Moore, 1978; Short and Strodbeck, 1965; Spergel, 1966). These research efforts were either generally grounded in prior theory or interested in testing new theoretical explanations of gang delinquency. By the 1970s, however, interest in gangs had become passe and some wondered if gangs had met their demise (Bookin-Weiner and Horowitz, 1983).

It was not until the urban gang violence of the early and mid-1980s that academic and media attention once again focused on the gang problem. As with most of the early gang studies, the majority of recent gang research has relied on observational methods and has produced a wealth of information about specific gangs and their members (e.g., Campbell, 1991; Hagedorn, 1988; MacLeod, 1987; Sullivan, 1989; Vigil, 1988). Relatively few gang research projects have used survey methods, however. Notable examples of survey research on gangs include Bowker and Klein (1983), Esbensen et al. (1993), Fagan (1989), Klein (1971), Morash (1983), Thornberry et al. (1993), and Winfree et al. (1991). With the exception of Fagan's (1989) reliance on a snowball sample of gang members, the other studies cited relied on more representative samples of youths.

In addition to observational and survey methods, other gang researchers have relied on law enforcement records to examine gang offenses and to describe gang members. Klein and Maxson (1989) and Spergel (1990) dis-

---

Reprinted with permission from *Criminology*, Vol. 31, No. 4 (1993): 565–586.

cussed the extent to which official data provide rather subjective assessments of gang behavior.[1]

While research design and methods of data collection have been varied and the generalizability of results has been questioned, concern has also been raised with regard to the applicability of the old gang knowledge to the new gang situation. Hagedorn (1988), for instance, noted the changing nature of the ethnic–racial composition of inner cities and the lack of contemporary research to address the current status of gangs. While being rather critical of prior gang research, he noted that "the theories of the fifties and sixties were rigorously examined by sociologists and for the most part failed to stand the test of empirical verification" (p. 27). A number of other gang commentators have echoed the need for further theoretical and empirical examination of gang formation and behavior. Interestingly, one point of consensus in the voluminous gang literature is the high rate of criminal activity among gang members. Regardless of methodology and design, the consensus is that gang members commit all kinds of crimes at a greater rate than do nongang members.

The call for more empirical analysis of gangs in conjunction with the consistent finding of high rates of offending by gang members provided the impetus for conducting the analyses reported here. Despite almost a century of gang research, an important question (and the one guiding this research) remains: Are gang members more delinquent because of their gang affiliation or were they predisposed to delinquent activity prior to their gang initiation? That is, is the gang unit a criminogenic peer group, do delinquent youths seek out gangs, or do both processes occur? Using longitudinal data from the first four years (1988–1991) of the ongoing Denver Youth Survey (DYS),[2] we examine the temporal ordering of gang membership and involvement in delinquent activity.

Study Description

Sample and Ecological Areas

In order to ensure sufficient numbers of serious or chronic juvenile offenders in a household sample of Denver, we identified "high-risk" neighborhoods from which to select prospective respondents.[3] Based on the results of earlier studies, we selected thirty-five variables from the 1980 census data representing seven conceptual areas: family structure, ethnicity, socioeconomic status (SES), housing, mobility, marital status, and age composition. Using a factor analysis of variables within each of these seven conceptual domains, we identified 11 distinct factors. Four of the theoretically derived concepts identified above produced two distinct factors. The socioeconomic domain, for example, resulted in the identification of an upper SES (e.g., high education, household income over $40,000, and professional and managerial occupations) and a lower SES factor (e.g., families in poverty, incomes under $10,000, and laborer occupations).

We subsequently ran a cluster analysis to identify and combine similar block groups of the city. Seven distinct clusters emerged, three of which we very loosely identified as being "socially disorganized." The first cluster or grouping of block groups was economically disadvantaged; it had high rates of poverty and unemployment and high numbers of unemployed school-dropout youths. It also had a high racial mix (white, African-American, and Hispanic), and high rates of single-parent households and persons per room (density). The second cluster was also economically disadvantaged, although not as severely as the first: it had a highly mobile population, many unmarried persons and few intact families, and many multiple-unit dwellings. The third cluster was a predominantly minority cluster (African-American) with higher than average rates of single-parent and unmarried-person households and a high rate of persons per room.

The geographic areas covered by these clusters include areas identified by arrest data from the Denver Police Department as having high crime rates. Using arrest data, we identified those neighborhoods within the socially disorganized areas that were in the upper one-third of the crime distribution.[4] These socially disorganized, high-crime areas became the neighborhoods for inclusion in the study sample. Although this sample selection precludes generalizations to the total disorganized areas, it ensures that youths living in these areas are likely to be in highly criminogenic environments as well, and it is to these disorganized, high-crime areas that findings apply. A more detailed description of the sampling design and the social ecology analysis is provided in Esbensen and Huizinga (1990).

Selection of Respondents

The overall design of the ongoing research project is based on a prospective, sequential longitudinal survey. The longitudinal survey involves a sequence of annual personal interviews with a probability sample of five birth cohorts. At the point of the first annual survey, the birth cohorts were seven, nine, eleven, thirteen, and fifteen years of age. Assuming the period effects between adjacent cohorts are not too large, the use of these birth cohorts (samples) results in overlapping age ranges during the first four years of the study, which allows examination of developmental sequences across the full span from age seven to eighteen.

To identify study participants, a stratified probability sample of 20,300 households was selected from the 48,000 in the targeted households. Then, a screening questionnaire was used to identify those households that contained an appropriately aged respondent (i.e., seven, nine, eleven, thirteen, or fifteen years old). This sampling procedure resulted in 1,527 completed interviews in the first year (a completion rate of 85 percent among identified eligible youths); the youths were distributed across the five cohorts. Fifty-two percent of the sample are male, 48 percent female; 33 percent are African-American, 45 percent Hispanic, 10 percent Anglo, and 12 percent "other" (primarily Asian and native American).

Annual retention rates for the first four annual in-person interviews have been high by prevailing standards, 91 percent to 93 percent,[5] and complete data covering all four years are available for 85 percent of the original sample (some youths not interviewed in a given year are located and interviewed in later years). In this paper, only data from the three oldest cohorts are used for the full analyses because of the distinctly different developmental stages represented by the two youngest cohorts (aged seven and nine during the first annual data collection), for whom gang involvement was not a major factor. Data for the nine-year-old cohort, however, were included in the specific analyses for years three and four, when these youths were aged eleven and twelve.[6]

Methods

Definitions of Gangs and Gang Membership

Arriving at a definition of the term *gang* is no simple task; considerable debate exists regarding an appropriate definition (see Covey et al., 1992). We have adopted the position espoused by Miller (1974) and Klein and Maxson (1989), that is, in order to be considered a gang, the group must be involved in illegal activity.

Considerable data about gang membership were collected during the survey's ninety-minute, in-person interviews. One early finding from this line of questioning was that approximately 5 percent of youths in the DYS indicated that they were gang members in any given year (thirty-nine in wave one, thirty-seven in wave two, forty-one in wave three, and seventy-six in wave four). Respondents were asked early in the interview if they were "members of a street or youth gang." All those responding affirmatively were later asked a series of questions about their gangs. Examination of this follow-up information indicated that what some of the youths described as gangs could best be defined as informal youth groups, or in some instances, church groups, that did not necessarily include involvement in delinquent behavior. As mentioned above, to be considered a gang member, the youth had to indicate that the gang was involved in illegal activity. An affirmative response to either of two follow-up questions (i.e., perceived gang involvement in fights with other gangs and participation in illegal activities) was used to exclude nondelinquent gangs from the analysis. While the exclusion of respondents who indicated their gang was not involved in these activities reduced the number of potential gang members to twenty-seven in wave one, thirty-three in wave two, thirty-two in wave three, and sixty-eight in wave four, this process permits a more stringent and, arguably, more accurate description of juvenile *delinquent* gang membership and activity. The thirty-two gang members in wave three represent 2.7 percent of the general sample of youths aged eleven to seventeen, and the sixty-eight gang members in wave four represent 6.7 percent of the youths when they were twelve to eighteen years of age. From this, one might conclude that gang membership is a relatively infrequent phenomenon in Denver, even among this "high-risk" sample of urban youths.

What are these gangs like? Descriptive data provided by respondents paint a picture of what Yablonsky (1959:109) referred to as "near groups"— groups characterized by limited cohesion, impermanence, shifting membership, and diffuse role definition, but at the same time that had some level of identification as a gang, as evidenced by having a gang name and use of gang colors and initiation rites. Year four data are representative of the descriptive information provided across the four years of data collection: 97 percent of the members indicated their gang had a formal name (thirty-seven gangs were identified by the sixty-eight gang members); 86 percent indicated their gang had initiation rites; and 97 percent reported that their gang had symbols or colors. With regard to shifting membership and impermanence, when asked what role they would like to have or what role they expect to have in the gang someday, over 60 percent of year four gang members indicated that they would like to *not* be a member and expected *not* to be a member sometime in the future.

Self-reported delinquency data were also collected from all respondents. The measures are improved versions of our earlier work (e.g., Huizinga and Elliott, 1986) and avoid some of the problems of even earlier self-report inventories. The measures exclude traditional trivial offenses, such as defying parental authority, and include serious offenses often excluded from early self-report inventories (e.g., rape, robbery, and aggravated assault). Additionally, follow-up questions were included as integral parts of the measures. These follow-up questions allow for determination of the seriousness and appropriateness of initial responses. If, for example, a respondent indicated that he or she had committed an aggravated assault during the prior year but follow-up information revealed that it was accidental and that the victim truly was not injured, the original response would be changed to zero.

For analysis purposes, our delinquency and drug use measures focus on those behaviors often considered to be of greatest concern. To this end, we developed four levels of delinquency: (1) street offending, (2) other serious offending, (3) minor offending, and (4) nonoffending. We used a subset of the street offenses to create a measure of drug sales[7] in order to address the concern that gangs are disproportionately involved in drug distribution (e.g., Fagan, 1989). One gang expert has even suggested that youth gangs of the

1990s have established a national network of drug distribution similar to the "mafia's" alcohol distribution network during prohibition (Taylor, 1990).

Street offenses focus on serious crimes that occur on the street and are often of concern to citizens and policymakers, alike. *Other serious offenses* includes behaviors that, while not in the street crime category, are nevertheless considered as serious delinquency. *Minor offenses* refers primarily to status offenses and other public nuisance type behaviors. These categories of delinquent behavior generally reflect the seriousness weighting used by Wolfgang et al. (1985). We dichotomized *drug use* into alcohol use and "other drug use," including marijuana and other illicit drugs. For the analyses reported below, all youths were categorized based on their most serious level of involvement in delinquency and drug use. Thus, if an individual reported committing a minor, a serious, and a street offense in a given year, that individual was classified as a street offender. . . .

Results

Gang Member Demographics

Gangs have traditionally been thought of as being a predominantly male phenomenon, and relatively few studies have concentrated on female gang members (exceptions include Bowker and Klein, 1983; Campbell, 1990, 1991; Giordano, 1978; Harris, 1988; Morash, 1983; Quicker, 1983). This has resulted in considerable ignorance concerning not only the role of female gang members, but also the number of females involved in gang activity. Campbell (1991) reports a long and rich history of female gangs and female members in male gangs; she suggests that at one point approximately 10 percent of New York City gang members were female, and that female membership might have been as high as 33 percent in one gang. Fagan (1990) reported female gang membership to be approximately 33% in his survey.

The demographic characteristics of both gang and nongang members are presented in table 14.1. As seen there, the DYS data confirm that a significant proportion of all gang members are female—a fact not generally acknowledged in media presentations of gangs. Cross-sectional analysis of DYS gang data reveals that females constituted from 20 percent to 40 percent of gang members during the four-year study period. Thus, while there is evidence that gang members are primarily males, there is reason to believe that females are more involved in gangs than is generally acknowledged. One caveat, however, is that while female gang membership may well be greater than that presented in the popular press, female gang members are less likely to report high levels of involvement in delinquent activity. In wave three, for example, female gang members reported an average individual offending rate of 14.0 on the general delinquency scale, and male gang members reported an average offending rate of 36.9 offenses on that scale.

Table 14.1   Demographic Characteristics of the Denver Youth Survey Sample

	Year 1		Year 2		Year 3		Year 4	
	Gang	Nongang	Gang	Nongang	Gang	Nongang	Gang	Nongang
Sex								
Male, *N*	15	441	27	397	24	555	53	511
Column %	54%	52%	80%	52%	74%	52%	80%	50%
Female, *N*	12	400	7	390	8	514	13	516
Column %	46%	48%	20%	48%	25%	48%	20%	50%
Total *N*	27	841	33	801	32	1102	68	1027
Race								
Af.-Am., *N*	7	320	14	283	15	385	28	371
Column %	26%	38%	42%	37%	48%	36%	42%	36%
Hisp., *N*	16	374	14	352	14	470	35	443
Column %	60%	45%	43%	46%	42%	44%	52%	43%
White, *N*	0	71	2	65	0	104	2	103
Column %		9%	7%	8%		10%	3%	10%
Other, *N*	4	75	1	67	2	110	2	110
Column %	14%	9%	8%	9%	7%	10%	3%	11%
Total *N*	27	830	33	801	32	1102	68	1026
Age, Birthyear								
1972, *N*	14	256	11	226	11	228	18	227
Column %	52%	30%	33%	30%	35%	22%	27%	22%
1974, *N*	10	291	17	268	11	275	20	257
Column %	38%	35%	52%	35%	33%	26%	31%	25%
1976, *N*	3	294	5	273	10	276	24	257
Column %	10%	35%	16%	36%	32%	26%	36%	25%
1978, *N*	—	—	—	—	0	291	5	285
Column %						27%	7%	28%
Total *N*	27	830	33	801	32	1102	68	1027

Note: These data are weighted to represent the stratified sample. As a result, the integral values are approximates and do not always provide the exact percentage.

As with gender, it is often assumed that gang members are youths from ethnic-racial minority backgrounds (e.g., Fagan, 1989; Spergel, 1990). A 1989 survey of law enforcement officials in forty-five cities across the nation found that African Americans and Hispanics made up 87 percent of gang membership (cited in Gurule, 1991). Due to the nature of the DYS sample (78% of the sample is African-American or Hispanic), it is not possible to address the ethnic distribution of gang membership, although it does appear that African-American and Hispanic youths tend to be overrepresented in the DYS gang subsample (ranging from 85% to 94% of gang members in the various years). Given the disproportionate number of minority youths in the sample, however, it should be expected that the majority of gang members would also be African-American or Hispanic.

Gang membership does appear to be somewhat associated with age. In year four, for example, 27 percent of gang members were eighteen years old, 31 percent were sixteen, 36 percent were fourteen years old, and 7 percent were twelve. Given this age distribution, at what age do youths join gangs? Gang members were asked when they joined their gang. Analysis of these responses for year four revealed that most did not join until their teenaged years, although a few respondents did indicate that they joined the gang before the age of twelve.

Gang Delinquency

Are gang members more involved in delinquency than nongang members? Examination of table 14.2 results in a firm yes for males and a qualified yes for female gang members.[8] Both prevalence and individual offending rates for gang members and nongang members are reported for four types of delinquent behavior and two types of drug use during year four. It is important to examine prevalence rates first in that this identifies the number of active offenders involved in each specific behavior.

The prevalence rates for male and female gang members are significantly greater than those for their nongang counterparts. Gang membership is almost synonymous with involvement in all types of delinquency. Male gang members, for example, reported a prevalence rate of .85 for street offenses and .83 for other serious offenses. This is substantially higher than the prevalence rates of .18 and .32, respectively, for nongang males. The difference in prevalence rates is even more pronounced for females; .76 of female gang members

Table 14.2 Year Four Prevalence and Individual Offending Rates (IOR) of Gang and Nongang Members Controlling for Sex

| | Males | | | | | | Females | | | | | |
| | Gang | | | Nongang | | | Gang | | | Nongang | | |
Offense Type	N	Prev.	IOR	N	Prev.	IOR	N	Prev.	IOR	N	Prev.	IOR
Street	53	.85*	22.3**	511	.18	8.3	13	.76*	5.9	515	.07	2.7
Drug Sales	53	.29*	22.8**	511	.03	30.5	13	.18*	10.5	515	.01	6.8
Serious	53	.83*	31.8**	510	.32	10.0	13	.61*	5.1	516	.18	10.0
Minor	49	.87*	29.0**	500	.56	11.6	13	.93*	18.7	499	.54	10.1
Alcohol Use	53	.71*	48.4**	510	.35	24.1	13	.85*	36.9	516	.32	16.7
Other Drug Use	52	.52*	46.8**	491	.13	20.0	13	.69*	11.9	516	.13	23.6

* p <.05 (chi-square).
** p <.05 (T test, separate variance estimate of t).

reported involvement in street offending compared with .07 for non-gang females. For each type of behavior, the prevalence rate for female gang members is consistently greater than that for male nongang members. Gang members during year four report being involved in a variety of delinquent activities; with male prevalence rates ranging between .29 for drug sales and .93 for minor offending, these youths clearly do not specialize in any one type of activity. Nongang members had much lower rates of involvement in all types of delinquent activities and drug use than did the gang members, as evidenced by prevalence rates of .01 and .03 for females and males, respectively, involved in drug sales, and nongang prevalence rates of .07 and .18 for female and male involvement, respectively, in street-level offending (compared with .76 and .85 for female and male gang members).

With respect to the individual offending rates, however, there are no statistically significant differences between female gang and nongang members. Nongang females who were involved in delinquent activity, whether assault, theft, or drug use, reported nearly the same level of activity. Male gang members, however, had individual offending rates, that were two to three times greater than those of nongang males involved in each specific activity, with the exception of drug sales. To illustrate the value of examining both prevalence and individual offending rates, we interpret the street-level offending data for males. While there were only fifty-three male gang members, 85 percent of them (forty-five members) reported involvement in street offenses. Those forty-five gang members reported committing an average of 22.3 offenses per person. This translates into 1,003 (45 × 22.3 = 1,003.5) offenses.[9] For the nongang members, only 18 percent of the 511, or ninety-two males, reported committing street crimes. And, they reported committing only 8.3 offenses per person, for a total of 764 offenses. Thus, while male gang members accounted for only 33 percent of street offenders in year four, they reported committing 57 percent of street offenses.

Additional analyses were conducted to determine if the level of gang involvement was associated with levels of offending. Gang members were categorized as core or peripheral members based on their responses to the question, How would you describe your position in the gang? All those indicating that they were leaders or one of the top persons were classified as core members. All others were considered as peripheral members. No age or sex differences were found between the core and peripheral members. More important, and perhaps somewhat surprising, introduction of this control did not result in any statistically significant differences between the two levels of gang involvement and self-reported delinquency. That is, the peripheral members reported the same level of delinquent activity as did the core members.

With respect to gang activity, gang members were asked a series of questions about the kinds of activities in which the gang was involved. Given our definition of gangs and desire to describe *delinquent gangs*, the responses listed below confirm that in addition to being delinquent gangs, the *perception* of gang members is that members of their gangs are involved in a wide range of illegal activity. While fights with other gangs is the most frequently mentioned form of illegal activity, approximately three-fourths of the gang members reported that their gang was involved in the following: robberies, joyriding, assaults of other people, thefts of more than $50, and drug sales. Clearly, illegal activities are a prominent part of the *perceived* gang experience, and these descriptions coincide with the self-reported levels of delinquency discussed above. It is interesting, however, that only 30 percent of male and 18 percent of female gang members indicated in the self-report inventory that they themselves were involved in drug sales during the preceding year.

Longitudinal Analyses

With four years of longitudinal data available for 85 percent of the original sample, it became possible to examine the stability of gang membership. Consistent with the research literature (e.g., Hagedorn, 1988; Klein, 1971; Short and Strodbeck, 1965; Thornberry et al., 1993; Vigil, 1988; Yablonsky, 1959, 1963), we found gang membership to lack stability.[10] Of the ninety gang youths for whom we have complete data for all four years, 6 percent belonged for three years, and only 3 percent belonged for all four years.

A major purpose of this paper is to address the temporal ordering of delinquency and gang membership. That is, are gang members more delinquent prior to becoming gang members or is the heightened level of delinquent activity contemporaneous with gang membership? And, perhaps equally important, what is the delinquency level of gang members in years following their departure from the gang? Answers to these questions help identify gang influences on behavior and address the often-debated theoretical issue of "feathering versus flocking." Table 14.3 summarizes the relationship between gang membership and street-level offending during the four years examined. This particular analysis is restricted to those youths in the three oldest cohorts for whom complete longitudinal data were available ($N = 730$).

Annual prevalence data illustrate that, overall, gang members were particularly likely to be involved in street offenses during the year in which they were gang members, with lower levels of involvement both before and after their time in the gang. However, the indication is that regardless of their year of membership, youths who have been gang members at some point in time, have higher prevalence rates for street offending than do youths who have never belonged to a gang. Among year one gang members, 72 percent were classified as street offenders. By years two, three, and four, when these youth were no longer in a gang, the percentage of those youths who were street offenders had decreased substantially and was only slightly higher than the prevalence rate for nongang youths. For year two gang members, 23 percent

Table 14.3 Prevalence of Street Offending Among Gang and Nongang Members Controlling for Year of Membership (N = 730)

Year of Gang Membership[a]	N[b]	Prevalence of Street Offending			
		Year 1	Year 2	Year 3	Year 4
Nongang	640	70	72	94	80
		.11	.11	.15	.13
Year 1 Only	10	7	1	2	3
		.72	.09	.20	.28
Year 2 Only	9	2	6	3	3
		.23	.65	.32	.35
Year 3 Only	10	1	2	8	5
		.09	.21	.77	.53
Year 4 Only	31	3	8	12	23
		.10	.25	.39	.74
Years 3 and 4	10	4	7	9	9
		.44	.73	.91	.88
Years 2, 3, and 4[c]	5	3	3	5	5
Years 1, 2, 3, and 4[c]	3	2	3	3	2

Note: These data are weighted to represent the stratified sample. As a result, the integral values are approximates and do not always provide the exact percentage.

a. These refer to consecutive years of membership. An additional 12 youths reported gang membership during 2 nonconsecutive years.

b. The N reflects those cases for which four years of complete data are available. For gang members, complete four-year data are available for 90 of 112 (80%) youths. For nongang youths, complete four-year data are available for 640 of 729 (88%) youths.

c. Samples are too small to allow calculation of reliable prevalence estimates.

were classified as street offenders in year one, sixty-five in year two (when they were gang members), and then 32 percent and 35 percent, respectively, in the two subsequent years when they were no longer in the gang. For youths who were gang members during year three or year four, a gradual increase in the number of street offenders can be seen prior to their joining the gang, and then a sharp increase in the prevalence rate over the year immediately preceding gang membership (from 21% to 77% for year three gang members and from 39% to 74% for year four members). The prevalence rates of street offending for stable gang members, that is, those reporting gang membership for two or more consecutive years, exceed those of the transient, one-year only members.

In table 14.3 we controlled for the actual years of gang membership and the prevalence of street offending, which permitted examination of stable and transient members. Due to the low number of stable gang members and interest in other delinquency measures, in table 14.4 we report differences in the prevalence rate between gang members and nongang youths for two types of delinquency (street-level offending and other serious offenses) and illicit drug use. In this table, the behavior of gang members in a specific year is tracked for the four-year study period. This means that the stable gang members are included in multiple years, which inflates the overall pattern. However, we thought it inappropriate to exclude stable members from the analysis.

In table 14.4, *year of gang membership* refers to all those individuals who reported belonging to a gang that year. *Prevalence of offending* refers to whether these individuals reported engaging in any of the specified behaviors in each year. Consistent with the detailed findings for street offending reported in table 14.3 prevalence rates for each type of behavior are highest during the gang member's year of actual gang membership. For example, among the year three gang members, 43 percent committed street offenses in year one, 55 percent in year two, 90 percent in year three, and 77 percent in year

Table 14.4 Prevalence of Street Offending, Serious Offending, and Illegal Drug Use among Gang and Nongang Members

| Year of Gang Membership | Sample Size | | Prevalence of Offending | | | | | |
| | | | Street Offenses | | Serious Offenses | | Illicit Drug Use | |
	Gang	Nongang	Gang	Nongang	Gang	Nongang	Gang	Nongang
Year 1 Membership								
Year 1 Behavior	25	835	.85*	.15	.93*	.36	.42*	.13
Year 2 Behavior	25	766	.41*	.15	.61*	.32	.52*	.15
Year 3 Behavior	21	782	.39*	.20	.51	.36	.36*	.14
Year 4 Behavior	22	779	.40*	.19	.48	.30	.27	.19
Year 2 Membership								
Year 1 Behavior	32	757	.50*	.13	.66*	.37	.29*	.13
Year 2 Behavior	33	764	.69*	.13	.89*	.30	.47*	.13
Year 3 Behavior	30	737	.59*	.18	.68*	.35	.44*	.14
Year 4 Behavior	30	729	.63*	.18	.70*	.28	.39*	.18
Year 3 Membership								
Year 1 Behavior	31	768	.43*	.13	.53	.37	.23	.13
Year 2 Behavior	29	736	.55*	.14	.67*	.32	.42*	.13
Year 3 Behavior	32	1059	.90*	.15	.75*	.32	.60*	.10
Year 4 Behavior	30	1026	.77*	.15	.66*	.27	.42	.15
Year 4 Membership								
Year 1 Behavior	61	733	.33*	.13	.54*	.35	.13	.13
Year 2 Behavior	60	695	.51*	.12	.73*	.29	.34*	.14
Year 3 Behavior	65	983	.58*	.14	.65*	.31	.37*	.10
Year 4 Behavior	67	1026	.83*	.12	.79*	.25	.56*	.13

* $p < .05$ (chi-square).

four. Each of these prevalence rates is substantially greater than the comparable annual rate for those youths who were not gang members in year three, all of which were between .13 and .15 In separate analyses controlling for gang membership status (i.e., transient and stable), similar differences between gang and nongang youths were found, although the differences between transient members and nongang youth were less pronounced.

Examination of these prevalence rates across years permits an assessment of the temporal relationship between gang membership and delinquency. While some people believe that "birds of a feather flock together," others believe in a socialization explanation (e.g., Elliott and Menard, in press). In table 14.4, there is some evidence to support the selection or "birds of a feather" explanation. Gang members have higher prevalence rates of involvement in delinquency in years preceding their gang membership. Year three gang members, for example, have a higher rate of participation in street offending (.43 compared with .13), but not other serious offenses or illicit drug use, in year 1 than do nongang members. By year two, the prevalence rates for year three gang members are higher than those of the nongang members for all three behaviors, and in year three, the largest discrepancy is noted.

While rates of participation are, in fact, higher in years preceding and during gang membership, table 14.4 also reveals that these rates of delinquent activity decline in years subsequent to gang membership.[11] By year four, the year one gang members are more similar to those youths who reported never having belonged to a gang, although they still report statistically significant higher rates of participation in street offending (40% compared with 19%).

The preceding discussion focused on the prevalence of street offending and other types of delinquency among gang and nongang members. Of equal importance, and essential to the understanding of the level of delinquent behavior, is examination of individual offending rates, or lambda (i.e., average number of offenses per active offender) for these two groups (table 14.5). As with prevalence rates, the individual offending rates of gang members are substantially greater than those of nongang members.[12] As with prevalence rates, gang members clearly have higher offending rates than do nongang members, but this is especially pronounced during the year in which the youths reported being a gang member (e.g., in year two, gang members categorized as street offenders committed an average of 31.2 street offenses each, compared with 7.6 such offenses for nongang members).

Table 14.5 also reveals that the mean number of street offenses committed by gang members in years preceding their joining the gang is significantly higher than that of nongang members, but that in the years following their departure, there is a dramatic reduction, although they remain more delinquent than their nongang counterparts. By year two, for example, there were no statistically significant differences between the year one gang members and

Table 14.5   Individual Offending Rates of Street Offending, Serious Offending, and Illegal Drug Use Among Gang and Nongang Members

| | Individual Offending Rates | | | | | |
| Year of Gang Membership | Street Offenses | | Serious Offenses | | Illicit Drug Use | |
	Gang	Nongang	Gang	Nongang	Gang	Nongang
Year 1 Membership						
Year 1 Behavior	29.2*	6.8	31.4*	8.8	47.4*	15.8
Year 2 Behavior	12.9	6.8	15.0	7.9	34.1	14.9
Year 3 Behavior	7.2	5.9	9.7	5.9	13.1	14.8
Year 4 Behavior	10.7	5.2	17.6*	5.6	26.4	10.9
Year 2 Membership						
Year 1 Behavior	19.7*	4.5	17.3*	7.1	13.0	12.2
Year 2 Behavior	31.2*	7.6	32.2*	11.1	38.2*	17.4
Year 3 Behavior	9.2	8.5	15.3*	6.3	21.0	17.3
Year 4 Behavior	10.8	9.2	11.4	8.1	19.6*	14.9
Year 3 Membership						
Year 1 Behavior	13.9*	2.0	12.7*	5.1	10.6	7.1
Year 2 Behavior	20.9*	2.0	24.8*	7.2	22.3*	8.0
Year 3 Behavior	34.5*	5.7	29.8*	8.3	56.8*	23.3
Year 4 Behavior	22.9*	4.2	29.4*	6.6	38.8	20.1
Year 4 Membership						
Year 1 Behavior	8.8*	1.8	9.1*	3.8	3.6	6.2
Year 2 Behavior	13.4*	1.7	22.1*	4.0	11.2	9.2
Year 3 Behavior	14.4*	2.8	13.3*	5.6	27.0*	11.6
Year 4 Behavior	19.7*	6.7	28.1*	10.0	39.5*	21.7

* $p < .05$ (*T* test, separate variance estimate of *t*).

those who were not gang members in year one. Similarly, by year three, there were no statistically significant differences for street offending and illicit drug use between the year two gang and nongang members.

A popular perception is that gang members are frequent drug users. During their year of membership, gang members reported significantly higher rates of marijuana and other illegal drug use. However, unlike the delinquency measures, drug use prior to and subsequent to gang membership, generally, was not found to be statistically different from the drug use of nongang youths.

In sum, while gang members had higher rates of involvement than nongang members in street offending and other serious offending not only during the year in which they were gang members but also in the years preceding membership, the rate is particularly high and pronounced during the gang years. These higher rates of individual offending, however, decrease substantially once the youths leave the gang. In analyses not presented, this trend is especially pronounced for males in the sample. Illegal drug use fits the same pattern—it is highest during the gang year. However, drug use by gang members is not significantly different from that of nongang members in years when they are not affiliated with a gang.

Summary and Discussion

In the preceding analyses, we addressed three issues: (1) the prevalence and demographic characteristics of gang members in a general survey of urban youths; (2) the relationship between delinquency and drug use among gang youths; and (3) the temporal relationship between offending and gang membership. With regard to the number of urban youths who belong to gangs, two observations should be made. First, even in a sample of high-risk urban youths, gang membership is a statistically infrequent phenomenon. Second, depending on the definition of gang used, different estimates of gang membership are obtained. Prior to controlling for the criminal conduct of gangs, estimates of gang membership were in excess of 5 percent during each study year. However, when the analysis was restricted to youths who belonged to *delinquent* gangs, slightly less than 3 percent of the total sample during years one through three could then be classified as gang members. By year four, when the cohorts were aged twelve to eighteen years, the number of youths reporting to be members of delinquent gangs had increased to almost 7 percent. Such definitionally induced discrepancies in prevalence of gang membership highlight the need to establish consensus on an operational definition of gangs.

As has been repeatedly argued by Klein and Maxson (1989) and more recently by Spergel and Chance (1991), there is considerable need for a uniform definition of gang and gang behavior. Whether from a research or policy perspective, it is important that a common consensus be reached. While the earlier calls for a uniform definition emphasized jurisdictional differences among law enforcement agencies, our research suggests that a common definition should be employed by survey researchers. A uniform definition of gangs and gang behavior would be a point of departure for a better understanding of a phenomenon that may well be substantially distorted because of a lack of a common means for studying, describing, and regulating gang behavior.

The importance of general surveys is highlighted by examination of the demographic characteristics of gang members. Contrary to much prior research on gangs, females were found to be quite active in gangs (approximately 25 percent of gang members during the four-year study period were female). While this is higher than the prevailing stereotype, it is consistent with Fagan's (1990) and Campbell's (1991) estimates. Why is it that so many studies fail to report any substantial involvement of females in gangs? It may be, as Campbell (1991:vii) suggests, that writings about gangs, as well as other social science topics, historically have been written by men about men. Thus, female gang membership may well have been systematically underreported in prior research endeavors. A casual examination of early gang research provides some evidence for this argument. Cohen (1955) and Cloward and Ohlin (1960), for example, excluded females from their research and conceptualizations.

A second possibility is that the reliance on official data or purposive samples of gang members has resulted in a biased representation of not only gang membership, but gang behavior as well. Yet another possible explanation may be associated with the sampling or site selection in the DYS and other general surveys. In any localized survey project, it is possible that a particular site or sample is atypical and nonrepresentative of other populations or sites. However, given the similarity of findings between Fagan's (1990) three-city study and the DYS, the high percentage of female gang members may be an accurate accounting of gang membership in the late 1980s. A fourth possibility is that there has been a historical change in female delinquency or in the role of females in gangs. With respect to this issue, Huizinga and Esbensen (1991) reported no change in self-reported levels of offending among two samples of urban females, one from 1978 and the other from 1989.

Another characteristic of gang membership found to be contrary to widely held, media-promoted stereotypes is the notion that youths become gang members for life. While media accounts generally portray gangs as surrogate families for disenfranchised youths, this view is not supported by our research nor by the majority of gang research of the past three decades (e.g., Fagan, 1989; Hagedorn, 1988; Klein, 1971; Short and Strodbeck, 1965; Thornberry et al., 1993; Vigil, 1988; Yablonsky, 1959, 1963). Very few of the youths in the DYS survey reported being in a gang for more than one year. And, many of those youths in a gang indicated that they would like *not* to be a gang member and expected to leave the gang in the future. It appears that the majority of gang members are peripheral or transitory members who drift in and out of the gang.

With regard to involvement in delinquent activity, gang members were found to be considerably more active in all types of delinquency, including drug sales and drug use, than were nongang members. It is important, however, to provide a caveat concerning gang involvement in drug sales. As concluded by Klein et al. (1991), while drug sales/distribution is an activity engaged in by individual gang members, we did not find evidence that drug sales was an organized gang activity involving all gang members. That is, although 80 percent of the year four gang members indicated that the gang was involved in drug sales, only 28 percent of these very gang members reported that they sold drugs. Further, drug sales is only one of a variety of illegal activities in which the gang is involved. As reported by Fagan (1989), we found that all of the gangs were involved in what Klein (1984) has called "cafeteria-style" delinquency.

The temporal relationship between offending and gang membership is important, and one that can best be examined with longitudinal data of a general population. Participant observation of existing gang members relies on selective retrospective information and generally excludes comparison groups. Cross-sectional surveys cannot examine the developmental sequences that we believe are necessary to explain the process of gang recruitment.

The longitudinal analyses reported here indicate that involvement of gang members in delinquency and drug use is rather strongly patterned. While gang members had higher rates of involvement than nongang members in street crime and other serious forms of offending even before joining the gang, their prevalence and individual offending rates were substantially higher during the actual year of membership. Similar results were also reported in a study of high-risk youths in Rochester, New York (Thornberry et al., 1993). Their findings for "stable" gang members mirrored those reported here. Their "transient" gang members, however, did not appear to have significantly higher rates of offending than nongang members in years prior to or following gang membership. Our findings, in conjunction with those from the Rochester study, lead us to conclude that it is not solely individual characteristics that are associated with higher levels of involvement in street crime. Rather, there may well be factors within the gang milieu that contribute to the criminal behavior of gang members.

Thus, while the high prevalence and individual offending rates prior to gang membership may lead one to espouse the view that they are supportive of a social control perspective, which maintains that people select others of similar values as friends (e.g., Hirschi, 1969), that may be premature. Given that the highest rates of offending occurred during gang years, these data may be more supportive of a learning perspective, which maintains behavior is learned within particular groups and settings (e.g., Burgess and Akers, 1966; Elliott and Menard, in press; Sutherland and Cressey, 1970). A third possibility is what Thornberry et al. (1993:59) have referred to as an "enhancement" model, in which both processes are operative. Without a test of theoretically relevant variables, such conclusions are mere projection. The temporal ordering of such key factors as peer group norms and values and respondent behavior must be examined prior to going beyond the mere speculation stage. Elliott and Menard (in press) have documented with National Youth Survey data that the acquisition of delinquent friends generally precedes the onset of delinquency. The data we have presented suggest that delinquent involvement precedes gang membership. It is here that we do not want to make the tempting juxtaposition and equate gang membership with delinquent friends, for it may well be that gang membership is but a more formalized form of co-offending that was initiated within a delinquent peer group in prior years. Answers to such theoretically important issues should be tested fully, and we hope that our research provides a basis for subsequent work on this issue.

From a policy standpoint, our findings suggest, at least tentatively, that gang intervention strategies should focus not only on decreasing the influence of gangs on individual gang member behavior, but also on the conditions that foster gang development. Although gang members are more highly delinquent than their nongang peers, the trend toward increasing delinquency is prevalent at least two years prior to gang initiation. An important aim should thus be to retard this initial escalation of delinquent activity and disrupt gang effects before peer group behavior becomes formalized within the gang environment.

Notes

1. One common problem, for example, is whether any crime committed by a gang member should be labeled a *gang crime* regardless of the circumstances surrounding the offense. Using law enforcement data from Chicago and Los Angeles, Maxson and Klein (1990) examined gang homicide rates by applying the different definitions of "gang-related" criminal activity used in those two cities. Using the more narrow definition of gang-related homicides employed by the Chicago police (i.e., "a killing is considered gang-related only if it occurs in the course of an explicitly defined collective encounter between two or more gangs"; Maxson and Klein, 1990:77) would reduce the gang homicide rate in Los Angeles by about half. The fact that such discrepancies in prevalence rates can be derived simply by different definitional criteria should cause researchers, theorists, and policymakers substantial discomfort.

2. This research is part of the Program of Research on the Causes and Correlates of Delinquency, with companion projects at the University at Albany-SUNY and the University of Pittsburgh.

3. An apparently recent development in American gang structure or organization is that gangs are no longer confined to "chronic" gang cities but are making an appearance in "emerging" gang cities, often small and medium-sized cities with no history of gang activity (Spergel, 1990:182). According to Lou Lopez, former commander of the Denver Police Department Gang Intervention Program, "the gang influence can be traced back to the late 1970s when Denver Police officers started to notice young Hispanic youth dressed in 'chollo' attire" (Lopez, 1989:i).

4. A number of block groups defined as socially disorganized did not have high crime rates, and, therefore, were excluded from the sample. Conversely, block groups that had high crime rates but were not socially disorganized according to our analysis also were excluded from the high-risk sample.

5. Given that the survey was conducted in "high-risk" neighborhoods with high rates of mobility, these high retention rates are a testament to the diligence and expertise of the field staff involved in tracking respondents throughout the survey.

6. Some concern may be raised by the relatively young age range included in this sample (i.e., ages eleven through eighteen). We acknowledge that others have documented the recent trend of youths remaining in gangs well into their twenties and even thirties. Clearly, the DYS sample is an adolescent sample and may not be representative of gangs in general. As a result of the sampling frame, this sample may contain more "transient" members than would an older sample. Analyses of transient and stable members, however, did not produce different results. This age issue will be addressed as subsequent data waves become available.

7. The drug sale measure consists of two items from the street offending scale. We ran specific analyses to verify that these drug sale items were not "driving" the street offender results.

8. Throughout the analyses reported in this paper, we truncated the self-reported frequency of offending at 99 in order to minimize the effect of "outliers." We also limited the frequency analysis to active offenders and thus use the terms individual offending rates and lambda interchangeably throughout the text to refer to the average offending rate among active offenders. For a discussion of lambda, consult Blumstein et al. (1988).

9. Given what is known about the extent of co-offending among juveniles, it is exceedingly difficult, if not impossible, to make a reasonable transition from offender-specific data to offense data. For example, the fact that twenty youths reported committing an aggravated assault does not necessarily mean that twenty assaults were committed. For discussion of this co-offending issue, consult, for example, Elliott et al. (1985), Fagan (1990), Johnson (1979), and Krohn (1986).

10. In their study of high-risk youth in Rochester, for example, Thornberry et al., (1993) found that 55 percent of gang members were members for only one year.

11. Analyses in which the sample was disaggregated by gender produced similar results for males. Female gang members, however, only had higher prevalence rates than female nonmembers during the actual year of membership.

12. Once again, analyses disaggregated by gender reveal that these differences are more pronounced for male gang members than female gang members. While males seem to be on a trajectory of increasingly higher rates of offending in years prior to gang initiation, as with prevalence rates, females appear to have higher rates of offending primarily only during their actual year of gang membership.

References

Asbury, Herbert. (1927). *The Gangs of New York*. New York: Capricorn.

Blumstein, Alfred, Jacqueline Cohen, and David Farrington. (1988). Criminal career research: Its value for criminology. *Criminology* 26:1–35.

Bookin-Weiner, Hedy and Ruth Horowitz. (1983). The end of the gang: Fact or fad? *Criminology* 21:585–602.

Bowker, Lee H. And Malcolm W. Klein. (1983). The etiology of female juvenile delinquency and gang membership: A test of psychological and social structural explanations. *Adolescence* 18:740–751.

Burgess, Robert L., and Ronald L. Akers. (1966). A differential association-reinforcement theory of criminal behavior. *Social Problems* 14:128–147.

Campbell, Anne. (1990). Female participation in gangs. In C. Ronald Huff (ed.), *Gangs in America*. Newbury Park, CA: Sage.

———. (1991). *The Girls in the Gang*. 2d. ed. Cambridge, MA: Basil Blackwell.

Cloward, Richard A. And Lloyd E. Ohlin. (1960). *Delinquency and Opportunity: A Theory of Delinquent Gangs*. New York: Free Press.

Cohen, Albert. (1955). *Delinquent Boys: The Culture of the Gang*. Glencoe, IL: Free Press.

Covey, Herbert C., Scott Menard, and Robert J. Franzese. (1992). *Juvenile Gangs*. Springfield, IL: Charles C. Thomas.

Elliott, Delbert S. and Scott Menard. (In press). Delinquent friends and delinquent behavior: Temporal and developmental patterns. In David Hawkins (ed.), *Current Theories of Crime and Deviance*. New York: Springer-Verlag.

Elliott, Delbert S., David Huizinga, and Suzanne S. Ageton. (1985). *Explaining Delinquency and Drug Use*. Beverly Hills, CA: Sage.

Esbensen, Finn-Aage and David Huizinga. (1990). Community structure and drug use: From a social disorganization perspective. *Justice Quarterly* 7:691–709.

Esbensen, Finn-Aage, David Huizinga, and Anne W. Weiher. (1993). Gang and non-gang youth: Differences in explanatory variables. *Journal of Contemporary Criminal Justice* 9:94–116.

Fagan, Jeffrey. (1989). The social organization of drug use and drug dealing among urban gangs. *Criminology* 27:633–669.

———. (1990). Social processes of delinquency and drug use among urban gangs. In C. Ronald Huff (ed.), *Gangs in America*. Newbury Park, CA: Sage.

Giordano, Peggy C. (1978). Girls, guys, and gangs: The changing social context of female delinquency. *Journal of Criminal Law and Criminology* 69:126–132.

Gurule, Jimmy. (1991). The OJP initiative on gangs: Drugs and violence in America. *NIJ Reports* 224:4–5.

Hagedorn, John M. (1988). *People and Folks: Gangs, Crime and the Underclass in a Rustbelt City*. Chicago: Lakeview Press.

Harris, Mary G. (1988). *Cholas: Latino Girls and Gangs*. New York: AMS.

Hirschi, Travis. (1969). *Causes of Delinquency*. Berkeley: University of California Press.

Huizinga, David and Delbert S. Elliott. (1986). Reassessing the reliability and validity of self-report delinquency measures. *Journal of Quantitative Criminology* 2: 293–327.

Huizinga, David and Finn-Aage Esbensen. (1991). Are there changes in female delinquency and are there changes in underlying explanatory factors? Paper presented at the Annual Meeting of the American Society of Criminology, San Francisco.

Johnson, Richard E. (1979). *Juvenile Delinquency and Its Origins*. Cambridge: Cambridge University Press.

Klein, Malcolm W. (1971). *Street Gangs and Street Workers*. Englewood Cliffs, NJ: Prentice-Hall.

———. (1984). Offense specialization and versatility among juveniles. *British Journal of Criminology* 24:185–194.

Klein, Malcolm W. and Cheryl L. Maxson. (1989). Street gang violence. In Neil A. Weiner and Marvin E. Wolfgang (eds.), *Violent Crime, Violent Criminals*. Newbury Park, CA: Sage.

Klein, Malcolm W., Cheryl L. Maxson, and Lea C. Cunningham. (1991). "Crack," street gangs, and violence. *Criminology* 29:623–650.

Krohn, Marvin D. (1986). The web of conformity: A network approach of the explanation of delinquent behavior. *Social Problems* 33:s81–s93.

Lopez, Lou. (1989). *Gangs in Denver*. Denver, CO: Denver Public Schools.

MacLeod, Jay. (1987). *Ain't No Makin' It: Leveled Aspirations in a Low-Income Neighborhood*. Boulder, CO: Westview Press.

Maxson, Cheryl L. and Malcolm W. Klein. (1990) Street gang violence: Twice as great or half as great? In C. Ronald Huff (ed.), *Gangs in America*. Newbury Park, CA: Sage.

Miller, Walter B. (1958). Lower class culture as a generating milieu for gang delinquency. *Journal of Social Issues* 14:5-19.

———. (1974). American youth gangs: Past and present. In Alfred Blumberg (ed.), *Current Perspectives on Criminal Behavior*. New York: Knopf.

Moore, Joan W. (1978). *Homeboys: Gangs, Drugs, and Prison in the Barrios of Los Angeles*. Philadelphia, PA: Temple University Press.

Morash, Merry. (1983). Gangs, groups, and delinquency. *British Journal of Criminology* 23:309-331.

Puffer, J. Adams. (1912). *The Boy and His Gang*. Boston: Houghton Mifflin.

Quicker, John C. (1983). *Homegirls: Characterizing Chicano Gangs*. San Pedro, CA: International University Press.

Short, James F. And Fred L. Strodbeck. (1965). *Group Processes and Gang Delinquency*. Chicago: University of Chicago Press.

Spergel, Irving A. (1966). *Street Gang Work: Theory and Practice*. Reading, MA: Addison-Wesley.

———. (1990). Youth gangs: Continuity and change. In Norval Morris and Michael Tonry (eds.), *Crime and Justice: An Annual Review of Research*. Chicago: University of Chicago Press.

Spergel, Irving A. and Ronald L. Chance. (1991). National youth gang suppression and intervention program. *NIJ Reports* 224:21-24.

Sullivan, Mercer L. (1989). *Getting Paid: Youth Crime and Work in the Inner City*. Ithaca, NY: Cornell University Press.

Sutherland, Edwin H. And Donald R. Cressey. (1970). *Criminology*. New York: Lippincott.

Taylor, Carl S. (1990). Gang imperialism. In C. Ronald Huff (ed.), *Gangs in America*. Newbury Park, CA: Sage.

Thornberry, Terence, Marvin D. Krohn, Alan J. Lizotte, and Deborah Chard-Wierschem. (1993). The role of juvenile gangs in facilitating delinquent behavior. *Journal of Research in Crime and Delinquency* 30:55-87.

Thrasher, Frederick M. (1927). *The Gang: A Study of One Thousand Three Hundred Thirteen Gangs in Chicago*. Chicago: University of Chicago Press.

Vigil, James D. (1988). *Barrio Gangs: Street Life and Identity in Southern California*. Austin: University of Texas Press.

Winfree, L. Thomas, Teresa Vigil, and G. Larry Mays. (1991). Social learning theory and youth gangs. A comparison of high school students and adjudicated delinquents. Paper presented at the Annual Meeting of the American Society of Criminology, San Francisco.

Wolfgang, Marvin, Robert M. Figlio, Paul E. Tracy, and Simon I. Singer. (1985). *The National Survey of Crime Severity*. Washington, DC: U.S. Government Printing Office.

Yablonsky, Lewis. (1959). The delinquent gang as a near group. *Social Problems* 7: 108-117.

———. (1963). *The Violent Gang*. New York: Macmillan.

Appendix A: Self-Report Delinquency and Drug Use Scales

Street Delinquency

1. Stolen or tried to steal money or things worth more than $50 but less than $100.
2. Stolen or tried to steal money or things worth more than $100.
3. Stolen or tried to steal a motor vehicle.
4. Gone into or tried to go into a building to steal something.
5. Attacked someone with a weapon or with the idea of seriously hurting or killing them.
6. Used a weapon, force, or strongarm methods to get money or things from people.
7. Physically hurt or threatened to hurt someone to get them to have sex with you.
8. Been involved in gang fights.
9. Snatched someone's purse or wallet or picked someone's pocket.
10. Stolen something from a car.
11. Sold marijuana.
12. Sold hard drugs.
13. Knowingly bought, sold, or held stolen goods or tried to do any of these things.

Other Serious Delinquency

1. Stolen or tried to steal money or things worth more than $5 but less then $50.
2. Stolen or tried to steal money or things worth less than $5.
3. Gone joyriding.
4. Hit someone with the idea of hurting them.
5. Thrown objects such as rocks or bottles at people.
6. Had or tried to have sexual relations with someone against their will.
7. Carried a hidden weapon.
8. Purposely damaged or destroyed property that did not belong to you.
9. Purposely set fire to a house, building, car, or other property or tried to do so.
10. Used checks illegally or used a slug or fake money to pay for something.
11. Used or tried to use credit or bank cards without the owner's permission.

Minor Delinquency

1. Avoided paying for things such as movies, bus or subway rides, food, or computer services.
2. Lied about your age to get into someplace or to buy something.
3. Ran away from home.
4. Skipped classes without an excuse.
5. Hitchhiked where it was illegal to do so.
6. Been loud, rowdy, or unruly in a public place.
7. Begged for money or things from strangers.
8. Been drunk in a public place.
9. Been paid for having sexual relations with someone.

Alcohol Use

1. Drank beer.
2. Drank wine.
3. Drank hard liquor.

Marijuana

1. Used marijuana or hashish.

Other Drugs

1. Used tranquilizers such as valium, librium, thorazine, miltown, equanil, mepro-
   bamate.
2. Used barbiturates, downers, reds, yellows, blues.
3. Used amphetamines, uppers, ups, speed, pep pills, or bennies.
4. Used hallucinogens, LSD, acid, peyote, escaline, psilocybin.
5. Used cocaine, or coke other than crack.
6. Used crack.
7. Used heroin.
8. Used angel dust or PCP.

15

"Crack," Street Gangs, and Violence

Malcolm W. Klein, Cheryl L. Maxson and Lea C. Cunningham

Crack, or "rock" cocaine as it was first known in Southern California, exploded in south central Los Angeles before expanding to other places. Although Inciardi (1988) claims a longer history for crack, the early 1980s can be taken as its point of major initiation. The first major media report appeared in November 1984—"South Central Cocaine Sales Explode into $25 'Rocks'" (*Los Angeles Times*, November 25, 1984). The first article on crack cocaine in the professional literature (Klein and Maxson) appeared in 1985.

Although the history of Hispanic gangs in Los Angeles goes back to the first quarter of this century and that of black gangs to the early 1950s (Klein, 1971; Vigil, 1988), their drug involvement was principally an issue of use, not control of distribution. Significantly, the police and press reports of the Los Angeles crack explosion were that it was intimately tied to gangs and to gang involvement in distribution. The now infamous Crips and Bloods, black gangs prominent in the south central area, were soon singled out, and reports began to emerge of their exporting crack to other cities. Members of a national panel of experts reported, among other things, "growing proof that drugs are contributing to the alarming increase in gang violence" and that the Drug Enforcement Administration "has confirmed the presence of Los Angeles street gang members in forty-nine cities" (McKinney, 1988). Statewide data for California were notably similar in the increasing prevalence curves for gang-related and drug-related homicides over the past ten years (Bureau of Criminal Statistics, 1988).

These are but a few of the indications of a growing belief about a close relationship among crack, gangs, and violence. It is that relationship that is the subject of this paper, and fittingly, it is from the investigative files of the police and sheriff's departments in Los Angeles that the data are taken. These data permit research on the confluence of gang activity and crack distribution, which,

Reprinted with permission from *Criminology*, Vol. 29, No. 4 (1991): 623–650.

according to many enforcement and media reports, has led to unprecedented levels of violence. With other research beginning to yield data on crack elsewhere in the country (Belenko and Fagan, 1987, Inciardi, 1988; Mieczkowski, 1988; Skolnick, 1988), the Los Angeles data provide an early context for understanding some of the empirical and conceptual issues involved.

Further, our research procedures contrast considerably with those reported above, which provides some potential for useful debate. Other crack researchers, to date, have relied principally on ethnographic procedures, but we have employed statistical analyses of data taken from detailed police arrest and investigation files. Both types of data have limitations for establishing prevalence rates of drug sales, but they do complement each other. For example, our conclusions will be seen to be similar to those of Fagan (1989). In this paper, however, it is not prevalence that is at issue, but the specific question of gang involvement and its consequences. It is the gang versus nongang comparison in crack sales that relates to our hypotheses.

The adequacy of our established procedures to address these issues has been documented elsewhere (Klein et al., 1986). The gang/nongang designation, as determined from the extensive gang enforcement units in Los Angeles, has shown major differences in the character of gang and nongang violence (Maxson et al., 1985). Discriminant analyses suggested little impact on these differences attributable to biases in the police reporting, recording, and investigative processes from which gang/nongang designations are derived.

The use of official data to represent the behavior of law violators is always problematic, but extensive work on self-report versus official indicators of crime in the United States and abroad consistently shows concordance (Elliott et al., 1985; Hindelang et al., 1981; Klein, 1989). This has also been demonstrated for drug data (Bonito et al., 1976). There is no evidence in the published literature that this concordance is differentially related to the distinction between gang and nongang youths (Tracy, 1979). Finally, in a study of crack arrests in New York City, Belenko and Fagan (1987) cite several indications of the reliability of their arrest statistics: (a) all officers are *required* to flag any case involving crack, thus at least increasing the reliability of arrest records; (b) 95.9 percent of the arrests were subsequently identifiable in the pre-arraignment files developed for the New York City Criminal Justice Agency; and (c) the reliability is sufficiently high to reveal a series of significant differences between powder cocaine and crack arrestees, the latter being more often male, black, and young and having few verified community ties and less extensive prior records (p. 1, fn. 1; pp. 10–11, fn. 2).

Contrasting Hypotheses

Because our research was designed in a period of ferment, ambiguity, and excitement, it addressed a mixture of immediate practical concerns, longer term policy issues, and conceptual questions raised by our past research on street gangs. Specifically, enforcement and media reports, echoed by political officials, proffered two propositions.

First, due to the advantages of crack over the traditional form of powdered cocaine,[1] neighborhood- and street-level distribution was given to and accepted by local street gangs. The presumed organizational and territorial characteristics of street gangs made them ideal for rapid, organized, and controlled distribution.

Second, widespread gang involvement in distribution would yield substantive differences in various aspects of crack sales incidents, especially an increase in violence associated with them. Gang members, it was asserted, have a high violence potential in any case, and mid-level distributors would employ gang members specifically to enforce their rules and to control territorial "rights."

These organizational and violence propositions, however, contrast significantly with hypotheses that can be derived from the sociological literature on street gangs and from the criminological literature on the relationship between drugs and violence. For instance, several decades of gang research have documented that street gang organization tends to be loose, cohesiveness low, and leadership unstable (e.g., see Hagedorn, 1988; Huff, 1989; Klein, 1971; Short and Strodtbeck, 1965; Vigil 1988; Yablonsky, 1963). Traditional gangs combine poorly connected fringe members with high turnover and a smaller number of close-knit cliques of heterogeneous criminality (Klein, 1971). Only a few of the cliques might provide a basis for concentrated drug involvement (Short and Strodtbeck, 1965; Spergel, 1964).

Thus, although some potential exists for limited exploitation of gang cliques for purposes of crack distribution, a reasonable hypothesis, contrasting with police and press reports, is that street gangs would not become the principal mechanism for crack distribution in their neighborhoods. Some involvement would be predictable, but levels of street gang cohesiveness and organization, and ephemeral gang leadership, would work against a gang's development of effective sales networks.

The second common proposition, that gang involvement is a precursor of greater violence in crack distribution, is less obviously opposed by the literature. It is clear that gang law violators are more criminal and proportionately violent than are nongang offenders (Maxson et al., 1985; Tracy, 1979), but a fair summary of the extensive literature on the drug/violence connection is that this relationship involving drug *use* is weak and inconsistent (e.g., see Blum, 1972; Gandossy et al., 1980), although that involving drug *distribution* is perhaps stronger (Gropper, 1984). This latter conclusion, however, is based on a far more sparse ethnographic and anecdotal literature (see, e.g., McBride, 1981). At the time we undertook our research on crack and gangs, there was no literature on which to base directional hypotheses about the crack/violence

276

connection and, therefore, no empirical base for accepting local enforcement claims about that connection. To the contrary, our hypothesis of limited gang involvement leads as well to a secondary hypothesis of minimal increases in distribution violence attributable specifically to gangs in the crack trade.

In sum, then, public reports of serious gang involvement and consequent increased violence associated with crack distribution accompanied a widely reported increase in crack availability in high gang areas of south central Los Angeles. Those reports are contrasted here with hypotheses derived from the sociological literature on gangs and the drug/violence connection. These hypotheses, of limited gang involvement and gang-derived violence, given the crack explosion, yield two general data predictions in the context of increased crack cocaine sales arrests:

1. Street sales incidents would not show control of crack distribution by street gangs.
2. Evidence would not demonstrate major changes in sales-related violence or in other variables attributable to street gang involvement in sales, either over time or as compared with nongang crack sales.

To state the conclusions early, cocaine sales arrests did increase dramatically. However, accelerations in gang involvement, while evident, were not at the levels we had been led to expect by enforcement and press reports; neither were the differences in sales-related violence. The data are more consistent with predictions derived from the sociological literature. But we must caution the reader about two restrictions. First, the data refer only to arrests. Undetected drug transactions may follow different patterns (but see Fagan, 1989), and they can best be approached by ethnographic and biographical procedures. Second, the data refer to a period ending on December 31, 1985. Since that time, police and press reports have rather consistently reported a continued increase in Los Angeles of crack sales, gang involvement, and violence. Notably, however, some police officials are now acknowledging that gang involvement is mostly limited to special cliques or "drug gangs." Press reports have generally been slow to acknowledge these developments.

We begin our presentation of the study findings by reporting on the extent of cocaine sales incidents and the levels of gang involvement in those incidents. We then turn to the issue of whether gang involvement seems to make a difference. We document which case characteristics—incident, participant, and drug—distinguish gang-involved incidents from others and address whether those characteristics changed while levels of gang involvement in cocaine sales were increasing. Finally, we investigate the concern of violence associated with gangs and crack sales by utilizing two data sources. We report on indicators of violence from the cocaine sales incidents, but we rely chiefly on homicide data to assess gang/drug/violence connections. We report on drug aspects of gang and nongang homicides and look for evidence of increased drug involvement in violent incidents over this time period.

Levels of Gang Involvement in Cocaine Sales

Underlying the aim of assessing the level and increase in gang involvement was the assumption that, as reported in the press, there had indeed been a major increase in cocaine sales since 1982. We begin our analysis by documenting that increase and then describe levels of gang involvement in sales incidents.

Five stations—three from the Los Angeles Police Department (LAPD) and two from the Los Angeles County Sheriff's Department (LASD)—with the highest combinations of cocaine sales arrests and reported gang activity in south central Los Angeles were selected for data collection. The purpose was not to be representative of any geographic area, but rather to capture the phenomena of interest at their points of highest concentration. Arrest logs in the five stations were reviewed for cases having at least one arrest for sale of cocaine (Health and Safety Code, section 11352) or possession for sale (section 11351). Simple possession for use was not included. The average cocaine seizure in our cases was about 13 grams, and cash seizures averaged several hundreds of dollars. Thus, logging *sales* charges was seldom a function of charging high on simple drug *use* arrests. Details of the data extraction procedures are contained in the project's technical report (Klein et al., 1988).

Dramatic increases in the number of cocaine sales arrest cases were evident. In 1983, 233 such cases appeared across all five stations. In 1984, the number rose to 542, an increase of 133 percent. In 1985, the number increased to 1,114, an increase of an additional 106 percent or 375 percent above the 1983 numbers.[2] Note that these figures refer to *cocaine* sales arrest cases and not specifically to sales of cocaine in its *crack* form. Although our research design was framed in the context of the growth of the crack phenomenon and our expectations cite crack sales only, our analyses preceded an investigation of the presence of crack versus the powder form of cocaine in these incidents.[3]

Did gang involvement increase disproportionately? The answer, determined by using the extensive LAPD and LASD gang rosters,[4] is affirmative, but not nearly to the extent expected by our law enforcement informants. Defining gang involvement as the attribution of gang status to at least one arrestee in a case, gang-involved cases constituted 8.6 percent of all cocaine sales cases in the five stations in 1983, 20.8 percent in 1984, and 24.9 percent in 1985. The percentage increases are 142 and 20 percent, or 213 percent overall from 1983. Figure 15.1 illustrates how these data represent a major increase in gang involvement, yet a decelerating rate of change, and a 1985 level—25 percent—far lower than the informal estimates suggested to us by many of our police collaborators. During this three-year period, the explosion

Figure 15.1: Proportion of Cocaine Sales Arrest Incidents with Gang Members in South Central Los Angeles During First Years of "Crack" Explosion (1983–1985)

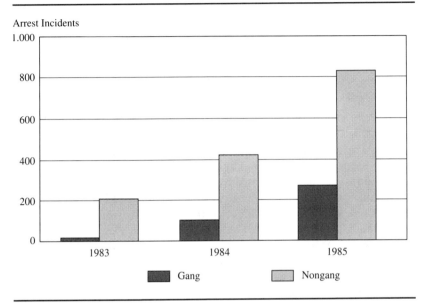

$x^2 = 31.25$
d.f. $= 2$
$p < .001$

in cocaine sales was engaging a number of street gang members, but it was in no way dominated by gang involvement. Our literature-based hypothesis of limited gang involvement is supported.

Two less obvious but possibly alternative measures of increased gang involvement were considered: the proportion of gang members per case and the proportion of members of the *same* gang in a case (indicating recruitment and use of clique structures). For both measures, the enforcement expectation would be an increase over time. To apply these indicators with the reliability afforded by sufficiently large numbers, the time dimension was divided into the four half years starting with the first half of 1984; 1983 case numbers (twenty gang cases) were too low for this analysis. For instance, the proportion of roster-identified gang members among all arrested suspects (including those charged with offenses other than cocaine sales) for each case was calculated for all gang cases with more than one suspect. About 65 percent of the 384 gang cases had multiple suspects. Table 15.1 presents the data.[5]

We also analyzed data for members of the same gang. The numbers are far smaller (only 18% of all gang cases) because only cases with more than one identified gang member and all gang names known are appropriate to the

Table 15.1   Mean Proportion of All Arrestees Who Were Identified Gang
Members for Four Half-Years (Gang Cases with Multiple Suspects
Only)

Period	Mean Proportion	Standard Deviation	N
First half 1984	.603	.288	24
Second half 1984	.593	.270	48
First half 1985	.551	.245	79
Second half 1985	.575	.246	89

analysis. The same-gang proportions dropped steadily from .78 to .53, a direction opposite to that required by the police/press reports but supportive of our contrasting, literature-based hypothesis.

Neither set of data offers support for an increasing level of gang involvement per case over the two-year period being measured. Indeed, if there is any trend at all, it is toward a *lower* level of gang member involvement on an event basis. Although the cocaine business was increasing dramatically and gang members were becoming more involved, they were not becoming a larger proportion of all who were involved. Rather, there is evidence of an increasing *nongang* presence even in gang-involved cases.

Correlates of Increased Gang Involvement

In order to assess the correlates, and presumably the effects, of increased gang involvement in cocaine distribution, detailed information was collected from the case files for each incident. As noted, the year 1983 was omitted because it had too few gang cases (20) to provide reliable estimates of gang/nongang differences. For 1984 and 1985, all cases from the five stations that had at least one roster-identified gang member arrestee were collected. An equal number of cases without gang arrestees was selected randomly in proportion to each station's contribution to the nongang total for each year.

Case records were located in station files, centralized storage facilities, and on microfilm. A pilot comparison of the availability of relevant information from different record sources yielded no substantial differences. Occasionally, case records could not be located and others were dropped when case materials indicated no arrests for cocaine sales. Those cases were not replaced because the nonsampled cases were exclusively nongang.

We turn next to the data comparing the characteristics of 384 gang incidents and 357 nongang cases to assess the possible effects of gang member involvement. We begin by looking at characteristics that distinguished gang and nongang homicides in prior research in order to determine whether those features also differentiate the two groups of cocaine sales incidents. We then turn to unique aspects of drug sales events and examine what gang/nongang differences emerge. Finally, to assess gang impact we investigate changes in case characteristics occurring in this period of increased gang involvement.

General Characteristics of Gang and Nongang Incidents

In previous research (Maxson et al., 1985) comparing gang-involved and nongang *homicides*, several variables were identified that significantly differentiated between them. Gang homicides were more likely to take place on the street, involve firearms, and include more suspects with different demographic profiles than nongang homicides. In the cocaine sales incidents, we found no evidence of gang/nongang differences in location and presence of firearms. About two-thirds of the incidents had street locations and about one-quarter had mentions of firearms, but neither varied significantly by gang involvement. However, statistically significant differences in *participant* characteristics paralleled those found previously for homicide cases. Cocaine sales incidents with gang involvement had slightly more suspects (2.16 vs. 1.81), and the suspects were more likely to be male, black rather than Hispanic, and younger (22.7 vs. 26.9 years) than cases without gang members involved.

Differences in Drug Characteristics in Gang and Nongang Cocaine Sales

Keeping these confirmatory findings in mind, we can ask now whether gang and nongang cases differed overall with respect to special features of cocaine sales or possession-for-sale incidents, leaving aside for the moment the question of changes over time.

"Crack House" Involved. About one-third of all sales incidents took place in dwellings of some type, but crack houses—fortified residences redesigned for the purpose of retail sales of rock or crack cocaine and, therefore, known in Los Angeles as rock houses—were mentioned specifically in less than 6 percent of all cases, 5 percent in gang and 6 percent in nongang incidents. Police and press reports on gang involvement stressed these crack houses as symbolic of the intrusion of gang control into crack distribution. There, gang members could be assigned specific roles, such as lookout or enforcer, and could make use of their weaponry. Our doubts, based on previous findings of low cohesiveness and organizational potential among street gangs, led to a prediction of far lower gang domination of crack house operations than suggested by our police and media informants.

Clearly, reports of widespread use of gang-manned crack house cocaine distribution centers are contradicted by the data reported here. Street or car sales locations were twice as prevalent as house or apartment locations, and type of location did *not* vary with gang involvement. If dwellings were perceived by law enforcement personnel as crack houses, they rarely labeled them as such in official reports.

Fortifications. The surprisingly low level of crack house mentions could be an artifact of police recording practices. The recording of special fortifications—barred windows or doors, reinforced entrances, and so on—has more relevance to officers attempting a forced entry into a known sales location. Such fortifications were mentioned in 16 percent of gang and 17 percent of nongang incidents, or about half of the cases with home or apartment locations. With so many homes in the area having burglar bars, the 16 to 17 percent level of mention of fortifications is surprisingly low. Coupled with the lack of gang/nongang differences in frequency, we conclude that well-fortified crack houses, and their associated threats to officer safety and evidence retrieval, were the exception rather than the rule during this two-year period. The absence of gang-nongang differences again supports the hypotheses derived from the sociological gang literature.

Source of Information. This category refers to the means by which the police were alerted to the potential arrest situation. "Traditional" narcotics unit operations, such as receipt of information from paid or "turned" informants, citizen complaints, or anonymous tips, might be expected to be less common in gang-related cases because the openness of street gang activity might lead to more police-observed sales incidents and lead-up events (accidental discoveries in responding to calls on nondrug offenses). But the data reveal no such differences. About two-thirds of the arrest incidents were responses to prior information regarding drug activity. There were no gang/nongang differences relative to either existence of prior information or the source of prior information.

Cocaine Involvement. Two measures were assessed here: cocaine taken in evidence and the mean amount of cocaine seized by the police. With cocaine mentioned very high in both sets of cases (96 and 97%), no differentiation is possible. But in these cases, the mean amount of coke seized also does not differ significantly. It is over twice as high in nongang cases (19.04 vs. 8.50 grams), which clearly does not support the expectation that gang involvement would yield more serious sales levels, but the variance is so high that the difference is not statistically significant. Even removal of "the outliers," the few cases involving very large drug seizures, failed to yield a significant difference between gang and nongang cases.

Crack. Because the arrest logs that provided the sampling frame did not differentiate between forms of cocaine, it is only in the individual case files that one can find data about the presence of crack specifically (called "rock" in Los Angeles police files). As expected, however, crack was the predominant form involved. Gang cases more commonly included mention of crack, 92 percent compared with 81 percent, and the difference is statistically significant. However, the mean amount is actually, although not statistically, lower in gang cases (6.62 grams) than in nongang cases (8.49 grams). Thus, the 11 percent difference in prevalence is accompanied by a lower, but chance, difference in amount of crack involved. We are not dealing here with a major difference between gang and nongang cases.

Other Drugs. All incidents were also coded for involvement of other drugs in order to assess whether gang sales events yielded higher levels of polydrug presence. Here again, no differences emerged. The marijuana percentages were 18 and 20 percent, and the next most common drugs, heroin and PCP, together were mentioned in only 4 percent of each set of cases.

Cash Taken. The files included the seizure of money as well as drugs. The percentage of cases with cash taken was significantly higher in gang cases (63 vs. 53%), but the actual amounts were not (means of $1,136 in gang cases and $764 in nongang cases). Thus, gang cases are somewhat more likely to involve crack and cash seizure, but the amounts obtained do not vary significantly with gang involvement. Further, the mean amounts of drugs and cash taken indicate the generally low levels of the distribution hierarchy involved in these incidents. Gangs had little effect at this level of the drug business.

Multiple Handlers. Two enforcement-predicted characteristics of gang involvement that were expected to be measurable in case files were violence and organization. Our police collaborators were quite certain that gang cases were more violent, and we will report data on that later. They also thought that what gangs brought advantageously to crack distribution was their intrinsic organization. Indeed, two Los Angeles area courts have officially labeled street gangs as "unincorporated organizations," thereby making them more vulnerable to civil and criminal charges for court-order violations and conspiracy charges.

The case files were carefully coded for what we termed "multiple handlers." The term was used because of the relative absence of the role-specific argot reported in New York research reports (Goldstein, 1981)—"enforcers" "lookouts," "holders," and so on. Nevertheless, Los Angeles files did describe suspect activities that could be reasonably interpreted as division of labor in street sales. Some suspects warned of police surveillance or approach; some sold crack; some held money nearby; and some kept drugs or money in a nearby home, apartment, or car. Thus, one could describe distribution roles or "multiple handlers" in those incidents involving more than one suspect.

Multiple handlers should appear more commonly in gang-involved cases if gang organization is a factor in crack distribution. Given the fact that there were fewer than two suspects per case, however, a difference might be hard to find. And indeed, multiple handlers were coded in only 18 percent of all cases. They were more common in gang than nongang cases—21 vs. 15 percent, significant at the .05 level. However, this effect is likely the result of the more common appearance of multiple participants in gang cases. When we look at mentions of multiple handlers only among cases with more than one suspect, the gang/nongang difference is no longer statistically significant. Multiple handlers appear in 30 percent of gang cases with multiple suspects and in 24 percent of comparable nongang cases.

What do these comparisons mean? First, the vast majority of these cocaine arrest cases involved crack, but they yielded low numbers of suspects and low levels of drugs and cash. The crack phenomenon, as revealed in formal arrest activity, is increasingly widespread but undramatic. Second, there were few recorded differences between gang and nongang cases, and fewer still of any importance, as summarized in table 15.2. Thus, there is little support for hypotheses derived from police and press reports of gang involvement; contrary expectations from the sociological literature hold up better. One could suggest that the drug parameters overwhelm the gang parameters. There is little evidence, certainly, that gang membership brings anything special to the crack trade.

Table 15.2   Summary, Gang/Nongang Differences in Sales Arrest Incident Characteristics

Variable	Police/Press Prediction	Sociology of Gangs Prediction	Result*
Crack House Involved	gang > nongang	no difference	no difference
Fortifications	gang > nongang	no difference	no difference
Source of Information	gang > nongang in traditional sources	no difference	no difference
Mean Amount of Cocaine	gang > nongang	no difference	no difference
Presence of Crack	gang > nongang	gang > nongang	gang > nongang
Mean Amount of Crack	gang > nongang	no difference	no difference
Presence of Other Drugs	gang > nongang	no difference	no difference
Cash Seized	gang > nongang	no difference	gang > nongang
Mean Amount of Cash	gang > nongang	no difference	no difference
Multiple Handlers	gang > nongang	no difference	gang > nongang
Multiple Handlers in Cases with 1 + Suspects	gang > nongang	no difference	no difference

*Based on chi-square statistics for categoric variables, *t*-test statistics for interval-level variables.

Differences over Time

Did the increase in gang involvement yield concomitant growth in characteristics of cocaine sales incidents? As reported by the police and the media, the answer is in the affirmative. If it is actually in the negative, however, the sociologically derived hypotheses would be supported.

The issue was approached in two ways. First, a series of bivariate analyses was undertaken, comparing gang and nongang cases in the four half years covered, in which the numbers of gang and nongang cases were, respectively, 36 and 38, 70 and 71, 131 and 117, and 147 and 131. The second approach applied analyses of covariance to the case characteristics as dependent variables, to ask whether the impact of gang involvement "worsened" over time as the level of gang involvement increased. It is the contribution of the gang-time *interaction* to the overall variance that is important in this analysis.

Looking at the bivariate analyses first, did case characteristics change over time and did gang/nongang differences in each change over time? As seen in table 15.3, the division of cases into the four time periods produces far lower cell sizes to be used for tests of statistical significance, especially in the earlier time periods. We report these tests cautiously, therefore, and look for broad and consistent patterns of change over time.

Location. Over the four time periods, sales arrest incidents moved more into the streets. The street proportion moved from 55.5 percent to 60 percent to 59 percent to 68 percent. This trend could be explained equally well by changing law enforcement operational strategies as by changes in cocaine sales activity. The gang/nongang differences were not significant in any of the four periods.

Presence of Firearms. Guns reclaimed in arrest incidents are carefully recorded by the police. When present, they were coded for our analysis except for about fifteen cases in which their location was so remote as to be inaccessible to the participants. Over the four half years, the proportion of cases with guns present decreased, somewhat surprisingly, from 34 percent to 27 percent to 24 percent to 21 percent. However, this change could be largely an artifact of the increase in street location noted above. The presence of firearms was recorded in the files of 8.8 percent of arrests at street locations and at 55.6 percent of residence locations. Gang/nongang differences were not significant in any of the four time periods. However, the decreasing presence of guns is more pronounced in gang (39 to 17%) than in nongang (29 to 24%) cases.

Mean Number of Firearms. Within those cases in which guns were present, the mean number also decreased consistently, if slightly; the numbers

Table 15.3   Characteristics in Gang and Nongang Cocaine Sales Events Over Four Time Periods

Incident Characteristics	First Half 1984			Second Half 1984			First Half 1985			Second Half 1985		
	Nongang N = 38	Gang N = 36	P	Nongang N = 71	Gang N = 70	P	Nongang N = 117	Gang N = 131	P	Nongang N = 131	Gang N = 147	P
Location Type												
Street	21 (55%)	20 (56%)	ns	47 (66%)	36 (51%)	ns	67 (57%)	79 (60%)	ns	83 (63%)	107 (73%)	ns
Dwelling	14 (37%)	16 (44%)		21 (30%)	30 (43%)		43 (37%)	43 (33%)		43 (33%)	33 (22%)	
All Other	3 (8%)	0		3 (4%)	4 (6%)		7 (6%)	9 (7%)		5 (4%)	7 (5%)	
Guns Present	11 (29%)	14 (39%)	ns	15 (21%)	23 (33%)	ns	30 (26%)	29 (22%)	ns	32 (24%)	25 (17%)	ns
Mean Guns per	(N = 11)	(N = 14)	ns	(N = 15)	(N = 23)	ns	(N = 30)	(N = 29)	ns	(N = 32)	(N = 25)	ns
Incident with Guns	1.54	2.57		1.73	2.22		1.7	2.2		1.69	1.76	
Prior Investigative Information	19 (51%)	16 (53%)	ns	45 (65%)	42 (62%)	ns	71 (63%)	86 (70%)	ns	90 (71%)	98 (70%)	ns
Cash Seized	16 (40%)	24 (67%)	*	36 (52%)	43 (61%)	ns	63 (54%)	80 (61%)	ns	74 (56%)	96 (65%)	ns
Mean Cash Amount	$837	$2,637	ns	$457	$1,050	ns	$1,120	$750	ns	$585	$1,120	ns
Crack/Rock Present	23 (60%)	31 (86%)	*	56 (79%)	60 (86%)	ns	102 (87%)	124 (95%)	*	107 (82%)	139 (95%)	**
Mean Number Participants Charged for Sales	1.58	1.75	ns	1.79	2.14	ns	1.73	2.1	ns	1.53	1.75	*

Participant Characteristics	First Half 1984			Second Half 1984			First Half 1985			Second Half 1985		
	Nongang N = 60	Gang N = 63	P	Nongang N = 127	Gang N = 150	P	Nongang N = 203	Gang N = 275	P	Nongang N = 200	Gang N = 258	P
Gender Male	49 (82%)	61 (97%)	**	115 (91%)	136 (91%)	ns	172 (85%)	252 (92%)	*	168 (84%)	246 (93%)	**
Race					(N = 149)		(N = 202)	(N = 274)				
Black	31 (52%)	38 (60%)	*	88 (69%)	104 (70%)	ns	125 (62%)	199 (73%)	*	122 (61%)	180 (70%)	**
Hispanic	23 (38%)	25 (40%)		36 (28%)	45 (30%)		75 (37%)	75 (27%)		72 (36%)	78 (30%)	
Other	6 (10%)	0		3 (3%)	0		2 (1%)	0		6 (3%)	0	
Mean Age	27	22.6	**	25.9	21.5	**	26.9	21.8	**	27.2	21.6	**
Prior Arrest Record	38 (63%)	57 (90%)	**	95 (75%)	121 (81%)	ns	136 (67%)	227 (83%)	**	137 (69%)	225 (87%)	**
Mean Violence Priors	.53	.67	ns	.52	.78	ns	.43	.67	*	.42	.69	**
Mean Drug Sales Priors	.63	.63	ns	.74	.48	ns	.87	.75	ns	.82	.66	ns
Mean Drug Possession Priors	1.1	.65	ns	.62	.63	ns	.76	.65	ns	.76	.67	ns

Note: Chi-square statistics for categoric variables, t-test for interval-level variables.

* p < .05
•• p < .01

were 2.12, 2.03, 19.95, and 1.72 guns per incident. This decrease, too, could well be due to the increase in street location. Gang/nongang differences were not significant in any of the four periods, although in each period the gang mean surpassed the nongang mean slightly. Even more than the trend for firearm presence, the decrease in number of guns was all in gang (2.57 to 1.76) rather than nongang (1.54 to 1.69) cases.

Number of Participants. Despite the increase in gang involvement over time, and the relationship between gangs and the number of incident participants, there was no appreciable increase in the average number of participants arrested for cocaine sales in our incidents over the four time periods. In each time period, there were slightly more participants in gang cases, but significantly so only in the last half of 1985.

Gender. The proportion of male arrestees is always high in these incidents. It hovers around 85 percent for nongang and 93 percent for gang cases. These percentages did not vary substantially over time. Gang/nongang differences were statistically significant in all but the second time period (second half of 1984), but there is no pattern of increased differences over time.

Ethnicity. The presence of "Anglos" in these cocaine incidents was virtually nonexistent; participants were principally black. However, the arrestees in gang cases were proportionately more often black than were nongang arrestees. Nevertheless, the percentage of blacks never exceeded 73 percent, despite the expectation that crack sales in our five-station area was almost exclusively a black phenomenon. Although the ethnic differences attained statistical significance in all but the second period, the proportion of blacks never differed by more than 11 percent between gang and nongang cases.

Age. Cocaine sales arrestees were modally in their twenties. Means were about twenty-seven years for nongang participants and twenty-two years for gang participants.[6] There was no appreciable change over time. As expected, gang members were significantly younger in all four time periods.

Prior Offenses. The arrest histories were gathered from central data files maintained by the county, supplemented as necessary from state-derived rap sheets. From 63 to 75 percent of the nongang members arrested in the four time periods were found to have prior records. For gang members, the percentages ranged from 81 to 90 percent, confirming the expectation that gang members brought a more extensive criminal arrest background to the drug sales situation, despite their younger ages. Changes over time showed no particular pattern, such as enlisting more or less serious offenders. The gang/nongang differences were significant in all but the second time period.

Prior Violence. Gang members, as just noted, are somewhat more likely to have arrest histories, and they have more violent histories, as suggested by our police collaborators and prior research (Tracy, 1979). The proportion of gang members with arrests for violent charges was higher in all four time periods, significantly so in the last two periods. With the exception of the first period, the gang/nongang difference in violence records exceeded the difference in the proportion with prior records of all kinds; that is, the greater propensity toward violence was not merely a function of more extensive criminal behavior generally. Gang participants were more likely to have prior records and more likely even beyond that to have been arrested for assaults, weapons violations, and the like. The same holds true for robbery. Thus, we can reasonably expect to find more evidence of violence in the gang-involved sales incidents in our sample.

Prior Drug Arrests. The final bivariate comparison has to do with prior arrests for sales and for possession of drugs. Here, we found no particular trend over time, and no significant gang/nongang differences during the four time periods for either sales or possession. However, in the eight comparisons (four periods × sales and possession), the nongang proportion with prior arrests equals or exceeds the gang proportion in seven and fails by only one percentage point in the eighth. This is in marked contrast to both the overall and the violence priors. This finding suggests that cocaine sales incidents throughout the two years were more in the hands of offenders experienced in drug matters, even when involving gang members. It is a point raised earlier, and to be raised again.

The ten bivariate analyses yield some tentative conclusions. First, although there was an increase in street locations and a decrease in firearms presence (the latter, probably redundant, a function of the increasingly open locations), there were no other noteworthy changes over time despite the demonstrated increase in gang involvement. This does not indicate any major impact of gang involvement on the qualitative nature of the cocaine sales incidents under study.

We can add confidence to this conclusion by noting that results of bivariate comparisons of drug-specific characteristics are quite similar—few gang/nongang differences and minimal change over time. The same pattern appears with crack involvement. A higher likelihood of crack and cash taken in gang cases was evident in several time periods, but there is no indication that these gang patterns increased over time in comparison with nongang cases.

Second, *incident* characteristics do not differ between gang and nongang cases (location, weapons, number of participants), but participant characteristics do (gender, ethnicity, age, prior records except for drugs). Despite an occasional anomaly during the second time period, this seems to suggest that what gang members bring with them does not have much impact on the nature of the sales incidents themselves. We have already shown that the *level* of gang involvement in 1984 and 1985 was generally overstated. Now we can add that the concomitants of gang involvement may also have been overstated by police and press.

Interaction Effects

Following the bivariate analyses, we undertook a series of analyses of covariance to see if we could tease out time or gang/time interaction effects on aspects of cocaine sales incidents. As noted earlier, the enforcement expectations were for substantial gang main effects; these hypotheses suggested that time main effects would be confounded by the increase in gang involvement in cocaine sales. Therefore, gang/time interaction was of particular interest to this study.

We selected a set of dependent variables that were most likely to show the gang/time interaction: street location, amount of cocaine and cash taken into evidence, mean age of suspects, and several aspects of the suspects' prior arrest records. The results were consistent with those of the bivariate analyses. Gang, time, and the gang/time interaction term explained very little variance in the dependent variables. Only on street location were the effects for time ($F = 7.64$) and the gang/time interaction ($F = 4.12$) statistically significant. For most of the dependent variables, R^2s ranged only from .01 to .06. The only exceptions were attributable to the strong main effects on suspect age. The R^2 for mean age of suspects charged with cocaine sales offenses was .15, but neither time nor the gang/time interaction term contributed significantly to the explained variance. Another exception is mean age of onset of criminal record, which is lower for gang members. Although the R^2 for this variable was .64, only mean age of suspects contributed to the explained variance. In this case, there were no significant main effects for either gang or time, nor was the gang/time interaction effect significant.

Consistent with the bivariate analyses, there were significant gang effects on some aspects of cocaine sales incidents (i.e., amount of cash, mean age of suspects, and prior arrest histories). The low amount of explained variance in the dependent variables indicates that factors other than gang and time should be examined, but the available data did not contain indices of such other variables. To test the notion of other, more explanatory variables, we turned to the example of jurisdictional differences in law enforcement field activity, investigation procedures, and case recording as well as possible jurisdictional differences in the nature of cocaine sales activity. Although such information was not collected specifically from the case files, our experience in the stations and interviews with officers suggested there would be such differences between our two cooperating departments.

To explore this possibility, we used a dummy variable for jurisdiction (LAPD v. LASD) as a proxy measure for unspecified jurisdictional differences. We selected street location, total number of suspects, and the amount of cocaine taken into evidence as dependent variables that would be most likely to show a jurisdictional effect. The amount of variance explained with jurisdiction included was quite similar to the initial results with only gang and time included. Time/jurisdiction interactions did not contribute significantly to the explained variance.

Thus, whatever may be the major factors that contribute to the variance in our data, they have not been tapped in this research. Gang involvement, time, jurisdictions, and their interactions yield relatively little. One might better turn to such issues as neighborhood or areal characteristics and the complex of variables that describe the drug distribution system. But that would constitute a very different project, geared toward very different questions.

Violence and Cocaine Sales

When crack became a media event in Los Angeles, it was partly because of events that seemed to tie crack, gangs, and violence together. Most prominent was an incident in which a raiding group killed five young men in a brief burst of gunfire. This was variously described in the press as a gang retaliation, a drug territory retaliation, and both. The advent of gang participation in the fast burgeoning crack distribution system was an open invitation to speculations about gang-induced violence, based on assumptions about the nature of gang activity and about crack distribution (Hagedorn, 1988; Klein and Maxson, 1989; Reuter, 1988). Gang members might bring a greater familiarity with, or "propensity" for, violent approaches to conflict resolution. They may have more ready access to illicit firearms and automatic weapons. Such characteristics could be seen by drug distributors as prime qualifications for the "enforcer" or protective functions required by the large amounts of cash and drugs reputedly linked to crack house operations. The gang member armed with a shotgun pointed at the buyer purchasing crack through a small slot in an interior door was the picture often presented in our early law enforcement interviews.

Further, it was reported that gang members were recruited into drug operations specifically for their preexisting territorial claims over neighborhoods targeted for drug distribution. According to this view, coopting gang members into drug sales networks would reduce the potential for violence stemming from gang vs. drug territorial struggles. Others claimed that bringing gang members into drug distribution would merely carry ongoing gang rivalries into the drug scene; drug operations of one gang would be targets for rival gang retaliations.

There were two ways we could use available data to respond to these speculations. The first was to seek indices of violence in the sales arrest incidents already described. The second was to investigate aspects of drug involvement in homicides.

Violence in Cocaine Sales Incidents

The indices of violence available in cocaine sales incidents were few, for at least two reasons. First, most incidents involved sales of small volume. Front-line distributors are unlikely targets for violence-generating buyer rip-offs, and single sales transactions or arrests of front-line distributors are unlikely to involve turf disputes and retaliations. Indeed, a significant proportion of the incidents were "buy-bust" operations with narcotics officers as the buyers. Moreover, if a drug transaction precipitated violence and injury, the case typically would be investigated as a homicide or assault. Such charges would likely supersede drug sale charges and, therefore, not appear in narcotics arrest logs, the source of our population of incidents.

Second, most arrests were by narcotics or patrol officers whose primary purpose is to gather evidence useful in the prosecution of narcotics offenses. They are less concerned about intergang rivalries, rumors of impending or ongoing territorial conflicts, and gang-related motives. Gang unit officers typically have more concern for such matters, and they often pay less attention to drug paraphernalia and sales evidence. Therefore, we found that these arrest incidents presented few opportunities to investigate violence associated with cocaine sales. Indeed, occurrences of violence during these incidents were rare—7 percent in gang and 3 percent in nongang cases—and usually involved resisting arrest, rather than the type of drug-associated violence implied by our contrasting hypotheses.

Nevertheless, we can extract indices of violence *potential* from the cocaine sales arrest incidents. Once again, it is the comparison of gang with nongang cases and changes in the differences over time that address the issue of the gang/crack/violence connection. Relevant data were presented earlier, but we review them briefly here to provide the context for the supplemental data gathered to address gang/crack/violence relationships.

The presence of firearms, it will be recalled, did not distinguish gang from nongang cases, although the average number of guns in incidents with firearms did. Further, as crack sales flourished over time, the proportion of incidents with firearms decreased from 34 percent in the first half of 1984 to 21 percent in the second half of 1985. The levels are not high, and decline. The numbers of weapons also decreased steadily per incident with weapons, from 2.12 to 1.75. Decreasing trends in both presence and number were more evident among gang cases. Finally, proportion of gang members with prior arrests for violence remained relatively stable over time, which argues against the position that gang members were increasingly recruited by cocaine distributors to serve as their "muscle."

An additional point about the presence of firearms can be made. In the early stages of the project period, when there was much excitement about crack houses (the authors went on a ten-house raid with a sheriff's task force in a single evening), it was said that over a thousand crack houses were active on any given day. Further, we were told consistently that *every* crack house contained guns or that "almost every" busted crack house yielded guns of various kinds.

In our combined samples of 741 cases, crack houses were mentioned in only 39 cases (5%). Fortifications, a defining characteristic of crack houses, were mentioned in 121 (16%) cases. Clearly, this sets something of a ceiling on the "always a weapon" issue and therefore on weapons as harbingers of potential violence. Firearms were seized in 58 percent of the cases with crack house identifications and also in 58 percent of the cases in which fortifications were mentioned. Thus, again, the presence of weapons was greatly exaggerated by our police collaborators. After all, it is commonly estimated that over 50 percent of American homes contain guns of some type.

None of these findings is conclusive about violence levels in cocaine sales, but they represent what is available. At best, they offer little support for the widely reported phenomenon of gang involvement in cocaine sales and violence during the 1984–1985 period.

Drug Involvement in Homicide

Because we anticipated that narcotics investigation files would be unlikely to yield much evidence of violence, we determined in the planning of the research to turn elsewhere. Sampling assault, weapons, and robbery incidents unfortunately would have taken far more resources than available funds would permit. We chose instead to use the most dramatic violent incidents—homicides—to address the question from the reverse direction: Is there evidence over our two-year period of more drug, cocaine, or crack involvement in gang than nongang homicides investigated in the five-station area?

Prior research had made us very familiar with homicide files. We had already developed data extraction and coding procedures for them. Further, if the drug/violence connection was increasingly obvious as dealers and distribution networks grew and came more into direct competition and conflict, it was most likely to be manifested in homicide.

A total of 123 1984–1985 gang homicides in the five-station area were available for data collection. For more than a decade, LAPD and LASD gang units have designated homicides as "gang" based on incident characteristics, knowledge of gang-related motives, and gang membership of either victims or suspects. In general, designation practices have been consistent over time in both jurisdictions (Klein et al., 1986). We matched the 123 gang homicides with 136 nongang homicides sampled randomly in proportion to each station's

Table 15.4   Characteristics in Gang and Nongang Homicides (1984–1985)

Incident Characteristics	Nongang N = 136	Gang N = 123	P
Location Type			
Street	39 (29%)	82 (67%)	
Dwelling	65 (48%)	17 (14%)	**
All Other	32 (23%)	24 (19%)	
Guns Present	87 (64%)	112 (91%)	**
Mean Number Participants			
on Suspect Side	1.50	3.71	**
(Missing)	(7)	(1)	
Suspect Characteristics	Nongang N = 464	Gang N = 615	P
Male	438 (94%)	600 (98%)	**
Mean Age	27.7	20.0	**
(Missing)	(64)	(108)	

Note: Chi-square statistics for categoric variables, t-test for interval-level variables.
** p < .01

contribution to the five-station nongang homicide total for each year. Our first analysis, reported in table 15.4 addressed the validation of gang/nongang differences found in our earlier homicide research (Maxson et al., 1985), assuring us that we were still dealing with consistent gang definitions. Five parameters were chosen for this purpose: location, presence of firearms, number of participants on the suspect's side, proportion of male suspects, and mean age of suspects. In all five comparisons, the gang/nongang differences were statistically significant, in the expected direction, and of the magnitude seen previously. Thus, we have the basis for valid comparisons with respect to the drug issues, of which we present four.

First, the most gross comparison is simply that of any drug involvement. In gang homicides, 84 of 123, or 68 percent of the cases showed evidence of drug involvement—paraphernalia, drug use or sales by victim or suspect, evidence of drugs at the scene, etc. The number of nongang homicides was 76 out of 136, or 56 percent. Thus gang homicides are somewhat more likely to reveal drug involvement than nongang homicides.

Second, when we compared gang homicide cases with and without drug involvement (see table 15.5), we found few statistically significant differences with respect to the gang parameters—location, firearms present, and participant characteristics. Yet, when we compared nongang homicide cases with drug and without drug involvement, we found notable differences with regard to location, firearms present, number of suspect participants, and mean age.

293

Table 15.5   Characteristics in Gang and Nongang Homicides (1984–1985) with and without Drug Involvement

Incident Characteristics	Nongang N = 136			Gang N = 123		
	Nondrug N = 60	Drug N = 76	P	Nondrug N = 39	Drug N = 84	P
Location Type						
Street	8 (13%)	31 (41%)		25 (64%)	57 (68%)	
Dwelling	37 (62%)	28 (37%)	**	4 (10%)	13 (15%)	ns
All Other	15 (25%)	17 (22%)		10 (26%)	14 (17%)	
Guns Present	29 (48%)	58 (76%)	**	33 (85%)	79 (94%)	ns
Mean Number Participants on						
Suspect Side	1.31	1.66	*	3.26	3.93	ns
(Missing)	(2)	(5)		(0)	(1)	

Suspect Characteristics	Nongang N = 464			Gang N = 615		
	Nondrug N = 136	Drug N = 328	P	Nondrug N = 167	Drug N = 448	P
Male	125 (92%)	313 (95%)	ns	162 (97%)	438 (98%)	ns
Mean Age	30.3	26.6	**	20.1	19.9	ns
(Missing)	(21)	(43)		(34)	(74)	

Note: Chi-square statistics for categoric variables, t-test statistics for interval-level variables.
* p < .05
** p < .01

Of interest is that the differences were consistently in the direction of character-istics seen more often in gang than nongang homicides: more commonly street locations, firearms present, involving more participants and of younger ages. We interpret these second-order differences to mean that drug involvement has little impact on the *nature* of gang homicides—perhaps the import of "gang-relatedness" overwhelms the relevance of drug involvement. On the other hand, drug involvement is less common among nongang homicides, but when it is present, characteristics of the incident are quite distinct from those of other nongang cases. These results do not support the notion that gangs have unique and strong drug/violence connections.

Third, gang and nongang homicide files were coded for drug parameters, such as type of drug involved, mention of participant drug use or involvement in drug sales, and specification of explicit drug-related motives for the homi-cide (e.g., dealer rip-off, drug territory dispute). A gang-induced violence connection, as suggested by police and the press, should yield drug differences favoring the gang homicides. Cocaine was involved in 60 percent of the 160 homicides with any indication of drug involvement. Just over half of those 95 cases included specific mention of the rock form of cocaine—crack. There were no differences in type of drug among gang and nongang incidents.

About two-thirds of the drug homicides included an aspect of drug sales rather than merely drug use. Gang homicides were no more likely to involve drug sales than nongang homicides. Finally, a drug-related motive was indicated in just 27 percent of gang homicides with drug involvement, but in 47 percent of the nongang drug incidents, a statistically significant difference.

These results support the contention that despite the relative frequency of drug involvement in gang homicides, its *relevance* is more limited than public reports would suggest. The drug dimension of these homicides is perhaps a function of gang member involvement in drug sales, but it is not often a *motive* for homicide. The more frequent mention of drug-related motives in nongang homicides could explain the differences in incident characteristics noted among nongang homicides when drugs are involved.

Finally, there is the time dimension. With the increasing gang involvement in cocaine distribution and all the expectations for a concomitant rise in violence, gang homicides in the area should have shown a proportional increase in drug involvement, at least as compared with nongang homicides. Table 15.6 reports the data.

In some ways, these data are the most interesting in this section. Gang homicides manifest essentially no change in drug involvement, contrary to police expectations, but the *nongang* homicides show a dramatic change. The clear suggestion is that the portion of the gang world that got involved in severe violence was already tinged with drug connections, but that nongang homicide came to be drug tinged as the cocaine problem exploded. The gang/drug connection was already there; the cocaine explosion brought more violence to the *nongang* portion of the growing drug arena.

These are, of course, strong conclusions to be based on such indirect indications as drug mentions in homicide cases. The reader may wish to consider them with caution. We state them with some clarity in order to highlight the possibilities, and because they are directly contrary to police and press

Table 15.6   Drug Involvement in Gang and Nongang Homicides over Four Time Periods

	1984		1985	
	First Half	*Second Half*	*First Half*	*Second Half*
Gang[a]	71%	74%	67%	65%
Nongang[b]	43%	36%	72%	64%

a. $\chi^2 = .63$; d.f. $= 3$; $p =$ ns.
b. $\chi^2 = 12.62$; d.f. $= 3$; $p < .01$.

suggestions. The drug/homicide connection, to judge from all four of the above comparisons, is not basically a gang phenomenon. Gang homicides were not affected over time by the drug scene, but nongang homicides were. More broadly, Fagan (1989) has noted similar patterns in a three-city comparison. He reported relative independence among levels of gang membership, drug dealing, and violence and concluded, "One must look to factors other than drug involvement to explain violence among gang members" (p.19).

The fit between these suggestions and the data reported earlier is quite good. For the period of 1984 and 1985, the initial and major growth period for crack sales in Los Angeles, the purported gang connection seems in most respects to have been considerably overstated. The implications for violence similarly seem to have been overstated. The more parsimonious hypotheses suggested by the professional literature are the ones supported by our data.

Conclusion

Arrests logged by narcotics officers in five districts of two large jurisdictions indicate that the growth in crack sales from 1983 to 1985 was very dramatic. Although the growth was accompanied by a major increase in street gang member involvement, the increase was primarily at the low volume, street level of sales. This parallels findings from New York (Fagan and Chin, 1989a), although the New York selling groups were not described in street-gang terms. Gang members seemed neither to have played a predominant role nor to have brought much extra violence or organizational character to crack distribution. We conclude, in line with the hypotheses derived from the literature, that the world of crack in Los Angeles belonged principally to the regular drug dealers, not to street gangs.

We should note also that more research is needed on this topic because of the unique situation of gangs in cities like Los Angeles, and because the crack and gang phenomena have spread rapidly throughout the country. Our data fit well with some of those of Belenko and Fagan (1987) in New York and of Mieczkowski (1988) in Detroit. In particular, Fagan and Chin (1989b) reported data on violence, gangs, and drug distribution that complement our data on the absence of a violence connection due to gangs.

But Skolnick (1988), using interviews with officials and a purposive sample of 39 inmates and wards in the California correctional system, claims a far greater involvement of gangs—especially in Northern California—in crack distribution, and at a higher organizational level. Skolnick's conclusions captured the approval of enforcement officials such as then California Attorney General Van de Kamp (Los Angeles Times, November 15, 1988). Our data were originally downplayed by Los Angeles officials because they do not go beyond 1985 and because of continuing reports of close gang/crack/violence connections (McKinney, 1988). But with new information and analysis of heir own data by Los Angeles enforcement officials, the atmosphere in which)ur questions about the intensity of the gang/crack connection were not well received is now changing. The direct relevance of Skolnick's purposive correctional cohort to the issue of gang domination of street sales is unclear, and more careful analyses by the local police have revealed specialized "drug gangs" with peripheral relevance to traditional street gangs. In Los Angeles, as in many other cities, drug and gang problems may well intersect, but they do not thereby become a single, comprehensive social problem. Research on their confluence requires analysis of the gang and drug parameters separately, as well as in combination. In particular, assessments of an involvement must go beyond simplistic, undifferentiated depictions of street gangs to use the considerable knowledge base on street gangs available from the criminological literature of the past three decades.

Notes

1. Advantages, in addition to relatively easy distribution and disposability, included lower sales price and easier addiction. The Los Angeles price varied between $10 and $25 per quarter-gram "rock." This low price, the flood on the market, the ease of rock manufacture, transportation, carrying, hiding, and the rapidity and intensity of the high all conspired to make the rock form of cocaine preferable to the powdered form.

2. The cocaine sales arrest *incident* is the primary unit of analysis in this study. However, comparable increases can be seen in the number of *arrests* for these charges in the five stations. In 1983, the logs showed 380 arrests on cocaine sales charges. In 1984, arrests numbered 820, an increase of 116%. In 1985, the number rose to 2,123, a 159% increase over 1984 and a 459% increase over the 1983 arrest totals.

3. When the case file coding was completed, we found in fact that 87% of the incident case files reported the crack form of cocaine, with an average seizure of about 7.5 grams. These data are based on very thorough investigative techniques by the narcotics units, including laboratory determination of amounts seized and confirmation of the material as cocaine. Successful prosecution depends on such data, and the narcotics units were very concerned about having good cases for filing with the district attorney. Our observations within the stations confirmed the assiduousness with which these drug determinations were made.

4. Full details on this and other aspects of the data collection and coding are omitted due to space limitations. They are included in the full report available on request from the authors. Also, see Maxson et al. (1985) and Klein et al. (1986).

5. This measure of gang involvement was also examined by month. Despite the low number of cases in many of these time periods, the results are consistent with the analysis by six-month time periods reported in Table 15.1, that is, no evidence for an increasing level of gang involvement.

6. The mean gang age of twenty-two years speaks to two issues of interest. First, it yields no support for the claim by some that drug distributors have been

employing juveniles in order to avoid adult prosecutions of dealers. Second, it reinforces the recognition that gangs in the 1980s are "street gangs," not juvenile gangs. The average age of gang homicide suspects, in Chicago and Los Angeles, is nineteen.

References

Belenko, Steven and Jeffrey Fagan. (1987). *Crack and the Criminal Justice System*. New York: New York City Criminal Justice Agency.

Blum, Richard H. (1972). *The Dream Sellers*. San Francisco: Jossey-Bass.

Bonito, Arthur J., David N. Nurco, and John W. Shaffer. (1976). The veridicality of addicts' self-reports in social research. *The International Journal of the Addictions* 11:719–724.

Bureau of Criminal Statistics. (1988). *Homicide in California, 1988*. Sacramento, CA: Office of the Attorney General.

Elliott, Delbert S., David Huizinga, and Susan S. Ageton. (1985). *Explaining Delinquency and Drug Use*. Beverly Hills, CA: Sage.

Fagan, Jeffrey. (1989). The social organization of drug use and drug dealing among urban gangs. *Criminology* 27:633–669.

Fagan, Jeffrey and Ko-lin Chin. (1989a). Initiation into crack and cocaine: A tale of two epidemics. *Contemporary Drug Problems* 16:579–618.

_____. (1989b). Violence as regulation and social control in the distribution of crack. Presented at National Institute of Justice Technical Review Meeting on Drugs and Violence, Rockville, Md.

Gandossy, Robert P., Jay R. Williams, Jo Cohen, and Henrick J. Harwood. (1980). *Drugs and Crime: A Survey and Analysis of the Literature*. Washington, DC: U.S. Department of Justice.

Goldstein, Paul J. (1981). Getting over: Economic alternatives to predatory crime among street users. In James A. Inciardi (ed.), *The Drug-Crime Connection*. Beverly Hills, CA: Sage.

Gropper, Bernard A. (1984). Probing the links between drugs and crime. *NIJ Reports/SNI* 188 (November).

Hagedorn, John. (1988). *People and Folks: Gangs, Crime and the Underclass in a Rustbelt City*. Chicago: Lakeview Press.

Hindelang, Michael J., Travis Hirschi, and Joseph G. Weis. (1981). *Measuring Delinquency*. Beverly Hills, CA: Sage.

Huff, C. Ronald. (1989). Youth gangs and public policy. *Crime and Delinquency*. 35:524–537.

Inciardi, James A. (1988). *Crack Cocaine in Miami*. Newark: University of Delaware.

Klein, Malcolm W. (1971). *Street Gangs and Street Workers*. Englewood Cliffs, NJ: Prentice-Hall.

Klein, Malcolm W. (ed.). (1989). *Cross-National Research in Self-Reported Crime and Delinquency*. Dordrecht: Kluwer.

Klein, Malcolm W. and Cheryl L. Maxson. (1985). Rock sales in South Los Angeles. *Sociology and Social Research* 69:561–565.

_____. (1989). Street gang violence. In Neil A. Weiner and Marvin E. Wolfgang (eds.), *Violent Crime, Violent Criminals*. Beverly Hills, CA: Sage.

Klein, Malcolm W., Margaret A. Gordon, and Cheryl L. Maxson. (1986). The impact of police investigations on police-reported rates of gang and nongang homicides. *Criminology* 24:489–512.

Klein, Malcolm W., Cheryl L. Maxson, and Lea Cunningham. (1988). *Gang Involvement in Cocaine "Rock" Trafficking*. Social Science Research Institute. Los Angeles: University of Southern California.

Maxson, Cheryl L., Margaret A. Gordon, and Malcolm W. Klein. (1985). Differences between gang and nongang homicides. *Criminology* 23:209–222.

McBride, Duane C. (1981). Drugs and violence. In James A. Inciardi (ed.), *The Drugs-Crime Connection*. Beverly Hills, CA: Sage.

McKinney, Kay C. (1988). Juvenile gangs: Crime and drug trafficking. *Juvenile Justice Bulletin* (September). U.S. Department of Justice, Office of Juvenile Justice and Delinquency Prevention.

Mieczkowski, Tom. (1988). Crack distribution in Detroit. Paper delivered at the annual meeting of the American Society of Criminology, Chicago.

Reuter, Peter. (1988). *Youth Gangs and Drug Distribution: A Preliminary Enquiry*. Washington, DC: Rand.

Short, James, F., Jr. and Fred L. Strodtbeck. (1965). *Group Process and Gang Delinquency*. Chicago: University of Chicago Press.

Skolnick, Jerome H. (1988). The social structure of street drug dealing. BCS Forum. Bureau of Criminal Statistics. Sacramento: Office of the Attorney General.

Spergel, Irving. (1964). *Racketville, Slumtown, Haulburg: An Exploratory Study of Delinquent Subcultures*. Chicago: University of Chicago Press.

Tracy, Paul E. (1979). *Subcultural Delinquency: A Comparison of the Incidence and Seriousness of Gang and Nongang Member Offensivity*. Philadelphia: University of Pennsylvania Center for Studies in Criminology and Criminal Law.

Vigil, James D. (1988). *Barrio Gangs*. Austin: University of Texas Press.

Yablonsky, Lewis. (1963). *The Violent Gang*. New York: Macmillan.

16

Differences Between Gang
and Nongang Homicides

Cheryl L. Maxson, Margaret A. Gordon, and Malcolm W. Klein

A common and relatively unchallenged assertion in the literature of criminology is that delinquency is primarily a group phenomenon. Traceable to the early work of Shaw and McKay (1931) and reinforced by their Chicago colleagues (Sutherland, 1955; Thrasher, 1963; Tannenbaum, 1966; Lohman, 1966), the group delinquency assertion has since been repeated often enough to constitute a truism in our field. Oblique challenges to the assertion by the Sherifs (1967) and by Korn and McCorkle (1959) have been joined by only one direct challenge (Klein, 1969) which was based on definitional rather than empirical grounds.

While the assertion of the preponderance of group delinquency has generally been accepted, the form of group delinquency, or what the nature of "group" brings to delinquency, remains a relatively barren field of research. Yablonsky (1963) stressed the violent consequences of low-cohesion gangs with megalomanic leadership. Jansyn (1966) and Klein and Crawford (1967) drew opposite conclusions about the causal directions between gang cohesiveness and delinquency, the former on the basis of an ethnography of a gang clique and the latter on the basis of more distant observations of five large clusters of gangs.

Tracy (1981) has demonstrated with Philadelphia police data that gang members commit more offenses across the board than do nongang members. Klein (1971), Cohen (1969), and Erickson and Jensen (1977) have described the kinds of offenses more and less likely to be committed in the company of others. Different sources (gang and survey respondents) and methodologies (official arrest versus self-reports) in these latter three studies yield findings with significant but moderate agreement. Yet the character of group delinquency events is not yet well documented; we need the sorts of descriptive

Reprinted with permission from *Criminology*, Vol. 23, No. 2 (1985): 209–222.

data about these events that will increase our understanding of the group nature of youthful offending.

Several directions toward this end may be taken, of which the work reported here on gang violence is one. If "the group" has a significant effect on the form and magnitude of delinquent events, the street gang is a particularly convenient context in which to demonstrate it. While gang-related incidents need not necessarily involve large numbers of participants and nongang crimes may include more than a single assailant and victim, gang incidents are more likely to be group affairs, and thus to illuminate group delinquency processes. Our concern is not whether and how much group or gang delinquency takes place, but rather the difference gangs make in the character of events—in particular, violent events leading to homicide.

During the late seventies, Los Angeles County witnessed a dramatic increase in gang violence (a 75% jump in gang-related homicides from 1978 to 1980, rising to a reported total of 351 in 1980). This evoked an energetic response by the law enforcement community to combat gang crime. While Los Angeles presents an extreme case, it is hardly unique either in its concern with the extent and seriousness of gang violence (Miller, 1975) or in the growth of law enforcement specialists to respond to it (Stapleton and Needle, 1982). Yet few researchers have investigated the differences between gang and nongang violence. In light of the group nature of events, variation can be anticipated, but the extent and nature of this variation remains largely unexplored.

Cohen's (1969) comparison of essential patterns of delinquency exhibited by organized gangs and spontaneously formed groups yielded differences with reference to the content of the event (that is, type of offense, motive, and use or display of weapons), aggregated characteristics of offenders, and aggregated characteristics of victims. However, these findings concerned incidents referred to Philadelphia's Gang Control Unit that were originally presumed to be gang incidents; that is, the "group" events were misclassified as gang events. Thus, the differences between Cohen's gang and group incidents presumably would be less substantial than those emerging from comparisons of gang incidents and the more inclusive category of nongang incidents investigated here.

Spergel (1983) compared aggregated demographic characteristics of the participants in gang and nongang homicides. In particular, he found that gang-related homicides involve persons younger than did other types of homicides. Finally, Tracy (1981), in a follow-up of the 1945 Philadelphia birth cohort, reported that the incidence and seriousness of official and self-reported offenses among gang members were significantly greater than among nongang subjects in Philadelphia.

In this paper, we have two purposes in mind. The first is to fill the gap in the criminological literature on how gang-related homicides differ from other homicides. The second is to address whether gang-related homicide warrants distinctive public concern as well as specialized law enforcement responses (see Dahmann, 1982). Using bivariate and discriminant analyses, we can assess how different the two types of homicides are from each other, the nature of the differences, and the relative effect of each of the variables in producing these differences.

Methods

The following analyses utilize data collected from law enforcement investigation files on over seven hundred gang- and nongang-designated homicides within the jurisdiction of the Los Angeles Sheriffs Department (LASD) and the Los Angeles Police Department (LAPD) between 1978 and mid-1982.[1] Due to differences in sampling procedures[2] as well as jurisdictional differences in investigation and recording practices, it was necessary to treat the LASD and the LAPD cases as separate samples. To maximize the comparability between gang and nongang incidents, all homicides included in these analyses have at least one named suspect between the ages of ten and thirty.[3]

Findings

The homicide incident descriptors can be roughly divided into characteristics of the setting (broadly defined) and characteristics of the participants. In both categories, major gang/nongang differences emerge.

Turning first to the LASD data, the setting descriptors (table 16.1) indicate that the where and how of homicide is clearly related to gang/nongang distinctions. Gang killings are far more likely to take place in public settings, particularly on the street. They are somewhat more likely to involve automobiles and shooting out of a vehicle. They are more likely to involve guns and more weapons overall in the incident.

Gang murders are more likely to include additional offenses, particularly attempted homicide and assault with a deadly weapon. Note, however, that the number of additional offenses among such cases does not differ between gang and nongang events. Gang cases are more likely to inflict injuries in addition to the homicide, although the difference in the number of injured victim companions per injury case does not reach statistical significance. There are more gang cases with unknown suspects (again, the number of unknown suspects among these cases does not differ) and more cases involving intimidation or fear of retaliation. The only other exception to the pattern of gang/nongang setting differences among the LASD cases is the time of day. The majority of both gang and nongang homicides occur at night, between 10 p.m. and 6 a.m.

In sum, most setting variables differentiate between gang and nongang

Table 16.1 Setting Characteristics for Restricted Gang and Nongang Samples (LASD)

Characteristics	Restricted Gang (N = 226)[a]	Nongang (N = 200)[a]	Association and Significance[b]
Location			.390**
Street	48%	14%	
Other Public	27%	34%	
Residence	24%	53%	
Automobile			.267**
None	34%	43%	
Car Involved	44%	53%	
Shooting Out of Car	22%	4%	
Time of Day			n.s.
Daytime	11%	13%	
Afternoon/Evening	33%	34%	
Nighttime	57%	53%	
Weapons			
Guns Present	80%	60%	.212**
Knives Present	31%	37%	n.s.
Other Weapons			
Present	31%	23%	n.s.
Mean Total Number			
of Weapons	2.23	1.68	.160**
Associated Offenses			
None	27%	48%	
One	43%	28%	.212**
More Than One	29%	24%	
Mean Number Per	(n = 164)	(n = 105)	
Case with Offense	1.55	1.71	n.s.
Type of Associated Offense	(n = 164)	(n = 105)	
Per Case with Offense[c]			
Other Homicide (e.g.			
Attempt, Conspiracy)	45%	22%	.230**
Robbery	20%	34%	−.166**
ADW	57%	39%	.178**
Other	23%	50%	−.282**
Injuries in Addition to Homicide			
Cases with Injuries	30%	10%	.243**
Mean Number Injured	(n = 67)	(n = 20)	
Per Injury Case	1.69	1.35	n.s.
Unknown Suspects			
Cases with Unknowns	19%	7%	.169**
Mean Number Per Case	(n = 43)	(n = 14)	
with Unknowns	2.74	1.71	n.s.
Fear of Retaliation Present	33%	10%	.287**

a. Most variables refer to the total number of cases (226 and 200) minus missing information on up to 7 cases. Where Ns differ by reason of subsampling, the different Ns are indicated.

b. Levels of association in the last column were determined as appropriate by Phi, Cramer's V, or Pearson's r, respectively, for 2 × 2 tables, 2 × N tables, and interval-level data. Significance levels were determined as appropriate by chi-squares or t-tests.

c. Associated offense types are not mutually exclusive categories.

  * $p < .05$

** $p < .01$

homicides. Gang homicides appear to be considerably more visible and more violent. Yet the differences are not so striking as one might have expected. For example, drive-by shootings, presumably the quintessence of gang killings, occur in only 48 of 226 cases. Similarly, fear of retaliation is noted in 33 percent of the gang cases—one might have anticipated a higher figure—but also in 10 percent of the nongang cases. The difference in presence of various weapons is also less striking than might have been expected.

Variables not typically examined by researchers, such as presence and type of associated offenses, injuries to other victims, and unknown suspects also emerged in this analysis (admittedly with low coefficients of association) and help to fill out a picture of the gang homicide setting. As compared with the nongang setting, it is less dramatically different than is often depicted, but more broadly different than is generally recognized (that is, more gang/nongang differences, but smaller than commonly assumed). This finding suggests a generally qualitative as well as quantitative difference.

The second aspect of possible differences is in the characteristics of the homicide suspects and victims (table 16.2). The participant variables even more clearly distinguish gang from nongang cases, a point easily illustrated by reference to the measures of association. Gang homicides involve two and a half times as many participants. Participants in gang incidents are twice as likely never to have had known prior contact between victims and suspects, and are less than one third as likely to have had a clear prior relationship. Homicide victims and suspects charged with homicide are about five years younger in gang incidents, despite the age restrictions placed on the sample (ten to thirty years). Gang suspects and victims in the LASD jurisdiction are far more likely to be Hispanic and almost never white, in contrast to the more even ethnic breakdown in nongang cases.

The ethnicity difference is not surprising; Los Angeles has long been known for its Hispanic gangs in contrast with the white ethnic gang activity observed in cities such as Chicago or Boston. The relationship difference may be surprising to some, because in decades past, gangs were generally portrayed as preying primarily on well-known adversaries. The presumption that warring gang members know each other at least by reputation, if not by sight and name, seems untenable. Among gang-designated homicides with clear gang-on-gang motives or behavior during the incident, 54 percent show no evidence of any prior personal contact. In these gang homicides, the relationship between opponents appears to be based on gang affiliation rather than enmity between familiar individuals. In spite of rising public concern about innocent bystander victims, we found mention of only four such cases (all gang-related).

Turning now to the LAPD data, a number of setting factors differentiate between gang and nongang incidents (table 16.3). However, it is notable that the distinctions are not as uniform nor as large as those observed in the LASD data. Presence or type of associated offense are not differentiating factors in

Table 16.2 Participant Characteristics for Restricted Gang and Nongang
Samples (LASD)

Characteristics by Case[a]	Restricted Gang (N = 226)	Nongang (N = 200)	Association and Significance[b]
Participants			
Total	8.96	3.59	.344**
On Suspect Side	4.07	1.79	.386**
On Victim Side	4.70	1.79	.262**
Relationship			
No Prior Contact	54%	24%	.496**
Minimal Familiarity	28%	8%	
Clear Prior Contact	19%	68%	

Characteristics by Individual[a]	Restricted Gang	Nongang	Association and Significance[b]
Gang Affiliation, Homicide Suspects	(n = 458)	(n = 238)	.800**
No Mention	11%	92%	
Possibly Gang	12%	5%	
Clearly Gang	78%	3%	
Gang Affiliation, Homicide Victims	(n = 236)	(n = 209)	.539**
No Mention	45%	94%	
Possibly Gang	7%	1%	
Clearly Gang	47%	4%	
Mean Age	(n = 458)	(n = 238)	
Homicide Suspects	19.16	24.02	−.371**
	(n = 236)	(n = 209)	
Homicide Victims	23.50	29.00	−.198**
Gender			
Homicide Suspects	(n = 458)	(n = 238)	
% Male	97%	87%	.174*
Homicide Victims	(n = 236)	(n = 209)	
% Male	92%	82%	.145**
Ethnicity, Homicide Suspects	(n = 458)	(n = 238)	.505**
Black	24%	42%	
Hispanic	74%	30%	
White	1%	27%	
Other	1%	1%	
Ethnicity, Homicide Victims	(n = 236)	(n = 209)	.498**
Black	12%	32%	
Hispanic	83%	39%	
White	3%	29%	
Other	3%	—	

a. Participants and Relationship refer to involved individuals on the crime scene (226 and 200) minus missing
information on up to 9 cases. Variables describing demographic characteristics of police-designated
victims and suspects are reported by individual rather than by case and refer to homicide victims (236 and
209) and suspects charged with homicide (458 and 238) rather than victims or suspects of associated
offenses.
b. Levels of association in the last column were determined as appropriate by Phi, Cramer's V, or Pearson's
r, respectively, for 2 × 2 tables, 2 × N tables, and interval level data. Significance levels were
determined as appropriate by chi-squares or t-tests.
* p <.05   ** p <.01

Table 16.3 Setting Characteristics for Restricted Gang and Nongang Samples (LAPD)

Characteristics	Restricted Gang (N = 135)[a]	Nongang (N = 148)[a]	Association and Significance[b]
Location			.153**
Street	49%	34%	
Other Public	22%	27%	
Residence	29%	39%	
Automobile			.288**
None	37%	53%	
Car Involved	42%	44%	
Shooting Out of Car	21%	3%	
Time of Day			n.s.
Daytime	14%	12%	
Afternoon/Evening	41%	39%	
Nighttime	45%	48%	
Weapons			
Guns Present	83%	68%	.173**
Knives Present	24%	37%	−.140*
Other Weapons			
Present	12%	15%	n.s.
Mean Total Number			
of Weapons	1.63	1.57	n.s.
Associated Offenses			
None	52%	62%	
One	33%	29%	n.s.
More Than One	15%	9%	
Mean Number Per	(n = 65)	(n = 56)	
Case with Offense	1.27	1.48	n.s.
Type of Associated Offense	(n = 65)	(n = 56)	
Per Case with Offense[c]			
Other Homicide (e.g.			
Attempt, Conspiracy)	51%	41%	n.s.
Robbery	38%	29%	n.s.
ADW	28%	25%	n.s.
Other	23%	23%	n.s.
Injuries in Addition to Homicide			
Cases with Injuries	21%	14%	n.s.
Mean Number Injured	(n = 28)	(n = 20)	
Per Injury Case	1.54	1.15	n.s.
Unknown Suspects			
Cases with Unknowns	23%	10%	.174**
Mean Number Per Case	(n = 31)	(n = 15)	
with Unknowns	3.19	2.08	n.s.
Fear of Retaliation			
Present	33%	13%	.304**

a. Most variables refer to the total number of cases (135 and 148) minus missing information on up to 6 cases. Where Ns differ by reason of subsampling, the different Ns are indicated.

b. Levels of association in the last column were determined as appropriate by Phi, Cramer's V, or Pearson's r, respectively, for 2 × 2 tables, 2 × N tables, and interval data. Significance levels were determined as appropriate by chi-squares or t-tests.

c. Associated offense types are not mutually exclusive categories.

* p < .05
** p < .01

the LAPD data, and consequently the presence of other victim injuries does not separate gang from nongang cases. As in the LASD data, street location and presence of firearms and automobiles are more likely in gang killings.

To a greater extent than was the case with the setting variables, the LAPD participant characteristics in table 16.4 do differentiate between gang and nongang cases. Victim ethnicity is the only exception. In contrast with the LASD, LAPD homicides have a preponderance of black participants as well as high proportions of Hispanic participants, but very few white suspects or victims, even in nongang cases. The participant variables show a general pattern of lower coefficients of association in the LAPD data than is true in the LASD tables, but the jurisdictional difference in the participant data is nowhere near as striking as it is with respect to setting characteristics.

Discriminant analysis was utilized to assess the differentiation between designated gang and nongang cases in a multivariate context.[4] This technique produces a linear combination of discriminating variables (a discriminant function) that best separates the groups from each other.[5] In both the LASD and LAPD data, the proportion of variance in the discriminant function (eta^2) accounted for by the two groups (gang and nongang) is surprisingly high (.48 and .38), given the complexity and ambiguity of the file materials and the exploratory nature of the research. Classification based on the discriminant function is successful in 82 percent of LASD cases and 79 percent of LAPD cases.[6]

The standardized discriminant function coefficients shown in table 16.5 reflect the relative importance of the variables in distinguishing between gang and nongang homicides. All coefficients are statistically significant; the direction is relative to the signs of the group centroids. In the LASD data, two participant variables—mean age and ethnic status of suspects—are clearly the most important, followed by street location, number of participants on the suspect side, and presence of a gun; variables pertaining to characteristics of the suspects, rather than of the victims, predominate.

Results from the LAPD and LASD analyses are generally similar. Confirming the observations made from the bivariate tables, the LAPD discrimination between gang and nongang cases is lower. Both sets of analyses indicate a strong overall capacity for the participant variables to discriminate between gang and nongang cases, and this is particularly true of variables describing designated suspects and other participants on the suspect side. The characteristics of the homicide setting tend to be of secondary importance to the participant characteristics.[7]

Conclusions

Both the cross-tabular and discriminant analyses display substantial differences between gang and nongang homicides; several items of particular interest may

Table 16.4   Participant Characteristics for Restricted Gang and Nongang
Samples (LAPD)

Characteristics by Case[a]	Restricted Gang (N = 135)	Nongang (N = 148)	Association and Significance[b]
Participants			
Total	6.96	3.77	.281**
On Suspect Side	3.82	1.92	.254**
On Victim Side	2.83	1.83	.225**
Relationship			
No Prior Contact	49%	27%	.469**
Minimal or Indirect			
Relationship[c]	31%	8%	
Clear Prior Contact	20%	65%	
Characteristics by Individual[a]	*Restricted Gang*	*Nongang*	*Association and Significance[b]*
Gang Affiliation,	(n = 251)	(n = 165)	.724**
Homicide Suspects			
No Mention	15%	88%	
Possibly Gang	10%	4%	
Clearly Gang	75%	8%	
Gang Affiliation,	(n = 136)	(n = 148)	.524**
Homicide Victims			
No Mention	51%	96%	
Possibly Gang	9%	1%	
Clearly Gang	40%	2%	
Mean Age			
Homicide Suspects	(n = 251)	(n = 165)	
	19.40	23.68	−.332**
Homicide Victims	(n = 136)	(n = 148)	
	23.67	31.06	−.305**
Gender			
Homicide Suspects,	(n = 251)	(n = 165)	
% Male	97%	88%	.185*
Homicide Victims,	(n = 136)	(n = 148)	
% Male	95%	89%	.114**
Ethnicity, Homicide	(n = 251)	(n = 165)	.140*
Suspects			
Black	55%	65%	
Hispanic	45%	34%	
White	—	1%	
Other	—	—	
Ethnicity, Homicide	(n = 136)	(n = 148)	n.s.
Victims			
Black	43%	56%	
Hispanic	53%	39%	
White	4%	4%	
Other	1%	1%	

a. Participants and Relationship refer to involved individuals on the crime scene (135 and 148) minus missing
   information on up to 9 cases. Variables describing demographic characteristics of police-designated victims
   and suspects are reported by individual rather than by case and refer to homicide victims (136 and 148) and
   suspects charged with homicide (251 and 165) rather than victims or suspects of associated offenses.
b. Levels of association in the last column were determined as appropriate by Phi, Cramer's V, or Pearson's
   r, respectively, for 2 × 2 tables, 2 × N tables, and interval data. Significance levels were determined as
   appropriate by chi-squares or t-tests.
c. "Indirect" relationship was a new coding category developed for LAPD cases; victim and suspect
   interacted only as a result of a mutual third party contact, e.g., brother or girl friend of victim.
   * p < .05   ** p < .01

Table 16.5   Standardized Discriminant Function Coefficients[a]

LASD		LAPD	
Mean age of suspects	−.491	Mean age of suspects	.736
Hispanic suspects	.415	Mean age of victims	.342
Street location	.322	Black suspects	.248
No. of participants, suspect side	.307	Gun present	−.238
Gun Present	.278	Proportion male suspects	−.218
Mean age of victims	−.237	No. of participants, suspect side	−.196
Proportion male suspects	.185	No prior contact, victims and suspects	−.189
No prior contact, victim and suspects	.164	Automobile present	−.188
No. of participants, victim side	.156	No. of participants, victim side	.063
Associated violent offenses	.152		
Mean age difference, victims and suspects	.113		
[Group Centroids: nongang, −1.040; gang, .907]		[Group Centroids: nongang, .825; gang, −.866]	
Wilkes Lambda	.52	Wilkes Lambda	.62
Canonical Correlation	.70	Canonical Correlation	.62
Eta^2	.48	Eta^2	.38
Classification Success:		Classification Success:	
Nongang	79%	Nongang	71%
Gang	84%	Gang	87%
Overall	82%	Overall	79%

a. Direction of coefficient is relative to sign of group centroid.

be highlighted. For instance, some may be surprised by the relatively common instances of gang homicides involving participants on each side with no prior personal contact, but also by the relative absence of "innocent bystander" victims. Greater automobile involvement fits the general picture of modern mobile street gangs, as do the preponderance of intra-ethnic relationships between opposing sides and the preponderance of minority group and male involvement. Finally, while gang suspects and victims are, as expected, considerably younger than their nongang counterparts, they are older than might be expected of "youth gang" members. In the absence of good historical data, it is nevertheless our impression that gang homicide participants described here are older than their counterparts of two or three decades ago.

There can be little doubt, given the data presented here, that gang homicides differ both quantitatively and qualitatively from nongang homicides. Most distinctly, they differ with respect to ethnicity, age, number of participants, and relationship between the participants, properties clearly related to the *group* nature of the events.

Gang homicide settings also differ from those of other settings. They are more likely to involve public areas, automobiles, firearms, and, in the LASD data, associated nonhomicide offenses and injuries to other victims.

The contribution of group processes to the higher incidence of these features is well worth further research.

Finally, given these differences, gang incidents seem to present unique problems to investigators and may well benefit from the specialized skills and experience of experts on gangs. The public nature of gang homicides, reluctance of victims, witnesses, and informants to provide information (either through fear of retaliation or gang loyalty), and the lack of prior contact between victims and offenders suggest that investigators might profit from knowledge about the character of such offenses and access to relatively sophisticated gang intelligence (territories, rivalries, membership rosters, and descriptions). Location, automobile involvement, and gun presence suggest potential points of intervention. While the data presented here refer to homicide, analysis of nonhomicide violent incidents (see footnote 7) indicates marked similarities between the two offense types regarding the nature of gang/nongang differences. Therefore, the implications of the differences between gang and nongang homicides for specialization in law enforcement can be more broadly drawn as gang/nongang *violence* differences. Given the nature of these differences, investigative specialization may be justified in police departments of cities having large gang populations.

Implications for public concern regarding gang homicides are less clear. It is evident that gang incidents are generally more chaotic, with more people, weapons, offenses, and injuries out in the open, among people less familiar with each other. However, the small number of "innocent bystander" victims suggests that the potential threat of gang violence to the general public is not substantial.

Notes

1. See Klein, Maxson, and Gordon (1984) for a detailed description of research methodology. Los Angeles enforcement agencies employ a comprehensive definition of gang-related incidents that generally assigns gang status to any event principally involving a gang member or gang motive on either the suspect or victim side.

2. Within the LASD, all gang homicides between 1978 and mid-1982 were included. In LAPD, limited resources and a larger number of gang murders precluded collection of all gang homicides over the four-and-one-half-year period. Accordingly, all gang homicides between 1979 and 1981 that occurred in three high gang activity stations were collected in LAPD. In both jurisdictions, nongang homicides were selected according to a random sampling design stratified by rate of gang homicide per station. See Klein et al. (1984) for a full description of jurisdictional differences.

3. Restricting the sample in this manner represents a potential bias, but upon investigation, it appears that the loss in numbers is more of a problem than is bias. The gang/nongang comparison was made twice in LASD (the jurisdiction with the larger loss of eighty-six cases), once with the full gang population, and once with the restricted gang sample (selection of nongang cases was restricted from the outset).

Among a total of ninety-three variables, there was a difference in conclusion (statistical significance) with respect to only seven variables, and most of these were related to the omission of unknown suspects affecting investigation variables not included in the analyses presented here.

4. Discriminant analysis assumes equal covariance matrices across the groups (Klecka, 1980; Pedhazur, 1982), a condition not met here. However, logistic regression does not make this assumption (Press and Wilson, 1978), so we have applied this technique to our data as well. The resulting model of gang/nongang differences was quite fully substantiated. Similarly, the comparison of results of a quadratic classification analysis (Huberty, 1984) with results of our classification rates yields no substantial difference. Both of these alternative techniques indicate that the unequal covariance matrices across the groups are not a significant problem for our analysis.

5. A multistaged procedure was used to select variables for the discriminant analysis. A significant ($p < .05$) bivariate relationship between the variable and gang designation was the first and most basic criterion for selection. Choices among highly correlated variables were made on the basis of the strength of bivariate relationships, as well as conceptual considerations. Partial correlations between variables controlling for the number of participating suspects and victims were also considered. In contrast to the bivariate analyses described in Tables 16.1 through 16.4, demographic characteristics refer to *all* designated victims, including those injured but not killed, and all designated suspects, whether charged with homicide or an associated offense or not charged at all, including "unknown" suspects. Ethnicity variables are dummy coded for presence of suspects predominantly Hispanic (LASD) or black (LAPD).

6. These numbers should be viewed cautiously because classification of the same cases from which the discriminant function was derived results in an upward bias of classification success rates; the degree of bias varies with sample size and the number of discriminating variables (Morrison, 1974).

7. Information on violent nonhomicide incidents (that is, felony assault, robbery, shooting into an inhabited dwelling, and rape) was collected from two LASD stations with high gang activity in order to compare gang/nongang homicide differences to a broader assortment of violent offenses. Analyses of the sample of 280 gang and 243 nongang violent incidents indicated substantial differences between the two types of nonhomicide cases. The bivariate analysis revealed a similar pattern of differences (predominance of participant differences), but the coefficients of association were quite often lower. In the discriminant analysis, the nonhomicide eta^2 and classification success rate were substantial, but lower than in homicide cases, suggesting less distinction between the character of gang and nongang violent nonhomicide events. The ordering of variables, according to their coefficients, and the content of the variables were somewhat different than was the case in the homicide discriminant analysis, but characteristics of the suspects (in particular, age) were similarly important to the differentiation of gang from nongang violent incidents.

References

Cohen, Bernard. (1969). The delinquency of gangs and spontaneous groups. In Thorsten Sellin and Marvin Wolfgang (eds.), *Delinquency: Selected Studies*. New York: Wiley.

Dahmann, Judith. (1982). *An Evaluation of Operation Hardcore: A Prosecutorial Response to Violent Gang Criminality* (draft). Washington, DC: National Institute of Justice.

Erickson, Maynard and Gary Jensen. (1977). Delinquency is still group behavior!: Toward revitalizing the group premise in the sociology of deviance. *Journal of Criminal Law and Criminology* 68: 262–273.

Huberty, Carl. (1984). Issues in the use and interpretation of discrimination analysis. *Psychological Bulletin* 95: 156–171.

Jansyn, Leon. (1966). Solidarity and delinquency in a street corner group. *American Sociological Review* 31: 600–614.

Klecka, William. (1980). *Discriminant Analysis*. Beverly Hills: Sage.

Klein, Malcolm. (1969). On the group context of delinquency. *Sociology and Social Research* 54: 63–71.

————. (1971). Street Gangs and Street Workers. Englewood Cliffs, NJ: Prentice-Hall.

Klein, Malcolm and Lois Crawford. (1967). Groups, gangs, and cohesiveness. *Journal of Research in Crime and Delinquency* 4: 63–75.

Klein, Malcolm, Cheryl Maxson, and Margaret Gordon. (1984). *Evaluation in an Imported Gang Violence Deterrence Program: Final Report* (draft). Washington, DC: National Institute of Justice.

Korn, Richard and Lloyd McCorkle. (1959). *Criminology and Penology*. New York: Holt.

Lohman, Joseph. (1966). County communities, the City of Pleasant Hill, and the unincorporated area of Lafayette (mimeo). Berkeley: University of California.

Miller, Walter. (1975). *Violence by Youth Gangs and Youth Groups as a Crime Problem in Major American Cities* (draft). Washington, DC: National Institute for Juvenile Justice and Delinquency Prevention.

Morrison, Donald. (1974). Discriminant analysis. In Robert Ferber (ed.), *Handbook of Market Research*. New York: McGraw-Hill.

Pedhazur, Elazar. (1982). *Multiple Regression in Behavioral Research*. New York: Holt, Rinehart, and Winston.

Press, S. James and Sandra Wilson. (1978). Choosing between logistic regression and discriminant analysis. *Journal of the American Statistical Association* 73: 699–705.

Shaw, Clifford and Henry McKay. (1931). *Social Factors in Juvenile Delinquency, Report on the Causes of Crime No. 3*, Vol. II. Washington, DC: U.S. Government Printing Office.

Sherif, Muzafer and Carolyn Sherif. (1967). Group process and collective interaction in delinquent activities. *Journal of Research in Crime and Delinquency* 4: 43–62.

Spergel, Irving. (1983). Violent Gangs in Chicago: Segmentation and integration. Unpublished manuscript. Chicago: School of Social Service Administration, University of Chicago.

Stapleton, Vaughan and Jerry Needle. (1982). *Police Handling of Youth Gangs*. Sacramento: American Justice Institute.

Sutherland, Edwin. (1955). *Principles of Criminology*. 5th ed. Philadelphia: Lippincott.

Tannenbaum, Frank. (1966). Point of view. In Rose Giallombardo (ed.), *Juvenile Delinquency: A Book of Readings*. New York: Wiley.

Thrasher, Frederic. (1963). *The Gang: A Study of 1,313 Gangs in Chicago*. University of Chicago Press.

Tracy, Paul. (1981). Subcultural delinquency: A comparison of the incidence and seriousness of gang and non-gang members' offensivity. Unpublished, Center for Studies in Criminology and Criminal Law. Philadelphia: University of Pennsylvania.

Yablonsky, Lewis. (1963). *The Violent Gang*. New York: Macmillan.

17

Gang Homicide, Delinquency,
and Community

G. David Curry and Irving A. Spergel

Earlier discussions, using lower class culture and subculture frameworks (Cloward and Ohlin, 1960; A. Cohen, 1955; A. Cohen and Short, 1958; Miller, 1958), tend to obscure distinctions between gang and delinquent group behavior (Kornhauser, 1978). A few theorists and researchers (Cartwright and Howard, 1966; Kornhauser, 1978; Miller 1975; Morash, 1983; Thrasher, 1963) indicate that the gang is a broader concept than the delinquent group. Gang behavior is nondelinquent as well as delinquent. It has even been suggested that the gang can perform an organizing and stabilizing function in slum communities (Suttles 1968; Whyte, 1943). Although there is a wealth of theory about delinquency, including theories about delinquent subcultures and groups, a number of recent reviews of the research literature emphasize individual characteristics (Baldwin, 1979; Currie, 1985; J. Wilson and Herrnstein, 1985). Most criminologists and sociologists, however, continue to demonstrate that delinquency, particularly among lower class youths, tends to be companionate or group in nature (Empey, 1978; Erickson and Jensen, 1977; Samecki, 1986; Shaw and McKay, 1969; Zimring, 1981). Recently, there has been renewed interest in ecological studies and the relation between delinquency or crime rates and community characteristics, such as poverty, race-ethnicity, housing, family structure, and population age (Reiss and Tonry, 1986). In particular, there is growing interest in the stable and dynamic aspects of each of these community characteristics over time (Bursik, 1986, Bursik and Webb, 1982; Heitgerd and Bursik, 1987; Schuerman and Kobrin, 1986).

We define group delinquency as law-violating behavior committed by juveniles in relatively small peer groups that tend to be ephemeral, i.e., loosely organized with shifting leadership. The delinquent group is engaged in various forms of minor or serious crime. We define gang delinquency or crime as

Reprinted with permission from *Criminology*, Vol. 26, No. 3 (1988): 381–405.

law-violating behavior committed both by juveniles and adults in or related to groups that are complexly organized although sometimes diffuse, sometimes cohesive with established leadership and membership rules. The gang also engages in a range of crime but significantly more violence within a framework of norms and values in respect to mutual support, conflict relations with other gangs, and a tradition often of turf, colors, signs, and symbols. Subgroups of the gang may be differentially committed to various delinquent or criminal patterns, such as drug trafficking, gang fighting, or burglary. The concepts of delinquent group and youth gang are not exclusive of each other but represent distinctive social phenomena (see also Miller, 1982; Thrasher, 1963).

The inconsistency of earlier research is compounded by its use of youth agency samples, participant-observation, and self-report methodologies. Perhaps it is theoretical and methodological shortcomings, as much as changes in social behavior, that lead to different perspectives of gang behaviors over time (Gilbert, 1986). Based on observations in the 1950s and 1960s, researchers (Klein, 1971; Miller 1958; Short and Strodtbeck, 1965) reported that property crime was highly prevalent, but little serious violence was committed by youth gangs. A few took strong exception (Spergel, 1964; Yablonsky, 1962), but all to some extent failed to distinguish clearly between gangs and nongang delinquent groups. More recent research emphasizes the use of official as well as informant data and systematically compares the official deviancy of gang members with that of delinquent group members. In the 1970s and 1980s, scholars have emphasized the serious and violent nature of gang behavior (Klein and Maxson, 1987; Maxson et al., 1985; Miller, 1975, 1982; Spergel, 1984, 1986). Findings over time have consistently indicated that the delinquency of gang members is more extensive, violent, serious, and persistent (B. Cohen, 1969a, 1969b; Friedman, et al., 1975; Robin, 1967; Tracy, 1982, 1988).[1] Only Cartwright and Howard (1966) attempted an ecological analysis, which partially succeeded in distinguishing between gang and delinquency rates. Unfortunately, their sample was limited to 16 gangs participating in a special YMCA youth gang project. Still, they found evidence that the socioeconomic characteristics of gang neighborhoods were different, in fact somewhat better, than those of other delinquent groups.

Classic delinquency theory and research also do not clearly or systematically distinguish between "the poverty belt" and social disorganization, particularly the problems of shifting, newcomer, immigrant colonies (Shaw and McKay, 1969; Thrasher, 1963). Recent authors of participant-observation research in many cases (Campbell, 1984; Horowitz, 1983; Moore, 1978) also fail to make this distinction. At least in reference to inner-city communities, social disorganization and poverty are sometimes treated as equivalent concepts (W. Wilson, 1987). We, however, treat social disorganization as a weakening of social control associated with the disruption of a stable social and cultural life (Collins and Makowski, 1983; Farrell and Swigert, 1982; Janowitz, 1978,

1983; Thomas and Znaniecki, 1920). By poverty, we refer to the economic conditions and deprivation that persist over time within a given population. We argue that delinquency is more closely associated with poverty and that gang crime, especially gang homicide, is more closely associated with social disorganization.

Variables in Analysis

Using community-level data on Chicago community areas, we examine two conceptual differences. The first is the distinction between gang crime and delinquency as community-level phenomena. The second is the difference between theoretical associations of each of the former patterns of social disorganization and poverty in community areas. Our interest is in the stable or quasi-stable and dynamic aspects of the ecological system, which may be at the heart of explaining different, mainly community-level, crime patterns as well as their changes over time. Our research differentiates two patterns of gang activity and delinquency; one associated with the chronic poverty of ghetto life and the other with the social disorganization that comes with population resettlement and a period of cultural isolation. The first pattern is more common in Chicago's black communities, the second, more common in Chicago's Hispanic communities.

Our analysis is based on aggregate or community-level data because (1) individual-level data are not available and, more important, (2) the phenomena of interest are ecological or aggregate level in nature. The ecological fallacy has been avoided by carefully restricting our conclusions to the community as the unit of analysis rather than to individual community residents or gang members. We are interested primarily in gang and delinquency problems in their relation to other community-level characteristics, as well as in their relation to each other.

Gang Crime and Delinquency

A key methodological issue is the operational definition of the gang problem. With a variety of options available (California Council on Criminal Justice, 1986; Klein, 1971, Miller, 1982; Spergel, 1984; Thrasher, 1963) some empirical if not theoretical consensus exists that the measure should be based on official police statistics (Klein and Maxson, 1987) and the most serious criminal offenses (Maxson et al., 1985; Miller 1975, 1982). The Gang Crime Unit of the Chicago Police Department focuses on high-profile gangs engaged in the serious, mainly assaultive crime that grows out of gang function or gang-related motivation.[2] We chose to use the gang homicide statistics maintained by this unit. Though this statistic remains the tip of the gang problem iceberg, it is the one that has been most consistently and systematically measured across

Chicago's community areas over time. It is the type of measure that is used in policy and program assessments of the extent and seriousness of the gang problem in other cities and states across the country. This measure is selected for the periods 1978–81 and 1982–85, in order to be coordinate with available 1980 census and delinquency rate data. We aggregate gang homicide rate for the entire eight-year period for the first part of our analysis and disaggregate the two four-year periods for our subsequent analysis of change in the gang problem.

Gang membership and participation tend to be age-specific behavior involving youths and younger adults, but the victims of gang violence involve a somewhat wider age range, all members of the community. In actuality, for Chicago, gang homicide offenders and victims are concentrated at the upper edge of the youth and younger adult categories. Since 1978, the average age of gang homicide offenders has been nineteen; the average age of victims, twenty (Spergel, 1986). This age concentration is consistent with findings from other cities (Maxson et al., 1985; San Diego Association of Governments, 1982). We compute gang homicide rate on the basis of its impact on the population of the total community area, i.e., as the number of gang-related homicides per 100,000 population in the total community area.

Delinquency rates are the number of reported police arrests per 100,000 age-eligible male population (ages ten to sixteen), but it includes a variety of minor illegal acts and even possibly status offenses. We selected what we consider to be the best available measures of serious delinquency available, burglary-theft and violent offenses. This combined measure conforms with other measures used in ecological analyses of delinquency in Chicago's community areas (Bursik, 1986; Bursik and Webb, 1982; Heitgerd and Bursik, 1987). Although an earlier Chicago study (Spergel, 1986) showed that only 20 percent of gang homicides are committed by offenders under seventeen years of age, we reemphasize our concern with showing that gang activity is distinct from juvenile delinquency, at least in its distribution across the community areas of Chicago.

Ordinarily, one would expect high delinquency and high crime areas to be distributed the same way across communities. Areas with the highest serious delinquency rates should be the areas with the highest serious general crime, including gang crime. One would also expect to find the highest juvenile violence rates highly correlated and predictive of gang crime rates. Our findings will show that this is not necessarily so, however. Also, gang homicide and nongang homicide rates have not varied correlatively across the city in its local communities over time. Although Hispanic gang homicide rates are very high, nongang homicide rates are closer to those of whites. Black gang homicide rates have been consistently lower than those of Hispanics, but their nongang homicide and general crime rates have been consistently higher in the city (Block, 1987; Spergel, 1986).

Table 17.1   Kurtosis and Skewness Statistics for Five Measures of Quality of Community Life: Before and After Transformation

	Kurtosis	Skewness
Delinquency Rate	0.790	1.056
(Square Root)	−0.268	0.236
Gang Homicide Rate	1.211	1.523
(Square Root)	−0.798	0.568
Percent Living Below Poverty Level	0.435	2.938
(Logged)	−0.815	−0.221
Mortgage Investment Per Unit	11.696	2.938
(Logged)	0.684	−0.597
Unemployment Rate	4.461	1.750
(Logged)	−0.654	0.335

Standard error for kurtosis = 0.548.
Standard error for skewness = 0.277.

Gang homicides and serious delinquent acts fit the classic definition of rare events generally associated with the Poisson distribution. An analysis of skewness and kurtosis reveals the nonnormality of the distributions of these two variables (table 17.1). Transforming these variables by taking their square roots brings them more into conformity with the assumptions of normality required for dependent variables in ordinary least squares regression and multivariate analysis (Kirk 1982; Walker and Lev, 1953). Gang crime is measured by the square root of gang homicide rate, and delinquency by the square root of delinquency rate.

Social Disorganization and Poverty

The ETHNIC variable is used to categorize Chicago communities by race and ethnicity. Its values are assigned by a rather simple set of algorithms. Communities that are over 70 percent white according to the 1980 census are identified as "white" (n = 31, 41.3%); communities over 70 percent black as "black" (n = 27, 36%); and communities in which the number of Hispanic residents outnumber whites or blacks as Hispanic communities (n = 5, 6.7%). These Hispanic communities are either predominantly Puerto Rican or Mexican in composition. These communities include the most recent arrivals to the city's population, and they are most likely to fit the classic social disorganization model of areas inhabited with residents who are marginally integrated into the city's organizational and political life. Only twelve of Chicago's seventy-five community areas (16%) do not fit one of these categories. These community areas are extremely diverse and perhaps the source of a great deal of the social change in the urban system. We group them as "mixed" for the purposes of our analysis.

In recent decades, the segregated racial-ethnic pattern of community populations has become a more stable component of the ecological process in Chicago. The white population (40% of the total) is considerably older than the black (40%) and Hispanic (14%) populations. It is relatively stable in certain communities, particularly on the southwest and northwest sides of the city. The highly segregated black population has been growing older and has experienced gradual expansion. The Hispanic population, including mainly low-income Mexican-Americans and a substantial, smaller and even poorer, Puerto Rican group, is relatively new to Chicago. These Hispanic groups are rapidly expanding into all areas of Chicago, although they are currently concentrated in a few "interstitial" communities or "ports of entry" near the center of the city. Our measure of social disorganization is simply and grossly the concentration of Hispanics in a community.

A measure of the percentage of the population who had lived in the same residence for five years at the time of the 1980 census could have been used in place of percentage Hispanic. We rejected it for several reasons, though it is in fact positively correlated with percentage Hispanic. On an empirical level, the five-year residency variable does not significantly enter into a regression equation for gang homicide rates once percentage Hispanic is in the model. More important, our theoretical intention in this analysis has been to separate community mobility that is a part of inner-city poverty (W. Wilson, 1987) from the more traditional view of social disorganization as it has been, more often but not exclusively, associated with immigrant populations, per se.

We are, at this point, primarily concerned with separating social disorganization as it exists in the Hispanic communities of Chicago from chronic poverty as it exists in the black communities. As measures of poverty, we consider three interrelated measures of the quality of community life: the 1980 unemployment rate, percentage of the population living below the poverty level as recorded by the 1980 census, and average mortgage investment per owner-occupied housing unit. All three variables demonstrate the skewness and kurtosis associated with the distribution of economic resources within U.S. society (table 17.1). Taking the natural logarithm of each diminishes these difficulties for parametric analyses.

Community Life, Gang Homicide, Delinquency, and Ethnicity

Reiss (1986:1) has correctly noted that "our sense of personal safety and potential victimization by crime is shaped less by knowledge of specific criminals than it is by knowledge of dangerous and safe places and communities." Though dilapidated buildings and graffiti serve as warning signs for the uninformed, the racial-ethnic composition and identity of neighborhoods often function as guides for safe movement for many urban residents (Suttles, 1968). In the case of gang crime, the role of neighborhood or territory (Ley, 1975; Thrasher, 1963) is especially important, yet some researchers attribute the degree to which this is true to ethnic and cultural differences across communities (Dolan and Finney, 1984; Horowitz, 1983; Moore, 1978; Suttles, 1968; Williams and Kornblum, 1985). We think that it is necessary to look first at delinquency and gang homicide within the general context of the quality of community life. Second, it is important to demonstrate the degree to which the quality of community life, at least in Chicago, is defined by the race or ethnicity of community residents.

The Quality of Community Life

Excluding the ethnic-race variable for the moment, the five variables in the analysis, measures of gang homicide rate, delinquency rate, unemployment rate, percentage living below the poverty level, and mortgage investment per dwelling, can each be viewed as a separate measure of the community life.[3] A straightforward principal components analysis of these variables over the seventy-five community areas of Chicago produces only one significant eigenvalue (table 17.2). Using that one factor, it becomes possible to arrange the seventy-five community areas from ''best'' to ''worst'' along a single continuum defined by the generated factor scores. This eigenvalue accounts for 75.3 percent of the variance of these five variables across communities. At the top of the list is a community that is 98.2 percent white. Its percentage of persons living below the poverty level was the lowest in the city for the 1980 census. Unemployment is ninth lowest in the city and mortgage investment per dwelling is ninth highest. It had no gang homicides over the eight-year period, and its low delinquency rate is the sixty-fourth highest in the city. At the other end of the list is a community that is 98.9 percent black. Its gang homicide rate, unemployment rate, and percentage of people living below the poverty level

Table 17.2 Factor Analysis of Five Measures of Quality of Community Life

	Factor Score	Communality
Percent Living Below Poverty Level (Logged)	0.952	0.907
Mortgage Investment per Unit (Logged)	−0.803	0.645
Unemployment Rate (Logged)	0.918	0.843
Delinquency Rate (Square Root)	0.887	0.786
Gang Homicide Rate (Square Root)	0.763	0.583

Eigenvalue = 3.764; percent of variance = 75.3.

Table 17.3   Means and Multiple Comparison Tests of Five Variables for Four
Types of Racial-Ethnic Communities in Chicago

	White (31)	Black (27)	Hispanic (5)	Mixed (12)
Percent Living Below				
Poverty Level	1.810	3.305	3.233	2.837
(Logged)	(BHM)	(W)	(W)	(W)
Mortgage Investment	7.825	6.401	7.126	7.630
per Unit (Logged)	(BHM)	(W)	(W)	(W)
Unemployment Rate	1.782	2.831	2.755	2.192
(Logged)	(BH)	(WM)	(WM)	(BH)
Delinquency Rate	6.555	11.266	9.826	9.472
(Square Root)	(B)	(W)		
Gang Homicide Rate	0.851	3.347	7.076	2.958
(Square Root)	(H)	(H)	(WBM)	(H)

Note: Letters below means are results of Scheffe's S test at 0.05 level:
   W - Significantly different from white communities.
   B - Significantly different from black communities.
   H - Significantly different from Hispanic communities.
   M - Significantly different from mixed communities.

in 1980 fall within the ten highest in the city, just as its mortgage investments
fall in the bottom ten. The delinquency rate for the lowest scoring community
area (Oakland) on the list is over eleven times that of the delinquency rate of
the community area (Edison Park) with the highest quality of life in the city.
It is telling that 85.2 percent of the communities classified as black by the
ETHNIC variable are below the median in the quality of community life
ranking. Ninety-three percent of the white communities fall above the median,
and all five Hispanic communities fall below.

   The racial-ethnic character of communities, however, takes us beyond
a unilinear view of the quality of community life in Chicago. The means of
the four types of racial-ethnic neighborhoods on the five variables used in
the analysis are shown in table 17.3. Scheffe's S (Kirk, 1982) provides a
nonorthogonal *a posteriori* comparison of multiple means and enables us to
identify communities that are significantly different from each other for each
variable. The additional imposition of the harmonic means computation (Hull
and Nie, 1981) produces the groupings of community types identified by the
letters beneath each mean in the table. These represent subsets of community
types whose highest and lowest means do not differ more than would be
expected at the 0.05 level of statistical significance. It is obvious that the
means produce different groupings of the racial-ethnic communities depending
on which variable is examined.

   In terms of percentage of the population living below the poverty level and mortgage investment per housing unit, the white communities cannot be grouped with the other three types. Unemployment separates the white and mixed communities from the Hispanic and black communities. With respect to delinquency, the white and black communities cannot be grouped together, but the Hispanic and mixed communities cannot be significantly distanced from either of these two extremes. When it comes to gang homicide, however, it is the Hispanic community that is distinctively different from the other three types. Most important, however, a multivariate analysis of variance for differences in several means across groups produces a Hotelling's t squared of 3.56 (observed level of significance less than 0.01) for the four types of communities.

Discriminant analysis is an effective technique for delineating the multivariate dimensions that separate units within a system of classification (Bock, 1986; Finn, 1974; Green, 1976; Jones and Bock, 1960; Tatsuoka, 1971). The discriminant analysis of the three ethnically distinct types of community (white, black, and Hispanic) provides the two significant discriminant functions in table 17.4. Most important to our interests is the emergence of a second significant dimension of community differentiation. The first expected dimension of discrimination (accounting for 76.2% of the variance) among the communities is significantly related to the measures of delinquency and the three socioeconomic measures of quality of community life. The second discriminant function, though accounting for a much smaller portion of the variation among community types (23.8%), is significantly related to the gang homicide rate and mortgage investment (in the case of mortgage investment, the sign is in an opposite direction from its relationship to the first discriminant function).

Table 17.4 Discriminant Analysis Results for Five Community Measures for White, Hispanic, and Black Communities of Chicago

| | Standardized Canonical Discriminant Function Coefficients | |
	Function 1	Function 2
Eigenvalue	2.954+++	0.923+++
Percent of Variance	76.19	23.81
Square Root of Gang Homicide Rate	0.076***	1.122***
Square Root of Delinquency Rate	−0.383**	−0.639
Natural Logarithm of Poverty Rate	0.519***	0.089
Natural Logarithm of Unemployment Rate	0.760***	0.058
Natural Logarithm of Mortgage Investment per Dwelling	−0.060***	0.649***

**Variables significantly correlated with each function at .01 level.
***Variables significantly correlated with each function at .001 level.
+++Chi-square test based on transformation of Wilke's lambda is significant at the 0.001 level.

Figure 17.1: Discriminant Analysis of ETHNIC Scattergram of Communities on Gang and Nongang Dimensions of Community Life

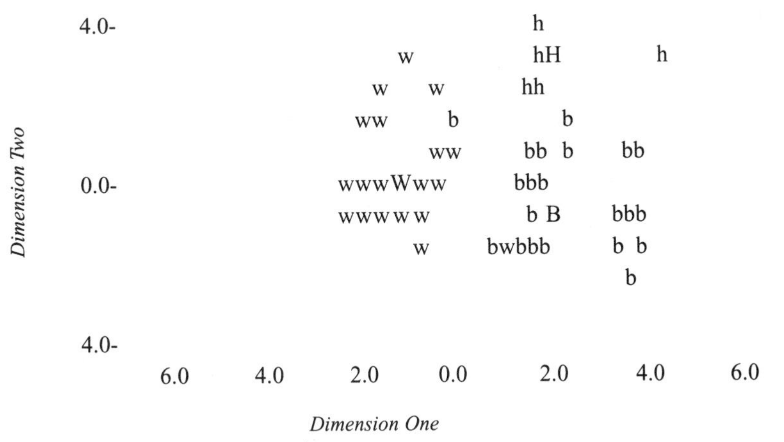

Ethnic/Racial Codes for Communities

w = white
h = Hispanic
b = black

W = Group centroid for white communities
B = Group centroid for black communities
H = Group centroid for Hispanic communities

A graph of the communities and their group centroids (figure 17.1) shows that it is the separation of the Hispanic communities from the others that produces this dimension. Hispanic communities have high gang homicide rates in comparison to white and black communities and mortgage value measures that fall somewhere between those of white and black communities.

A strong test of any discriminant analysis is the extent to which the discriminant functions permit correct reassignment of the units of analysis to the original categories—classification analysis. How effectively can the racial-ethnic identity of community areas be assigned on the basis of the area's measures on the quality of community life indices? As seen in table 17.5, 93.7 percent of the three racially-ethnically distinct neighborhoods can be correctly classified on the basis of their variation on the five variables included in the analysis as represented by the two discriminant functions. Moreover, classification analysis reveals something about the heterogeneous group of neighborhoods that we have so far lumped together in the mixed category. Six are closest in social characteristics to the white communities, five are

Table 17.5   Results of Classification Analysis Based on Two Discriminant
Functions

Actual ETHNIC Classification	Predicted ETHNIC Classification		
	White	*Black*	*Hispanic*
White	30 (97%)	1 (3%)	0 (0%)
Black	2 (7%)	24 (89%)	1 (4%)
Hispanic	0 (0%)	0 (0%)	5 (100%)
Mixed	6 (50%)	5 (42%)	1 (8%)

classified with the black communities, and one with the Hispanic communities.[4]

Gang and Nongang Delinquency

A Measure of Poverty

In order to compare the community forces associated with gang and nongang delinquency, it is in the interest of parsimony to apply factor analysis to the three economic measures to produce a single variable vested with the communality that is captured in their single factor score that we here label POVERTY. Keeping the uniqueness associated with each of the three separate economic measures met our need for distinguishing among types of communities in our discriminant analysis. As we turn our attention to the two measures of the quality of community life with which we are most concerned, parsimony and clarity benefit from our using a single measure of poverty. Moreover, in studying the differences and the relationships between gang crime and nongang delinquency, we find regression analysis most useful. By working with a single measure of poverty instead of three, we gain two degrees of freedom. Finally, we have reached a point in our analysis at which it is convenient to regard poverty as the communality shared by percentage of the population living below the poverty level, unemployment rate, and mortgage investment.

Using a principal components analysis of our three measures to generate a factor score gives us a single measure that we call POVERTY (table 17.6) associated with the only significant eigenvalue. POVERTY accounts for 85 percent of the variation in our three measures of poverty across the seventy-five community areas. Regressing POVERTY on percentage black and percentage Hispanic reveals the statistical significance of both predictors (table 17.7). The distribution of poverty in Chicago is a function of the distribution of black and Hispanic minority populations.

Social Contexts of Gang Crime and Nongang Delinquency

Regressing our measure of delinquency rate and our measure of gang homicide rate on POVERTY, percentage Hispanic, and percentage black suggests different explanatory models for gang crime and nongang delinquency (table 17.7). Neither percentage black nor percentage Hispanic significantly predicts delinquency rate when POVERTY is included in the regression equation. On the other hand, although gang homicide rate is not directly related to percentage

Table 17.6   Principal Components Analysis of Three Measures of Poverty

	Factor Score	Communality
Percent Living Below Poverty Level (Logged)	0.913	0.834
Mortgage Investment per Unit (Logged)	−0.900	0.810
Unemployment Rate (Logged)	0.955	0.912

Eigenvalue = 2.556; percent of Variance = 85.2.

Table 17.7   Multiple Regression Analyses Results

Dependent Variable	Independent Variable	Regression Coefficient	Beta	R^2
POVERTY	% Black	0.022**	0.919	0.747
	% Hispanic	0.022**	0.405	
Delinquency Rate	% Black	0.002	0.032	0.617
(Square Root)	% Hispanic	0.005	0.026	
	POVERTY	2.436**	0.757	
Gang Homicide Rate	% Black	0.001	0.009	0.562
(Square Root)	% Hispanic	0.644**	0.432	
	POVERTY	1.392**	0.573	
Gang Homicide Rate	% Black	−0.001	−0.332	0.483
1978–81	% Hispanic	0.058**	0.531	
(Square Root)	POVERTY	0.735*	0.415	
Gang Homicide Rate 1982–85 (Square Root)	Gang Homicide Rate 1978–1981 (Square Root)	0.517**	0.482	0.651
	% Black	0.001	0.029	
	% Hispanic	0.006	0.048	
	POVERTY	0.813**	0.429	
Gang Homicide	% Black	0.002	0.051	0.269
Rate, Residual	% Hispanic	−0.008	−0.094	
Change Score	POVERTY	0.642*	0.474	

*Significant at .05 level.
**Significant at .01 level.

black, it is significantly predicted by percentage Hispanic even when POVER-TY's significant effect is taken into account. Hence, we find that nongang delinquency rates vary significantly from community to community with the distribution of poverty but not with the distribution of minority populations. Gang homicide rates, as delinquency rates, are related to poverty. And like nongang delinquency rates, gang homicide rates do not vary from community to community with the distribution of black population. Gang homicide rates do vary from community to community with the distribution of Hispanic population.

The regression model for nongang delinquency rate suggests poverty as a theoretical explanation. The regression model for gang homicide rate suggests a dual explanation of poverty and social disorganization.

The Question of Interaction

The relationship between nongang delinquency rate and gang homicide rate holds for all seventy-five community areas, but it is reasonable to ask if relationships between these measures are the same within different ethnic-racial groups of communities. In order to test whether there is an interaction between ETHNIC category and POVERTY, an analysis of covariance was conducted for differences in delinquency rate and gang homicide rate treating POVERTY as a covariate. As can be seen in table 17.8 a significant interaction between race-ethnic group and POVERTY accounts for the significant differences in delinquency rates from different ETHNIC communities. Though there is also a significant interaction between ETHNIC type and neighborhood for gang homicide rate, there remains a significant main effect associated with ETHNIC type after that interaction is taken into account. This supports the conclusions of our regression analysis, but gives us some additional pieces of interesting information.

Table 17.8 Analysis of Covariance of Gang and Nongang Delinquency Measures

Dependent Variable	Covariate Effect (POVERTY) F Statistic	Main Effect (ETHNIC) F Statistic
Delinquency Rate (Square Root)	117.10***	0.973
Gang Homicide Rate (Square Root)	62.96***	10.958***
Residual Score of 1982–85 Period vs. 1978–81	24.88***	0.834

***Significant at .001 level.

Figure 17.2: Regression Lines by Community Type for Delinquency Rate on POVERTY

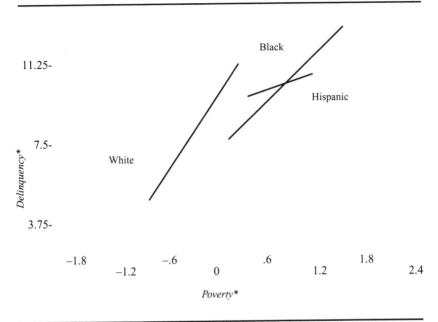

*Delinquency is the square root of 1980 delinquency rate. POVERTY is the factor score produced by the single significant eigenvalue of a principal components analysis of unemployment rate, percentage of residents living below the poverty level in 1980, and dollar mortgage investment per dwelling.

Our interpretation of the results of the analysis of covariance is enhanced by graphic examination of the slopes of the regression lines for the different racial-ethnic categories of communities (Tatsuoka, 1971). In white, black, and Hispanic communities, the positive slopes of the regression lines of delinquency rate on POVERTY vary in steepness, but the differences are not significant (figure 17.2). In each type of community, greater poverty is associated with higher rates of delinquency.

The interaction between the effect of poverty on gang homicide and type of ethnic-racial community shown in table 17.8 can be seen in figure 17.3. In Hispanic communities, the association between poverty and gang homicide rate is not evident. The gang violence stemming from the social disorganization of immigrant life overshadows the visible impact of poverty on gang homicide rate. In black communities, the steep positive slope of the regression of gang homicide rate on POVERTY underscores the strength of that relationship.

Figure 17.3: Regression Lines by Community Type for Gang Homicide on
POVERTY

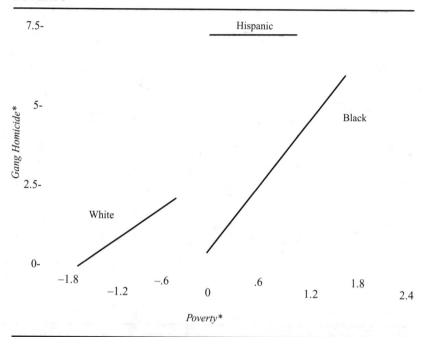

*Gang homicide is the square root of gang homicide rate per 100,000 community residents 1978–1985.
POVERTY is the factor score produced by the single significant eigenvalue of a principal components
analysis of unemployment rate, percentage of residents living below the poverty level in 1980, and dollar
mortgage investment per dwelling.

The Process of Change and Gang Crime

The importance of change in the urban ecological system has been especially
well demonstrated for general crime and delinquency data (Bursik, 1986;
Bursik and Webb, 1982; Heitgerd and Bursik, 1987; Reiss, 1986; Schuerman
and Kobrin, 1986). Given our gang homicide data for each community for
two separate four-year periods—1978–81 and 1982–85, it is possible to offer
some tentative findings on the dynamic pattern of gang crime. If we look at
the means for the community gang homicide rate 1978–81 and the same rate
1982–85 broken down by ETHNIC area (table 17.9), there is a small decline
in gang crime in white (already very low) and Hispanic communities but an
increase in black and mixed communities.

We examine next the residual change score for each community (Bursik,
1986; Bursik and Webb, 1982; Elliott and Voss, 1974; Heitgerd and Bursik,
1987). The residual change score for gang homicide rate is computed by
regressing the square root of the gang homicide rate for the second period on

Table 17.9   Gang Homicide Measure Means by ETHNIC Community for Two
Time Periods

Ethnic Composition of Community	1978–1981	1982–1985
White	0.6419	0.4238
Black	1.7183	2.6271*
Hispanic	5.4106	4.5022
Mixed	1.7154	2.1718

*Difference significant at 0.01 level in paired t-test.

the square root of the gang homicide rate for the first period. Gang homicide rate for 1978–81 explained 48.9 percent of the variation in gang homicide rate for the period 1982–85. This speaks to the stability of gang homicide patterns in Chicago's community areas. Regressing the residual change score for gang homicide rate on POVERTY, percentage Hispanic, and percentage black, a change in the structure of gang crime did indeed occur over the two periods (table 17.7). Although percentage Hispanic is a significant predictor of the gang homicide measure in the 1978–81 period, it is not a significant predictor of the residual change score for gang homicide as measured in the 1982–85 period.

Although POVERTY explains only 25 percent of the variation in the change in gang homicide rates over the two periods, 73.3 percent of the cases fall within the confidence interval for predicted single cases from the regression equation (Dillon and Goldstein, 1984; Gilley, 1986).[5] Interestingly, ten cases fall above and ten cases fall below the interval. A breakdown of these twenty outlying cases by ETHNIC is shown in table 17.10. Equal numbers of black communities fall above and below the confidence interval. One white community shows more of an increase than is expected for its poverty level; three, less. One Hispanic community shows more of an increase than expected; two, less. Four of the mixed community areas show more of an increase in gang homicide rate than is predicted by poverty level and only one, less. Clues to the identity of the unincluded variable(s) contributing to the large unexplained variation in the change score for gang homicide rate may possibly be found through a more qualitative study of the twenty communities.[6]

Summary and Conclusions

The gang problem is concentrated in certain communities, particularly (but not necessarily) in low-income, public-housing projects and poor black and low-income Hispanic sections of the city. The gang problem is disproportionately more serious and more frequent in Hispanic rather than in black communi-

Table 17.10   Community Areas Lying Above and Below Single-case 95 Percent Prediction Intervals for Regression of Change Score of Gang Homicide Rate on Poverty Level by Ethnic Type

Ethnic Composition of Community	Above	Below
White	1	3
Black	4	4
Hispanic	1	2
Mixed	4	1

ties. The problem appears to have been growing more severe in black than in Hispanic communities over two time periods. Although we believe there are processes of population and institutional change involved in the distribution of gang crime, we also emphasize the degree to which relatively stable social patterns characterize the distribution of the gang problem in the urban ecological system. There is a need for more detailed research on the patterns of change in the gang problem at the ecological level, just as there is need for longitudinal research on the gang problem at the individual level (Farrington et al., 1986).

Our analysis suggests that poverty (the social adaptation to chronic deprivation) and social disorganization (the settlement of new immigrant groups) are most strongly related to the distribution of delinquency and gang homicide in Chicago's communities. Poverty is the strongest predictor of delinquency rate in community areas. The concentration of the Hispanic population is most strongly associated with gang homicide in the 1978–81 period. Ethnicity and race also indirectly combine with poverty variables to explain the delinquency problem in Hispanic community areas, but the occurrence of gang homicide in such communities appears unrelated to poverty. Overall, the patterns of gang homicide and delinquency problems appear to be quite different, particularly in the interaction of poverty and ethnic-race variables. This finding is consistent with theory and research that suggest a distinction between delinquent and gang structures (B. Cohen, 1968a, 1969b; Kornhauser, 1978; Robin, 1962; Thrasher, 1963; Spergel, 1984). This finding is inconsistent with those classic theories and studies that draw little distinction between delinquent and gang behavior or subcultures (Cloward and Ohlin, 1960; A. Cohen, 1955; A. Cohen and Short, 1958; Miller, 1958; Short and Strodtbeck, 1965).

Our inability to separate the impact of specific socioeconomic measures at the aggregate level does not permit us to support or refute many competing theories of gang and nongang delinquency, such as relative deprivation, or its near-equivalent anomie theory in Mertonian terms, and unemployment theory, particularly at the structural level. Pressures leading to deviant behavior, particularly delinquency, in urban society may result from the lack of economic means available to achieve minimal standards of living. At the same time, social disorganization as it affects recently arrived groups in the urban area may be a key force in generating gang structures and violent gang behaviors as social alternatives to nongang delinquency. We may observe this in the spread of gang problems to suburban communities, smaller cities, and areas of the country, mainly the South and West, that have been subjected to large population in-migrations in recent years (Miller, 1982). Analyses over time show that changes untapped by our variables may be at work, especially in the black, but also in the Hispanic, communities of Chicago. Increases in gang violence in the black communities in the late 1960s and the 1980s and in the Hispanic communities in the 1970s (Block, 1987) may be associated not only with population shifts but with sharp changes in the structure of organizational and leadership resources available to these groups (W. Wilson, 1987).

Gangs are residual social subsystems often characterized by competition for status and, more recently, income opportunity through drug sales. They are organizations concerned with territoriality, status, and controlling human behavior. For disadvantaged youths, uncertain in the face of the unstable urban social world, the gang is responsive and provides quasi-stable, efficient, meaningful social, and perhaps economic, structures. In gang membership, there is the opportunity to obtain the psychic rewards of personal identity and minimal standards of acceptable status and sometimes the material benefits of criminal income. The value of research on gang phenomena as distinct from but related to delinquency is beyond question, both for social theory and public policy. Social disorganization and poverty rather than criminal organization and conspiracy may better explain the recent growth and spread of youth gangs to many parts of the country. Moreover, community organization and social opportunity in conjunction with suppression, rather than simply suppression and incapacitation, may be more effective policies in dealing with the social problem.

Notes

1. An exception is the work of Morash (1983), whose definition of the gang does not include possession of a name, tradition, or complex structure, or the commission of delinquent behavior, all criteria employed generally in the definition of other researchers.

2. For the eight-year period covered in this analysis, incidents of gang crime reported by the Chicago Police Department include simple and aggravated assaults, simple and aggravated batteries, robbery, homicide, and unauthorized use of a weapon. Since 1986, arson, theft, burglary, and vice (including drug offenses) have been added to this reporting system. A preliminary examination of these statistics indicates that

violent offenses continue to dominate as a majority of all offenses identified as "gang-related."

3. We gave serious consideration as a component of this research to some measures of age structure. Results obtained from males 5–14, 15–17, 18–20, and 21–24 as a proportion of total population yield either nonsignificant or ambiguous results. The unraveling of the complex relationship of the age-sex structure of a community to its patterns of gang crime and delinquency is not attempted here.

4. Among the mixed neighborhoods, Hyde Park, Rogers Park, Hermosa, Albany Park, Lake View, and Near North Side are in social distance closest to the white neighborhoods. As has been noted (Bursik, 1986), the Near North Side, with the poverty of its public-housing population overshadowed by the wealth of its neighbors and one of the highest gang homicide rates in the city, stretches the community area as a unit of analysis to its worst extreme. South Deering, Morgan Park, South Chicago, New City, and Armour Square (where Chinatown is located) are in social distance closest to the city's black communities. The analysis includes only Uptown, with the city's five Hispanic communities.

5. Computations for this application are from Gilley (1986). They can be obtained in SPSS using the REGRESSION SAVE subcommand to obtain measures of the predicted values (PRED), their standard errors (SEPRED), and the centered leverage values (LEVER). COMPUTE statements are then used to generate the following variables: MSE (mean square residual) = SEPRED**2/(1/N+LEVER). SESINGLE (standard error for each case) = SQRT(MSE+SEPRED**2). U(L)SINGLE (upper [lower] confidence interval for each single case's value on the dependent variable) = PRED + (−) t*SESINGLE. N is the sample size and t is the appropriate value of Student's t for the desired confidence interval.

6. We believe that communities with rapid changes in population numbers and composition are most destabilized and probably suffer a higher than expected rate of increase in gang homicide. Communities that have been relatively stable in their population and institutional character probably experience lower increases in gang homicide than might be expected by socioeconomic status alone. This concept is in keeping with elements of *internal* social disorganization that characterize impoverished communities (W. Wilson, 1987). In this analysis we have no variable that captures this kind of instability. Some of these elements may be delineated through longitudinal individual-level research, such as that currently being conducted on preadolescent youths in inner-city Hispanic and black Chicago communities (Spergel, 1987).

References

Baldwin, John. (1979). Ecological and areal studies. In Norval Morris and Michael Tonry (eds.), *Crime and Justice: An Annual Review of Research*. Vol. 1. Chicago: University of Chicago Press.

Block, Carolyn Rebecca. (1987). Homicide in Chicago: Aggregate and Time Series Perspectives of Victim, Offender and Situation (1965–1981). Urban Insights Series No. 14. Chicago: Center for Urban Policy.

Bock, R. Darrell. (1986). *Multivariate Statistical Methods in Behavior Research*. Chicago Scientific Software.

Bursik, Robert J., Jr. (1986). Ecological stability and the dynamics of delinquency. In Albert J. Reiss, Jr., and Michael Tonry (eds.), *Communities and Crime. Crime and Justice: A Review of Research*. Vol. 8. Chicago: University of Chicago Press.

Bursik, Robert J., Jr. and Jim Webb. (1982). Community change and patterns of delinquency. *American Journal of Sociology*. 88:24–42.

California Council on Criminal Justice. (1986). *State Task Force on Youth and Gang Violence*. Final Report. Sacramento: California Council of Criminal Justice.

Campbell, Anne. (1984). *The Girls in the Gang*. Oxford: Basil Blackwell.

Cartwright, Desmond S. and Kenneth I. Howard. (1966). Multivariate analysis of gang delinquency: I. Ecological influences. *Multivariate Behavioral Methodology* 1: 321–371.

Cloward, Richard A. and Lloyd E. Ohlin. (1960). *Delinquency and Opportunity*. Glencoe, IL: Free Press.

Cohen, Albert K. (1955). *Delinquent Boys: The Cultures of the Gang*. Glencoe, IL: Free Press.

Cohen, Albert K. and James F. Short, Jr. (1958). Research on delinquent subcultures. *Journal of Social Issues* 14: 20–37.

Cohen, Bernard. (1969a). The delinquency of gangs and spontaneous groups. In Thorsten Sellin and Marvin E. Wolfgang (eds.), *Delinquency: Selected Studies*. New York: Wiley.

———. (1969b). Internecine conflict: The offender. In Thorsten Sellin and Marvin E. Wolfgang (eds.), *Delinquency: Selected Studies*. New York: Wiley.

Currie, Elliott. (1985). *Confronting Crime: An American Challenge*. New York: Pantheon Books.

Dillon, William R. and Matthew Goldstein. (1984). *Multivariate Analysis: Methods and Applications*. New York: Wiley.

Dolan, Edward F., Jr. and Shan Finney. (1984). *Youth Gangs*. New York: Julian Messner.

Elliott, Delbert S. and Harwin L. Voss. (1974). *Delinquency and Dropout*. Lexington, MA: Lexington Books.

Empey, Lamar T. (1978). *American Delinquency: Its Meaning and Construction*. Homewood, IL: Dorsey Press.

Erickson, Maynard L. and Gary F. Jensen. (1977). Delinquency is still group behavior: Toward revitalizing the group premise in the sociology of deviance. *Journal of Criminal Law and Criminology* 68:388–395.

Farrell, Ronald A. and V.L. Swigert. (1982). *Deviance and Social Control*. Glenview, IL: Scott Foresman.

Farrington, David P., Lloyd E. Ohlin, and James Q. Wilson. (1986). *Understanding and Controlling Crime*. New York: Springer-Verlag.

Finn, Jeremy D. (1974). *A General Design for Multivariate Analysis*. New York: Holt, Rinehart & Winston.

Friedman, C.J., Frederika Mann, and Albert S. Friedman. (1975). A profile of juvenile street gang members. *Adolescence* 11:527–533.

Gilbert, James. (1986). *A Cycle of Outrage: America's Reaction to the Juvenile Delinquent in the 1950's*. New York: Oxford University Press.

Gilley, Sheri. (1986). Prediction intervals in SPSS. SPSS Internal Memo. Available from authors upon request.

Green, Paul E. and J. Douglas Carroll. (1976). *Mathematical Tools for Applied Multivariate Analysis*. New York: Academic Press.

Heitgerd, Janet L. and Robert J. Bursik, Jr. (1987). Extracommunity dynamics and the ecology of delinquency. *American Journal of Sociology* 92: 775–787.

Horowitz, Ruth. (1983). *Honor and the American Dream*. New Brunswick, NJ: Rutgers University Press.

Hull, Hadlai, C. and Norman H. Nie. (1981). *SPSS Update 7-9*. New York: McGraw-Hill.

Janowitz, Morris. (1978). *The Last Half Century*. Chicago: University of Chicago Press.

_____. (1983). *The Reconstruction of Patriotism*. Chicago: University of Chicago Press.

Jones, Lyle V. and R. Darrell Bock. (1960). Multiple discriminant analysis applied to "ways to live." *Sociometry* 23: 162–176.

Kirk, Roger E. (1982). *Experimental Design: Procedures for the Behavioral Sciences*. 2nd ed. Belmont, CA: Brooks/Cole.

Klein, Malcolm W. (1971). *Street Gangs and Street Workers*. Englewood Cliffs, NJ: Prentice-Hall.

Klein, Malcolm W. and Cheryl L. Maxson. (1987). Street gang violence. In Marvin E. Wolfgang and N. Weiner (eds.), *Violent Crimes, Violent Criminals*. Beverly Hills, CA: Sage.

Kornhauser, Ruth R. (1978). *Social Sources of Delinquency*. Chicago: University of Chicago Press.

Ley, David. (1975). The street gang in its milieu. In G. Gappert and H. M. Rose (eds.), *The Social Economy of Cities*. Beverly Hills, CA: Sage.

Maxson, Cheryl L., M.A. Gordon, and Malcolm W. Klein. (1985). Differences between gang and nongang homicides. *Criminology* 23: 209–222.

Miller, Walter B. (1958). Lower class culture as a generating milieu of gang delinquency. *Journal of Social Issues* 15: 5–19.

_____. (1975). Violence by Youth Gangs and Youth Groups in the United States. Draft. Washington, DC, National Institute of Juvenile Justice and Delinquency Prevention.

_____. (1982). *Crime by Youth Gangs and Groups as a Crime Problem in Major American Cities*. Washington, DC, National Institute of Juvenile Justice and Delinquency Prevention.

Moore, Joan W. (1978). *Homeboys*. Philadelphia, PA: Temple University Press.

Morash, Merry. (1983). Gangs, groups, and delinquency. *British Journal of Criminology* 23: 309–331.

Reiss, Albert J., Jr. (1986). Why are communities important in understanding crime? In Albert J. Reiss, Jr., and Michael Tonry (eds.), *Communities and Crime*.

Crime and Justice: A Review of Research. Vol. 8. Chicago: University of Chicago Press.

Reiss, Albert J., Jr. and Michael Tonry (eds.). (1986). *Communities and Crime. Crime and Justice: A Review of Research.* Vol. 8. Chicago: University of Chicago Press.

Robin, Gerald. (1967). Gang member delinquency in Philadelphia. In Malcolm W. Klein (ed.), *Juvenile Gangs in Context: Theory, Research, and Action.* Englewood Cliffs, NJ: Prentice-Hall.

San Diego Association of Governments. (1982). *Juvenile Violence and Gang-Related Crime.* San Diego, CA: Association of Governments.

Sarnecki, Jerzy. (1986). *Delinquent Networks.* Report 1. Research Division. Stockholm: National Council for Crime Prevention.

Schuerman, Leo and Solomon Kobrin. (1986). Community careers in crimes. In Albert J. Reiss, Jr., and Michael Tonry (eds), *Communities and Crime. Crime and Justice: A Review of Research.* Vol. 8. Chicago: University of Chicago Press.

Shaw, Clifford R. and Henry D. McKay. (1969). *Juvenile Delinquency and Urban Areas.* Rev. ed. Chicago: University of Chicago Press.

Short, James F. and Fred L. Strodtbeck. (1965). *Group Process and Gang Delinquency.* Chicago: University of Chicago Press.

Spergel, Irving A. (1964). *Racketville, Slumtown, and Haulburg.* Chicago: University of Chicago Press.

_____. (1984). Violent gangs in Chicago: In search of social policy. *Social Policy Review* 58: 199–226.

_____. (1986). The violent gang problem in Chicago: Local community approach. *Social Service Review* 60: 94–131.

_____. (1987). School community gang crime prevention. Research proposal. Washington, DC, U.S. Department of Education, Office of Educational Research and Improvement.

Suttles, Gerald D. (1968). *The Social Order of the Slum.* Chicago: University of Chicago Press.

Tatsuoka, Maurice. (1971). *Multivariate Analysis.* New York: Wiley.

Thomas, W.I. and Florian Znaniecki. (1920). *The Polish Peasant in Europe and America.* Chicago: University of Chicago Press.

Thrasher, Frederic M. (1963). *The Gang: A Study of 1,313 Gangs in Chicago.* Abridged with a new introduction by James F. Short, Jr. Chicago: University of Chicago Press.

Tracy, Paul E. (1982). Gang membership and violent offending. Preliminary Results from 1968 cohort study. Draft. Philadelphia, Pa., Center for Studies in Criminology and Criminal Law, University of Pennsylvania.

_____. (1988). Subcultural delinquency: A comparison of the incidence of gang and nongang member offenses. In Marvin E. Wolfgang, Terrence P. Thornberry and Robert M. Figlio (eds.), *From Boy to Man, From Delinquency to Crime.* Chicago: University of Chicago Press.

Walker, Helen M. and Joseph Lev. (1953). *Statistical Inference.* New York: Holt, Rinehart & Winston.

Whyte, William F. (1943). *Street Corner Society*. Chicago: University of Chicago Press.

Williams, M.T. and William Kornblum. (1985). *Growing Up Poor*. Lexington, MA: Lexington Books.

Wilson, James Q. and Richard J. Herrnstein. (1985). *Crime and Human Nature*. New York: Simon and Schuster.

Wilson, William J. (1987). *The Truly Disadvantaged: The Inner-City, the Underclass, and Public Policy*. Chicago: University of Chicago Press.

Yablonsky, Lewis. (1962). *The Violent Gang*. New York: Macmillan.

Zimring, Franklin E. (1981). Kids, groups, and crimes: Some implications of a well-known secret. *Journal of Criminal Law, Criminology, and Police Science* 72: 867–885.

18

Routine Activities and a Subculture of Violence: A Study of Violence on the Street

Leslie W. Kennedy and Stephen W. Baron

Research using the routine activities perspective indicates that the degree of exposure that individuals experience following certain lifestyle patterns increases property and personal crime victimization (Jensen and Brownfield, 1986; Kennedy and Forde, 1990a; 1990b). Kennedy and Forde (1990a, 1990b) report that young, unmarried males who frequent bars, go to movies, go out to work, and spend time out of the house walking or driving around are the most vulnerable to assaults and robberies. Jensen and Brownfield (1986) suggest it is the "criminogenic potential" of certain routines that accounts for their "victimogenic potential." They argue that individuals heavily involved in certain lifestyle patterns are not merely more available and in close proximity to potential offenders, but are more involved in activities that are likely to be associated with offensive behavior, as well (Jensen and Brownfield, 1986).

Members of delinquent groups follow some of the risky lifestyles outlined above but have been overlooked by researchers studying routine activities. These groups have most often been studied using theories focusing on subcultural norms that guide their members' behavior. In particular, the violent behavior of delinquent groups is explained as stemming from norms that promote conditions under which violence is expected or required of members. In this article, the assumptions made in subcultural theories about the etiology of violence in street groups will be examined. These assumptions will then be contrasted to those of routine activities theory that provides alternative explanations for the emergence of violence. Particular attention will be paid to the experience of "punks," who have developed a reputation for violent action connected with countercultural beliefs. The offender and victimization experience of this group will be assessed using these perspectives.

Reprinted by permission of Sage Publications, Inc. from the *Journal of Research in Crime & Delinquency*, Vol. 30, No. 1 (February 1993): 88–112.

Subculture of Violence

The concept of subculture has been used extensively by criminologists to account for violent behavior. Wolfgang and Ferracuti's (1967) subculture of violence theory proposes that variations in the use of violent behavior stem from the adherence to subcultural normative systems that support and encourage violence. The subculture of violence does not completely oppose the dominant culture, nor is it characterized by violence in every situation. Instead, the violent subculture promotes a relatively greater number of conditions under which violence is expected or required of its members. Subcultural norms serve as guides for the perception and interpretation of certain situations (the jostle, the derogatory remark, the appearance of a weapon) where violence is viewed as an appropriate response to the cues provided. Difficult problems and frustrating experiences are perceived and reacted to as "menacing, aggressive stimuli" to which violence becomes a quick definitive response that is socially rewarded. People who do not follow the norms are criticized or ridiculed by others in the subcultural group. In fact, Wolfgang and Ferracuti portray the subculture as one in which nonviolence is actually forbidden in certain situations. The juvenile who fails to live up to his gang's requirements (for example, the member who does not defend his honor) incurs an immediate, and perhaps irrevocable, loss of status and is forced to find new friends and form new alliances.

In this tradition, Horowitz (1983; Horowitz and Swartz, 1974) suggests that gang violence revolves around insult and honor. Horowitz argues that honor is a normative code that "stresses the inviolability of one's manhood and defines breaches of etiquette . . . in an adversarial idiom" (1983, p. 80). Honor sensitizes gang members to violations that are interpreted as "derogations of the self" and must be responded to with physical violence. Horowitz distinguishes between types of orientations toward honor: "Self-image promoters" who intentionally and frequently provoke violent incidents to demonstrate courage, power, and importance; and "self-image defenders" who do not provoke incidents but appraise situations as insulting and act accordingly.

In a more recent formulation of a subculture of violence theory, Luckenbill and Doyle (1989) suggest that violence is the product of three successive events. The first, naming, involves the determination that an experience has been injurious and attributing the injury suffered to the fault of another individual. In the second event, claiming, the victim must express a grievance to and demand reparation from the harmdoer. In the third, the harmdoer must reject the victim's claim in whole or in part. According to Luckenbill and Doyle, the rejection of a claim transforms the interaction into a dispute to which the victim may respond in a number of ways including perseverance and the use of force. Thus violent incidents can be generally viewed as transactions in which offenders use force to settle a dispute stemming from a negative

338

outcome. The subculture of violence fosters naming, claiming, and aggressiveness. Individuals within the subculture of violence are more likely to "perceive a negative outcome as injurious, and are more willing to express a grievance to and demand reparation from the harmdoer." They are more willing to persevere and use force in settling the dispute. Again it is in those situations where the "fundamental properties of self are attacked" (Luckenbill and Doyle, 1989, p. 426) that violence is most called for.

A survey of the literature focusing on delinquent groups reveals similar properties to those outlined above. Cohen and Short (1958) describe a conflict-oriented subculture where the most prized virtue is "heart" and courage in fighting. The status of the gang is determined by members' willingness to engage in, and their prowess in, physical conflict. Cloward and Ohlin (1960) have also outlined a conflict subculture where adolescents create criteria for status through the manipulation of violence. Again, the acquisition of status is not simply a consequence of skill in the use of violence. It also requires the willingness to risk injury, defend personal integrity, and maintain gang honor. Two of Miller's (1958) lower-class cultural concerns emphasize violent behavior. The "trouble" concept implies that violence can be recognized as a prestige-conferring behavior, and the qualities required in the "toughness" concept include physical prowess and bravery in physical combat.

We can summarize the subculture of violence perspective as follows: Violent behavior stems from the adherence to norms that define violence as a necessary response to actions that are derogatory to the self. Individuals adhering to these norms are more likely to perceive situations as insulting, and are more willing to use violence as a response. The subcultural norms are backed up with social rewards and punishments: Individuals who abide by the norms are admired and respected by other members of the subculture, and those who do not conform are ridiculed, criticized, and/or expelled.

Critiques of the Subculture of Violence

Those who have examined the explanatory power of the subculture of violence perspective have come up with a fairly pessimistic assessment of its worth (Ball-Rokeach, 1973; Erlanger, 1974). Ball-Rokeach (1973) concludes that there is little empirical evidence for the subcultural theory based on degree of self-esteem, violence in the form of fighting, and the conferral of esteem by others for using violence. She suggests that "the subculture of violence thesis, at best, is incomplete and at worst invalid as an explanation of violent behavior" (Ball-Rokeach, 1973, p. 748). Erlanger (1974) also reports evidence that is inconsistent with the subculture of violence thesis and Hartnagel (1980) reports only partial support at best, for the theory. Kornhauser (1978) notes that there is limited evidence for the idea that violent norms are transmitted by gangs. More recent homicide research has also failed to generate much support for the subculture of violence theory (Loftin and Hill, 1974; Parker, 1989; Sampson, 1987; Williams and Flewelling, 1988; Williams, 1984).

Hagan (1984) has argued that the subcultural approach suffers from its emphasis on juvenile gangs and the exaggerated perception of the organizational structure of gangs. Most research suggests that gangs are loose affiliations with minimal cohesion and low membership stability (Jansyn, 1966; Klein and Crawford, 1967; Short and Strodtbeck, 1965; Suttles, 1968) that make it difficult to construct distinctive subcultural norms.

As Nettler (1974) notes, the basic problem with the subcultural approach is its tendency to infer (rather than identify independently) subcultural values from subcultural behaviors. He argues that subcultural theories explain subcultural behaviors by reference to the behaviors themselves. "It is as though one were to say that 'people are murderous because they live violently'" (Nettler, 1974, p. 152). As Hagan (1984) points out, such statements are not false, but rather are descriptive of what we already know. Hagan (1985) suggests that given this weak empirical evidence that groups adhere to deviant subcultures, where violence is considered an integral part of the group's functioning, the possibility exists that the violence may be situationally specific, depending on opportunity and circumstance.

Routine Activities Theory

Routine activities theorists view street crime as a product of opportunity that arises in the ongoing activities that occur on the street. The probability of being a victim of crime increases with the convergence in space and time of three factors: motivated offenders, suitable targets, and an absence of capable guardians (Cohen and Felson, 1979; Felson and Cohen, 1980; Lauritsen, Sampson, and Laub, 1991; Sampson and Wooldredge, 1987; Sampson and Lauritsen, 1990). Sampson and Lauritsen (1990; Lauritsen et al., 1991) suggest that these conditions can lead to an increase in crime independent of the structural or cultural conditions that might motivate individuals to engage in crime. The lifestyles that lead one to bar behavior and to being on the street lead to situations in which these factors coincide to present offenders with opportunities to commit crime (Jensen and Brownfield, 1986; Kennedy and Forde, 1990a, 1990b).

Routine activities theorists suggest further that the chances of victimization may increase through the "principle of homogamy" (Sampson and Lauritsen, 1990). Individuals increase their likelihood of victimization the more frequently they come into contact with, or associate with, members of demographic groups that contain a disproportionate share of offenders. It is argued, for example, that young males leading "risky lifestyles" out on the street, are more likely to become victims of crime because they are more likely to come in contact with, and associate with other young males who are themselves involved in offending (Kennedy and Forde, 1990b; Sampson and Lauritsen, 1990; Lauritsen et al., 1991).

The routine activities theory also suggests that criminal and deviant lifestyles directly increase victimization because of the nature of offending itself. Jensen and Brownfield (1986) have argued that "offense activity can be considered as a characteristic of lifestyles or as a type of routine activity which increases the risk of victimization because of the motives, vulnerability, or culpability of people involved in those activities" (p. 87). They suggest that it is the "criminogenic potential" of certain routines that accounts for their "victimogenic potential." Individuals heavily involved in certain lifestyle patterns are not merely more available and in close proximity to potential offenders but are more involved in activities that are likely to be associated with offensive behavior as well (Jensen and Brownfield, 1986).

In terms of violent behavior, Sampson and Lauritsen (1990; Lauritsen et al., 1991) point out that assaultive behavior requires more than one person, "so that the risk of becoming a victim given that one is the initial offender (e.g., struck the first blow) is at a maximum" (Lauritsen et al., 1991, p. 268). They also suggest that most assaults take place in contexts (bars, etc.) where the probability of retaliation is high. In fact, a number of studies have gone so far as to imply that victimization leads to greater delinquent offending behavior (Fagan, Piper, and Cheng, 1987; Singer, 1981, 1986).

It has also been argued (Lauritsen et al., 1991; Sampson and Lauritsen, 1990; Sparks, 1982) that offenders are ideal targets because they can be victimized with impunity. "Offender victims" are less likely than "nonoffender victims" to report to police in fear of implicating themselves. Further, if they do report their victimizations, offender victims may have less credibility with the police than those victims without offending histories. As a result, offenders can be viewed as attractive to other offenders. Routine activities theory also stresses the importance of ecological factors in explaining victimization (Garofalo, 1987; Lauritsen et al., 1991). Proximity to crime has an effect on victimization. Thus the levels of crime in certain areas are viewed to represent an important structural determinant of risk.

Finally, routine activities theorists suggest that predatory crime is a matter of rational choice (Felson, 1986; Felson and Cohen, 1980; Seigal and Senna, 1991). Felson (1986) has argued that in order to understand criminal opportunity, we need to know the decisions made by offenders, targets, and guardians as well as the situations of physical convergence that result from these decisions. He notes that human choice enters at many steps in the process. Choice theorists indicate that law-violating behavior occurs when an offender decides to take a chance violating the law after considering his or her own personal situation (need for money, learning experiences), personal values (conscience, moral values, need for peer approval) and situational factors (how well the target is protected; whether people are at home, etc.) (Cornish and Clarke, 1986; Seigal and Senna, 1991). The decision to commit a crime or entry into a delinquent lifestyle is a matter of personal decision making. This suggests that routine activities are shaped by, and in turn shape, choices.

The routine activities theory can be summarized as follows: The probability of victimization increases with the convergence in space and time of motivated offenders, suitable targets and the absence of capable guardians. Choice in turn influences individuals routines and their actions on convergence. Individuals leading risky lifestyles in dangerous locations increase their likelihood of victimization through their association and contact with other offenders. The nature of offending behavior also increases individuals' vulnerability for victimization as circumstances influence outcomes. Finally, risk is increased by the proximity to crime in certain areas.

The Study

The case study of a delinquent street group provides an opportunity to compare the explanatory power of the routine activities approach with the subcultural approach. This type of group seems appropriate for a number of reasons. First, most of the work using the routine activities perspective has relied on official crime statistics, demographic variables, and data from victimization surveys so lacks grounding in ethnographic data. Second, the delinquent group at first glance appears to follow many of the patterns outlined above. The participating individuals are regularly on the street in an ecological area where they are regularly at risk. They lead the risky lifestyles that present opportunities for crime and victimization, and they associate with, and come into contact with, members of demographic groups that contain a disproportionate number of offenders. Members of delinquent groups are also involved in a great deal of violence both as victims and offenders and it would appear that group members could function as guardians for one another. Finally, the group would seem to be an appropriate sample for comparing the routine activities and subcultural approaches because prior research on this type of group has focused on the subcultural norms that guide members' behavior.

To explain the experience of violence within street groups, a field study was undertaken with a group of punk rockers known for their violent behavior.[1] An initial assessment of the characteristics of the downtown core of a mid-size city in Western Canada preceded the investigation. This review identified various territories or turfs, including one area populated by a group of punks (with a group of skinheads near by).[2] Entry into the group was initiated by one of the researchers (who had adopted long unkempt hair, a black leather jacket, torn jeans, work shirt, T-shirt, and high-top runners for appearance in the field) approaching five youths who appeared to be punk rockers. Although these youths were attired in a punk style, the researcher felt it important to establish their group status. This was done by asking if they gathered at this location daily. The five acknowledged that they met at this location on a daily basis. With their group status determined, the researcher identified himself and explained the nature of the research to the group. He explained that in order to properly carry out his research he would need to spend a great deal of time with the group and would also like to interview the various members if they consented. He told them that participation in the interviews was voluntary and he stressed that they would be able to withdraw from an interview at any time or refuse to answer any questions. These five members seemed excited about the prospect of being subjects in a research project. They questioned the researcher about his academic background and institution and after satisfying their curiosity, they agreed to let the researcher "hang around." In a matter of days, the members of the group came to expect the researcher's presence. He knew that he had made a successful entry when he deviated from his normal arrival time and was questioned by a number of members about his tardiness.

The five members that were approached on the first day in the field were helpful in introducing the researcher to the other members of the group. In fact, he was able to develop a good rapport with a number of the members far in advance of an actual interview. Members seemed to enjoy introducing the researcher to others often reciting the research explanation and consent statements they had been given when approached. This put the newly approached members at ease and allowed interviews to progress with ease. After interviewing most of the group the introductions ceased. Some members who had yet to be interviewed approached the researcher inquiring if they would be interviewed. Others, aware of the researchers' motives, consented to interviews when approached.

In addition to the punks' street corner turf, data collection took place inside a restaurant about two blocks away and about four blocks away in front of a fast-food restaurant that was also a gathering place for "skaters."[3] All three locations were on the periphery of the turf of another group in the downtown core, the "rockers."[4]

The data were gathered through a combination of unstructured interviews with all thirty-five punk members and field notes kept on members' activities, interactions, and physical appearance. Although the researcher had an initial list of open-ended questions formulated before entry into the field, the interviews and observations lent to the generation of further questions in the attempt to more fully understand the members' behavior. There was no consistent sequence of questions in the interviews. The researcher often had to adapt to the flow of the conversation by taking the liberty to explore other facets that the subjects seemed to believe were important. The interviews were recorded, with permission, using a microcassette recorder. Completed interviews were selectively transcribed within a twenty-four-hour period to ensure against ethical problems. To preserve anonymity, subjects were given pseudonyms and identifying information was left out. All interviews were usable, although some subjects chose not to respond to specific questions. It was discovered that getting members to answer every question was difficult if not impossible. Some members had no answers to certain questions. Others did not wish to answer certain questions. Still others answered questions in a hostile manner that cued the researcher not to pursue questions in that area.

A total of sixty consecutive days was spent in the field interviewing subjects. Time in the field ranged from five to fifteen hours a day, depending on the degree of activity. The researcher maintained subsequent contact by returning to the field one or two days a week for an additional two months, after which contact was limited to attending the local punk gigs (concerts).

The strong rapport the researcher developed with members far in advance of an interview facilitated data collection. However, interviewing was at times difficult. Subjects usually carried on their daily activities during interviews, resulting in interruptions from other members and panhandling. Subjects sometimes broke off the interview to pursue more exciting activities with other group members (although the researcher was usually asked along). Over time the members began to treat the researcher as a member of the group. This rapport hampered research in the last phases of the study. After the initial interviews, the researcher continued to ask questions developed from the prior interviews and observations. Questioning sometimes became difficult because the researcher was now considered a punk and his questions were dissonant with everyday group activities. He therefore resorted to asking a group member one or two questions during informal conversation and recording the responses at the earliest opportunity, a method that also provided a reliability check of the members' previous responses. The appearance the researcher had adopted for the field also created problems where local police officers assumed he was a member of the group. Fortunately, no complications occurred.

Background

The group under study has been referred to as punk because of its style or physical appearance. The style is associated with punk rock music and its more recent incarnation "hard core." The group was comprised of a network of individuals who dressed in a certain style and met at certain locations on a daily basis. It did not include those individuals who had adopted the punk style but were not members of the network. The members had established group boundaries and dismissed those outside the group as "poseurs." The group for the most part dressed in black jeans and T-shirts, a variety of heavy black boots and jackets (denim or leather) decorated with slogans and band names. Females sometimes deviated from this by wearing skirts and blouses. Hair styles, mainly dyed black, ranged from mohawks (usually worn down), to shaggy spikes, to dreadlocks. Researchers have argued that punks can be distinguished from other youth groups by their social and political consciousness (Hall and Jefferson, 1976; Brake, 1980, 1985; Muncie, 1981; Frith, 1985). The punks under study did suggest that they were more creative, intelligent, and politically aware than others (Baron 1989a). They also claimed that they were less violent than other groups (Baron 1989b). However, the researcher found no coherent political ideology within the group. What seemed to link the group was a libertarian ideology. The members were into "doing their own thing," which meant no restrictions (Baron 1989a). A survey of a group of skinheads (a group known for its racist beliefs) revealed a similar type of group outlook. Further, impressions from time spent in the field and from conversations with street workers suggest that the behavior of the other groups (skinheads, skaters, and rockers), including their involvement in violence, differs little from the group under study. Other than looking different, listening to different types of music, and perhaps adhering to slightly different beliefs, these groups were similar to one another. Thus we believe that the punks are representative of youths spending time on the street.

The punk group contained thirty-five members at the time of the field study (twenty-one males, fourteen females) who ranged in age from fourteen to twenty-nine (only two members were above nineteen), with a mean and median age of seventeen. Length of participation in the group ranged from four weeks to five years, with a mean of approximately two years. The majority of the members had established independence from their parents. Only twelve members of the group resided in their parents' homes. Fourteen members of the group rented their own residences. Three of these were supported by their parents, three others supported themselves through low-wage employment, and seven members relied on the state for support. One member who rented her own residence would not disclose how she supported herself. Nine members of the group lived on the street, did not work, and relied on various methods of survival including illegal activities. The street experience was quite common. Nine of the fourteen members who were renting their own apartments had lived on the street, including four who moved off the street during the field study. Three others living at home at that time had also lived on the street previously. This brings the total to twenty-one members who had at some point in time lived on the street.

Seventeen of the twenty-three members who did not live at home were males, as were the majority of those who had lived or were presently living on the street. In addition, those who received state support were male. In contrast, eight of the twelve members who lived "at home" were female. The members who lived on the street or state support relied on panhandling to gain funds for food. However, they also begged for food and stole food. Other methods of gaining funds included scamming,[5] thieving, and rolling (mugging). When all else failed they went to the soup kitchens. Members for the most part squatted in small groups. Favorite targets were those buildings that were uninhabited or abandoned. Buildings under construction also provided shelter. Other shelter was to be found in parkades, in outdoor storage areas, in stairwells, and under stairs.

The members of the group usually began gathering at their street corner locations in the early afternoon and "hung around" in the downtown core until the early hours of the morning. They moved between their "hangouts" but their main activity was to stand or sit around and talk, waiting for something to happen.

Findings

As outlined above, the routine activities-lifestyle approach implies that victimization is more likely to occur in ecological areas where there is increased risk. Further, it is argued that victimization will increase the more individuals associate with, or come into contact with, members of demographic groups that contain a disproportionate number of offenders. It has already been noted that the members of the group under study met regularly at street corner locations in the downtown core of the city. This area contains numerous commercial facilities found to be associated with victimization (i.e., bars, theaters) (Kennedy and Forde, 1990a). These facilities attract members of similar demographics as the group under study, suggesting an increased risk. This demographic group becomes even larger when the members of the other downtown groups (skinheads, skaters, rockers) are included. Thus the group is in an ecological area known for increased risk; an area that contains and attracts a large number of potential offenders. The fact that a number of the members make their home on the street can only serve to increase their vulnerability.

On entry into the field it became immediately apparent that members were involved in a great deal of violence, both as victims and offenders. Interviews revealed that they rolled, or mugged, people for money and other attractive items, and were involved in violence with members of other delinquent groups and the general public. Most members carried weapons, usually knives or canes. Some boasted of guns, but these were never carried. Instead they were hidden back at the squat or at friend's house. During the field study there were on average two violent incidents a week. To determine if the violence was valued within the group (i.e., a subcultural norm) members were questioned about the violence. The responses were varied but provide us with a number of interesting insights. A number of the members did not view the group as violent. In fact, there were some who had never been involved in a violent incident during their participation in the group, and others who had only been victims of such incidents.

> No like it's not violent. I'm like mellow all the time.

> They think we're all violent and shit. I'm not violent. I mean people literally hate me because of the way I look. Literally hate me. They beat my fuckin' face in.

But further investigation confirmed that there was variation in violent participation with some members viewing others as more violent. Some members admitted participation in fights but refused to admit that they were prone to violence. Many argued that their violence arose out of the circumstances that they were placed in by participating in the group out on the street.

> I wasn't violent before. It's just hanging around with these guys, it's the situations around. You have to be.

> We're not violent. We're mellow. I mean anything that happens is because we have to do it.

They suggested that having moved into a new cultural context with different norms, rules, and expectations they accordingly followed a new set of routine activities. In turn, these routines appeared to shape and influence members' behavioral choices. Although most members went out of their way to describe why they tried to avoid violent confrontation they appeared to recognize the potential for victimization in these situations and had concluded that they were more likely to be victimized if alone and outnumbered, or if at a disadvantage in size or skill. Certainly, because of their lifestyle and exposure to other offenders they had a greater chance of being in situations where this was the case.

> I usually don't get into fights. I try to avoid it. You get good at it. Like on the street there's no chance if it's five on one. You have to be smart enough to get away. Life is short. Do what you can because you haven't got much time.

> Why fight? Even though I've only been beat up three or four times in last 3 years, there's always somebody bigger, tougher, smarter, that will get you and you chance that every time you get into a fight.

However, the members' responses also revealed that as targets they made rational choices to protect themselves. The fear of physical and psychological harm (via a loss of respect) (Jankowski, 1991) led members to respond with violence. Although respect was at stake, the instigating provocations were far more severe than those outlined by Wolfgang and Ferracuti (1967). The members seemed to require more than the jostle or a derogatory remark to signal a violent response. But at a certain point the members refused to "be humiliated" and retaliated or engaged in a "first strike" to gain the upper hand in what they perceived as an unavoidable confrontation.

> The point is to avoid fighting, even if you back down. No big deal. But I won't be humiliated. But I'll let a guy punch me a couple times. I mean

347

he goes away happy and I get a bloody nose and will recover in a few days, unless you become a beating bag and then you have to do something about it.

I don't want to get into fights and stuff, people beating the shit out of each other. Now I have people coming on to me because they think I'm mellow. I don't like to fight but I'm not the type person that of a person who turns their head when somebody comes on to me. I don't like it if I can.

The researcher was quite surprised at the amount of verbal abuse that members absorbed without retaliatory measures. Passersby frequently made derogatory remarks about members sexual preferences and "manliness." The members' appearance also made them the center of attention. Individuals passing by the group often stared and often made negative comments. This type of response was more noticeable when members were alone, away from the group, walking the downtown streets. When asked about this abuse most members replied that it did not bother them, that it was part of the territory.

I don't give a shit. It doesn't bother me. Why do people dress like this if it bothers them. You sure won't be a punk for long.

No it doesn't bother me. I don't give a shit. I look at people and think, "yeah, it's cheaper than a movie." I've noticed when people get involved they're worried about other people staring at them. If they're worried about being stared at, they shouldn't be dressing like this. I think, "who gives a shit, let them look."

There are at least three explanations why members failed to respond to these provocations. First, many of these incidents took place on the busy street limiting the optimal opportunity to respond violently. Second, most of these incidents were unknown to the rest of the group, meaning members could not be rewarded or punished for their responses. As we will see below, the presence of other group members is an important factor in our understanding of how episodes escalate to violence. Third, fear inhibited responding. In fact, fear consciously influenced some members' routines (Vigil and Long, 1990). Members who feared victimization guided their behavior to limit their attractiveness. They rarely ventured out alone without the guardianship of other members. It is likely that those who had never been involved in violence were rarely without guardianship. Thus as Jankowski (1991) illustrates, fear both inhibits, and acts as a catalyst for, violence.

From the above responses, we see emerging an intersection between the theoretical frameworks guiding our analysis. Subcultural norms appear to influence routine activities that in turn influence the conditions and situations where violence can occur. But the escalation to violence is contingent on the rational choices that actors make in those situations. To examine this idea more fully we now analyze the violence initiated by the members of the group.

Instigation of Violence

As outlined earlier, a number of the members of the group participated in violence by rolling or mugging people. Rolling was a source of income for the members and also served as a quick method of obtaining other desirable articles (leather jackets, boots, T-shirts, skateboards). Members openly acknowledged that some of them precipitated violence through their actions to gain material goods. These events also served to enhance members' reputations within the group, particularly among those who also participated in these events (Jankowski, 1991; Vigil and Long, 1990). Those members who regularly rolled people were viewed as "hard core" or tough. However, a number of the members felt that those who attempted to construct "hardcore" images had become parodies of themselves in their attempts to live up to the ideal punk image. This variation of support for violence suggested that the mutual support violent offenders felt in association with each other was more loosely structured than has previously been thought (Singer, 1986).

The following responses provide us with evidence that suggests that the punks were motivated offenders in instrumental violence.

> The violence here is provoked. I mean putting a cane up to someone's head and asking for their money is provoked. I mean mugging people is provoked.

> To roll someone is to beat the shit out of someone till they don't know what's going on and then take their stuff.

The members appeared to make rational choices as to who they chose as targets. The targets were desirable in that they had desirable items, were alone, and lacked guardianship. Often the punks manipulated the attractiveness of victims by enticing them into areas where they would be alone and lacking guardianship. Targets were almost always approached by more than one member of the group and first asked for their boots or jacket or money. Often an offer to trade items was made. For example, a punk may have offered to trade his jacket with the victim. However, all these incidents possessed the potential for escalation into violent crime. Many times the victim refused to part with his property or refused to make a trade. Resistance on the part of the victim changed the circumstances whereby violence was needed to secure the desired item.

When asked about their targets, members informed the researcher that their targets or victims were "geeks." The term geek suggested a subcultural neutralization of the victim's humanity. Geeks were unworthy of respect or fear. They were lower on the cultural totem pole than any of the other groups that gathered downtown. A geek was unfit even to be a member of a rival group. This implied that the choice of victims was influenced by attributions generated from within the subcultural group. Members rationally chose targets whom had come to be perceived as weak, compliant, and unlikely to go to the police.

Members of the other groups that gathered downtown were also prime targets. Again the rational choice of these groups as targets was influenced by subcultural neutralizations and the idea of victimization with impunity. Although certainly not seen as weak as a geek there was the consensus that the members of these groups were inferior to the punks in a number of ways. More important, the offenders believed they could rob or assault these victims without the fear of being reported to the police. This certainly influenced offenders' initial choice of victims and contributed to the decision to move to more violent means to secure the desired items on those occasions where victims resisted the demands of their offenders.

> I wanted his shirt, so we were following behind. Then he got on his skate (skateboard) so we ran him down. I said "heh I really like your shirt, I'll trade you my ring." He said no, so I said "I'll trade you my Jesus Christ Superstar shirt." He said no. So I said "which do you value more, your shirt, or your life." He goes, my life. I said "Well give me your shirt." He says he can't I just got it. So I thought OK he's just a little shit and there's two of us, he's got a lot guts so we just left him alone. Then we just started kicking the fucking shit out of him and trying to get the shirt, but it was all fucking ripped and shit by the time we got it.

Subcultural norms called for violence in these situations. First, violence was instrumental in getting the desired items. Realizing that the items were not forthcoming without force, members made the rational choice to use violence to secure the items. Second, violence was called for in reaction to the harm done to the members' reputations. The resistance presented a challenge to the hard-core image that each member had constructed. The insult was amplified by the fact that the offenders perceived offering the victim a reasonable nonviolent alternative (i.e., a trade). The fact that the insult was made to more than one person meant that members had to save face in front of each other and attempt to validate their hard-core image. Within this group situation each member possessed a sanctioning power over the other. Members could either reward each other for a violent response, or punish the member who did not react appropriately to the insult. The need to gain the social and material rewards led members to opt for violence in these situations. Thus third parties were influential in the escalation to violence. Felson, Ribner, and Seigal (1984) have noted that third parties serve as allies that sometimes instigate conflict, or engage in the physical attacks. The dynamics of these disputes contain important elements that prevent individuals from pulling back from violence and suggest that group norms deescalating violence once it begins are weak.

Once again our discussion has benefited from the intersection of our guiding explanatory frameworks. We can see that members' routine activities, shaped by their subcultural participation, increase the likelihood that they will be involved in situations where the potential for escalation to violence is at a maximum. To a certain extent they are encouraging violence by daring victims to resist them. If so, subcultural norms influence the choices members make to engage in violence. Because of the audience of peers, these are the situations where members have the most to gain by engaging in violence. If the episode does not escalate to violence, the offender has still demonstrated power over his victim thereby increasing his reputation. Third parties and their support for violence appear to be extremely important in understanding how one responds to provocation.

Dangerous Locations, Offender Behavior, and Victimization

The above review has demonstrated how choices are constrained by places and people and are also shaped by cultural norms. Routine activities are constrained by cultural milieu, as are choices. In light of their participation in the subcultural group, and the routine activities that evolve, it is not surprising that the punks also find themselves in situations where they are potential victims. The subcultural norms that influence routines and offending opportunities also contribute to the members' vulnerability to victimization. It is also important to examine how choice operates in these situations, the influence it has on outcomes, and the circumstances whereby the initial offender becomes the victim. We investigate this theme further by examining the conditions under which the punks themselves were victimized.

An examination of the punks' victimization experiences revealed that they were similar to their offender experiences. The only difference is that they were now the victims. Members noted that in most situations they encountered more than one adversary, were alone, and lacking guardianship. This made them attractive targets to the other delinquent groups in the downtown core. And like the victims that they themselves pursued, the punks often reacted with violence in a situation where they were outnumbered and at a distinct disadvantage. Judging from comments that appeared earlier, it seems that mediation was the favored tactic in the dyadic situation, or to let the offender push them around for a short period and hope the altercation would be diffused. If there were no third parties, the chances of a compromise were increased. If the situation progressed, the members made the choice out of fear of physical harm to react with violence. In contrast, when members faced a number of

351

adversaries, the situation often escalated to violence. The same dynamics that led to a group of punks, reinforced by each other, to instigate violence against adversaries, worked against them in situations where they were outnumbered and were perceived to have insulted the reputation of their adversaries. Again, members often reacted out of fear, using a first-strike approach.

> There were three guys. I had a cane and I broke it over his head and then I had two pieces to break. He thought I wasn't going to do anything. But they beat the shit out of me.

> These two guys were chasing me and they got me cornered, then one guy starts taking off his jacket so I bend this aluminum siding and rip it off and swing it at him and they both take off.

On a number of occasions the members reported that they got the upper hand in these altercations. That is, although they were the intended victims, the punks often became offenders as the situation changed and superior skill enabled them to beat up the original aggressors. This supports the notion offered by Sampson and others (Lauritsen et al., 1991; Sampson and Lauritsen, 1990; Sparks, 1982) "that the risk of becoming a victim given that one is the initial offender (e.g., struck the first blow)" is a real possibility.

> Thursday like I got hassled . . . I thought this is cool, everyone in this neighborhood knows who I am. These two rockers come up and I have a 56-pound puppy which is half rottweiler. I mean not nice dogs. So they're so stupid they hassle me. I mean one kicks my dog. Like this dog has always been mellow but if its owner is threatened it freaked out. So my dog is chewing on one guy's leg and I take off my belt and hit the other guy in the face. So they ended up taking off.

> I was standing outside the soup kitchen and this guy starts hassling me. Then he starts doing this martial arts stuff. So I think to myself this guy is going to kill me, the only chance I have is to kick him in the balls, which he may block. So I kick him in the balls and he goes down so I keep kicking him. Then when I go inside the soup kitchen I notice I've got skin on my boots.

A closer examination of these incidents indicated that the initial offenders miscalculated the attractiveness of their punk victims. The punks often were more skilled than anticipated, or produced a weapon. The appearance of guardians (other punks) also made the initial punk victim less attractive as a target. These guardians often appeared "to even things up" and increased the likelihood that the original aggressor would become the victim. The willingness of group members to come to each other's aid suggested the development of subcultural protective norms.

> These three rockers were bugging this chick and then they went after
> Damien which is stupid, right? So three guys jump him so me and Alan
> jump in and beat the shit out of them and they run away like and get into
> a cab. We throw a rock at the cab and it breaks the back window and
> so it stops and we haul them out and like a riot almost breaks out.

> We beat up these pongos, right? They came after us and Damien goes
> "come on I'll take you all on. It doesn't matter if I get it, I'll take one
> of your heads with me." And Carl had this knife and they were freakin'
> out he has a knife so they took off.

Although the male members of the group were involved in most of the
violent incidents, the females were not excluded. During the study one female
was threatened with a knife by two male members of the rocker group and another was rolled by three female members of the rocker group. There was also
one incident reported where three punk females attacked a rocker female in a
fastfood restaurant. However, most females had little experience with fighting.

> No I've never been in a fight in my life. I wouldn't know what to do. I
> just stay away from people who don't like me. If they don't like me they
> don't like me. I have a lot of friends down here that if someone hassled
> me there could be trouble because I have friends behind me.

Although the number of events involving females were too small to make firm
conclusions, it appeared that for the most part, the incidents were similar to
those involving the male members of the group.

In sum, we see that punks are both offenders and victims. Their victimization arises in situations similar to those that give rise to their offending behavior. Members' routines, influenced by their subcultural participation, exposed
them to victimization by rational offenders. Alone and lacking capable guardianship, they are seen as attractive targets to potential aggressors. The situation
is influenced by subculture and choice. Violence is more likely when there
is more than one offender, as third parties, representing a source of reinforcement, serve as allies and help instigate conflict. The victims respond rationally
to situational violent cues in kind, often out of the fear of physical harm. The
outcomes of these violent altercations are difficult to predict because many
times the original aggressor becomes the victim as circumstances change with
the entry of guardians, unforeseen weapons, or superior fighting skills.

Drugs, Alcohol, and Violence

Drugs and alcohol also played an important role in the victim/offender experiences of group members. There appeared to be rules governing drinking and
drug taking within the group and the behavior tolerable within certain settings

while under the influence. For example, every weekend the members of the group attended the local punk gigs that also attracted the members of the other downtown groups and therefore, provided opportunities for intergroup violence. The party atmosphere of the gigs provided great excitement for the members as they drank, smoked, and danced. The major activity at these gigs was "slam dancing" (also referred to as "slamming," "moshing," "skanking," and "thrashing") where participants ran into, and rebounded off of, one another. Slamdancing took place in the pit, the area directly in front of the stage. Participation in the dancing was normative. Members were ostracized for failing to participate.

The intensity and viciousness of the slam in the pit depended on the speed of the music. Often members of other downtown groups, or punks not members of the group under study (referred to as "poseurs"), violated slam etiquette by dancing overly aggressively. Punk group members usually responded by slamming more vigorously with feet and elbows in an attempt to injure the offenders. The fights that usually ensued, were often indistinguishable from the slam dancing that spawned them, and often grew to include members of the various groups (or in the case of the "poseurs," a fragmented group). The resulting fights would eventually attract bouncers and police who would disperse the youths and shut down the concert if still in progress. Members of the various groups would gather outside, exchange threats, and then slowly go on their way. Although members talked with great excitement as they stood around, these incidents never progressed once outside the venue and the researcher got the impression that the members did not really want them to progress any further.

The members understood the setting as one that was orchestrated around symbolic violence. The members were expected to become intoxicated and act aggressively. They entered the setting with the expectations of participating in this controlled violence and understood the potential for escalation as altercations were a regular part of the dancing. Members used these settings to enhance their reputations at minimal risk to themselves.

The violence at these gigs also served an integrative function for the group. In these settings, members were expected to be on the look out for trouble, guard each others' backs, and be prepared to help out at the first sign of trouble. There was a feeling of "us against them." The potential for conflict between the various groups demonstrated this further. It was "showing up" or "being there" for the group that was important because police and venue security deterred escalation to conflict. Here members could save face by remarking on how they would have come out on top of the altercation had it proceeded, and how the other groups backed down. Thus within these settings we see evidence of subcultural norms guiding members' behaviors; norms requiring participation in controlled, but potentially serious, aggression, and strong group norms concerning protection.

On other occasions where members were ingesting drugs or alcohol, there was little evidence of aggressive behavior. These were times of collective relaxation. Group members behaving aggressively toward each other on these occasions was almost unheard of. Group norms discouraged such behavior. In the field, intragroup aggression within this type of setting happened only twice and involved the same offender both times. As the researcher left the field he noticed this member's participation had grown sporadic. In sum, intoxication did not lead directly to aggressive behavior. As both Zinberg (1984) and Fagan (1990) have illustrated, drinking norms require different behaviors from group members in different settings.

Discussion and Conclusions

Our examination of a delinquent street group has revealed the need to incorporate an integrative approach to help explain violent offending and victimization. It appears that routine activities theory with a choice component and subcultural theory complement one another. Behavior is sometimes guided by choice, sometimes influenced by cultural norms and processes, and at other times by routine activities. On many occasions various aspects of these three components interact to influence behavioral outcomes. To begin with, the data indicate that members' choices to enter into the subcultural group influence their routine activities. Their cultural context encourages them to follow routines where they associate with, or come into contact with, groups that contain a disproportionate number of potential offenders. Thus the convergence of victims and offenders is influenced by a cultural component. This subcultural component also influences offending experiences. Members' responses suggest that they rationally choose targets based on the items, and guardianship, that the targets possess. In addition, cultural definitions and neutralizations influence target attractiveness. Targets gain attractiveness when they are deemed by the group as worthless, weak, and unlikely to go to the police. Targets fitting these criteria can be victimized with impunity. Thus the convergence of victims and offenders is influenced not only by subcultural norms guiding routines, but also subcultural norms guiding choice.

The escalation to violence is contingent on subcultural definitions of what is acceptable and tolerable within these interactions. These interactions are also forums for certain group members to promote images or construct reputations. The loss of respect, the instrumental need to gain desired items, and the influence of third parties all interact to explain the instigation and advocacy of violence. In the course of their offending behavior, members come to perceive some actions by victims as insulting to the reputations they have constructed. The victim insults all the offenders by refusing to trade items, or refusing to give up items under circumstances where he (rarely she) is at an obvious disadvantage. Each member reacts with violence, saving face and avoiding possible sanctions. Further, violence is a choice made to secure items that are not forthcoming. Violence, therefore is a desired reaction that gains social and material rewards within these situations.

The dynamics of these disputes contain important elements that prevent individuals from pulling back from violence. Further, by participating in these incidents, members increase the likelihood of violent confrontation. To a certain extent they were encouraging violence to gain and keep a reputation. Episodes that do not escalate to violence still demonstrate the members' power over their victims and increase or substantiate their reputations.

In the dyadic situation, where members are alone and faced with single violators, the provocation required for violent responses is severe. Where members perceive a confrontation to be unavoidable, they respond to physical attack in kind, or engage in a first strike to gain the upper hand in the dispute. Their entry into the subculture influenced their routine activities, exposing them to situations where the chances of victimization are increased, but their decision to engage in violence appeared to be made on the basis of rational choice: Respond or be beaten.

The role of the subculture and third parties accentuated the importance of insider versus outsider. Many times members became guardians for individuals under attack. This suggests that their affiliation served to establish norms of protection where members are expected to intervene on each others' behalf during conflict situations. Under certain circumstances the conflict appears to provide an integrative function for the group. We have also seen that punks tend to victimize those that are outside of their social network. It is this same affiliation that promotes the control of conflict. Given their risky lifestyles, the group attempts to avoid victimization by all. By restricting their relationships to those of the same approximate age, and in this case stylistic group, the members can avoid some of the most obvious sources of conflict. As Suttles (1968) and Thrasher (1927) argue, these groups reduce the likelihood of intragroup conflict, and offer protection against intergroup conflict. In the absence of other sources and guarantees of safety, the group emerges as a grouping whose behavior can be anticipated (Suttles, 1968). It is this guardianship that helps explain why a small number of members had never been involved in violent episodes. Although these members are certainly not interested in constructing a hard-core reputation, we might predict that because of their group experiences they would react rationally out of fear if they found themselves in a situation without guardianship. The variation in the mutual support for violence suggests that violent subcultures are much more loosely structured than has previously been thought (Singer, 1986).

The results suggest that we must examine more fully how choices, routines, and cultural milieu interact to affect one another. The evolution of events leading to assaults or robberies may depend on conflict styles that vary by individual personality and the social situation that individuals confront (Hocker and Wilmot, 1985, p. 38). Hocker and Wilmot assume that people develop patterned responses to conflict. Decisions about style are made on the basis of past experience and learning. People learn conflict styles by observing others' behavior and trying different responses. These responses may be molded by the routine activities that people are involved in during their daily living. However, we might add that these responses and experiences and even routines are influenced by culture. Culture will impinge on the routines people adopt, the exposure to others' conflict styles, and the expectations about decisions in certain situations. Bernard (1990) argues that social groups transmit rules specifying levels of aggression in certain situations and support those rules with the awarding and withholding of status and prestige. The rules are acquired through vicarious learning and maintained through reinforcement and instrumental learning. Thus culture, routines, and choice may actually promote certain conflict styles. Routine activities theory must include a choice component and draw on ideas from the subcultural literature to determine how conflict styles mediate the impact of exposure to high-risk situations.

Notes

1. The group has been the focus of attention from a number of different groups. Local press coverage has evolved from a portrayal of the group as harmless, to the depiction of a group that is disturbing the public because of their lifestyle. Merchants have complained that the congregation of the group and its members' behaviors (spitting, swearing, panhandling, violence) frightens potential shoppers. Some members of the public have expressed similar views. Last, the group has drawn attention from a number of groups expressing concern about the increasing number of youths living on the street.

2. The "skinheads" or "skins" are stylistically a copy of those in Britain. They wore "Doc Marten" work boots, rolled-up jeans, suspenders, and flight jackets. Their heads were shaved and most had an array of tattoos.

3. The skaters wore long shorts (with long-johns underneath in the winter), high-top runners, wore their hair short with long bangs, and rode or carried skateboards wherever they were.

4. The rockers could be identified by their long hair, black T-shirts (emblazoned with pictures of their favorite bands), jeans, and black leather jackets.

5. A scam refers to a con. However, members used the term more generally to mean anything involving deception. For example, asking someone if they would like to buy some fireworks to entice them into an alley where they would be robbed was called a scam. The members' favorite scam was to cut up dots from lottery tickets, wrap them in cigarette paper and sell the creations to the naive as LSD.

References

Ball-Rokeach, S. (1973). "Values and Violence: A Test of the Subculture of Violence Thesis." *American Sociological Review* 38:736–49.

Baron, Stephen W. (1989a). "The Canadian West Coast Punk Subculture: A Field Study." *Canadian Journal of Sociology* 14(3):289–316.

_____. (1989b). "Resistance and Its Consequences: The Street Culture of Punks." *Youth & Society* 21(2):207–37.

Bernard, Thomas J. (1990). "Angry Aggression Among the Truly Disadvantaged." *Criminology* 28:73–95.

Brake, Mike. (1980). *The Sociology of Youth Culture and Youth Subcultures*. London: Routledge & Kegan Paul.

_____. (1985). *Comparative Youth Culture*. London: Routledge & Kegan Paul.

Cloward, Richard A. and Lloyd E. Ohlin. (1960). *Delinquency and Opportunity*. Glencoe, IL: Free Press.

Cohen, Albert K. and James F. Short, Jr. (1958). "Research in Delinquent Subcultures." *Journal of Social Issues* 14(3):20–37.

Cohen, Lawrence E. and Marcus Felson. (1980). "Social Change and Crime Rate Trends: A Routine Activity Approach." *American Sociological Review*. 44(4): 588–608.

Cornish, Derek B. and Ronald V. Clarke. (1986). *The Reasoning Criminal*. New York: Springer-Verlag.

Erlanger, H.S. (1974). "The Empirical Status of the Subculture of Violence Thesis." *Social Problems* 22:280–92.

Fagan, Jeffrey. (1990). "Intoxication and Aggression." Pp. 241–320 in *Drugs and Crime, Crime and Justice: A Review of Research*, Vol. 13, edited by M. Tonry and J.Q. Wilson. Chicago: University of Chicago Press.

Fagan, Jeffrey, Elizabeth S. Piper, and Yu-Teh Cheng. (1987). "Contributions of Victimization to Delinquency in Inner Cities." *Journal of Criminal Law and Criminology* 78(3):586–609.

Felson, Marcus. (1986). "Linking Criminal Choices, Routine Activities, Informal Control, and Criminal Outcomes." Pp. 119–28 in *The Reasoning Criminal*, edited by Derek B. Cornish and Ronald V. Clarke. New York: Springer-Verlag.

Felson, Marcus and Lawrence E. Cohen. (1980). "Human Ecology and Crime: A Routine Activities Approach." *Human Ecology* 4:389–406.

Felson, Richard B., S.A. Ribner, and M.S. Seigal. (1984). "Age and Effects of Third Parties During Criminal Violence." *Sociology and Social Research* 68:452–62.

Frith, Simon. (1985). "The Sociology of Youth." Pp. 301–68 in *Sociology: New Directions*, edited by Michael Haralobos. Ormskik: Causeway.

Garofalo, James. (1987). "Reassessing the Lifestyle Model of Criminal Victimization." Pp. 23–42 in *Positive Criminology*, edited by Michael R. Gottfredson and Travis Hirschi. Newbury Park, CA: Sage.

Hagan, John. (1984). *Disreputable Pleasures*. Toronto: McGraw-Hill.

_____. (1985). *Modern Criminology: Crime, Criminal Behavior, and Its Control*. New York: McGraw-Hill.

Hall, Stuart and Tony Jefferson. (1976). *Resistance Through Ritual: Youth Subcultures in Post-War Britain*. London: Hutchinson.

Hartnagel, T. (1980). "Subculture of Violence: Further Evidence." *Pacific Sociological Review* 23(2):217–42.

Hocker, Joyce L. and William W. Wilmot. (1985). *Interpersonal Conflict.* 2nd ed. Dubuque, IA: Brown.

Horowitz, Ruth. (1983). *Honor and the American Dream.* New Brunswick, NJ: Rutgers University Press.

Horowitz, Ruth and Gary Swartz. (1974). "Honor, Normative Ambiguity, and Gang Violence." *American Sociological Review* 39:238-51.

Jankowski, Martin Sanchez. (1991). *Islands in the Street.* Berkeley: University of California Press.

Jansyn, L.R. (1966). "Solidarity and Delinquency in a Street Corner Group." *American Sociological Review* 29:653-68.

Jensen, Gary F. and David Brownfield. (1986). "Gender, Lifestyles, and Victimization: Beyond Routine Activity." *Violence and Victims* 1(2):85-99.

Kennedy, Leslie W. and David R. Forde. (1990a). "Routine Activities and Crime: An Analysis of Victimization in Canada." *Criminology* 28(1):137-52.

_____. (1990b). "Risky Lifestyles and Dangerous Results: Routine Activities and Exposure to Crime." *Sociology and Social Research* 74(4):208-11.

Klein, M. and L.D. Crawford. (1967). "Groups, Gangs, and Cohesiveness." *Journal of Research in Crime and Delinquency* 4:63-75.

Kornhauser, Ruth Rosner. (1978). *Social Sources of Delinquency.* Chicago: University of Chicago Press.

Lauritsen, Janet L., Robert J. Sampson, and John Laub. (1991). "The Link Between Offending and Victimization Among Adolescents." *Criminology* 29(2):265-91.

Loftin, Colin, and Robert H. Hill. (1974). "Regional Subculture and Homicide." *American Sociological Review* 39:714-24.

Luckenbill, David F. and Daniel P. Doyle. (1989). "Structural Position and Violence: Developing a Cultural Explanation." *Criminology* 27(3):419-35.

Miller, Walter B. (1958). "Lower Class Culture as a Generating Milieu of Gang Delinquency." *Journal of Social Issues* 14(3): 5-19.

Muncie, John. (1981). *Politics, Ideology and Popular Culture.* Walton Hall, Milton Keynes: Open University Press.

Nettler, G. (1974). *Explaining Crime.* New York: McGraw Hill.

Parker, Robert Nash. (1989). "Poverty, Subculture of Violence, and Type of Homicide." *Social Forces* 67(4):983-1007.

Sampson, Robert J. (1987). "Urban Black Violence: The Effect of Male Joblessness and Family Disruption." *American Journal of Sociology* 93:348-82.

Sampson, Robert J. and Janet L. Lauritsen. (1990). "Deviant Lifestyles, Proximity to Crime, and the Offender-Victim Link in Personal Violence." *Journal of Research in Crime and Delinquency* 27(2):110-39.

Sampson, Robert J. and John Wooldredge. (1987). "Linking the Micro- and Macro-Level Dimensions of Lifestyles Routine Activity and Opportunity Models of Predatory Victimization." *Journal of Quantitative Criminology* 3:371-93.

Seigal, Larry J. and Joseph J. Senna. (1991). *Juvenile Delinquency.* 4th ed. St. Paul: West Publishing.

Short, James F., Jr. and Fred L. Strodtbeck. (1965). *Group Process and Gang Delinquency.* Chicago: University of Chicago Press.

Singer, S. (1981). "Homogeneous Victim-Offender Populations: A Review of Some Research Implications." *Journal of Criminal Law and Criminology* 72:779-88.

———. (1986). "Victims of Serious Violence and Their Criminal Behavior: Subcultural Theory and Beyond." *Victims and Violence* 9(1):61-69.

Sparks, R. (1982). *Research on Victims of Crime.* Washington, DC: U.S. Government Printing Office.

Suttles, Gerald. (1968). *Social Order of the Slum.* Chicago: University of Chicago Press.

Thrasher, Frederick M. (1927). *The Gang.* Chicago: University of Chicago Press.

Vigil, James Diego and John M. Long. (1990). "Etic and Emic Perspectives on Gang Culture: The Chicano Case." Pp. 55-68 in *Gangs in America*, edited by C. Ronald Huff. Newbury Park, CA: Sage.

Williams, Kirk. (1984). "Economic Sources of Homicide: Reestimating the Effects of Poverty and Inequality." *American Sociological Review* 49:283-89.

Williams, Kirk and Robert Flewelling. (1988). "The Social Production of Criminal Homicide: A Comparative Study of Disaggregated Rates in American Cities." *American Sociological Review* 53:421-31.

Wolfgang, Marvin E. and Franco Ferracuti. (1967). *The Subculture of Violence.* London: Tavistock.

Zinberg, N.E. (1984). *Drug, Set, and Setting: The Social Bases of Controlled Use.* New Haven, CT: Yale University Press.

Part 5
Different Contexts, Different Gangs

This section takes a slightly different direction than those that have gone before. Much of the literature on gangs in the United States—and elsewhere, for that matter—focuses almost exclusively on youth street gangs. In this section we will look at a variety of different gangs: and it is in this way we see even more clearly the difficulty that our definitions present us (see especially part 1).

The first selection deals with women associated with outlaw motorcycle gangs. In some of the recent research on motorcycle gangs, these groups (virtually all composed of adult members) have been likened to organized crime families. The article by Hopper and Moore examines the various roles played by women in these organizations, and the article presents a useful comparison with articles by Campbell and by Harris in part 3.

The next article in this section, by Fong and Vogel, presents research on prison gangs within the institutions of the Texas Department of Corrections. While no one would assert that the Texas situation is typical, other states have experienced gang-related problems in their prisons as well. This article shows some problems caused by prison gangs in Texas and explores the nature, composition, and organizations of these gangs. One of the major concerns facing law enforcement authorities in states like Texas is the connection between prison gangs and street gangs. For a vivid portrayal of the prison gang problem and connections with street gangs you might want to get a copy of *Blood In, Blood Out (Bound by Honor)* or *American Me* on videocassette.

In the last article, Pincomb and Judiscak examine the Jamaican posses. In some ways these groups resemble adolescent street gangs. However, in other ways their activities depart fairly significantly from youth gangs. The Jamaican posses have been linked with a variety of criminal activities, but especially with drugs and many gun crimes in the cities in which they are found. Pincomb and Judiscak explore the problems created by these groups and the dilemmas facing law enforcement authorities in dealing with them.

Questions to Consider

As you finish reading this section, consider the following questions:

1. In the article by Hopper and Moore, do you believe that outlaw motorcycle gangs are similar to or different from youth street gangs?
2. Are the roles played by women in outlaw motorcycle gangs similar to those of females in youth street gangs? Why or why not?
3. What seem to be the connections, if any, between street gangs and prison gangs? What features seem to distinguish prison gangs from youth street gangs?
4. Are the Jamaican posses like any other gangs you have read about? That is, do they in any way resemble African-American, Hispanic, or Asian gangs, or are they completely different and separate?

19

Women in Outlaw Motorcycle Gangs

Columbus B. Hopper and Johnny Moore

This chapter is about the place of women in gangs in general and in outlaw motorcycle gangs in particular. Street gangs have been observed in New York dating back as early as 1825 (Asbury, 1928). The earliest gangs originated in the Five Points district of lower Manhattan and were composed mostly of Irishmen. Even then, there is evidence that girls or young women participated in the organizations as arms and ammunition bearers during gang fights.

The first gangs were of two types: those motivated primarily as fighters and those seeking financial gain. Women were represented in both types and they shared a remarkably similar reputation with street gang women more than one hundred years later (Hanson, 1964). They were considered ''sex objects'' and they were blamed for instigating gang wars through manipulating gang boys. The girls in the first gangs were also seen as undependable, not as loyal to the gang, and they played inferior roles compared to the boys.

The first thorough investigation of youth gangs in the United States was carried out by Thrasher (1927) in Chicago. Thrasher devoted very little attention to gang girls, but he stated that there were about half a dozen female gangs out of 1,313 groups he surveyed. He also said that participation by young women in male gangs was limited to auxiliary units for social and sexual activities.

Short (1968) rarely mentioned female gang members in his studies, which were also carried out in Chicago, but he suggested that young women became gang associates because they were less attractive and less socially adequate compared to girls who did not affiliate with gangs.

According to Rice (1963), girls were limited to lower status in New York street gangs because there was no avenue for them to achieve power or prestige in the groups. If they fought, the boys thought them unfeminine; if they opted for a passive role, they were used only for sexual purposes.

Reprinted by permission of Sage Publications, Inc. from *Journal of Contemporary Ethnography*, Vol. 18, No. 4 (January 1990): 363–387.

Ackley and Fliegel (1960) studied gangs in Boston in which girls played both tough roles and feminine roles. They concluded that preadolescent girls were more likely to engage in fighting and other typically masculine gang actions while older girls in the gangs played more traditionally feminine roles.

Miller (1973, 1975) found that half of the male gangs in New York had female auxiliaries but he concluded that the participation of young women in the gangs did not differ from that which existed in the past. Miller also pointed out that girls who formed gangs or who were associates of male gangs were lower-class girls who had never been exposed to the women's movement. After studying black gangs in Los Angeles, Klein (1971) believed that, rather than being instigators of gang violence, gang girls were more likely to inhibit fighting.

The most intensive studies of female gang members thus far were done by Campbell (1984, 1986, 1987) on Hispanic gangs in New York City. Although one of the three gangs she studied considered itself a motorcycle gang, it had only one working motorcycle in the total group. Therefore, all of the gangs she discussed should be thought of as belonging to the street gang tradition.

Campbell's description of the gang girls was poignant. The girls were very poor but not anomic; rather, they were true believers in American capitalism, aspiring to success as recent immigrants always have. They were torn between maintaining and rejecting Puerto Rican values while trying to develop a "cool" streetwise image.

As Campbell reported, girl gang members shared typical teenage concerns about proper makeup and wearing the right brands of designer jeans and other clothing. Contrary to popular opinion, they were also concerned about being thought of as whores or bad mothers, and they tried to reject the Latin ideal that women should be totally subordinate to men. The basic picture that came out of Campbell's work was that gang girls had identity problems arising from conflicting values. They wanted to be aggressive and tough, and yet they wished to be thought of as virtuous, respectable mothers.

Horowitz (1983, 1986, 1987) found girls in Chicano gangs to be similar in basic respects to those that Campbell described. The gang members, both male and female, tried to reconcile Latin cultural values of honor and violence with patterns of behavior acceptable to their families and to the communities in which they existed.

The foregoing and other studies showed that girls have participated in street gangs as auxiliaries, as independent groups, and as members in mixed-gender organizations. While gangs have varied in age and ethnicity, girls have had little success in gaining status in the gang world. As reported by Bowker (1978, Bowker and Klein, 1983), however, female street gang activities were increasing in most respects; he thought that independent gangs and mixed groups were increasing more than were female auxiliary units.

Unlike street gangs that go back for many years, motorcycle gangs are relatively new. They first came to public attention in 1947 when the Booze

Fighters, Galloping Gooses, and other groups raided Hollister, California (Morgan, 1978). This incident, often mistakenly attributed to the Hells Angels, made headlines across the country and established the motorcycle gangs' image. It also inspired *The Wild Ones*, the first of the biker movies released in 1953, starring Marlon Brando and Lee Marvin.

Everything written on outlaw motorcycle gangs has focused on the men in the groups. Many of the major accounts (Eisen, 1970; Harris, 1985; Montegomery, 1976; Reynolds, 1967; Saxon, 1972; Thompson, 1967; Watson, 1980; Wilde, 1977; Willis, 1978; Wolfe, 1968) included a few tantalizing tidbits of information about women in biker culture but in none were there more than a few paragraphs, which underscored the masculine style of motorcycle gangs and their chauvinistic attitudes toward women.

Although the published works on outlaw cyclists revealed the fact that gang members enjoyed active sex lives and had wild parties with women, the women have been faceless; they have not been given specific attention as functional participants in outlaw culture. Indeed, the studies have been so one-sided that it has been difficult to think of biker organizations in anything other than a masculine light. We have learned that the men were accompanied by women but we have not been told anything about the women's backgrounds, their motivations for getting into the groups or their interpretations of their experiences as biker women.

From the standpoint of the extant literature, biker women have simply existed; they have not had personalities or voices. They have been described only in the contemptuous terms of male bikers as "cunts," "sluts," "whores," and "bitches." Readers have been given the impression that women were necessary nuisances for outlaw motorcyclists. A biker Watson (1980: 118) quoted, for example, summed up his attitude toward women as follows: "Hell," he said, "if I could find a man with a pussy, I wouldn't fuck with women. I don't like 'em. They're nothing but trouble."

In this article, we do four things. First, we provide more details on the place of women in arcane biker subculture, we describe the rituals they engage in, and we illustrate their roles as money-makers. Second, we give examples of the motivations and backgrounds of women affiliated with outlaws. Third, we compare the gang participation of motorcycle women to that of street gang girls. Fourth, we show how the place of biker women has changed over the years of our study and we suggest a reason for the change. We conclude by noting the impact of sex role socialization on biker women.

Methods

The data we present were gathered through participant observation and interviews with outlaw bikers and their female associates over the course of seventeen years. Although most of the research was done in Mississippi, Tennessee,

Louisiana, and Arkansas, we have occasionally interviewed bikers throughout the nation, including Hawaii.[1] The trends and patterns we present, however, came from our study in the four states listed.

During the course of our research, we have attended biker parties, weddings, funerals, and other functions in which outlaw clubs were involved. In addition, we have visited in gang clubhouses, gone on "runs" and enjoyed cookouts with several outlaw organizations.

It is difficult to enumerate the total amount of time or the number of respondents we have studied because of the necessity of informal research procedures. Bikers would not fill out questionnaires or allow ordinary research methods such as tape recorders or note taking. The total number of outlaw motorcyclists we studied over the years was certainty several hundred. In addition to motorcycle gangs in open society, we also interviewed and corresponded with male and female bikers in state and federal prisons.

The main reason we were able to make contacts with bikers was the background of Johnny Moore, who was once a biker himself. During the 1960s, "Big John" was president of Satan's Dead, an outlaw club on the Mississippi Gulf Coast. He participated in the rituals we describe, and his own experience and observations provided the details of initiation ceremonies that we relate. As a former club president, Moore was able to get permission for us to visit biker clubhouses, a rare privilege for outsiders.[2]

Most of our research was done on weekends because of our work schedules and because the gangs were more active at this time. The bikers usually had a large party one weekend a month, or more often when the weather was nice, and we were invited to many of these.

At some parties, such as the "Big Blowout" each spring in Gulfport, there were a variety of nonmembers present to observe the motorcycle shows and "old lady" contests as well as to enjoy the party atmosphere. These occasions were especially helpful in our study because bikers were "loose" and easier to approach while partying. We spent more time with three particular "clubs," as outlaw gangs refer to themselves, because of their proximity.

In addition to studying outlaw bikers themselves, we obtained police reports, copies of Congressional hearings that deal with motorcycle gangs, and indictments that were brought against prominent outlaw cyclists. Our attempt was to study biker women and men in as many ways as possible. We were honest in explaining the purpose of our research to our respondents. They were told that our goal was only to learn more about outlaw motorcycle clubs as social organizations.

Dilemmas of Biker Research

Studying bikers was a conflicted experience for us. It was almost impossible to keep from admiring their commitment, freedom, boldness, and fearlessness;

at the same time, we saw things that caused us discomfort and consternation because bikers' actions were sometimes bizarre. We saw bikers do things completely foreign to our personal values. Although we did not condone these activities, we did not express our objections for two reasons. First, we would not have been able to continue our study. Second, it was too dangerous to take issue with outlaws on their own turf.

Studying bikers was a risky undertaking for us, even without criticizing them. At times when we were not expecting any problems, conditions became hazardous. In Jackson, Tennessee, for example, one morning in 1985 we walked into an area where bikers had camped out all night. Half asleep and hung over, several of them jumped up and pulled guns on us because they thought we might be members of a rival gang that had killed five of their "brothers" several years earlier. If Grubby, a biker who recognized us from previous encounters, had not interceded in our behalf, we could have been killed or seriously injured.

Bikers would not humor many questions and they did not condone uninvited comments. Even seemingly insignificant remarks sometimes caused a problem. In Biloxi on one occasion, we had an appointment to visit a biker clubhouse late on a Saturday afternoon in 1986. When we were admitted into the main room of the building, two women picked up four pistols that had been on a coffee table and scurried into a bedroom. Several men remained in front of a television set, watching a wrestling match.

Because we looked upon professional wrestling as a humorous sham, one of us made a light reference to it. Immediately the bikers became tense and angry; it was clear that another sarcastic comment would have resulted in our being literally thrown out of the clubhouse. In this way, we accidentally learned that some bikers take television wrestling seriously. It would have been a bad mistake to have questioned them about their reasons for liking the dubious sport. There was a human skull on a pole in front of their clubhouse but we thought it better to ignore it!

For practical purposes, both male and female bikers worship the Harley Davidson motorcycle. One Mississippi group that we studied extensively had an old flathead "Hog" mounted on a high tree stump at the entrance to their clubhouse. When going in or out, members bowed to the old Harley or saluted it as an icon of the highest order. They took it very seriously. Had we not shown respect for their obeisance, our relationship would have been terminated, probably in a violent manner.

It was hard to fathom the chasm between bikers and the rest of us. Outlaw cyclists have no constraints except those their club mandates. When a biker spoke of something being "legal," he was referring to the bylaws of his club rather than to the laws of a state or nation. A biker's "legal" name was his club name that was usually inscribed on his jacket or "colors." Club names were typically one word, and this was how other members and female associates referred to a biker. Such descriptive names as Trench Mouth, Grimy, Animal, Spooky, and Red sufficed for most bikers we studied. As we knew them, bikers lived virtually a tribal life-style with few restraints. The freedom they enjoyed was not simply being ''in the wind''; it was also emotional. Whereas conventional people fear going to prison, the bikers were confident that they had many brothers who would look out for them inside the walls. Consequently, the threat of confinement had little influence on a biker's behavior, as far as we could tell.

Perhaps because society gave them so little respect, the bikers we studied insisted on being treated with deference. They gave few invitations to nonmembers or ''citizens'' and they were affronted when something they offered was refused. Our respondents loved to party and they did not understand anyone who did not. Once we were invited to a club party by a man named Cottonmouth. The party was to begin at 9:00 P.M. on a Sunday night. When we told Cottonmouth that we had to leave at seven in the evening to get back home, we lost his good will and respect entirely. He could not comprehend how we could let anything take precedence over a ''righteous'' club party.

Bikers were suspicious of all conversations with us and with other citizens; they were not given to much discussion even among themselves. They followed a slogan we saw posted in several clubhouses: ''One good fist is worth a thousand words.'' Studying outlaw cyclists became more difficult rather than easier over the course of our study. They grew increasingly concerned about being investigated by undercover agents. In 1989, ''1 percent''[3] of bikers *never* trusted anyone except their own kind. At times, over the last years of our study, respondents whom we had known for months would suddenly accuse us of being undercover ''pigs'' when we seemed overly curious about their activities.

Our study required much commitment to research goals. We believed it was important to study biker women and we did so in the only way open to us—on the terms of the bikers themselves. We were field observers rather than critics or reformers, even when witnessing things that caused us anguish.

Problems in Studying Biker Women

Although it was difficult to do research on outlaw motorcycle gangs generally, it was even harder to study the women in them. In many gangs, the women were reluctant to speak to outsiders when the men were present. We did not hear male bikers tell the women to refrain from talking to us. Rather, we often had a man point to a woman and say, ''Ask her,'' when we posed a question that concerned female associates. Usually, the woman's answer was, ''I don't know.'' Consequently, it took longer to establish rapport with female bikers than it did with the men.

Surprisingly, male bikers did not object to our being alone with the women. Occasionally, we talked to a female biker by ourselves and this is when we were able to get most of our information and quotations from them. In one interview with a biker and his woman in their home, the woman would not express an opinion about anything. When her man left to help a fellow biker whose motorcycle had broken down on the road, the woman turned into an articulate and intelligent individual. Upon the return of the man, however, she resumed the role of a person without opinions.

The Place of Women in Outlaw Motorcycle Gangs

Although national[4] outlaw motorcycle clubs of the 1980s had restricted their membership to adult males (Quinn, 1983), women were important in the outlaw life-style we observed. We rarely saw a gang without female associates sporting colors similar to those the men wore.

To the casual observer, all motorcycle gang women might have appeared the same. There were, however, two important categories of women in the biker world: "mamas" and "old ladies." A mama belonged to the entire gang. She had to be available for sex with any member and she was subject to the authority of any brother. Mamas wore jackets that showed that they were the "property" of the club as a whole.

An old lady belonged to an individual man; the jacket she wore indicated whose woman she was. Her colors said, for example, "Property of Frog." Such a woman was commonly referred to as a "patched old lady." In general terms, old ladies were regarded as wives. Some were in fact married to the members whose patches they wore. In most instances, a male biker and his old lady were married only in the eyes of the club. Consequently, a man could terminate his relationship with an old lady at any time he chose, and some men had more than one old lady.

A man could require his old lady to prostitute herself for him. He could also order her to have sex with anyone he designated. Under no circumstances, however, could an old lady have sex with anyone else unless she had her old man's permission.

If he wished to, a biker could sell his old lady to the highest bidder, and we saw this happen. When a woman was auctioned off, it was usually because a biker needed money in a hurry, such as when he wanted a part for his motorcycle or because his old lady had disappointed him. The buyer in such transactions was usually another outlaw.

Rituals Involving Women

Outlaw motorcycle gangs, as we perceived them, formed a subculture that involved rituals and symbols. Although each group varied in its specific cere-monies, all of the clubs we studied had several. There were rites among bikers that had nothing to do with women and sex but a surprising number involved both.

The first ritual many outlaws were exposed to, and one they understandably never forgot, was the initiation into a club. Along with other requirements, in some gangs, the initiate had to bring a "sheep" when he was presented for membership. A sheep was a woman who had sex with each member of the gang during an initiation. In effect, the sheep was the new man's gift to the old members.

Group sex, known as "pulling a train," also occurred at other times. Although some mamas or other biker groupies (sometimes called "sweetbutts") occasionally volunteered to pull a train, most instances of train pulling were punitive in nature. Typically, women were being penalized for some breach of biker conduct when they pulled a train.

An old lady could be forced to pull a train if she did not do something her old man told her to do, or if she embarrassed him by talking back to him in front of another member. We never observed anyone pulling a train but we were shown clubhouse rooms that were designated "train rooms." And two women told us they had been punished in this manner.

One of the old ladies who admitted having pulled a train said her offense was failing to keep her man's motorcycle clean. The other had not noticed that her biker was holding an empty bottle at a party. (A good old lady watched her man as he drank beer and got him another one when he needed it without having to be told to do so.) We learned that trains were pulled in vaginal, oral, or anal sex. The last was considered to be the harshest punishment.

Another biker ritual involving women was the earning of "wings," a patch similar to the emblem a pilot wears. There were different types of wings that showed that the wearer had performed oral sex on a woman in front of his club. Although the practice did not exist widely, several members of some groups we studied wore wings.

A biker's wings demonstrated unlimited commitment to his club. One man told us he earned his wings by having oral sex with a woman immediately after she had pulled a train; he indicated that the brothers were impressed with his abandon and indifference to hygiene. Bikers honored a member who laughed at danger by doing shocking things.[5]

The sex rituals were important in many biker groups because they served at least one function other than status striving among members. The acts ensured that it was difficult for law enforcement officials, male or female, to infiltrate a gang.

Biker Women as Money-Makers

Among most of the groups we studied, biker women were expected to be engaged in economic pursuits for their individual men and sometimes for the entire club. Many of the old ladies and mamas were employed in nightclubs as topless and nude dancers. Although we were not able to get exact figures on the proportion of "table dancers" who were biker women, in two or three cities almost all of them were working for outlaw clubs.

A lot of the dancers were proud of their bodies and their dancing abilities. We saw them perform their routines in bars and at parties. At the "Big Blowout" in Gulfport, which is held in an open field outside of the city, in 1987 and 1988 there was a stage with a sound system set up for the dancers. The great majority of the two thousand people in attendance were bikers from around the country so the performances were free.

Motorcycle women who danced in the nightclubs we observed remained under the close scrutiny of the biker men. The men watched over them for two reasons. First, they wanted to make sure that the women were not keeping money on the side; second, the cyclists did not want their women to be exploited by the bar owners. Some bikers in one gang we knew beat up a nightclub owner because they thought he was "ripping off" the dancers. The man was beaten so severely with axe handles that he had to be hospitalized for several months.

While some of the biker women limited their nightclub activities to dancing, a number of them also let the customers whose tables they danced on know they were available for "personal" sessions in a private place. As long as they were making good money regularly, the bikers let the old ladies choose their own level of nightclub participation. Thus some women danced nude only on stage; others performed on stage and did table dances as well. A smaller number did both types of dances and also served as prostitutes.

Not all of the money-making biker women we encountered were employed in such "sleazy" occupations. A few had "square" jobs as secretaries, factory workers, and sales persons. One biker woman had a job in a bank. A friend and fellow biker lady described her as follows: "Karen is a chameleon. When she goes to work, she is a fashion plate; when she is at home, she looks like a whore. She is every man's dream!" Like the others employed in less prestigious labor, however, Karen turned her salary over to her old man on payday.

A few individuals toiled only intermittently when their bikers wanted a new motorcycle or something else that required more money than they usually needed. The majority of motorcycle women we studied, however, were regularly engaged in work of some sort.

Motivations and Backgrounds of Biker Women

In view of the ill treatment the women received from outlaws, it was surprising that so many women wanted to be with them. Bikers told us there was never a shortage of women who wanted to join them and we observed this to be true. Although it was unwise for men to draw conclusions about the reasons mamas and old ladies chose their life-styles, we surmised three interrelated factors from conversations with them.

First, some women, like the male bikers, truly loved and were excited by motorcycles. Cathy was an old lady who exhibited this trait. "Motorcycles have always turned me on," she said. "There's nothing like feeling the wind on your titties. Nothing's as exciting as riding a motorcycle. You feel as free as the wind."

Cathy did not love motorcycles indiscriminately, however. She was imbued with the outlaw's love for the Harley Davidson. "If you don't ride a Hog," she stated, "you don't ride nothing. I wouldn't be seen dead on a rice burner" (Japanese model). Actually, she loved only a customized bike or "chopper." Anything else she called a "garbage wagon."

When we asked her why she wanted to be part of a gang if she simply loved motorcycles, Cathy answered:

> There's always someone there. You don't agree with society so you find someone you like who agrees with you. The true meaning for me is to express my individuality as part of a group.

Cathy started "putting" (riding a motorcycle) when she was fifteen years old and she dropped out of school shortly thereafter. Even with a limited education, she gave the impression that she was a person who thought seriously. She had a butterfly tattoo that she said was an emblem of the freedom she felt on a bike. When we talked to her, she was twenty-six and had a daughter. She had ridden with several gangs but she was proud that she had always been an old lady rather than a mama.

The love for motorcycles had not dimmed for Cathy over the years. She still found excitement in riding and even in polishing a chopper. "I don't feel like I'm being used. I'm having fun," she insisted. She told us that she would like to change some things if she had her life to live over, but not biking. "I feel sorry for other people; I'm doing exactly what I want to do," she concluded.

A mama named Pamela said motorcycles thrilled her more than anything else she had encountered in life. Although she had been involved with four biker clubs in different sections of the country, she was originally from Mississippi and she was with a Mississippi gang when we talked to her. Pamela said she graduated from high school only because the teachers wanted to get rid of her. "I tried not to give any trouble, but my mind just wasn't on school."

She was twenty-four when we saw her. Her family background was a lot like most of the women we knew. "I got beat a lot," she remarked. "My daddy and my mom both drank and ran around on each other. They split up for good my last year in school. I ain't seen either of them for a long time."

Cathy described her feelings about motorcycles as follows:

I can't remember when I first saw one. It seems like I dreamed about them even when I was a kid. It's hard to describe why I like bikes. But I know this for sure. The sound a motorcycle makes is really exciting— it turns me on, no joke. I mean really! I feel great when I'm on one. There's no past, no future, no trouble. I wish I could ride one and never get off.

The second thing we thought drew women to motorcycle gangs was a preference for macho men. "All real men ride Harleys," a mama explained to us. Generally, biker women had contempt for men who wore suits and ties. We believed it was the disarming boldness of bikers that attracted many women.

Barbara, who was a biker woman for several years, was employed as a secretary in a university when we talked to her in 1988. Although Barbara gradually withdrew from biker life because she had a daughter she wanted reared in a more conventional way, she thought the university men she associated with were wimps. She said:

Compared to bikers, the guys around here [her university] have no balls at all. They hem and haw, they whine and complain. They try to impress you with their intelligence and sensitivity. They are game players. Bikers come at you head on. If they want to fuck you, they just say so. They don't care what you think of them. I'm attracted to strong men who know what they want. Bikers are authentic. With them, what you see is what you get.

Barbara was an unusual biker lady who came from an affluent family. She was the daughter of a highly successful man who owned a manufacturing and distributing company. Barbara was thirty-nine when we interviewed her. She had gotten into a motorcycle gang at the age of twenty-three. She described her early years to us:

I was rebellious as long as I can remember. It's not that I hated my folks. Maybe it was the times [1960s] or something. But I just never could be the way I was expected to be. I dated "greasers," I made bad grades; I never applied myself. I've always liked my men rough. I don't mean I like to be beat up, but a real man. Bikers are like cowboys. I classify them together. Freedom and strength I guess are what it takes for me.

Barbara did not have anything bad to say about bikers. She still kept in touch with a few of her friends in her old club. "It was like a family to me," she said. "You could always depend on somebody if anything happened.

I still trust bikers more than any other people I know.'' She also had become somewhat reconciled with her parents, largely because of her daughter. ''I don't want anything my parents have personally, but my daughter is another person. I don't want to make her be just like me if she doesn't want to,'' she concluded.

A third factor that we thought made women associate with biker gangs was low self-esteem. Many we studied believed they deserved to be treated as people of little worth. Their family backgrounds had prepared them for subservience.

Jeanette, an Arkansas biker woman, related her experience as follows:

> My mother spanked me frequently. My father beat me. There was no sexual abuse but a lot of violence. My parents were both alcoholics. They really hated me. I never got a kind word from either of them. They told me a thousand times I was nothing but a pain in the ass.

Jeanette began hanging out with bikers when she left home at the age of fifteen. She was twenty-five when we talked to her in 1985. Although he was dominating and abusive, her old man represented security and stability for Jeanette. She said he had broken her jaw with a punch. ''He straightened me out that time,'' she said. ''I started to talk back to him but I didn't get three words out of my mouth.'' Her old man's name was tattooed over her heart.

In Jeanette's opinion, she had a duty to obey and honor her man. They had been married by another biker who was a Universal Life minister. ''The Bible tells me to be obedient to my husband,'' she seriously remarked to us. Jeanette also told us she hated lesbians. ''I go in lesbian bars and kick ass,'' she said. She admitted she had performed lesbian acts but she said she did so only when her old man made her do them. The time her man broke her jaw was when she objected to being ordered to sleep with a woman who was dirty. Jeanette believed her biker had really grown to love her. ''I can express my opinion once and then he decides what I am going to do,'' she concluded.

In the opinions of the women we talked to, a strong man kept a woman in line. Most old ladies had the lowly task of cleaning and polishing a motorcycle every day. They did so without thanks and they did not expect or want any praise. To them, consideration for others was a sign of weakness in a man. They wanted a man to let them know who was boss.

Motorcycle Women versus Street Gang Girls

The motorcycle women in our study were similar to the street gang girls described by Campbell and Horowitz because their lives were built around deviant social organizations that were controlled by members of the opposite sex. There were, however, important differences that resulted from the varying natures of the two subcultures.

As our terminology suggests, female associates of motorcycle gangs were women as opposed to the teenage girls typically found in street gangs. The biker women who would tell us their age averaged twenty-six years, and the great majority appeared to be in their mid-twenties. While some biker women told us they began associating with outlaws when they were teenagers, we did not observe any young girls in the clubs other than the children of members.

Male bikers were older than the members of street gangs and it followed that their female companions were older as well. In one of the outlaw clubs we surveyed, the men averaged thirty-four years old. Biker men also wanted women old enough to be legally able to work in bars and in other jobs.

All of the biker women we studied were white, whereas street gang girls in previous studies were predominantly from minority groups. We were aware of one black motorcycle gang in Memphis but we were unable to make contact with it.[6]

Biker women were not homogeneous in their backgrounds. While street gangs were composed of "home boys" and "home girls" who usually grew up and remained in the areas in which their gangs operated, the outlaw women had often traveled widely. Since bikers were mobile, it was rare for us to find a woman who had not moved around a lot. Most of the biker women we saw were also high school graduates. Two had attended college although neither had earned a degree.

While Campbell found girls in street gangs to be interested in brand name clothes and fashions, we did not notice this among motorcycle women. In fact, it was our impression that biker ladies were hostile toward such interests. Perhaps because so many were dancers, they were proud of their bodies but they did not try to fit into popular feminine dress styles. As teenagers they may have been clothes-conscious, but as adults biker women did not want to follow the lead of society's trend setters.

Biker women were much like street gang girls when it came to patriotism. They were proud to be Americans. Like biker men, they had conservative political beliefs and would not even consider riding a motorcycle made in another country.

As another consequence of the age difference, biker women were not torn between their families and the gang. Almost all of the old ladies and mamas were happy to be rid of their past lives. They had made a clean break and they did not try to live in two worlds. The motorcycle gang was their focal point without rival. Whereas street gang girls often left their children with their mothers or grandparents, biker women did not, but they wanted to be good mothers just the same. The children of biker women were more integrated into the gang. Children went with their mothers on camping trips and on brief motorcycle excursions or "runs." When it was necessary to leave the children at home, two or three old ladies alternately remained behind and looked after all of the children in the gang.

The biker men were also concerned about the children and handled them with tenderness. A biker club considered the offspring of members as belonging to the entire group, and each person felt a duty to protect them. Both male and female bikers also gave special treatment to pregnant women. A veteran biker woman related her experience to us as follows:

> Kids are sacred in a motorcycle club. When I was pregnant, I was treated great. Biker kids are tough but they are obedient and get lots of love. I've never seen a biker's kid who was abused.

As mentioned, the average biker woman was expected to be economically productive, a trait not emphasized for female street gang members or auxiliaries. It appeared to us that the women in motorcycle gangs were more thoroughly under the domination of their male associates than were girls described in street gang studies.

The Changing Role of Biker Women

During the seventeen years of our study, we noticed a change in the position of women in motorcycle gangs. In the groups we observed in the 1960s, the female participants were more spontaneous in their sexual encounters and they interacted more completely in club activities of all kinds. To be sure, female associates of outlaw motorcycle gangs have never been on a par with the men. Biker women have worn "property" jackets for a long time, but in the outlaw scene of 1989, the label had almost literally become fact.

Bikers have traditionally been notoriously active sexually with the women in the clubs. When we began hanging out with bikers, however, the men and the women were more nearly equal in their search for gratification. Sex was initiated as much by the women as it was by the men. By the end of our study, the men had taken total control of sexual behavior, as far as we could observe, at parties and outings. As the male bikers gained control of sex, it became more ceremonial.

While the biker men we studied in the late 1980s did not have much understanding of sex rituals, their erotic activities seemed to be a means to an end rather than an end in themselves, as they were in the early years of our study. That is to say, biker sex became more concerned with achieving status and brotherhood than with "fun" and physical gratification. We used to hear biker women telling jokes about sex but even this had stopped.

The shift in the position of biker women was not only due to the increasing ritualism in sex; it was also a consequence of the changes in the organizational goals of motorcycle gangs as evidenced by their evolving activities. As we have noted, many motorcycle gangs developed an interest in money; in doing so, they became complex organizations with both legal and illegal sources of income (McGuire, 1986).

When bikers became more involved in illegal behavior, they followed the principles of sex segregation and sex typing in the underworld generally. The low place of women has been well documented in the studies of criminal organizations (Steffensmeier, 1983). The bikers did not have much choice in the matter. When they got involved in financial dealings with other groups in the rackets, motorcycle gangs had to adopt a code that had prevailed for many years; they had to keep women out of "the business."

Early motorcycle gangs were organized for excitement and adventure; money-making was not important. Their illegal experiences were limited to individual members rather than to the gang as a whole. In the original gangs, most male participants had regular jobs, and the gang was a part-time organization that met about once a week. At the weekly gatherings, the emphasis was on swilling beer, soaking each other in suds, and having sex with the willing female associates who were enthusiastic revelers themselves. The only money the old bikers wanted was just enough to keep the beer flowing. They did not regard biker women as sources of income; they thought of them simply as fellow hedonists.

Most of the gangs we studied in the 1980s required practically all of the members' time. They were led by intelligent presidents who had organizational ability. One gang president had been a military officer for several years. He worked out in a gym regularly and did not smoke or drink excessively. In his presence, we got the impression that he was in control, that he led a disciplined life. In contrast, when we began our study, the bikers, including the leaders, always seemed on the verge of personal disaster.

A few motorcycle gangs we encountered were prosperous. They owned land and businesses that had to be managed. In the biker transition from hedonistic to economic interests, women became defined as money-makers rather than companions. Whereas bikers used to like for their women to be tattooed, many we met in 1988 and 1989 did not want their old ladies to have tattoos because they reduced their market value as nude dancers and prostitutes. We also heard a lot of talk about biker women not being allowed to use drugs for the same reason. Even for the men, some said drug usage was not good because a person hooked on drugs would be loyal to the drug, not to the gang.

When we asked bikers if women had lost status in the clubs over the years, their answers were usually negative. "How can you lose something you never had?" a Florida biker replied when we queried him. The fact is, however, that most bikers in 1989 did not know much about the gangs of twenty years earlier. Furthermore, the change was not so much in treatment as it was in power. It was a sociological change rather than a physical one.

In some respects, women were treated better physically after the transition than they were in the old days. The new breed did not want to damage the "merchandise."

An old lady's status in a gang of the 1960s was an individual thing, depending on her relationship with her man. If her old man wanted to, he could share his position to a limited extent with his woman. Thus the place of women within a gang was variable. While all women were considered inferior to all men, individual females often gained access to some power, or at least they knew details of what was happening.

By 1989, the position of women had solidified. A woman's position was no longer influenced by idiosyncratic factors. Women had been formally defined as inferior. In many biker club weddings, for example, the following became part of the ceremony:

> You are an inferior woman being married to a superior man. Neither you nor any of your female children can ever hold membership in this club or own any of its property.

Although the bikers would not admit that their attitudes toward women had shifted over the years, we noticed the change. Biker women were completely dominated and controlled as our study moved into the late 1980s. When we were talking to a biker after a club funeral in North Carolina in 1988, he turned to his woman and said, "Bitch, if you don't take my dick out, I'm going to piss in my pants." Without hesitation, the woman unzipped his trousers and helped him relieve himself. To us, this symbolized the lowly place of women in the modern motorcycle gang.

Conclusion

Biker women seemed to represent another version of what Romenesko and Miller (1989) have referred to as a "double jeopardy" among female street hustlers. Like the street prostitutes, most biker women came from backgrounds in which they had limited opportunities in the licit or conventional world, and they faced even more exploitation and subjugation in the illicit or deviant settings they had entered in search of freedom.

It is ironic that biker women considered themselves free while they were under the domination of biker men. They had the illusion of freedom because they lived with men who were bold and unrestrained. Unlike truly liberated women, however, the old ladies and mamas did not compete with men; instead, they emulated and glorified male bikers. Biker women thus illustrated the pervasive power of socialization and the difficulty of changing deeply ingrained views of the relations between the sexes inculcated in their family life. They believed that they should be submissive to men because they were taught that males were dominant. While they adamantly stated that they were living the life they chose, it was evident that their choices were guided by values that they had acquired in childhood. Although they had rebelled against the strictures of straight society, their orientation in gender roles made them align with outlaw bikers, the epitome of macho men.

Notes

1. We briefly observed the Alii ("Chiefs"), a native Hawaiian gang, located on the island of Hawaii, the "Big Island." Motorcycle gangs on the island of Oahu may have developed before the California clubs. Lord (1978) described a club that volunteered its services during the attack on Pearl Harbor in 1941. The bikers, wearing their colors, carried messengers and officers on motorcycles from one place to another because automobiles could not move efficiently during the traffic jams caused by the battle. This display of patriotism was not the only instance. Sonny Barger, the president of the Oakland chapter, sent President Lyndon Johnson a letter offering to send the Hells Angels to Vietnam. Some outlaws were active in "Toys for Tots" drives and blood drives. These activities were seldom noted that led bikers to the slogan: "When we do right, nobody remembers; when we do wrong, nobody forgets."

2. Bikers presented "courtesy cards" to people that they believed deserved the privilege of biker acceptance. "Big John," as Moore was called by outlaws, had cards from outlaw motorcycle clubs throughout the country.

3. Some years ago, an officer of the American Motorcycle Association, in defense of motorcycling, stated that 99% of all motorcyclists were decent and honorable people and that only 1% gave the rest a bad name. Since that proclamation, outlaws have proudly worn the 1% patch.

4. A national club had chapters in different regions of the country. For more details on gang vocabulary and argot and the distribution of specific gangs, see Hopper and Moore (1983, 1984).

5. Although the initiation ceremony was the culmination of a biker's efforts to become a member of a club, it usually required a period of a year or more before a man would be made a member in full standing. During this time, a person was a "probate." He rode with the gang, and to the public he appeared to be a regular member, but a probate was not trusted until he proved himself worthy of complete membership. He did this by showing his courage and disregard for danger.

6. Motorcycle gangs in the 1980s emphasized race. White gangs often were members of the Aryan Brotherhood. Earlier bikers were sometimes racially integrated. They developed their racial division after many bikers got into prisons where they adjusted to intraracial groups that banded together for protection. Being white, we were unable to develop relationships with a black group.

References

Ackley, E. and B. Fliegel. (1960). "A social work approach to street-corner girls." *Social Problems* 5: 29–31.
Asbury, H. (1928). *The Gangs of New York*. New York: Alfred A. Knopf.

PART 5 / DIFFERENT CONTEXTS, DIFFERENT GANGS

Bowker, L. (1978). *Women, Crime, and the Criminal Justice System.* Lexington, MA: D. C. Heath.

Bowker, L. and M. Klein. (1983). "The etiology of female juvenile delinquency and gang membership: a test of psychological and social structural explanations." *Adolescence* 8: 731–751.

Campbell, A. (1984). *The Girls in the Gang.* New York: Basil Blackwell.

Campbell, A. (1986). "Self report of fighting by females." *British Journal of Criminology* 26: 28–46.

Campbell, A. (1987). "Self-definition by rejection: the case of gang girls. *Social Problems* 34: 451–466.

Eisen, J. (1970). *Altamont.* New York: Avon Books.

Hanson, K. (1964). *Rebels in the Streets.* Englewood Cliffs, NJ: Prentice-Hall.

Harris, M. (1985). *Bikers.* London: Faber and Faber.

Hopper, C. and J. Moore. (1983). "Hell on wheels: the outlaw motorcycle gangs." *Journal of American Culture* 6: 58–64.

Hopper, C. and J. Moore. (1984). "Gang slang." *Harpers* 261: 34.

Horowitz, R. (1983). *Honor and the American Dream.* New Brunswick, NJ: Rutgers University Press.

Horowitz, R. (1986). "Remaining an outsider: membership as a threat to research rapport." *Urban Life* 14: 238–251.

Horowitz, R. (1987). "Community tolerance of gang violence." *Social Problems* 34: 437–450.

Klein, M. (1971). *Street Gangs and Street Workers.* Englewood Cliffs, NJ: Prentice-Hall.

Lord, W. (1978). *Day of Infamy.* New York: Bantam.

McGuire, P. (1986). "Outlaw motorcycle gangs: organized crime on wheels." *National Sheriff* 38: 68–75.

Miller, W. (1973). "Race, sex, and gangs." *Society* 11: 32–35.

Miller, W. (1975). *Violence by Youth Gangs and Youth Groups as a Crime Problem in Major American Cities.* Washington, DC: U.S. Government Printing Office.

Montgomery, R. (1976). "The outlaw motorcycle subculture." *Canadian Journal of Criminology and Corrections* 18: 332–342.

Morgan, R. (1978). *The Angels Do Not Forget.* San Diego: Law and Justice.

Quinn, J. (1983). Outlaw Motorcycle Clubs: A Sociological Analysis. M.A. thesis: University of Miami.

Reynolds, F. (1967). *Freewheeling Frank.* New York: Grover Press.

Rice, R. (1963). "A reporter at large: the Persian queens." *New Yorker* 39: 153.

Romenesko, K. and E. Miller. (1989). "The second step in double jeopardy: appropriating the labor of female street hustlers." *Crime and Delinquency* 35: 109–135.

Saxon, K. (1972). *Wheels of Rage.* Privately published.

Short, J. (1968). *Gang Delinquency and Delinquent Subcultures.* Chicago: University of Chicago Press.

Steffensmeier, D. (1983). "Organization properties and sex-segregation in the underworld building a sociology theory of sex differences in crime." *Social Forces* 61: 1010–1032.

Thompson, H. (1967). *Hell's Angels.* New York: Random House.

380

Thrasher, F. (1927). *The Gang: A Study of 1,313 Gangs in Chicago*. Chicago: University of Chicago Press.

Watson, J. (1980). "Outlaw motorcyclists as an outgrowth of lower class values." *Deviant Behavior* 4: 31–48.

Wilde, S. (1977). *Barbarians on Wheels*. Secaucus, NJ: Chartwell Books.

Willis, P. (1978). *Profane Culture*. London: Routledge & Kegan Paul.

Wolfe, T. (1968). *The Electric Kool-Aid Acid Test*. New York: Farrar, Straus & Giroux.

20

A Comparative Analysis of Prison Gang Members, Security Threat Group Inmates, and General Population Prisoners in the Texas Department of Corrections

Robert S. Fong and Ronald E. Vogel

Introduction

This chapter examines differences between prison gang members and security threat group inmates identified by the Texas Department of Corrections (TDC). Although prison gangs have been administratively segregated from general population inmates within the TDC, security threat group members—which include KKK, Aryan Nation, Aryan Circle, Crips, Cubans, Banditos and Nuestra Familia among others—are mixed in the general population. Even though security threat groups have not yet developed the internal structures or membership size necessary to be classified as prison gangs, their potential for development has not gone unnoticed. Realizing the potential problems associated with additional prison gangs, concerned correctional officials are closely monitoring identified security threat groups. However, little is known regarding how these groups differ from prison gangs and how the members in both groups differ from general population inmates. Based on the records maintained by the TDC, this study focuses on these questions.

Background

To understand the development of prison gangs in Texas, it is instructive to briefly examine the history that fostered their development. Although the conditions that initially led to the creation of many prison gangs have changed,

Reprinted with permission from *The Journal of Gang Research*, Vol. 2, No. 2 (Winter 1995): 1–12.

history warns us that new pressures or forces have the potential for spawning the development of new prison gangs.

Historically, prison officials were unbridled in their ability to exercise discretion over the lives of inmates. This authority was legally derived (e.g. *Ruffin v. Commonwealth* 62 Va, 1871; *Price v. Johnson* 334 U.S. 266) and maintained by the courts through a "hands off" philosophy. As a result, living conditions in many prisons were extremely poor and legally unchecked. However, in 1961 the U.S. Supreme Court ruled that inmates could seek monetary damages or injunctions against state officials accused of civil rights violations (*Monroe v. Pape* 365 U.S. 167). Three years later in *Cooper v. Pate* (378 U.S. 546), the Supreme Court expanded its earlier decision by allowing prisoner complaints to be heard against state prison officials. This ruling opened the "flood gates" for prisoners seeking redress for intolerable prison conditions and stimulated litigation to remedy their complaints. The reforms that followed improved many aspects of prison life but also, in some instances, undermined the traditional authority of some prison systems, which created a more dangerous environment (Marquart and Crouch, 1985; Statsney and Tynauer, 1982). For example, with the court-ordered dismantling of the building tender system in the Texas Department of Corrections, prison violence increased and an atmosphere developed where inmates found it necessary to form into groups for self-protection, power and dominance. These groups quickly formed into prison gangs complete with organizational structures and significant power within the prison system (Fong, 1990). Although prison reforms were not the cause of prison gang development in Texas, the erosion of traditional control mechanisms fostered their growth.

Although prison gangs have existed since the 1950s, research on these groups has been hampered by their secretive nature as well as the difficulty in gaining access to reliable data (Fong, 1990; Fong and Buentello, 1991). Nevertheless, prison gang research has increased during the past several years and researchers have slowly obtained insights into the operations of these organizations. For example, in a nationwide study, Camp and Camp (1985) revealed the presence of prison gangs in thirty-three jurisdictions. Specifically, they identified 114 gangs with an estimated membership of 13,000. Because of the proliferation of these organizations and the disruption associated with their activities, it is not surprising that prison gangs are classified among the newest and most dangerous crime syndicates in the nation (Emerson, 1985; Buentello, 1986; Fong and Buentello, 1991).

Prison gangs share several common but unique characteristics, which include: organization along racial and ethnic lines (Irwin, 1980; Camp and Camp, 1985; Beaird, 1986); a hierarchical structure with well-defined lines of authority and responsibility (Camp and Camp, 1985; Buentello, 1986; Fong, 1990); recruitment based on the "homeboy" preprison experience (Camp and Camp, 1985; Beaird, 1986; Buentello, 1986; Fong, 1990); lifetime commitment with absolute loyalty–"blood in, blood out" (Camp and Camp, 1985; Buentello, 1986; Fong, 1990); adherence to a strict code of silence (Irwin, 1980; Buentello, 1986; Fong, 1990); clearly defined illicit activities that include but are not limited to contract murder, extortion, drug-trafficking, gambling, homosexual prostitution, and protection rackets (President's Commission on Organized Crime, 1983; Camp and Camp, 1985; Beaird, 1986; Buentello, 1986; Fong, 1990); achieving their goals through brutal and violent means if necessary (Holt, 1977; Camp and Camp, 1985; Buentello, 1986; Fong, 1990); hate and distrust of each other (Irwin, 1980); and expansion of their crime base to the streets (Emerson, 1985; Freelander, 1985; Buentello, 1986; Elizondo and Glass, 1989; Edwards, 1989; Fong, 1990; Fong and Buentello, 1991).

The Research Problem

One aspect of prison gangs that has not been examined in the literature is the extent to which they differ from or are similar to security threat groups and/ or general population inmates. For example, it has been suggested that because security threat groups have the potential of developing into full-blown prison gangs, their evolution and activities merit scrutiny by prison officials as well as social scientists. According to Texas prison officials, security threat groups are characterized by small numbers, a lack of organization within the prison, and affiliation with a gang, group, or organization that has a power base external to the prison environment. What is not known is how similar or dissimilar security threat groups are in comparison to prison gangs and/or general population inmates with regard to a variety of demographic characteristics such as custody level, the number of times spent in solitary confinement, the number and type of offenses for which time is being served, length of prison sentence, and the number of days currently served in prison.

Answers to the above questions will not demonstrate whether or not security threat groups will evolve into prison gangs but they will increase our understanding of some differences between these groups when compared to general population inmates. Therefore, the intent of this exploratory and descriptive study is to provide the reader with additional information on prison gangs and security threat groups.

Limitations of the Study

The variables and data utilized for analysis were drawn from unclassified prison records, which were not perfectly designed for answering social science research questions. Also, some of the variables used in this study are problematic in terms of operational definition and interpretation. These problems are addressed and discussed in the following pages.

Methodology

Three independent data sets were used to answer the questions previously outlined. All the data used for this analysis were provided by the Texas Department of Corrections (TDC) and included all relevant variables kept in the TDC's computer system on prison gangs and disruptive group members between 1989 and 1990.

Group Selection

The first group selected for analysis included all *security threat group members* identified by the Texas Department of Corrections (N = 102). To ensure group size equivalence, 103 TDC *prison gang members* were randomly drawn from the total known population (N = 1,229). The third group involved 103 randomly selected *general population inmates* drawn from a larger random sample of TDC inmates (n = 1,016), which was developed in 1991. Because security threat group members are included in the general population, care was taken to remove them from the sampling frame before the (1991) random sample was selected.

Study Variables

The following list of variables were selected for analysis in this study.

    Race
    Education (EDUC)
    IQ score (IQ)
    Placement in solitary confinement (SOL)
    Custody level (CUST)
    Offense category (UCR)
    Number of offenses (OFFN)
    Maximum prison term (MAX)
    Flat time served (FLAT)

Race, education, and IQ were demographic variables included for descriptive purposes and were not expected to reveal differences between the groups. Although the results are self-explanatory, it should be noted that in terms of education, a test score of 6.3 is interpreted as a sixth grade, third month educational level. Testing for IQ and educational level is completed as part of the intake process at the TDC.

Placement in solitary confinement reflects the number of times inmates were placed in isolation. In the TDC, an inmate must be found guilty of a major institutional rule and have a disciplinary hearing before being placed

385

in solitary confinement. Individuals may be placed in solitary confinement for up to fifteen days for each charge. If any inmate is found guilty of multiple charges arising from the same incident, they may be administratively sentenced to serve consecutive solitary terms. However, such incidents are rare.

The number of times inmates are placed in solitary confinement is a reasonable measure of serious prison infractions and is appropriate for exploring group differences.

Custody level is a classification status ordinarily assigned to inmates when they enter the TDC. The classification is determined by the conviction offense as well as several other factors such as escape risk, sexual deviance, arson risk and gang affiliation. However, custody levels are not fixed, can change over time and reflect the behavior of inmates in the prison environment.

There are seven custody levels, which are divided as follows: three high risk (maximum) categories, one medium, and three low (minimum) classifications. For the purposes of this research, the custody levels have been collapsed into three categories (high, medium, and low).

Using custody level as a variable in our analysis is problematic because it fluctuates and interacts with other variables. For example, solitary confinement, a measure of prison infractions, is directly related to custody level; as solitary confinement increases, custody level increases. A separate analysis revealed a significant relationship between custody level and solitary confinement with each group (gangs, threat groups, and general population inmates). Realizing the problems with this variable, the authors have included it in the analysis with the warning that care needs to be exercised in interpreting the results.

Offense category is based upon the most serious offense for which an inmate was serving time. If multiple offenses were being served consecutively, only the most serious offense was reported. This variable has obvious flaws as it does not take into account the original charge, which may have been reduced through plea bargaining, or other serious offenses, which impact upon sentence length. As such, the utility of this variable is marginal.

Number of offenses refers to the number of charges for which an inmate was serving time in the TDC. Many inmates in this study were found to be serving multiple prison terms consecutively or concurrently. Specific information on the multiple offenses for which inmates were serving time was not available.

Maximum prison term represents the longest prison term to which an inmate was sentenced. Because the state of Texas has determinate sentencing, this variable was used as a crude indicator of the seriousness of the offense(s) committed.

Flat time served represents the number of days that an inmate has served in the TDC. This variable reveals the exact number of days served excluding good time earned. The interaction of this variable with the maximum prison term is fairly obvious and will be discussed in the following pages.

Results

The analyses used for this study included crosstabs and related procedures as well as analysis of variance. The analyses revealed a number of statistically significant results, which are presented below.

Demographic Variables

Race was examined for all three groups in this study and included blacks, whites, and Hispanics; no other ethnic groups were found. The gang group (n = 103) contained 20 percent whites, 30 percent blacks, and 70 percent Hispanics, while the security threat group (N = 102) revealed an entirely different pattern with 82 percent white, 13 percent black, and 5 percent Hispanic. The general population inmate group (n = 103) consisted of 32 percent whites, 51 percent blacks, and 17 percent Hispanics.

The majority of prison gangs in the TDC are Hispanic, which explains their overrepresentation in the gang sample. Security threat group members are predominantly white and belong to such well known groups as the KKK, Aryan Circle and Aryan Nation. The general population sample more accurately reflects the composition of the overall inmate population in the Texas prison system.

The educational levels of all three groups were examined for descriptive purposes. Although statistical significance was found between the general population inmates ($\overline{X}$ = 6.9 years) and the security threat groups ($\overline{X}$ = 5.5 years), the differences lack substantive utility. The average years of education for the prison gang members was 5.9.

IQ's were calculated for each sample with no significant differences found between the groups. The average IQ for the general population group was 92.1. Similarly, the security threat group had a calculated mean of 91.6, followed by prison gang members with a reported mean of 90.

Placement In Solitary Confinement (SOL)

The average number of times general population inmates were placed in solitary confinement ($\overline{X}$ = 1.06) was less than either the security threat group prisoners ($\overline{X}$ = 3.87) or the prison gang members (X = 4.53) (table 20.1).

Table 20.1   Times in Solitary Confinement by Group

Source	D.F.	Sum of Squares	Mean Squares	F Ratio	F Prob.
Between Groups	2	697.0210	348.5105	12.3780	.0000
Within Groups	305	8587.4985	28.1557		
Total	307	9284.5195			

Multiple Range Test Duncan Procedure
(*) Denotes pairs of groups significantly different at the .010 level

		G G G
		r r r
		p p p
		2 1 3
Mean	Group	0 0 0
1.0680	Grp20	
3.8725	Grp10	*
4.5340	Grp30	*

Comparing the means of these groups, a one-way analysis of variance F ratio was calculated and found to be significant.

The Duncan multiple comparison procedure revealed differences between the general population inmates and the security threat groups as well as the general population and the prison gangs. Statistically significant differences were not found between the gang and security threat groups. Because the variable (SOL) was not normally distributed, crosstabs were performed by dividing the dependent variable into two categories (never placed in solitary confinement; placed in solitary confinement one or more times) and analyzed with the three possible combinations of the independent variable (groups). As can be seen from tables 20.2 and 20.3, this analysis revealed the same pattern found in the one-way analysis of variance. Significant differences were not found between the security threat group inmates and the prison gang members.

In terms of individuals being put in solitary confinement for prison infractions, the security threat groups are as likely as prison gang members to receive this punishment. The general population inmates differ from either of these two groups and are less likely to receive this type of discipline.

Custody Level (CUST)

The three groups showed significant differences on high, medium, and low custody levels. However, only the security threat groups inmates and general population prisoners were comparable in relationship to custody level because identified prison gang members are automatically placed in administrative

Table 20.2   Solitary Confinement by Group

Count Exp Val Row Pct Col Pct	Threat Groups 1	General Population 2	Row Total
No Solitary 1	34 49.3 34.3% 33.3%	65 49.7 65.7% 63.1%	99 48.3%
Solitary 2	68 52.7 64.2% 66.7%	38 53.3 35.8% 36.9%	106 51.7%
Column Total	102 49.8%	103 50.2%	205 100.0%

	Value	DF	Significance
Chi-square	18.19319	1	.00002
Phi	.29790		

Table 20.3   Times in Solitary Confinement by Gang

Count Exp Val Row Pct Col Pct	Prison Gangs 1	Threat Groups 2	Row Total
No Solitary 1	28 46.5 30.1% 27.2%	65 46.5 69.9% 63.1%	93 45.1%
Solitary 2	75 56.5 66.4% 72.8%	38 56.5 33.6% 36.9%	113 54.9%
Column Total	103 50.0%	103 50.0%	206 100.0%

	Value	DF	Significance
Chi-square	26.83547	1	.00000
Phi	.36093		

Table 20.4   Custody Level by Group

Count Exp Val Row Pct Col Pct Tot Pct		Threat Groups 1	General Population 2	Row Total
CUSTODY				
HIGH	1	38 24.4 77.6% 37.3% 18.5%	11 24.6 22.4% 10.7% 5.4%	49 23.9%
MEDIUM	2	19 13.9 67.9% 18.6% 9.3%	9 14.1 32.1% 8.7% 4.4%	28 13.7%
LOW	3	45 63.7 35.2% 44.1% 22.0%	83 64.3 64.8% 80.6% 40.5%	128 62.4%
Column Total		102 49.8%	103 50.2%	205 100.0%

	Value	DF	Significance
Chi-square	29.72606	2	.00000
Lambda	.36275		

segregation. Custody levels of prison gang members are not comparable to the other two groups.

Of the two groups remaining in the analysis, the results revealed that general population inmates are significantly different from security threat group members. It can be seen from table 20.4 that security threat groups have more members in high custody levels and fewer in low custody levels when compared to general population prisoners.

Number of Offenses (OFFN)

The total number of offenses for which group members were serving sentences was also analyzed. Most inmates were serving sentences as a result of being convicted for one offense (prison gang members 45%; security threat group inmates 54%; and general population prisoners 55%). Although the range was from one to eight convicted offenses, only 3 percent of the general population inmates, 7 percent of the gang group members, and 9 percent of the security threat group prisoners were serving time for more than three offenses. The differences in number of offenses for which individuals were serving time were not statistically significant when groups were compared.

Offense Categories (UCR)

The type of offenses for which inmates were serving the most time were analyzed and explored for group differences. Examining the frequencies, it was interesting to note that all three groups were extremely similar in terms of murder convictions (prison gang members 11.7%; security threat group inmates 12.7%; general population prisoners 12.6%). A similar pattern was found, although not as pronounced, for those inmates convicted of robbery (prison gang members 34.9%; security threat group inmates 31.3%; general population prisoners 27.2%). Drug offenses were among the least number of crimes for which individuals were serving the most time when comparing prison gang members (4.9%) and the security threat group inmates (5%). The general population sample revealed that 21.4% were serving the longest sentences for drug offenses.

Exploring relationships between the groups, all seventeen offense categories were collapsed into crimes against property and crimes against persons. The analyses revealed that the security threat groups and the general population inmates were significantly different in relationship to the collapsed offense categories.

Table 20.5   Offense Type for Crime Serving the Most Time by Group

Count	Threat Groups	General Population	Row Total
	1	2	
Against Persons 1	73	58	131 63.9
Against Property 2	29	45	74 36.1
Column Total	102 49.8%	103 50.2%	205 100.0%

	Value	DF	Significance
Chi-Square	5.17226	1	.02295
Phi	.15884		

Table 20.6   Maximum Prison Term in Years

Group	Mean	Median	Mode	Std. Dev.
Security Threat	33.89	22.5	100	30.76
Prison Gangs	42.51	25	100	35.43
General Population	34.15	20	20	29.60

Table 20.7   Flat Time Served in Days

Group	Mean	Median	Mode	Std. Dev.
Security Threat	1679	1581	2628	1295
Prison Gang	1923	1729	1484	1192
General Population	1294	746	432	1275

It is clear that the majority of offense types for which inmates were serving the most time were for crimes against persons.

Maximum Prison Term (MAX)

The maximum term of imprisonment was based on the longest sentence for which individuals were convicted. The frequencies revealed that prison gang members were serving more life sentences (20.4%) when compared to either the security threat groups (10.8%) or the general population inmates (4.9%). The median for the prison gang members was 25 years, the security threat groups 22.5 years and the general population inmates 20 years. Although some variation was found in the frequency distribution between the groups, there were no statistically significant differences.

Flat Time Served (FLAT)

Flat time served is the number of days that inmates have spent in prison regardless of the amount of good time credited to their sentence. As table 20.7 reveals, prison gang members have spent more days in prison ($\overline{X} = 1923$) when compared to security threat groups ($\overline{X} = 1679$) or general population inmates ($\overline{X} = 1294$).

A one-way analysis of variance revealed a significant F ratio (F = 6.581, p = .0016) between the dependent variable (FLAT) and our groups. A multiple comparisons test found the significant difference between the general population and prison gang groups. By categorizing the dependent variable (three years or less; four years or more), less assumptions were violated but the

Table 20.8   Flat Time Served by Groups

Count Row Pct Col Pct Tot Pct	Threat Group 1	General Population 2	Row Total
Up to Three 1 Years Served	40 37.7 39.2 19.5	66 62.3 64.1 32.2	106 51.7%
Greater Than 2 Three Years Served	62 62.6 60.8 30.2	37 37.4 35.9 18.0	99 48.3%
Column Total	102 49.8%	103 50.2%	205 100.0%

	Value	DF	Significance
Chi-Square	12.68591	1	.00037
Phi	.24876		

level of measurement reduced and statistical power lost. Nevertheless, prison gang members were not found to be statistically different from security threat groups in terms of the number of years that they spent in prison. However, both groups were significantly different from general population inmates who served comparatively less time in prison.

Conclusion

Several concluding observations can be made regarding the similarities and dissimilarities between prison gangs, security threat groups, and general population inmates. First, the analysis did not reveal significant differences between the groups in terms of education, IQ scores, number of offenses for which time was being served, and the maximum prison term. Even though hypotheses were not formulated for this exploratory study, it was interesting to note that the number of offenses and the maximum prison terms of inmates failed to show significant differences. In light of the violent reputation of prison gangs and security threat groups, it would have been reasonable to hypothesize that these groups would differ significantly (i.e. longer maximum prison terms for prison gang members and security threat groups in comparison to general population inmates). Even though a comparison of means test and crosstab analyses revealed little, it must be noted that prison gang members and security

Table 20.9   Flat Time Served by Groups

Count Row Pct Col Pct Tot Pct	Prison Gangs 1	General Population 2	Row Total
Up to Three 1 Years Served	32 32.7 31.1 15.5	66 67.3 64.1 32.0	98 47.6%
Greater Than 2 Three Years Served	71 65.7 68.9 34.5	37 34.3 35.9 18.0	108 52.4%
Column Total	103 50.0%	103 50.0%	206 100.0%

	Value	DF	Significance
Chi-square	22.49962	1	.00000
Phi	.33049		

threat groups were sentenced to proportionally more life terms when compared to general population inmates.

Overall, security threat groups were significantly different from general population inmates with respect to solitary confinement, custody level, offense categories, and flat time served. Security threat groups were not significantly different from prison gangs in terms of solitary confinement, offense categories, maximum time served, and flat time served. These findings suggest that security threat groups are different from general population inmates and that they are more similar to prison gang members on several dimensions. The results indicate that security threat groups are adequately named and policies regarding their scrutiny warranted. Whether or not security threat groups will develop into full blown prison gangs is a matter of conjecture and policies must be formulated to curtail their development. We believe that if the environment in which Texas prison gangs developed and proliferated is replicated, it is reasonable to suggest that security threat groups are well situated to quickly grow and develop.

In summary, correctional systems throughout the United States are encouraged to develop policies and strategies designed to closely monitor the activities, growth, and development of security threat groups. As reforms alter the traditional limits of supervisory power within prisons, fertile environments can be produced for the swift emergence of prison gangs. Proactive unrestrictive actions may curtail the need for ''get tough'' reactive approaches if appropriate preventive policies are formulated.

References

Beaird, Lester H. (1986). Prison gangs: Texas. *Corrections Today* 18 (July): 18.

Buentello, Salvador. (1986). Texas Syndicate: A Review of Its Inception, Growth in Violence and Continued Threat to the Texas Department of Corrections. Unpublished manuscript, Texas Dept. Of Corrections, Huntsville, TX.

Camp, George M. and Camille Camp. (1985). *Prison Gangs: Their Extent, Nature and Impact on Prisons.* (Grant No. 844–NI–AX–0001). U.S. Dept. of Justice, Office of Legal Policy. Washington, DC: U.S. Government Printing Office.

Crouch, Ben M. and James W. Marquart. (1990). Resolving The Paradox of Reform Litigation, Prisoner Violence and Perceptions of Risk. *Justice Quarterly* 7 (1): 103–123.

Edwards, Thomas. (1985). Prison Gang Violence Spilling into the Streets. *San Antonio Express News* 19 (July): A1.

Elizondo, David and Stephanie Glass. (1989). Murder Spree Sends Police Scrambling. *San Antonio Light* 9 (November): A2.

Emerson, Ryan Q. (1985). Black/White/Latino: Prison Gangs. *American Survival Guide* (August): 14–19.

Fong, Robert S. (1990). The Organizational Structure of Prison Gangs: A Texas Case Study. *Federal Probation* LIV (4): 36–43.

Fong, Robert S. and Salvador Buentello. (1991). The Detection of Prison Gang Development. *Federal Probation* 55 (1): 66–69.

Freelander, Doug. (1985). Warfare Spreading to the Streets: McCotter. *Houston Post* 10 (September): A3.

Holt, N. (1977). Prison Management in the Next Decade. *Prison Journal* 57: 17–19.

Irwin, John. (1980). *Prisons in Turmoil.* Boston, MA: Little, Brown.

Marquart, James W. and Ben M. Crouch. (1985). Judicial Reform and Prisoner Control: The Impact of *Ruiz v. Estelle* on a Texas Penitentiary. *Law and Society Review* 19: 557–586.

Statsney, Charles and Gabrielle Tynauer. (1982). *Who Rules the Joint?* Lexington, MA: Lexington Books.

21

The Threat of the Jamaican Posses to the United States in the 1990s

Ronald A. Pincomb and Daniel L. Judiscak

Introduction

Among the ethnic gangs that threaten American inner cities, none has had the impact of the Jamaican posses. These posses were spawned in the ghettos of Kingston, Jamaica, as mercenary street fighters for the People's National Party (PNP) and the rival Jamaica Labour Party (JLP). The U.S. Bureau of Alcohol, Tobacco and Firearms has been tracking the posses since their U.S. mainland debut in the early 1980s, and in a recent document they reported that the gangs have killed forty-five hundred people in the United States since then (BATF, 1988).

Organized firearms and narcotics trafficking by Jamaican nationals is an emerging crime problem that has been identified by law enforcement agencies as reaching epidemic proportions. Their criminal acts cross all levels of jurisdictional responsibility because of the types of crimes committed and their multistate and international locations of activity. Jamaican organized criminal groups, commonly known as posses, are involved in the trafficking of narcotics, illegal acquisition and trafficking of firearms, money laundering, fraud, kidnapping, robbery, and murder. The Jamaican posses are among the country's newest and most violent organized crime groups. Born in the poverty and political turmoil of Kingston, Jamaica, these gangs adopted the name *posse* because of their fondness for American western films and because the word connotes the potential for use of violence to enforce political will (Kenney, 1994). Each of the posses is an alliance of autonomous core groups spread throughout the country which utilize continuing criminal conspiracies to attain the goals of accumulation of wealth and individual power through illegal, quasi-legal, or legal means.

Organization Strength

The continual exchange of information among enforcement agencies constantly changes the complexion of the problem from what was previously estimated.

At this time, there may be as many as forty posses, involving more than 20,000 members (Gay and Marquart, 1993), and associates operating in the United States and Canada. Areas of concentrated activity in the United States are along the Eastern seaboard, parts of the Midwest, and the Southwest. The most prominent group, the "Shower Posse" with more than 5,000 members, is based primarily in Miami and New York, but it has expanded its activities to the metropolitan areas of Philadelphia, Boston, Cleveland, Dallas, Hartford, Chicago, Los Angeles, Denver, and Toronto, Ontario. In addition, other prominent posses are operating in Kansas City, Houston, Washington, D.C., Atlanta, and other cities.

The majority of Jamaican posse members are convicted felons, illegal aliens, or both. Gang members start their criminal careers in Jamaica and frequently become fugitives from that country. Many fugitives who had fled elsewhere, including to the United States, hold mid- to high-level positions in a posse. Street-level narcotics and firearms dealers utilized by the gang are recruited from Jamaican communities within the United States or from the geographic neighborhoods of Jamaica. The expansion and increase in the number of posses can be attributed to opportunism and the lucrative market of narcotics trafficking, especially in crack cocaine. The Jamaicans' cocaine business has become their principal criminal enterprise, largely supplanting smuggling and distribution of marijuana, which traditionally had been their primary criminal activity. It is estimated by some that they control 30 to 40 percent of the U.S. crack trade (Kenney, 1994).

History

As background into the formation of Jamaican posses, one has to look into the history of Jamaican governmental politics prior to the 1980 elections, and to the economy of Jamaica. Another important aspect of Jamaican gang formation revolves around public housing projects in Jamaica.

Tivoli Gardens was the first public housing project built in Jamaica. Conceived in the 1960s, it was an ambitious effort to deliver jobs and housing to the Kingston ghetto of Trench Town. At the time, Edward Seaga was one of the leaders in the ruling conservative Jamaica Labour Party (JLP). Seaga had the sense to award the Tivoli Gardens construction jobs, and later the housing, to JLP supporters. When this happened, politics became an outlet for survival; political access meant access to jobs and housing. The existence of the gangs preceded politics and there had always been turf wars; however, when the housing projects were built, the gangs became politicized. Tivoli Gardens became a power base for the JLP and the home of the Shower Posse.

Seaga's JLP planned more housing, but not all of it had been completed by 1972 when the JLP lost a national election to the socialist People's National Party (PNP) and Michael Manley became prime minister. Manley called for sweeping socialist reforms; however, one thing he did not reform was the housing project scheme started by the JLP. When Manley built the housing project called Arnett Gardens, he copied Seaga's Tivoli Gardens plan by awarding his supporters the construction jobs and housing. Just as Tivoli Gardens became a power base for Seaga and the JLP, Arnett Gardens became a power base for Manley and the PNP. It also became known as the Concrete Jungle and the home of the Jungle or Spangler Posse.

Manley's government swung Jamaica to the left and developed ties with Communist and Third World countries. He solidified PNP support in several Kingston neighborhoods, among them the community in central Kingston known as Tel Aviv, the home of the Tel Aviv Posse.

According to Jamaican historian Basil Wilson (1988), of John Jay College in New York City, each community had its organized leadership with the leaders usually being gunmen who have the respect of the ghetto community. The "top ranking gunmen" may be called upon to settle disputes. They may decide if there will be peace or war, and they served as role models for a generation of ghetto youth.

By the time Manley called an election in 1976, most of the neighborhoods of Kingston were politicized and the various posses were so volatile that Manley declared a state of emergency, rounding up the "top ranking gunmen" and putting them into detention. Despite this effort at peace, violence erupted. Jamaican reggae hero and superstar Bob Marley was wounded by automatic-weapons fire prior to a concert in downtown Kingston.

Manley won the 1977 election, but the Jamaican economy did not improve. Two years later, Seaga put his supporters on a war footing with JLP loyalists in Miami, sending hundreds of thousands of dollars worth of guns which were distributed in the ghettos of Kingston in the months before the 1980 elections.

As soon as Seaga won the 1980 elections, he moved quickly to consolidate control of the posses, and to stop the violence that many observers believe he had fostered. According to Walter Thelwell, Lecturer, University of the West Indies, Seaga targeted the "top ranking gunmen" who controlled the warring posses, paying some of the "ranking" to work for him during his administration (Payne, 1994: 80–81).

Seaga also encouraged other gunmen to emigrate to the United States, where they continued to engage in two traditional enterprises of Jamaican posses: selling marijuana and cocaine. The case of Jim Brown, who became "top ranking gunman" of Tivoli Gardens, is an example. In October 1984, Brown came to Miami on a visitor's visa in the name of Lester Lloyd Coke. Ten months later, when Coke was arrested for marijuana trafficking, his true identity was discovered, which revealed that he was wanted for at least twelve murders in Jamaica. Despite repeated attempts to extradite Coke to Jamaica, Jamaican government officials refused to accept Coke back, or to initiate extradition proceedings. Coke was not returned to Jamaica until March 1986, when he was deported after an investigation of Jamaican gangs revealed that he was the leader of Miami's Shower Posse. Coke (or Brown) ultimately was released from custody in Kingston after being acquitted of one of the twelve murders. He also has been hailed as a hero in Jamaica after thousands of supporters paraded in Kingston following his release.

Jamaican gang task forces in several United States cities are trying to determine if posse drug money is still being sent back to Jamaican political parties gearing up the 1984 national elections. In Kansas City, like other jurisdictions, millions of dollars are being generated by narcotics sales, and there is nothing here in the United States that indicates outward wealth. Even people high up in the hierarchy of Jamaican posses do not exhibit immense wealth and are living relatively modestly. Some American posse operations have abandoned the strictly political alignment observed in Jamaica in favor of business ties, which increase the ability to make huge amounts of money, especially in crack cocaine. What they have not abandoned, however, is the gunfighter mentality encouraged by Hollywood westerns and Jamaican political strife.

Violence

As recently as 1985, law enforcement officials in various jurisdictions blamed Jamaican posses for over three thousand homicides nationwide (Goode, 1993). Motives attributed to Jamaican-related murders are: (a) enforcement among the ranks in the posse, (b) retaliation for "rip-offs," (c) competition over customers, and (d) territorial disputes between posses. Sometimes the motives for these shootings merely involve "saving face" over such minor incidents as making insulting remarks (Gay and Marquart, 1993).

In the past few years, the posses have killed a hundred people in New York, twelve in Washington, D.C., thirty-one in Houston, fifteen in Dallas, and nineteen in Kansas City. In south Florida, where five rival posses are currently vying for power, the gangs have murdered at least one hundred fifty people. In Rochester, New York, Jamaican gangs have all but sewn up control of the marijuana and cocaine businesses; and in Toronto, Canada, police are watching a female-run gang known as the Junkie Posse, which is smuggling drugs from Miami.

Wherever the Jamaican posses establish themselves, they subscribe to what are seen as status symbols in Jamaica. They prefer to drive Volvos, Mercedes, BMWs, or Nissan Maximas; they drink Heineken beer, and they covet top quality 9-millimeter weapons.

Jamaican organized criminal gangs have smuggled thousands of high-powered handguns and rifles from Miami to Jamaica in an ongoing scheme to arm drug dealers and criminals who are linked to the island's two dominant political parties. Hundreds of guns recovered by Jamaican police have been traced to southern Florida and other posse jurisdictions.

Traced to a Miami gun shop was an Uzi machine gun used last year in an ambush on a Jamaican police station by organized crime posse members. In this attack three police officers were killed and six were wounded. Investigators later found that the men who bought the weapon also purchased thirty other assorted guns in south Florida, three of which were recovered in Kansas City when the headquarters of the Jamaican gang operating there was raided.

There is a generation of Jamaican youth that has been corrupted and totally hardened. They have grown up on violence. The gangs have come out of a context in which life is cheap and the ultimate goal in life is money and power. The Jamaican criminal gangs' drive for wealth is linked to Jamaica's importance in the international drug trafficking picture. Historically, Jamaica has been a significant trans-shipment point for bulk quantities of cocaine and marijuana from Colombia to the continental United States. The geographic proximity of Jamaica to both the United States and the drug-producing countries of Central and South America makes it attractive to traffickers as a base of operation, transit point, and sanctuary for fugitives.

In recent years, however, Jamaica's role in international drug trafficking has increased dramatically, due primarily to its development as a major marijuana production source for the United States. It is estimated that between 17 and 20 percent of marijuana entering the United States is now being grown in Jamaica. Increased law enforcement pressure has forced traffickers to focus on Jamaica as an alternative to the high frequency routes of the Yucatan Channel, the Windward Passage, and the Bahamas.

Increasingly, the Caribbean coastal areas of Jamaica are being used by trafficking organizations as jump-off points for marine routes to the United States. The port at Kingston and the fishing ports in the north are particularly popular areas for moving bulk quantities of cocaine and marijuana on fishing vessels and pleasure craft. These drug-laden craft travel either directly to Florida or to intermediate stops in the Bahamas and the Cayman Islands.

Additionally, intelligence indicates that traffickers are increasing their use of Jamaica as a transfer point to move drugs on private aircraft using the same routes, that is, the Cayman Islands, Bahamas, and ultimately to the United States.

While Jamaica's geographic location is important in the overall international drug trafficking scene, the full impact of Jamaican posse activity is realized in street level narcotics distribution. The majority of posse street-level dealers are recruited from the large Jamaican communities within the United States, particularly Miami and south Florida, and New York City. American blacks are also utilized, usually in lower-level positions.

The expansion of, and increase in, the number of posses operating within the United States can be attributed to opportunism. A mid- to upper-level posse member will recognize the lucrative market of narcotics trafficking, especially in crack house operations, split from the original posse, and recruit workers from the Jamaican community to set up operations in another location. This type of division is actually encouraged by the posses because it expands their operations. Yet these factions operating in different cities are still tied to the leaders of the larger, more organized posses.

Organizational Structure and Composition

Immigration and Naturalization Service officials at the new evolving INS Academy state that federal authorities are beginning to witness a three-tiered structure emerging within the posses. At the top is a leader, or several leaders, who control the policy decision making but remain somewhat insulated from street-level activity. The second tier consists of subleaders or lieutenants who transport drugs, guns, and money to the leaders. The underbosses also smuggle illegal aliens into the United States. The third tier consists of street-level drug dealers who often become involved in violent confrontation as a result of drug trafficking territorial disputes.

The bulk of the criminal enterprises is cellular in structure. It is common for new factions to emerge under separate leaders within the same posse. Leadership fluctuates and can be shared at any one time by two or more members (see figure 21.1). In the "Shower Posse" of the late 1980s, leadership was shared between Vivian Blake and Lester Lloyd Coke. Vivian Blake, who allegedly established an extensive drug network in the United States, was the most powerful leader of the American faction of the Shower Posse, while Lester Coke was the leader of the smaller faction of the posse that operated in Jamaica.

The upper echelon of the posses are usually Jamaican nationals who have lived in the United States since the early 1970s and have legal status. More than 70 percent of the lower echelon are, however, illegal aliens.

Distribution Network

In its early formulation in the U.S., Jamaican posses trafficked almost solely in marijuana. The present trafficking trend is predominately cocaine and crack with the establishment of crack house operations in a number of United States cities. Crack is distributed through a three-level operation: the lowest is the street-level or crack house, next is distribution centers or stash houses, and highest is a control center or safehouse location. With this organizational structure, a posse can possibly control fifty crack houses in one city making nine million dollars a month (Abadinsky 1993).

At the street level, rental houses or apartments are used as outlets, usually rented by American females used as fronts by the organization. They are staffed

Figure 21.1: Jamaican posses. There are similar groups in Philadelphia, Boston, Cleveland, Dallas, Hartford, Conn., Denver, Toronto, Ontario, Kansas City, Houston, Washington, DC., and Atlanta.

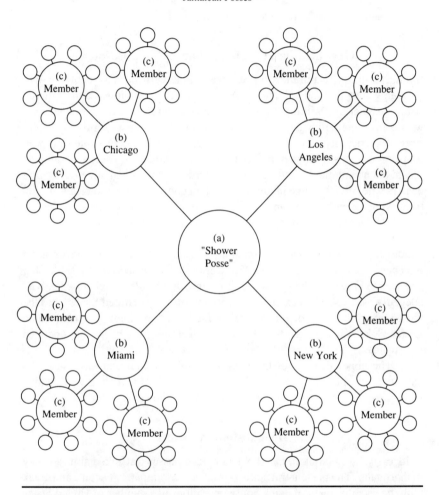

Jamaican Posses

by armed Jamaicans recruited in Miami or New York, or armed Americans recruited into the organization at the lowest level.

Distribution centers are used to store larger amounts of narcotics and weapons. Cooking and packaging of crack cocaine usually is done at these locations. When a distribution point is in need of resupply, the drugs are moved from the stash house to the crack house. The stash house may be the residence of a high ranking member of the organization.

The safehouse or control point in each jurisdiction orchestrates the resupply of street-level crack houses. Individuals at this location primarily will be high-ranking members of an independent gang organization or key members in a large posse.

The loss of any portion of the operation will not shut down the organization completely. The loss of one or many distribution points or crack houses is not damaging overall, as these locations and workers are expendable. The loss of a distribution center, while more damaging, is not fatal to the organization, as the organization is designed to be continuing in nature.

In addition to trafficking in illegal drugs, firearms trafficking is a major crime committed in each geographic area settled by Jamaican posses. Posses utilize weapons acquired for intimidation, protection, and enforcement of rules within the organization. Firearms are acquired by Jamaican posse members through illegal means, by straw purchase (using another citizen as a cover for an unusual or questionable transaction) of firearms and through firearms thefts. As an example, an investigation by the Bureau of Alcohol, Tobacco, and Firearms in Miami revealed seventeen individuals aligned with the Shower Posse illegally purchased 143 firearms. Fifty of these firearms have been recovered in narcotics-related arrests around the United States. In Kansas City, four burglaries since 1980 resulted in the thefts of 369 firearms. Thirty-four of these firearms have been recovered in the possession of Jamaican drug dealers.

In 1984, the seizure of twenty firearms by the Jamaican Constabulary Force began the investigation of Jamaican posses by the U.S. Bureau of Alcohol, Tobacco, and Firearms. According to Jamaican authorities, several methods are used in illegally transporting firearms into Jamaica. These include:

- Through commercial shipment in containers (i.e., drums containing detergent, food products, parts and machinery from Miami to Jamaica).
- Jamaican female merchants known as ''higglers,'' who travel frequently to Miami, are the principal couriers of illegal firearms. They obtain commodities or consumer products in small amounts for resale in street stalls or boutiques, and conceal their contraband in these commodities. They are experts at packaging and concealment and utilize diversionary tactics at customs check points to expedite the inspections at border crossings.
- Flights of small planes into primitive landing sites. These planes allegedly bring firearms in and take marijuana out.

These methods also may be used by Jamaican posses to transfer large sums of money from drug operations back to Jamaica. Although an accurate figure cannot be pinpointed, the amount of money obtained by posses through drug trafficking in the United States makes it a multi-million dollar operation. Payments to key posse members in other cities are often made by wire transfer or Western Union when the payment is under $10,000. Amounts over $10,000 are delivered by couriers in cash. According to the El Paso (Texas) Intelligence

Center (EPIC), money seized from Jamaican nationals on commercial airlines during the first three months of 1987 was double what was seized from Jamaican nationals in all of 1986.

Enforcement Problems

The investigation of Jamaican posses and their distribution of crack has become the top drug enforcement problem facing law enforcement in some major U.S. cities. Jamaican organized crime investigations face some unique problems that require the assistance of federal law enforcement agencies. Members and associates of Jamaican organized crime groups use fictitious names and addresses. Fingerprint checks and photographs are usually the only way to determine the actual identity and criminal history of a posse member—if that individual has been arrested in the U.S.; otherwise, he is often treated as a first offender regardless of his criminal history in Jamaica. At the street level, investigators and witnesses know members only by nicknames which may or may not change, depending on which U.S. city the member happens to be in at the time.

Jamaican criminals are also highly mobile and move from one jurisdiction to another and internationally at will. When associates are arrested, other members will flee the area and blend in with the large Jamaican communities in Miami and New York, or return to Jamaica. The Metro Dade (Florida) Police Department alone has nearly three hundred outstanding felony warrants on Jamaican posse members.

Jamaican posse members are a close-knit group with established relationships, some going back to childhood. Because of their close associations and their general distrust of Americans, it is difficult to infiltrate a posse with undercover officers. Posse members use the Caribbean patois dialect among themselves to communicate and confront each other usually on a face-to-face basis. Audio projection equipment is the only way to keep them totally under surveillance.

While the problems identified here make law enforcement investigations difficult, many successful investigations have been conducted by cooperating task force operations in the last year. The development and execution of a national strategy against Jamaican posses is a major challenge facing drug and arms enforcement professionals today. Continued coordination and exchange of information among law enforcement agencies will hopefully clarify the interrelationships among the posses, identify their leadership, and assist in successful prosecution of members of Jamaican organized crime.

The prevailing view of investigators and other experts is that the posses have come "farther, faster" than any other organized criminal group now active in the United States. The fact that they maintain close ties with the Colombian drug cartels and are also expanding their contacts with American street gangs like the Crips suggests that the Jamaicans are highly likely to be a continuing problem (Kenney, 1994).

References

Abadinsky, H. (1993). *Drug Abuse: An Introduction.* Chicago, IL: Nelson-Hall.

Bureau of Alcohol, Tobacco, and Firearms. U.S. Treasury Department. (1988). *Jamaican Organized Crime.* Washington, DC: U.S. Government Printing Office.

Gay, B.W., and Marquart, J.W. (1993). Jamaican Posses: A New Form of Organized Crime. *Journal of Crime and Justice* 26 (2), 1993: 139–170.

Goode, E. (1993). *Drugs, Society, and Behavior.* Guilford, CT: Dushkin Pub. Group.

Kenney, D.J. (1994). *Organized Crime in America.* Belmont, CA: Wadsworth.

Payne, Anthony J. (1994). *Politics in Jamaica.* Rev. ed. New York: St. Martin's Press.

Wilson, B. (1988). Telephone Interview, November 1988.

Part 6
Gang Policies—Prevention, Intervention, and Enforcement

One of the basic questions asked by students and the general public alike is "So what?" In other words, once we know something about gangs, what can we do with that knowledge? This section will examine the three primary strategies for dealing with gangs and gang behavior: prevention, intervention, and enforcement. In the broadest possible terms we can say that families, schools, social service agencies, law enforcement agencies, and other community organizations all share responsibility for implementing the numerous policies designed to prevent gang formation and involvement. When these strategies fail, intervention programs (like gang mediation) or enforcement activities are called for. Unfortunately, in most communities, the first and most common response to gang activity is enforcement. Many citizens (and, at times, even the police themselves) see the presence of gangs as calling for a suppression response. As many people come to realize, gangs do not exist for one reason, and one solution will not be sufficient to address gang problems in most communities.

In the first article, Curry and Thomas report on the results of agency surveys in twenty-one urban areas as part of the National Youth Gang Intervention and Suppression Program. They were looking for four different policy dimensions or responses for dealing with gangs: (1) availability of staff training, (2) policies for dealing with youth gangs, (3) written policies, and (4) attempts to influence legislation relating to youth gang problems. Based on this nationwide gang research project, Curry and Thomas recommend five policies for dealing with gangs:

1. There should be increased linkages among agencies within communities.
2. The concept of "structural equivalence" should be employed in community organizational strategies.
3. Network analysis should be used to study the relations among local agencies.
4. The quality of information should be increased to actors within local networks.
5. A national network for addressing gang problems should be considered.

In some ways Curry and Thomas help us begin to think about dealing with gangs in a more systemic way and at a more "macro" level.

In the second article, Hagedorn revisits an issue discussed in part 2 by Jackson and by Simons and Gray: the impact of deindustrialization (or the postindustrial economy) on youth gang formation. He utilizes three research projects conducted in Milwaukee, Wisconsin, to examine this issue. Hagedorn particularly focuses on poor African-American neighborhoods, where he finds that the problem is not a lack of working people but a lack of "effective social institutions." In terms of public policy, Hagedorn recommends that communities need to emphasize the creation of jobs and investments in underclass neighborhoods. Effective policies should also include elements aimed at "family preservation and community control of social institutions." Hagedorn notes that his research, and the policy suggestions that flow from it, are consistent with the notion of social disorganization theory. Thus, more effective community institutions are the key to dealing with social problems such as gangs (which are symptoms of broader and more pervasive social problems).

As previously mentioned, one of the first-line responses to gangs in virtually every community is an increased law enforcement presence and a suppression response. Jackson, in her article on the police as social control instruments for dealing with gangs, studied U.S. cities with populations of 25,000 or more to see how urban decline (between 1970 and 1980) and youth gang problems were related to the financial commitment to policing. She draws two conclusions from her research. First, as cities experience urban decay, more money is allocated to police services. Second, cities with gang activity spend more per capita on policing than cities without gang problems. The implications of such research are significant. Law enforcement efforts are a logical response to gang activities, and they demonstrate to the public that something is being done. However, we must be cautious in assuming that a law enforcement response alone will ever get at the root of gang problems. Broad-based social problems like gang behavior warrant broad-based solutions employing a variety of intervention styles and types.

In a look at possible intervention approaches, Thompson and Jason consider one school-based program in an effort to identify promising strategies for dealing with gangs. Through the use of a quasi-experimental design, Thompson and Jason found that fewer of the youngsters participating in the program they examined joined gangs than those who did not participate in the same program. However, their results were not statistically significant owing to small numbers of subjects and other factors. This chapter is particularly useful because the authors explore many of the methodological problems facing gang researchers (as they themselves experienced these problems).

In the final chapter, Clark presents strategies for working with youngsters involved in deviant subcultures. The groups she identifies as deviant subcultures include Satanists, neo-Nazi skinheads, and violent street gangs. Her recommendations include ways to prevent alienation, and she stresses the importance of families, schools, and peer groups. Clark also notes that prevention may not be effective in some cases, so treatment and intervention programs should be in place to meet the needs of youngsters involved in deviant subcultures. She emphasizes that, to be effective, clinicians must be armed with knowledge about the different groups and understand the levels of fear these youngsters experience. From her viewpoint, alienation is the key factor to understand when one deals with the youngsters who participate in deviant subcultures.

Questions to Consider

As you finish reading this section, consider the following questions:

1. At the most basic level, what do we need to know about gang formation and persistence? Do we now have some understanding of why youngsters join and continue to belong to gangs?
2. Who seems to deal most effectively with gang problems? Are successful programs and policies transferable to other areas?

3. Is the gang problem really a cluster of problems? If so, is it likely that a single solution is not available to us?
4. How can families, schools, police, and community agencies/organizations most effectively deal with gangs?
5. Can we arrest gangs out of existence? Should we expect the police to be social workers in dealing with gangs? What is the most appropriate role for the police?

22

Community Organization and Gang Policy Response

G. David Curry and Rodney W. Thomas

Introduction

We reanalyze the sociometric data gathered by the National Youth Gang Intervention and Suppression Program for twenty-one communities included in the program's national survey that have more than four agencies participating in a community-level program to deal with youth gang-related problems. Our goals are (1) to examine differential distributions of prestige and involvement across types of agencies and (2) to study the relationship between network structure and the diffusion of formalized gang policy response.

Gangs as a Community Problem

Wherever the gang problem is identified, the problem is more likely to be viewed as a community-level problem as opposed to an individual-level problem or a national-level problem. This perspective has its roots in the rich history of gang research. For Thrasher (1927), the gang was a social phenomenon associated with interstitial areas of the city. Whyte (1943) confesses that he selected his Cornerville community because he thought it "looked like" a gang community should. Shaw and McKay (1972) explained the distribution of youth gangs and delinquency in terms of social ecology and the patterns of urban population migration. Spergel's (1964) late fifties' comparison of three New York City communities found distinct variations in delinquent subcultures, illegitimate as well as legitimate opportunities, and the existence and level of organization of fighting gangs across communities. In his analyses of delinquency in Chicago community areas, Bursik and his coauthors (Bursik

Reprinted with permission of Plenum Publishing Corporation from *Journal of Quantitative Criminology*, Vol. 8, No. 4 (1992): 357–374.

and Webb, 1982; Heitgerd and Bursik, 1987; Bursik, 1986) have shown that patterns of delinquency can in large part be correctly attributed to other community-level variables. In a study of gang homicide and delinquency rates, Curry and Spergel (1988) found differences in the ecological distribution of the two types of phenomena that are associated with the ethnicity of neighborhoods and poverty. Even the definition of what is a gang or a gang problem varies across urban areas (Horowitz, 1990; Spergel and Curry, 1992).

Community Organization as a Gang Intervention Strategy

The repeated identification of youth gang and delinquency problems with community-level variables has led most researchers to focus at least some part of their policy recommendations on the community-level coordination of public and private agencies. Thrasher (1927) called for coordinated gang intervention campaigns involving law enforcement, court, corrections, schools, and social service agencies. In Thrasher's perspective, communities with greater numbers of and more highly organized gangs were "disorganized." Thrasher's gangs were former playgroups that became organized through conflict with other existing gangs and conventional institutions within their communities. Within this theoretical perspective, many potential gangs never become organized, because conventional community organization is too strong, or only become organized in ways that meet with the approval of the well-organized conventional community.

The "disorganized" community as a context for the growth and spread of gangs is also examined by Shaw and McKay (1972). It is not, they argue, that communities with higher levels of gang delinquency are "disorganized" but that these communities are differentially organized. In the community with a high level of gang-related and other crime, the illegitimate opportunity structure of the community may be as well or better organized than the legitimate opportunity structure. Characteristic of such communities are those where schools, police, and social service agencies do not have lines of communication with one another and, just as importantly, with the residents of the community.

Two of the communities studied by Spergel (1964) are particularly illustrative of the negative implications of the relationship between community organization and gang activity. Slumtown is portrayed as one of the most impoverished and "rundown" in New York. Its residents, predominantly Puerto Rican immigrants, appear as isolated from their neighbors as they are from the major institutions that affect their lives. The primary delinquent opportunity available to youths is participation in fighting gangs that are predominantly offensive in nature. Prowess in conflict serves as the only immediately available source of status for the gang participants. Gang members are portrayed as committed to their gangs only to the degree that commitment serves to build their own reputations and are alienated from neighborhood adults and nondelinquent youths. The delinquent and nondelinquent youths of Slumtown face a future that is almost completely devoid of legitimate or profitable illegal opportunities.

In contrast, Spergel's Racketville is a predominantly Italian community. The legal and illegal opportunity structures in the community are well integrated. Police officers and racketeers are depicted as being on cordial terms. Youths belong to fighting gangs that Spergel characterizes as more defensive in nature. Members of the same gang are likely to form lifetime friendships. Neighborhood adults often perceive the gangs as protecting their communities from non-Italian invaders. Relations between delinquent and nondelinquent youths are not hostile. Gang members from Racketville mature out of the gang into a "well-integrated" legitimate and illegal opportunity structure. While Spergel feels that community organization and opportunity provision are key to dealing with the delinquency problem in Slumtown, he offers no such prescription for Racketville.

Spergel's (1964) conclusions underscore the need to conform delinquency response programs to particular community conditions. In his section on organization, Spergel (1964: 183–187) describes programs centered around interagency communication and coordination. More detail is provided in Spergel's *Community Problem Solving: The Delinquency Example* (1969). Here Spergel (p. 213) describes community coordination as "the regularized and the reciprocal character of communication and action of organizations to meet individualistic organizational objectives." Spergel's most recent contributions to the practical applications of the community organization approach to dealing with the gang problem are two technical assistance manuals, *General Community Design* (1991b) and *Community Mobilization* (1991a). Community mobilization builds on organization and coordination. "The process depends on cooperation, 'cutting through' denial and apathy, as well as managing interorganizational suspicion and conflict, so that the process leads to changes in awareness and improved response to the problem" (Spergel, 1991a).

The National Youth Gang Survey Data

Here we reanalyze network data gathered by the National Youth Gang Suppression and Intervention Program, a cooperative project of the Office of Juvenile Justice and Delinquency Prevention and the University of Chicago. The total National Youth Gang Survey data set consists of the responses to 254 agency-level in-depth interviews. Agencies surveyed were located in forty-five cities and six one-agency sites (Spergel and Curry, 1990, 1992). The survey focused on youth-based criminal gangs and, for the most part, did not seek information on prison gangs, skinhead groups, Satanist sects, or drug organizations except to the degree that such groups overlap with youth gangs. Site-based selection criteria for the survey were "the presence and recognition of a youth gang problem; the presence of a youth gang program; the existence of a program for at least a year; an articulated set of program goals; and evidence of more than a simplistic unitary response to the problem.'' For our analysis, we use the twenty-one urban areas for which there are four or more agencies participating in youth gang prevention, intervention, or suppression programs. Table 22.1 shows the breakdown of agencies by site and agency type.

Spergel and Curry (1990) divide the cities in the survey into chronic and emerging gang problem cities. They identify chronic gang problem cities as those having had a long history of gang problems and emerging gang problem cities as those which recognized and began to deal with the gang problem since 1980. Gangs in chronic gang problem cities or contexts tend to be better organized and involved in more serious violence and drug trafficking activity. Emerging gang problem cities are on the average smaller cities. Spergel and Curry found that the perceived effectiveness of gang strategies varies across city types, with only community organization as a primary strategy resulting in enhanced effectiveness ratings in both kinds of cities. Eight of our twenty-

Table 22.1   Urban Area and Agency Type for Agencies Included in the Analysis ($n = 178$)

Urban Area	n of Agencies	Mean Prominence	Agency Type	n of Agencies	Mean Prominence
Albuquerque	6	3.4	Law enforcement	30	16.9
Chicago	15	8.4	Prosecution	17	9.6
Columbus	8	4.5	Court	13	7.3
El Monte	5	2.8	Probation	25	14.0
Indianapolis[a]	6	3.4	Corrections	4	2.2
LA City	12	6.7	Parole	4	2.2
LA County	20	11.2	School security	7	3.9
Louisville[a]	6	3.4	School other	13	7.3
Miami[a]	15	8.4	Youth services	38	21.3
Milwaukee[a]	8	4.5	Comprehensive		
Minneapolis[a]	7	3.9	services	3	1.7
New York	15	8.4	Family services	8	4.5
Pamona	5	2.8	Grass roots	4	2.2
Philadelphia	5	2.8	Defense	1	0.6
Sacramento[a]	4	2.2	Planning	10	5.6
San Diego	10	5.6	Private		
San Francisco	10	5.6	commercial	1	0.6
Salt Lake City[a]	4	2.2			
Santa Ana	8	4.5			
Stockton	6	3.4			
San Jose	7	3.9			

a. Emerging gang problem cities.

Table 22.2   Binary Matrix of Youth Gang Agency Relations for Western City

1	2	3	4	5	6	7	8	9	10		Prominence
0	0	0	0	0	0	0	0	0	0	(1) Law Enforcement 1	0.84
1	0	0	0	0	0	0	0	0	0	(2) Law Enforcement 2	0.69
1	1	0	1	0	0	1	0	0	0	(3) Prosecution	0.28
1	1	1	0	0	0	0	0	0	0	(4) Probation	0.48
1	1	1	1	0	0	0	1	0	0	(5) Planning 1	0.04
0	0	0	0	1	0	1	1	0	0	(6) Planning 2	0.11
0	0	0	1	0	0	0	0	0	0	(7) Youth Service 1	0.47
1	1	0	1	0	1	1	0	0	1	(8) Youth Service 2	0.08
1	1	0	1	0	0	0	0	0	0	(9) Youth Service 3	0.09
1	1	0	1	0	0	1	1	1	0	(10) Youth Service 4	0.03

one urban areas are identified as emerging gang problem cities by Spergel and Curry (1990). These eight are designated in table 22.1. The other thirteen urban areas are labeled as chronic gang problem cities.

In order to construct our social network data, we use an item from the survey that asked each respondent, "With what other organizations is your agency in most contact in terms of dealing with the gang problem?" For each respondent, the identification of another respondent is treated as a choice. No mention of a respondent is treated as a nonchoice. For each urban area, a binary matrix of sociometric choice data was produced, with each row constituting an agency's choices and each column an agency's pattern of being identified.

Table 22.2 shows the binary matrix for Western City, a pseudonym for one of the cities included in the analysis. Row one of the matrix represents the choices of Law Enforcement Agency 1. Law Enforcement Agency 1 listed no local agencies in response to the question of contacts in dealing with the gang problem. Looking down the first column of the matrix, we can see that Law Enforcement Agency 1 was listed as a contact by Law Enforcement Agency 2, Prosecution, Probation, Planning Agency 1, and three of the youth service agencies included in the survey. The binary matrix in table 22.2 translates into the sociogram in figure 22.1.

Measuring Community Organization

Spergel and Curry (1990), using data from the national survey of 254 agencies involved in gang programs, found that community organization as a stated primary agency strategy was positively associated with perceived effectiveness in dealing with the problem. Measuring the actual level of community organization, as opposed to stated commitment to this strategy, is, however, more problematic. We have chosen to use three measures taken from network analysis research—social cohesion, structural equivalence, and prominence.

Figure 22.1: Western Gang Agency Network

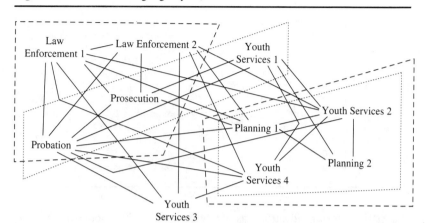

The application of quantitative analysis to the study of personal and organizational links within communities is well established. The theoretical foundations of what is today network analysis are attributed to social philosophy, sociology, and social anthropology. The German neo-Kantian philosopher, Georg Simmel (1971), insisted that the study of society be based on a distinction between social form or the structure of social relations and social content or the substantive or cultural characteristics of these relations. Though noted for his skepticism on the quantification in sociology, Pitirim Sorokin (1927/1959, p. 3) asserted that the ways in which human beings speak of ''social distance'' ''indicate that there is . . . 'social space'.'' A. R. Radcliffe-Brown (1952: 189–190) argues that ''the most fundamental part'' of social anthropology must be not the study of culture but the study of the ''complex network social relations'' by which human beings are connected. Radcliffe-Brown's dedication to a focus on social structure was based on his belief that these relations can be discovered by ''direct observation.'' The measurement and analytic techniques that we utilize here to measure community organization emerge from the unification of three sometimes overlapping streams of research in contemporary social science that have grown out of this multidisciplinary focus on social structure—community power studies, studies tying network linkages of community elites and organizations to collective decision-making, and application of exchange theory to community systems.

Case studies based on interviews of community elites in Atlanta (Hunter, 1953) and New Haven (Dahl, 1961) set the stage for the debate between ''elitists'' and ''pluralists'' about ''who governs'' that defined two decades of research on community power (Janowitz, 1978). The community power literature led to quantitative approaches that framed the questions about community power in terms of a political economy in which diverse ethnic and interest groups translated resources into public goods (Clark, 1973, 1975; Coleman, 1971; Laumann, 1973; Curry, 1976). Systematic random surveys of relatively large urban populations provided the data for these analyses that utilized regression and other multivariate techniques.

In an appendix to Laumann's (1973) *Bonds of Pluralism*, McFarland and Brown provided a "systematic introduction" to smallest space analysis, a method specifically developed to quantify social distance. Distances between community elites were measured on the basis of mutual recognition, the transfer of money or information, and the level and duration of interaction. The structures of these systems of distances (networks) were examined in the context of their impact on consensus on salient community issues and political policy outcomes (Laumann and Pappi, 1976; Laumann et al., 1977). Concern with networks of linkages among elites increasingly gave way to analyses of networks of linkages among organizations or "corporate actors" (Coleman, 1974; Laumann et al., 1978). Illustrative of this kind of analysis is Spergel and his colleagues' (1982) study of the adoption of status offender policies as a function of the network of linkages between juvenile justice and social service agencies.

Coleman (1957, 1973, 1990) introduced and has systematically developed the perspective that social behavior can be effectively modeled as a system of exchange anchored in purposive action by individuals and organizations. The introduction of Coleman's "political market" assumptions into the analysis of community-based networks of organizational linkages extends the measurement of community organization beyond the limits of sociometric modeling and the unidimensional measurement of social distance. Quantitative studies of community organization utilizing multidimensional characteristics of social structure as a system of interorganizational linkages translate microlevel variables into macrolevel measures that deal with questions of community influence in entirely new levels of complexity (Marsden and Laumann, 1977; Burt, 1982; Marsden, 1990). Here we apply these methods in an elementary way to the organizational reaction of communities to perceived gang crime problems. First, however, a closer examination of the three kinds of network measures that we utilize in our analysis is warranted.

Social Cohesion

Initially, the role of social networks in the diffusion of innovation emphasized the role of direct or indirect network contact or cohesion. Coleman et al. (1966), in their study of a population of 130 physicians, concluded that the physicians' pattern of adoption of the drug tetracycline constituted evidence for social contagion through informal networks. The assumption of cohesion is that direct and indirect contacts between network participants facilitate similar behavior.

In our study of the adoption of formal antigang policies, we measure cohesion by clique membership. According to Burt (1983), ''a clique is a set of actors with cohesive bonds to one another and without cohesive bonds to other actors in the network.'' We used the software program STRUCTURE (Burt, 1989) to generate clique structures for our twenty-one cities.

To return to our specific example, two cliques are identified by the STRUCTURE program for the sociometric data from Western City shown in figure 22.1. In the figure, each clique is enclosed by a dotted line. One clique consists of prosecution, probation, and one youth service agency. The other clique consists of the two planning agencies and two of the youth service agencies.

Structural Equivalence

In a reanalysis of the Coleman et al. data on medical innovation, Burt (1987) demonstrated that structural equivalence rather than cohesion drove the medical innovation process. Structurally equivalent actors in networks are not brought together by their direct ties to one another. Actors that are structurally equivalent play similar roles in the overall structure of relations in the network. This places structurally equivalent actors in similar positions to receive or distribute information or other resources.

Our sets of structurally equivalent actors was constructed from the Euclidean distance matrices produced by the STRUCTURE software (Burt, 1989). To be included in a structurally equivalent set, actors from the same community must have resulted in an item scale reliability correlation of 0.85 or higher. For Western City, two sets of structurally equivalent actors are identified in figure 22.1 (enclosed in the dashed lines). The four criminal justice agencies share structurally equivalent positions defined by their locations in relation to the other actors in the network. A second structurally equivalent position is shared by the two planning agencies and two of the youth service agencies.

Prominence

According to Knoke and Burt (1983), ''an actor is prominent within a network to the extent that his relations make him particularly visible relative to other actors in the system.'' A number of conceptual distinctions concerning just what prominence is and how to measure it exist in the literature (Burt, 1982; Knoke and Burt, 1983). For our analysis, following Knoke and Burt (1983, p. 205), we use primary form to measure prominence. Primary form is a measure of prominence that takes into account both the visibility of an actor in a network and the pattern of the actor's reciprocation of relationships with other actors. For instance, an actor in a network who is more likely to be listed as a contact by many other actors has a higher primary form score. When we refer to prominence below, we mean the primary form scores generated by the STRUCTURE software (Burt, 1989). For Western City (table 22.2), we can see that Law Enforcement Agency 1 has the highest level of prominence score followed by Law Enforcement Agency 2. Probation and Youth Services Agency 1 also have relatively high prominence in comparison to the other agencies in the network.

Measuring Policy Response to the Gang Problem

We measure policy response to the gang problem using four items related to the development of formal policies for dealing with youth gang problems. These are (1) having training on gangs available to staff members, (2) having an agency gang policy, (3) having a policy in writing, and (4) successfully initiating or modifying legislation related to the gang problem. These measures were selected because they were items included in the survey that reflect systematic development and application of formal policy. (We considered including items on having internal or external advisory boards, but neither of these two items was revealed by factor analysis or Rasch modeling to fit into the kind of unidimensional measure of policy adaptation that we were seeking.) Fitting these four variables to a Rasch model reveals their suitability for use as a scale. The item separable reliability is 0.99. This gives us a variable measuring degree of policy response to the gang problem that ranges from 0, for none of these policy measures implemented, to 4, for all four. We make no assumptions here about the quality of individual policies, either in terms of program effectiveness or in terms of political fairness, which might be the concern of labeling or conflict theorists. Table 22.3 displays descriptive

Table 22.3 Descriptive Statistics for Policy Response Variable

Scale item		Frequency			Calibration
Training available		118 (66.3%)			−3.35
Gang policy		93 (52.2%)			−0.92
Written policy		60 (33.7%)			1.26
Legislation		40 (22.5%)			3.01
Distribution on policy response scale					
0	46	25.8%	1	39	21.9%	2	27	15.2%
3	46	25.8%	4	20	11.2%			
		Mean, 1.75		SD, 1.38	

statistics for our policy response variable including Rasch model calibration coefficients for each item.

Policy Response and Network Measures

Our first concern is the relationship between variation in policy response and network structure. In order to estimate the variation in policy response that is explained by clique membership and structural equivalence, we conduct a general linear model (GLM) analysis of variance of policy response using as our independent variables clique membership and structural equivalence set membership. Table 22.4 presents the GLM results. Both membership in cliques and structural equivalence explain significant portions of the variation in policy response adoption. There is no significant interaction effect for joint membership in cliques and structural equivalence. For these twenty-one urban area networks, structural equivalence and clique membership combined account for 54.1 percent of the variation in gang policy response adoption across agencies. The unbalanced design complicates any comparison of the relative strengths of the two elements of network structure. Using the Type III sums of squares estimates, we can see that there is no significant interaction between clique membership and equivalence structure. (Unlike the more commonly used Type I sums of squares, Type III sums of squares do not normally add up to the model sums of squares.) In addition, from F tests based on these orthogonal sums of squares, we know that each component of network structure makes its own statistically significant independent contribution to explaining variation in the adoption of formal gang policy responses. Controlling neither

Table 22.4   General Linear Model Analysis of Variance Results for Policy Response Adoption by Structural Equivalence and Clique Membership

	df	Sum of Squares	Mean Sum of Squares	F
Network structure	63	182.7	2.90	2.13**
Error	116	154.9	1.36	
Total	177	337.6		
$R^2 = 0.54$				
Structural equivalence	23	50.9[a]	2.60	1.91*
Clique membership	11	28.6	2.21	1.63*
Interaction	3	1.4	0.47	0.35

a. Type III sums of squares do not normally add up to the model sums of squares.
 *Significant at 0.05 level.
**Significant at 0.0001 level.

Table 22.5   Structural Equivalence, Clique Membership, and Average Policy Response Score

	n	Average Policy Score	t Statistic
Member of structurally equivalent subset of actors	89	1.64	1.03
Not structurally equivalent to other actors	89	1.85	
Member of clique	133	1.93	3.63*
Not member of a clique	45	1.19	

*. Significant at 0.001 level.

for city gang problem status—chronic versus emerging nor for prominence of actors affects these results.

It is important to note that while network structure accounts for the variation in policy response adoption, being in a structurally equivalent position or a clique does not necessarily mean that an agency will have adopted a greater number of gang policy responses. To make our point, let us return to the Western City network presented in table 22.2 and figure 22.1. The two members of the Western City network that are not structurally equivalent to other actors—Youth Services Agencies 1 and 3—report three and four policy adoptions, respectively, for a mean policy response score of 3.5. The four structurally equivalent actors in structural position 1—the four criminal justice agencies—all report three policy responses, for a slightly lower average policy response score. The four agencies sharing the second structurally equivalent position—two planning agencies and two youth service agencies—have an average policy response score of 0.75. These four agencies also constitute a clique. The three agencies that are not involved in the two cliques identified for the city have policy response scores of 3. Clique number 1—the prosecutor's office, probation, and Youth Service Agency 1—has an average policy response score of 3.3. For one network, it is clear that being in a clique or being in a structurally equivalent position may impede as well as enhance policy response adoption.

Table 22.5 shows the comparisons for all actors in structurally equivalent positions and all actors not in structurally equivalent subsets of actors. We found that eighty-nine, or 50 percent, of the actors involved in these twenty-one networks were located in a structurally equivalent position to at least one other actor. The average policy response score (1.6) is not significantly different from the policy response scores of actors with no structurally equivalent actors (1.9).

A comparable computation for clique membership shows that, in general, being in a clique is associated with adopting a greater number of formal policy responses to the gang problem. Of our 178 agency respondents 133, or 74.7 perecnt, can be identified as a member of a clique within their local gang program network. The average policy response score for clique members (1.93) is significantly greater than the average score for respondents who are not involved in a clique (1.18) at the 0.001 level of statistical significance.

The Role of Prominence

As noted above, when the variation accounted for by structural equivalence and clique membership is controlled, prominence is not a significant predictor of policy response. An alternative hypothesis is that, in networks built around dealing with gang problems, agencies with a greater number of formal youth gang policy adoptions have greater prominence than agencies that have fewer. Without involving other measures of network structure, there does exist a significant relationship between prominence and policy response score ($r = 0.202$, significant at the 0.01 level). An increasing result emerges, however, if we examine this statistic separately for chronic and for emerging gang problem cities. For respondents from chronic gang problem cities, the correlation between prominence and policy response is still significant at the 0.01 level ($r = 0.229$). For respondents from emerging gang problem cities, the correlation is weaker and not statistically significant at the 0.05 level ($r = 0.1253$).

Western City (table 22.2) was not the only city for which law enforcement agencies appeared to be much more prominent than other kinds of agencies. The average prominence score for law enforcement agencies in chronic gang problem cities is 0.46; the comparable average for other agencies besides law enforcement is 0.20. The t statistic for the two means is 3.50, which is statistically significant at the 0.01 level. Looking at emerging cities, the difference in the two average prominence scores for law enforcement agencies (0.28) and other agencies (0.21) is not statistically different at the 0.05 level. Law enforcement agencies are, therefore, found to have significantly greater network prominence only in the thirteen chronic gang problem cities. The difference in prominence between law enforcement agencies and other agencies is not significant for respondents from the eight urban areas with emerging gang problems.

One additional concern is whether the higher prominence accorded law enforcement agencies in the chronic gang problem city networks can be regarded as a function of law enforcement's leadership in adopting formalized gang policy measures or must be attributed to some other independent source of prominence associated with being a law enforcement agency. The seventeen law enforcement agencies in the chronic gang problem cities have a policy response score average (2.17) higher than that for the other 103 agencies

Table 22.6   Regression Results for Prominence Score[a]

Independent Variable	b	β	t Statistic
Policy response	0.026	0.184	2.25*
Law enforcement	0.245	0.415	5.07**

a. $n = 120$; $R^2 = 0.223$
 *Significant at 0.05 level.
 **Significant at 0.001 level.

(1.74), but the difference is not statistically significant. Table 22.6 presents the results from regressing prominence on policy response score and a dummy variable for law enforcement agency. Together the two variables account for 22.3 percent of the variation in prominence. Both variables are statistically significant predictors of prominence. The prominence associated with being a law enforcement agency when level of policy response is controlled is the more statistically significant predictor. Therefore, we do find evidence for an independent prominence attached to law enforcement agencies in dealing with the gang problem. We do not find evidence of a similar effect in the eight emerging city networks.

Summary and Conclusions

We have conducted network analyses of respondent agencies from twenty-one urban areas. The data were collected by the National Youth Gang Intervention and Suppression Program in its 1989 national survey of sites with organized responses to youth gang problems. We utilized data from only the sites with four or more respondent agencies.

From the network analyses, we generated three measures of network structure: clique membership, subsets of structurally equivalent actors, and prominence within the network. Four formal policy measures—having training available, having a gang policy, having a written policy, and influencing legislation on gangs—were used to construct a gang policy response scale. GLM analysis of variance reveals that 54 percent of the variation in gang policy adoption can be attributed to clique membership and structural equivalence. In comparison to clique membership, structural equivalence accounts for the greater proportion of explained variation (83.7%).

In and of itself, being in a structurally equivalent subset of actors is not associated with a higher gang policy response score. As can be seen by examining the average policy response scores for each structurally equivalent subgroup and each clique, there are cases in which members of the network who are not in either a clique or a structurally equivalent subgroup have the greater number of formal policy responses to the gang problem. There is, however, a general tendency for members of cliques to have higher levels of gang policy response than nonmembers of cliques.

We found a positive association between prominence in a network and level of policy response for respondents from networks in urban areas defined as having chronic gang problems. In chronic gang problem urban areas, law enforcement agencies hold on the average more prominent positions in their respective networks. In his survey of Ohio school principals, Huff (1989) found that schools feel that gangs are a problem for which the police have the "primary responsibility." This condition does not hold for the eight networks identified as dealing with emerging gang problems.

Policy Implications

Developing and strengthening connections among diverse agencies has always been an important dimension of pursuing a community organization strategy in dealing with delinquency and youth gang problems (Spergel, 1964, 1969). The logic of this conclusion stems from the traditional identification of gang problems as community problems. Our findings provide additional empirical support for the promise of such a strategy. How the community organization focus can become integrated into a national response to the gang crime problem through programs and research is the subject of the following more specific recommendations.

1. Increasing linkages between agencies within communities is, in general, a good thing. While there are cases revealed in this analysis where isolated cliques demonstrate a collective absence of formal policy innovation, in general, clique members show higher levels of policy adoption than agencies operating in isolation. A national gang program must include a programmatic expansion of communication across agencies of all kinds within communities as well as mechanisms to allow more effective citizen input into those agencies. A variety of organizations ranging from criminal justice institutions to social service agencies involved in one large all-encompassing clique is an ideal standard by which coalition construction efforts in communities can be evaluated.

2. Utilize the concept of structural equivalence in carrying out community organization strategies. Our findings show that the structure of local networks has just as significant (if not greater) an impact on the dissemination of gang program policies as the structure of cliques. The mobilization of community organizations in a way that exploits equivalent or even competitive network positioning is a strategically more demanding approach than that proposed in Recommendation 1. A greater investment in initial as well as subsequent information gathering is needed. Assessment of community network structure must proceed or, at least, accompany program implementation. Programs that attempt to increase overall linkages among organizations, while at the same time taking advantage of preexisting network structure, will inevitably generate changes in those structures. Reassessment of the structure of network relations must become a routine component of evaluation plans and must be considered in measuring the effective achievement of other program goals.

3. Use research, particularly network analysis, to study the nature of local interagency relations. Updated network information can become a valuable resource in the effort to mobilize communities to deal with a wide range of social problems, including gang-related crime. The research on gangs as community-level phenomena cited above conceptualize gang crime as symptomatic of a wider range of problems rooted in social organization, citizen participation, and uneven economic development. Network analysis measures generated from community organizational linkages constitute variables that must be incorporated into explanatory models of social problems including those of what is currently perceived to be a geographically expanding gang crime problem.

4. Increase the quality of information being supplied to crucial actors in local networks. We have shown here that the structure of local community networks can enhance or impede the diffusion of policy innovation in response to youth gang crimes. If local networks are going to be used to spread policy innovation in response to gang crime, it is important that the information that is spread be accurate and subject to scientific verification. Especially if Recommendation 5 is followed, an increase in the dissemination of information on the causes of the gang crime problem and the effectiveness of reactions to the problem must occur as a coordinated research effort thoroughly imbued with the principles of peer review, open debate, and systematic collaboration and evaluation.

5. Begin to think in terms of a national-level network. If we are going to develop a locally based national program to deal with the gang problem, we need to be aware of the national-level networks that are developing around these efforts. This study has examined local networks within selected community contexts. A more ambitious effort will be required to model and measure the impact of the currently emerging and rapidly changing network of federal and local agencies engaged in the national-level response to the gang problem. Such a model will be required if we are to assess effectively and evaluate accurately the progress of the federal programs striving to deal with the problem at a national level.

The National Youth Gang Intervention and Suppression Program at the

University of Chicago in cooperation with the Office of Juvenile Justice and Delinquency Prevention, from which the data used here were obtained, is currently disseminating results of its five-year research and development project. Two departments of the U.S. government—the Department of Health and Human Services (DHHS) and the Department of Justice—have initiated national-level programs to assist communities in dealing with local gang crime problems. This current analysis has been conducted as part of the DHHS's Administration for Children and Families research program into the prevention of gang- and drug-related crime. Another part of this project has involved gathering network analysis data on agencies dealing with juvenile crime in Washington, DC. The first author is currently engaged in research in cooperation with the National Institute of Justice on the interorganizational networks that exist among law enforcement agencies dealing with gang problems in major cities. Other researchers, usually in cooperation with one of the federal agencies noted above, are gathering data on the networks that exist among other kinds of agencies dealing with the gang problem. Maxson and Klein (National Institute of Justice, 1991) are studying the national patterns of gang migration and linkages between gangs in different cities. While our recommendations are not exhaustive, they are already, to varying degrees, elements of the gradually coalescing national program for dealing with the gang crime program. Regardless of what we recommend here, network analysis as a tool in the national program to study and deal with gang crime problems will receive further utilization.

References

Bursik, R.J. (1986). Ecological stability and the dynamics of delinquency. In Reiss, A.J., Jr., and Tonry, M.H. (eds.), *Crime and Community*. Chicago: University of Chicago Press.

Bursik, R.J., Jr., and Webb, J. (1982). Community change and patterns of delinquency. *American Journal of Sociology* 88: 24–42.

Burt, R.S. (1982). *Toward a Structural Theory of Action: Network Models of Social Structure, Perception, and Action*. New York: Academic Press.

Burt, R.S. (1983). Cohesion versus structural equivalence as a basis for network subgroups. In Burt, R.S., and Minor, M.J. (eds.), *Applied Network Analysis*. Beverly Hills, CA: Sage. Pp. 262–282.

Burt, R.S. (1987). Social contagion and innovation: Cohesion versus structure equivalence. *American Journal of Sociology*. 92:1287–1335.

Burt, R.S. (1989). *Structure Assistant*. New York: Columbia University.

Burt, R.S., and Minor, M.J. (1983). *Applied Networks Analysis*. Beverly Hills, CA: Sage.

Clark, T.N. (1973). *Community Power and Policy Outputs*. Beverly Hills, CA: Sage.

Clark, T.N. (1975). Community Power. *Annual Review of Sociology* 1: 271–295.

Coleman, J.S. (1957). *Community Conflict*. New York: Free Press.

Coleman, J.S. (1971). *Resources for Social Change*. New York: Wiley Interscience.

Coleman, J.S. (1973). *The Mathematics of Collective Action*. Chicago: Aldine.

Coleman, J.S. (1974). *Power and the Structure of Society*. New York: Norton.

Coleman, J.S. (1990). *Foundation of Social Theory*. Cambridge, MA: Harvard University Press.

Coleman, J.S., Katz, E., and Menzel, H. (1966). *Medical Innovation*. New York: Bobbs-Merrill.

Curry, G.D. (1976). Utility and collectivity: Some suggestions on the anatomy of citizen preferences and urban public policy. In Clark, T.N. (ed.), *Citizens and Preferences and Urban Policy*. Beverly Hills, CA: Sage.

Curry, G.D., and Spergel, I.A. (1988). Gang homicide and delinquency. *Criminology* 26: 381–405.

Dahl, R.A. (1961). *Who Governs?* New Haven, CT: Yale University Press.

Heitgerd, J.L., and Bursik, R.J. (1987). Extra-community dynamics and the ecology of delinquency. *American Journal of Sociology* 92: 775–787.

Horowitz, R. (1990). Sociological perspectives on gangs: Conflicting definitions and concepts. In Huff, C.R. (ed.), *Gangs in America*. Newbury Park, CA: Sage. Pp. 37–54.

Huff, C.R. (1989). Youth gangs and public policy. *Crime and Delinquency*, 35:537.

Hunter F. (1953). *Community Power Structure*. Durham, NC: North Carolina University Press.

Janowitz, M. (1978). *The Last Half-Century: Societal Change and Politics in America*. Chicago: University of Chicago Press.

Knoke, D., and Burt, R.S. (1983). Prominence. In Burt, R.S., and Minor, M.J. (eds.), *Applied Network Analysis*. Beverly Hills, CA: Sage. Pp. 195–222.

Laumann, E.O. (1973). *Bonds of Pluralism: The Form and Substance of Urban Networks*. New York: Wiley.

Laumann, E.O., and Pappi, F.U. (1976). *Networks of Collective Action: A Perspective on Community Influence Systems*. New York: Academic Press.

Laumann, E.O., Galaskiewicz, J., and Marsden, P.V. (1977). Community influence structures: Replication and extension of a network approach. *American Journal of Sociology* 83: 594–631.

Laumann, E.O., Galaskiewicz, J., and Marsden, P.V. (1978). Community structure as interorganizational linkages. *Annual Review of Sociology* 4: 455–484.

Marsden, P.V. (1990). Network data and measurement. *Annual Review of Sociology* 16: 435–463.

Marsden, P.V., and Laumann, E.O. (1977). Collective action in a community elite: Exchange, influence resources, and issue resolution. In Liebart, R.J., and Imersheim, A.W. (eds.), *Power, Paradigms, and Community Research*. London: Sage.

National Institute of Justice. (1991). National Institute of Justice Research and Development Awards Fiscal Year 1991. Washington, DC: U.S. Dept. of Justice, Office of Justice Programs.

Radcliffe-Brown, A.R. (1952). *Structure and Function in Primitive Society*. New York: Free Press.

Shaw, C.R., and McKay, H.D. (1972). *Juvenile Delinquency in Urban Areas*. Chicago: University of Chicago Press.

Simmel, G. (1971). *On Individuality and Social Forms*. Chicago: University of Chicago Press.

Sorokin, P.A. (1927/1959). *Social and Cultural Mobility*. New York: Free Press.

Spergel, I.A. (1964). *Racketville, Slumtown, Haulburg*. Chicago: University of Chicago Press.

Spergel, I.A. (1969). *Community Problem Solving: The Delinquency Example*. Chicago: University of Chicago Press.

Spergel, I.A. (1991a). *Community Mobilization*. National Youth Gang Suppression and Intervention Program, Technical Assistance Manual, School of Social Service Administration in Cooperation with the Office of Juvenile Justice and Delinquency Prevention, U.S. Dept. of Justice. Chicago: University of Chicago Press.

Spergel, I.A. (1991b). *General Community Design*. National Youth Gang Suppression and Intervention Program, Technical Assistance Manual, School of Social Service Administration in Cooperation with the Office of Juvenile Justice and Delinquency Prevention, U.S. Dept. of Justice. Chicago: University of Chicago Press.

Spergel, I.A., and Curry, G.D. (1990). Strategies and perceived agency effectiveness in dealing with the youth gang problem. In Huff, C.R. (ed.), *Gangs in America*. Newbury Park, CA: Sage. Pp. 288–309.

Spergel, I.A., and Curry, G.D. (1992). The National Youth Gang Survey: A research and development process. In Goldstein, A., and Huff, C.R. (eds.), *Gang Intervention Handbook*. Champaign-Urbana, IL: Academic Press.

Spergel, I.A., Lynch, J.P., Reamer, F.G., and Korbelik, J. (1982). Response to organization and community to a deinstitutionalization strategy. *Crime and Delinquency*. 28: 426–449.

Thrasher, F.M. (1927). *The Gang*. Chicago: University of Chicago Press.

Whyte, W.F. (1943). *Street Corner Society*. Chicago: University of Chicago Press.

23

Gangs, Neighborhoods, and Public Policy

John M. Hagedorn

Are today's youth gangs part of an "underclass"? What policies should communities adopt to control their gang problem? Based on recent gang research and experience in reforming Milwaukee's human service bureaucracy, we can address these questions and suggest practical local policies that go beyond the usual nostrums of "more cops" and "more jobs."

In the last few years a number of researchers have suggested that today's gangs have changed in some fundamental ways and may be part of an urban minority "underclass" (Moore, 1985; Short, 1990b; Taylor, 1990; Vigil, 1988). The nature of the "underclass," however, has been the subject of controversy (Aponte, 1988; Gans, 1990; Jencks, 1989; Ricketts, Mincy, and Sawhill, 1988; Wilson, 1991). This paper uses data gathered from three different Milwaukee studies over the past five years to examine the changing nature of Milwaukee's gangs, the characteristics of Milwaukee's poorest African-American neighborhoods, and the relationship between gangs and neighborhoods.

For the first study, completed in 1986, forty-seven of the founding members of Milwaukee's nineteen major gangs, including eleven of the nineteen recognized leaders, were interviewed (Hagedorn, 1988). That study described the origins of Milwaukee gangs, their structure and activities, and documented how gangs came to be seen as a social problem. It also tracked the education, employment, drug use, incarceration experience, and the level of gang participation of the 260 young people who founded the nineteen gangs, including the 175 founders of twelve African-American male gangs.

A brief follow-up study in spring of 1990 looked at the patterns of drug abuse and the structure of gang drug dealing in three African-American gangs. This pilot study tracked the employment, incarceration, and drug use status

Reprinted with permission from *Social Problems*, Vol. 38, No. 4 (November 1991): 529–540. © 1991 by the Society for the Study of Social Problems.

of the thirty-seven founding members of the three gangs since the original study. It began a process of exploring the relationship between Milwaukee gangs and drug dealing businesses or "drug posses."

Finally, as part of a human services reform plan, Milwaukee County commissioned a needs assessment in two neighborhoods where several of Milwaukee's gangs persist (Moore and Edari, 1990b). Residents were hired to survey heads of households drawn from a probability sample of 300 households in ten census tracts in two neighborhoods. These neighborhoods had a high percentage of residents living in poverty and a clustering of social problems associated with the "underclass."

This article first looks at how Milwaukee gangs have changed due to deindustrialization. Second, the paper explores some volatile social dynamics occurring within poor but still heterogeneous African-American neighborhoods. Finally, based on the analysis of gangs and their neighborhoods, other underclass research, and on the author's own experience in reforming the delivery of social services, the article suggests several local policies to strengthen and assist community institutions with gang troubles.

Macro-Economic Trends and Gangs in Milwaukee

The underclass has been conceptualized as a product of economic restructuring that has mismatched African-American and other minority workers with radically changed employment climates (Bluestone and Harrison,1982; Kasarda, 1985; Sullivan, 1989). Milwaukee epitomizes this mismatch: between 1979 and 1986 over 50,000 jobs were lost or 23 percent of Milwaukee's manufacturing employment (White et al., 1988:2–6). African-American workers were hit especially hard. In 1980, prior to the downturn, 40 percent of all African-American workers were concentrated in manufacturing (compared to 31 percent of all city workers). By 1989, research in five all-black Milwaukee census tracts found that only about one quarter of all black workers were still employed in manufacturing (Moore and Edari, 1990b). African-American unemployment rates in Milwaukee have reached as high as 27 percent over the past few years.

Another way to view economic changes in the African-American community is to look at social welfare over the last thirty years. Like European immigrants before them, African-Americans came to Milwaukee with the hopes of landing good factory jobs (Trotter, 1985), and large numbers succeeded. But as industrial employment declined and good jobs were less available, reliance on welfare increased (Piven and Cloward, 1987:83). In 1963, when black migration to Milwaukee was still rising, fewer than one in six of Milwaukee's African-Americans were supported by AFDC. However by 1987, nearly half of all Milwaukee African-Americans and two thirds of their children received AFDC benefits. Seven out of every ten Milwaukee African-

Table 23.1   Employment and Adult Gang Involvement

	Percent Black Male	Percent Hispanic Male	Percent White Male	Percent Female
Full Time	9.7	10	10	8.6
Part Time	14.0	0	40	11.4
Unemployed	70.3	82.5	40	63.0
Involved with the				
Gang as an Adult	81.1	70	100	8.6
Totals				
N = 260	N = 175	N = 40	N = 10	N = 35

Americans in 1987 were supported by transfer payments of some kind accounting for half of all 1987 black income in Milwaukee County (Hagedorn, 1989a).

Coinciding with reduced economic prospects for African-Americans, Hispanics, and other working people, gangs reemerged in Milwaukee and other small and medium-sized cities across the Midwest. While the popular notion at the time was that these gangs had diffused from Chicago, gangs in Milwaukee and the Midwest developed from corner groups and breakdancing groups in processes nearly identical to those described by Thrasher fifty years before (Hagedorn, 1988; Huff, 1989). The economy may have been changing, but the way gangs formed had not.

In 1986 we interviewed 47 of the 260 Milwaukee gang founders or members of the initial groups of young people who started the nineteen major gangs in the early 1980s. At the time of our interviews, the founders were in their early twenties and at an age when young people typically "mature out" of gang life. We asked the 47 founders to report on the current status of all the members who were part of the gang when it started. To our surprise, more than 80 percent of all male gang founders were reported as still involved with the gang as twenty to twenty-five year old adults.

We concluded at the time that the *economic basis* for "maturing out" of a gang—those good paying factory jobs that take little education, few skills, and only hard work—was just not there anymore. As Short wrote in a review of gang literature, "There is no reason to believe that boys hang together in friendship groups for reasons that are very different now than in the past. . . .What has changed are the structural economic conditions . . ." (Short 1990a).

Moore (1991) has also documented economic effects of deindustrialization on the "maturing out" process of Chicano gangs. She finds that members of recent gang cliques in East Los Angeles are less likely to have found good jobs than members of older gang cliques. She concludes, "It is not that the men from recent cliques were more likely to have dropped out of the labor

Table 23.2   1990 Status of Thirty-Seven Founding Members of Three
African-American Gangs

Involved in Regular Sales of Cocaine	Used Cocaine Routinely Since 1987	Spent Time in Prison	Presently Working Full Time	Murdered
59%	76%	86%	19%	8%
N = 22	N = 28	N = 32	N = 7	N = 3

market, nor were they more likely to be imprisoned. It may be that they could not get full-time, stable jobs.''

The difficulty in finding a good job today is offset by the abundance of part-time jobs in the illegal drug economy. In preparation for a proposal to the National Institute on Drug Abuse to examine the impact of drug abuse and drug dealing on Milwaukee's gangs, we updated our rosters on the current status of the thirty-seven founding members of three African-American gangs. By 1990, less than one in five (19%) of the founders, now in their mid to late twenties, were engaged in full-time work. However, three times as many of the founders (59 percent) graduated from the gang into drug ''posses'' or high-risk small businesses selling drugs. ''High risk'' is perhaps an understatement. Almost all of the thirty-seven (86%) had spent significant time in prison since 1986, most for drug offenses. Three quarters (76%) had used cocaine regularly within the last three years, and three had been murdered. While five of the thirty-seven were said to be working as entrepreneurs (called ''hittin' 'em hard''), the others involved with drug distribution worked part time (''makin' it'') or sporadically (''day one''), and continued to live on the margins.

As Don, a leader of the 1–9 Deacons told us in 1985: ''I can make it for two or three more years. But then what's gonna happen?'' The answer to Don's question is now clear. The lack of access to good jobs has had a direct effect of making illegal drug sales, no matter how risky, more attractive to Milwaukee's gang founders as an occupation for their young adult years.

Frederick Thrasher pointed out sixty years ago: ''As gang boys grow up, a selective process takes place: many of them become reincorporated into family and community life, but there remains a certain criminal residue upon whom gang training has, for one reason or another, taken hold'' (Thrasher, 1963:287). The loss of entry level manufacturing jobs appears to have turned Thrasher's ''selective process'' on its head. Today most of the young adult gang founders rely on the illegal economy for guarantees of survival. It is only the ''residue'' who, at this time in Milwaukee, are being ''reincorporated into family and community life.''

There are also some indirect effects of economic changes. In Milwaukee, most of the founders still identify somewhat with their old gang and often hang out in the same neighborhoods where they grew up, coexisting with a new generation of gang youth. This mixing of older members of drug "posses" with younger siblings and other young gang members has produced disturbing intergenerational effects. Older gang members with a street reputation employed in the fast life of drug dealing are modeling dangerous career paths for neighborhood youth. These intergenerational effects also appear in Anderson's latest work (1990). He finds that "old heads," older residents who upheld and disseminated traditional values, are being replaced by *new* "old heads" who "may be the product of a street gang" and who promote values of "hustling," drugs, and sexual promiscuity (p. 103). This "street socialization" may contribute to reproducing an underclass rather than socializing young people into conventional lifestyles (Short, 1990b; Vigil, 1988).[1]

In summary, contemporary gangs have changed from the "delinquent boys" of fifties literature: There is a growing relationship between the youth gang, illegal drug-based distribution, and survival of young adult gang members in a post-industrial, segmented economy. Clearly, powerful *economic* forces are affecting contemporary gangs as Wilson and other underclass theorists would predict. But when we take a closer look at the impact of economic, demographic, and institutional changes on processes within Milwaukee's poorest African-American neighborhoods, the situation becomes more complicated.

Gangs and Neighborhood Segmentation

Gangs have always been associated with neighborhoods, and African-American gangs have been no exception. Thrasher found "Negroes" had "more than their share" of gangs (Thrasher, 1963:132) as far back as the 1920s. In the neighborhood that Suttles studied, gangs were functional "markers" or signs by which neighborhood youth could know who may be harmful and who is not and thus were an important part of a neighborhood's search for order. Suttles' black gangs were not in any significant way distinct from white ethnic gangs (Suttles, 1968:157). Similarly, the black Chicago gang members that Short and Strodtbeck (1965:108) studied were quite similar to nongang black youth, though they were more lower class than white gang members. Until the 1960s, the sociological literature largely viewed black gangs as functional parts of black neighborhoods.

But things have been changing. Perkins, summarizing the history of black Chicago gangs, wrote that gangs first became disruptive to their communities in the 1960s due to the influence of drugs, corrupting prison experiences, and the failure of community-based programs (Perkins, 1987:40–42). Cloward and Ohlin theorized that housing projects and other big city "slums" tended to be disorganized and "produce powerful pressures for violent behavior among the young in these areas" (Cloward and Ohlin, 1960:172). They correctly predicted that "delinquency will become increasingly violent in the future as a result of the disintegration of slum organization" (p. 203).

Increasing violence in central cities has prompted angry responses from residents. Cooperation by broad elements of the black community with police sweeps of gang members in Los Angeles and elsewhere and the founding of "mothers against gangs" and similar organizations throughout the country are examples of community hostility toward gangs. Gangs today are seen by both law enforcement and many community residents as basically *dysfunctional*. Today's gangs are a far cry from the "Negro" street gangs of Suttle's Addams area which contained the "best-known and most popular boys in the neighborhood" (Suttles, 1968:172).

Based on our Milwaukee interviews, we concluded that gang members reciprocated the hostility of "respectables." While the gang founders were hostile toward police and schools as expected, they also severely criticized African-American community agencies which they felt were mainly "phoney." The black founders agreed their gangs were dysfunctional for their neighborhoods: two thirds of those we interviewed insisted that their gang was "not at all" about trying to help the black community. Some were shocked at even the suggestion that their gang would be concerned about anything but "*green* power" (i.e., money). The role model of choice for many of the founders we interviewed was not Dr. Martin Luther King, Jesse Jackson, or any African-American leader, but Al Capone.

One explanation for this intra-community alienation in Milwaukee is the peculiar way black gangs formed. Gang formation in Milwaukee coincided with desegregation of the schools: a one-way desegregation plan that mandatorily bused only black children. While gangs originally formed from neighborhood groups of youth in conflict with youth from other neighborhoods, busing complicated the situation. School buses picking up African-American students often stopped in many different neighborhoods, mixing youth from rival gangs and transforming the buses into battlegrounds. Gang recruitment took place on the buses and in the schools as well as from the neighborhood. The black founders told us in 1985–86 that a majority of the members of their gangs no longer came from the original neighborhood where the gang formed.

Consequently, when the gang hung out on neighborhood corners, they were not seen by residents as just the "neighbors' kids" messing up. "I'll tell your Mama" did not work when no one knew who "mama" was or where she lived. Informal social controls were ineffective, so calling the police became the basic method to handle rowdiness and misbehavior as well as more serious delinquency. Hostility between the gangs and the neighborhood increased with each squad car arriving on the block.

A second explanation for intra-community hostility is provided by 1989 research in five of Milwaukee's poorest and all-black census tracts (Moore and Edari, 1990b) where several of the gangs I had studied were founded. These neighborhoods exhibit many of the criteria of an "underclass" area, but they also differ in many respects from very poor ghetto neighborhoods described by Wilson and others.

Household income of the tracts was very low—1980 census data (*before* the eighties downturn) show more than 30 percent of the families in the five tracts living below poverty. The five tracts experienced a 42 percent population loss between 1960 and 1985. In 1989, when the interviews were completed, most (53.8%) respondents received AFDC and nearly 20 percent (19%) did not have a phone. A majority of residents in the five tracts presently live below the poverty line. The tracts certainly qualify as "underclass" areas by standard definitions (Ricketts and Mincy, 1988).

But these neighborhoods are not uniformly poor. One quarter of the residents (28.6%) owned their own home—15 percent less than the city-wide average, but still a stable base within a very poor neighborhood. Half of the household heads lived at their current residence for five or more years. While stable employment had drastically declined in these tracts since 1980, still nearly one third of working respondents had held their current job for ten or more years. Unlike the "densely settled ghetto areas" Sampson describes (1987:357) where residents have "difficulty recognizing their neighbors," 80 percent of the Milwaukee respondents said the best thing about their neighborhood *was* their "neighbors." Nearly three in five (59.2%) visited with neighbors at least once a week.

More striking were strong kinship ties, supporting earlier work by Stack (1974) and others. Nearly half of all respondents visited their parents every day and over 90 percent visited parents monthly. An even higher percentage visited siblings at least once a month. Finally, more than three quarters belonged to families that held family reunions—and 77 percent of those respondents regularly attended those reunions. Even child protective clients, who are among the most transient residents, had extensive kinship networks (Moore and Edari, 1990a).[2]

But the neighborhoods are not regarded positively by most residents. Less than one-fifth (19.7%) said the neighborhood was a "good place to live," and 52 percent said they would move if they could. While respondents liked their neighbors as the best thing about their community, the top three worst things were said to be drugs (64%), violence (52%), and gangs (20%). About half said things had gotten worse the past two years, and a majority (54.5%) believed things will continue to get worse. And the problems were not "around the corner" or in an adjacent neighborhood, but right on the blocks where the interviews took place. The interviewers were often told by respondents to not go to a certain house or to avoid a certain side of the street because of dangerous drug or gang problems.

The area also has few basic social institutions. Zip code 53206 is a twenty by twenty square block area with 40,000 residents in the heart of Milwaukee, containing the census tracts where the interviews took place. This area has no large chain grocery stores. There are no banks or check-cashing stores in the entire zip code area. Bars and drug houses are in plentiful supply and the area has the highest number of Milwaukee drug arrests. Still, in 1989, this zip code area did not have a single alcohol/drug treatment facility. Even community agencies are located overwhelmingly on the periphery of 53206, circling the neighborhoods they serve, but not a part of them.[3] Community programs, churches, and social workers were seldom mentioned by survey respondents as a resource to call in times of neighborhood trouble.[4]

In summary, while these poor African-American neighborhoods have characteristics of Wilson's notion of the underclass, they also exhibit important differences. On the one hand, central city Milwaukee neighborhoods have been getting poorer due to deindustrialization and have experienced substantial population loss. They are home to the poorest and most troubled of all Milwaukee's residents. The area's lack of basic institutions is reminiscent of descriptions by Thrasher (1927) and Shaw and McKay (1969) and supports aspects of Wilson's underclass thesis.

On the other hand, large numbers of working class African-American families still reside in these neighborhoods. Some want to leave but cannot because of residential segregation (Massey and Eggers, 1990) or lack of affordable housing. But many stay because they want to. Rather than neighborhoods populated overwhelmingly by a residue left behind by a fleeing middle and working class, as Wilson has described, Milwaukee's "underclass" neighborhoods are a checkerboard of struggling working class and poor families, coexisting, even on the same block, with drug houses, gangs, and routine violence.

This ecological coexistence explains much of the intra-community tension between poor and working families and underclass gangs. Clearly when drug deals gone bad turn into midnight shoot-outs, residents of a neighborhood will be scared and angry. Contrary to Wilson's claim, events in one part of the block or neighborhood are often of vital concern to those residing in other parts (Wilson 1987:38). With a lack of effective community institutions, residents can either ignore the gunshots in the night, arm themselves for self-protection, call 911—or give in to the fear and despair by moving out.[5]

While Milwaukee neighborhoods are not the socially disorganized underclass areas reported by Wilson, neither are they the highly organized neighborhoods described by Whyte (1943) or Suttles (1968). Milwaukee's poor neighborhoods have segmented and an uneasy peace reigns between nervous factions. Suttles (1968) saw the 1960s Addams area as representing "ordered segmentation," where firm boundaries between ethnic neighborhoods helped make "a decent world within which people can live" (p. 234). Instead, Milwaukee's neighborhood segments have become a prime source of instability.

This picture of neighborhood segmentation is consistent with Anderson's portrait of "Northton," a poor African-American community in a large eastern city (Anderson, 1990). "Old heads" in Northton are not so much missing, as they have become demoralized and their advice shunned (pp. 78–80). Respectable residents are confronted by a growing street culture that increases community distrust of young people, victimizes neighborhood residents, and lures children into dangerous activities (p. 92). Police simplistically divide the neighborhood between the "good people" and those linked to drug trafficking (pp. 202–203). Conflict between neighborhood segments inevitably increases, and "solidarity" is sacrificed to the imposed order of police patrols, vigilante justice, and prisons.

These heterogeneous but segmented neighborhoods in "Northton" and Milwaukee may be characteristic of many "underclass" communities across the United States (Jencks, 1990). How to stabilize such neighborhoods is one of the major policy debates of the nineties.

Gangs, Neighborhoods, and Public Policy

In light of these findings, what do we make of this contradictory picture of gangs and their neighborhoods? What policies ought to be followed? The data suggest the drug economy flourishes in large part because of the absence of good jobs. It is hard to argue with the response from a 1986 interview:

Q: OK, we're at the end here. The Governor comes in. He says, Darryl, I'm gonna give you a million dollars to work with gangs. Do what you want with it.
A: Give 'em all jobs.

But while jobs are certainly needed, there is no reason to believe hundreds of thousands of good paying, entry-level jobs will appear anytime soon from either the private or public sector. In the absence of sufficient jobs, pressure will continue to mount for more police and more prisons as the policy option of choice to curtail violence. This militarization of our neighborhoods is inevitable unless community residents and public officials can be persuaded that alternative policies are plausible and can be effective. But what alternative policies should be advocated?

One popular option is to work with city hall and call for more federal resources to come to cities. While we clearly need more resources, a more critical issue is how money is spent. As Spergel says in summarizing his recommendations in the National Youth Gang Survey "the implications of our findings is that more resources alone for police or even human service programs would not contribute much to dealing effectively with the youth gang problem" (Spergel and Curry, 1990:309). In the absence of institutional reform and guarantees that resources will get to those that need it, more resources alone will not necessarily contribute to solving gang problems.[6]

The development of effective policy will require a struggle within cities over where new and existing programs are physically located, who will be served, and how the massive public bureaucracies (which gobble most resources intended for the poor) should be structured. Rather than proposing specific new model gang programs or narrowly calling for a federal office of gang control (Miller, 1990), our data suggest a focus on strengthening neighborhood social institutions. Our experience in reforming Milwaukee's human service system suggests that we should adopt four policies to strengthen neighborhood-level social control.

1. *Public spending and private investment must be concentrated in the most impoverished areas.* This does not mean spend more human service dollars "for" the underclass by funding well intentioned programs run by middle-class white providers located on the periphery of the poorest neighborhoods. Rather, I suggest we should insist that money be spent mainly on programs physically located *in* underclass neighborhoods, run by people with ties to the neighborhoods they intend to serve. This policy has the effect of targeting programs for the underclass while also strengthening minority agencies or creating new agencies within very poor neighborhoods. These agencies provide not only services but also can provide jobs for neighborhood residents. As employment opportunities increase and better funded local agencies become centers for social action, pressures for working- and middle-class residents to flee should decrease.

For example, in Milwaukee, close examination of where human service dollars were spent by zip code exposed that less than 1 percent of $100 million of Department of Health and Human Service contract dollars in 1988 was spent on programs located in two of Milwaukee's poorest zip code areas (53206 and 53204). These two areas contain only 8 percent of Milwaukee County's population but are home to 25 percent of Milwaukee's human service clients. These figures were used by our reform administration to direct several million dollars in purchase contracts to agencies physically located in the two zip code areas, helping build an institutional infrastructure. Boarded up buildings are being rehabilitated to house the new agencies, employing neighborhood youth in the rehabbing effort.

Redirecting existing money is not an easy task. When we sent more than "crumbs" to neighborhood organizations, the mainly white traditional agencies—which are located down town or in integrated, more stable neighborhoods—howled "reverse discrimination" and lobbied against us. Funding new programs is a zero sum game: if agencies located in poor neighborhoods are to get funded, agencies located elsewhere stand to lose. Those providers will almost certainly have more political power and connections than poor neighborhood organizations.

438

But as our research shows, while very poor neighborhoods have been devastated by economic and demographic changes, they also have important strengths to build on. The residents who live in poor neighborhoods need stable, well-funded agencies and institutions in which to participate. This recommendation is a call for sustained local political struggle over *where* money is spent to better stabilize impoverished neighborhoods.

2. *Programs should be fully evaluated to see if they are having a positive impact on gangs or those most in need.* It is not only important where the money is spent, but it is also critical whether anyone besides the agency or bureaucracy benefits. The inability of traditional agencies to serve the "hard to reach" has a long history: the Chicago Area Project (Schlossman, Zellman, and Schavelson, 1984) was initiated to fill just such a gap. Geis cites the 1960s New York City Youth Board as an example of the need for innovative programming to replace the traditional agencies which were unable "to respond readily to new ideas and approaches" (Geis, 1965:43). And some programs do "work." Lizbeth Schorr lists numerous contemporary programs that have been effective and could be replicated (Schorr, 1988).

Large public bureaucracies are seldom concerned with formal results of programs. Once programs are funded, their continuation is often all that is offered as proof of effectiveness. In Milwaukee, research on agencies which received more than $20 million worth of contracts to work with delinquents discovered the Department of Social Services kept no records at all of client outcomes of these programs. Funding decisions were based almost solely on routine approval of the re-funding of those agencies funded the year before (Hagedorn, 1989b).

Programs thus continue with no regard for their effectiveness for clients. Lindblom points out the apparent absurdity that "In an important sense, therefore, it is not irrational for an administrator to defend a policy as good without being able to specify what it is good for" (Lindblom, 1959:84). James Q. Wilson, in a forum on "Can Government Agencies be Managed?" recommended the novel idea that managers be judged on program results, a prospect he doubted would happen because "It is in no one's interest in Washington, D.C.," to do it (Wilson, 1990:33). Many organizational theorists have pointed out that program evaluation serves only ceremonial functions for public bureaucracies (Meyer and Rowan, 1981; Weick, 1976). If sociologists are not among those insisting that social programs be evaluated and show results for the clients they are intended to serve, who will?

3. *Fund family preservation programs.* One of the most encouraging developments in the past decade in social work has been family preservation programs (Nelson, Landsman, and Duetelman, 1990). These short-term, intensive, empowerment model programs, which focus not on an individual client, but rather the needs of the entire family, have been remarkably successful.[7] In dozens of states and cities, these programs, many of them modeled

after the successful "homebuilders" projects funded by the Edna McConnell Clark Foundation, have reduced out of home placements and helped families learn how to stay together during a crisis.

Families where an older sibling is involved with gangs may be ideal candidates for these types of intensive, coordinated efforts. Our data show that many child protective clients have extensive family networks whose strengths could be utilized by intensive interventions. Milwaukee received a $1 million grant from the Philip Morris Companies to fund a "homebuilders" model program. An agency located in one of the poorest areas of the city was awarded the contract to implement the program and collaborate with the public school system. As noted above, there was considerable resistance to the program from elements within the social welfare bureaucracy, where family-based, results-oriented programming was viewed as a threat to business as usual (Nelson, 1988). Yet, strategies were developed to confront the opposition, and the program was implemented.

4. *Finally, large public bureaucracies should become more neighborhood based and more open to input from clients and the neighborhoods they serve.* Reminiscent of the 1960s community control movement (Altshuler, 1970), current research suggests that social control is least effective when imposed by outside forces. Community controls are strengthened most when informal community level networks are voluntarily tied to external bureaucracies and other resources (Figueira-McDonough, 1991).[8] Public dollars for social programs today are largely used to support "street level bureaucrats" whose structure of work often makes it difficult to deliver services that improve the quality of life of their clients (Lipsky, 1980). Diverse reform trends in policing, education, and social services all stress more community involvement in public bureaucracies (Chubb and Moe, 1990; Comer, 1972; Goldstein, 1977; Kamerman and Kahn, 1989). These reforms, insofar as they increase client and neighborhood control and break down existing bureaucratic barriers, merit support.

While Lipsky and others comment that it will be difficult to reform public bureaucracies in the absence of a social movement (Lipsky,1980:210; Wineman, 1984:240), unfavorable conditions should not be an excuse for inaction. The Milwaukee experience of creating multidisciplinary teams of human service workers, moving them into the neighborhoods, and creating neighborhood councils to increase accountability is one example of such a reform.

Conclusion

Deindustrialization has altered the nature of gangs, creating a new association between the youth gang, illegal drug-based distribution, and survival of young adult gang members in a postindustrial, segmented economy. While it would be a mistake to see all gangs as drug-dealing organizations, the lack of opportunity for unskilled delinquents creates powerful strains on gang members to become involved in the illegal economy. Without a major jobs program, illegal trade in drugs and related violence seem likely to continue at unacceptable levels (Goldstein, 1985; Johnson et al., 1989).

Although neighborhood changes are clearly relevant to gang activities, Wilson's characterization of the underclass as living in neighborhoods from which middle and working class African-Americans have fled and abandoned social institutions (Wilson, 1987:56) does not fully apply in cities like Milwaukee. Instead, there are deteriorating neighborhoods with declining resources and fractured internal cohesion. In cities like Milwaukee, it is not the absence of working people that define underclass neighborhoods but more the absence of effective social institutions. Without community controlled institutions, conventional values will have diminished appeal, neighborhoods will segment, solidarity will weaken, and working residents will continue to flee. The research on Milwaukee is consistent with the basic tenet of social disorganization theory, that the lack of effective institutions is related to crime and delinquency. The data support Spergel and others who call for "community mobilization and more resources for and reform of the educational system and job market" (Spergel and Curry, 1990:309) as the most effective approach to gang control.

This article does support Wilson and others who call for massive new federal jobs programs. While lobbying for new state and federal job programs, social scientists should also focus on ways to encourage private and public investment in poor neighborhoods and advocate for more community control of social institutions. This means a stepped up involvement by academics in the workings of the large public bureaucracies which control resources needed to rebuild these communities.[9]

In the words of C. Wright Mills, bureaucracies "often carry out series of apparently rational actions without any ideas of the ends they serve" (Mills, 1959:168). All too often the ends public bureaucracies serve are not helpful for poor communities. This article can be read as a call for social scientists to step up the struggle to make public bureaucracies more rational for the truly disadvantaged.

Notes

1. Moore (1991) also finds a mixing of gang cliques in Los Angeles gangs. Short's (1990) 1960 Nobles were mainly employed in the early 1970s when they were restudied, in contrast to Vicelords, virtually all of whom had more prison experience, many of whom still identified with the Vicelords and were involved in illegal operations more than a decade after they were first studied.

2. Child protective clients, however, more than other residents, turned to police for help with problems than asking help from their relatives or neighbors.

3. In contrast, zip code 53204, a predominantly Hispanic area home to several Hispanic gangs, is dotted with community agencies, banks, merchants, and grocery stores. While this neighborhood is an area of first settlement for Mexican immigrants, it does not have the characteristics of social disorganization of the predominantly African-American 53206 neighborhoods. Those who use "percent Hispanic" as a proxy for social disorganization should take note of these findings (cf. Curry and Spergel, 1988:387).

4. There are other institutions in the area with a high profile, particularly law enforcement. But the strong police presence plays to a mixed review. While most residents (38.3%) called the police for any serious problems in the neighborhood before they called relatives or friends, one in eight (12.1%) listed police as one of the three top "bad things" about the neighborhood. Police are still viewed with suspicion and fear in African-American communities.

5. It must be remembered however, that the illegal drug economy, while disruptive, is also sustained by local demand. Workers in drug houses assert that most Milwaukee cocaine sales are to people within the neighborhood, not to outsiders (in contrast to Kornblum and Williams [1985:11]). But when illegal activities bring trouble to the neighborhood, particularly violence, police are often welcomed in ousting drug dealers and combating gang problems (Sullivan, 1989:128).

6. City hall may be as capable today of using academics against Washington for its own purposes as Washington in the sixties was adept in using academics to attack city hall (Gouldner, 1968; Piven and Cloward, 1971).

7. Recent control group evaluations have questioned these programs' effectiveness in reducing out of home placements. The main conclusion from the evaluations is the incapacity of social service bureaucracies to refer the appropriate clients to the programs. The evaluations found family preservation programs are so effective that social workers try to place families in the programs even though they do not fit project guidelines (cf. Feldman, 1990; Schuerman et al., 1990; Yuan, 1990). These evaluations also point out the important role social scientists can play in insisting programs be properly implemented.

8. This was also Suttles' conclusion: as community ties to external forces increased, so did its internal social control—it became more "provincial" (1968:223–224). Social disorganization and social control, Sullivan also points out, is not linear, but varies widely between poor neighborhoods (Sullivan, 1989:237).

9. This recommendation is not a call for revisiting the Chicago Area Project which relied on private financing and performed a "mediating role" with local institutions (Schlossman and Sedlak, 1983; Sorrentino, 1959), nor is it a call for a new war on poverty with built in antagonism between city hall and short lived federally funded agencies (Marris and Rein, 1967; Moynihan, 1969). Rather, it is a call for academics to directly engage in local struggles over how and where large public bureaucracies distribute existing resources.

References

Altshuler, Alan A. (1970). *Community Control, The Black Demand for Participation in Large American Cities.* New York: Pegasus.

Anderson, Elijah. (1990). *Streetwise: Race, Class, and Change in the Urban Community.* Chicago: University of Chicago Press.

Aponte, Robert. (1988). "Conceptualizing the underclass: An alternative perspective." Paper presented at Annual Meeting of the American Sociological Association. August. Atlanta, Georgia.

Bluestone, Barry, and Bennett Harrison. (1982). *The Deindustrialization of America: Plant Closings, Community Abandonment, and the Dismantling of Basic Industry.* New York: Basic Books.

Chubb, John E., and Terry M. Moe. (1990). *Politics, Markets, and America's Schools.* Washington, DC: The Brookings Institute.

Cloward, Richard, and Lloyd Ohlin. (1960). *Delinquency and Opportunity.* Glencoe, IL: Free Press.

Comer, James P. (1972). *Beyond Black and White.* New York: Quadrangle Books.

Curry, G. David, and Irving A. Spergel. (1988). "Gang homicide, delinquency, and community." *Criminology* 26:381–405.

Feldman, Leonard. (1990). "Evaluating the impact of family preservation services in New Jersey." Trenton, NJ: New Jersey Division of Youth and Family Services.

Figueira-McDonough, Josefina. (1991). "Community structure and delinquency: A typology." *Social Service Review* 65:68–91.

Gans, Herbert J. (1990). "The dangers of the underclass: Its harmfulness as a planning concept." Working paper 4. New York: Russell Sage Foundation.

Geis, Gilbert. (1965). *Juvenile Gangs.* Washington, DC: President's Committee on Juvenile Delinquency and Youth Crime.

Goldstein, Herman. (1977). *Policing a Free Society.* Cambridge, MA: Ballinger Publishing.

Goldstein, Paul J. (1985). "The drugs-violence nexus: A tripartite conceptual framework." *Journal of Drug Issues* 15:493–506

Gouldner, Alvin. (1968). "The sociologist as partisan: Sociology and the welfare state." *American Sociologist* (May): 103–116.

Hagedorn, John M. (1988). *People and Folks, Gangs, Crime, and the Underclass in a Rustbelt City.* Chicago: Lakeview.

———. (1989a). *Roots of Milwaukee's Underclass.* Milwaukee, WI: Milwaukee County Dept. of Health and Human Services.

———. (1989b). *Study of Youth Released from Residential Treatment, Day Treatment, and Group Homes in 1989.* Milwaukee, WI: Milwaukee County Dept. of Health and Human Services.

Huff, C. Ronald. (1989). "Youth gangs and public policy." *Crime and Delinquency* 35:524–537.

Jencks, Christopher. (1989). "Who is the underclass—and is it growing." *Focus* 12: 14–31.

Johnson, Bruce, Terry Williams, Kojo Dei, and Harry Sanabria. (1989). "Drug abuse in the inner city." In *Drugs and the Criminal Justice System,* ed., Michael Tonry and James Q. Wilson. Chicago: University of Chicago Press.

Kamerman, Sheila B., and Alfred J. Kahn. (1989). "Social services for children, youth, and families in the United States." Greenwich, CT: The Annie E. Casey Foundation.

Kasarda, John D. (1985). "Urban change and minority opportunities." In *The New Urban Reality*, ed., Paul E. Peterson, 33–65. Washington, DC: The Brookings Institution.

Kornblum, William, and Terry Williams. (1985). *Growing Up Poor.* Lexington, MA: Lexington Books.

Lindblom, Charles E. (1959). "The Science of 'Muddling Through'." *Public Administrative Review* 19:79–88.

Lipsky, Michael. (1980). *Street-Level Bureaucracies: Dilemmas of the Individual in Public Service.* New York: Russell Sage.

Marris, Peter, and Martin Rein. (1967). *Dilemmas of Social Reform, Poverty and Community Action in the United States.* Chicago: University of Chicago Press.

Massey, Douglas S., and Mitchell L. Eggers. (1990). "The ecology of inequality: Minorities and the concentration of poverty. 1970–1980." *American Journal of Sociology* 95:1153–1188.

Meyer, John M., and Brian Rowan. (1981). "Institutionalized organizations: Formal structure as myth and ceremony." In *Complex Organizations: Critical Perspectives*, ed., Mary Zey-Ferrell and Michael Aiken, 303–321. Glenview, IL: Scott, Foresman.

Miller, Walter. (1990). "Why the United States has failed to solve its youth gang problem." In *Gangs in America*, ed. C. Ronald Huff, 263–287. Beverly Hills, CA: Sage.

Mills, C. Wright. (1959). *The Sociological Imagination.* London: Oxford University Press.

Moore, Joan W. (1985). "Isolation and stigmatization in the development of an underclass. The case of Chicano gangs in East Los Angeles." *Social Problems* 33:1–10.

———. (1991). Going Down to the Barrio. Philadelphia, PA: Temple University Press.

Moore, Joan W., and Ronald Edari. (1990a). "Survey of Chips clients: Final report." Milwaukee, WI: University of Wisconsin–Milwaukee Urban Research Center.

———. (1990b). "Youth initiative needs assessment survey: Final report." Milwaukee, WI: University of Wisconsin–Milwaukee.

Moynihan, Daniel P. (1969). *Maximum Feasible Misunderstanding: Community Action in the War on Poverty.* New York: Free Press.

Nelson, Douglas. (1988). "Recognizing and realizing the potential of 'family preservation.'" Washington, DC: Center for the Study of Social Policy.

Nelson, Kristine, Miriam J. Landsman, and Wendy Deutelman. (1990). "Three Models of Family-Centered Placement Prevention Services." *Child Welfare* 69:3–21.

Perkins, Useni Eugene. (1987). *Explosion of Chicago's Black Street Gangs.* Chicago: Third World Press.

Piven, Frances Fox, and Richard A. Cloward. (1971). *Regulating the Poor: The Functions of Public Welfare.* New York: Pantheon.

———. (1987). "The contemporary relief debate." In *The Mean Season: The Attack on the Welfare State.* ed. Fred Block, Richard A. Cloward, Barbara Ehrenreich, and Frances Fox Piven, 45–108. New York: Pantheon.

Ricketts, Erol, and Ronald Mincy. (1988). "Growth of the underclass: 1970–1980."

Washington, DC: Changing Domestic Priorities Project, The Urban Institute.

Ricketts, Erol, Ronald Mincy, and Isabel V. Sawhill. (1988). "Defining and measuring the underclass." *Journal of Policy Analysis and Management*, 7:316–325.

Sampson, Robert J. (1987). "Urban black violence: The effect of male joblessness and family disruption." *American Journal of Sociology* 93:348–382.

Schlossman, Steven, and Michael Sedlak. (1983). "The Chicago Area Project revisited." Santa Monica, CA: Rand Corporation.

Schlossman, Steven L., Gail Zellman, and Richard Schavelson. (1984). *Delinquency Prevention in South Chicago*. Santa Monica, CA: Rand Corporation.

Schorr, Lisbeth. (1988). *Within Our Reach*. New York: Doubleday.

Schuerman, John R., Tina L. Pzepnicki, Julia H. Littell, and Stephen Budde. (1990). "Some intruding realities." Chicago: University of Chicago, Chapin Hall Center for Children.

Shaw, Clifford R., and Henry D. McKay. (1969). *Juvenile Delinquency and Urban Areas*. Chicago: University of Chicago Press.

Short, James F. (1990a). "Gangs, neighborhoods, and youth crime." Houston, TX: Sam Houston State University Criminal Justice Center.

————. (1990b). "New wine in old bottles? Change and continuity in American gangs." In *Gangs in America*, ed. C. Ronald Huff. 223–239. Beverly Hills, CA: Sage.

Short, James F., and Fred L. Strodtbeck. (1965). *Group Process and Gang Delinquency*. Chicago: University of Chicago Press.

Sorrentino, Anthony. (1959). "The Chicago Area Project after 25 years." *Federal Probation* 23:40–45.

Spergel, Irving A., and G. David Curry. (1990). "Strategies and perceived agency effectiveness in dealing with the youth gang problem." In *Gangs in America*, ed. C. Ronald Huff, 288–309. Beverly Hills, CA: Sage.

Stack, Carol B. (1974). *All Our Kin*. New York: Harper Torchbook.

Sullivan, Mercer L. (1989). *Getting Paid: Youth Crime and Work in the Inner City*. Ithaca, NY: Cornell University Press.

Suttles, Gerald D. (1968). *The Social Order of the Slum*. Chicago: University of Chicago Press.

Taylor, Carl. (1990). *Dangerous Society*. East Lansing: Michigan State University Press.

Thrasher, Frederick. (1927/1963). *The Gang*. Chicago: University of Chicago Press.

Trotter, Joe William. (1985). *Black Milwaukee: The Making of an Industrial Proletariat, 1915–1945*. Chicago: University of Illinois Press.

Vigil, Diego. (1988). *Barrio Gangs*. Austin: University of Texas Press.

Weick, Karl E. (1976). "Educational organizations as loosely coupled systems." *Administrative Science Quarterly* 21:1–19.

White, Sammis, John F. Zipp, Peter Reynolds, and James R. Paetsch. (1988). "The Changing Milwaukee Industrial Structure." Milwaukee: University of Wisconsin–Milwaukee. Urban Research Center.

Whyte, William Foote. (1943). *Street Corner Society*. Chicago: University of Chicago Press.

Wilson, James Q. (1990). "Can government agencies be managed?" *The Bureaucrat* 9:29–33.

Wilson, William Julius. (1985). "Cycles of deprivation and the underclass debate." *Social Service Review* 59:541–559.

_____. (1987). *The Truly Disadvantaged*. Chicago: University of Chicago Press.

_____. (1991). "Studying inner-city social dislocations: The challenge of public agenda research." *American Sociological Review* 56:1–14.

Wineman, Steven. (1984). *The Politics of Human Services*. Boston: South End Press.

Yuan, Ying-Ying T. (1990). "Evaluation of AB 1562 in-home care demonstration projects." Sacramento, CA: Walter R. McDonald and Associates.

24

The Police and Social Threat: Urban Transition, Youth Gangs, and Social Control

Pamela Irving Jackson

Introduction

During the past twenty years our understanding of the police as a social control mechanism responding to threats to the established order has sprouted and taken root. Social threats, other than crime, have been conceptualized in terms of the presence of threatening populations (measured as minority group size), the occurrence of threatening events (such as riots and non-violent civil disturbances), the degree of contact between heterogeneous populations (greater where there is less residential segregation), and the level of income inequality (reflected in the Gini index or the ratio of black to white median income) (cf. Jacobs, 1979; Liska, Lawrence, and Benson, 1981; Jackson, 1989).

There is reason to expect that two contemporary characteristics of U.S. cities, socioeconomic decline and youth gangs, both apparent early in the 1980s, are similarly viewed as threatening to the social order and that they contribute to municipal fiscal commitment to policing. In the mid-1970s and early 1980s, population losses and decreases in labor market opportunities in manufacturing and wholesale trades disrupted cities' social and economic foundations. They were inescapable manifestations of the nation's transition from a manufacturing to a service based economy. Consequent high levels of unemployment and poverty, coupled with the visibility of low income urban minority populations (cf. Kasarda, 1985) were viewed as harbingers of change for the worse in U.S. cities.

Such visible reminders of the demise of the city center could well spark support for law enforcement efforts to maintain order. Formal social control

Reprinted with permission from *Policing and Society*, Vol. 2 (1992): 193–204. © 1992 Harwood Academic Publishers.

mechanisms become most important during times of transition, when informal normative structures and processes erode. As police chief Anthony Bouza (1990: 20) notes in his recent book, *The Police Mystique*, there is tremendous pressure on police to keep " 'street conditions' under wraps;'' to control conditions that "communicate a distressing sense of decline . . . troubling to citizens.''

While the criminogenic influence of the urban transition and decline consequent to postindustrial economic change has received serious scrutiny in recent research, still relatively unexplored is the impact of these conditions on public fiscal commitment to policing, after the effect of crime on police resources is taken into consideration. This paper begins that exploration. It is expected that even after controls for municipal crime rates and other related community characteristics, urban socioeconomic decline will influence municipal expenditures for policing. When urban residents feel threatened by the changing economic and demographic circumstances around them, they may provide greater fiscal support for the police in a misguided attempt to restore the stability of the past.

As a recent U.S. Department of Justice Bulletin (Bryant, 1989: 1) indicates, fear that another urban problem, youth gangs, is out of control has led to intensive law enforcement and prosecution efforts. Bouza (1990: 235) points out that public fear of gangs provides "another invitation to roust black kids without examining the conditions of their lives.'' The Justice Department Bulletin cites testimony by Frank Radke of the Chicago Police Department to a national conference on youth gangs indicating that "we are arresting more gang members than ever before; we are getting more convictions than ever before; and we are getting longer sentences than ever before. But ironically, we have more gangs than ever before. Arrest and prosecution are not the deterrent that we expected them to be.'' The message of the bulletin is in its title which states that a "Communitywide Response [is] Crucial for Dealing With Youth Gangs.'' Nonetheless, it is clear that a "preoccupation with delinquency control, rather than its prevention'' (Short, 1990: 1) has characterized this period of urban change. As a result, it is likely that perceived youth gang problems have an independent impact on municipal appropriations for policing, even after the crime rate is taken into consideration.

Method and Hypotheses

Population and Data

This study of the impact of urban transition on public fiscal commitment to policing is based on a multivariate analysis of quantitative data from all U.S. cities of 25,000 or more in 1970 and 1980. Additional analyses of the impact of perceived youth gang problems on police expenditures were conducted in a subset of these cities. The U.S. Census of Population (1970, 1980), the Uniform Crime Report (Federal Bureau of Investigation, 1980), the Law Enforcement Assistance Administration (1978, 1981), and the 1981 National Juvenile Assessment Center survey regarding youth gangs (Needle and Stapleton, 1983) were the sources of data.

Urban Socioeconomic Decline

Population decline in large urban centers in the 1970s heralded economic deterioration, as employment opportunities in manufacturing and wholesale operations moved to less densely settled sunbelt locations and to less developed nations. Urban centers have increasingly been left to unskilled minority individuals as better educated members of the work force have relocated to improve their employment and living conditions.

Several authors have elaborated on the extent to which informal social controls erode in the face of such population turnover. Taylor and Covington (1988: 533) quote McKenzie (1968 [1921]: 62) in citing the "striking instability of local life" under conditions of high mobility. Bursik (1988: 521, 527) refers to the work of Kornhauser (1978), Berry and Kasarda (1977), and Greenberg with others (1982a, 1982b, 1985) in describing several consequences of population turnover that together undermine the effectiveness of informal social controls in maintaining order and stability: deterioration of "institutions pertaining to internal control," reduction in the "development of primary relationships," erosion of informal surveillance and direct intervention. The focus of this paper is on the extent to which socioeconomic transitions known to destabilize the social order of city life also predict municipal commitment to the formal social control represented by policing even after their effect on the crime rate has been taken into account.

Percent city population change (1970–80), and percent of city residents born in the state where they are now residing (1980) are included in the analysis as measures of short and long term demographic change. Such measures have been viewed by others as a reflection of "a declining city syndrome" (Clark, 1985: 254; Muller, 1975; and Peterson, 1976) and of "urban distress" (Clark, 1985: 259; Nathan and Dommel, 1977). The percent change in civilian labor force opportunities in manufacturing between 1970 and 1980, and in wholesale and retail trades 1970–1980, also included in the analysis, represent economic instability.

The loss of such employment opportunities for unskilled laborers in central cities as a result of the national economic shift toward a service based economy requiring technologically sophisticated training for many new positions have created a mismatch between the skill levels of employees and the positions available in urban centers. (In fact, recent evidence indicates that growth in jobs with low educational requirements has been limited to the suburbs and exurbs [cf. Kasarda, 1985].) It is expected that in cities with the largest declines in population and in opportunities for unskilled labor, the level of fiscal support for policing will be greater even after the influence of these factors on the crime rate and the influence of other known determinants of municipal police expenditures have been controlled. This hypothesis will be investigated for all cities of 25,000 or more.

Reported Youth Gangs

Youth gangs represent another threat to urban dwellers. In a summary of their recent examination of youth gang program effectiveness in forty-five cities, Spergel and Curry (1990: 299–300) note that suppression (arrest, incarceration, and supervision) is the most common primary strategy in response to the problem of youth gangs, while provision of opportunities (jobs, job training, and education) is the least frequently chosen tactic. Although they later indicate that "in cities or areas with chronic youth gang problems, agencies perceive there is a significant reduction in the problem mainly when the primary response strategy is the provision of social opportunities" (Spergel and Curry, 1990: 306), a law enforcement response is most often invoked when citizens feel threatened by youth gangs. Police chief Bouza (1990: 234–235) corroborates this proposition, pointing out that "summer jobs, dropout programs, recreational centers, and other costly projects" are generally avoided as solutions to youth problems in favor of the "action" inherent to a law enforcement response.

To test the impact of the youth gang threat on collective fiscal support for policing, the National Juvenile Justice Assessment Center's data (Needle and Stapleton, 1983) on the existence of youth gangs in a random, representative sample of sixty U.S. cities of 100,000 or more is used. These cities constitute a subset of the larger population of cities on which this study is based. In each of the sixty cities police department gang control and youth personnel were interviewed concerning the existence, size, and activity of street gangs. On the basis of this information Center staff classified the magnitude of the gang problem as minor, moderate, or major (Needle and Stapleton, 1981: 20). This three-point index of reported youth gang activity is included in the present investigation. Using the sixty cities for which data are available, a multivariate analysis of the influence of the perceived gang problem on the proportion of city government expenditures spent on policing will be conducted controlling for other recognized determinants of police allocations.

Other City Characteristics

Since crime fighting, traffic control, and emergency service calls are major police activities, several structural and budgetary characteristics of cities contribute to per capita levels of police spending. Many of these variables can also be expected to be related to the measures of demographic and economic decline, requiring the use of ordinary least squares regression to develop a multivariate model.

City revenue per capita (1980) is included in the model as a measure of a community's fiscal ability to pay for policing. The total index crime rate per capita (1980) (FBI), a measure of the level of the direct contact predatory crime (Cohen and Felson, 1979) that most occupies police crime fighting attention, represents to some degree the need for policing. Percent poor is also included as an indicator of a city's fiscal situation, but could, in addition, be expected to increase the demand for policing since the poor are more likely than others to rely on the police for the provision of emergency services. City population size and density influence the need for policing through their effects on traffic control problems and service related demands. Percent unemployed and the ratio of black to white median income have recently been included as police resource determinants because it is expected that unemployment and inequality make people more difficult to control by loosening the conventional bonds circumscribing individuals' behavior and by undermining the legitimacy of the established order (cf. Jacobs, 1979, 1982). Percent black is included directly, as is percent Hispanic since they have been found to influence the level of policing resources, even after the crime rate and other community characteristics are controlled (Jackson and Carroll, 1981; Jackson, 1985).

As suggested above, the indicators of demographic and economic decline included in the model may be related to the relative size of the black and Hispanic populations in a city, as well as to city revenue per capita, interracial inequality, population size, density, and the level of poverty. Use of the multivariate model will permit determination of the extent to which any observed impact of socioeconomic decline on police spending levels is spurious.

Dependent Variables

In assessing the impact on public fiscal commitment to policing of the 1970s decade of transition in urban centers and of the early 1980s youth gang threat, two measures of police expenditures in U.S. cities are used: per capita police expenditures, and police expenditures as a proportion of total city government expenditures in 1981. The per capita total police expenditures indicator is used in determining the influence of demographic and economic decline on the level of municipal commitment to social control. The measure has been deployed many times before as an indicator of public fiscal commitment to policing (cf. Jackson, 1989). Since youth gang threat, to be studied in the sixty city subsample, is a phenomenon with newspaper headline potential, its influence on the proportion of total city government expenditures allocated to policing is investigated.

Results

Bivariate associations between variables included in the analysis (in table 24.1) indicate little cause for concern about problems associated with multicolinearity. The independent variables are not highly intercorrelated, but do appear to be related to police expenditures. Cities with a lower percentage of population born in the state, population decline between 1970–1980, and decline in the proportion of wholesale and retail positions have greater per capita police expenditures. Control variables in the analysis, including indicators of racial composition, unemployment, and population size and density are significantly related to both per capita police expenditures and to one of the measures of urban decline. Other control variables, such as interracial income inequality help to specify the model as direct or indirect influences on police expenditures.

For the sixty city subsample to be used in the investigation of the youth gang threat, it is evident that the measure of a perceived gang problem has a positive bivariate association with the proportion of city government expenditures allocated to policing in 1981 ($r = .29$), and with several other city characteristics. The multivariate results below help to determine whether or not the associations of the police appropriations measures with socioeconomic decline and youth gang problems are spurious.

The ordinary least squares regression results (in table 24.2) provide further support for the hypothesis that urban decline fosters greater public fiscal support for policing, even after controls for the municipal crime rate. As expected city revenue per capita and the overall crime rate have the greatest impact on end of the decade municipal police expenditures, with population density and the negative impact of percent poor next in importance. Following them in order of statistically significant explanatory impact on total police expenditures per capita are decline in wholesale/retail positions, percent black, percent unemployed, lower proportions of city residents born in the state, and decline in the number of manufacturing positions in the city. This model including sociodemographic change and decline during the 1970s explains over 50 percent of the variance in per capita police expenditures at the end of the decade.

Decline in wholesale, retail and manufacturing positions, as well as long-term population transition (reflected in low proportions of city residents born in the state in which they are now residing), may disorganize communities to the point where informal mechanisms of social control no longer seem sufficient to maintain order. Despite the fact that their impact on the crime rate has been controlled in the multivariate equations, these indicators of demographic transition and economic decline exert a significant positive influence on collective fiscal commitment to the formal social control that police provide.

In the subsample for which the youth gang data are available, the significant bivariate association between reported gang presence and the proportion of city government spending devoted to policing holds in the multivariate

Table 24.1 Zero Order Correlation Matrix with Means and Standard Deviations (All cities ≥ 25,000, N = 563) (Pearson's r)

	(1)	(2)	(3)	(4)	(5)	(6)	(7)	(8)	(9)	(10)	(11)	(12)	(13)	(14)	(15)	X	S.D.
1. Police Expenditures Per Capita	—	.33^c	.35^c	.00	.21^c	-.20^c	-.19^c	.22^c	.23^c	-.06	-.27^c	-.06	.49^c	.50^c	.29^c	45.3	21.5
2. Percent Black		—	.13^b	-.17^c	.41^c	-.11^b	-.23^b	.12^b	.69^c	-.28^c	-.20^c	-.06	.43^c	.21^c	-.24^c	15.5	17.0
3. Density			—	.26^c	.13^b	-.16^c	-.23^c	.28^c	.17^c	.11^b	-.15^c	-.13^b	.05	.21^c	.14^c	4271.5	3488.9
4. Percent Hispanic				—	-.04	-.35^c	.23^c	.08	.20^c	.21^c	-.07	.25^c	.07	-.14^c	.46^c	8.2	13.3
5. Percent Unemployed					—	.24^c	-.30^c	.05	.57^c	-.03	.09	-.28^c	.22^c	.10^a	-.04	7.0	3.0
6. Residents Born in State						—	-.37	-.06	.14^c	-.04	.11^b	-.28^c	-.25^c	.01	-.36^c	60.4	16.0
7. Percent Population Change							—	-.03	-.18^c	.07	.04	.22^c	-.06	-.21^c	.13^b	6.8	21.8
8. Population Size								—	.13^b	-.08	-.06	.00	.10	.32^c	-.26^c	131.7	370.5
9. Percent Poor									—	-.25^c	-.12^b	.03	.44^c	.19^c	-.02	10.4	5.4
10. Black/White Income										—	-.04	-.07	-.23^c	-.11^b	.01	.7	.2
11. Wholesale/Retail Change											—	-.29^c	-.17^c	-.16^c	-.02	-.1	2.2
12. Manufacturing Change												—	.12^b	-.03	.31^c	-2.7	4.0
13. Index Crime Rate													—	.26^c	-.05	79.9	27.7
14. City Revenues Per Capita														—	.08^a	528.8	316.4
15. Perceived Gang Problem^{d,e}															—	.9	1.1

a. p < .05
b. p < .01
c. p < .001
d. Perceived Gang Problem correlations based on 52 cases.
e. Police Expenditures as a Percent of City Government Expenditures used in Gang Presence/Police Expenditures Correlation.

Table 24.2   Regression Equation for Per Capita Police Expenditures on 1970–80
Transition and Other Social Characteristics of Cities (All Cities
$\geq 25,000$, N = 563) (Standardized Regression Coefficients)

Constant	14.665
City Revenues Per Capita	.336^c
Residents Born in State	−.137^c
Black/White Income	.015
Wholesale/Retail Change	−.148^c
Percent Unemployed	.139^c
Population Size	.015
Density	.196^c
Percent Hispanic	.005
Index Crime Rate	.333^c
Manufacturing Change	−.086^b
Percent Population Change	−.040
Percent Black	.145^c
Percent Poor	−.191^c
R^2	.51^c

a. p (for one-tailed test) < .05
b. p < .01
c. p < .001

regression equation despite controls for other variables expected to influence
the impact of gangs on policing, including the crime rate, racial and ethnic
heterogeneity, per capita city revenues, percent poor and inequality. Per capita
city revenues and percent poor both have a negative statistically significant
impact on the percent of city revenues devoted to policing. After them, the
positive significant impact of reported youth gang presence follows that of
percent black and the crime rate in order of explanatory importance. Overall,
this model including perceived youth gang problems explains 51 percent of
the variance in the relative size of the 1981 budgetary law enforcement commitment for the subsample where the data on gangs is available.

Implications

These results have implications for three areas of concern: (1) the role of the
police in responding to perceived societal threats; (2) the capacity of postindustrial societies to respond to urban dislocations triggered by the economic shift
from a manufacturing to a service based economy; and (3) the effectiveness
of the municipal response to youth gang problems.

Police and Social Threat

The fact that demographic and economic transition in cities influences public
fiscal commitment to policing independently of its effect on crime and other

454

relevant city characteristics underscores once again the public's reliance on police to stem change. This is a source of great concern, since police are not trained, equipped, or staffed sufficiently to successfully resolve or confront these strains. City governments had just begun to recognize this when the threats inherent to urban decline became apparent.

With the racially turbulent 1960s behind them, municipal police departments in the United States had set aside by the late 1970s their riot preparations and demonstration control strategies. In response to public demand they had begun to redefine themselves as community relations officers. Overnight, it seemed, police administrators sought to transform the force and its image. They moved away from the "tough" cop model described by Mayor Rizzo in his pre-election loss assertion that the Philadelphia Police Department could "invade Cuba and win" (*Evening Bulletin*, Aug. 14, 1979), favoring instead the "community relations officer" described by newly appointed Philadelphia Police Commissioner Solomon in his promise to start "building up a mutual respect between the people of Philadelphia and the police department" (*Philadelphia Inquirer*, Jan. 13, 1980) (cf. Jackson, 1989: 77, 118).

Times had changed. A decade of civil rights demands initially backed by the White House, and the increasingly minority composition of U.S. cities helped: (1) to usher out those members of the old guard who condoned police brutality as a regrettable, but necessary evil; (2) to rein in police use of deadly force; and (3) to diversify the police force, in terms of race, ethnicity, gender, and sexual preference. New demands for police accountability and responsiveness emerged, as did recognition of "their problems with the minorities

Table 24.3 Regression Equation for Police Expenditures as a Percent of City Government Expenditures on Perceived Gang Problem (1981) and Other Social Characteristics of Cities (N = 52) (Standardized Regression Coefficients)

Constant	12.449
Perceived Gang Problem	.212[a]
Black/White Income	.024
Index Crime Rate	.254[b]
Density	.206
Percent Black	.715[c]
Percent Hispanic	.226
Population Size	.220
City Revenue Per Capita	−.789[c]
Percent Poor	−.713[c]
R^2	.51[c]

a. p (for one-tailed test) $< .05$
b. $p < .01$
c. $p < .001$

they've been sent to police and their resentment toward an overclass that has issued the *sub rosa* marching orders" (Bouza, 1990: 6).

Unstated pressure to control the underclass has been recognized as dangerous, encouraging excessive and illegal behaviors. Police cannot solve the current problems of urban decline any more than they could resolve the riots and disturbances of the 1960s. Yet the results of this study indicate that the transitions associated with such decline trigger public fiscal commitment to policing.

Responding to Urban Dislocations

In a recent National Institute of Justice document, Williams and Murphy (1990: 12) point out the Commission on the Cities' finding that after a brief period of improvement, the conditions that led to the deterioration of ghetto communities are actually getting worse. " 'Quiet riots,' the report concludes, are occurring in America's central cities: unemployment, poverty, social disorganization, segregation, housing and school deterioration, and crime are worse now than ever. . . ."

Wilson (1987) has also drawn attention to these conditions, suggesting their link to rising violent crime rates, increasing rates of out-of-wedlock births, and greater reliance on welfare in inner city communities. Citing the problems of black male joblessness, Wilson addresses the need for a full employment policy combined with a federally sponsored job training program geared toward retooling unskilled labor sufficiently to create a flexible workforce for a postindustrial economy.

Police chief Bouza (1990: 22), however, reminds those who argue for such policy solutions to these problems that "citizens want the cop back on the beat;" they want "action now." "The frightened and impatient citizen's eyes glaze over with frustration and ill-concealed hostility," he explains, "at the mention of cultural, social, or especially, economic forces channeling the underclass into lives of crime. . . . Long-term strategies for the prevention of crime are lost in a desire for the prompt removal of undesirables."

Research has shown that within the currently feasible range of police resource levels cities cannot control their crime problem through law enforcement (cf. Greenberg et al., 1983; Loftin and McDowall, 1982). Certainly police have an indispensable role in managing and processing those involved in crime, and in helping citizens to deal with its aftermath. However, their efforts in detecting and preventing crime simply cannot stem its tide. As we have known for almost half a decade, the causes of crime are considerably beyond the effectiveness of detection and prevention. Public reliance on policing to resolve the consequences of demographic change and economic decline in urban areas may prevent both inquiry into and implementation of more effective strategies for responding to the urban dislocations of postindustrial economic growth.

Municipal Response to Youth Gang Problems

In assessing "why the U.S. has failed to solve its youth gang problem," Miller (1990) cites lack of a coordinated national policy as a chief determinant, fueled by "a pervasive reluctance to face squarely the issue of the social context of gang crime" (Miller, 1990: 277). However, Miller (1990: 281) goes on to label as "misdirected, inefficient, and uneconomical," the position that "the totality of lower-class life must be changed to affect gangs. However desirable such change might be. . . ." He cites instead the need for "carefully targeted programs with specific objectives" and argues for further investigation of the effectiveness of specific programs along the lines of recent work by Spergel, Curry, Ross, and Chance (1989).

Sullivan's (1990) new study of Brooklyn gangs leads him, as Short (1990b: 666) points out, to argue that improvement of social control and enhancement of economic opportunity be seen as complementary, rather than alternative and opposed strategies for reducing youth crime. Another key element in Sullivan's perspective is that involvement of the poor in increasing community safety will have important effects on disadvantaged communities as well as on the individuals within them. Short (1990: 667) goes on to support this argument, noting that youth gangs "are more likely to be a factor in the reproduction of the underclass . . . when they become institutionalized in local communities. . . ."

While work by Miller (1990), Short (1990b), Sullivan (1990), and Moore (1988) suggests the importance of law enforcement in preventing gang "owner-ship" of communities, these recent investigations also indicate that in the long term, resolution of conditions fostering gang development is critical in reducing the significance of youth gang problems in cities. Law enforcement in and of itself is insufficient "when young people cannot find good jobs in conventional society . . ." (Short, 1990b: 667).

Since the research presented in this paper suggests that municipal fiscal commitment to policing is greater in cities where youth gang problems are perceived, the centrality of police in the societal response to this issue cannot be ignored. In light of the public's reliance on the police as a first line of defense against gangs, integration of police sponsored gang control efforts with opportunity building and community empowerment strategies may be the most fruitful approach to long term repair of those community conditions that foster youth gangs.

Summary and Conclusions

Two central conclusions can be drawn from the data analysis in this study. The first involves the impact of demographic and economic decline on municipal support for policing. The results indicate that sociodemographic change and decline in U.S. urban centers in the 1970s contributed to municipal fiscal commitment to policing even after the city's crime rate, financial, and demographic characteristics are statistically controlled. Decline in wholesale/retail and manufacturing positions in the city from 1970–80 and long term population transition increase the collective financial commitment to the municipal police effort.

The second conclusion of the analysis has to do with the influence of recognized youth gangs on the level of the urban police effort. The magnitude of a city's youth gang problems as perceived by knowledgeable sources is related to the level of its public investment in policing. Cities with youth gang problems spend more per capita on policing.

Overall, these results suggest that transition and decline in the demographic and economic base of urban centers, as well as the specter of youth gangs trigger funding for formal social control in the form of municipal police even when the crime rate, revenues and other city characteristics are held constant. Police are called upon to manage the social threats that rise from the ashes of urban decay. They are also the first to discern the gap between management and amelioration of such problems (cf. Bouza, 1990).

Recognition of the extent to which police efforts are city residents' first line of defense against the threats of urban decline will facilitate a more accurate assessment of the resources, training, and public support necessary to permit police and police related agencies to help lay the groundwork necessary to rebuild the city's infrastructure. It may be that successful strategies of urban revitalization can be constructed on an integrated set of social control, economic growth, and opportunity enhancement initiatives.

References

Berry, Brian J.L. and John D. Kasarda. (1977). *Contemporary Urban Ecology.* New York: Macmillan.

Bouza, Anthony V. (1990). *The Police Mystique.* New York: Plenum.

Bryant, Dan. (1989). *Communitywide Responses Crucial for Dealing with Youth Gangs.* Washington, DC: U.S. Dept. of Justice, Juvenile Justice Bulletin.

Bursik, Robert J., Jr. (1988). "Social Disorganization and Theories of Crime and Delinquency: Problems and Prospects." *Criminology* 26 (4): 519–551.

Clark, Terry Nichols. (1985). "Fiscal Strain: How Different Are Snow Belt and Sun Belt Cities?" Pp. 253–280 in *The New Urban Reality*, ed. P.E. Peterson. Washington, DC: Brookings.

Cohen, Lawrence E. and Marcus Felson. (1979). "Social Change and Crime Rate Trends." *American Sociological Review* 44: 533–607.

Evening Bulletin (Philadelphia). (1979). "Mayor is Eager to Battle Charges." Aug. 14.

Federal Bureau of Investigation. (1980). *Annual Report of the Federal Bureau of Investigation.* Washington, DC: U.S. Government Printing Office.

Greenberg, David F., Ronald C. Kessler, and Colin Loftin. (1983). "The Effect of Police Employment on Crime." *Criminology* 21 (3): 375–394.

Greenberg, Stephanie, William M. Rohe, and Jay R. Williams. (1982a). "The Relationship Between Informal Social Control, Neighborhood Crime and Fear: A Synthesis and Assessment of the Research." Paper presented at the annual meetings of the American Society of Criminology, Toronto.

————. (1982b). "Safe and Secure Neighborhoods: Physical Characteristics and Informal Territorial Control." In *High and Low Crime Neighborhoods.* Washington, DC: National Institute of Justice.

————. (1985). *Informal Citizen Action and Crime Prevention at the Neighborhood Level.* Washington, DC: National Institute of Justice.

Jacobs, David. (1979). "Inequality and Police Strength: Conflict Theory and Coercive Control in Metropolitan Areas." *American Sociological Review* 44: 913–925.

————. (1982). "Inequality and Economic Crime." *Sociology and Social Research* 66: 12–28.

Jackson, Pamela Irving. (1989). *Minority Group Threat, Crime, and Policing.* New York: Praegar.

————. (1985). "Ethnicity, Region, and Public Fiscal Commitment to Policing." *Justice Quarterly* 2 (2): 167–194.

Jackson, Pamela Irving and Leo Carroll. (1981). "Race and the War on Crime: The Sociopolitical Determinants of Municipal Expenditures in 90 U.S. Cities." *American Sociological Review* 46: 290–305.

Kasarda, John D. (1985). "Urban Change and Minority Opportunities." Pp. 33–68 in P.E. Peterson (ed.), *The New Urban Reality.* Washington, DC: Brookings.

Kornhauser, Ruth R. (1978). *Social Sources of Delinquency.* Chicago: University of Chicago Press.

Law Enforcement Assistance Administration. (1978). *Expenditures and Employment Data for the Criminal Justice System.* Washington, DC: U.S. Government Printing Office.

Liska, Allen E., Joseph J. Lawrence, and Michael Benson. (1981). "Perspectives on the Legal Order: The Capacity for Social Control." *American Journal of Sociology* 87: 413–426.

Loftin, Colin and David McDowell. (1982). "The Police, Crime, and Economic Theory: An Assessment." *American Sociological Review* 47:393–401.

Mackenzie, Roderick D. (1968). "The Neighborhood." (1921). In A. H. Hawley (ed.), *Roderick D. McKenzie on Human Ecology.* Chicago: University of Chicago Press.

Miller, Walter B. (1990). "Why the United States Has Failed to Solve Its Youth Gang Problem." Pp. 263–287 in C. Ronald Huff (ed.), *Gangs in America.* Newbury Park, CA: Sage.

Moore, Joan. (1988). "Gangs and the Underclass: A Comparative Perspective." Pp. 3–17. In John M. Hagedorn, *People and Folks: Gangs, Crime and the Underclass in a Rustbelt City.* Chicago: Lake View Press.

Muller, Thomas. (1975). *Growing and Declining Urban Areas: A Fiscal Comparison.* Washington, DC: Urban Institute.

Nathan, Richard P. and Paul R. Dommel. (1977). "The Cities." Pp. 283–316 in Joseph A. Peckman (ed.), *Setting National Priorities: The 1978 Budget.* Washington, DC: Brookings.

Needle, Jerome A. and Wm. Vaughn Stapleton. (1983). *Report of the National Juvenile Justice Assessment Centers: Police Handling of Youth Gangs.* Washington, DC: U.S. Dept. Of Justice.

Peterson, George E. (1976). "Finance." Pp. 35–118 in William Gorham and Nathan Glazer (eds.), *The Urban Predicament.* Washington, DC: Urban Institute.

Philadelphia Inquirer. (1980). "At the Police Department: A New Broom Sweeps Fast." Jan. 13.

Short, James F. (1990a). "Gangs, Neighborhoods, and Youth Crime." *Criminal Justice Research Bulletin,* 5 (4).

_____. (1990b). "Cities, Gangs, and Delinquency." *Sociological Forum* 5 (4): 657–688.

Spergel, Irving A. and G. David Curry. (1990). "Strategies and Perceived Agency Effectiveness in Dealing with the Youth Gang Problem." Pp. 288–309 in C. Ronald Huff (ed.), *Gangs in America.* Newbury Park, CA: Sage.

Spergel, Irving A., G. David Curry, R.A. Ross, and R. Chance. (1989). *Survey of Youth Gang Problems and Programs in 45 Cities and 6 Sites.* (Technical Report No. 2, National Youth Gang Suppression and Intervention Project). Chicago: University of Chicago, School of Social Service Administration.

Sullivan, Mercer L. (1990). "Getting Paid": *Youth Crime and Work in the Inner City.* Ithaca, NY: Cornell University Press.

Taylor, Ralph B. and Jeanette Covington. (1988). "Neighborhood Changes in Ecology and Violence." *Criminology* 26 (4): 553–589.

U.S. Bureau of the Census. (1970). *Characteristics of the Population, 1980.* Washington, DC: U.S. Government Printing Office.

Williams, Hubert and Patrick V. Murphy. (1990). "The Evolving Strategy of Police: A Minority View." *Perspectives on Policing* 13 (January).

Wilson, William Julius. (1987). *The Truly Disadvantaged: The Inner City, the Underclass, and Public Policy.* Chicago: University of Chicago Press.

25

Street Gangs and Preventive Interventions

David W. Thompson and Leonard A. Jason

The problem of youth street gangs in urban areas is both a long-standing and costly one. In addition to the direct costs to individual victims resulting from assaults, property damage, and robberies, the community as a whole pays significantly for gang-related law enforcement, trials, and other judicial proceedings, as well as for gang offenders' imprisonment and rehabilitation. For example, Adams (1967) reported that the correctional costs alone for a hundred gang members followed for a six-year period reached $658,435.00 (based on 1963 costs). No one can place a dollar amount on the loss of life and the physical and emotional suffering experienced by gang members and their victims alike, or on the loss to society of gang members' potential skills and contributions. In addition to the gang-affiliated victims, many uninvolved persons are victimized by gang activities simply by coincidence. Recent news reports of murders due to mistaken identities or gang affiliations are salient reminders of this fact.

Because of methodological difficulties, an accurate estimate of the magnitude of the gang problem is difficult to obtain. Concerns, however, are growing. Chicago, for example, has experienced a significant increase in the number of youth gangs since the mid-1970s (Chicago Crime Commission, 1983). The Chicago Police Department (1983) recently reported the existence of at least 110 gangs, ranging in size from ten to more than four thousand members, in Chicago. These gangs actively recruit new members, some as young as seven or eight years old. Public schools are prime targets for gang recruitment. A 1981 survey of Chicago public schools (Clark, 1981) reported that nearly 40,000 school children had been attacked or threatened at some time by gang members, and instances abound of youngsters afraid to attend classes because of the presence of gang recruiters. Therefore, interventions

Reprinted by permission of Sage Publications, Inc. from *Criminal Justice and Behavior*, Vol. 15, No. 3 (September 1988): 323–333. © 1988 American Association for Correctional Psychology.

aimed at preventing youth street gang membership might well be based in the public schools.

There are a variety of theoretical formulations of gang behavior, but no single theory has achieved general acceptance (Thompson, 1986). The most well-known theories include opportunity theory (Cloward and Ohlin, 1960) and subcultural theory (e.g., Cohen, 1955). The former postulates that youths turn to gang behavior because of frustration in obtaining goals through conventional channels, while the latter theory asserts that the youths' behavior is not deviant within their subculture. Weis and Hawkins (1981) offered a model of delinquency which is relevant to the prevention of gang membership. Their dynamic multivariate model suggests that the different "causes" of delinquency (including street gang membership) have different effects at different points in a youngster's life. They further suggest that prevention attempts must provide opportunities for involvement in conventional activities, interaction with conventional others, and the application of requisite skills that make the involvement and interaction rewarding (Weis and Hawkins, 1981). In other words, prevention programs must teach requisite social and educational skills when they are absent and then facilitate their use and subsequent reinforcement in an appropriate manner. Despite the fact that this social development theory is relatively young, research evidence exists both for and against it (e.g., Roff and Wirt, 1984; Suzuki, Nishimura, and Takahashi, 1982).

A review of the theoretical and research literature concerning gang behavior suggests that the current paucity of knowledge in this area stems in large part from methodological difficulties inherent in investigating gangs. It is clear that gang behavior is more complex than previously postulated. The formulation of more complex (e.g., multivariate) models of gang behavior requires experimental designs and data collection techniques significantly more sophisticated than those reflected by the current literature. For example, no reliable method of determining gang membership has been published, with most researchers depending on either self-report data or police department records, which have been found (Klein, 1971) to be seriously inaccurate. Determining the relationship between delinquent activities and gang behavior is difficult, as youth often deny gang membership, leaving police officers to classify offenses as gang-related or not using only their best judgment. Finally, accurate data collection demands interaction with dangerous and violent gang members who rarely cooperate with researchers.

A variety of interventions have targeted youth street gangs and gang membership (see Klein, 1971, for a comprehensive review). The majority employ street workers (also referred to as "detached workers") and are grounded in the belief that, since gang members do not respond well to in-house agency programs, to be effective the programs must be taken to the youth (Klein, 1971). Most of these programs devote little, if any, attention to evaluating their effectiveness. Methodologically adequate evaluations are sorely lacking, and when the methodology is adequate they often conclude that the popular detached worker programs are ineffective and even counterproductive (e.g., Klein, 1969).

The most promising interventions to date, such as Klein's (1966) Lincoln Heights project, seem to be those that assist youth in developing more appropriate social relationships and engaging in alternatives to delinquent behavior. Consistent with community psychology principles, a preventive intervention that enables youth who are at risk of joining gangs to channel their energies into more productive activities instead is to be preferred over an intervention that works with established gang members. The costs of an effective prevention program are likely to be substantially lower than the direct and indirect costs of crime, rehabilitation, and corrections. Moreover, it appears that preventing new members is a highly effective strategy for eliminating gangs altogether (Klein, 1971).

The current article reports the results of such a preventive intervention, BUILD (Broader Urban Involvement and Leadership Development), which was based on social development theory. Currently, BUILD is the only non-profit agency in the Chicago area focusing entirely on the problem of youth street gangs. The agency's service mission is to involve and assist a specific group of young people to become productive individuals. It attempts to accomplish this goal by channeling individual gang members' talents and leadership abilities into more productive and socially acceptable activities. BUILD currently works with 29 youth gangs on Chicago's North Side (about 25 percent of the identified youth gangs in the city) and includes two components: (a) prevention, which focuses on identifying youth most likely to become involved with youth street gangs and involving them in alternative activities designed to divert them from gang membership, and (b) remediation, a detached-worker program that targets identified members of the twenty-nine street gangs within BUILD's service area.

To date, no objective evaluation of BUILD's prevention programs has been reported. The present study serves as an example of how a gang prevention program can be evaluated from a community psychology perspective.

Method

Intervention Sites

BUILD staff and the authors identified public grade schools in the neighborhoods served by BUILD, as well as the names of the gangs who generally recruited new members from each particular school. Pairs of schools in which the same gang was known to be conducting recruiting activities were subsequently identified; one school in each pair was selected by BUILD staff to serve as an experimental school and the other as a control school. (This selection was made on the basis of BUILD's experience with the individual schools and on the perceived receptivity of each school principal both to the intervention and to program evaluation efforts. Unfortunately, random assignment of schools to conditions was not possible.) Permission was received to conduct the evaluation project within each superintendent's district. School principals were then contacted, the program explained to them, and permission requested to conduct the evaluation according to the procedure described below. Data from youth attending a total of six schools (three experimental and three control) were included in the final analyses. These schools represented a cross section of the neighborhoods served by BUILD.

Subjects

The subjects were 117 eighth graders (seventy male, forty-five female, two unidentified). The children's schools were in lower and lower-middle class neighborhoods, and the children met the following criteria: (a) Each participant attended one of the public schools included in the project. (b) Gang informants reported that the youngster was not a member of the gang. (BU I LD's remediation program employs street workers who maintain close contact with the various street gangs. By these means, BUILD compiles and continuously updates confidential membership rosters of the gangs. Prior to the intervention, the names of the targeted youth were checked against these rosters to ensure that they were not gang members.) (c) The youngster was identified as being at risk for gang membership on the basis of subjective teacher report and by the determination of BUILD staff members. Although attempts by the researchers to quantify these ratings were not successful, reports by teachers and staff indicated that they based their judgments on the extent to which youth associated with known gang members, the manner in which they dressed, and on personal knowledge of the youngsters' private lives.

Procedure

Targeted youth in the three experimental schools participated with the rest of their classes in a series of twelve classroom sessions conducted by BUILD staff over twelve weeks as part of a regularly scheduled series of presentations in the school. These sessions were designed to inform them about the dangers and consequences associated with street gang membership and to assist them in developing alternative strategies to gang involvement.

Classroom Sessions. The initial classroom session involved an introduction to BUILD and an explanation of the prevention curriculum. The second session focused on the definition of a gang, why gangs exist, and the enumeration of gang characteristics. In the third classroom session, a guest speaker

464

from BUILD's remediation program addressed the issues of gang recruitment, peer pressure and how to resist it, and persons to whom a student could talk if attempts were made to recruit him or her.

The fourth classroom session consisted of "It's Too Late for Me," a movie portraying the experiences of a youngster who becomes involved in gangs and focusing on the consequences for the youth of this involvement. The following session involved a structured discussion of the film. The sixth session featured a guest speaker from the Cook County State's Attorney's office, who spoke on gang violence and presented case histories and crime statistics.

The seventh, eighth, and ninth sessions concentrated on substance abuse in the gang context. The tenth session considered careers, and included such guest speakers as the chief of security of a major electronics corporation, an insurance agent, and several police officers from the neighborhood. All of the speakers were from minority racial backgrounds, and their talks stressed the fact that, despite initial economic disadvantages, it was possible to obtain an education and achieve professional success. In addition to this, the presenters discussed the obstacles and difficulties that they, as minorities, had faced while accomplishing these goals.

The next session was devoted to values clarification and included role-playing, written exercises, and group discussions. The final session consisted of a review of the previous sessions, and a wrap-up discussion by BUILD staff.

After-School Program. Following the twelve classroom sessions, the targeted youth in the experimental schools were invited by the BUILD prevention staff to participate in an after-school athletics program conducted by BUILD in their neighborhood. This program consisted of organized sports clinics and competition and encouraged intragroup cooperation. In addition to the neighborhood-based activities, the after-school program facilitated the travel of these youth out of their neighborhood to participate in events and activities with similar groups from other locations. These after-school programs continued throughout the school year. Also, the targeted experimental group youth were invited to participate in a series of job skills training workshops conducted by the agency, as well as social/recreational activities (e.g., pizza parties) and educational assistance programs sponsored by BUILD. Agency field workers recorded the names of all youth who participated in each event, as well as the date, time, and nature of the event. Targeted youth in the control schools were not invited to participate in the after-school program.

At the end of the school year, gang membership was again determined by comparing targeted youths' names with gang rosters provided by gang members involved with BUILD's remediation program.

Table 25.1   Gang Membership by Experimental Condition

		Gang Membership	
Condition	n	Member	Nonmember
Control	43	4	39
Experimental	74	1	73

Probability of obtaining the distribution of gang membership (or a more extreme one) by chance alone (using Fisher's Exact Test) = 0.056.

Results

For data analysis purposes, the targeted youth were divided into three groups according to their participation in the intervention: No-Treatment (control group youth), $n = 43$; Classroom Sessions (experimental youth who participated in *only* the classroom sessions and not the after-school program, $n = 36$; and after-school (experimental youth who participated both in the classroom sessions and in at least one after-school program activity), $n = 38$.

Gang membership data were analyzed using Fisher's Exact Probability Test (Siegel, 1956) for 2 × 2 contingency tables. The data were grouped according to gang membership (member versus nonmember) and condition (control group versus experimental group). The results of this comparison are given in table 25.1. Whereas none of these youth had been gang members at the beginning of the program, four control and one experimental group youth (all males) joined gangs during the year. Using Fisher's Test, the probability of obtaining this distribution or a more extreme distribution by chance alone was 0.06. Although not statistically significant, this strong trend suggests that targeted youth who did not participate in either the classroom sessions or the after-school program may have been more likely to join street gangs than youth who participated in the programs.

None of the After-School group had subsequently joined gangs during the year. When this group was separately compared with the No-Treatment and with the Class Sessions group, though, the results did not approach statistical significance.

Discussion

Methodologically sound research in gang intervention is sparse, and the results conflictual. Based on several studies (Klein, 1969, 1971), it was predicted that youth who participated in the prevention program would be less likely to join street gangs than would nonparticipants. The present investigation's results tended to support this prediction. While four of the forty-three control group youth joined gangs, only one of the seventy-three experimental subjects joined a gang.

The statistically nonsignificant results obtained were likely a result of the low frequency with which targeted control and experimental youth were identified as having joined street gangs. This low level of gang membership may in turn have been due to inaccuracy in identifying youth who were truly at risk for gang membership. Instruments that accurately discriminate between potential gang members and nonmembers need to be developed and validated, and a risk index needs to be developed that will more accurately identify youth who are likely to join street gangs. Increased accuracy in the identification of youth who are at risk for gang membership would lead to better sampling and increased statistical power, resulting in more accurate evaluations of the effectiveness of preventive interventions.

A number of methodological difficulties complicate the interpretation of the results. The lack of random assignment to experimental conditions, for example, raises questions of sampling biases. That is, differences in the principals' willingness to permit student participation in the experimental program may have reflected other, qualitative differences in the regular school programs. The questionable reliability of gang informants poses additional questions concerning the accuracy of the data. Finally, variables such as self-selection and motivational differences were not addressed in the study. The children were offered the opportunity to participate in the after-school activities but, as participation was voluntary, their attendance may have been reflective of their motivation.

Despite the study's methodological difficulties and the consequent lack of certainty in interpreting the findings, however, the current investigation does, we believe, contribute meaningfully to the literature on youth street gangs. Although numerous gang intervention projects have been implemented over the years, few have been evaluated. Of those that have been assessed, very few have proven to be effective in addressing the problem of street gangs. As in the present study, those that were effective demonstrated their major impact on the recruitment of new members, rather than on the activities of current gang members. The current research suggests an alternative to the street-work interventions most frequently utilized with gangs. Moreover, it addresses the problem by attempting to identify youth who are at risk for gang membership and then intervene with them on a larger scale (classroom by classroom) rather than on an individual basis.

The present study serves as an example of how a community psychology approach can be utilized to address gang delinquency. Although the investigators were asked to evaluate the effectiveness of an existing program rather than design a new intervention, they were successful in measuring the effects of a multifaceted program on a transient and often poorly identified population. Moreover, the research yielded suggestions for subsequent research programs (e.g., for improved identification of at-risk children) within the agency. Despite the study's limitations, community psychologists were able to help an agency evaluate its programs and interpret the results in an area where such feedback is rarely found.

References

Adams, S. (1967). A cost approach to the assessment of gang rehabilitation techniques. *Journal of Research in Crime and Delinquency*, 4, 166–182.

Chicago Crime Commission. (1983). Untitled document distributed at the 1983 Conference of the Chicago Crime Commission, Chicago, IL.

Chicago Police Department. (1983). *Identification of Chicago street gangs*. Internal report. Chicago: Robert J. Simandl.

Clark, J.H. (1981). *A report of the Gang Activities Task Force*. Chicago Board of Education, Chicago.

Cloward, R.A., and Ohlin, L.E. (1960). *Delinquency and opportunity*. Glencoe, IL: Free Press.

Cohen, A.K. (1955). *Delinquent boys*. Glencoe, IL: Free Press.

Klein, M.W. (1971). *Street Gangs and street workers*. Englewood Cliffs, NJ: Prentice-Hall.

Klein, M.W. (1969). Gang cohesiveness, delinquency and a street-work program. *Journal of Research in Crime and Delinquency* 6, 135–166.

Klein, M.W. (1966). *A structural approach to gang intervention: The Lincoln Heights Project*. Proposal submitted to the Office of Juvenile Delinquency and Youth Development.

Roff, J.D., and Wirt, R.D. (1984). Childhood aggression and social adjustment as antecedents of delinquency. *Journal of Abnormal Child Psychology*, 12, 111–126.

Seigel, S. (1956). *Nonparametric statistics for the behavioral sciences*. New York: McGraw-Hill.

Suzuki, S., Nishimura, H., and Takahashi, Y. (1982). An analysis of the conditions conducive to delinquency involvement among high school students: II. On their weakened bonds to family and school. *Reports of the National Research Institute of Police Science*, 23, 147–165.

Thompson, D.W. (1986). Preventing youth membership in urban street gangs: The evaluation of a behavioral community intervention. *Dissertation Abstracts International*, 47, 3987B.

Weis, J.G., and Hawkins, J.D. (1981). *Preventing delinquency*. Office of Juvenile Justice and Delinquency Prevention, U.S. Depart. of Justice. Washington, DC: U.S. Government Printing Office.

26

Deviant Adolescent Subcultures: Assessment Strategies and Clinical Interventions

Cynthia M. Clark

Alienation and Youth

The adolescent experience is one of great change. It has been defined as a period of rapid psychosocial and biological growth between childhood and adulthood. In the process, many teenagers have difficulty coping effectively in our rapidly changing social climate. According to Bronfenbrenner (1986) societal forces that produce alienation are growing in strength and scope. He states that family, school, and other institutions that play important roles in human development are rapidly being eroded.

American society is an important influence on adolescents' development, relationships, adjustment, and behavior. Society's expectations mold adolescent personalities, influence their roles, and guide their future (Rice, 1978). Thus, alienation presents a serious threat to the successful resolution of the adolescent identity crisis. To be alienated is to lack a sense of belonging; to feel cut off from family, friends, school, or work (Bronfenbrenner, 1986). Because a sense of belonging and self-identity is central to the adolescent experience, feeling alienated and unwanted may severely compromise psychosocial development.

Adolescents seek comfort from those who welcome them and who reinforce their sense of belonging. Unfortunately, some youths may turn to deviant subcultures, such as gangs and cults (in this chapter, ''cult'' refers to Satanic cult involvement), in order to satisfy their need for approval, belonging, and self-worth.

Social control theory postulates that if adolescents feel alienated and

Reprinted with permission of Libra Publishers, Inc. from *Adolescence*, Vol. 27, No. 106 (Summer 1992): 283–293.

unattached, they may not internalize basic societal norms and may resort to deviance and nonconformity (Empey, 1982). According to Lloyd (1985), youths who feel alienated may succumb to depression, cynicism, delinquency, and substance abuse, and may choose to align with deviant subcultures. Youth-serving professionals report increasing numbers of adolescents who are involved with deviant subcultures. Three of the most destructive groups are the Satanists, the neo-Nazi skinheads, and violent street gangs.

Satanism

Bodemann (1974) describes Satanism as a blatant attack on society's dominant value system. Satan in Hebrew means "adversary," and Satanists systematically supplant what is held holy with the blasphemous. Satanism is devil worship—the antithesis of the Judeo-Christian belief system. Adolescents who practice Satanism often make up rituals as they go along, learning their craft from peers, occult books, album covers, movies, videos, and "heavy metal" rock bands which use Satanic lyrics in their music. Satanism is a destructive religion that advocates violence, death, and revenge. Curran (1989) describes Satanism as "a hole in the ground that some adolescents stumble into because they have been wandering, desperate, angry and alone."

Satanism can range from experimentation with devil worship to serious and chronic involvement. The depth of involvement may be measured using the "Continuum of Deviant Cultism," developed by the author, and based on the patterns of drug-using behaviors described in the Second Report of the National Commission on Marijuana and Drug Abuse (1973). (See figure 26.1.)

It should be noted that the vast majority of adolescents do not participate in Satanism. However, when an adolescent is involved, careful consideration should be given to the type and level of involvement. The patterns depicted in the model are descriptive in nature and do not necessarily imply that an adolescent will move through all these levels. A number of sequences are possible. Some youths will remain at the lower levels, while others may progress through each level, enter further along the continuum, or skip levels.

Neo-Nazi Skinheads

According to *Klanwatch* ("Hate, Violence and White Supremacy," 1989), the neo-Nazi skinheads are the most violent group of white supremacists this country has seen in a quarter century. They espouse bigotry, hatred, and violence toward minorities, and have been responsible for the worst racial assaults that have occurred in the past two years. The skinhead phenomenon originated in the 1970s in England, where gangs of menacing-looking, head-shaven, tattooed youths wearing combat boots began to be seen in the streets ("Shaved for Battle," 1987).

Figure 26.1: Continuum of Deviant Cultism

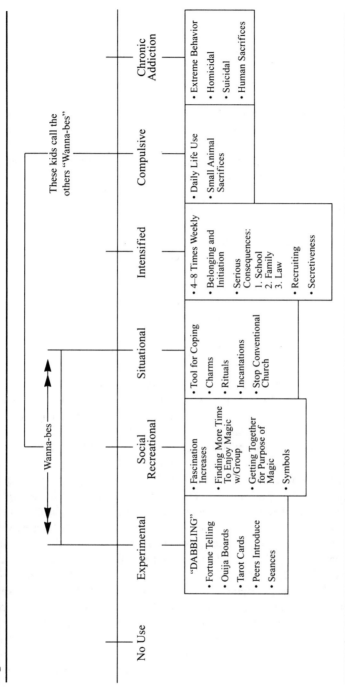

Today in America, skinheads resemble their British counterparts. They often shave their heads and wear rolled-up Levi's, black leather jackets, suspenders (called braces), and Doc Marten boots, and have tattoos and symbols representing white supremacy, neo-Nazism, and racial violence. American skinheads are very dangerous; most members are aged sixteen to nineteen, and bolster their courage with alcohol, methamphetamine, and cocaine. They tend to come from broken homes, and a high proportion were abused as children ("Skinhead Nation," 1988). Their weapons include knives, baseball bats, and their steel-toed boots. Their crimes range from gang beatings to murder. They have carried on a campaign of reckless terrorism against minorities, Jews, and gays ("Skinheads/Satanists," 1988).

A 1988 nationwide survey of neo-Nazi skinheads indicated continued membership growth and a persistent propensity for engaging in violence—mainly against racial and religious minorities. The gangs are composed overwhelmingly of teenagers, many as young as thirteen and fourteen years of age ("The Skinheads," 1988). It is alarming to note that the skinheads provide a recruitment pool for other organized white supremacy groups, such as The Order, the National Socialist Vanguard, and the White Aryan Resistance (WAR). White supremacy groups draw from skinhead gangs in an effort to recruit "soldiers devoted to the cause."

Violent Street Gangs

Gangs have probably received more attention than any other delinquent groups. These are groups that claim a turf, associate regularly, and are generally organized around illegal behavior. Gangs vary in size and are typically composed of same-sex and same-ethnic-group members. Although street gangs are predominantly male, female street gangs do exist (Lloyd, 1985), and some professionals believe they are growing in number.

Friedman et al. (1975) reported that a "high proclivity for violence" was a powerful predictor of gang membership. Other motivators include protection (usually from other gangs), companionship, camaraderie, and excitement. According to Lloyd (1985), alienation from parents is an initial cause of adolescents' turning toward delinquency and gang membership. More specifically, Friedman et al. (1975) found that acts of shouting at, cursing, and striking parents (primarily fathers) occurred more often among gang members than nongang members. Defiance of parents was found to be highly associated with gang affiliation, as was premeditated aggression and formal acts of violence. Other factors which ranked high in gang membership attributes were truancy, substance abuse, and failure to experience guilt (Friedman et al., 1975). Gangs directly challenge the established authority of social institutions, and it is likely that the gang will become the most important influence in a member's life.

Approximately twenty years ago in south central Los Angeles, a group of youths began assaulting, robbing, and intimidating anyone who had the misfortune to cross their path. They called themselves "Crips," identified with the color blue and the word "cuzz," and adopted a blue bandanna and a hand sign as identifying symbols (Dawkins, 1989). As the Crips became bolder and more intimidating, they instilled fear in some and admiration in others. This resulted in the formation of other neighborhood street gangs who either aligned with the Crips or became their rivals. One gang that was formed to protect themselves was the "Bloods." They identified with the color red and adopted a red bandanna and their own hand sign as symbols of their allegiance (Dawkins, 1989). Today, the Crips and Bloods remain rivals, and the hatred and often deadly violence has grown. Their numbers are increasing and gang membership is moving from larger cities to other areas—not because they have been forced out by the police, but by choice. They are motivated primarily by the desire to establish a larger market for crack cocaine.

Socioeconomic factors contribute to gang affiliation; members share similar backgrounds and characteristics. A dysfunctional family system, low self-esteem, poor academic performance, and poor vocational training are common traits. Parents' educational level is low, and many gang members lack positive male role models (Dawkins, 1989). Such adolescents are at risk for joining a gang because it offers an instant "family"—providing companionship, loyalty, identity, and status.

Huerter and Dawkins have developed a "Youth Gang Continuum" that describes the types and levels of gang participation (see figure 26.2). *Peripheral* gang members are youths who are on the fringe, but are at risk for deeper involvement. *Associates* are individuals who seek status and recognition by identifying with the gang when it is advantageous to them. *Hardcore* members express their identity through deeper gang allegiance and are involved in violent behaviors and criminal acts. They attempt to remain "behind the scenes," having less powerful members do the actual "dirty work." Thus, it is important to evaluate the level of involvement. Adolescents at all levels, however, are at risk, making intervention essential.

Psychosocial Assessment

The author has developed an assessment strategy that assists in determining a young person's involvement with deviant subcultures. Since only one or two symptoms are not conclusive, it is imperative to consider the whole person before diagnosing the adolescent as being involved in a gang or cult. It is also important to realize that some adolescents may be involved in both. In their desperation to belong and to feel worthwhile, some may join a gang and also worship Satan ("Skinheads/Satanists," 1988).

Adolescents who are involved in a gang or cult demonstrate various

473

Figure 26.2: Youth Gang Continuum

Peripheral		Associate		Hardcore	
		Wanna-be's →		*Baby Gangsters*	
Fringe	Peripheral	Social	Situational	Intensified	Compulsive

• No Involvement
• May Be Seen as Involved
• Location of Residence
• Friends
• Ethnicity
	• Youth Affected by Others' Involvement
	• Knows Persons Involved
	  – Family
	  – Friends
	• Does Not Wear Colors
	• Onlooker
	• Some Danger
	• Adolescents At-Risk
	  – Dysfunctional Family System
	  – Lowered Self-Esteem
	  – Absent or Poor Male Role Models
	  – Parental Substance Abuse
		• Participates and Identifies w/Gang when Advantageous
		• Joins for Protection
		• Fluid Movement
		• Flees at Threat of Danger
		• Colors Worn When Advantageous
		• No True Loyalty
		• Practices Gang Behaviors
			• Participates and Identifies Only w/Gang Members
			• Desires Recognition as a Gang Member
			• Behaves for Recognition and Approval
			• Recruited
			• Builds Reputation
			• Moniker (street name)
			• Colors
			• Graffiti
			• Hand Signs
			• Sagging (wearing pants low on hips)
			• Violence Increases
			• Need For Protection Increases
				• Initiation
				• Criminal Acts
				• Tattoos
				• Main Identity
				• May Change Moniker
				• Drive-By Intimidation
				• Recruits New Members
				• Serious Consequences
				  – Family
				  – School
				  – Law
				  – Death
				• Professional
				• Avoids 'B' or 'C' words (Crips avoid 'B' words, Bloods avoid 'C' words)
					• Idolized (father image)
					• Thrives on Totality of the Gang
					• Power/Control
					• May Form Own Gang
					• Intense Loyalty
					• Reputation and Status
					• Often Born into the Gang
					• Greater Threat to Law Enforcement
					• May Leave Street Scene
					• High Roller
					• Loyal to the Color Green (color of money)

(Turning Point — between Situational and Intensified)

symptoms. Some adolescents withdraw and become more secretive, especially as their involvement increases. Some change friends and develop a new vocabulary. Others demonstrate various dysfunctional behaviors, such as drug and alcohol abuse, truancy, runaway behavior, and serious family conflicts. Many of these adolescents have difficulty expressing their anger appropriately and often act out violently.

These adolescents frequently have a dismal outlook on life and display a lack of humor and spontaneity. They experience feelings of hopelessness about the future. Depression with suicidal ideation and/or gestures (e.g., cutting oneself and self-mutilation) is frequently present. These adolescents have difficulty developing and maintaining intimate and flexible relationships. Their peer relationships are frequently superficial and centered around their mutual experience of gang or cult activity.

Substance abuse is a hallmark of deviant subculture involvement. Satanists are heavy users of hallucinogenic drugs, while gangs are more likely to abuse alcohol and stimulants. Some adolescents who have been involved with gangs or cults report sexual promiscuity, sexual deviance, and engaging in sexual games and pornographic filmmaking. Other areas of concern include intense cruelty to animals (usually without a sense of remorse), animal sacrifice, and church desecration. These adolescents prefer lyrics from bands that glorify racism, violence, sexism, and gloom. While the music in and of itself is not the problem, the obsession with this music can be damaging. The families of gang- or cult-involved adolescents are frequently chaotic and detached. There may be significant abuse in the family, with a history of child neglect and poor attachment.

As with most conditions, it is critical that the whole spectrum of needs and symptoms be considered, and the individual carefully evaluated before a diagnosis of gang or cult involvement is reached.

Prevention

An effective way to deal with adolescent involvement with deviant subcultures is to prevent alienation from occurring in the first place. Three important areas of prevention are family, school, and peers.

In the family, there must be an established parental structure where communication is open and where roles and rules are clear. Communication can be enhanced through family meetings, outings, and open discussions. Children should be encouraged to ask questions, voice their opinion, and be involved in family decisions. Supportive parenting techniques enhance self-esteem and reinforce a sense of belonging and empowerment.

Schools that develop experiential programs and place less emphasis on competition help students develop a sense of mastery and efficacy (Johnson and Johnson, 1984). Building self-esteem and teaching solid decision-making skills are instrumental in preventing a sense of alienation. Schools that provide student assistance programs and network with the community have been shown to be effective (Griffin and Svendson, 1986).

Adults need to provide alternative activities for adolescents who might otherwise become involved in more deviant forms of recreation. Parents should take an interest in their children's friends, since reinforcement of an adolescent's involvement with a positive peer group helps encourage its continuation. Parents should provide structure and limits in the promotion of acceptable behavior.

Capitalizing on children's strengths, teaching coping skills, and providing them with an arena for success helps teach skill mastery and promotes feelings of accomplishment, and may prevent delinquency and subculture involvement. Providing physical and mental challenges may stretch the adolescent's ability to think and cognitively grapple with concepts, which may ultimately build a sense of importance and efficacy.

Treatment and Intervention

When prevention has not been effective, an adolescent may require clinical treatment and intervention. The clinician should be knowledgeable about adolescent gang and cult involvement. It is important to know the language of the deviant group in order to avoid confusion. For example, some groups often reverse the meaning of words. In order to build rapport and encourage the teenager to trust the therapy process, the clinician should avoid overreaction to the content and be an active and interested listener. Although the therapist should be direct in dealing with this kind of delinquency, it is important to first establish rapport before dealing intimately with the patient. Clinical experience indicates that it may take weeks or months on an outpatient basis before the adolescent is ready to reveal the intimate details of his or her gang or cult involvement. Secretiveness is a requirement for gang or cult membership, and the more involved the adolescent, the greater the degree of secrecy. Thus, the first several weeks of therapy may be spent on the more salient symptoms of drug involvement, family conflict, runaway behavior, and low self-esteem.

It is crucial to assess the adolescent's level of fear. One question that should be asked early in therapy is, ''Are you afraid for your life?'' This is asked in order to determine the degree of criminal involvement and whether law enforcement agencies should be contacted. Underlying issues have to be addressed; the therapist should not get lost in the details of the ''war stories,'' but should focus on the patient's internal struggles. Attention should be paid to lowered self-esteem, ineffective coping strategies, and compromised development.

Asking when the cult/gang involvement began can elicit useful information. Often, participation was precipitated by a traumatic event, which can be a clue to the treatment approach.

Even if the therapist is considering the use of group therapy, it is crucial that some individual work be done first. Group therapy should take place only after motivation for personal change has developed, and there is a sincere desire to assist others. Group therapy is best facilitated by the use of cotherapists, with emphasis on psychosocial problems rather than details of the rituals or criminal acts. All members of the group should be made aware of the format and rules, which includes respect for each member's confidentiality. Once the group process begins, the cotherapists should focus on keeping the group on task, but leave plenty of time for closure so that members can become less affectively charged. It is important that a therapy group of this nature not be followed by another highly affective group, but rather one that is less intense.

In many cases, it is important to involve the family once the adolescent has made some progress. The family then can hear from both the therapist and the adolescent about the progress that has been made and the means through which the adolescent plans to recover. Family therapy should also focus on all family members—their dynamics, roles, rules, and means for resolving family conflict. There may be instances in which an adolescent is from a multigenerational gang or cult where other family members are involved. This complicates therapy because the family reinforces the activity and usually resents and fears clinical intervention.

When an adolescent is attempting to surrender a major coping strategy (such as membership in a cult or gang), healthy alternatives must be developed. These are determined according to the individual's needs, and should be practiced while still in the therapeutic arena. It is important that adolescents who suffer from alienation develop a productive relationship with at least one adult whom they consider to be a positive role model. It is also important for adolescents to develop relationships with peers who share similar interests and who support their recovery. Many adolescents who have been developmentally compromised because of drug or alcohol use or gang or cult involvement may need help in developing various skills. Teaching effective coping strategies and appropriate decision-making and social skills reinforces self-sufficiency and enhances self-esteem.

Occasionally, an adolescent is so disturbed that hospitalization is required in order to prevent self-destructive behavior. However, inpatient treatment should not be too rigid. Although destructive behaviors should not be permitted, there should be some leniency regarding attire and makeup. This permits the treatment team to observe the adolescent's unique expression of feelings and thoughts, and thus plan treatment accordingly. Emphasis should be placed on empowering the adolescent, which fosters accountability and responsibility. The peer culture also can be utilized to initiate change and promote new behaviors.

The inpatient setting provides a rich forum for observation and clinical assessment. It is a safe place to practice new behaviors and to help the adolescent deal with the sense of dissatisfaction and anger toward self and others. The inpatient arena also offers the unique opportunity to ''tag team'' with other members of the staff and provide a multidisciplinary approach for promoting recovery.

Summary

Alienation is a contributing factor in adolescents' participation in Satanism, the neo-Nazi skinhead movement, and violent street gangs. Many of their needs are met by gang and/or cult affiliation, including a sense of belonging, self-worth, companionship, and excitement. Emphasizing prevention may minimize deviant subculture involvement, but some adolescents require clinical intervention, ranging from a few outpatient sessions to lengthy inpatient hospitalization. Therapists must be knowledgeable about adolescents' involvement, empathic to their circumstances, and sophisticated in the approach to treatment.

References

Bodemann, Y.M. (1974). Mystical, satanic and chiliastic forces in counterculture movements: Changing the world—or reconciling it. *Youth & Society.* 5(4), 433–447.

Bronfenbrenner, U. (1986, Feb.). Alienation and the four winds of childhood. *Phi Delta Kappan*, pp. 430–436.

Curran, D.K. (1989, Aug.). Why troubled teens might turn to Satanism. *The American School Board Journal*, pp. 12–15.

Dawkins, D.O. (1989). *Hangin', bangin', and rollin': L.A. gangs in Denver.* Unpublished manuscript.

Empey, L. (1982). *American delinquency: Its meaning and construction.* Chicago: Dorsey Press.

Friedman, C.J., Mann. F., and Friedman, A.S. (1975). A profile of juvenile street gang members. *Adolescence*, 10(40), 563–605.

Griffin, T., and Svendson, R. (1986). *The Student Assistance Program: How it works.* St. Paul, MN: Hazelton.

Hate, violence and white supremacy. (1989, December). *Klanwatch: A Decade in Review*, pp. 1–8.

Johnson, D., and Johnson, R. (1984). *Circles of learning: Cooperation in the classroom.* Washington, DC: Association for Supervision and Curriculum Development.

Lloyd, M. (1985). *Adolescence.* New York: Harper & Row.

National Commission on Marijuana and Drug Abuse. (1973). *Drug use in America: Problem in perspective* (Second Report of the National Commission on Marijuana and Drug Abuse). Washington, DC: U.S. Government Printing Office.

Rice, F. (1978). *The adolescent: Development, relationships and culture.* Boston: Allyn and Bacon.

Shaved for battle: Skinheads target America's youth. (1987, Nov.). *Anti-Defamation League Special Report*, pp. 1-6.

Skinhead Nation. (1988, December). *Rolling Stone*, pp. 55-65.

Skinheads/Satanists mix racism, ritual crime. (1988, August). *Klanwatch Intelligence Report*, p. 4.

The Skinheads: Update on "Shaved for Battle." (1988, February). *Anti-Defamation League Fact Finding Report*, pp. 1-5.

Index

INDEX

INDEX

history of, 397–399
organizational strength, 396–397
origin, 396
structure and composition, 401
violence by, 399–401
Joe Fong Gang (San Francisco), 236
Junkie Posse, 399
Juvenile court, class-based stereotypes in,
182–183
Juvenile crime, predicting, 67–70

King, Martin Luther, Jr., 434
KKK (Ku Klux Klan), 382
Klanwatch, 470

Latin Gang Member Recognition Guide for
the City of Phoenix, 184
Law enforcement; *see also* Police
anti-gang strategies, 47–48
and Chicano gangs, 182–201
data on gangs, 34–48
and Jamaican gangs, 404–405
problem of defining gangs, 39–41
prominence of, 422–423
Lexical definitions, 5–6
Lions (Chicago), 140
Location, of drug sales, 285
Long-term population change, 88
Los Angeles, 79, 167
gang capital of the world, 150
gang membership, 109–110
Mexican-American gangs, 150–163
Los Angeles County, gang violence, 300
Los Angeles County Sheriff's Office, 278,
292, 302, 307
Los Angeles Police Department, 23, 278,
292, 302, 307
reports on gang crime, 42
Louisville Police Department report on
organized crime, 42
Lower-class youth, and economic
opportunity, 114–123
Loyalty, 156–157

Male dominance, 157
Manley, Michael, 397–398
Manson, Charles, 139
Marianismo, 143–146
Marijuana
from Jamaica, 400
Jamaican distribution network, 401–403

Marley, Bob, 398
Maximum prison term of prison gang
members, 386, 392
Mexican-American gangs, 150–163
legal processing of, 182–201
Mills, C. Wright, 441
Milwaukee, 102
gang formation and school
desegregation, 434
gangs, neighborhoods, and public
policy, 437–440
intra-neighborhood alienation, 434
macro-economic trends and gangs, 430–
441
neighborhood segmentation, 433–437
Minor offenses, 256, 272
Monroe v. Pape, 383
Monte Carlo simulations, 191
Moore, Johnny, 366
Motherhood, teen pregnancies, 141–142
Motorcycle gangs; *see* Outlaw motorcycle
gangs
Multiple handlers, drug dealers, 283–284

National Commission on Marijuana and
Drug Abuse, 470
National Incident-Based Reporting System
(FBI), 34–35
National Institute of Justice, 35
Gang Survey, 34, 40, 41, 46, 47–48
National Institute on Drug Abuse, 432
National Juvenile Justice Assessment
Center, 82, 86, 450
National-level network, 425–426
National Strategy for Youth Development
Project, 117
National Youth Gang Intervention and
Suppression Program, 411, 423, 426–
427
survey data, 413–415
National Youth Gang Survey, 267, 437
Neighborhoods
police response, 437–440
revitalization programs, 437–440
segmentation of, 433–437
Neo-Nazi skinheads, 470–472
Nuestra Familia, 382
New gangs
age factors, 101–102
data on, 104–105
research on, 101–110

487